The NBA Finals
A Fifty Year Celebration

Roland Lazenby

MASTERS PRESS

A Division of Howard W. Sams & Co.
A Bell Atlantic Company

Published by Masters Press
A Division of Howard W. Sams & Company, A Bell Atlantic Company
2647 Waterfront Pkwy E. Dr, Suite 300, Indianapolis, IN 46214

96 97 98 99 00 01   10 9 8 7 6 5 4 3 2 1

Library of Congress Cataloging-in-Publication Data

Lazenby, Roland
        The NBA finals : a 50 year celebration / Roland Lazenby.
                p. cm.
        ISBN 1-57028-103-3
        1. National Basketball Association--History. 2. Basketball--Tournaments--United
States--History. I. Title.
GV885.515.N37L387 1996   96-32312
796.323'64'0973--dc20   CIP

This book is not an official publication of, nor is it endorsed by,
the National Basketball Association.

Acknowledgments

I have a number of people to thank for making this project possible. First, Tom Bast at Masters Press believed in it, then turned it over to Heather Lowhorn to edit it and guide it through the publishing process, aided by Tom Doherty, Holly Kondras and all the gang at Masters. I also want to thank David Levin and Mike Shank for research help. Especially important were Lindy Davis at *Lindy's Sports Annuals* and Larry Canale at *Tuff Stuff* magazine, both of whom have offered support. Then, of course, there's my wife Karen and children Jenna, Henry and Morgan, who make the most special contributions of all.

*To all the guys who played the game when the lights
weren't so bright and the money wasn't so good.*

Boston battles New York at Madison Square Garden in 1955.

Contents

Foreword

When I was named the Most Valuable Player of the 1989 NBA Finals, my hometown of Natchitoches, Louisiana, honored me with Joe Dumars Appreciation Day. It was a wonderful day, with a parade, a luncheon, and many other honors. Yet at the same time it left me feeling uncomfortable. I tried to explain my feelings in my address to the crowd. "The most important thing about today," I said, "is that these people have something to be proud of. I'm just the vehicle. I can't get caught up

in what I'm doing. I know that 70 million people in 60 different countries watch the NBA Finals on television, so I know that's important. Twenty years ago, somebody did the same thing, and twenty years from now, somebody else will still be doing it. I'm just passing through."

Having reviewed this history of the league's world championship series, I'm more convinced than ever that my words of 1989 were true. A marvelous array of athletes has come through the NBA Finals. I am very honored and very thankful to be merely one of them. This collection of text and photographs brings together a half a century of their efforts. I can feel the drama and intensity of their battles even across the decades.

Pro basketball hasn't always been a glamour game, but in its own tough way, it has always been a wonderful one. I commend this book to you as a testament to the people — the players, the coaches, the owners, the support people, the media — who have nurtured the game over the years. We are all the richer for their efforts.

Joe Dumars

Introduction

Let history record that the very first NBA Finals were inaugurated by a superstar effort.

April 16, 1947: The Chicago Stags, coached by Harold Olsen, vs. the Philadelphia Warriors, led by owner-coach Eddie Gottlieb. Philadelphia took it, 84-71, as Joe Fulks, the league's first scoring champion, pumped in a dazzling 37 points.

The wire-service man could hardly contain his enthusiasm in describing Fulks' second-half scoring outburst of 29 points. "Fulks picked up steam in the third quarter, and then really poured it on in the final session as he delighted a crowd of 7,718 with the greatest exhibition of shooting ever seen on the arena floor," reported the anonymous scribe. Indeed, Fulks had a startling (for the time) 21 points in the last quarter, hitting his first eight shots from the floor.

The Warriors went on to win the title in five games (with Fulks scoring 13, 26, 21, and 34 in the remaining four games), establishing for all time the idea that the best basketball in the world was that played in the NBA, or its forerunner, the Basketball Association of America, and that the premier demonstration of the product would take place in its championship series.

The world at large didn't pay much attention. It still wasn't paying enough attention a decade later when the Boston Celtics won their first world championship with a scintillating 125-123 double-overtime triumph over the St. Louis Hawks. And it still wasn't paying sufficient attention in 1970 when the noble Willis Reed hobbled onto the Madison Square Garden floor in Game 7 and turned the rostrum over to Walt Frazier, whose 36 points and 19 assists paced New York to a 113-99 victory and its first championship.

Inattention is no longer the NBA's problem. The Finals are now one of America's premier sporting events, and the interest has also become global. The number of foreign journalists covering the NBA Finals grows annually. It's not the World Cup — yet — but it is an event which commands the attention of many millions who have never seen Michael and Mars do a sneaker commercial.

Lord, but it's too bad somebody hadn't invented videotape 40 years ago. Then we'd have preserved the wonderful 1951 Finals, when the Rochester Royals won the first three games over the Knicks, lost the next three, and then won their first and only title with a 79-75 victory in Game 7. The Knicks were 14 down in the second period, but rallied to tie the game at 75-all with 59 seconds remaining. Bobby Davies drove to the hoop, drew a foul from Tricky Dick McGuire, and sank two big free throws to break the deadlock. To this day, no team has ever come closer to pulling off the ultimate comeback of climbing out of an 0-3 hole.

Two franchises have dominated the Finals. First there were the Mineapolis Lakers, the original NBA dynasty. Featuring George Mikan in the middle, the Lakers won it all in 1949, 1950, 1952, 1953, and 1954. Then came the long, distinguished reign of the Boston Celtics, who won 11 championships in 13 years starting in 1957. The '80s were highlighted by another Laker squad, this one located in

Syracuse won the first two games at home. Fort Wayne won the next three games in Indianapolis, sending the Nationals of coach Al Cervi back home needing two victories to win the championship. Game 6 was titanic. Syracuse's Wally Osterkorn and Fort Wayne's Don Meineke tangled in the second period, bringing fans onto the court. George yardley, later to become a Nat but then the scoring mainstay of Charlie Eckman's Pistons, had 31, but Dolph Schayes had 28 as the Nats won it, 109-104. Game 7 truly went down to the wire. The score was tied at 91 apiece with 12 seconds left when George King sank a clutch free throw

1964

1970

Los Angeles. The Lakers had a tough series in 1952 with the luckless Knicks. One year after their inspired comeback against Rochester, the Knicks pushed Mikan & Co. to a seventh game, but Mikan's 22 points sparked his team to an 82-75 victory in the deciding game.

One of the great series of the league's first decade took place in 1955, when Syracuse and Fort Wayne waged war for seven games. The series was conducted under the same 2-3-2 homesite format employed today, as opposed to the longstanding 2-2-1-1-1 arrangement.

and then stole the ball to preserve a 92-91 Syracuse victory. Think that one wouldn't lead SportsCenter in this day and age?

Two years later the Celtics brought home the first title for Red Auerbach, launching the basketball world into a tyranny it had never known. Year after year teams tried to find the answer to Bill Russell, not to mention Bob Cousy, Bill Sharman, Tom Heinsohn, Sam Jones, John Havlicek, and the other Boston stars, many of whose number hang proudly from the Boston Garden rafters today. The only teams successful in their quest were the 1958 St. Louis Hawks and the 1967 Philadelphia 76ers, both coached by Alex Hannum. The former needed an ankle injury to Russell and 50 points from Bob Pettit to win in six games, while the latter did it on the strength of Wilt Chamberlain's finest all-around performance.

The Celtics needed seven games in 1960 (St. Louis), 1962 (Los Angeles), 1966 (Los Angeles), and 1969. By far, the biggest scare came in 1962, when L.A.'s Frank Selvy missed an open 15-footer from the left baseline that would have won Game 7 in regulation. Given a

The Lakers won Games 1 and 2 in the Fabulous Forum, and no team had come back from an 0-2 deficit to win a playoff series. But the old boys banded together to write NBA history, finishing the job with a 110-108 seventh-game decision in the Forum.

Sixteen years later another L.A. team would avenge that loss for its ancestors, upsetting a favored Boston team seeking a repeat title by winning a climactic Game 6 in the Boston Garden, where no Laker team had ever won a championship. An excited Kareem Abdul-Jabbar said he felt like Johnny Podres, proving that you can take the boy out of Brooklyn, but

1984

1989

reprieve by the gods, the Celtics prevailed in OT, as Russell scored 30 points and hauled in 40 rebounds.

The most satisfying of all Celtic titles, however, came in 1969. The aging Celtics had finished fourth in the regular season, and were faced with the prospect of winning the title without one home-court advantage in any series. They knocked off Philadelphia and New York to get out of the East, earning the right to face L.A. for the championship.

you can't take Brooklyn out of the boy.

Kareem's inspired play that year was only one of many brilliant displays in the Finals. Who could ever forget Magic Johnson's spectacular Game 6 against Philadelphia in 1980? With Kareem nursing a sprained ankle, the rookie Magic played all five positions and scored 42 points to make L.A. a champion. And how about Bird's virtuoso play in 1984, when he played basketball the way it's supposed to be played to bring championship number 15 to Boston?

But perhaps the most unexpected, curious, and heartwarming of all NBA champs were the 1975 Golden State Warriors, season-long overachievers who upset a powerful Washington Bullets squad in four dramatic games. Before the season had begun, the Warriors had lost Cazzie Russell, Clyde Lee, and Jim Barnett without compensation. But Rick Barry led by example all season, and a band of assorted castoffs and no-names kept doing things they weren't supposed to do.

They were down, three games to two, against Chicago in the Western Conference finals, heading back to Chicago. They never lost another game. In five of their final six games they trailed by a minimum of 11 points. At the start of the fourth quarter in Game 4 against the Bullets, coach Al Attles had five subs on the floor. When it was all over, and the heavily favored Bullets had been swept in four games, Washington's Mike Riordan said, "They beat us in areas you don't find on the scouting reports."

In order to earn the championship ring, that's very often what you must do in this game. The NBA Finals have a way of bringing out the best in the best. It started that way with Joe Fulks, and every year it keeps getting better and better.

Bob Ryan

I.
In The Beginning

The year was 1946, and the operative word was boom.

Economic boom.

Housing boom.

Baby boom.

Even, in its own quiet way, a basketball boom.

The end of World War II had brought the return home of hundred of thousands of G.I.s. Money that had once been directed at the war effort suddenly began flowing into the American economy. First it was a trickle, then a rush, as the nation moved out from the shadow of catastrophe. Sick of war bonds and weapons plants and rationing, people turned their thoughts to rebuilding their lives.

After five years of struggle and sacrifice, the public hungered for fun. New products seemed to emerge overnight. Polaroid cameras. 33 1/2 long-playing records. Wash-and-wear shirts. Most fascinating of all was the television set, although there were only about 100,000 tubes (with seven- and twelve-inch screens) in American households (and bars) in 1946. Even so, programmers were already looking to sports. A Joe Louis fight was aired in June 1946, and the World Series followed the next year.

And if things weren't brand new, they were innovative. Suddenly ice cream came in eight flavors, and Americans gobbled up 714 million gallons of it in 1946, apparently much of it by pregnant women.

The biggest product, of course, was babies. Nearly 3.5 million were born in 1946 alone, and the numbers would spiral from there, blowing out all government projections on population. By the 1960s, there would be an extra thirty million Americans, all of them young and eager for excitement.

Looking back, it seems logical that the National Basketball Association, itself a child of this baby boom, would grow and mature with the generation. But back in 1946, starting another pro basketball league seemed like a crazy thing to do. Sure, fans flocked to college basketball games. But pro ball was another matter. The business climate was as tough as the play on the court. Teams and entire leagues struggled through a life-and-death search for cash flow. They attracted a small core of dedicated fans, but beyond that, the public at large paid them little attention. Their media coverage usually amounted to a paragraph or two on the back sports pages.

There was already the National Basketball League, which had franchises in Chicago, Pittsburgh, Fort Wayne, Rochester, Oshkosh, Sheboyhan, and Indianapolis. Founded in 1938, the NBL had struggled through the lean years of World War II with some franchises faltering in midseason.

Even so, a group of executives gathered in New York in June 1946 to discuss the formation of a new league. For the most part, they were arena owners and professional hockey managers, and they figured basketball was a good way to keep the building busy on off nights. They hoped to bring the charm of the college game to a new pro circuit.

Whereas the NBL had largely out-of-the-way settings, the new league began with franchises in eleven major cities (once television grabbed hold, these areas would become known as "media markets," of course). With teams in New York, Boston, Philadelphia, Providence, Toronto, Washington, Chicago, Cleveland, Detroit, Pittsburgh, and St. Louis, this new circuit called itself the Basketball Association of America, or the BAA.

The league hustled to begin play that fall of 1946 as newly selected coaches scrambled to find players. Each team was limited to a payroll of $55,000, which meant an average annual contract of about $5,000 per player. (Some earned $7,500 or more.) Because the NBL was allowed to pay more, many of the big-name college players went to the older

In 1949 the BAA and the NBL merged to become the NBA. In the center is Maurice Podoloff, first NBA president, and Eddie Gottlieb is on the left.

league. But with the war ending, there was a surplus of players for both the colleges and the pros. In that climate, the BAA coaches finally got their teams together, and on November 1, 1946, the New York Knicks beat the Toronto Huskies, 68-66, in the league's first regular-season game.

Like the pro leagues that had preceded it, the BAA soon found its share of troubles. Franchises opened and closed overnight in those first few years. Before its second season, the new league had lost teams in Detroit, Cleveland, Pittsburgh, and Toronto. To replace them, it added Baltimore out of the old American League (a small professional league that started in the 20s).

Pro basketball was learning the same lesson as pro football. Competing leagues meant bidding wars for talent, which meant certain economic failure as operating costs skyrocketed. In 1948, the proud old National Football League had agreed to merge with its upstart rival, the All-America Football Conference. The same fate awaited pro basketball.

Just before the 1948-49 campaign, the four strongest teams in the NBL — Minneapolis, Rochester, Fort Wayne, and Indianapolis — left their league to join the BAA's Western Division. The following season, the six surviving teams from the NBL joined the BAA, creating a three-division alignment that was renamed the National Basketball Association.

In no way did the merger mean that the lean times were over. Pro basketball would need time to mature and prosper. But those early years had provided a beginning. And like the rest of the Baby Boom, the NBA was off and toddling.

1.
The Philadelphia Story
Fulks, Gottlieb and the Warriors

1947

When the NBA, then known as the Basketball Association of America, opened for business in 1946-47, Arnold "Red" Auerbach was the 29-year-old rookie head coach of the Washington Capitols. He would later move on to coach the Boston Celtics teams that dominated pro basketball for two decades. But Auerbach's Capitols weren't a bad club either. In fact, they put together a home winning streak that left them with the best record in the new league and seemed a good bet to win the title. But then something happened that left Auerbach fuming for decades.

First, he had a run-in with the referees, something that would become a common refrain over Auerbach's glorious career.

But even worse, the Basketball Association of America in its first season of operation had adopted a wacky playoff system that required the divisional champions to play each other in the first round.

"It was terrible," George Senesky, who played guard for the 1946-47 Philadelphia Warriors, said of the format. "I don't know how they came up with that."

Actually the answer is quite simple. Because most of the team owners were hockey men, they based their first basketball playoffs on an old hockey system. Strangely, it called for

New York battles Chicago during regular-season BAA play in 1946.

the first-place teams in each of the BAA's two divisions to play each other in the first round. The second- and third-place teams did likewise. Such a set-up meant that one of the two best teams in the league would be automatically eliminated in the first round.

11

Using contacts he had made while he was in the Navy, Auerbach had rounded up some of the best players available and brought them to Washington to play for his Capitols in those days just after the war. Bones McKinney played the post, and Auerbach's Navy buddy, Bob Feerick, worked the corners as a forward, while Fred Scolari, a friend of Feerick's from the West Coast, ran at guard. With those three as a nucleus, the Caps had ripped off a league-best regular-season record of 49-11, including a 29-1 home mark at Washington's Uline Arena (which had a seating capacity of only 4,000).

Red Auerbach coached the Washington Capitols to a 49-11 regular-season record in 1947.

Yet with Auerbach fuming about the officiating and the strange playoff system, the Caps stumbled in the postseason. They were upset in their first-round match-up four games to two by the Western Division champions, the Chicago Stags, who had finished the regular season 11 games worse than Washington.

Auerbach and his players had to take a seat and watch the emergence of the Philadelphia Warriors, a team that had finished 14 games behind Washington in the standings. No wonder that the hypercompetitive Auerbach was still fuming about the circumstances a half century later.

The Warriors, though, say their record was bad only because they had struggled early in the season. By the time the playoffs rolled around, they had meshed and captured second place in the Eastern Division, and that in turn put them in position to claim the league's first championship.

In some regards, it's only fitting that the Warriors wound up taking the first NBA title. After all, they were coached by Philadelphia basketball legend Eddie Gottlieb. Depending on whom you talk to, Gottlieb is remembered as either the "father of pro basketball," or the world's biggest tightwad. He probably couldn't have been one without being the other in those lean early years.

Promoter. Coach. Owner. Entrepreneur. All of those tags fit Gottlieb. Since 1918, shortly after he graduated from South Philadelphia High School, "Gotty" had been infatuated with basketball as a business. Back then, he and a group of his young Jewish buddies had formed a team, and Gottlieb talked the South Philadelphia Hebrew Association into sponsoring it. They drew their name, the SPHAs, from the sponsor's acronym on their jerseys (in Hebrew letters, of course). It wasn't long before the association dropped its sponsorship, but Gotty and the boys kept the acronym name anyway.

The SPHAs came to be quite a hustle. Gottlieb spent most of his time working out deals and promotions, anything to draw a few spectators. While running his team, Gottlieb grew up with the pro game. He nurtured it through the days of two-handed dribbles and center jumps after every bucket. As time went on, he figured ways to promote it and even make a little money from it. He staged games in dance halls and armories and athletic clubs. Sometimes the goals had backboards, sometimes they didn't. That didn't matter so much back then. What mattered is that Eddie Gottlieb kept the books balanced and the bills paid.

As his players used to say, "Gotty" had a knack for counting the house. From the bench, he could scan the stands and figure whether the draw was 500, 800 or 1,000. In time, there was nobody who knew more about promoting basketball than Eddie Gottlieb. He worked his SPHAs to the highest level of the game, which in those days wasn't very high. Fans had shown marginal interest in pro basketball in the 1930s, but Gottlieb found he could attract a decent crowd if he combined the games with a dance afterward, the only problem being that quite often the "fans" were obviously more interested in the dance. It wasn't unusual to have girls in heels interrupt play with an inadvertent stroll across the floor.

Back then, the game was played in three periods. Gottlieb's boys would play a period, then the fans would dance a while. They they'd play another period.

The SPHAs played most of their games at Philly's old Broadwood Hotel. "The floor was slick, a lot of dance wax on it," recalled Robert "Jake" Embry, owner of the Baltimore Bullets. "The players were used to sliding and shooting. They'd dribble, slide about five feet and shoot."

Under these circumstances, Gottlieb built his SPHAs to a competitive level with the great barnstorming teams of the era, the New York Celtics and the Harlem Rens. He also entered his teams in a variety of leagues, the Philadelphia league, the several versions of the Eastern League, and the old American League. Eventually, the SPHAs dominated the American League, winning seven championships in the 15 years the league operated.

Thus, Gottlieb was more than ready in June 1946, when the Basketball Assocation of America organized to play what the owners hoped would become big-time pro basketball. Because New York promoter Ned Irish had made a fortune staging college basketball during the 1930s and '40s, many owners in the new BAA hoped to build their teams with name college players. "Gotty" knew better. In putting together his Warriors, he went after the tough old pros, the guys who had spent their weekends playing for a few bucks in the hardscrabble coal towns and the tough city neighborhoods of the Northeast.

For this reason as well, it was only fitting that the Warriors won the first championship. They did it by and large by using players who had stuck with the game when the money wasn't so good. Matt Guokas (father of pro coach and TV color analyst Matt, Jr.) was a prime example. He was 31 years old with a wealth of low-paying pro experience when Gottlieb selected him as the backup center for the Warriors in 1946. Guokas' salary was only $5,000 (about the league average), but at the time that seemed like manna from heaven, recalled Joan Guokas, the player's wife. "For the first time, Matt could play and not hold a day-time job. He could play without having to spend 12 hours a day on his feet."

The Warriors' first superstar was "Jumpin'" Joe Fulks from Kentucky.

To fill out his Warriors roster, Gottlieb used several guys who had played for his SPHAs, including George Senesky, guard Petey Rosenberg, center Art Hillhouse and utility player Jerry Fleishman.

Gottlieb's team also featured the first superstar of pro basketball, but in 1946 he was neither a tough old pro nor a big-name college player. The "superstar" was an intense, quiet hillbilly from western Kentucky, "Jumpin' " Joe Fulks, the guy credited with popularizing the jump shot.

Rosenberg was running a service team in Hawaii during the war when he spotted Fulks playing for an opposing Marine team. His shooting was stunning. "Whenever he played, he would pop them in," Rosenberg said. "I wrote Gotty a letter and said if you get ahold of this guy you got a hell of a player."

"Gotty" got ahold of him.

But when Fulks came to the Warriors, his new teammates weren't quite sure what to make of him.

"It took me a month and a half before I could understand him," Warriors forward Howie Dallmar said of Fulks' accent.

"He had that Kentuckyish way about him," Guokas, one of Fulks' early admirers, admitted.

"He didn't look like an athlete," Senesky said. "He was kind of hunched over. But as soon as we saw him in practice you could tell."

It didn't take long for the rest of the league to tell, either. The 6'5' Fulks averaged 23.6 points per game that first season, which qualified as a legitimate feat. It wasn't quite the equivalent of a four-minute mile or a 60-home run season, but it was close.

"That was a lot of points in those days when you didn't have the time clock," Dallmar said.

Fulks couldn't run fast or jump very high. But his one- and two-handed jump shots left fans marveling. Gottlieb, ever the promoter,

sensed this and did his best to make Fulks a superstar. The owner/coach never came out and told his players to give Fulks the ball. But it was understood by the Warriors. Gottlieb often left Fulks in games to make sure his average stayed high. A high-scoring star had marquee value, and while Gottlieb may not have been the most technical of coaches, he sure understood promotions.

"Gottlieb always liked a big scorer," Paul Seymour recalled. "He figured that's what he had to have to draw the people."

For his part, Fulks was well-suited for this particular brand of stardom. He loved to shoot. "He was a gunner," Dallmar said. With a .305 shooting average, he was one of the most accurate players in the league in that early era of dimly lit gyms, imperfect balls and no dunks.

"He would hoist that ball high above his head with two hands," Guokas said of Fulks' shot. "It was touch, not a rifle. It was so soft you could almost see the lettering on the ball. He did very little faking and dribbling, and we didn't set a lot of picks and screens for him, but in the movement of the ball, he would get his shots. Joe's gait was on the slow side, but meaningful. He knew where to get to."

He was just the new sensation that pro basketball needed. "The league was new, and they were looking for heroes," Senesky explained. "Joe's style was revolutionary. Everybody else was shooting two-handed set shots, and here was this guy shooting one-handed jump shots, off balance and from all angles. It was new for

> **O**n the jerseys, you could see the salt marks on them after a while. You had to hang it up in your room after the games so it would dry out. There was no equipment manager. You were responsible. But nobody complained about it. We were so glad to have the opportunity, so glad to be there.

Philadelphia's George Senesky drives past Chicago's Don Carlson in the 1947 NBA Finals.

fans in the East. It was exciting. People took to him right off."

Despite his unique skill, his shooter's ego and his lack of athleticism, Fulks wasn't entirely one-dimensional. "He was a hell of a rebounder, too," Senesky said. "When he took the ball off the board, he'd hook it under his arm, and you'd never get it away from him. He had strong wrists."

To go with him, Gottlieb had Angelo Musi, a 5'9" guard with a smooth set shot out of Temple, and Senesky, a 6'2" defensive guard and former All-America out of St. Joe's. The starting center was Hillhouse, a 6'7", 220-pounder who had played college ball at Rutgers and Long Island University. Another St. Joe's product, Guokas, at 6'2", was the backup in the post. Rosenberg, Fleishman, and Ralph Kaplowitz kept Gottlieb company on the bench until the regulars got tired.

There was only one problem. "We weren't that big," Senesky said. "We actually had a team with six backcourt men. Eddie needed somebody else, so he got ahold of Dallmar."

The 6'5" Dallmar filled the bill in another manner, as well. He had been a big college name. At Stanford, he had been named the most outstanding player of the 1942 NCAA tournament, which Stanford had won. Then, during the war, he had played for the University of Pennsylvania, while stationed there for service training. He was a popular figure in Philadelphia. Most important, he was a good all-around player who would eventually lead the league in assists even though he played in the frontcourt.

"Without Howie we probably would have finished last," Senesky said.

Gottlieb's coaching was what one might expect from someone long on promotional skills and short on Xs and Os. He coaxed teamwork out of his people but let them play their individual games. "He was a good upstairs man," Rosenberg said of Gottlieb. "But as far as coaching, the guys were good enough. He didn't have to tell them much."

"He was not what you would call a fundamentals coach," Dallmar agreed. "He wanted

to get people to work together. And he had a knack for substituting at the right time. He had more notes in his pockets about so many things."

Somehow, Dallmar said, Gottlieb could reach into his pocket and pull out just the right note at the right time. And if the notes failed, "Gotty" was always ready with an outburst, particularly in the huddle during timeouts.

Eddie Gottlieb was called a "good upstairs man."

"Eddie had a short fuse at times and was very vociferous," Dallmar said. This anger would often be directed at an assigned "goat," usually Jerry Fleishman.

"Jerry was used to it," Senesky said. "So it didn't bother Jerry. The rest of us were always glad it wasn't us."

While his coaching may have been suspect, Gottlieb had his promotional approach down to a science. He dressed his team in satin uniforms with an Indian logo. The Warriors wore gold and blue on the road, white shirt, gold pants at home, with PHILA across the front of the jersey.

Yet for all the satin and gold at game time, the day-to-day life of the players was a bit ragged. Training methods were what you might expect of 1946. At home, the teams usually employed a trainer of sorts, "but on the road, each guy took a roll of tape with him," Senesky said. "You knew how to tape your own ankles."

And as nice as the jerseys looked, there was no such thing as a clean road uniform. "You couldn't wash them; they had to be drycleaned," Senesky said. "On the jerseys, you could see the salt marks on them after a while. You had to hang it up in your room after the games so it would dry out. There was no equipment manager. You were responsible. But nobody complained about it. We were so glad to have the opportunity, so glad to be there."

Out of an average $5,000 salary, a player

would take home about $3,800, which wasn't bad pay for the times. "A lot of us always thought it was going to get better the next year," Senesky said. "The best ticket was $2.50, and 50 cents of that was tax. The owners weren't making money either."

Because they mostly played in hockey rinks, the BAA teams competed on temporary floors over the ice, which meant the building had to be kept cool. If things got too hot, condensed moisture would collect on the hardwood, making the play slippery and dangerous. Thus bench warmers had to be just that, huddled in overcoats with newspapers under their feet for insulation.

"After a while you got used to it," Senesky said.

As for their play over the first part of the season, the Warriors were as cold and stiff as the arenas they played in. "We started off badly," Senesky said. "But in February we caught hold and started to win. A lot of us had been in the service and gotten muscle bound. By January we were starting to get our legs back."

Under the playoff system, the first-place teams played a best-of-seven first-round series, while the other brackets played best-of-three. St. Louis and Chicago tied in the West, but Chicago edged out the regular-season title in a one-game playoff with St. Louis. The Washington Capitols were favored against the Stags in the tough first round, but Auerbach's team lost the first two games at home and went down four games to two.

Meanwhile, the Warriors and St. Louis split the first two games, and their series came down to a critical third game in St. Louis on Easter Sunday. "It was hard to beat them out there," Senesky said. The Warriors had gotten blown out in Game 2 in St. Louis, 73-52. But Game 3 was another story. "We just overwhelmed them," Dallmar said. St. Louis fell, 75-59.

The New York Knicks had won their third place series with Cleveland, 2-1. But the Warriors beat the Knicks in the next round, advancing to the finals with a 12-point win at

home in Game 1, then a 72-53 waltz in New York to take the best-of-three series, 2-0.

The Warriors' rise to the Finals had been nice, but anybody who followed pro basketball figured Chicago as the favorite. "Chicago always seemed to have the best players," Senesky said. "They had 10 good men. They paid well. Max Zaslofsky was their big scorer, from the back court."

Zaslofsky was a big Jewish kid, a New Yorker who had played some college ball at St. John's. He averaged 14.4 points per game (fifth in the league) and shot .329 from the floor (also fifth in the league). "He had a beatiful two-hand set shot, right from the chest," Guokas said of Zaslofsky. "He could release very quickly."

Gottlieb was a teetotaler, but as the picture brightened for the Warriors that spring, he made a private bet with Philadelphia team president Peter Tyrell that if the team won the title he would celebrate with a Manhattan.

Right off the bat, the Warriors gave Gotty reason to wet his whistle. The Stags' coach, Harold Olson, who had had a successful program at Ohio State, liked his teams to run. They averaged 77 points per game, the highest in the league. The numbers for Philadelphia, 68.6, weren't nearly as impressive. But all that flipflopped in the Finals.

The concept of home-court advantage hadn't settled in the minds of the strategists in 1947. So when scheduling conflicts occurred in Chicago, the Stags agreed to shift the site of one game to Philadelphia. "We got a break in that final series with Chicago," Senesky said. "They weren't able to use Chicago Stadium for one game so we played an extra one at our place."

If there was such a thing as a pro basketball town in 1947, Philadelphia was it, mainly due to Gottlieb's years of relentless promotions. The Warriors usually played in front of a packed house at the old Philadelphia Arena on Market Street. The fans had a reputation for making the referees miserable in those days before security escorts off the floor after games. The Arena was quite a pit.

The Champion Warriors. Seated, from left, are Jerry Rulio, Angelo Musi, Pete Tyrell, Pete Rosenberg, and Jerry Fleishman, Standing from left, are Cy Kaselman, George Senesky, Ralph Kaplowitz, Howard Dalimar, Art Hillhouse, Joe Fulks, Matt Guokas, and Eddie Gottlieb.

A crowd of 7,918 packed it on April 16 as the series opened. The Warriors rewarded them by never trailing. They took a 34-20 lead at intermission, then watched Fulks lace in 29 in the second half. He hit his first eight shots of the fourth period and added five free throws to finish with 37 on the night for what the Associated Press called "the greatest shooting exhibition ever seen on the arena floor."

Musi added 19 as the Warriors walked away, 84-71. The Stags, meanwhile, had taken an incredible 129 shots, hitting just 26 for 20 percent from the field.

Fulks cooled off considerably the next night for Game 2. Still, it didn't matter. Five Warriors finished in double figures, including Dallmar with 18 and Fleishman with 16. It was just enough to allow Philadelphia to nurse a lead that got no larger than eight points most of the game. The Stags even took a brief advantage at 69-68, but Hillhouse was the man in the fourth period. The big center scored seven of Philly's last 10 points, as the Warriors claimed a 2-0 edge in games with an 85-74 win.

The series then moved to Chicago, and the weather seemed good, so the Warriors decided to take a commercial airlines flight. As it turned out, the commercial carrier was hop-ing to set a record for the flight to Chicago, by covering the 800 or so miles in less than four hours. Thoughts of setting records soon ended after the plane was airborne.

"We were up in the air about five to 10 minutes when we smelled smoke," Senesky said. "I asked Dallmar if he had put a cigarette out on the floor. Then all this black smoke filled the plane."

The Warriors had to return to the airport and switch to another plane. They were a little shaken but resumed their trip to Chicago unscathed. After arriving safely, they did immediate damage the next night, April 19, as Fulks returned to form and led the Warriors with 26. With about four minutes left, Philly led by 10, but the Stags closed fast. The Warriors held on to win, 75-72, for a 3-0 lead.

They almost iced it the next game. Chicago held a 13-point lead heading into the fourth. Fulks had spent most of the third quarter on the bench with four fouls, but he returned in the fourth as Philly made a run. They might have pulled off the sweep if he hadn't fouled out with two minutes left and the Warriors down two. Fulks finished with 21, and Senesky led all scorers with 24. But Chicago's Zaslofsky and Don Carlson scored 20 and 18 points respectively, and the Stags kept their hopes alive with a 74-73 win.

The scene then shifted back to Market Street, where Fulks again showed his form in Game 5. He hit for 34, Musi for 13 and Senesky for 11. But it was Dallmar, the assist man, who salvaged a close game. With less than a minute left and the score tied at 80, he hit the big bucket.

"I know that I scored the winning basket, which gave me a total of two points for the game," Dallmar, who went on to a career coaching at Stanford, said when asked for his recollections. "It was from outside. I think it bounced about four times before it went in."

Fleishman added a late free throw, and the Warriors brought home a trophy for the new game's old town. Each of the players received a $2,000 bonus, quite a boost in those days, and a ring with a diamond chip in it.

Dallmar recalls being quite impressed with the money in a time when the members of the all-star team got nothing more than a tie clasp and an autographed photo of commissioner Maurice Podoloff.

As for Gottlieb, the victory meant a toast. After the game, he retreated to an office in the Arena for the Manhattan.

"He didn't even sip it," Senesky recalled with a laugh. "One gulp and it went down."

2.
The Minor Miracle
Baltimore's '48 Bullets

1948

Expansion teams must spend hundreds of millions of dollars to join the modern NBA. They select slick names, outfit their teams in snazzy uniforms, and dream up lovable mascots, all in hopes of creating a party atmosphere that will draw massive crowds to fancy arenas. Even though they do all this, they still lose. They lose a lot. And, more often than not, they lose for a long time.

Yet, things haven't always been so tough. For example, back in the good old days of pro basketball the 1947-48 Baltimore Bullets became "the expansion team that won the title," although they didn't exactly fit the pattern. The Bullets had actually operated for years as a successful "minor league" team before being invited to join the Basketball Association of America, the forerunner of the NBA, in 1947.

Four teams had folded after the BAA's first season, and the surviving seven clubs were desperate for competition. So the survivors pulled Baltimore into the fold to "round out" the divisions. At the time, the Bullets seemed like fresh enough meat. But they wound up embarrassing the other "established" teams, which speaks volumes about the BAA's level of competition in its second season.

In all fairness, it should be pointed out that the Bullets may have been a minor league

team prior to joining the BAA, but they were the ultimate minor league team. They had won four consecutive titles in the old American League during the 1940s. Bullets' owner Robert "Jake" Embry, who also owned a piece of the Baltimore Colts, and Bill Dyer, a local sports broadcaster who managed the team, aspired to build the Bullets into a big-league franchise. They had wanted to join the BAA in its first year, but the new league balked because of the Bullets' shoddy building, the old Coliseum on North Monroe Street in one of Baltimore's poorer neighborhoods.

"It was a real dump," Embry admitted. "You could only get 4,000 in if you stood them in all the corners."

Undaunted by their initial rejection, the Bullets decided to impress the BAA by upgrading the schedule and the roster. The American League played only 30 games or so each season, so Baltimore added an ambitious barnstorming schedule that upped their 1946-47 season to 70 games. From Sheboygan to Paterson, even out to the state of Washington, the Bullets hunted down any challenger. And they whipped most of 'em. They finished the season at 60-10. Their biggest accomplishment was a split with the National League's Chicago American Gears and rookie sensation George

Paul Hoffman, chasing a loose ball vs. New York, was a scrapper at guard for Baltimore.

Mikan, arguably the best team in pro basketball at the time.

If the Bullets could lay claim to any big-league pretensions, they did so because of player/coach Buddy Jeannette. The Bullets had lured him away from the National League's Fort Wayne Pistons, where Jeannette and Bobby McDermott had pushed that team to back-to-back league championships. Having Jeannette, an NBL star on their roster, also helped Baltimore impress the BAA. The new league needed all the stars it could get.

"That's when we really started getting good, when we got Buddy Jeannette in '46," Embry said.

When the BAA finally called in '47, the Bullets were ready and willing, even if the conditions weren't ideal. Their addition made for an awkward alignment. Philadelphia, Boston, Providence and New York played in the Eastern Divison. Washington and Baltimore joined Chicago and St. Louis in the "Western." The Bullets, though, were just happy to be in the circuit, tenuous as it was.

With the league's first-year losses, the BAA's surviving owners had decided to cut the schedule from 60 games down to 48. They had hoped it would save travel expenses, but all it did was cut revenues and create more problems. Because their payroll wasn't large, the Bullets weathered these tough times and actually made a little money, Embry recalled.

Still, their home court gave them the image of a hard-times outfit. The Celtics played in Boston Garden. The Knicks used either the 69th Regiment Armory (fresh with newly installed seats) or Madison Square Garden. The Stags had Chicago Stadium.

And the Bullets had their "Coliseum."

Its primary function was as a skating rink. Jeannette laughed when he recalled it. "I'll tell you how bad it was," he said. "When they quit using it as an arena, they made a garage out of it."

The Coliseum had a floor you couldn't forget. "It was never finished," recalled Paul "Bear" Hoffman, a scrapper who played guard for the Bullets. "It was raw wood. They would roller skate on it the night before we played on it." Floor burns took on a new meaning for Hoffman, who had played his college ball at Purdue in the big-time atmosphere of the Big Ten.

Yet the Coliseum wasn't a home without its comforts. "I don't think the place could hold 4,000 people," said Paul Seymour, who played part of the season with the Bullets. "It was a dingy, dirty place. But with the crowd being on top of you, it seemed like 50,000." If nothing else, the supporters appreciated the Bullets, Hoffman said. "We were close to our fans. We knew practically everybody there."

Only good basketball teams draw such affection, and the Bullets were worthy. At the core of the roster as the season opened were Jeannette, a 5'11" guard, and 6'6" forward Mike Bloom, a two-time MVP of the old American league. At 33, Bloom had a little mileage on him, but he still had his set shot and a nose for defense that made him a crowd favorite.

Basketball was a guard-dominated game in that era before the development of the fully athletic big man. So right before the season, the Bullets loaded up some extra ammunition by signing another veteran guard, Joseph Francis "Chick" Reiser, away from the NBL's Pistons. He was one of the premier set shooters in that age of two-handed, long-range gunners. Reiser boosted the Bullets' offense by averaging 11.5 points that season.

"He was probably the best two-handed set shooter that I ever played with, and he shot from way out," Hoffman said of Reiser. "He was a tough kid out of New York. He didn't play college ball. He came up right off the streets. He was a tough old pro."

Except for rookies Hoffman and Red Meinhold and 19-year-old Seymour, the other Bullets fit that same mold. "Most of those guys hadn't even been to college," Embry said. "Just tough old pros out of that barnstorming era."

On paper, Jeannette could qualify as a college boy. He had attended little Washington & Jefferson. But to watch him play, you'd never have known it. He carried that old pro image. Eight seasons of barnstorming had weathered him. At age 30, he was still a slashing driver, enough of a scorer to average 10.7 points the hard way. Going to the hoop in those days meant the risk of life and limb, but Jeannette was fearless. "Buddy wouldn't back down," Seymour said. "He would smile and take his lumps and get back up."

And he still had enough left to do the coaching. "Buddy was a good player/coach, which was a tough combination," Hoffman said. "But he got it done."

"He was loose," Seymour said. "He had to drink with the boys and still do the things you were supposed to do."

As with most teams of the era, Baltimore ran an offense that approached a three-guard

alignment, with the 6'2" Hoffman, a rookie, filling the third slot. An all Big Ten performer four years in a row at Purdue, he willed another 10 points per game into the basket. Plus he was always good for plenty of spirit and defense. "He was like a bull on the court," Embry said of Hoffman. "Nobody got in his way when he headed for the basket. He was a big strong boy, looked like a linebacker."

At center, Baltimore went with 6'8" Clarence "Kleggie" Hermsen, an NBL veteran who had played his college ball at Minnesota. The stat sheet shows that he led the team in scoring with 12 points a game, but Hermsen's real value was his key role in the Bullets' passing and cutting offense. They played the offense typical of the times, focused on the pivot, with a lot of cutting to the basket. "Chick and I set up the big guys," Jeannette explained. "We'd throw it in to them and then get it back heading to the basket. We used the pivot man quite a bit that way."

After an opening night loss, the Bullets started their season with a nine-game winning streak. But from there, the calendar turned into a roller coaster ride. The winning streak was followed by a five-game losing skid. The team righted itself, but progress was erratic.

Although the Bullets had a winning record, they fell to third in the Western standings. That didn't sit well with Jeannette, who was used to winning championships. Shortly, the local papers told of trade rumors that the Bullets had offered Mike Bloom to Chicago for Max Zaslofsky. Instead, they acquired 6'8" Grady Lewis from St. Louis to give them a little muscle in the frontcourt.

Still, the Bloom trade rumors persisted, and eight games later the

Buddy Jeannette handled the tough combination of being player/ coach for the Bullets.

team arranged a deal: Bloom went to the Celtics for their leading scorer, 6'8" Connie Simmons, who was only 22 years old. Good as it looked on paper, the trade brought an outburst from the Coliseum regulars.

"Bloom was a fan favorite," Hoffman said. "When Buddy traded him, it was like a revolt." Four decades later, Bloom still smarted from the trade. "It was a personality clash between Jeannette and myself," he said in a 1990 interview.

"We had a chance to get a bigger guy," Jeannette said of the trade. "Connie played a different type of ball. Mike was a good outside shooter, but he was no help on the boards."

Bloom said the Bullets could have won it with him anyway. But Jeannette and the others saw Simmons as the team's missing ingredient. "When Connie came with us it just started to take off. We got on a roll the last month," Hoffman said. "We got in the playoffs and it just kept going."

The Bullets went on to finish the season 28-20 in a three-way tie for second place in the four-team Western Division. The defending champion Philadelphia Warriors won the Eastern with a 27-21 record, worse than all four teams in the Western.

The Bullets faced the well-financed New York Knicks in the first round, a best-of-three series. Three decades later, Embry still chuckled at the recollection of the New York entourage coming down to Baltimore on a specially chartered train set up by Knicks owner Ned Irish. The Knicks represented the strength and wealth of the league. Eager to show off his team, Irish had even persuaded columnist Red Smith to come along with the crowd of sportswriters on the train. He seemed confident, Embry said, that the Knicks would advance. The teams split the first two games, and the Knicks even held an eight-point lead with two minutes left in the decisive Game 3, but the Bullets scored 10 quick points to win at the buzzer, claiming the series 2-1.

"Ned Irish never did forgive Baltimore from that point on," Embry said. "He had to ride back to New York on that train and listen to the writers giving him trouble about the loss."

Yet, just when it seemed like high times for the Bullets, they faced a defection by a major player. In the modern NBA, most guys would trade their shoe money for a chance to start on a team that had just gotten a playoff win. But things were a little different in 1948. Back then the business pro basketball looked very iffy. Right after the New York series, Paul Hoffman decided to quit the team immediately. He had been persuaded by his new wife that it was time to find a job that didn't keep him on the road so much. The news, of course, sent Bullets management into a panic. The team was preparing to leave for Chicago for the next series. Hoffman informed Embry by phone that he wouldn't be making the trip. Embry first expressed disbelief, then went through a round of entreaties. Hoffman, though, refused to budge. He was giving it up, he said.

Finally the owner decided to call in league commissioner Maurice Podoloff to speak with Hoffman. The commissioner played the heavy. Podoloff told Hoffman he would be blacklisted if he didn't join the team. The Bullets' flight to Chicago had already left, but Hoffman would still have time to make the game if he took the last available train, the commissioner said.

> # The 66-63 final was one of the most impressive comebacks in history, only nobody paid much attention to pro basketball in those days. The story merited a few paragraphs on the back page of the New York Times.

You better show up at the station, Podoloff warned emphatically before he hung up.

"Sure enough he showed up," Embry said. "That night in Chicago he played a great game. He scored 16 points, I think. But that was really touch and go. I was fit to be tied about that situation because we couldn't have won without him."

With Hoffman back in the fold, the Bullets promptly swept the Stags, 2-0, to earn a place in the league championship series against the defending champion Philadelphia Warriors, who had survived a grueling series with St. Louis. If anything, the Warriors had strengthened their lineup from the previous season with the addition of center Chuck Halbert (from Chicago), who joined a Philadelphia lineup that featured Joe Fulks, Howie Dallmar and George Senesky. "When you got Fulks and Halbert and Dallmar under the basket and Senesky outside, you got a pretty good ballclub," Hoffman said.

With the divisional title, the Warriors also had the home-court advantage. "We knew we had to win at least one game in Philadelphia," Jeannette said. That didn't happen in Game 1, won by the Warriors, 71-60, before a less-than-capacity crowd of 7,201.

Things turned worse for the Bullets in Game 2 when Philadelphia rolled out to a 41-20 halftime lead. "In those days, if you got behind that far, the game was over," Jeannette said. "There was no 24-second clock to help you comeback. But somehow we did. We took our time and made our shots and caught 'em. I don't know if we were so good or Philly was so bad."

Joe Fulks, the Philly gunner, helped matters by continuing to shoot and miss. And the Bullets helped themselves by driving to the hole for good shots. Newspaper accounts said the home crowd "sat stunned" when Baltimore took a late lead. First, the Bullets had cut the gap to 48-40 in the third quarter. Then the last period was all Baltimore. "We were up by one with four seconds to go, and I tipped in a missed free throw," Hoffman recalled.

The 66-63 final was one of the most impressive comebacks in sports history, only

Connie Simmons, (left) who came to Baltimore in a trade with Boston, led the Bullets into the playoffs. Fulks added rebounding skills to his shooting ability.

nobody paid much attention to pro basketball in those days. The story merited a few paragraphs on the back page of the New York Times.

Still, it was the momentum the Bullets were looking for. "That pepped us up," Jeannette said. "Then we made sure we won 'em at home."

For their part, the Warriors had simply run out of energy with drawn-out battles in the early rounds of the playoffs. "What killed us was the series with St. Louis," guard George Senesky said of Philadelphia. "We had gone back and forth on the train, and it was a 24-hour trip. We could have flown and saved some energy if the weather had been better."

Baltimore took the two games at its "Coliseum," by scores of 72-70 and 78-75. Back in Philadelphia, the Warriors prevailed in Game 5, 91-82, but they still had to return to Baltimore for Game 6 trailing 3-2 in games. There, on April 21, the "minor leaguers" took the title with an 88-72 blowout.

"I remember the last game with Philly," Jeannette said. "George Senesky hit me in the mouth and split my lip open. We were ahead and holding the ball. He took a swipe at the ball and hit me in the mouth. Right after the game I had to go get my mouth sewed up. A couple of stitches. Then we went out and had a few beers."

The evening was nothing fancy. Just another good time at the neighborhood deli where the team always gathered. "There wasn't much celebration," Jeannette said. "None of that crap of shooting champagne over everybody. That was just another game to us."

Each Bullet player earned $2,000 in playoff bonus money. And Gunther Brewery, one of the team's sponsors, gave player/coach Jeannette a TV set. The Brewery gave the rest of the team a pen and pencil set, a disparity that left the Bullets still hooting decades later.

There were no big endorsements and contract upgrades like the modern superstars got, Jeannette said. "But I wouldn't trade all of my experiences for any of their million-dollar contracts. We were a good team. We won in every league we played in."

Not bad for an "expansion" team.

3.
Broad Shoulders and a Narrow Lane

He led the Minneapolis Lakers to five NBA championships in six years, but George Mikan sure didn't look like a dominator. At least not with the wire rim glasses and the wavy hair. He looked more like a book worm.

Which he was (he would earn a law degree while playing pro ball). He was also an accomplished pianist. The lenses in his glasses were a quarter inch thick.

He once said trying to see without them was like driving a car without wipers during a rainstorm. His eyesight had been reason enough to get him cut from the basketball team at Catholic High in Joliet, Illinois. But Mikan was so tall (he had grown six inches while convalescing from a broken leg as an adolescent), people kept telling him he should play the game. Plus, a scholarship could pay for his education. He wanted to go to Notre Dame, but that was a costly proposition in 1942.

Instead, he enrolled in classes at DePaul, with the idea that he would catch the train down to Notre Dame over Christmas break and try out for the team. The war was on, and just about every college coach was looking for athletes. Mikan was too tall and too blind to go into the service. So he figured that Notre Dame coach George Keogan might be interested.

"He's too awkward, and he wears glasses," Keogan supposedly said after watching Big George work out.

"Keogan told me to return to DePaul, that I'd make a better scholar than a basketball player," Mikan recalled.

He took that advice, and went back to DePaul and resumed classes. But that spring he caught the eye of Ray Meyer, the school's new basketball coach.

"There's my future," Meyer said to himself.

Indeed, time would show that the big, unpolished prospect was the future of pro basketball, too.

Mikan underwent a miraculous development at DePaul, seemingly blossoming overnight into the premier player in college basketball, the big-time gate attraction during World War II. Remarkably, he developed agility while growing from 6'8" to 6'10". By the 1944-45 season, Mikan's junior year, he and Oklahoma A&M's Bob Kurland had become prototypes for what future generations would come to know as a "force." But when Mikan entered college in 1942, most coaches had little regard for tall players. Basketball was still the domain of the little man. Considered too awkward for the game, the big guys were called "goons."

**George Mikan —
an unlikely looking
star.**

Both Mikan and Kurland soon proved that they weren't goons. "George and I opened the door to the idea that the big man could play the game," Kurland said. "which in our day was, by eastern standards, played by guys 5'10", 5'11", who were quick, took the set shot, and so forth. We opened the door for what the game is to-day."

Mikan and DePaul won the 1945 National Invitational Tournament, in those days the college game's prized trophy. In one NIT game, Mikan scored 53 points, an incredible sum for the slow pace of 1940s basketball, and he twice won the NCAA scoring crown. All of this from a guy who hadn't been able to make the Notre Dame varsity three years earlier.

"He was an awkward kid at first," Ray Meyer once explained, "but he just kept improving. I guided him, but he had talent, and he just kept getting better and better. The superstars are like that. They have something inside."

Mikan had something outside, too: wide shoulders and a pair of bruising elbows. But he wasn't just a brute. Meyer, then a young, ambitious coach, sensed that he could develop Mikan. He hired a co-ed to give the center dancing lessons to improve his agility, and he set up drills with Mikan guarding a 5'5" teammate one-on-one, to teach Mikan to move his feet defensively. Jumping rope and shadowboxing were also part of the regimen, as was alternately playing catch with a tennis ball and a medicine ball. Then Meyer made him work on his shooting and faking. First 250 right-handed hooks each day. Then 250 left-handed. That grueling repetition would

become a staple of basketball how-to manuals as "The Mikan Drill." Soon Meyer's awkward protégé had developed a simple but punishing style around the basket, based on a solid drop step.

"George didn't have a lot of moves," explained Hall of Famer Jim Pollard, who teamed with Mikan to make the Minneapolis Lakers a dynasty. "He never fooled you very often. Some of those old centers gave great fakes. Not George."

Mikan would get position down low, drop his inside foot back, and pivot toward the hoop. As he did, he'd lead his motion with his inside elbow. "He didn't get called for the offensive foul because he had both hands on the ball," Pollard said. "He'd take it up in the air with both hands. If he took a hand off the ball and threw the elbow, he was going to get called for the foul. But George seldom did that. He was smart."

The foul lane was only six feet wide in those days, which allowed him to set up and score. "If you let Mikan get position, it was over," said Mike Bloom, a defensive specialist in the 1940s. "He would back in to the basket and go to work with those elbows."

"When he got you in that pivot, you couldn't do anything about it," agrees Horace "Bones" McKinney, who played against Mikan.

"Mikan was great with those elbows," said Paul Seymour, who played for the Syracuse Nationals. "He used to kill our centers. Used to knock 'em down, draw the foul, them help 'em up and pat 'em on the fanny."

The Chicago American Gears signed Mikan to an unprecedented five-year, $62,000-contract in the spring of 1946 after he had completed his college eligibility. He went right to work for them, even playing in the old Chicago Herald American tournament that spring, where he was named the MVP. But that fall Mikan claimed that the cash-thin Gears were cutting his paychecks short. In protest, he held out for 19 of the 44 regular-season games. Finally, he and the team worked out their differences in time for him to lead the Gears to the National League championship that spring of 1947.

His size and dominance had made Mikan an overnight sensation, and that gave American Gears owner Maurice White ideas. Why not start a new league just to showcase the big guy?

Needless to say, if White didn't have enough cash to run one club, he certainly didn't have enough to float a 24-team league. Within weeks of the opening the American Professional Basketball Leauge that fall of 1947, both the Gears and the league folded, leaving White with $600,000 in losses, a gigantic sum in that era.

It was the luck of the newly organized Lakers (they were formed from the old Detroit Gems franchise in the National League) to catch Big George in the National League dispersal draft.

Mikan joined the Lakers for their fifth game of the 1947-48 season, at Sheboygan. "I had never seen George," Jim Pollard recalled. "I didn't know what he was like at all. He walked into that locker room at Sheboygan, and I thought that was the biggest-looking dumb character that I'd ever seen for a guy that was barely 23 years old. He had these great big thick glasses, and he had this homburg hat on. I said to myself, 'What the hell's a guy 23-years-old doing wearing a homburg and a great big storm overcoat?'

"He walked in and said, 'Hi, fellas: I'm your new center.' I jumped up and said, 'Hi, George; my name's Jim.'

"When we got out on the floor [for our first game together], we threw him the ball over and over and said, 'Show us what you can do.' I played with that big horse for every game for seven years, and that's the only time I ever heard him say, 'Please don't throw me the ball; they're killing me.' The rest of us just threw him the ball and stood there. They ganged up on him and kicked the hell out of George that first night."

The Lakers lost their first five games with Mikan, making it immediately obvious that before they could rush off to harvest championships, they had to learn to play together. It wasn't easy, because Mikan's and Pollard's individual styles were so different. A gifted 6'6" player out of Stanford and California's AAU leagues, Pollard was a slashing driver, but Mikan clogged the middle, leaving his teammate little room to drive. "Pollard could really leap. He got hurt playing with Mikan," said Paul Seymour of the Syracuse Nationals.

"George was great if he stayed on his side of the lane," Pollard said. "But a lot of times, as soon as I got the ball on the wing, he would come over to my side of the lane. I would tell him, 'Stay over there a minute.' But that wasn't his style of play. When we first started playing together, I couldn't very well go to the middle because he was there.

"When I started to drive, he'd go to the basket. So he'd bring his man, 6'8", 6'10", down to the basket where they'd kick the hell out of me. At that time, George didn't know what I could do. He'd go to the basket, and I'd flip the ball to him and he'd miss it. I kept telling him, 'You better get your hands up because nine out of ten passes are going to hit you right in the face.' After a while, he learned to give me that one count, to give me that step and give me room to drive, and then he could come in. If his man switched off on me, I'd flip him the ball. It made it easier for George, too. But we had to learn that. It took us awhile."

From that awkward chemistry, Mikan and Pollard built a deadly pick-and-roll routine, which Lakers coach John Kundla called the J&G (Jim and George) play. Needless to say, it was the coach's favorite because most opponents couldn't stop it.

"It was a simple little play," Kundla said proudly. "But it was very successful."

The Lakers ran it again and again that season on their way to a league-best 43-17 record. In the playoffs, they moved aside Oshkosh, Tri-Cities, and Rochester to claim the National League championship.

"After we won, we had to hustle to catch a train out of Rochester," Pollard recalled. "On the way out, we picked up a couple of six-packs. We put 'em in the stainless steel-sink in the men's room on the train. Then we sat there and celebrated our first championship with the train rattling all around and the wheels rolling underneath."

In those days, the Lakers did just about all their traveling by train except when management chartered an occasional DC-3. With Minneapolis so far west of the other franchises, the scheduling was brutal. They rode all night to Chicago, then got off the train and grabbed a cab across the city to yet another station, where they caught the 8:00 a.m. train to Minneapolis. The league champions arrived home the next afternoon at 2:30, almost too tired to celebrate with the small group of family and friends waiting at the station.

Still, it was hard not to be elated. Mikan and Pollard had finally found a chemistry that worked.

1949

Just before the 1948-49 season, Minneapolis and three of the National League's best teams — Fort Wayne, Rochester, and Indianapolis — crossed over and joined the new league, the BAA, a move that would lead to the formation of the NBA. But it also brought howls of protest from the remaining National owners, who claimed the Lakers and other teams had sold out to the competing league. The National League gets no modern recognition, but it was far better than the BAA, said Syracuse Nationals owner Danny Biasone, who was often fond of pointing out that after the leagues merged, National teams won the first seven NBA championships.

The BAA, though, had the big money and the big markets, and it was able to force the National League into a merger.

By 1948, the BAA had franchises based in Boston, New York, Washington, Chicago, Baltimore, Philadelphia, and St. Louis. The BAA's best arenas, Boston Garden, Madison Square Garden, and Chicago Stadium, were the sports palaces of that era. The National League, on the other hand, was a decade older and had many of the name players. But its teams were located in smaller markets — Fort

Wayne, Syracuse, Rochester, Dayton and Oshkosh — with small, often dingy buildings. That situation changed overnight with the move of the four National teams, which took up residence in the BAA's Western Division with Chicago and St. Louis. The result was a nicely balanced 12-team league.

Pollard recalled how excited the Lakers were at finally getting to play in the big cities and arenas, particularly New York and Madison Square Garden. The new league had a big-time feel to it, and the Lakers quickly showed they belonged. The Rochester Royals won the Western Division regular-season crown with a 45-15 record, while Mikan and the Lakers finished just one game back at 44-16. The best Eastern Division team, the Washington Capitols (coached by Red Auerbach), finished 38-22.

Minneapolis closed the schedule with Mikan, the league's leading scorer, ringing up 48 and 51 points against New York, 53 against Baltimore, and 46 against Rochester,

"Bones" McKinney was one of many opponents who found it impossible to stop Mikan.

incredible totals in that era of 40-minute games. When it came to winning, the big, affable Mikan could be incredibly tough and just a little mean, Pollard recalled. "Toward the end of a ball game, if we were ahead by 20, George would come over to the bench and say, 'Let's beat 'em good. Let's kick the hell out of 'em so they don't want to play us ever again.' "

Despite the stats and appearances, the Lakers were far from a one-man team. First of all, they had Jim Pollard, the star from Stanford who in his second pro season averaged 14.8 points. Pollard was a multi-faceted player, an extraordinary leaper (although he was listed at 6'3 1/2" he was closer to 6'6") who could execute acrobatic dunks (mostly in practice; dunking in games was thought to be ungentlemanly in the 1940s).

"We used to know when Pollard had been in the building," Bones McKinney of the Washington Capitols recalled, "because the tops of the backboards would be clean where he raked them." Pollard was fast, too, McKinney said, "You couldn't press him either. He was too good moving with the ball. He'd get by you in a cat lick."

To go with Pollard and Mikan, there was 6'5" Arnie Ferrin, a 23-year-old rookie who had been named the most outstanding player in the 1944 NCAA tournament while leading the University of Utah to the national championship. Ferrin averaged 7.3 points in his first pro season. The other offensive threats were Herm Schaeffer, a veteran pro who averaged 10.4 points per game, and Don Carlson, a University of Minnesota product who scored at a 9.3 clip.

With this cast, Minneapolis powered into the 1949 playoffs. And now that it had two six-

> **G**eorge gloried in that 'I am number one' feeling. That's why he was so successful. He wanted that spot, wanted to be number one, wanted you to be a little bit fearful of him on the court.

team divisions, the NBA finally had an equitable playoff system that allowed the first place teams in each division to play the fourth, and the second-place teams to play the third. It probably didn't matter. The Lakers could have overwhelmed whoever happened into their path. They swept both Chicago and Rochester 2-0 on their way to a meeting with Auerbach's Capitols in the Finals. The Caps had a deep, talented team that still featured Bob Feerick, Bones McKinney, John Norlander and Fred Scolari. To them, Auerbach had added 6'8" Kleggy Hermsen, who had helped Baltimore to the title the previous year.

Washington, however, was undermanned in the playoffs, with Feerick, a double-figure scorer, knocked out of action by a knee injury. And Scolari, who had gotten banged up against New York in the Eastern Division Finals, was just returning. Still, the Caps made it a battle April 4 when the series opened at the Minneapolis Auditorium. Mikan powered around the basket for 42 points, but with a little more than a minute to go, the score was tied at 84. Then Carlson hit a pair of late free throws, which was enough to help boost the Lakers to an 88-84 win.

In Game 2 on April 6, Auerbach shifted his defense to deny Mikan the ball. That strategy worked on the big center, who scored only 10 points while taking nine shots from the field. But the rest of the Lakers got untracked — with Carlson and Schaeffer scoring 16 and 13 points — as Minneapolis took a 2-0 lead with a 76-62 win.

The series then moved to Washington's Uline Arena (with a seating capacity of about 4,000) on April 8 for Game 3, where Mikan again dominated, scoring 35 points and

Former Stanford star Jim Pollard was a multifaceted player.

leading the Lakers to a 94-74 win and a 3-0 lead. He scored another 27 points in Game 4, but Washington won 83-71, after Mikan broke his wrist.

"Kleggy Hermsen hit me up in the air while I was on a fast break," Mikan recalled. "I went up at the free-throw line and got hit by Kleggy and knocked into the first row of seats. I got hit from behind. It was a tackle."

Mikan said he still remembers falling back onto the court. "Red told them to drag me off the court and get the game going," he recalled with a laugh. "Hermsen made sure he fouled out quick after that. There's such a thing as retribution in sport. You didn't necessarily have to get back at someone because your teammates would."

Hermsen, a Minneapolis native, feared that if the series returned to Minnesota, the hometown crowd would want to lynch him for being involved in Mikan's injury.

"He was scared to death," McKinney recalled with a laugh.

But Mikan appeared in a cast two nights later for Game 5 in Washington. "That cast was hard as a brick; it fit right in with his elbows," McKinney recalled. "It would kill you. And it didn't bother his shooting a bit."

Mikan distinctly recalled that the Caps immediately went after his bad arm by attempting to hack the injured wrist. Even with the cast, Mikan scored 22 in Game 5, but Washington pulled to 3-2 with a 74-66 win. The Capitols, however, weren't ready to start crowing. They had to head back to Minnesota for Game 6. Because of scheduling conflicts with the annual sportsman's show, the game had to be shifted from Minneapolis to St. Paul. Playing in their twin city, the Lakers still packed in a crowd and won the championship

handily, 77-56. Mikan had scored 303 points in 10 playoff games, an unprecedented performance.

"George gloried in that 'I am number one' feeling," Pollard said. "That's why he was so successful. He wanted that spot, wanted to be number one, wanted you to be a little bit fearful of him on the court."

Mikan would get his wish time and again over the coming seasons. He would stay on top, and opponents would be quite fearful of him and his powerful drop step and leading elbow. His intensity would burn bright for five more seasons, all of them immensely fun for the Lakers. But then, almost as quickly as it had been put together, the team would fall apart. And in the aftermath the participants would have plenty of time to wonder why.

Sweet as it was, success bred its own sort of contempt for the Minneapolis Lakers. From time to time, problems arose between Pollard and Mikan, then-forward Vern Mikkelsen said. Both were great athletes, yet Mikan did most of the scoring and got most of the recognition. The little problems could have been big ones, "but Kundla handled that situation just beautifully," Mikkelsen recalled. "Our offense was built around George, and it would have been stupid not to use him."

One night the marquee outside Madison Square Garden read: "Tonite: Geo. Mikan vs. the Knicks." More than anything, that incident summed up his stature in those early years of the game. He was the league's draw, just as he had been for college basketball. "Accolades were something that I had no control over," Mikan said.

The real rub, of course, was Pollard. He was a masterful player, a former leading scorer in the AAU leagues, and he admitted that the attention given to Mikan bothered him. "The thing about Mikan, everything revolved around him, and he got too much publicity and he tried to do too much himself because of it," Pollard said. "But he was a hell of a competitor. We'd get through a game and his question was,

'Did we win?' That was the idea of the whole game. That made us all on George's side, because he was a winner.

"I used to get on George's case all the time. George and I always argued. But when we stepped on the floor, George and I always played to win, the hell with who got the points."

The biggest irritation was Mikan's refusal to pass the ball when he was double-teamed, Pollard said. "It wasn't that he was selfish. It was more a matter of pride." During one season, Mikan suddenly began passing out of the double teams, and the Lakers went on an eight-game winning streak, with everybody scoring in double figures. "Then we went to New York, and George always wanted to put the big show on in New York," Pollard said. "George had 38 or 39 points that night, and no one else was in double figures. We lost, and afterward we went drinking with friends. Mikan was at one end of the bar drinking. I told the guy I was drinking with to go up there and ask Mikan how we could have an eight-game winning streak with everybody happy

and then come here and lose. My friend went over and asked him that, and then George roared, 'I'm gonna kill that goddamn Pollard.' 'You'll never catch me, George,' I yelled back at him. That was our way of picking on George. He was the bellwether of our club, and we all picked on him."

Pollard admitted the friction between the stars was "something that could have torn the team apart. But Kundla kept a very even keel, and he didn't pick on anybody. He seldom made a big deal out of offensive mistakes. But boy, would he get upset about defense."

"Kundla gets no recognition, and he should be in the Hall of Fame," Mikan agreed. "He did a great job of molding the team, taking care of the players' idiosyncrasies."

Keeping the Lakers' abundant talent controlled and focused took its toll on Kundla, a shy, quiet man who by every January was gulping milk to combat the ulcers left over from his duty on a navy landing craft in the Pacific during the war. It wasn't that he couldn't get angry. He just didn't very often. "He had a very, very slow fuse, but when it

Slater Martin (top) joined Minneapolis for the 1949-50 season, as Mikan (left) and the Lakers rolled on.

finally erupted, then look out," Mikkelsen said.

Kundla was successful both because of and despite of his youth. His age allowed him to joke with his players, to engage in the silly fun experienced by adults who are paid to play games. Four decades later, the Lakers still couldn't agree on who rubbed the Limburger cheese in whose hat. Mikkelsen swore that reserves Tony Jaros and Bud Grant (he was a Laker reserve for a couple of seasons before going on to coach the NFL's Minnesota Vikings) ruined several of Kundla's hats. Kundla, though, was sure that he was the one who pulled the cheese trick on somebody else.

Kundla also recalled the time his players stuffed pornography in his luggage, which his wife found later.

Then there was the infamous train ride early one very cold morning to a game against the Fort Wayne Pistons. Because of the extreme cold, the Lakers' train experienced several delays, and it soon became apparent they weren't going to make the game on time. At Milwaukee, a messenger boarded the train with a telegram from Pistons owner Fred Zollner, telling the Lakers that he would send the Pistons' team plane for them.

"They were the envy of the league because they flew to all the games," Vern Mikkelsen said of the Pistons.

The Lakers got off the train, but no one realized that Kundla had gone to the dining car to drink milk for his ulcer. As the train pulled out of the station, the players standing on the platform saw the coach looking plaintively out a window two cars back. Kundla didn't see his players and didn't know of the developments until a conductor later informed him.

As planned, the team caught the plane and made the game at North Side High School in Fort Wayne, where the Pistons played their home games. The Lakers, in fact, had a lead at intermission and had returned to the floor just before the start of the second half when

**The Syracuse Nationals featured 6'8"
forward Dolph Schayes from NYU.**

they heard a murmur from the crowd.

Kundla had walked in the gym door wearing his storm coat and toting his suitcase. "He walked in pretty sheepishly," Mikkelsen recalled. "At the time we were winning, but we wound up losing the game. We gave John plenty of trouble on that."

The Lakers were the kind of team that could laugh about losses, because there weren't that many. When tight situations arose, they always seemed to have an answer. "George Mikan had a tremendous, total confidence that he could get the job done," Mikkelsen said. "He would make believers out of us. Late in close games he always wanted the ball. The tremendous competitor that he was, he would say, 'Let me have the ball. I'll get it done.' More often than not, he did."

II.
Quiet Times, Quiet Changes

As American decades go, the 1950s retain a whitebread image — wholesome but just a bit bland. It was a time of duck tails and drive-ins and bobby socks. Cars grew fins, radio was still king, and everybody liked Ike. The mood was sleepy and easygoing. Life seemed to stand still.

At least it did if you believed the image.

In reality, the 1950s was decade of sweeping changes. Only most of them occurred quietly, without the noise and hype and excess that accompanied events in the 60s. Across the spectrum, American society jazzed itself up. Rock 'n' roll was born from a parentage of rhythm and blues, country and western, and the big band sound. Frank Sinatra gave way to Elvis. And the big screen got steamier with Marilyn Monroe's heavy-breathing presence. Americans barely knew it, but they were already moving to a new beat.

So was pro basketball.

The game was experiencing a quiet, understated revolution. Big things happened, but that didn't necessarily mean headlines.

Especially if the subject was integration.

The fact had long been established that blacks had much to offer to basketball. First, there had been the famed New York Rens (named after the Renaissance Casino in Harlem), the great all-black barnstorming team that since the 1920s had competed with the all-white barnstorming teams, the New York Celtics and the Philadelphia SPHAs.

Following on the Rens' heels came the Harlem Globetrotters, a concoction of ballhandling wizardry and showmanship that made fun out of competition. Having witnessed these exhibitions, the NBA owners and coaches of the 1950s knew that black athletes could play. But as businessmen, the owners had concerns about how black players would be received by the public and by white teammates. It helped, of course, that Jackie Robinson had integrated major league baseball in 1947 and that in the previous decades there had been some limited integration of high school and college teams, mostly in northern and western states. It also helped that the Rochester Royals had added Dolly King to their roster in 1946-47, thus integrating the old NBL.

But America was still blatantly and deeply segregated in 1950, and the NBA still had no black players. That changed shortly after the league draft opened that spring in a Chicago hotel room. During the second-round picks, Walter Brown, the owner of the Boston Celtics, stood and announced the selection of Charles Cooper of Duquesne.

The room grew still.

Then, according to several accounts, another owner asked, "Walter, don't you know he's a colored boy?"

"I don't give a damn if he's striped, plaid, or polka dot," Brown supposedly retorted. "Boston takes Charles Cooper of Duquesne!"

Toward the bottom round of that same draft, the Washington Capitols quietly took Earl Lloyd of West Virginia State, a second black player.

Brown's comment would help to dash the old attitudes concerning black players, although he and Celtics coach Red Auerbach weren't making the move out of a great urge to cure social ills. They simply sought the best competitive edge they could get by getting the best players. Winning was a bottom line that nearly everyone understood, and it answered its own questions about competence.

Earlier that same year, Auerbach had heard that the Globetrotters' big man, Nat "Sweetwater" Clifton, was unhappy with team owner Abe Saperstein. Auerbach sought out Clifton in Pennsylvania and signed him to a Celtics contract. But then the league got involved, not because of the color issue, but because of business. The team owners, several of whom also owned arenas, did not want to anger the Globetrotters, who were good attractions for their buildings, according to Auerbach. "I had him signed and the league wouldn't accept it." he said later.

Brown, as a diplomat and a partner of the other owners, told Auerbach to back off. The coach reluctantly agreed.

Less than two months later, the Knicks signed Clifton to a contract. Knicks owner Ned Irish was able to do so because he worked out compensation to the Globetrotters. He arranged for their appearances in Madison Square Garden.

With the introduction of these three players, a gradual process of integration occurred, with an average of one or two black players on each roster. Some teams remained all white. Most importantly, integration opened the door in 1956 for a truly revolutionary player, Boston's Bill Russell. His presence gave owners and managers an inkling of the vast contributions black players could make to professional basketball. In time, they would bring a style, a savvy and an audience that would help define the modern game.

Pro basketball's development also got an assist from another unlikely source, a short little man named Danny Biasone, who owned the Syracuse Nationals. He would champion the 24-second shot clock, virtually insisting on it as a means of changing the game's stalling, fouling, and low-scoring nature — a style of play that fans of the game were becoming increasingly frustrated with.

Beyond the shot clock, the 50s brought other developments to the game. The foul lane was widened from six to twelve feet to take away some of the big man's advantage inside.

Just as important, says Paul Seymour, was the emergence of the jump shooter. First there was "Jumpin'" Joe Fulks in Philadelphia, who shocked the league by scoring 61 points in a game in 1949. His jump-and-pop example was followed by another Warrior, Paul Arizin. Then came Hal Greer in Syracuse and Sam Jones in Boston. Before long, the entire league was leaping.

Seymour, who both played and coached in the NBA, contended that a player traveled when he took a jump shot, his leap adding the extra, illegal step. But officials allowed it anyway, and that opened the door for all that followed. Dunks and treys and a variety of spectacular moves in a game that seemed to rush ever onward and upward.

Charles Cooper became the first black drafted into the NBA.

4.
Time On Your Side

There was no shotclock in pro basketball in the late 1940s, which meant the game was interminably slow, particularly if the Minneapolis Lakers were involved. George Mikan or Jim Pollard would control a defensive rebound, then the league champions would begin their methodical assault on the opponent's goal. At the offensive end, the Lakers would hold the ball and wait for Mikan to lumber upcourt and take position down near the basket. Only then would they go to work. Even at this pace Mikan's spectacles would often fog up, and play would be stopped while he toweled off and wiped the lens dry. After he had dominated the league for a couple of years, opponents grew impatient with these pauses to refresh. They complained that if Big George wanted to wipe his glasses, the Lakers should call a timeout.

That was only fair, the league decided.

So John Kundla shifted his timeout strategies to make sure his center had a clean windshield. He also kept a spare set of Mikan's specs in his coat pocket. No one would accuse the young Laker coach of not knowing who punched his meal ticket. The entire offense was built around Mikan, and in two years of competition no one had been able to stop him when the game really mattered.

Coach John Kundla of the Lakers is usually accorded nothing more than a footnote in basketball history.

But, as strong as the Lakers seemed after winning two straight championships, they were a machine with a definite need for replacement parts in the spring of 1949. Herm Schaeffer was a smart ballhandler and a good passer, but his age beginning to show. And even in his youth, he was pudgy and slow. In the frontcourt, Don "Swede" Carlson was the last of pro basketball's six-foot forwards. He had been crafty and tough enough to average about eight points a game over three seasons in Minneapolis. Of playing with Mikan, Carlson once said, "I used to like to pass him the ball, cut around him and then listen to the sound the guy guarding me made when he ran into George." But the game was changing rapidly in 1950. The players were getting larger.

"If he stood up straight, he was 6'1"," Pollard said of Carlson. "As the game got bigger, they moved him out."

George Mikan was slowed by a hairline fracture of his ankle near the end of the regular season.

Knowing that the team needed to upgrade, Max Winter and Sid Hartman found three good picks in the 1949 draft. The top prizes were thought to be 6'7" forward Vern Mikkelsen, a power player out of Minnesota's little Hamline College, and Bob "Tiger" Harrison, a guard from the University of Michigan.

Almost as an afterthought, the Lakers drafted 5'9" guard Slater "Dugie" Martin out of the University of Texas. Martin had been an All-American in the high-speed offense run by Texas, but few thought he was big enough to survive in the pro game. His best offer had come from the Phillips 66ers, one of the top AAU teams of the era, but the 66ers wanted Martin to hold down an office job in addition to his playing duties. Martin would later explain that he just couldn't stomach the idea of sitting behind a desk.

So he accepted a low-grade, $3,500 offer from the Lakers, where his value was held suspect by Kundla, who had little say in the team's personnel moves. Martin had scored easily in the up-tempo offense he played in college, but how would this slightly built Texan fit into the Lakers' plodding floor game? At first the answer was, not very well at all. Kundla gave Martin scant playing time, and when he did play, the little guard seemed overwhelmed. Muscular Frankie Brian of the Anderson Duffy Packers scored 40 points against him in an early game, a severe blow because Martin's long suit was supposed to be his defense. On offense, he was caught in a tug-of-war between the coach and the star. Kundla inserted him into a game at St. Louis

with the idea that he would pass the ball to Mikan, then cut to the hoop. But the center angrily told the rookie guard not to cut because he was clogging the middle. Martin was intimidated by Mikan and kept quiet when Kundla called him to the bench for not following instructions.

"Kundla didn't use me much until our next trip to St. Louis when Herm Schaeffer was hurt," Martin recalled. "Schaeffer, a nice fellow, came up to me in the locker room before the game. 'Don't be afraid to take your shots,' he said. 'You're letting the big guy cramp your style.' I had one of those lucky nights where everything I threw up went in. I hit eight straight shots from the floor. They came just in time to save my job."

Before long, the veteran Schaeffer had stepped aside and was teaching the rookie how to run the team. Martin soon showed that his quickness gave the Lakers another weapon. And his coach came to love the little guard's style. Both Martin and Kundla had served in the navy in the Pacific during the war. Both thought like coaches, and their mutual understanding grew from there. Martin, the high-scoring college player, became a low-scoring, ball-distributing pro guard, running the Lakers' lumbering offense. Later, after helping the Lakers to four championships, Martin would move on to the St. Louis Hawks and direct them to yet another title, accomplishments that would land him in the Hall of Fame.

"He wanted to win," Kundla said of Martin. "He didn't care who made the points."

With Martin in the lineup, Kundla kept the offense moving at a pace that matched Mikan's abilities, but this retooled group could also get up and move, with Martin running the break and Pollard on the wing. "If the fast break was there, they'd go on you," said Paul Seymour of the Syracuse Nationals. "But most of the time they waited for Mikan to come down the floor and then set things up."

"We didn't fastbreak that much," Pollard said, "because Mikan and Mikkelsen were not that quick, and you didn't want either one of them to dribble. But Martin always wanted to go. He was always looking for the fastbreak."

The rookie adjustment for Mikkelsen, the son of a Lutheran minister, was just as difficult as Martin's, and just as important to the team's development. At 6'7", 235 pounds, he had played center in high school and college, but he was forced to shift to forward in the pros, which meant that he played facing the basket for the first time in his career. The new position suited his skills. He could leap and knew how to get rebounding position. In adjusting, he developed a bit of an outside shot, although he made his living on the offensive glass.

"I didn't see the ball much," Mikkelsen said of his first few years in the league. "I didn't have to. Mikan and Pollard did most of the scoring. When they had an off night, I cleaned up on the boards."

Before the 1950 season was over these rookies would help make the Lakers into a blueprint for modern teams. Building around the 245-pound Mikan, the dominant center, and Pollard, the quick, acrobatic small forward, the Lakers transformed Mikkelsen into the original 'power' forward. And Slater Martin filled the role of a ballhandler, or what could come to be known as a 'point guard.' The 6'4" Harrison, meanwhile, found a place in the lineup as the off guard.

"We were the first team to have those types of players filling the roles," Pollard said, "and we became the model for all the modern teams that came after us."

There is a lingering perception today that the old Lakers couldn't play the modern game. Wrong, says Marty Blake, the former Hawks general manager who today serves as the NBA's director of scouting. "The Lakers were a great team. Mikan and Mikkelsen and Pollard and Martin — they could have played today. Mikkelsen would be making $2 million a year, for God sakes. These people today don't realize how good they were."

The Lakers were also the first fully athletic team capable of dunking at will, but the ethic of that era didn't allow for such overtly macho statements. "All of us could dunk except Slater Martin," Mikkelsen said. "But we weren't allowed to much, because Kundla wouldn't let us. It was frowned on as hotdogging."

> **A**ll of us could dunk except Slater Martin, but we weren't allowed to much because Kundla wouln't let us. It was frowned on as hotdogging.
>
> — Vern Mikkelsen

Pollard recalled getting a steal once and taking the ball in for a jam only to have it hit the back of the rim and sail out to half court, leaving him to endure an unusually vociferous ragging from Kundla during the timeout.

"They could all dunk," Kundla agreed. "But usually they just shot the ball. In practice they did a lot of dunking. But otherwise we kept away from that. You didn't want to embarrass another team or player. Wilt Chamberlain was the one who really started the dunking in games in the late '50s."

As if their talent wasn't enough, the Lakers also got a boost on their home floor, the Minneapolis Auditorium, where the court was narrow by a few feet. "That made them much more effective," said Dolph Schayes of the Syracuse Nationals. "We always had a difficult time with them. If you double-teamed George, then Mikkelsen would clean up. And Pollard was able to drive, and he was a great passer."

"They used to say that when Mikan, Mikkelsen and Pollard stretched their arms across that narrow court, nobody could get through," Syracuse coach Al Cervi said.

Paul Seymour laughed at the memory of trying to play against the Lakers' frontcourt.

Bob Davies (top and on the floor trying to stop a New York drive in the Finals) popularized the behind-the-back dribble.

"Those three big bastards made every court look narrow," he said. "Mikkelsen was a brute."

Sid Hartman smiled at the recollection. "Our front line played volleyball with an awful lot of teams," he said.

Nothing proved that more than the 1950 season, as the six surviving teams of the National League — Syracuse, the Anderson Duffy Packers, Tri-Cities Blackhawks, Denver Nuggets, Sheboygan Redskins and the Waterloo Hawks — merged with the BAA to form the National Basketball Association, a 17-team league aligned in three cumbersome divisions. Syracuse was placed in the Eastern Division but played most of its games against teams in the new Western Division, which was made up of the recently added National teams and the new Indianapolis Olympians.

The old Western Division, meanwhile, became the Central, where Minneapolis and the Rochester Royals battled to a tie with 51-17 records. The two teams had joined the BAA together and were placed in the Western Division, a move that kept them from meeting

in the title game, although they were clearly the league's best. Both had 33-1 home records, but with Mikan scoring 35 the Lakers won the tiebreaker game at Rochester, 78-76, to claim the divisional title. From there, the Lakers swept both Fort Wayne and Anderson 2-0 to meet Syracuse for the championship.

In addition to Seymour, the Nationals featured 6'7" Dolph Schayes out of NYU, Bill "Bullet" Gabor from Syracuse University and player/coach Al Cervi.

To say the least, Mikan presented problems for the Nationals. The two teams had battled during the regular season. Seymour laughingly recalled being infuriated during one game that spring because of an encounter with big George's elbows. "I had a goose egg on my head, I was on my ass on the floor, and the ref was pointing at me," said the 6'2", 180-pound Seymour. "I chased George right up into the stands. I don't know what I would have done if I had caught him."

For the Finals, the Nationals had the home-court advantage, but they faced the roughhouse challenge of Mikan. The series opened at State Fair Coliseum, just outside Syracuse, where the home boys had a 34-1 record. Mikan was his usual self, powering inside for 37 points, but the Nationals answered each time. In the closing minute, Syracuse had the lead, 66-64, but Bud Grant, a Minneapolis sub who would go on to fame as coach of the NFL's Minnesota Vikings, hit a hook shot to tie it.

Syracuse got the ball back but couldn't get an open shot. With time running out, Cervi took a pass from Alex Hannum and headed for the basket.

"Cervi decided to win it himself," Seymour said. "He went inside and threw up an underhand shot. Mikan just tapped it away."

"I was fouled and didn't get the call," Cervi said.

Minneapolis controlled the ball and rushed upcourt for a final shot, where "Tiger" Harrison, the rookie out of Michigan, nailed a 40-footer at the buzzer to give the Lakers a 1-0 lead in the series. "He went wild, he jumped up and down," coach John Kundla said of Harrison, who had played high school ball with Seymour.

But in the giddiness of the victory, the Lakers made a major mistake in the locker room. Kundla recalled that Mikan told reporters that he was allergic to all the smoke in the arena. Mikan, on the other hand, was adamant that the slip was Kundla's. Whatever the case, the story made the Syracuse papers the next morning.

"That next night all the fans came out smoking cigars," Mikan said.

"You could hardly see across the floor," Kundla agreed. "It was filled with smoke."

Allergic or not, Mikan muscled in another 32 points in Game 2, but that wasn't enough. The Nationals evened the series at 1-1 with a 91-85 win. Even so, the Lakers felt good. They had taken away the home-court advantage and headed back to Minnesota, where because of scheduling conflicts in the Auditorium the Lakers were again forced to move the game to St. Paul. There, on April 14 and 16, the Lakers'

frontcourt exerted their power and claimed decisive wins, 91-77 and 77-69.

Game 5 went back to smoky State Fair Coliseum, where Seymour scored 12 and played furious defense against Pollard, holding him to six points. "I hugged him and he had no place to go with Mikan clogging the middle," Seymour said of Pollard. Mikan scored 28, but Syracuse closed the gap to 3-2 with an 83-76 win.

The Nationals returned to Minneapolis for Game 6 determined to fight, which they did, but it didn't help much. The Lakers were unstoppable in the Minneapolis Auditorium, where they had never lost a playoff game.

Their strategy for Game 6 called for Seymour to hold down Pollard, which he did. But Mikan continued to dominate and scored 40. Eventually, the atmosphere evolved into a brawl. There were a variety of cards: Seymour vs. Pollard; Gabor vs. Martin; Gabor vs. Carlson. The officials ejected Cervi in the third period and fouled out four Lakers in the fourth.

It was all window dressing as the Lakers claimed their second NBA championship, 110-95. If you counted Mikan's two NBL titles, with Chicago and Minneapolis, he had been the center of four straight championship teams, and the competition soon realized that even making him take a time-out to wipe his glasses wasn't going to slow this Laker juggernaut.

1951

The Lakers ran off the league's best regular-season record in 1951. And, as he had the two previous seasons, Mikan won the scoring crown. But as the schedule came to a close, their luck turned bad. Mikan suffered a hairline fracture of his ankle. Even that didn't sideline him. Doctors placed his foot in a cast and used ethyl chloride to numb his pain.

"He played, but he was at half speed," Kundla said.

Half-speed of slow must have meant that the Lakers were almost motionless. They still moved into the Western Conference finals again where they met their old rivals, the

Rochester Royals. "It seemed we were always neck and neck, with every game going down to the wire," Kundla said.

Between 1949 and 1954, the Lakers won 267 games. The Royals won 266. Twice they finished ahead of Minneapolis in the regular-season standings. But in the head-to-head meetings, the Lakers usually won (over the four years, the Lakers won 38 against the Royals and lost 28).

"To me, our games with Rochester, that was the greatest basketball ever played," recalled Sid Hartman, the Minneapolis newspaperman who helped found the Lakers. "There was some science to it, some finesse to it."

As Royals guard Bob Davies once explained, Minneapolis had the good frontcourt; Rochester the good backcourt. The Royals presented a slick look, with fancy ballhandling, smooth passing and a lot of quickness. Davies ran the offense. A former MVP of the National League, he had once played 90 games for Rochester while coaching his former college team, Seton Hall, to a 24-3 record (imagine a modern college coach pulling that off). Teamed with Davies in the Royals' backcourt was one of his former Seton Hall players, All-American Bobby Wanzer. Red Holzman, who later coached the Knicks, was the backup. Wanzer was a great set shooter and Davies was a Hall-of-Fame caliber ballhander.

Davies was known as the first to use behind-the-back dribbles and no-look passes in game situations. "He hit a lot of guys in the face with the ball. But he was ahead of his time," said Rochester's owner/coach Les Harrison. "I encouraged that. I thought it was the coming thing. Davies started the behind the back dribble. Davies started the fastbreak. He was way out of line because he was so far ahead of the game. He hit 'em if they didn't look for the ball. Sure he was different. But it was the modern basketball that he was leading us to."

The players for both teams enjoyed a high regard for one another. But the front offices of the two clubs seemed to be engaged in a running blood feud. Rochester owner/ coach Les Harrison was a little rough around the

edges, but he cared a lot for the game and nurtured it in Rochester. Harrison had hired the first trainer in the league and had helped to break the National League color line in 1946 when he added Dolly King to the club's roster. When reporters questioned the move, Harrison told them, "If he can play, he can play."

"The BAA started, and we lost a couple of players to the BAA," Harrison recalled, "so I signed Dolly King and Pop Gates, and I told them, 'It's gonna be tough. You're gonna be shunned in a lot of cities.' And they were. And, Ben Kerner, the owner of the Buffalo franchise (which later became the St. Louis Hawks) called and said, 'Give me one of them and I'll suffer along with you.' I said, 'That's a good idea.' So I sent him Pop Gates. Pop was the better ballplayer, but Dolly was younger and bigger, and our team needed his size."

Taking King on the road was a problem in that age when racial segregation was legal. "We were playing in Indianapolis," Harrison recalled. "We got in the Claypool Hotel and they wouldn't serve us food in the restaurant. We made a big stink so they served us in the

Opening-game action at Madison Square Garden in the Eastern Division Finals, with New York vs. Syracuse.

storage room where the garbage was. So we suffered, and we ate. Years later, when I was voted into the Hall of Fame with Oscar Robertson, who was from Indianapolis, he said, 'Don't worry about the Claypool. That place burned down.' Which got everybody to laughing."

Outside of his motivational efforts, Harrison's coaching consisted of a lot of noise from the bench, directed mostly at the officials. But he cared a lot for the game and nurtured it in Rochester. The city's Edgerton Park Sports Arena was a barnlike place that held about 4,200. Harrison attracted a well-heeled crowd that wasn't afraid to get rowdy. Davies recalled that the first 10 rows of seats always seemed to be filled with people wearing fur coats. Saturday nights in Rochester brought the fans out in their finest dress, a foreshadowing of the NBA in the age of Yuppiedom.

"We had the crowds, but it was only about 3,800," Harrison recalled. "We weren't making any money. I couldn't pay attention to the team. Every time I looked at the crowd, I asked myself, "How much am I gonna lose tonight?" We just were living from hand to mouth and hoping we could get a break. We never could get a break."

Harrison had run various independent basketball teams for about a decade when he decided to put up $25,000 and join the National League for the 1945-46 season. The very next season the Basketball Association of America started, making the shaky business of pro hoops tremble all the more. Teams in both leagues struggled and died. To survive, the BAA began taking in National League teams, which had several big-name players.

"They started the BAA, and half of the teams folded up," Harrison said. "They needed teams for their league, and our National league had the superstars. The BAA had the arenas, so that's how we all got together. If they had had enough teams, they wouldn't have bothered with us because our teams were in small cities. But they needed us because we had Mikan, we had Bob Davies, we had Red Holtzman,

who would later coach the Knicks, we had the merchandise. They were lucky we joined them, but that's why they accepted us. They needed us to keep their league going. Without us, they would have been out of business."

The reformation of the National teams in the NBA left Rochester and Minneapolis battling in the same division. Because of his abrasive style, Harrison was viewed as a villain in Minneapolis. Sid Hartman alleged that Harrison once had tried to convince the Lakers' Herm Schaeffer that he was underpaid, an act for which the Lakers were always trying to retaliate.

"Les Harrison was a strange duck," Sid Hartman recalled.

In one regular season game at Rochester, the Lakers managed to tie the score on a buzzer-beating basket, then won in overtime. Afterward, they sat exhausted in the lockerroom and listened through the thin walls as Harrison screamed at Chickie Shapiro, his scorekeeper, for not sounding the buzzer soon enough.

Another time, the Royals were playing in Fort Wayne when Davies hit a long shot. As Davies fired it up, referee Pat Kennedy blew his whistle but somehow inhaled and sucked the ball of the whistle into his windpipe. He passed out and collapsed. Harrison then supposedly ran onto the floor and screamed at Kennedy, "Pat, Pat, quick before you die, did the bucket count?"

Harrison hated that he couldn't beat the Lakers for a championship. "Each year we'd be battling it out for the championship," he recalled. "We had a lot of talented basketball players, but they had George Mikan. That was a little bit of difference."

In 1947, Harrison had gone so far as to pay $25,000 to acquire 6'9" Arnie Risen from Indianapolis in an effort to battle Mikan. When that didn't do the trick, he added bulky forward Arnie Johnson to the mix.

"Mikan and Risen had great battles at center," Pollard said. "Risen couldn't stop George, but George had a heck of a time stopping Risen, too. And Arnie Johnson was a big bull, and he had great battles with Mikkelsen. Our game was all underneath the boards and battle like heck. Their game was all outside set shooting with Wanzer and Davies and Red Holzman."

The Royals had aged by 1951, but Harrison still had hopes of getting past the Lakers, even though his team was struggling midway through the season with a four-game losing streak.

"Everybody thought we were done," Harrison recalled. The team was on the road and very frustrated, so he decided to seek an unusual remedy. "I said, 'Let's stop at this beer joint,'" he recalled. "I told them, 'You can all get drunk. I'm the owner; I'm the coach. Don't worry about it. What we need is to relax. We can't have stuff hanging over us. We gotta forget about it all. Drink. Do whatever you want.'

Some drank, some didn't. But after that we won 13 straight. Then we lost a game and then won 14 more. We won 27 out of 28 games."

Although Harrison wouldn't recommend it for modern teams, the alcohol-induced streak propelled his Royals into another Western finals against Minneapolis. The Lakers quickly won the first game at home. But then Rochester coach Les Harrison moved Red

Rookie guard Myer Skoog joined the Lakers in 1951.

Holzman into the starting lineup, and the Royals took command. With Mikan slowed by the injury, the Lakers juggernaut collapsed quickly, losing the next three games. As disappointing as it seemed in Minneapolis, the loss was one of several events that ultimately favored pro basketball.

For years, college basketball had been far more popular. But in 1951, the college game was in the throes of a nationwide point-shaving scandal that hurt its appeal. It would later be revealed that a handful of pro players had shaved points while in college, a development that would lead to their banishment from the pro game, as well. But by and large the pro game was left untainted in 1951. And the problems of the college game immediately created a vacuum in basketball entertainment, particularly in New York, where the old Madison Square Garden fell into disfavor as a site for big-time college games.

To fill this void, the NBA stepped forward with the most entertaining Finals in its short history. First, it featured two New York teams, the surprise Knicks against the upstate Royals. The news value of this series cannot be underestimated. Basketball game stories didn't replace major league baseball on the sports front page. But they were no longer reduced to one or two back page paragraphs. Unquestionably pro basketball jumped a notch in the public eye. Even better, the Finals for the first time in its history went to a seven-game showdown, although the series at first appeared headed for a sweep.

For 1951, center Arnie Risen led the Royals in scoring at 16.3 points a game (just ahead of Davies at 15.2). Rochester also got good frontcourt scoring from 6'7" Jack Coleman (11.4) and bulky Arnie Johnson (9.4). Surprisingly, the Royals were one of the weaker rebounding teams in the league, although Risen averaged 12 a game and Coleman nine. Surviving that deficiency, they finished the schedule at 41-27, three games behind Minneapolis in the Western Division.

The Knicks, meanwhile, finished third in the Eastern, back of Boston and Philadelphia. But

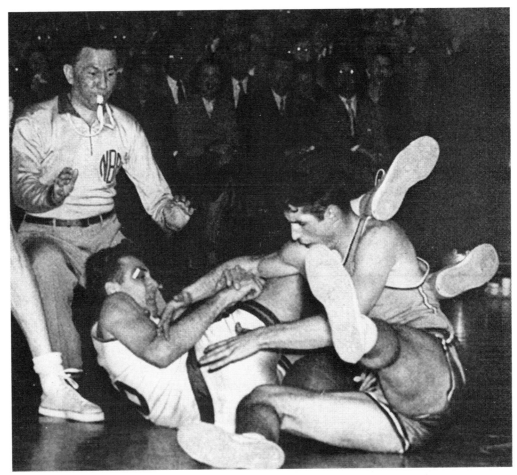

George Kaftan (left) of New York and Wally Osterkorn of Syracuse battle for a loose ball in the 1952 Eastern Finals.

they ripped Boston in the first round then edged Syracuse, 3-2, in the division finals. With ten minutes left in the fourth quarter of the fifth game, Syracuse led by twelve points. Somehow, though, New York overwhelmed them from there to earn a spot in the 1951 Finals against Rochester.

The Knicks were coached by the former college legend at St. John's, Joe Lapchick, a very popular figure in New York. They had no big man but operated adequately enough with 6'6" Nat "Sweetwater" Clifton, whom they had acquired from the Harlem Globetrotters. Clifton was actually the first black player signed to a contract in the NBA, although the Celtics had actually drafted Chuck Cooper earlier and Harrison had signed Dolly King for the old National League five seasons before. Clifton averaged about eight points and six rebounds. He has said many times that he could have put up better numbers had he not been confined to a limited role. He and Harry Gallatin, also 6'6", who averaged 12.8 points, did all the rough work, battling against the taller front lines around the league. Also up front was 6'8" Connie Simmons, who had helped Baltimore win the title three years earlier.

Richard (the original "Tricky Dick") McGuire, brother of Al and a former St. John's star, ran the Knicks' floor game and finished second (behind Philadelphia's Andy Phillip) in the league in assists with a 6.3 average. The bulk of the scoring was done by Max Zaslofsky, who came to the Knicks after the Chicago franchise failed, and 6'4 1/2" Vince Boryla, a second year player who led the team with a 14.9 average. Among the backups was Ernie Vandeweghe, (father of future NBA player Kiki) who also doubled as a medical student between practices and games.

That the Knicks made it to the Finals surprised and delighted both their followers at the 69th Regiment Armory and the New York media. No one really expected them to win the championship. Thus no one seemed surprised that they quickly fell behind Rochester 3-0 in games. First of all, they hadn't won a game in Rochester's Edgerton Park Sports Arena in three years. The string continued in Game 1, as they got blown out, 92-65. They were a little more respectable in Game 2, falling 99-84, but only a little. Davies had scored 24 and Risen 19 to lead the Royals.

The contest moved to the Armory, but the Knicks weren't much better at home, losing Game 3, 78-71, as Risen scored 27 inside. The series seemed over in the fourth quarter of Game 4 after New York blew a 17-point lead and trailed by six with under 10 minutes left. But as they had done against Syracuse in the earlier round, the Knicks awakened and outscored the Royals down the stretch. Lapchick had decided to start Vandeweghe in place of the struggling McGuire. And in the late going, other bench players — Tony Lavelli, George Kaftan and Ray Lumpp — came through in the clutch. Battling inside, Clifton and Gallatin helped push the score to a tie at 69. If there was a singular hero, it was Clifton, who scored and drew fouls in the closing minutes that carried New York to a 79-73 win.

Hopes still weren't high afterward. The Knicks trailed 3-1 and had to return to Rochester to try once more for a win. There, Simmons found the range, hitting nine of 13 from the floor, for 26 points. And Zaslofsky scored 24. But for a time, even that didn't appear to be enough.

Rochester led through the half (by as much as 10 in the third period), before the Knicks surged ahead. From there, Simmons maneuvered for a variety of hook shots, while Risen, who had five fouls, played softly. Zaslofsky hit a free throw for a three-point lead, but missed a running one-hander with 40 seconds left. Rochester controlled the rebound, but didn't have enough time to turn it around. Although much of the sports world didn't notice, the boys from New York had

pulled off the improbable, a win in Rochester, 92-89.

The Knicks went back to New York for Game 6 with just the right momentum. There, they won again, 80-73, with Vandeweghe playing near perfect ball and Zaslofsky scoring 23. McGuire, who had lost his starting job, added six assists and nine points.

Five days earlier, the Knicks had been on the verge of being swept. Abruptly, they found themselves headed back to Rochester tied at three games apiece, with nearly an even chance at the title.

That Saturday, April 21, they jumped it up in the Arena, where the Royals had rung up a 92-16 record in three NBA seasons. Rochester attempted to snuff New York's momentum quickly, taking a 13-3 lead out of the gate, then expanding it to 32-18. The Knicks found some life in the second quarter and pulled to 40-34 by the half. They kept close from there, finally tying it at 69 with a little more than six minutes left. Clifton fouled out moments later, but the Knicks took the lead at 71-70 on Gallatin's lay in. That lead moved to 74-72 with just under two minutes to go. But then Risen drew Simmons' sixth foul, and the Knicks had only Gallatin left in the frontcourt. Risen scored on a hook and a free throw to give Rochester the lead 75-74. Boryla tied it with a free throw at 1:29.

From there the momentum shifted. Davies drove and drew a blocking foul on McGuire (New York, of course, argued that it should have been a charging call). Davies made both free throws for a 77-75 lead, and according to the rules at the time, the teams faced a jump ball after foul shots in the final two minutes of a game. Rochester controlled the jump and Holzman ran out the clock until Coleman scored at the end for the 79-75 final. The celebration with Rochesters small group of loyal fans was a sweet memory for Harrison, who remained active in his 90s. "People call me and say, 'You did a great job. You made history,'" he said in a 1995 interview. "But I went broke. We struggled. We had one good year where we won the title. We figured we'd made a little money that year, but when we were through we had lost a couple thousand dollars. We didn't make any money. We kept hoping that it would get better.... It was losing for everybody all the time."

Harrison's one regret from 1951 was that his team never got any hardware to keep as a memento. "We never got a ring; we never got a trophy to show that we won the title," he said. "In 1985, we called up David Stern, the commissioner, and told the league office that we never got a trophy. They sent down Brian McIntyre, the league's public relations vice president, and he presented us a trophy. We finally got it."

1952

George Mikan returned from his ankle injury in the fall of 1951 and encountered a new game. In an obvious attempt to counteract his nearly unstoppable offense, the league rules committee had decided to widen the lane from six feet to 12.

That, in part, explains how Mikan lost the scoring title. With his average falling from 28.4 to 23.8 per game, he finished second behind Philadelphia's young jump shot specialist, Paul Arizin. While it stalled Mikan's statistical dominance, the lane widening had little effect on who took home the championship trophy.

"Actually, it opened up the lane and made it more difficult for them to defense me," Mikan said. "Opposing teams couldn't deter our cutters going through the lane. It moved me out and gave me more shot selection instead of just short pivots and hooks. I was able to dribble across the lane and use a lot more freedom setting the shot up."

Beyond that, it meant a few more points, a few more shots, for Pollard and Mikkelsen, both of whom averaged more than 15 points for the first time in their pro careers. Heading into his third season, Mikkelsen, in particular, was starting to find himself.

"Widening the lane opened the middle and allowed these marvelous one-on-one deals," he

New York's Kaftan gets the rebound, as the Knicks win Game 6 of the Finals.

explained. Mikkelsen had played center in high school and college, and the shift to forward in the pros meant that he was facing the basket for the first time in his career. In adjusting, he developed a bit of an outside shot, although he made his living on the offensive glass, which was another distinguishing aspect of the Lakers. Because of their frontcourt strength, they were the first great offensive rebounding team.

Each season, Slater Martin stood up at the opening of training camp and addressed the team in his Texas drawl. Had they all signed their contracts? he would ask. Then he would go on to explain that the only way they could earn more money would be to win the championship, and the only way to win the championship was to feed the ball to number 99, Big George.

But with the lane widened, the Lakers wouldn't be able to depend on their center as much. Sid Hartman knew the team needed better outside shooting, and he knew where to find it. Sitting on Rochester's bench was 6'2" Pep Saul, a two-handed set-shooting artist.

"We had been rotating Pollard outside, but we needed better shooting," Hartman said.

The newspaperman knew that Les Harrison would never agree to trade or sell Saul to the Lakers. "He wouldn't give us anything," Hartman said. "We had a bitter, bitter rivalry." Instead, Hartman called coach Clair Bee of the struggling Baltimore Bullets and told him that he would give him $5,000 for Saul.

"Do you think I can get him from Harrison?" Bee asked.

"You can get him for about $1,500 and keep the change," Hartman told him.

Which Bee promptly did, sending Saul to the Lakers just a few days after acquiring him from Rochester. "Harrison was furious when he realized what had happened," Hartman said. "He went to the league and protested, but he couldn't do anything. It was a legitimate

deal. Saul's outside shooting was just enough to open up our inside game. He helped us win three straight championships."

Minus their top young guard but $1,500 richer, the Royals had resumed their annual battle with the Lakers.

The season brought the resumption of the annual battle between the Royals and Lakers in the Western Division. Once again, Rochester nosed Minneapolis aside in the regular season, this time by a single game. Syracuse, Boston and New York were again the powers in the Eastern. And again, the Knicks finished third at 37-29 but prevailed in the playoffs. Their only roster change was the addition of Dick McGuire's feisty little brother, Al, a pesky defensive player who hustled because he couldn't often find the trigger on offense. (Primarily Al, who later coached Marquette to

Nat Clifton shows off his long reach for New York coach Joe Lapchich. The Knicks acquired Clifton from the Harlem Globetrotters.

an NCAA championship, was used as a fouler. In those days of strategic hacking, just about every club had one.) That didn't matter much because New York spread the scoring among seven players, all of whom averaged better than nine points per game.

In the Western playoffs, Minneapolis met Indianapolis in the first round. The Olympians had a fine team featuring Kentuckians Alex Groza and Ralph Beard, both of whom owned a piece of the club. But both stars would be implicated in the college point-shaving scandals and would later be banned from basketball, which would eventually lead to the folding of the Indianapolis franchise. This playoff match with Mikan and company would provide a last hurrah of sorts for Groza and Beard, two of the best young players in the game. They fell in two close games to the Lakers.

That led to another Lakers' showdown with the Royals. Gassed by the addition of Pep Saul, Minneapolis brushed aside Rochester, 3-1, to advance to the Finals, where by virtue of their superior record the Lakers had home-court advantage over the Knicks, who had again moved aside Syracuse in the Eastern finals.

The league's sixth championship series began April 12 in St. Paul (again there was a scheduling conflict that kept the Lakers out of Minneapolis), where the Knicks jumped out to a four-point first-quarter lead. The period was marred by a bit of controversy when Al McGuire drove the lane, hit his shot and drew a foul. Officials Sid Borgia and Stan Stutz didn't see the basket and sent McGuire to the line for two shots rather than the customary chance at a three-point play.

Knicks coach Joe Lapchick protested profusely, but the officials explained that they couldn't award the basket because they hadn't seen it. McGuire, meanwhile, made one of his two free throws, which left the Knicks feeling they had been robbed of a point. None of which would have mattered had the game not gone into overtime tied at 71. Pollard, who led the Lakers with 34, then hit four free throws in the closing minute to give Minneapolis a 83-79 win and a 1-0 lead in the series.

The Knicks vented their frustration in defense the next night. Clifton, Gallatin and Simmons dropped a web over the Lakers' frontcourt, holding Pollard to 13 and Mikan to 18, enough for a shocking 80-72 upset that evened the series and took away the Lakers' home-court advantage.

Minneapolis, however, snatched it back three days later in New York, moving ahead in the fourth period for an 82-77 win. But from there, the Lakers suffered a double loss in Game 4. First, Pollard injured his back, then the Knicks defense again snuffed Mikan, who could manage only 11 points. Still, New York needed an overtime to survive 80-79.

In St. Paul for Game 5, the Lakers could have stumbled without Pollard. But Mikkelsen and Mikan each scored 32, and Bob Harrison moved from guard to forward to replace Pollard. He scored 13 and Pep Saul added 15, as they drubbed the Knicks, 102-89, for a 3-2 lead in the series.

Having lost their defense and their respect in Game 5, the Knicks returned home to find the Armory only half-filled with 3,000 fans, the bulk of their followers apparently thinking the series was over. New York answered by playing the toughest game of the series, holding Minneapolis to just 68 points to even the series at three all with a 76-68 win. Zaslofsky scored 17 in the second half to drive New York's offense.

Each year, the Lakers were forced to stage their playoff games in St. Paul because a sportsmen's show at the Minneapolis Auditorium created a scheduling conflict. But for Game 7 on April 25 the Auditorium was open, which spelled doom for the Knicks, who hadn't won in 11 tries there spanning four seasons. The Lakers led by 12 after three and won in a swirl, 82-65, giving quiet John Kundla his fourth championship (counting the NBL, of course.)

1953

Both the Knicks and the Lakers thought the 1953 championship would again come down to the home-court advantage, and they played like it. Minneapolis won the Western regular season title with a 48-22 record. New York claimed the Eastern with a 47-23 finish, one game worse than the Lakers.

The saving grace of a long season came in the playoffs when the two best teams survived to meet again in the Finals. The '52-53 season had been a rough, foul-infested year for pro basketball, where strategy had moved toward fouling, as coaches attempted to play the percentages. Officials called an average of 58 fouls per game. Instead of shooting 1,500 or 1,600 free throws in a season, teams were shooting 2,300 or 2,400. It was ugly. And the playoffs were even worse. Boston and Syracuse engaged in a four-overtime battle featuring 107 fouls and 130 free throws. In that game, Bob Cousy scored 50, but 30 of them came from the line. Through the maze of flailing arms and the steady shrill of whistles, New York somehow finished off Boston in the Eastern Division, and the Lakers escaped Fort Wayne in the Western.

Mikan's average was down to 20.6 per game, second in the league behind Philadelphia center Neil Johnston. But Slater Martin had crept into double figures at 10.6 points, mostly by taking advantage of the defenses that always packed in around the Lakers' frontcourt. Martin would never take a shot unless it was an absolute necessity. Nevertheless, he hit .410 from the floor that season, eighth best in the league, an indication of just how many long set shots those old-timers took. In the championship series, the Knicks quickly established that they had a new confidence and were out to accomplish something. They stayed with the Lakers through three quarters of Game One in Minneapolis (played in a local armory, not the Auditorium, because of another scheduling conflict). At that point, according to the old script, the Knicks were supposed to wither sometime in the fourth. Instead, they produced a 30-point period that brought a surprise ending, 96-88, New York.

"We had had a tough time with Fort Wayne in the previous series and were a little weary," Kundla said of the defeat.

Just like that, the Lakers had lost their homecourt advantage. The next night they set out to mend things, and through the first half it appeared they would, with a 47-30 lead at intermission. But the Knicks caught up, then took a one-point lead in the third. And from there, the game adopted the character of the season. It became a free-throw shooting contest. Neither side allowed the other to shoot. So each team went to the line, and the Lakers settled it there, hitting nine of 13 while the Knicks made six of 10.

With a 73-71 win, the Lakers had evened the series at one all, but with a change in the championship format, the next three games were to be played in New York, a factor that seemed bad at the time. The circumstances, however, were decidedly extenuating. First, Mikan was an old hand at playing in the Big Apple, dating back to his college days and the double headers in Madison Square Garden. "They sort of liked me in New York," he recalled. "And I liked New York. Even today when I travel, people will come up to me and say, 'I saw you play in the Garden.'"

Second, the Lakers got an assist from the New York media.

"I can still see the clippings," Mikkelsen said. "The New York newspapers were all saying that the series wouldn't go back to Minneapolis. They were right. It didn't."

In what the Lakers viewed as their sweetest championship, they blasted the Knicks three straight in New York's old 69th Regiment Armory. The first half of Game 3 was experimenting with a turnaround jump shot. For help in handling their center, the Lakers had employed DePaul coach Ray Meyer, an old friend of Hartman's, as a consultant. "Ray had tremendous control over Mikan," Hartman explained. "Ray didn't say much during the first half while George was working his jump shot. He just sat there. But in the lockerroom at halftime, he said, 'George, take that jump shot and stick it up your ass.'"

52

The Lakers' Mikan and the Knicks' Harry Gallatin battle for a loose ball in this regular-season New York victory...

...But in the end, the Lakers celebrate another NBA title.

Properly admonished, Mikan ditched the jumpshot and went back to the old drop-step. With that, the Lakers turned on a fourth-quarter blowout that ended 90-75. The Knicks fought back in Game 4, which turned into another foul fest. With 28 seconds left and Minneapolis leading, 69-67, the Lakers' Jim Holstein went to the line and missed. But Minneapolis rookie guard Myron "Whitey" Skoog controlled the rebound and scored for a 71-67 lead. Connie Simmons hit two free throws for the Knicks to bring it to 71-69, and New York even got a final shot to tie it. But Harry Gallatin missed with a hook, and suddenly the Knicks were down, 3-1.

Kundla gave the team the next day off, so they toured Broadway's clubs after the game. Billy Eckstine was the music rage in those days, and Pollard, Mikkelsen and Jim Holstein used to croon his sweet bass tunes in the shower. That night, they caught him at a Broadway club. The singer finished his act and

"Nobody gave George anything...He earned his baskets."

came over to their table, even bringing Count Basie along to chitchat.

"That was some night," Pollard said.

The Lakers dragged back to their hotel rooms about 4:30 a.m., and Kundla waited until game day before he made them sweat it out in a one-hour practice.

Game 5 was set for Friday, April 10. The Lakers opened a solid lead in the second, then stretched it to 20 points in the third, only to see it slip away when Mikan developed foul trouble early in the fourth. Perhaps that's where party time caught up with the Lakers. The Knicks pushed back, paring the lead from 12 to five, then down to 84-82 with under two minutes left. But all they could do was foul, and the Lakers made enough of their free throws to stay ahead. Plus, with a jump ball after every late foul (as was the rule then), Mikan controlled the outcome. That was

enough for a 91-84 win and the Lakers' fifth title.

Which meant another trek to Broadway.

"That was an evening to remember," Mikkelsen said wistfully. "It was high-test stuff, even in those days."

Pollard recalled that only one local writer followed the team to New York, so at 4 a.m. they returned to their hotel to make a collect call to another reporter who had decided not to make the trip. "We just wanted to let him know what he had missed," Pollard said.

1954

The Lakers' sweet memories didn't end with 1953, although they went into the 1954 season with Mikan sporting an array of battle scars. Over his amateur and professional career, he had suffered two broken legs, broken bones in both beet, as well as fractures of his wrist, nose, thumb and three fingers. He once figured that he had received a total of 166 stitches.

Quite simply, opposing teams found the only way they could stop him was to get rough.

"Nobody gave George anything," Pollard said. "He earned his baskets."

The beating had begun to take its toll on Mikan's game, as his scoring average dipped to 18.1 points (third in the league behind Neil Johnston and Bob Cousy). One constant that remained was the bickering among the stars. The Milwaukee Hawks had a preseason series with the Lakers in 1953. "We played 'em seven straight games in the preseason and lost all seven," former Hawks GM Marty Blake recalled. "In the seventh game we were leading by 20 points, and John Kundla put on a press. We lost, and our owner, Benny Kerner, had me go out and buy a $10 trophy and give it to 'em."

The season opener that year was also against the Hawks, in Milwaukee, but the Lakers lost after Pollard and Mikan got into a shouting match in front of press row. Pollard recalled that Mikan failed to warn him about a pick, Pollard got whacked and his man scored easily. The next night they played in New York and the newspapers were filled with speculation that the Laker dynasty was coming to an end because of the feud.

Mikan and Pollard shared a laugh about the incident over breakfast, then went out and beat the Knicks soundly. "George and I were always very critical of each other, very frank," Pollard said. "But that helped our relationship, because nothing festered. We always got it off our chests."

This fussing duo carried the Lakers to the league's best record, a 46-26 finish, a feat they accomplished with the help of a big-scoring rookie, 6-foot-9 Clyde Lovellette, who had led Kansas to the 1952 NCAA title. With Mikan's career nearing its close, Lovellette was cast as the franchise's next great center.

Lovellette, in fact, had announced that he didn't want to play pro ball. Hartman figured that the Lakers, who were drafting last in the first round, really didn't need a player, so why not take a chance on Lovellette? When the Lakers announced his selection at the draft, New York Knicks owner Ned Irish immediately stopped the proceedings. It would be unfair, he protested, if the Lakers added Lovellette to their talented roster.

The pick stood, however, and the Laker machine rolled a little farther down the road.

Excessive fouling continued to mar the

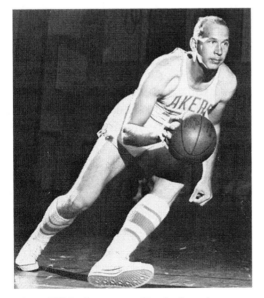

Vern Mikkelsen was the Lakers' power forward.

playoffs in 1954, but the real irritant was the format. Pro basketball faced tough economic circumstances. Although NBC had begun limited television broadcasts of games, the dearth of paying fans meant that eight of the league's 17 teams disappeared in a matter of two seasons. The Indianapolis Olympians folded before the '54 season, leaving only four teams in the Western Division while the Eastern still had five. Facing this imbalance, the owners went searching for a playoff system and came up with a three-team round robin for the first round, which gave no favor to the teams with the best regular-season records.

The Lakers survived in the Western bracket, but the Eastern Division produced a surprise. The Knicks had won the regular-season crown but were swept out of the way by the Nationals, who had tied Boston for second place during the regular schedule.

The Nats arrived at the Finals somewhat bloodied but unbowed after the brutal Eastern playoffs. Paul Seymour suffered a broken thumb and forwards Earl Lloyd and Dolph Schayes had broken hands. "The press took to calling us the 'bandage brigade,'" recalled Schayes. All would play, but a greater burden would fall on the other key Nationals — Bob Lavoy, Wally Osterkorn and Bill Kenville.

Many thought the injuries would bring the Finals to a swift conclusion. Instead, the league was treated to another seven-game series. It opened in Minneapolis on March 31, where the Lakers rolled along to a 79-68 win. Game 2 developed as another defensive standoff. The score at half was only 28-27, Syracuse. But guard George King got the Nats going in the third; they outscored the Lakers 16-1, for a 48-38 lead heading into the fourth. Minneapolis answered with its power game and bullied back. With 90 seconds left, the Nats took yet another casualty when King drove under the basket and met Mikan, who tried to block his shot and broke his wrist instead. King left the floor to become the newest member of the 'bandage brigade.' With 18 seconds left, Mikan took a pass from Holstein and scored to tie the game at 60.

Syracuse headed back downcourt with one final shot. With seven seconds left, Seymour took a set shot from 43 feet and swished it, giving the Nats a 62-60 win and stunning the crowd of 6,277. It was the first time the Lakers had lost a playoff game in the Minneapolis Auditorium, a streak that covered seven seasons. "It was a long shot," Schayes recalled. "He just got set and flung it up there."

Seymour remembered Pollard asking after the game why he would take such a shot with time on the clock for a closer attempt. "I was open," Seymour replied.

The Lakers easily claimed Game 3 in Syracuse's War Memorial Auditorium, but the Nationals evened it up four nights later in Game 4 with an 80-69 win. Their bad luck continued, however, as Billy Gabor went down with a knee injury that kept him out of the next two games.

The fifth game in Syracuse was all Lakers as they bulled inside for an 84-73 win. Down 3-2, the Nats headed back to Minneapolis, where they had just won their first game ever. The outlook for a second win there didn't seem promising. But with Schayes scoring 15 and Seymour 16, the Nats whipped up a miracle of sorts. They found themselves with the ball and the score tied at 63 in the closing seconds.

Coach Al Cervi had them hold the ball for a final shot, then called a timeout to set it up. The ball was supposed to go to anyone but Jim

Slater Martin added double-figure scoring to the Lakers' offense.

A fractured hand slowed Dolph Schayes in the Finals.

Neal, a 6-foot-11, 250-pound rookie backup center out of little Wofford College. Cervi had kept him on the roster, figuring he was good for five fouls a game. Neal played only 80 games in the NBA, but when his hour came along he made the most of it. His shot, a 27-footer from the right of the key, dropped through with four seconds left to give Syracuse the win, 65-63.

"It was a missed pass," Cervi said of the play. "Neal was at the top of the key and the ball came to him. He didn't know what to do with it, so he shoots it."

The Lakers were hardly panic-stricken, not with the seventh game in Minneapolis, and certainly not after four previous trips to the Finals. Jim Pollard stepped forward to lead them with 21 points. They got an early lead, and never relinquished it. Pollard scored nine of his total in the third period, when Minneapolis pulled ahead, 61-45 and rolled on to their sixth title in seven years.

It had been a great ride, but Mikan abruptly ended it after the season by announcing his retirement. Each season he had signed a one-year contract with the team. "We always sweated signing him at the end of every year," Hartman said. "His last year in the league he made $35,000."

But the center and the Lakers couldn't come to terms for the 1954-55 season, so at age 29 he retired. Some say it was none too soon. The league adopted a 24-second shot clock for the upcoming season, which didn't suit his style. Without him, Minneapolis finished 42-30, third best in the eight-team league, and still made it to the Western Finals, where they lost to Fort Wayne.

The team coaxed Mikan into attempting a comeback at mid season in 1955-56. Playing himself into shape, he averaged about 10 points over 37 games, and it was obvious his playing days were over. "It was stupid for him to come back," Hartman said. "He had taken a lot of punishment during his career. His knees were shot."

With its faster format, the pro game was racing off to a new level, leaving Mikan and

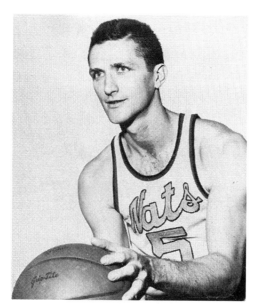

Paul Seymour was still the star in the Nats' backcourt.

his Lakers to exist in their own special amber. Yes, he had been a four-eyed, wavy-haired goon, but before age 30 he had mastered the pro game of his time, leading his teams to seven championships in eight seasons (including two National titles).

"Mikan ran the whole show," Larry Foust of the Fort Wayne Pistons once observed. "He was an athlete despite what some people say about his bulk, and nobody ever had better offensive moves under the basket. When George played, he owned that lane.

5.
Little Danny's Clock

Modern Basketball Arrives

1955

Danny Biasone revolutionized pro basketball, but unlike many of the game's other towering figures, he didn't do it with his physique. He was short and bald and a bit chunky. As a part owner of the Syracuse Nationals, he sat on the bench, rooting his team on. An Italian, he was fond of large hats and overcoats, which, some said, made him look like a Hollywood tough guy. But in person, he was a sweetheart with an easy smile. Few people disliked Danny Biasone. In turn, he liked just about everyone. About the only thing that seemed to upset him were the stall tactics of opposing teams.

"The stall game would kill him," recalled the late Charlie Eckman, a former NBA referee who later coached the Fort Wayne Pistons. "He used to go absolutely crazy."

For the better part of three years, Biasone argued that pro basketball needed a shotclock. To anyone who would listen, he extolled the benefits of his idea. Eager to prove his point, he ran tests, held discussions, and lobbied constantly.

"You need a clock," Biasone would tell the other owners after every foul-infested, low-scoring game. Otherwise, he said, coaches would continue to devise stalling tactics to keep even with tall, powerful teams like the Minneapolis Lakers. Some coaches would have their players foul. Others would freeze the ball. In Boston, where the frontcourt was weak, guard Bob Cousy controlled the tempo of many games by dribbling four or five minutes off the clock.

"It was a dull affair," Biasone recalled.

Finally the owners listened. For the 1954-55 season, the NBA relented and installed a 24-second shot clock. The league had decided on 24 seconds based on a test done by Biasone during the summer of 1954. He had gotten together some of his pros and a group of high school players for an experimental game and timed them with a stopwatch. Most shots were taken within 12 seconds, Biasone discovered. He decided to recommend 24 seconds because he figured that over a 48 minute game, each team would get a minimum of 60 possessions. The league's other owners decided Biasone's findings made sense, so they adopted a 24-second

Danny Biasone revolutionized basketball with the 24-second shot clock.

Al Cervi ended his playing career and focused on coaching the Nats.

shot clock for the 1954-55 season.

Almost immediately, the results proved Biasone had been right. Scoring jumped. Coaching and tactics became less of a factor. Pro basketball suddenly belonged to the players. Quickness and athletic ability were prized as they never had been before. Excessive fouling didn't disappear completely, but just about everyone concluded that the clock was good for the game.

It was also good for Biasone's team. Featuring a lineup brimming with rebounding and quickness, the Nationals claimed the league's ninth championship that spring of 1955.

"It was like we put in the game clock so we could win the title," joked Paul Seymour, the Nationals' guard and team leader.

In a 1990 interview, Biasone acknowledged that he had taken his share of ribbing over the years because his team won the title after he arranged the rules change. But throughout his life he remained immensely proud that he had fought to bring a shot clock to pro basketball. "It made the game," he said. "The results show that. It's the most exciting game going because of a clock."

Most pro basketball people agree with that assessment. "Danny Biasone saved the NBA with the 24-second rule, make no mistake about that," Eckman said.

Biasone had become involved in pro basketball almost as a lark. His primary livelihood was the Eastwood Sports Center, the sports bar he owned in the suburbs of Syracuse. It contained a lounge, 16 bowling lanes and a coffee shop.

On the side, he dabbled in semi-pro basketball in the days just after World War II. His intensity in the sport picked up after he scheduled a game between his Syracuse

club and the Rochester Royals of the National Basketball League. Then, at the last minute, the Rochester people backed out. "They cancelled on me," Biasone said. "So I joined the National Basketball League to force Rochester to come to Syracuse."

With relative pocket change and a lot of pluck, Biasone founded the Syracuse Nationals in 1946, which in time would evolve into one of the NBA's proudest franchises, the Philadelphia 76ers. But the NBA would never hold Biasone's heart. Truth be known, he preferred the old NBL. And he felt jilted in 1948 when four NBL teams jumped to the Basketball Association of America, a move that led to the forming of the NBA. Biasone said he felt as if his business partners had run out on him. But being the good businessman he was, Biasone joined the remainder of the NBL

Red Rocha drives against Boston.

the following season in merging with the other league to form the NBA.

"I haven't gotten over that to this day, for chrissakes," he said in 1990.

The salve Biasone found for these feelings of rejection and betrayal was winning. Their first year in the NBA, the Nationals ran up the league's best regular-season record, 51-13. But they lost to the Minneapolis Lakers 4-2 in the NBA Finals. Again in 1952, they stacked up the Eastern Division's best record, only to fall in the divisional finals. In 1954, they advanced to the NBA Finals for a second time, but there they ran into the Lakers once more and lost a seven-game series.

Through these frustrations and near misses, Biasone remained patient. NBA players and coaches alike seem to agree that a championship mindset begins with the team ownership. Biasone had that mindset. He was the kind of owner who was always around yet never in the way. Instead of discarding players and coaches in a search for the title, he kept the team together. "Danny Biasone felt the less changes you made the better," forward Dolph Schayes said. "The nucleus stayed together for many, many years."

This nucleus formed around another Italian, Al Cervi, who had served as Syracuse's player/ coach for several years before concentrating solely on coaching in 1954. He was from the tough old pro school, the kind of coach who would pound one of his players in one-on-one to prove a point.

"He had grown up the hard way and lived the hard way and coached that way, too," said

All Stars (from left) Larry Foust of Fort Wayne, Paul Seymour of Syracuse, Andy Phillip of Fort Wayne, and Dolph Schayes of Syracuse faced off in the East-West game, and later in the Finals.

Syracuse guard George King, who would later become the athletic director at Purdue.

As might be expected, Cervi's style didn't always sit well with his players. "He gave no quarter," Schayes said. "Al was a very aggressive coach. He led by example. We either loved him or hated him. We respected him, but he was difficult. He was one of those coaches who didn't use much psychology. If he had a grudge against you, you knew about it. We didn't say, 'Hey, we don't like Al,' or 'Let's not play hard.' We wanted to win. We were very aggressive. In that sense, the team reflected Al's personality. Cervi was one of a kind. He was one of the great competitors in the history of the game. He had a strong ego, and he never wavered. He was always the same from day one. He'd get you angry with things he said. He was egotistical. One of his favorite expressions was, 'You college guys, you couldn't guard your grandmother. I didn't go to college and I'm as good as you are. I'll play you one-on-one.' "

Cervi's theory was as rigid and successful as his personality. "You shoot fouls consistently, you play defense consistently, and you don't throw the ball away," he told his players.

Schayes adhered to part of that formula. A mere role player in college at New York University, he had developed as an offensive machine in the NBA. He had done so by working hours on his shooting, a factor that made him one of Biasone's favorites. He moved constantly to get open for his set shot, often running his defenders to exhaustion.

"I soon realized that I didn't have the size and strength to play inside, and frankly I didn't have the great pivot moves these other guys had," the 6'7" Schayes said of the style he developed as a pro. "I just felt if I kept moving, it was much easier to elude my man."

Danny Biasone saved the NBA with the 24-second rule, make no mistake about that.

In getting his shots, Schayes became incredibly skillful at drawing the foul. In fact, he was one of the few players in NBA history to make more free throws than field goals. "We used to tease him," Paul Seymour recalled, "that it must be great to be a Jewish star in a league with all those Jewish owners and officials."

Because of his excellent timing, Schayes also rebounded well, averaging better than 10 boards per game over the '54-55 season to go with his 18.5 points.

While Schayes starred offensively, he drew Cervi's ire with his defense. "Al didn't like Dolph too much," Seymour said. "Dolph wouldn't play defense. We used to call him 'No Hands.' "

"Dolph could play some defense," George King recalled with a laugh, "but he didn't worry much about that part of the game. Whenever we'd get on him when he didn't block out and play defense, he'd say, 'Goddamnit, let me tell you something. I'm gonna outscore the guy I'm playing. If the rest of you do that, we'll win.' "

Vern Mikkelsen of the Lakers said the scouting report on Schayes read, "Great outside shooter. Always seemed in perpetual motion. But he gave up position easily on defense."

Many of the defensive chores fell to the other forward, Earl Lloyd. "Lloyd became a prototypical defensive forward," Schayes said. "In those days, teams had a defensive forward and a scoring forward, a scoring guard and a defensive guard. Earl would take the best scorer on the other team. It was a selfless job."

"Earl the Squirrel, he was a great guy," Seymour said. "He did his job good, which was mostly defense, the sh--ty end of the stick. He had to play defense on the other team's toughest player, so he was called for a lot of fouls."

Cervi said he considered the 6'6" Lloyd and Red Rocha, a 6'9" stringbean veteran, to be the two very valuable unsung players on the squad, because they did the tough work in the frontcourt. Rocha had sat out the 1953-54 season with injury, when the Nats battled Mikan and the Lakers in the Finals. But he came back strong for '55, averaging 11 points and nearly seven rebounds per game. Cervi figured that just having Rocha and Lloyd on the floor gave him a three-basket edge. "Red Rocha was a greatly underrated player," Seymour agreed. "He could play defense, had a decent outside shot and never lost the ball."

The center was rookie Johnny "Red" Kerr, a 6'9" happy-go-lucky kid out of the University of Illinois. He knew how to play the post and averaged better than 10 points and six rebounds per game. "He could hook and he could rebound and he had a good knowledge of the game," Seymour said of Kerr. "But he was a playboy. He had a good time off the court."

The Nats had always been known for their excellent forwards and guards, Cervi said, but with Kerr, the team finally had a player who understood the pivot, not just someone who could score down low, but a big man who could pass and work the high post as well.

That frontcourt meshed well with a backcourt that offered both quality and depth. In Seymour, Cervi had a veteran guard who could play the game and understand it, too. He and George King both ranked in the top ten in the league in assists.

As a collegian, King had led the nation in scoring for two years at Morris Harvey in Charleston, West Virginia, where he played the post despite the fact that he was only six feet. His pro career hinged on him fitting a certain niche with the Nats. Like Seymour, he was a good shooter. But King was no great driver. He did, however, run the Syracuse break with skill. He was a dribble king, and during the exhibition season would treat the crowd to a halftime dribble show. Figure eights. Between the legs. Behind the back. All of it would seem routine in the modern era,

but back then it was showtime material.

To go with them was rookie Dick Farley, one of the early big guards at 6'4". He was a fine leaper and an excellent all-around player. The other scrapper was 6'2" Billy "the Kid" Kenville, a second-year pro out of St. Bonaventure. Both saw plenty of playing time and made major contributions. The depth they brought to the Nats' roster was essential now that the game had a clock.

George King filled a specific role for the Nats.

While the 24-second rule stepped up the action, it wasn't enough to generate more cash flow for the Baltimore Bullets, who struggled 13 games into the season, then collapsed, leaving the NBA as an eight-team league. Although other clubs faced the same fight for survival, the Nats thrived, packing the War Memorial almost nightly. (The team's financing would become secure when Biasone issued stock that brought in a broader base of investors.) This financial stability was matched by their play; they won the Eastern Division with a 43-29 record. In the Western, the Lakers struggled without Mikan and wound up the regular season three games behind the surprising Fort Wayne Pistons.

The most surprising thing about the Pistons, who won the Western with a 43-29 record, was their coach, Charlie Eckman, who had been an NBA referee but had no coaching experience whatsoever. In fact, Eckman had officiated the previous year's Finals and was considered a solid referee. All the same, he was viewed as somewhat overblown and full of bull. That perspective on him broadened after he went to the bench.

Opposing coaches and players were openly irritated that a mere ref had ascended to a head coaching job. "It was sort of a mockery," Paul Seymour said of Eckman's hiring. "Charlie was a real character. He was sort of wimpy, sort of portly, like most of those officials were back then. He was sort of a laugh. I guess at the time Fort Wayne needed a laugh."

The circumstances under which Eckman were hired were certainly laughable. Late in the '53-54 season he had officiated a game in Milwaukee between Minneapolis and Fort Wayne. The Lakers won, and Eckman recalled that afterward in a restaurant, he boastfully told George Mikan, "If I was coaching the Pistons, I'd beat you big clowns."

Pistons owner Fred Zollner, a wealthy man given to whimsical behavior, overheard the comment and remembered it. At the close of the season, he contacted Eckman, flew him to Miami for an interview and offered him the job.

"I said, 'You got yourself a boy,' " Eckman recalled.

Some had thought Zollner would give the coaching job to Rochester guard Bob Davies or to the Pistons' own veteran guard, Andy Phillip. "People thought Zollner was crazy, that he had gone off his trolley hiring a referee," Eckman said. "All the writers thought he was nuts."

Gifted with an immense capacity for gab, Eckman didn't help matters by constantly pumping out quips about how easy coaching was. But, compared with a referee's life, it was. "It was like a vacation, riding around on a plane and having a suite for a room," Eckman said. "As a referee, you were lucky to get a room. You spent your time riding around from game to game on them trains."

The ref's pay was $50 a game, plus $5 a day meal money and another $5 for incidentals. Saturdays usually meant calling two games. You might call an afternoon game in Philly, then jump on the train for New York to do the second half of a double header. Back then, though, coaching was a penthouse position in the NBA. Zollner offered Eckman a $10,000 contract that first year, which was great money in 1955.

But the biggest difference was the fans. "If you were refereeing, you had no friends," Eckman said. Each town seemed to have a character like the one in Syracuse, whom the officials took to calling the "Strangler," because of his penchant for choking refs. He'd stalk the transgressing official coming off the floor — there never seemed to be proper security, Eckman said — and get the ref in his clutches. "They all knew it," Eckman said, half facetiously alleging that Syracuse's management "kept him there for that purpose."

But once Eckman became a coach, the irate fans disappeared and the jeers turned to cheers. "What a feeling!" he said.

In retrospect, he should have kept up a few more pretensions about the difficulty of coaching, Eckman said. "The coaching strategy I made a farce of it, and it didn't sit well with some people. But we only had two plays and when we ran them I didn't even know where the ball was. We had no blackboards or papers or lines or Xs or Os or assistant coaches. We had no strategies. The only time pro players make plays is in practice. I was a cheerleader, and I kept everybody happy. It's a simple game."

But there were certain things Eckman had learned as a ref, and it helped him transform Fort Wayne from a third-place finish in the Western Division into an NBA Finals team. Mainly, he gained an understanding of individual matchups. "As a ref, you call 120 games and you get to see who can play who," he said. "I got to see the whole league. I knew who could play, who went to their right, who went to their left. There's a big difference." Fort Wayne's success caught opponents off guard. "The guys in the league thought that we'd be a joke, that we'd be cute," Eckman said. "Hell, we out-cuted them."

It helped that Eckman had inherited a talented club, albeit an underachieving one. In the post, he had hulking 6'9" 250-pound Larry Foust, a veteran out of LaSalle, who averaged 17 points and 10 rebounds for 1954-55. Foust had been one of the few players over the years capable of giving Mikan a decent matchup. The solid defensive forward was 6'6" Mel Hutchins, another veteran, out of

Brigham Young. The brother of Miss America Colleen Hutchins (who wed Ernie Vandeweghe of the Knicks), Mel averaged 12 points and nearly 10 rebounds a game to go with his excellent defensive play.

The backcourt was veteran as well, with a wealth of playoff experience. First, there was Max Zaslofsky, who had been to the Finals with both Chicago and New York. Then there was Phillip, one of the Illinois Whiz Kids, who had been to the Finals with Chicago. Also there was Frankie "Flash" Brian, who scored at a 9.7 clip per game.

And Eckman did take credit for at least one major coaching move. "I made one big change and that won me a pennant," he said. "I took George Yardley and made him a starter. He and Paul Birch (the former Pistons coach) didn't get along. But I had watched Yardley play in an exhibition game, and he could jump out of the building. And he could shoot. I had to have something that made me look like a coach. I told Yardley he was gonna start, and he couldn't thank me enough."

A 6'5" engineer out of Stanford who had played AAU ball, the sophisticated Yardley responded by averaging 17.3 points and nearly 10 rebounds per game. "He was a bald-headed skinny bastard, looked like an insurance man, anything but a basketball player," Eckman said. "But he could play." Eckman also had a nice array of bench players to choose from, including Bob Houbregs, Don Meineke, Paul Walther and Dick Rosenthal.

From their first-place regular-season finish, the Pistons met Minneapolis in the Western Finals and finished the Lakers there, 3-1, in a series that included two overtime wins by Fort Wayne. Their victory left the NBA faced with a promoter's nightmare. Fort Wayne vs. Syracuse. Two old NBL teams from two small cities. Both were nice places but hardly media centers. As a result, the Finals were even more obscure than usual, which was unfortunate, because the two teams battled through a classic seven-game series to perhaps the most dramatic finish ever.

It opened March 31 in Syracuse, where the Pistons took a 75-71 lead midway through the fourth period. Cervi sent Dick Farley into the game, and he scored four quick points and hit Red Rocha with an assist to put the Nats back in the lead for good. Syracuse won it 86-82 for a 1-0 lead. Foust had scored 26 for Fort Wayne, while Rocha led the Nats with 19.

Dick Farley was one of the first big guards.

Game Two on April 2 was cut from the same mold, as Syracuse won, 87-84, on a fourth-quarter surge led by Schayes, who finished with 24. The Nats had led by 11 at half, but with 30 seconds left, the Pistons had cut it to 85-84. With seven seconds left on the game clock and time running down on the shot clock, Rocha hit a 25-foot set shot for the final margin.

Pistons owner Fred Zollner offered the coaching job to Charlie Eckman.

From there, the series turned to Zollner's heartbreak. The owner of a piston factory, Zollner had nurtured basketball in the northern Indiana city since 1941. For years, the team had played its games in Fort Wayne's North Side High School, until Zollner had finally convinced the city to build an arena. But few people had figured the Pistons would be good enough to make it to the Finals. So the arena was scheduled for another event, a bowling tournament, that spring of 1955. Zollner was bitterly frustrated that the Finals had to be played in Indianapolis, where his team had only a marginal following. "He was really disappointed," Danny Biasone said of Zollner. "He said, 'I'm moving the team to Detroit.' And that's what he eventually did."

Only 3,200 fans showed up April 3 to see the Pistons win, 96-89, in Indianapolis. Hutchins rebounded like a madman and scored 22, as Fort Wayne opened as much as a 15-point lead in the second half. Rocha and Schayes scored 21 each for Syracuse, but the Pistons countered with balance.

Fort Wayne then evened the series at 2-2 in Game 4, also in Indianapolis, 109-102, despite 28 points by Schayes. The Nats were troubled by poor shooting, hitting just 32 of 103 shots from the field. At one point the Pistons led, 80-62.

Eckman, a former referee, decided the fans' cheers were better than the jeers.

Then on April 7, with Game 5 still in Indianapolis, the Pistons took a 15-point lead, only to see the Nats pull close again in the second half. Then in the third period, the action took a bizarre turn.

"We were playing them," Paul Seymour said. "All of a sudden there was an explosion. We jumped a mile. We thought a bomb went off. A guy behind the bench had gotten pissed off and thrown a chair. We turned around and it was this little bitty guy sitting there sheepishly."

"It went flying over our heads on the bench and went out on the floor," King said.

King said something curt to the guy who had thrown the chair, and the man was led away by police. The action resumed, and the Nats cut the lead to 72-71 with just over a minute remaining. Rocha, however, missed a key shot, and the Pistons' Frank Brian hit two free throws at the end.

Immediately fans crowded the floor and seemed intent on preventing the Nats from leaving. One guy in particular blocked their way, George King recalled.

"Cervi grabbed the guy by the front of the shirt and ripped it right off him," King said.

"I grabbed the guy by the neck," Cervi said. "When I yanked, his tie came away in my hand. 'Get out of my way,' I said. They opened up and I went through."

A short time later, King learned he had been charged with making threatening statements in connection with the chair-throwing incident. It seemed that the man who threw the chair was an off-duty policeman who obtained a warrant against King. The matter was settled when authorities said King could merely apologize for his language. King didn't think he had anything to apologize for, but team officials told him to do so just to get the matter behind them. King reluctantly agreed.

After all, the Pistons were returning to Syracuse trailing 3-2 in the series. Even so, the Nats had reason for confidence. The final two games would be played in the War Memorial, where the Pistons hadn't won in six seasons. They didn't play scared, though. Fort Wayne took an immediate lead and extended it to as much as 10 points in the first half of Game 6.

The tense atmosphere, however, had followed them from Indianapolis. In the second period, the Nats' Wally Osterkorn and the Pistons' Don Mieneke exchanged punches, an outbreak that brought the fans onto the War Memorial floor. After a time, police restored order and the game continued.

Shooting his jumper, Yardley fired the Pistons (he would finish the game with 31) and lifted them to a 74-68 lead at the end of the third. The Nats finally took the lead with just over four minutes left when Earl Lloyd hit a set shot. At the 90-second mark, the Pistons tied it at 103. But then Kerr hit a jump shot and Farley tipped in a miss. After hitting their free throws, the Nats evened the series at three all with a 109-104 win. Even the shot clock hadn't saved it from being a foulfest. Syracuse had been whistled for 31 transgressions, Fort Wayne for 33.

Game 7 was even more intense, although it didn't start out that way. The Pistons ran up a big lead, as many as 17 at one point in the second period. Cervi then pulled Seymour and

King and inserted Kenville and Farley in the Syracuse backcourt. "They picked us up and got us right back in it," Cervi said.

"Billy Kenville came in and sparked us and we closed the gap," Schayes said.

They closed to 53-47 by the half and pulled tight down the stretch. Schayes hit two free throws with 80 seconds left to give the Nats a 91-90 lead, but Yardley tied it moments later with a free throw. Then with 12 seconds left, King, a 61-percent free throw shooter, was fouled and went to the line for two. He missed the first and hit the second, giving Syracuse a 92-91 lead. Fort Wayne's Brian inbounded the ball to Phillip, who attempted to go left on Paul Seymour. Seymour nudged him enough to set up King for a steal. There was no call, and like that, the Nats had their first title.

"I bumped the crap out of Andy," Seymour admitted. "For years after that, whenever he'd see me, he'd tell me, 'You got away with the big foul.' I bumped him a little, King was there, and that was it."

Some thought it poetic justice, that Eckman, the former official, had been done in by the zebras.

"It was there," Eckman said of the foul. "(the official) choked up and lost his guts. Earlier in the game, when we were ahead by 17, he called a technical on Frankie Brian that got them going."

As for Danny Biasone, he was elated. "It was a tough game to lose," he said. "I would have felt bad myself."

Mostly, though, he was glad of the clock's role. "If it wasn't for the shot clock, it would have been the dullest game in history," he said. "Fort Wayne was up by 17. Under the old rules, they'd have gone into a stall. Then there'd have been a flurry of fouls."

All, it seemed, was happy in Syracuse. "The night we won the championship, they picked me up," Cervi recalled, "and I told myself, 'This is the time to get out.'"

He didn't follow his intuition, though, and would come to regret it.

1956

The Syracuse Nationals weren't the first team to self-destruct after a championship season, and they certainly wouldn't be the last. They had some conflicts going throughout the 1955-56 season, evidenced by their last-place finish in the Eastern Division.

Their 35-37 record, however, was good enough to get them into the playoffs, where they knocked off Boston in the first round, only to lose to Philadelphia in the Eastern finals, 3-2. When it was all over, the players voted unanimously to cut Cervi out of a share of playoff money.

George Yarkley, the NBA's first "Bird," starred for Eckman after being named a starter.

**Paul Arizin (top) and Neil Johnston
were capable veteran scorers.**

"It was one of those years in which we were catching hell from every side, including the coach," George King explained.

"It wasn't good," Dolph Schayes said. "The players resented a lot of things Cervi did."

Cervi agreed that it was his fault. After being tough for years, he had lightened up on his players, and it cost him. Plus, the team's multiple stockholders made it hard to keep control, he said. It seemed that every player had a different stockholder's ear.

"I blame myself," he said, "because I let go. They felt like I had an attitude where I was winning all the games and they were losing all the games."

Eckman, meanwhile, avoided such troubles by having a clause in his contract stating that his playoff bonus wouldn't be taken as a cut from the players' shares.

That was one of the keys to his success. Plus the fact that he picked his spots. "Never once," he said, "did I give them any hell or talk to them about a loss. You can't talk to a ball player after a game. They're too tired to listen."

Even so, Fort Wayne had its problems. Most of them stemmed from an incident that occurred the season before Eckman's arrival. Jack Molinas, a talented Pistons rookie, had been deeply involved in gambling and was forced out of the league (he would later become a major figure in the college point-shaving scandals of 1961). Fred Zollner was a deeply suspicious man, and the incident made him more so. Although there was no evidence to suggest any of his other players were doing business with gamblers, he seemed certain that was the case.

Zollner hired a former Fort Wayne police detective to shadow the team throughout the 1955-56 season, Eckman said. "Zollner had a private eye. All year he arrived ahead of us in most towns." Despite the distractions and the pressure on certain players that Zollner believed to be doing business, the Pistons made it back to the Finals. They got there by winning the weak Western Division with a 37-35 record, then nosing St. Louis in the divisional finals, 3-2.

Now in his third year, Yardley had developed into a star. "He could get rid of the ball as quick as anybody," Eckman said. "He wasn't big, but he could give that head fake. Bingo. The shot was up and gone."

The Pistons' talent, though, could carry them only so far. Like the Nats, Fort Wayne seemed to be shouldering too many troubles to win a championship. That honor would fall to a team, the Philadelphia Warriors, that had found an answer to its own troubles.

The Warriors had always seemed to have plenty of talent. First there was lantern-jawed center Neil Johnston, a 6'8" veteran out of Ohio State. His hook shot made him what you might call a mid '50s version of a scoring machine. For three straight seasons, 1952-55, he had led the league in scoring. To go with him, the Warriors had 6'4" Paul Arizin, the jump-shooting forward who had led the league in scoring in 1951 and finished number two behind teammate Johnston in '55.

But with the top two scorers in the league, the Warriors had finished dead last in the

Eastern in '55. It was obvious they needed something more. They got it in the draft that spring in the form of 6'6" Thomas Joseph Gola, the son of a Philadelphia policeman. Gola had played his college ball right in Philly at LaSalle. As a freshman, Gola had helped his team to the NIT championship and won a share of the MVP award for himself. Two seasons later, he carried LaSalle to the NCAA championship and was named the Final Four's Most Outstanding Player.

"I have never seen one player control a game by himself as well as Gola does," LaSalle coach Ken Loeffler told reporters.

The next year Gola again carried his team to the NCAA championship game, but there

Rookie Tom Gola was the perfect player to go with the big scorers and big egos.

the Explorers were done in by K.C. Jones, Bill Russell and the University of San Francisco. Regardless, his reputation remained intact, and the Warriors were thrilled to pick him up in the draft that spring. He had brought LaSalle instant success, and the Warriors figured he would do the same for them. They figured right.

"They won it because they got Gola," Charlie Eckman said.

He was the perfect player to go with big scorers and big egos. Eddie Gottlieb had retired as Philly's coach to focus exclusively on managing the franchise. His replacement was former Warriors guard George Senesky, who had been the kind of player to appreciate Gola's unique abilities.

"When Gola came, it changed the whole team," Senesky said. "He was the first big guy to convert from center in college to play backcourt in the pros. He was 6'6" and showed 'em it could be done. Tommy had been a center at LaSalle. He had played against bigger guys where he could shoot on them. Moving to guard required a transition. It took a little while. But after he went around the league once or twice, he learned. He didn't get beaten that much on defense by the smaller guys. But he would get quick fouls and missed some playing time because of it."

Long after his playing days were over, Gola remained proud of his adjustment. "There are certain guys who have to do the dirty job — take the ball out of bounds, play some defense," he told Billy Packer in a 1987 interview. "When I was in college, I played around the basket, but we had a five-man team so everybody handled the ball and everybody was equal. Nobody had to worry about getting the ball and everybody scored. When I got to the pros, we had great scorers, and I went into the backcourt. I played in the backcourt for 10 years and never had the opportunity to play the forward position. I think I could have scored a lot more in the forward position, but I ended up in the backcourt because of my defensive ability."

As a freshman at LaSalle, he had come in and helped focus his older teammates into a championship team. He did the same for the Warriors. "He didn't play like a rookie," Senesky said. "He was a leader. We had confidence in him. He got along well with everybody."

As might be expected, his college success meant that the basketball-sophisticated crowd in Philly was already deeply in love with Gola. His role with the Warriors only seconded the emotion. "Whenever he scored, the public address announcer would say, 'A goal by Goooalla.' He'd have the town going crazy," Eckman said.

Gola was paired in the backcourt with 6'2 ½" Jack George, a third-year pro who had spent part of his college career at LaSalle. George's height gave Philly the tallest backcourt in the league, enabling them to see over opposing defenses. George ranked second and Gola fourth in the league in assists. As a team the Warriors led the NBA in assists.

Arizin and Johnston, averaging about 24 and 22 points per game respectively, benefitted from the solid passing game. But even they didn't carry the burden alone. George and forward Joe Graboski each hit for about 14 points a game, and Gola averaged 10.8.

Gola's height boosted Philly's already substantial rebounding power. Johnston averaged better than 12 rebounds per game, and Graboski, a 6'8", 230-pound "old pro," pulled down about nine a game. Gola added about seven.

The primary people off the bench were Ernie Beck, George Dempsey and Walter Davis, each of them logging better than 1,000 minutes of playing time over the 72-game season.

Although he was no longer coaching, Philly president Eddie Gottlieb still led the league in worrying. "Eddie was great at stripping," Eckman recalled. "The coat would come off first. Then the tie. Over the course of a game, he'd sweat like a stuck hog." His duties still included making the league's schedule. Still the man with a pocketful of notes, Gottlieb somehow consulted the scraps of paper and put together the schedule in his head. "After a while, he was careful not to give himself too much of an edge," Boston's Red Auerbach recalled with a laugh.

With or without Gottlieb's scheduling, the Warriors were clearly the best team in the league in 1955-56. They finished with the best record, 45-27, six games ahead of Auerbach's Celtics.

They fought off Syracuse in the Eastern finals, which left them tired and tentative in

Game 1 of the league Finals. The series opened in Philadelphia, before a crowd of 4,100. What the fans saw was ugly but effective. The best defensive team in the league, the Pistons shut down the Philly offense in the second period, allowing just one field goal in nearly nine minutes. Midway through the period, the Pistons took a 37-22 lead.

Then Senesky put the 6'4" Ernie Beck in the game. A second year player out of Penn, Beck immediately went inside and did the job, both rebounding and scoring (he would finish with 23). "Beck was a good shooter," Eckman said. "He shot line drives right off his ear, like a catcher throwing to second base." By half, Philly had cut the lead to 49-40.

Beck led the Warriors with 11 points in the third, as they turned a nine-point deficit into a nine-point lead, 73-64, heading into the fourth. Hutchins, Foust and Bob Houbregs had pretty much disrupted Johnston's game. They held the Philly center to three field goals (one in the first half) for the game. But Beck and Arizin provided more than enough firepower, and Gola ran the show and did the defensive work. Fort Wayne fought back in the fourth but never got closer than four, the final margin at 98-94. Arizin had scored 28 for the Warriors, and Yardley matched that with 27 for Fort Wayne. The difference had been Beck's offense and Gola's floor play.

Game two was played in Fort Wayne, where the Pistons evened the series at one-all with an 84-83 win. The big points came on free throws from Yardley with 43 seconds left.

Ironically, a key defensive play came from Fort Wayne's Corky Devlin, who wasn't known for his defense. "Devlin was a good offensive player," Eckman said. "But not defense. He couldn't spell the word." Still, he intercepted a pass with 28 seconds left, then missed a shot, which gave the Warriors one final chance. Yardley, though, in the biggest defensive play of all blocked Arizin's shot underneath to preserve the win.

Arizin had again scored big, finishing with 27 points. "Arizin was asthmatic," Eckman said. "He was always clearing his nose.

The Warriors, who won the league's first title in 1947, celbrate their 1956 crown.

Everybody was scared to get close to him. They thought he had germs. I told them it was asthma, not germs. Yardley said Arizin was spittin' and slingin' snot on him. I told Yardley to spit back on him."

The close series brought the city of Philadelphia to life, and a record crowd of 11,698 packed Conventions Hall for Game 3. Arizin again wheezed his way to 27 points, and Johnston finally found his hook shot and added 20. Even so, the Warriors were down 51-48 at the half before finding just enough of an edge in the third period. They took a 2-1 lead with a 100-96 win. Foust put in 19 for Fort Wayne.

Game 4 was scheduled for April 5 in Fort Wayne, where Philadelphia hadn't won in four years. Although they had the series lead, the Warriors were clearly troubled. Senesky remembered that during a layover in Pittsburgh while traveling to Fort Wayne, Gola told his teammates, "Don't worry. We're gonna get the money."

"It was tough to win on the road back then," Senesky said. "But you had confidence in Tommy. You could rely on him. He wasn't gonna throw the ball away. You could just about always get a good shot out of him. He knew the game. He was a smart player."

The Warriors played smartly as a team in Game 4. None was smarter than Arizin, who was unstoppable for the fourth straight came. He hit just about everything he put up.

Reverse layups. Corner jump shots. Long sets. Short hooks. And he was eight for eight from the line to finish with 30 points.

The Warriors took a 106-100 lead with just under two minutes left. But Foust and Yardley hit field goals and Hutchins made a free throw to pull the Pistons to 106-105 with 40 seconds to go. Then George Dempsey made a free throw to move Philadelphia ahead, 107-105. As time expired, Devlin threw up a long prayer that went in. But the officials ruled it was after the buzzer.

To go with Arizin's 30, George added 20, Gola 19 and Johnston 18, to give Philly its first victory in Fort Wayne since February 1952.

Ahead 3-1, the Warriors headed home confident that they could close it out. Once there, they turned on the offense. Arizin scored 26 and Graboski 29. Yardley put in 30 for Fort Wayne, but it wasn't enough. Philly stayed strong down the stetch to give Gottlieb his second league title, 98-88.

In 10 playoff games, Arizin had scored 289 points. Only Mikan had scored more. It wasn't a bad close to the league's first 10 years. Philly, Baltimore, Minneapolis, Rochester and Syracuse had won titles. Almost overnight it seemed, the second decade was upon the league, and just about everyone anticipated the future. But little did they know, it already belonged to somebody else.

6.
Dynasty
Celtics and Hawks

1957

With no air conditioning, Boston Garden ran the range of temperatures. It could be cool and drafty or hot and steamy. Some say these conditions relied not so much on the weather but on what the Boston Celtics needed for a particular game. Regardless of the climate, the atmosphere was almost always oppressive in the dank, smelly building, with the umpteen NBA championship banners hanging in the rafters above the chipped and aged parquet floor. They called this atmosphere the "Celtic mystique," only it was far more tangible than that. Over the years, the tradition virtually hovered over an opponent's shoulder, weighing down his shooting percentage and deflating his confidence.

Detroit Pistons guard Isiah Thomas once said that winning a game there was one of the most difficult challenges of his pro career. In 1995, the Celtics played their last game in the grand old building and moved into a fancy arena nearby, leaving the Garden to an uncertain fate. Would it become a museum, or even worse, a parking lot? The latter seemed like an unthinkable fate for what many Celtic fans considered the ultimate hoops shrine.

Yet, unbelievable as it may seem for modern folks, there was actually a time when Boston didn't sit astride the basketball world, when the Celtics were just another struggling team in a struggling league, when Celtics mystique was as funky as Miami Heat.

There was even a time when Red Auerbach didn't talk so loud and walk so proud.

The time was the quirky fifties, when modern American society was in its pimply stage. Eisenhower had just offered the nation a balanced budget and won his second term in the White House. The civil rights fight was beginning to turn nasty down South. And the Soviet Union launched Sputnik and revealed it was also testing ICBMs. With his first LP and movie ("Love Me Tender"), Elvis Presley was steering the Baby Boom toward puberty. Ford was cranking Edsels off the assembly line. Zenith introduced its first 21" TV screen, but viewers still saw the world in black and white. The airwaves offered *The Ed Sullivan Show* and *The Honeymooners* and *Ozzie and Harriet* and *Leave It To Beaver* and *Dobie Gillis*. The cost of a first-class stamp ran four cents, and the average family of four needed about $60 a week to pay the bills.

But most of these developments mattered little to Arnold Jacob Auerbach as he neared his fortieth birthday. He was almost wholly consumed with winning basketball games, so much so that he left his wife and two daughters in Washington, D.C., eight months

Red Auerbach and Tom Heinsohn celebrate another Finals victory.

the Basketball Association of America formed in 1946. Though only 29, Auerbach had an eye for basketball talent. His time in the Navy had allowed him to line up some of the best players imaginable. Years later, his competitors would complain that Auerbach was successful because of the talent he found in the service.

"He had a great advantage during the war," Paul Seymour of Syracuse said of Auerbach.

Certainly, that was true. But just about everybody was in the service during World War II, and every basketball man scouted around for talent. It wasn't just blind luck that allowed Auerbach to emerge with a team. He immediately directed the Caps to a regular season divisional crown that first year. They lost in the playoffs, but Auerbach's reputation had been established. Across the league, opponents quickly learned that his wavy red hair was true to the stereotype.

"He was flamboyant, gutsy, on top of everything. And fiery. I mean really fiery," Celtics radio announcer Johnny Most said of the young Auerbach. "But the important thing about him was that he knew the rules better than the officials. And he pulled the rule book on the officials all the time because he knew them. And he had the bite of intimidation. Like when his team was not playing well or playing lethargically, he'd go out there and start to scream at the fans or the referee and get them on him."

After a falling out with the management in Washington, Auerbach coached the Tri-Cities Blackhawks for 1949-50, then moved to Boston for 1950-51. The Celtics had been losers in their first four seasons of operation, and team owner Walter Brown figured Auerbach was

out of each year and lived in an efficiency apartment in Boston while he coached the Celtics.

The son of a Russian immigrant, Auerbach had grown up in Brooklyn where his father operated a small laundry. A man steeped in work ethic, his father frowned upon time wasted with athletics. But the young redhead played high school basketball well enough to earn a junior college scholarship, then went on to play for Coach Bill Reinhart at George Washington University. After a stint in the Navy, Auerbach talked his way into the head coaching job of the Washington Capitols when gritty enough to change that. The young coach jumped at the chance. It was a perfect marriage. Auerbach had found an owner who wanted to win as badly as he did. Even more important, Auerbach, a man who trusted few people, had found a man he could trust.

"Walter Brown was one of the pioneers of professional basketball," Auerbach said. "He was a true sportsman. His word was his bond. He gave his whole material being and everything else to basketball. He was a guy who never knew basketball. He grew up in hockey. He came to the point where he loved basketball. That was his baby. He was one of the truly great men that affected my life."

Brown had the staying power when things were difficult financially in those lean early years. He didn't break and run under the pressure. "Holy Moses," Auerbach said. "He mortgaged his house and everything else. He had everything up with the basketball because he believed in it. See, I never had a written contract with him. When I came here I signed a contract. I didn't know him. After the first year we tore up the contract. We had a hand shake year by year. I'd say, 'What's the deal next year? What do you want?' Boom. Boom. We'd take five minutes and it was over. Nothing ever written down."

On occasion, Brown's good heartedness would extend beyond Auerbach's business sense. Red chiseled nickels and guarded Brown's money as if it were his own. "Walter Brown would fall in love with players," Auerbach recalled. "Some of the players would wait until I was out of town and play golf with him and sign with him and make more money. He was a great man. I always compare people to Walter Brown by saying, 'Yeah, he's got some of Walter Brown's traits, but he's no Walter Brown.' Which means he's no sportsman. Walter Brown dedicated his life to sports. He used to subsidize it out of his own pocket and he was never a real wealthy man."

The NBA was a league of eight to ten teams in the 1950s and hardly national. With franchises in Minneapolis, Fort Wayne, Rochester, and Syracuse, the focus was the Northeast and Great Lakes, and to some extent, the Midwest. It was a life of long train rides, cold gyms, dim lighting, lop-sided balls, fickle fans and fight-marred games. The atmosphere required a cunning and a toughness. There was little showboating. Most players disliked anyone doing any fancy leaping. "In those days, you couldn't leave your feet. They'd just knock you into a wall," recalled Slater Martin, who played for the Hawks and Lakers.

It was just the type of atmosphere that stimulated Auerbach's tough competitiveness. He threw the full force of his energy into the

Celtics owner Walter Brown (right) hired Auerbach to turn things around. Bob Cousy (below) was the Celtics' "Houdini of the Hardwood."

Bill Sharman helped give the Celtics the best backcourt in basketball.

job of building the Celtics. New Englanders cared little about basketball in the early fifties, choosing instead to spend their time with hockey. Asked his most important accomplishment in developing the Celtics, Auerbach had a ready answer: "Educating New England about basketball. The Bruins were here much before we were and being the cold climate and all, the colleges played hockey. It was the accepted thing. Take schools like Boston College. The number one sport was football and then hockey for years and years. But through a process we educated the people who became fans. That took quite a while. We made talks to the high schools, junior high schools. We did clinics all over. We would take a portable court and go to supermarket parking lots to conduct clinics and things like that, in order to teach our future fans."

Bob Cousy, the so-called "Houdini of the Hardwood," became another major factor in the popularization of basketball in New England, although he had to overcome Auerbach's skepticism to do it. For the Celtics' draft that spring of 1950, Brown suggested Auerbach pick Cousy, a 6'1" All-America guard at nearby Holy Cross. Cousy had a complete repetoire of fancy moves, from behind-the-back dribbles to no-look passes. Brown figured him as a selection that would please the fans. The coach, however, spurned the suggestion and made a regrettable comment to reporters that he had been hired to win championships, not to please "the local yokels." Boston selected Charlie Share, a seven-footer out of Bowling Green, in the first round and Chuck Cooper of Duquesne in the second. Cousy, meanwhile, was taken in the first round by Tri Cities, then quickly traded to the Chicago Stags. But that franchise folded, and as fortune would have it, Boston drew Cousy's name out of a hat in an expansion draft.

Auerbach cursed the bad luck. He had wanted veteran guard Max Zaslofsky.

But Auerbach believed deeply in the running game, the strategy he had learned while playing under Reinhart at George Washington. And Cousy wasted little time proving he was just the player to take the running game to a new level. He had a unique style to say the least. He could play the game on the go, and the rest of the Celtics weren't quite up to speed with him. Many times during that first season, his passes hit unexpecting hands and faces.

"Passingwise, Cousy was a fancy dancer," Syracuse coach Al Cervi said. "But there were a lot of times he threw the ball into the west wind."

With the turnovers mounting, Auerbach had a talk with his rookie ballhandler. "We came to an understanding," the coach said. "I told him, 'I don't care how you throw the pass. Between the legs. Over the head. Behind the back. I don't care. But somebody better catch it, because if they don't catch it, it's your fault.' I reasoned that the people we had were great athletes. They could catch the ball if they knew it was coming. What good did it do to fool the defenses, if you were fooling your own people at the same time?"

Cousy said his problems were no different than those faced by any rookie point guard adjusting to the pro game. "I was a little advanced in terms of unorthodox ball maneuvering," he said. "But what I was doing then every 12-year-old is doing now."

In time, the rookie guard and the regulars grew used to each other, and Cousy averaged 15.6 points on his way to winning NBA Rookie of the Year for 1951. It was the beginning of a career in which Cousy would lead the league in assists for eight straight years.

"He was the greatest innovator of the game," Johnny Most said of Cousy. "He had such a fabulous imagination. I think the greatest passer who ever lived. He could throw any kind of pass. The minute he touched the ball his head was up and he was looking down court looking for the open man. It was his philosophy to do it with the pass rather than the dribble. But if he had to dribble, if they forced the dribble, he could make you look like a fool. He really could. He had all the moves of a Globetrotter. And he never was lacking in confidence."

Just before hiring Auerbach, Walter Brown had signed Easy Ed Macauley, the 6'8", 190-pound center, who had spent the previous season with the St. Louis Bombers. An All-American at St. Louis University, Macauley was no intimidator, but he had a graceful offensive style and could run the floor. Together, Auerbach's first group of Celtics pushed Boston to a 39-30 finish for 1950-51.

Then the coach added another great player the next season, 1951-52, in Bill Sharman, the sharpshooter and defensive hawk out of Southern California who was playing baseball for the Brooklyn Dodgers. Sharman's ability at both ends of the floor gave the Celtics the best backcourt in basketball. He and Macauley had the speed and agility to go with Cousy. With this cast as the core of the franchise, the Celtics finished at .500 or above over the next three seasons. They were slick and fancy and something to watch (when they weren't freezing the ball against bigger stronger teams). But speed and flash weren't enough to get them past the division finals.

Then for 1954-55, the NBA adopted its 24-second shot clock, and to Auerbach's liking, the game became much speedier. Yet the new tempo made the Celtics' weaknesses even more obvious. Boston had the greyhound guards in Cousy and Sharman to run other teams off the floor, but they didn't have a powerful rebounding center who could pull the ball off the defensive boards and throw the outlet pass to start the fast break. Macauley was a fine shooter, but he simply didn't have the muscle and inside knack to fill that role. He was more of a forward.

> C**ousy was the greatest innovator of the game. He had such a fabulous imagination. I think the greatest passer who ever lived. He could throw any kind of pass. The minute he touched the ball his head was up and he was looking for the open man...He had all the moves of a Globetrotter. And he never was lacking confidence.**
>
> **— Johnny Most**

Auerbach had begun looking for that special inside player, when his old college coach, Bill Reinhart, told him of Bill Russell, then a sophomore center for the University of San Francisco. College basketball received little publicity in those days. There was no national television, no basketball poop sheets, no cable connection, no Dick Vitale touting the stars. Because he competed on the West Coast, Russell was largely unknown to the Eastern basketball establishment. Plus he was an unusual package. He was 6'9" and exceptionally athletic (he could run the 440 in 49 seconds). His sense of timing made him an excellent rebounder and shotblocker. Yet his offensive skills were unrefined to the point that much of his scoring came from guiding his teammate's missed shots into the basket. His knack for this "guiding" led to the development of offensive goal tending rules in college basketball.

Russell's reputation improved in 1955 as he and guard K.C. Jones led San Francisco to the first of consecutive NCAA championships. Still, his lack of offensive polish left most pro teams skeptical of his potential. Auerbach, however, knew Russell was just the player he was looking for.

"I had to have somebody who could get me the ball," Auerbach recalled. "I'd been tipped off about Russell by my college coach, Bill Reinhart. Bill said Russell was the greatest defensive player and greatest rebounder he'd ever seen."

Rochester had the first pick in the 1956 draft but planned to select Sihugo Green of Duquesne. St. Louis owned the second pick, but Hawks' owner Ben Kerner questioned how Russell would adjust as a pro. Plus he was put off by Russell's talk of a large contract. Auerbach's main competition for Russell would be the Harlem Globetrotters and the Minneapolis Lakers, the franchise with the third pick. The Globetrotters would offer plenty of money, but Russell was too proud a player to turn his basketball into a comedy routine. To get the second pick in the 1956 draft, the Celtics offered Macauley to the Hawks. Kerner wanted more. A couple of years earlier, Auerbach had employed the managerial craftiness he would come to be known for by drafting a pair of Kentucky blue chippers, Cliff Hagan and Frank Ramsey, although both were headed into the service. The Kentuckians were coming out just in time for the 1956-57 season, so Auerbach threw in Hagan to close the deal with the Hawks.

Walter Brown was also concerned that

Bill Russell came to Boston after proving his rebounding skills in college.

Macauley, a Boston favorite, would resent the trade. But Macauley was a St. Louis native, and he was faced with the health problems of his son. He assured Brown that he welcomed the opportunity to return home. With everyone happy, the trade went through smoothly, the only hitch being that Russell had made clear his intentions to play with the U.S. Olympic team in the Summer Games in Austrailia. He wouldn't join Boston until late December, and because of Olympic rules in effect then, he wouldn't be able to sign a contract until after the Games were over. The Celtics, however, weren't exactly shorthanded. A year earlier, they had drafted Jungle Jim Loscutoff, a muscled, 6'5" forward out of Oregon. And Ramsey, the 6'3" forward drafted out of Kentucky in 1954, was returning from a year in the service.

In addition, Auerbach had picked up two other jewels in the 1956 draft: Tom Heinsohn, a 6'7" forward out of Holy Cross, and K.C. Jones, Russell's teammate at San Francisco. Jones, a third-round pick, would do a stint in the Army and try pro football before joining the Celtics in 1958. But Heinsohn would become an immediate factor, and all three from that 1956 draft would eventually wind up in the Hall of Fame.

To bolster the backcourt depth, Auerbach signed Andy Phillip, the veteran with Finals experience at both Chicago and Fort Wayne. Dick Hemric, Jack Nichols, Lou Tsioropoulos and Togo Palazzi filled out the roster and provided more bench strength.

With Loscutoff and Heinsohn working the defensive boards, the Celtics got the ball out on the fast break that fall of 1956 and ran their way to a 16-8 record, three games ahead of the defending champions, the Philadelphia Warriors. Then that December 22, after having

NBA veteran Andy Phillip (above) and draft pick Heinsohn were also added for the 1956-57 season.

helped the U.S. win the Olympic gold, Russell joined the Celtics. (The young center reportedly had been offered $35,000 by the Globetrotters but turned that down to accept a $20,000 contract with Boston.) After getting stuck in his first Boston traffic jam and arriving late for the game, Russell scored only six points but pulled down 16 rebounds (in 21 minutes of playing time) to help Boston beat St. Louis. Maybe it wasn't obvious that first night, but the NBA would never be the same.

The impact on the Celtics was almost immediate. Russell struggled a bit the first few games, but his presence unshackled the rest of the team. The rookie center was such an awesome defensive rebounder that Heinsohn's and Loscutoff's roles shifted from battling on the boards. The forwards merely boxed out their men, then released quickly for the fast break while Russell was snaring the rebound

Cliff Hagan had been brought into the NBA by the Celtics before being traded to the Hawks.

and whipping the outlet pass to Cousy.

Sharman and Cousy, meanwhile, were ecstatic with this development, after having spent the previous seasons frustrated by the team's lack of inside power. Plus Russell's intimidating presence at center allowed them to gamble on defense. If they made a mistake, more often than not, Russell covered for them.

But the most pleased was Auerbach, who considered Russell's shotblocking to be one of the major innovations in the evolution of pro basketball. The young center exuded a confidence that bordered on arrogance. But as he later revealed in his book, Second Wind, Russell was far more insecure about his offensive skills than he let on. He was aware of his detractors. Across pro basketball, the coaches, the players, the writers all believed that the ideal big man was an offensive force.

But when Russell arrived, Auerbach called him in and told him not to worry about offense, that his primary responsibilities were rebounding and defense. The coach also promised that statistics, particularly scoring averages, would never be a part of contract discussions. Auerbach's understanding of Russell's unique skills was the single important element in the genesis of the Celtics dynasty.

Like Auerbach, Russell really cared only about winning. Player and coach didn't have to spend much time together to sense this in each other. "He was the ultimate team player," Cousy said of Russell. "Without him there would have been no dynasty, no Celtic mystique."

Beginning in his college days (he received little playing time until his senior year in high school) Russell had made shotblocking a science. By the time he reached the pros, he possessed a very special skill. He never swatted the ball so that it went out of bounds. Instead he brushed it, or caught it, or knocked it away, so that most times it remained in play and became a turnover, sparking the Celtics' fastbreak the other way. Such a defensive presence sent shock waves across the league.

"Nobody had ever blocked shots on the pros before Russell came along," Auerbach said. "He upset everybody."

The often-cited example is that of Neil Johnston, the Philadelphia center who dominated NBA scoring with his rather flat hook shot. Russell was so effective in blocking Johnston's shot that the three-time NBA scoring champion became ineffective and tentative on offense. Because he was basically a one-dimensional player, Johnston was unable to adjust. It was said that Russell's presence drove Johnston from the league, a claim that the Philadelphia center vehemently denied. Yet after the 1956-57 season, Johnston ceased to be a dominant offensive power.

"When Russell came into the league, that was the end of the hook shooters," said George Senesky, Johnston's coach at Philadelphia. "And Johnston shot his from way down. But Russell was pretty smart, too. When the game was essentially over, he would let Johnston score."

The addition of Russell, Ramsey and Heinsohn to the Boston roster made the Celtics almost unstoppable. Two weeks after Russell began play, Philadelphia owner Eddie Gottlieb protested that Boston's center was playing a one-man zone and goaltending. Other coaches and owners around the league joined the chorus. But Auerbach fended them off. "When we made the deal for Russell nobody thought he was going to be good," the Boston coach told reporters. "He has far exceeded everybody's expectations. None of his blocks of shots have been on the downward flight. He has marvelous timing. He catches the ball on the upward flight."

When the league supervisor of officials said Russell's play was clearly within the rules, Gottlieb dropped his beef. The age of a new athleticism had dawned, and everywhere coaches looked for a way to counter it. Mostly, other teams tried to muscle and bang Russell. But as tough and proud as he was, Boston's new weapon wasn't about to back down.

In other ways, Russell was not an average NBA rookie. A Celtics' tradition called for first-year players to haul the bag of practice balls from game to game. Heinsohn had been doing this chore and hoped he could pass it over to Russell when the center joined the team. But Russell's fierce frown made his teammates think better of asking. So Heinsohn carried on.

The Celtics finished the regular season 44-28, six games ahead of Syracuse in the Eastern Division, as Russell averaged 19.6 rebounds. Cousy led the league in assists and was voted the NBA's MVP. As the playoffs began, Heinsohn was selected the Rookie of the Year. In the lockerroom before the first playoff game, he opened the envelope containing the $250 rookie prize. Always a needler, Russell eyed the money and said that half of it should be his. At least half, some observers thought.

Boston pushed Syracuse out of the way rather easily in the Eastern finals. But St. Louis had battled to the Western Division championship after tying for first place during the regular season with only a 34-38 record. The Hawks, though, were a team that had jelled late and downed both Minneapolis and Fort Wayne in the playoffs.

Taken at face value, the Finals matchup didn't seem like much. The Celtics had finished the schedule 10 games better than the Hawks. But there was so much more to the 1957 NBA Finals than face value. The fortunes of the players and management of the Hawks and Celtics had become entwined over the years. Auerbach had worked for Kerner when the franchise was the Tri-Cities

Alex Hannum was the third coach for the Hawks in 1956-57.

Blackhawks. Macauley had played six seasons in Boston. Hagan had been brought into the league by the Celtics, then dealt to the Hawks. St. Louis had passed on drafting Russell. Charlie Share, who played in the St. Louis frontcourt, had been drafted by Boston and then released. Cousy, of course, had been the property of Kerner's Blackhawks, who had traded him to Chicago. Just about every player, it seemed, had a history with the other team.

The Hawks matched up well with Boston, too, despite their record. They had the incomparable Bob Pettit at forward, as well as Macauley, Hagan, Jack Coleman and Share in the frontcourt. Their guards were excellent, as well. Slater Martin ran the team (The Lakers had traded Martin to New York, but he remained there just a matter of weeks before the Hawks acquired him). At guard with him was Jack McMahon, a solid pro the Hawks had gotten from Rochester in a trade that included Coleman.

Bob Pettit scored 37 points in the opening-game victory for the Hawks.

About the only question mark was at coach. Ben Kerner set a record for coaching changes that only George Steinbrenner of the Yankees could admire. Red Holzman began the season with the job, but lasted only until early January with the team's record at 14-19. Kerner replaced him with Martin as interim player/coach. Slater, however, loved to play and had little interest in the other headaches.

Finally, the job fell to Alex Hannum, a Hawks' sub who had been claimed on waivers earlier in the season. He was a veteran journeyman with a good idea of the game. In other words, he let 'em play.

The Hawks proved they were ready to do that right off the bat in the Finals. Sharman scored 36 for the Celtics in the first game at the Garden, but Pettit scored 37, and Macauley and Martin added 23 apiece. With that kind of firepower, the Hawks pushed the home team to double overtime. Miraculously then, St. Louis won it, 125-123, on a long shot by Jack Coleman as the 24-second clock expired. The Celtics got the ball back but couldn't score.

Immediately, it was clear the matchup would be intriguing. St. Louis would do most of its scoring in the frontcourt with the offensive touch of Macauley and Pettit, who had been effective against Russell in Game 1. Most of Boston's offense came from the guards. St. Louis had excellent defenders and floor people in Martin and McMahon. Boston answered with defense in Game 2, held Pettit to 11 points and won 119-99 to tie the series at one.

Game 3 was another zinger, however. The St. Louis crowd in Kiel Auditorium had its rough edges, which included a reputation for racial and anti-Semitic epithets. (The Hawks would become the last all-white team to win a title.). Auerbach stirred this cauldron during pre-game warmups when he complained that one of the goals was too low. "I knew it was too low when Sharman and Cousy told me they could touch the rim," he explained. Auerbach took his complaint to the officials, who agreed to check the height. They found no problem. Kerner, though, had become overheated by the delay and stalked out onto the floor to scream that Auerbach was embarrassing him in front of the home fans.

Cousy dishes off to Heinsohn in Game 2 victory.

Auerbach ended the tirade with a shot to Kerner's mouth. "I was talking to the refs," Auerbach later explained. They chose not to throw him out, he said, because the incident occurred before the game. The blow brought blood but no permanent damage to Kerner, who was a friend to Auerbach both before and after the incident. "When I retired he gave me wonderful gifts," Auerbach said.

With this exchange as a backdrop, Game 3 began without further incident and quickly developed into a tense defensive struggle. Characteristic of such, there were numerous fouls and both teams did well at the line. But at the end, Pettit hit a long shot to give the Hawks a 100-98 win and a 2-1 lead. Boston came right back to win the fourth game, in St. Louis, 123-118, to tie the series again. Cousy scored 31 to counter 33 by Pettit. Then the Celts zipped St. Louis 124-109 in Game 5 for a 3-2 Boston lead. The series returned to St. Louis, where the Hawks waged another defensive battle and held Cousy to 15. Still, he could have won it with 12 seconds left and the score tied at 94, but he missed at the free-throw line. As expected, the Hawks gave Pettit the desperation shot, which missed, but Hagan tapped it in for a 96-94 win.

Tied at 3-3, the series returned to the Garden. Red Auerbach stood at the brink of a championship, the thing he had coveted for more than a decade. Like most coaches who had never won a title, he carried all the self doubts. When he had been a high school coach, he had put together a championship-caliber team that had been defeated. His good teams with the Washington Capitols had suffered the same fate. Those doubts continued while he struggled in Boston to put together a team. "I would look around at the other coaches," he recalled, "and I would say to myself, 'I still think I'm as good as they are.'" Yet as the 1957 Finals followed their excruciating path, he found the doubt returning. Here he was again in a championship game. What if he lost it again?

"I thought about it," he said. "Finally, I said, 'Oh sh--, what am I gonna do about those kinds

of things?' I just put it out of my mind. By that time, I had a lot of experience."

Even his experience didn't prepare him for what followed. Game 7 was a classic, except for the performance of the Boston backcourt. Cousy shot 2 for 20 and Sharman 3 for 20. Combined they made only 12.5 percent of their field goals. The championship load fell on the rookies, Russell (19 points and 32 rebounds) and Heinsohn (37 points and 23 rebounds).

The Celtics had jumped out early, but the Hawks wound up leading 28-26 at the end of the first. Boston went on a tear from there, moving up 41-32. Hagan put the Hawks back in it with a six-point outburst in the closing minutes of the half. They led, in fact, 53-51 at intermission. The Celtics found another edge late in the third, 73-68, and pushed that lead to eight points early in the fourth. The Hawks answered again with a 9-0 run to take the lead and held a four-point edge with less than two minutes left. Boston hit three free throws to trail 101-100. At less than a minute, St. Louis had the ball and Coleman took the shot to win it.

At this precious moment, Russell practiced his art. He blocked the shot and scored at the other end to give Boston a 102-101 lead. The Hawks couldn't score, and Boston again got possession. Desperate, the Hawks fouled Cousy, who had a chance to clinch the title at the line. He made one of two.

With the Celtics leading 103-101, Pettit sank two free throws in the closing seconds to send the game into overtime. Foul troubles caught up with the Hawks from there. McMahon went first, then Hagan fouled out. Still, St. Louis stayed close. As the first extra period wound down, Boston again held a lead, 113-111, but Coleman, who had won Game 1 for St. Louis, hit another clutch jumper for another overtime. With just seconds to go in the second extra period, Macauley went to the bench after fouling Loscutoff. The muscular forward hit two free throws for a 125-123 Boston lead. For their only hope to tie, the Hawks had to inbound the ball with a full-court pass to Pettit. Player-coach Alex Hannum, the last eligible player on the Hawks' bench, entered the competition for the first time in the series. He planned to bank the pass off the backboard and hope that Pettit could tip it in. Incredibly, Hannum banked the pass off the board to Pettit, but the final shot rolled off the rim.

The Celtics celebrated by shaving Russell's beard in the lockerroom, downing a few cold ones and going out to dinner. It was the first of the good times for Boston. Cousy remembered it as the most satisfying of all.

So did Auerbach. "It was hard," the coach said. "The first one is always the hardest, and it's also the most satisfying. Everywhere I went that following summer, I could tell myself, 'I'm the coach of the world champions.' And basketball is a world game."

1958

In his era, Bob Pettit epitomized basketball success. His statistics alone bear that out, although the numbers are only one indication of his greatness. Like George Mikan, he had the heart to overcome early adversity. Pettit was cut from his junior high team as a sophomore but made the varsity the following season after spending every spare minute he had at a backyard hoop.

This extra effort would become the hallmark of his career. Each plateau of success in life meant that more hard work would be needed to reach the next level, he once explained. He was driven by the need for personal satisfaction.

"When I fall below what I know I can do, my belly growls and growls," he said. This inability to digest mediocrity pushed him far beyond the sum of his talents.

"In his day, he was the best power forward that was," Red Auerbach said of Pettit. "Elgin Baylor was a close second. Pettit could do more things than Baylor, because he could play some center. And he was a better rebounder than Baylor. Pettit was Mr. Clean. Mr. All America. He was like John Havlicek, a clean liver, just a super guy. But very, very competitive. He would play all out, whether he was 50 points ahead, or 50 behind. It didn't matter. That's the only way he knew how to play — all out."

He entered college at Louisiana State as an unsung 6'7" player. But Pettit grew to a 6'9" center and retained his mobility. He averaged 27.4 points per game over his college career, outstanding numbers in the era of slower basketball and good enough to make Pettit a three-time All-America.

He was drafted by the Milwaukee Hawks in 1954, and once again found adversity. In training camp, he found that he couldn't outmuscle Charlie Share at center and was moved to forward. For the first time in his career, he had to play facing the basket. Pettit responded the way he had after being cut back in high school. He worked overtime to adjust

> **W**hen Russell arrived, Boston's veteran center Arnie Risen took him aside and talked about the ins and outs of the competition around the league. Another veteran on another team might not have imparted knowledge to a rookie about to take his starting job, Russell later noted, but Auerbach surrounded himself with people who only cared about winning.

his game. He became a starter for coach Red Holzman's Hawks, but the other forwards in the league had their turns at teaching him lessons. Vern Mikkelsen of the Lakers overpowered him. Dolph Schayes of the Syracuse Nationals befuddled him with slick offense. Maurice Stokes of the Cincinnati Royals moved around him with superior quickness. Pettit eventually found a way to counter all of them.

Holzman thought his rookie forward from the South was a bit too gentlemanly and one night threatened to cut him if he didn't punch somebody in a game against the Lakers. Pettit looked around for someone little to hit and finally took a swing at guard Slater Martin. He missed and thumped Mikkelsen in the chest instead.

"Please excuse me Mr. Mikkelsen," the rookie said quickly. The remark drew hoots that followed Pettit around that season.

Fortunately, his play outdistanced that rookie blunder. He averaged 20.4 points his first season (fourth best in the league) and finished third in rebounding. That performance earned him rookie of the year honors and presaged his stardom. He made the All-NBA first team for 10 of the 11 years he played. In 1956, he became one of only three players in NBA history to lead the league in both rebounding and scoring. (He retired in 1965 as the leading scorer in NBA history, although he knew the record wouldn't last long with Wilt Chamberlain in the league.)

As might be expected, it hadn't taken Pettit long to earn the respect of his "teachers." By his second year, he was an offensive weapon feared by opponents.

Auerbach rated Pettit (here taking the ball away from Boston's Arnie Risen) the best power forward in the game, better than Elgin Baylor.

Sam Jones was Auerbach's newest weapon for 1957-58.

"He kept coming at you," Schayes said. "There was no way you could stop him over the course of a game. He was just too strong."

The Hawks moved to St. Louis after Pettit's rookie season, and he soon became the favorite of crowds there. He came to be known as "Big Blue" because of his insistence on wearing a ratty old blue overcoat. That affection increased during the height of Pettit's career, from 1957-61, when he led the Hawks to four NBA Finals. Only once, in 1958, did they claim the trophy, losing the other three times to the Boston Celtics. Yet the effort was enough to establish St. Louis as one of the best clubs in league history. And although the franchise later moved to Atlanta, the Hawks' 1958 championship still stirs hearts in St. Louis.

The 1957-58 season was one in a chain of Pettit's outstanding campaigns. He averaged 24.6 points and 17.4 rebounds per game while boosting the Hawks to the Western Division crown with a 41-31 record.

By no means, though, were the Hawks a one-man team. Both Slater Martin and Jack McMahon returned at guard. "Jack was a prototypical New York City guard," Cousy said. "He was just a good, solid complimentary guard."

To go with this backcourt, the Hawks still had Ed Macauley, Chuck Share and Jack Coleman in the frontcourt. Also there was 6'4" forward Cliff Hagan, the team's other major point producer, averaging 19.9 points per game while shooting .443 from the floor, second best in the league. Despite his height, Hagan found a way to dominate inside. "He was the Adrian Dantley of his day," Auerbach said, comparing Hagan to one of his favorite modern players. "He played the game the same way. He was a

very powerful man. And a proud man. He was always a hard worker, and another Mr. Clean in Pettit's mold."

Hagan had begun perfecting his inside moves as a high school center in Owensboro, Kentucky. He joined the Celtics' Frank Ramsey at the University of Kentucky, where they starred on three of coach Adolph Rupp's best teams. Hagan had a wonderful hook shot and a rebounding fierceness that earned him consensus All-America honors in 1951-52.

"When Hagan took a hook shot, I knew that thing was going in," Ramsey said of his teammate.

Drawing their strength from these talents, the Hawks blasted the Pistons, 4-1, in the Western Division finals and advanced to the championship series for the second consecutive year.

The Celtics, meanwhile, dominated the Eastern Division with a 49-23 record. Russell led the league in rebounding with the unheard of average of 22.7 per game. Sharman led them in scoring with a 22.3 average. And Auerbach added his newest weapon, Sam Jones, a surprise first-round pick in the draft, out of little North Carolina Central. Auerbach's old friend, Bones McKinney, had tipped him off that this 6'4" guard was something special. In time, Jones would prove it. But for the present, he fit in nicely coming off the bench.

Russell's ankle injury might have cost Boston the 1958 title.

With Cousy leading the league in assists (7.1 per game), Boston ran past Syracuse to win the Eastern Division title by eight games. The players had voted Russell the league MVP, but the writers, showing their lack of understanding, put him on the All-NBA second team.

Most observers figured the Celtics probably would have won the 1958 title if Russell hadn't suffered an ankle injury in the third game of the series. Auerbach, however, found no comfort in that opinion.

"You can always look for excuses," he said. "We just got beat."

The results support that opinion. The Hawks upset the Celtics, with a healthy Russell, in Game One in Boston Garden, 104-102. Boston cracked back with a wipeout in Game Two, 136-112. Back in St. Louis, the Hawks held serve in Game Three when Russell injured his ankle, 111-108.

Then, without Russell, the Celtics evened the series with a 109-98 surprise in Game Four. Still, Boston was drastically undermanned in the frontcourt. Loscutoff had missed the entire season with an injury. And Russell's bad ankle left only Heinsohn and graybeard Arnie Risen to deal with the Hawks' power game. Even so, it was no cakewalk. St. Louis forced a 102-100 win in Boston Garden to take a 3-2 lead.

Back home in Kiel Auditorium on April 12, the Hawks weren't about to miss their opportunity. Pettit guaranteed that, turning in a solidly spectular performance. He scored 31 points in the first three quarters, then zoomed off in the final period, nailing 19 of his team's last 21 points. His last two, a tip-in with 15 seconds remaining, put the Hawks ahead, 110-107. The Celtics scored a meaningless bucket and could do no more. Ben Kerner's team finally had a title, 110-109.

Pettit's 50-point performance tied the single-game playoff scoring record set by Cousy against Syracuse in 1953. But Cousy's record had been set in a four-overtime game, an event so foul-plagued that he hit 30 of his points from the free throw line. In pure basketball prowess, Pettit's 50-point performance was stunning. Better yet, it had delivered his team a championship.

It was just the kind of effort Hawks fans had come to expect from "Big Blue."

1959

Even though the Hawks had won the 1958 title, there was a solid feeling across pro basketball that the Celtics were a superior team heading into the 1958-59 season.

About the only thing undermining the glorious beginning of Boston's dynasty was the undercurrent of race. The NBA and the Celtics were integrating ahead of society. There were few, if any, problems on the team. But Boston was a racially troubled town, as was all of America. Some sportswriters in Boston made little effort to mask their contempt for Russell. And road games were sometimes rough, particularly in St. Louis, where the fans delighted in their particular abuse. As with the rough play on the court, Russell wasn't about to back down. "Russ has always been extremely militant, and he is to this day," Cousy said. "He came

Frank Ramsey was the Celtics' first great sixth man.

into Boston with the proverbial chip on his shoulder. His militancy had been honed before he arrived. Of course, there were good reasons for the way he reacted, and I've said many times I would have been far more radical than he was. He couldn't play golf at the local courses. At one point, vandals broke into his house and defecated in his bed."

Russell's anger was justified, Johnny Most agreed. "I knew where he was coming from deep down. And for a lot of it, I didn't blame him. He faced a lot of irritating, irritating prejudice."

But his private manner with his teammates was as playful as his public face was scowling.

In Auerbach's system, winning was the only priority. For that system, the coach sought players who wanted to win as badly as he did. They weren't about to let racial differences interfere with that. Russell has said many times that above all, he knew he could trust his coach not to be petty. A master psychologist, Auerbach created an atmosphere of give and take, a unique mix of toughness and fun, where pranksters thrived amid grueling practices, an atmosphere that allowed exploding cigars and other silly gags to bring a soft edge to Auerbach's hard drive for winning. Within this system, the Celtics liked each other and got along, mainly because they all liked winning. When Russell arrived, Boston's veteran center Arnie Risen took him aside and talked about the ins and outs of the competition around the league. Another veteran on another team might not have imparted knowledge to a rookie about to take his starting job, Russell later noted, but Auerbach surrounded himself with people who cared only about winning.

That's not to say there weren't problems. The press had no sophisticated knowledge of basketball in those early years, and the reporters fawned over Cousy, the local hero, while virtually ignoring Russell's brilliance. Auerbach, however, sensed these injustices and constantly raved about Russell and other unrecognized players to reporters.

It was in this spirit that Frank Ramsey, the first of the Celtics' sixth men, grew in the public mind. Auerbach didn't invent the idea of the sixth man, but he tirelessly touted and promoted it to the writers covering Boston's games. In so doing, the coach wrapped his athletes in the ever increasing aura of team. After a time, it would become nearly inpenetrable.

The Celtics restarted their efforts in 1958-59, with the addition of Gene Conley, the veteran backup bruiser, and K.C. Jones, who teamed well with Sam Jones off the bench when Auerbach wanted to step up the defensive pressure. The league enjoyed a banner season, with the Knicks averaging crowds of better than

Elgin Baylor (left) and Bob Cousy

18,000 in New York. The Celtics, meanwhile, pulled in an average of 8,100. Again Russell and Cousy led the league in rebounds and assists, respectively. And again Boston powered to the Eastern Division title, this time by 12 games with a 52-20 record.

Despte winning the championship the previous season, St. Louis had undergone several major changes, the biggest of which was the retirement of Macauley. Also Hannum had left as coach because he wanted more control over the team, and owner Ben Kerner wouldn't give it to him. Kerner first hired Andy Phillip to coach the team, but he lasted only a few games into November. The mercurial owner then selected Macauley.

The team had changed its look in the frontcourt a bit with the addition of Clyde Lovellette, who had been picked up in a trade with Minneapolis. During the regular season, the Hawks were nearly as powerful in the West as the Celtics were in the East. Pettit had perhaps his best season ever, breaking the league scoring record by averaging 29.2 points. But the Hawks lost in the semifinals to the Minneapolis Lakers with rookie sensation Elgin Baylor, who had averaged 24.9 points in his first season.

Boston nearly suffered a similar fate against surprise Syracuse with Dolph Schayes. Their semifinal series went to seven games with a dramatic finish in Boston Garden. At one point, Celtics broadcaster Johnny Most got so excited he nearly lost his dentures over the rail of the upper press deck.

"We were down (by eight points) at the half," Most recalled, "and it looked as if the Celtics dynasty would be over before it ever got started. In the second half, it was the most perfectly played basketball game I've ever seen. Heinsohn often said it was the best game he ever played in."

The Celtics charged back in the third period, only to have Syracuse surge again before Boston finally won, 130-125. "I remember after the game that Cousy said they were gonna take Minneaplis in four straight, and they did," Schayes recalled.

The prediction seemed safe enough. In their last regular season meeting, in February, the Celtics had humbled the Lakers, 173-139 (the score was so large it caused Commissioner Maurice Podoloff to check into the possibility of point tampering. The game, though, was clean and thoroughly embarrassing to the Lakers). In

K.C. Jones arrived in 1958-59 to help off the bench.

fact, Boston had beaten Minneapolis eighteen consecutive times over the two previous seasons. Many considered it a miracle that John Kundla had gotten his team into the Finals. From their old crew during the Mikan era, the Lakers still had Vern Mikkelsen. Plus they had picked up Larry Foust, the former Piston. Hot Rod Hundley was the regular in the backcourt. They also got nearly 14 points per game from Dick Garmaker. This cast had finished the regular season at 33-39.

Despite their poor billing, they managed to keep every game close in the Finals. They just couldn't get a win. Boston won the first in the Garden, 118-115, then blasted to 2-0 with a 128-108 win. Game 3 was in St. Paul, where the Lakers fell, 123-120. Two nights later, April 9, Boston finished the sweep, 118-113, in Minneapolis.

It was the first sweep in Finals history.

1960

Pro basketball's familiarity bred its own sort of contempt in 1960. The NBA was an eight-team league, and over the 75-game schedule, opponents saw plenty of each other. The Celtics and Hawks, who knew each other well, got to know each other even better when they met for their third league Finals in four years.

"At the time, the Hawks were the most intense rivalry we had," Cousy said.

And, unlike Boston's fling with Philadelphia and New York, the St. Louis affair was a rivalry of pure competition. With Philadelphia

Slater Martin was the player Cousy most hated to face.

intensity never seemed to abate."

Cousy often looked forward to matching up with the bigger guards around the league, because his speed and quickness would usually win over their size and strength. Martin, though, was smaller than Cousy and matched his quickness. "Slater was the only one I used to call for help on," Cousy said. "I used to tell my big people to set picks as often as they felt like it."

Although Martin was an older veteran, Cousy said he never noticed a diminishing of his quickness. Nor a slackening of his fierce competitiveness.

But for the first time in his 11-year career, injuries began to nag Martin in 1960. "I'd never wrapped an ankle as long as I played basketball," he told writer Charles Salzberg. "Never had a sprained ankle, never put a piece of tape on it. I could get dressed for a game in 30 seconds. I'd put on my jockstrap, slip on the jersey, and I was ready to go."

He pulled a hamstring during the 1960 All-Star game in St. Louis, and that took a few weeks to heal. Then he pulled another leg muscle during the playoffs. But the team was in a tight series with the Lakers and needed a road win. Martin said Kerner asked him to play the next game with a shot of novacain to kill his pain. He agreed. The Hawks won. But Martin was left on crutches the next day and

and New York, the competition was almost as strong between the cities as the teams, Auerbach said. But St. Louis was too far away for that city rivalry. Whatever the two teams felt for each other was felt on the court. Nothing better epitomized this rivalry than the matchup of Cousy against the Hawks' Slater Martin.

"Slater was the guy I most disliked to play against, in terms of his skills matched against mine," Cousy said.

Quite often the younger guards around the league seemed eager to outplay Cousy because of his reputation, the Boston guard recalled. "You could practically see the saliva dripping out of the corners of their mouths. They had heard of Bob Cousy and were jacked up to take me on."

Experience had taught Cousy to remain steady against these young players, because they would tire by the second half and their intensity would abate. Martin, on the other hand, was a veteran, with a young guard's intensity. "In Slater's case," Cousy said, "the

Clyde Lovellette came to the Hawks from the Lakers with plenty of Finals experience.

was through for the season, his last in the league.

The Hawks squeezed past the Lakers and returned to the Finals once more to face the Celtics. Ed Macauley was now in his second season as the Hawks' coach. In a television interview after his team had eliminated the Lakers, Macauley predicted that St. Louis would whip Boston. But that was just his public comment. Privately, he

Russell scored 22 points and added 35 rebounds in the final game.

knew his team would be outmanned in the backcourt.

"We'll be lucky if we win one game," he later told his wife.

The St. Louis lineup had changed considerably since their '58 championship. Pettit and Hagan were still in the frontcourt. But Coleman, Share and Macauley were gone. McMahon's playing time had diminished (he appeared in only 25 games). And with Martin injured, Si Green and Johnny McCarthy ran the backcourt.

The Hawks' other new players, though, were plenty familiar to the Finals. Larry Foust (who had played with Fort Wayne) and Clyde Lovellette had been acquired from Minneapolis. Also Dave Pointek, a small forward, had been picked up from Cincinnati (the Royals had moved there from Rochester in '57). Bob Ferry was a rookie sub in the frontcourt, but he learned quickly.

Although this group had been strong enough win the Western Division with a 49-26 record, most observers, like Macauley, figured they'd never go the distance against the Celtics. After all, the Boston dynasty was off and running, and nothing seemed capable of stopping it. The Celtics had won an NBA-record 59 games for 1959-60. They accomplished this in the Eastern Division despite the dominating presence of 7'1" rookie Wilt Chamberlain, who had joined the Philadelphia Warriors after a stint with the Harlem Globetrotters.

Chamberlain's presence had an unprecedented effect on the league. The NBA was already attracting an average of 15 million viewers to its weekly broadcasts. But the addition of Wilt to the league prompted NBC to broaden its broadcast schedule. And owners upped the league schedule to 75 games to reap more revenues from the new exposure and popularity. Chamberlain responded to this billing by leading the league in scoring with a record 37.2 average. Despite that, Philadelphia still finished 10 games behind the Celtics in the standings and fell 4-2 to Boston in the Eastern finals. The young giant was so dismayed after the loss that he announced his retirement, which he, of course, later reversed. Certainly there was no shame in the loss.

Boston, after all, was a picture of depth and stability, with Russell and his 24 rebounds per game anchoring the team's performance. Sharman and Cousy started, but Sam Jones averaged about 20 minutes and 12 points as Sharman's backup. Heinsohn was in his prime and led the team in scoring at 21.7. In so doing, he had acquired the nickname of Ack-Ack, because he shot as rapidly and frequently as an anti-aircraft gun. Ramsey boosted the scoring totals by another 15 points. And Auerbach got a solid backup effort from K.C. Jones and Gene Conley, the 6'8", 255-pound former baseball pitcher.

True to expectations, Boston dominated the first game of the series, 140-122. But the Celtics got notice they were in for a scrap in Game 2, when the Hawks broke back and upset them, 113-103, in Boston Garden. To reaffirm their dominance, Boston thumped the Hawks again, 102-86, in Kiel Auditorium in Game 3. St. Louis won their second home game, 106-96, to send the series back to the Garden tied at 2-2. Boston again won big there, 125-102, which left things secure enough. Even if the Celtics lost Game 6 in St. Louis — which they did, 105-102 — they returned to the Garden for number seven.

There on April 9, they claimed their second consecutive championship and third overall with a comfortable win, 122-103. It was a day of big numbers for Auerbach's primary people. Russell scored 22 points to go with his 35 rebounds and four assists. The 6'3" Ramsey had 24 points and 13 rebounds, and Heinsohn added another 22 points and eight boards. All together, Boston outrebounded St. Louis, 83-47.

With Martin out of the lineup, Cousy had been able to maneuver unhampered. He finished with 19 points and 14 assists. All the same, St. Louis had nothing to be ashamed of. They had won three more games than Macauley figured they could.

1961

The people who knew Bill Sharman well called him Willie. It was a term of endearment but it didn't begin to indicate his toughness. His reputation today is that of one of the game's great early shooters. That, too, is misleading. Shooters are considered specialists, guys who languish on the perimeter where they take the open shots while everybody else mixes it up. In other words, shooters play soft.

There was never anything soft about Sharman's game.

He was rare, because not only was he a great shooter, but he was a tenacious defensive player as well. Cousy said he always figured he had the most intense killer instinct in basketball — until he met Sharman.

"Bill matched mine," he admitted.

Sharman wasn't known for excessive fighting. But when he did square off, whether the opponent was a seven-footer or just another guard, they were usually one-punch affairs.

"Willie didn't talk," Ed Macauley recalled. "When he'd had enough, you knew it."

His one-punch victims included 6'9", 230-pound Nobel Jorgensen of the Nats and Andy Phillip.

Sharman's skill at pugilism, though, was no greater than any of his other athletic abilities. He was good at everything he did. He lettered in five sports in high school in Porterville, California. Football, basketball, baseball, tennis and track. After retirement from pro basketball, he became a scratch golfer.

Tom "Satch" Sanders helped out on defense and on the boards.

"He's the best athlete I've ever been around," Cousy said, which is no small statement considering Cousy's substantial playing, coaching and broadcasting career.

After a stint in the Navy during World War II, Sharman played basketball at Southern Cal, where he was a 6'2" forward in a controlled offense, a background that didn't exactly prepare him for prominence in pro basketball. He gave pro baseball a try with the Brooklyn Dodgers organization before coming to the NBA with the Washington Capitols for 1951.

Auerbach picked him up after Washington folded, a development that allowed Sharman to prosper. Having been a forward in college, he wasn't a good ballhandler. In Boston, he played alongside Cousy, which allowed him to focus on his shooting and defense.

The Celtics ran a freewheeling system that allowed the players to play. Auerbach was unique among coaches in that he understood what it took to win, Cousy said. When you have talented players, you allow them to play. Boston had six basic plays and three variations of each of those for about 16 different options. But they relied on the freelance and transition situations as often as possible because they played best that way.

"Sharman was just perfect for it because he moved constantly," Cousy said. Other players around the league hated to defend him because he ran continuously.

"He would move in a circle, and eventually he would come free," Cousy said. "I almost

Sharman (guarding Lenny Wilkens) went out a winner in 1961.

knew where he was going before he got there." Most often he would circle and emerge on the weak side just as the defense was collapsing, which left him with an open shot. He was a quick shooter, hoisting the ball from his shoulders up.

"He was a complete technician in terms of the mechanics of the shot," Cousy said. "He never took a low percentage shot."

Those mechanics served him at the free throw line as well. For eight seasons he led the league in free-throw percentage. And for four seasons, 1956-59, he led the Celtics in scoring. He relinquished that role to Heinsohn in 1960 and '61, although Sharman continued to average better than 15 points a game.

But with each succeeding season, Sam Jones had become a bigger factor coming off the bench. And by 1961, Sharman was 35 and had played 11 seasons. The opportunity became available for him to coach the Los Angeles franchise in the new American Basketball Association. Sharman knew it made good sense to retire. It was a difficult decision.

"I didn't want to feel I was just hanging on to receive a paycheck," he said.

"He had a lot of pride, and great players are reluctant to stay too long," Auerbach said. "When it's a losing battle you look other places."

The Celtics sent Sharman out a winner that spring of 1961. They won 57 games during the regular season, 11 better than Chamberlain and Philadelphia. Their roster had changed only with the addition of rookie Tom "Satch" Sanders, a 6'6" rebounder and defensive forward out of NYU who fit nicely into Auerbach's system. With this regular crew, Boston steamrolled Syracuse 4-1 in the Eastern finals and awaited their opponents.

The Hawks had again dominated the Western, only Kerner had changed coaches again. The St. Louis owner had hired Paul Seymour, the former Syracuse coach, during the close of the previous season, only he didn't inform Macauley until after the playoffs were over.

Macauley later said he would have preferred to remain coach, but he agreed to move up to general manager. Seymour wanted the team to run a little more, and they finally had the guy to do that in rookie guard Lenny Wilkens out of Providence College. At first the Hawks veterans were cool to Wilkens, until they realized how well he could run the team. Pettit averaged a whopping 27.9 points, while Hagan and Lovellette each scored about 22 a game.

They might have made a better showing in the championship series if they hadn't gotten caught in such a fight with Los Angeles in the Western finals. Rookie Jerry West and Baylor pushed the Hawks through a seven game series before falling 4-3.

The St. Louis club arrived at Boston Garden April 2 after just completing their series with the Lakers the night before in St. Louis. As would be expected, they were blown out by the Celtics, 129-95. They improved a bit but still lost Game 2, 116-108. Their single victory was a tight win in Game 3 in St. Louis. But the Hawks lost Game 4 at home by 15 (119-104), then succumbed in Boston Garden to fall 4-1.

It was the Celtics' third straight title and fourth in five years. Sharman had certainly done his part, but Sam Jones was eager and waiting in the wings.

7.
Dynasty Continued
Old Celtics and New Lakers

The Boston Celtics emerged full-blown in the early 1960s. Russell and Heinsohn were in their prime. Sam Jones moved in as a starter and a scorer. The careers of Cousy and Frank Ramsey were winding down, but Red Auerbach always seemed to have the right answer to keep the transition of talent flowing smoothly.

K.C. Jones was gaining experience as a backup to Cousy, and in 1962, the Celtics drafted John Havlicek, a nice athlete but no superstar, out of Ohio State. Who could have seen that he would evolve into such a player? In retrospect, the development of the Boston dynasty was something to behold.

But at the time, it was no big deal. At least not in Boston.

The Celtics would win eleven NBA championships between 1957 and 1969. Yet throughout that great run, they seldom sold out Boston Garden. Year in, year out, the Celtics drew average crowds in the range of 8,000, leaving more than 5,000 empty seats most nights. Those numbers seem to confirm the notion that sometimes legends aren't all that impressive while they're being made. It's only with the passage of time that they become larger than life.

Between 1959 and 1966, Auerbach's Celtics won eight straight titles, a run unequaled by

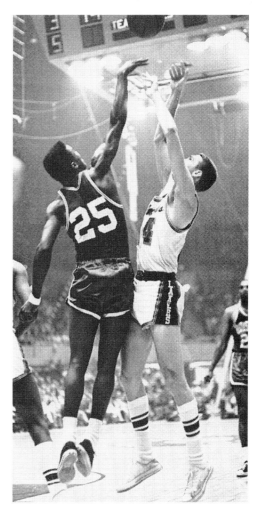

K.C. Jones (left) and Jerry West were two of the NBA's stars in the '60s.

95

West (left) had played for new Lakers coach Fred Schaus at West Virginia.

any professional team in any major sport. Yet each fall after winning a championship, the Celtics never had a sellout for their home opener. They didn't achieve a full house for their first game until November 1966, the season their consecutive streak ended.

"We were real fortunate from '57 on in winning championships," Auerbach said. "People in this area never realized what we did in those days. They would sort of say, 'Big deal.' Where if we were in any other area of the country, the accolades would have been tremendous. I'm talking about New York or New Jersey or Washington, wherever, Chicago, anyplace."

While the Celtics had been on the rise, the NBA's previous dynasty, the Minneapolis Lakers, had slumped into mediocrity. George Mikan had come back to the league in 1955-56 after a year of retirement, but he was unable to duplicate his former performance and retired for good after that season. Although they miraculously played their way into the 1959 Finals (where they were swept by Boston), the Lakers had struggled through

four straight losing seasons from 1957-60. And their attendance had sunk with their place in the standings. In turn, the team's always precarious cash flow grew even more precarious, forcing the owners into desperate considerations. By 1960, as the team struggled through a 25-50 season, the owners had begun selling off players to help meet the expenses. Then they learned that Major League Baseball was moving to the city. Bob Short, the team's principal owner, knew it would be too much competition. So he asked the league to allow him to move the franchise to Los Angeles, where the sports-minded city had recently built the 14,000-seat Los Angeles Sports Arena near the campus of the University of Southern California. At first the league owners voted down the request, 7-1. They were all worried about the increased travel costs for going cross country to play in California. Plus, the Knicks' Ned Irish had hopes of getting Elgin Baylor when the Lakers folded. But the same day they voted down the request, the owners learned that Abe Saperstein, the founder of the Harlem Globetrotters, had announced plans to form the American Basketball Association. None of them wanted the competition getting a head-start in the vast western market. So they voted again. The Lakers won the second time, 8-0, and were on their way to the city of the Angels.

The Lakers held the second pick in the draft that spring of 1960, and with it they selected Jerry West, a skinny, 6'3" forward out of West Virginia (The Royals, who had moved to Cincinnati, took Oscar Robertson out of the University of Cincinnati with the top pick). Because West could score and had lightning quickness, the Lakers figured he would make the adjustment to pro guard. To help ensure this adjustment, the team hired West's college coach, Fred Schaus, to replace Jim Pollard as the new head coach.

That summer, West was playing in the Olympics in Rome, when he learned of the team's move to Los Angeles from an issue of Stars and Stripes. He also learned from the same issue that the Lakers had hired Schaus.

Interesting, West thought.

To some observers, the hiring of Schaus may have seemed an unusual move for Short to take. But for those who knew, the decision made sense. In addition to his experience with West, Schaus brought a good list of credentials. He had been a solid pro player for five seasons with Fort Wayne, then had coached his alma mater, West Virginia, to the heights of college basketball. His 1959 Mountaineers, when West was a junior, had lost the NCAA championship by one point to the University of California, coached by Pete Newell.

It also helped that Schaus had coached another Laker veteran at West Virginia, fourth-year guard Rodney Clark Hundley, better known as "Hot Rod." If West was the obvious link between Schaus and the Lakers, Hundley was the spiritual connection. To Schaus and Hundley, basketball was an opportunity to put on a show. With his dribble-king wizardry, Hundley had played the prime attraction for Schaus in the mid 1950s (when West was an uptight freshman on the junior varsity). West Virginia basketball in those days was a forerunner to the Showtime basketball Schaus would eventually bring to the Lakers. With the pep bands blaring, his Moutaineer teams would dash onto the floor before each game and whip through a crisp series of warm-ups with a godawful blue-and-gold ball. Of course, it didn't come close to matching the hype of modern college basketball, but back in the '50s, the Mountaineer act qualified as fancy-dan. Schaus's basketball-as-entertainment approach struck a twangy chord with fans in the dreary, undeveloped mountain state and carried the Mountaineers to a run of Southern Conference titles.

It also goosed Hundley to hotdoggery's excesses. By the time West and Schaus joined him in Los Angeles, his legend was large and still growing. On the NBA's all-time, good-time team, Hundley was in serious contention for MVP (most vivacious partier). He seemingly knew every hot spot in every city. One typical night in St. Louis, Bob Short saw Hundley standing in front of the team's hotel waiting for a cab to take him off to another good time. Knowing that the Lakers had a game the next night and that Hundley needed his rest, Short tried to get the player to stay in his room. Reportedly, the owner even offered to have a beautiful woman sent up to keep him company.

"Bob, you know I don't work that way," Hundley supposedly said, draping his arm around Short's shoulder. "The thrill is in the chase, baby."

Hundley epitomized the fun-loving Lakers. Their life on the road was free and easy. They stuffed their off-court hours with laughs and card games and good times. The Lakers seemed right for Los Angeles. It was Hundley's kind of town. And Schaus was the Lakers' kind of coach.

All of which made for an awkward first-year adjustment for West, who described himself as painfully shy.

"There was not one inch, not one drop of showmanship in Jerry," Hundley once said of West.

He had grown up on the fringe of the coalfields in little Cheylan, West Virginia (near another little community, Cabin Creek, which would lead to Baylor dubbing West "Zeke from Cabin Creek"). He had traveled in his amateur basketball career, but those experiences did little to prepare him for what he encountered in Los Angeles.

"It was culture shock when I first started playing," West said, "coming from such a small place to such a big city."

Elgin Baylor led the Lakers into the 1960s.

Wilt Chamberlain was a scoring machine during the 1961-62 season.

To the veteran Lakers, he was Zeke, or "Tweetie Bird," a skinnier, hawk-nosed version of the Beverly Hillbillies. West, though, didn't like the names Baylor gave him, didn't like being kidded about his background. All he wanted to do was play basketball. His goal was to play the game as well as he could, and that meant perfect, if possible. And winning was the first test of perfection. If people wanted to watch, that was fine. He just didn't have much to say to them. "I'm not very social," he explained.

Crowds weren't much of a problem, though, in West's rookie season. The Lakers weren't very good. Although the Sports Arena seated 14,000, the Lakers averaged draws of about 5,000 in that first year on the L.A. scene. Early in the schedule, Schaus gave most of the playing time to the veterans, a situation that frustrated West. Schaus was concerned that bringing the rookie along quickly would place too much pressure on him and could end up ruining his confidence if he failed. West, however, wanted one thing. To play.

"I almost felt that I had to be so much better than the people I was playing with, that it was frustrating," West recalled.

Starting in front of West at ballhandling guard was Hundley. "He had fun and did a lot of funny things," Schaus said of Hundley. "But he was a fine player, too. He was a great dribbler and passer, and he played pretty fair defense. He was a scorer, but he was not the great shooter that Jerry West was."

For West, the time as a spectator was unbearable. He let Schaus know that he didn't like it. "I could not learn sitting on the bench," he said. "The only thing I could learn were bad habits. I had to get out there and get over those first year jitters." He knew he could compete on a higher level than the average player. But no matter how hard he tried, or how well he played in practice, his playing time seemed set. As badly as the team needed West's scoring, Schaus remained reluctant to place the burden on his rookie.

Finally, with the team's record sinking, Schaus gave West the nod. "All of a sudden things weren't very good," West said, "and I had a chance to step in and start, and I never gave it up."

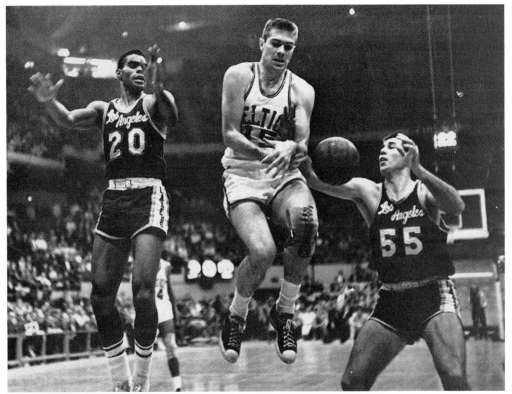

Boston's Tommy Heinsohn loses control as LA's Wayne Yates strips the ball.

The Lakers began a turnaround with West in the lineup, although it was nothing that the rookie guard engineered by himself. Baylor was in his prime, playing the forward spot in spectacular fashion. He led the team offensively and finished second in the league in scoring (behind Chamberlain) at a 34.8 points per game pace. With each passing game, it became more obvious they were something special. Baylor was the acrobatic wonder inside, and West gained confidence running the team. By the playoffs, they were solid.

The Lakers had finished second in the Western with only a 36-43 record. But they battled the Hawks through a seven-game series in the division finals before losing game seven in St. Louis, 105-103. The effort, though, had gotten them the attention of Los Angeles fans. In one season, they had found a home and a following. And West had finally gotten his beloved playing time. The more he played, the better he felt. In him there was a growing sense that he could perform at a higher level than just about any other player in the game.

It wouldn't be long before the rest of the league made that discovery, too.

1962

Wilt Chamberlain pushed the concept of individual achievement beyond imaginable limits during the 1961-62 season. He averaged 50.4 points per game and even scored 100 points against the Knicks in one game. He was able to do all this because Philadelphia owner Eddie Gottlieb wanted to boost his stardom, much as Gottlieb had boosted Joe Fulks years earlier. The owner had his big center play virtually every minute of every game.

Of the 3,890 minutes the Warriors played during the regular season, Chamberlain spent only eight on the bench. As his average suggests, he took 3,159 shots, nearly one every minute he played, which meant that he rang up a stunning 4,029 points.

The Celtics, meanwhile, contented themselves with team-oriented things. The league had expanded its schedule to 80-games, and the Celtics broke their own record by winning 60. Even with Chamberlain's golden numbers, the Warriors finished 11 games back, at 49-31. The Warriors, however, quickly closed the gap in the playoffs and battled Boston through one of those legendary seven-game semifinal matches.

The two teams didn't like each other and fought to prove it. In game seven in Boston Garden, the Warriors led 56-52 at the half and 81-80 after three quarters. With 10 seconds left and Boston holding a three-point lead, Chamberlain dunked over Russell and was fouled. He hit the free throw to tie the game at 107, but Sam Jones pumped in the winning jumper, 109-107, with two seconds left.

"I thought they'd be looking for me to go right, so I went left," Jones told reporters afterward. Russell had set a pick on Chamberlain and Jones had lofted the winning

It was one of those nights where Baylor's every effort seemed to guide him to just the right spot on the floor, West said. "He had that wonderful, magical instinct for making plays and doing things that you had to just stop and watch. He is without a doubt one of the truly great people who played this game."

Bob Cousy grabs the ball and moves away from West in playoff action.

the Army near Fort Lewis, Washington. As a result, he was able to appear in only 48 regular-season games. He made the lineup mostly on weekends or with an occasional pass, and when he did he was fresh, ready and virtually unstoppable. His 38.2 scoring average was second only to the prodigious Chamberlain.

When Baylor wasn't there, West had to carry the load, which pushed him to do more with his game. Early in his career, West was less secure in his abilities and often deferred to Baylor on offense. Like many great athletes, West was high-strung, sensitive and somewhat temperamental, Schaus said.

"I didn't feel I was competent enough to be consistent," West said of his early years in the pros. "I would have outlandish scoring games, but maybe the rest of my performance would not be what it should."

At times, West tended to brood over the flaws in his game, Schaus said. "When he was not playing well, he'd kind of go into a shell. He wouldn't talk to anybody, not the coaches or his own teammates. If he wasn't playing well, he was tough to live with."

"I was nervous all the time," West said. "But then again, I was a nervous player. That's where I got my energy from."

In that regard, the Lakers' looseness made them the perfect team for West, particularly in 1962. "It was an enjoyable year," Baylor recalled. "Our camaraderie was great. On and off the court, we did things together. We enjoyed one another. As a team we gave the effort every night."

Even if you were a bit uptight, it was hard not to enjoy time with the likes of Hundley, reserve forward Tommy Hawkins, veteran guard Dick Barnett and second-year forward Rudy LaRusso. Known in Boston as "Rough House Rudy" (the nickname courtesy of Celtics radio man Johnny Most), LaRusso was a 6'8", 220-pound youngster out of Dartmouth who quickly found a niche as the Lakers' resident enforcer. Mostly he just liked to have fun. His antics had once included a down-on-the-floor, rolling-around wrestling bout with a huge

shot over Philadelphia's center. "I figured that if I could get the ball over Chamberlain's head, Russell could probably tip it in even if I missed."

Once again, the Celtics returned to the Finals and met there the Lakers, who were coming off a wonderful season. With their success in the '61 playoffs, the Lakers had gathered a quick following in Los Angeles, and they fast became popular with the Hollywood crowds. The courtside celebs in those days were Doris Day, Danny Thomas and Pat Boone. Not exactly Jack Nicholson, Arsenio Hall and Dyan Cannon, but 1962 was a different time. Dinah was celebrity enough to attract the stargazers, and Lakers games became a place to be seen.

For the team itself, it was one of those golden, fun-loving seasons in which almost everything seemed to go right. Even their only real setback during the regular season had its advantages. Baylor began the year like a terror but was called into reserve duty with stuffed tiger at a Detroit airport gift shop. The scene was so outrageous that it demanded a rematch on another road trip to Motown.

"They were just a bunch of real characters," West said of his teammates. "The players then were closer than they are today. There was no reason to be jealous of anyone. No one was making any kind of money at all. We traveled differently back then." They shared cabs and rooms and time back then. Schaus kept this chemistry going by rotating the road rooming schedule. And unlike some teams, the coach paid no attention to the race of the roommates.

Even with Baylor's intermittent schedule, this harmony translated into success. They won the Western with a 54-26 record, 11 games better than Cincinnati, and whipped Detroit 4-2 in the division finals series.

In a sense, the Lakers were relieved when Boston defeated Philadelphia. "In all honesty, we had no post game," Schaus explained. They had no means of slowing Chamberlain's overwhelming offensive presence. Russell was equally dominating as a defensive player, but he didn't present the same problems for the Lakers as Wilt did. In the post, Los Angeles

alternated 6'8" Jimmy Krebs and 6'11" Ray Felix. Krebs could score, and Felix could muscle around, do a little rebounding and play defense. "Krebs was effective against the Celtics," Schaus said, "because he was a perimeter pivot man. When we sent him outside to shoot, he brought Russell away from the basket." With Russell unable to hang in the lane, the Lakers worked their offense and sometimes got decent shots.

And the Lakers had someone to take them; the two young superstars seemed fearless. "Both West and Baylor had fantastic playoffs," Schaus recalled.

Even so, the Celtics won big to open the series in the Garden, 122-108. But the Lakers broke back the next night with a 129-122 upset that sent them back home tied. A record crowd of 15,180 packed the Sports Arena. They were rewarded for their support in the closing seconds when West scored four points to tie the game at 115. Then Sam Jones tried to inbounds the ball to Cousy with four seconds remaining. West stole the ball and drove for the winning layup, 117-115. Auerbach contended it was impossible for West to dribble

Frank Ramsey gets a hand on the ball as LA's Rudy LaRusso can't get off a shot.

30 feet to score with only three seconds left.

The Lakers bench had feared as much. Everyone there shouted for West to pull up and shoot. But he kept digging for the goal and laid the ball in as the buzzer sounded.

"I had deflected the ball on the run," West explained in a 1990 interview. "I knew I would have enough time, because I knew what the shot clock was. Quite often I'm surprised today that more young players don't pay attention to the shot clock."

Frank Selvy's missed shot allowed the Celtics to take Game 7 into overtime.

The crowd went wild with the play, but the Celtics promptly killed any thoughts of prolonged jubilation in L.A. by taking Game 4, 115-103. They headed back to Beantown with the series tied at two. There, it was all Baylor. He scored 61 points (the record for an NBA Finals game) and had 22 rebounds, while the Celtics' defensive specialist, Satch Sanders, contemplated another line of work. "Elgin was just a machine," Sanders said later.

Boston had attempted to double-team him in the past, but Baylor passed the ball too well for that to work. In fact, nothing did. The Lakers took the fifth game, 126-121, and headed home with a 3-2 lead.

Asked about his big scoring night, Baylor said, "All I remember is that we won the game. I never thought about how many points I had."

It was one of those nights where Baylor's every effort seemed to guide him to just the right spot on the floor, West said. "He had that wonderful, magical instinct for making plays and doing things that you had to just stop and watch. He is without a doubt one of the truly great people who played this game. I hear people talking about forwards today. I don't see many that can compare to him."

The Celtics, though, again doused the jubilation in Los Angeles by tying the series

with a 119-105 win in the Sports Arena. On Wednesday night, April 16, they faced each other in Game 7 in Boston. The Celtics took a 53-47 lead at the half, despite the fact that Sam Jones was only one of 10 from the floor. The Lakers knew that a prodigious night from Baylor had delivered them earlier, and to win, they would have to have another one. He took 18 shots in the first half, and made eight of them.

The Celtics maintained their lead through most of the third and were ahead 73-67 heading into the period's final minute. But West then scored seven in a row to help tie the game at 75 as the fourth opened. From there, it only got wilder.

The Celtics first rushed up by six, then fell back into a tie at 88, with six minutes left. Then Boston went back up by three again. Then Heinsohn fouled out, joining Sanders and Loscutoff on the pine. Each of them had fallen trying to stop Baylor, who already had 38.

But Russell scored on a stickback seconds after that, and Boston breathed a bit at 96-91. Mistake. West canned a jumper, and Baylor hit one of two free throws. 96-94. Boston then added two Russell free throws, and West answered with another jumper. 98-96. Then Sam Jones blocked Frank Selvy's shot and hit two free throws at the other end. 100-96. LaRusso picked up an offensive foul with a minute to go, and the Lakers seemed doomed.

Selvy, though, saved them momentarily by getting a rebound and driving the length of the floor for a layup. Seconds later, he repeated the act, driving the length of the floor, missing the shot, then getting the rebound and scoring to tie the game at 100.

The Celtics got the ball back with 18 seconds left. Ramsey tried a driving hook shot in traffic and missed. LaRusso clutched the rebound, and the Lakers had a shot to win it. Schaus called timeout with five seconds to go.

The coach set up Baylor as the first option, West as the second and whoever else was open as the third. Hundley, who was in the game to handle the ball, had dreamed the night before that he made the winning shot. And Hundley quickly moved into the opening for a good shot. West and Baylor were covered.

But Selvy was open on the left baseline. Cousy, who was guarding him, had gambled for a quick double on West. Hundley sent the pass to Selvy, and Cousy rushed back to cover him. It was a seven- or eight-foot shot, one that Selvy made eight out of 10 times, Schaus said.

It hit the rim and fell away, to be known forever as the shot that could have ended Boston's dynasty and the Lakers' agony before it ever began.

"I would trade all my points for that last basket," Selvy told reporters afterward. "It was a fairly tough shot. I was almost on the baseline."

The ball came off the rim, and Russell, who would finish with 30 points and 40 rebounds, wrapped it in his arms for overtime.

The Celtics escaped with their fourth straight title in the extra period as they built a five-point lead and won, 110-107. Sam Jones scored five of his 27 points in the extra period. Frank Ramsey finished with 23. And the Lakers could only think of what could have been.

"Selvy thought Bob Cousy fouled him," Baylor said. "I thought Cousy fouled him. He took the shot from a spot where he was very proficient. Cousy said he never fouled him. I was in a position to get the offensive rebound. But somebody behind me shoved me out of bounds right into the referee. There was no foul call there, either. I looked around and saw Russell and Sam Jones were behind me."

Baylor said that some years later he got a copy of the game's film and confirmed what he had suspected. Sam Jones had shoved him out of bounds, away from the rebound. Jones later joked about it with him and admitted pushing him, Baylor said.

In the locker room, Selvy and Hundley were anguished. Hundley lamented that he should have taken the shot, just as he dreamed.

"There's been a lot of publicity about him missing the shot," West said of Selvy, who had

once scored 100 points for Furman in a college game. "But he hit a couple of shots that got us tied up in the first place."

Still, West said, it's hard not to think what could have been, because if the Lakers had won that would have changed the whole course of pro basketball history.

Not to mention what it would have done to lessen what would become the Lakers' overwhelming frustration in the Finals.

Don't worry about it, Hundley finally told Selvy with a laugh, you only cost us about $30,000.

"I'm sure that has bothered Frank to this day," Schaus said.

1963

"The Boston Celtics are an old team," *Sports Illustrated* declared in March of 1963. "Tired blood courses through their varicose veins."

The Celtics, of course, would win their sixth title that spring and five more over the next six seasons. But *SI*'s underestimation of Boston's strength still had some basis in fact. It seemed that each February of his career Bob Cousy blasted the NBA for seasons that were too long with games that had no meaning. Finally weary, Cousy announced that he would

Written off as an old and tired team, the Celtics still had many championship seasons ahead of them.

retire after the 1962-63 season. Observers saw his leaving as a major loss to the Celtics. And they didn't see the wheel's of Auerbach's cunning turning.

The previous spring, he had drafted John Havlicek out of Ohio State in the 1962 draft. Auerbach had never seen Havlicek play until camp that summer. "I remember I was stunned," Auerbach later told reporters. "All I could think of was, Ohh. Have I got something here? Are they going to think I'm smart."

But Havlicek was just one of several changing faces in the team's evolution. Later Auerbach's would get Don Nelson and Bailey Howell and several more key pieces to the puzzle. Plus Cousy's leaving meant the Jones duo of K.C. and Sam would become a larger factor. Most important, though, the Celtics had Bill Russell.

"Russell is the most dominant individual who ever played a team sport," Schaus said in 1990.

Bob Cousy

Built around this incredible player, the team's changes were made without problem. The coach and center had come to lord over the NBA, and Auerbach toasted each victory with a cigar. Where most people spent their lives chasing success, hoping for little more than to brush their fingers across her elusive hemline, Auerbach nestled in success's arms and had the audacity to light up afterward like a satisfied lover. "At first I didn't like Red Auerbach," a rival NBA coach once said. "But in time I grew to hate him."

"Red was hated around the league," Paul Seymour said in 1990. "He wasn't a very well liked guy. He always had the talent. He was always shooting his mouth off. If you walked up to him in the old days, he was more than likely to tell you to get lost."

Having a great player like Russell made Auerbach a coach, said former Syracuse coach Al Cervi. "He's the biggest phony who ever walked the streets of America."

Auerbach was an early master at working the refs and officials. His foot stomping and tirades, usually punctuated by a lit cigar at the end of the game, had begun to wear on his opponents by the mid 1960s. Plus, the NBA was getting more television exposure, and his antics weren't always pleasant to view.

"Red was a very astute judge of talent," Schaus, who battled Auerbach in the Finals, said in 1990. "When you have a lot of stars, you have to keep them happy and playing as a team. Red did that. I didn't like some of the things he did and said when I competed against him. Some of the things he said would bother me. But the guy who wore No. 6 out there bothered us more. You had to change your complete game because of Russell."

For West, Auerbach on the sidelines was more entertainment than irritation. "Red was outspoken," West said. "His sideline antics were funny. I happened to like him very much. When you talk to his ex-players, they all have great respect for him. I don't know how many players would tell you that about their former coaches."

Some coaches tried to intimidate the officials throughout the game, Auerbach said. "You work the refs only when you feel you're right. You got to pick your spots. Sure I was active. You had to be active. But it wasn't all the time."

As for the enmity from other coaches that still burned nearly three decades later, Auerbach said, "Any time you're winning, you get criticism. Nothing instigates jealousy like winning. When you're winning, they look for a thousand reasons for taking potshots. You don't pay attention. You just keep doing what you're doing."

This debate over Auerbach flared regularly over the winter and spring of 1963. His relationship with official Sid Borgia carried a particular spite. The Boston press took to calling Borgia "Big Poison."

"I'm convinced," Auerbach said after one game, "that it would be the highlight of his career if he refereed the game in which we lost the championship. He doesn't like me, he doesn't like Cousy and he doesn't like the Celtics."

Sparked as it was, this controversy still didn't translate into a crowd at the gate. If anything, the Celtics were so efficient, their fans almost acted as if they were boring. Regular season attendance dropped to 6,800. "Once we started to win, we almost did it too easily," Cousy said.

Boston again claimed the Eastern Division with a 58-22 record and then faced Oscar Robertson and the Cincinnati Royals in a seven-game shakedown in the Eastern finals. They survived a game seven shootout in Boston Garden, 142-131.

As his career neared a close, Cousy became more anxious. He even needed Nembutal to sleep, he told reporters. "People don't know what they're talking about when they say the older you are the less you notice the tension. Each day you have to prove yourself all over again."

The Lakers also had to prove themselves again by beating St. Louis in a seven-game Western final. West had been out with an injury for seven weeks at the close of the season, and although he was back in the lineup for the playoffs, the team still hadn't worked out all the kinks.

Schaus, though, offered no excuses. After all, they had a score to settle from last year. "If my guys aren't up for Boston, then, by heaven, they'll never be up for anyone," he told reporters. Auerbach allowed that his team was tired and ripe for plucking.

The Lakers were up, but Boston still eased by Game 1 in the Garden, 117-114. Game 2 wasn't much different. The Celtics took a 2-0 series lead, 113-106.

Back at their Sports Arena, the Lakers retaliated with a blowout, 119-99, only to see the Celtics take firm command by sneaking away with Game 4, 108-105. Up 3-1, Auerbach was as confident as ever. "We've never lost three games in a row," he told reporters.

The Lakers headed back to Boston and found the stuff to survive. Heinsohn was

Tom Heinsohn

ejected, Cousy fouled out with 12 points and the L.A. duo went wild. Baylor had 43, West 32, as L. A. pulled to 3-2, 126-119.

The loss fueled speculation that the Celtics had run out of gas, that the younger Lakers were about to surge ahead. "No," Russell said, "Los Angeles is not going to do any such thing."

Cousy seemed genuinely surprised by the question. "We are not the oldest men alive," he told reporters.

In Los Angeles, a throng estimated at more than 5,000 converged on the Sports Arena hoping to buy playoff tickets. When they found there was none, the scene turned angry. The Lakers quickly calmed things by offering closed-circuit TV seats at $2.50 a head. By Game 6, 6,000 such theater seats had been taken, to go along with the 15,000 arena sellout. "We were aware we were testing the future of pay television," Lakers General Manager Lou Mohs told reporters.

The crowd at the Sports Arena April 24 rode on a tide of hope that the Lakers could turn it around. For some reason, Doris Day came to courtside in a green suit. Danny Thomas puffed on a cigar, while Pat Boone, in a snazzy red jacket, blew bubbles.

And Bill Russell did his usual thing. He made rebounds a scarce commodity. It was Havlicek who had the hot hand, scoring 11 straight points during one first-half stretch that put Boston up by 14 at the half. The lead had dipped to nine with 11 minutes left in the fourth period when Cousy tripped and sprained his left ankle. He didn't return until the five-minute mark. By then, the Lakers had cut the Boston lead to one. At 2:48, the Celtics were holding on, 104-102. Then Heinsohn stole

Bill Russell goes up to stop West's shot in Game 6.

a West pass to LaRusso, drove and scored. From there, Cousy worked the clock as he had in the old days. He dribbled out the last seconds of his career and threw the ball high into the rafters of the space-age arena. Then he and Auerbach hugged as the final touch on a 112-109 win.

"Please," Auerbach crowed to the press, "tell me some of these stories about Los Angeles being the basketball capital of the world."

"It's nice to be playing with the old pros," Russell said. "The old, old pros."

There was no champagne or beer in the Boston locker room. Why celebrate? Heinsohn replied when asked about it. "We've won five in a row."

The Lakers' fans still applauded their team anyway. The team hadn't won the trophy, but it had picked up the dividend. Over the course of the season, the Lakers had taken in $1

million at the gate, then the largest sum in league history. Bob Short's gamble had paid off. Pro basketball had arrived. And not just in Los Angeles.

1964

With Cousy's retirement, Auerbach shifted strategy a bit, K.C. Jones recalled. "Red always added up what the starters would score. I was not a shooter, and Red figured with Cousy gone on offense we would lose seven or eight points. We made that up by increasing our defensive intensity."

There were some adjustments, Heinsohn said. "Cousy was the greatest ever running the fast break. We still ran with the ball, but we didn't run the same way because K.C. was now the middle man in the break. He wasn't the same type of passer as Cousy. But with Sanders and Russell and the Joneses, we had four excellent defensive players."

Auerbach also had another series of crafty personnel moves to crow about, the addition of veteran center Clyde Lovellette and 6'6" Willie Naulls in the frontcourt. Naulls would provide double-figure scoring as a key substitute for three important years, and Lovellette gave them some good games, too. Auerbach also added Larry Siegfried, Havlicek's teammate out of Ohio State who would mature into a double-figures scorer in a few seasons.

The big change for 1963-64 came with the league's balance of power. Maurice Podoloff had retired as commissioner and was replaced by Walter Kennedy. In an even bigger move, the Warriors had left Philly to move to

Bill Russell

San Francisco, where they took charge in the Western, with what appeared to be one of the most powerful teams in NBA history.

But that was on paper, as Auerbach pointed out. "I've seen a lot of great teams, at least on paper, that won nothing."

Warriors coach Alex Hannum called it his "muscle and hustle team."

Chamberlain was the chief muscle. But there was plenty more. There was 6'11", 230-pound Nate Thurmond, a rookie out of Bowling Green who had yet to develop offensively. Then there were 6'8" Wayne Hightower, a fine shooter, and 6'6", 215-pound Tom Meschery, who helped in the muscle department. The crafty backcourt showed Al Attles, Guy Rodgers and Gary Phillips, but they were no match for the Joneses and Havlicek.

"That was a powerful, physical team," Auerbach said. "Chamberlain and Thurmond were two of the best centers in the game."

Boston, meanwhile, again won the Eastern Division with a 59-21 record, then dismissed Cincinnati and Robertson in the Eastern finals 4-1. The Royals simply had no one to contend with Russell, who averaged 29 rebounds for the series. K.C. Jones, described by one reporter as a "polite man of 31," did the other key job, denying Robertson the ball and slowing down his nearly unstoppable game.

The Warriors finished first in the Western with a 48-32 record, two games better than St. Louis. Then they took the Hawks in a seven-game Western final, which gave Boston the opportunity to wait nine days before the Finals opened.

But the Warriors were no match for Boston in the big show. Frank Ramsey, all of 6'3", psyched Thurmond on defense, and the Celtics waltzed to the lead. Chamberlain was a power, but Russell forced him into taking a fallaway jumper. In one sequence in Game 1, a 108-96 Boston win, Russell blocked Wilt's shot, only to see Thurmond get the loose ball and take it back

up. Russell blocked that one, too.

"He never stops throwing you something new," an impressed Rodgers said afterward.

It was Wilt's first Finals appearance, and the intimidation factor set in for Game 2, as the Celtics took the 2-0 lead, 124-101. Then the Warriors returned to San Francisco for Game 3, gathered their poise and enforced a little intimidation of their own. The primary target was Heinsohn, who was having a rough series. The Warriors rode this to a 115-91 win in Game 3.

But Heinsohn found his shot in the crucial Game 4. With his team down, 52-51, Heinsohn went on a scoring binge that led them to a 71-60 lead. The Warriors charged back as Chamberlain dominated the boards with 38 rebounds. Still, the Celtics eased by, 98-95, and

Chamberlain beats out Boston's Tom Sanders for a rebound in Game 5.

headed back to Boston with a 3-1 lead.

Chamberlain scored 30 in the Garden, but Boston held an 11-point lead early in the final period. The Warriors closed furiously to 101-99, with 19 seconds remaining. Then Russell rebounded a Heinsohn miss and jammed it back through, propelling Boston to a 105-99 win.

They took the series, 4-1, for their sixth consecutive championship. "A lot of teams have come and gone since we first beat St. Louis in '57," Ramsey told reporters.

Auerbach had won seven championships and never been named coach of the year. Still, he pushed on.

During the season, he had fined several players for a transgression of team rules. They asked him to reconsider. "Get lost," he replied, "if you don't know by now that the Celtics are a dictatorship. I am a dictator and it's about time you found out."

Asked about his style, he told reporters: "Look, I don't worry about handling them. I worry about how they handle me. I'm not here as a doormat. Let them adjust to me. Anybody who comes to this team better take a little time to figure out what I'm like and learn to please me."

Despite his gruffness, he had a real flair for sales, and even represented several products on the side as he coached. "Selling keeps me alert during the season," he explained. "I meet clients when I'm on the road."

With this seventh title, it began to appear as if Boston might never lose. Auerbach projected that much. "The thrill never goes from winning," he said. "But maybe the reasons change. First, it was just trying to win a title. Now it is a question of going down as the greatest team of all time. That stimulates you."

The closing of the '64 season brought the retirement of Loscutoff and Ramsey. Loscutoff had once sworn that as soon as he turned in his uniform he was going to belt Auerbach. Using the psychological ploy he was known for, the coach had determined that he couldn't criticize Cousy, Ramsey or Russell. They just

couldn't or wouldn't take it. So he had used Heinsohn or Loscutoff to tonguelash when he needed to communicate displeasure with the team's play.

But Loscutoff's intentions were never realized. Like the rest of the Celtics, he loved Auerbach more than he hated him.

"His whole theory behind basketball is never get too close to the players' wives," Loscutoff said of his coach.

He couldn't make good coaching decisions if he knew a player's family well, Auerbach explained. "You can't be emotionally involved and impartial at the same time."

1965

Walter Brown died in August 1964, leaving Auerbach alone to guide the Celtics on to greatness. Brown's passing and the fact that a new group of young officials had come into the league brought the Boston coach to tone down his act somewhat.

He still prowled the sidelines while clutching a tightly rolled game program. And he still picked his spots. He just didn't pick them as often or as loudly. In some ways it didn't matter. Every time he stirred from the bench during a road game, the boos followed him.

LaRusso was one of the few LA veterans left when the Lakers met the Celtics in 1965.

In the spring of 1965, he appeared on a television talk show and seem startled when the audience clapped politely. "How come they applauded?" he asked the host. "It makes me feel uneasy."

Still, he conceded his image had changed. Going into the 1965 playoffs, he had been fined less than $1,000 by the league, an unusually low figure for him. By no means was he sanitized, though "If you get obnoxious, you get incentive," he told his players. And he regularly offered young coaches tips on how to get ahead — place the scorer's and timer's table near your bench at home, and when you're on the road, wait until the other team has taken the floor for warm-ups to request their basket. Anything that disconcerted the opponent was viewed as an asset.

While he talked these precepts, he employed them less and less as he neared the end of his coaching career. Red had mellowed, the writers covering the Celtics concluded.

Still, there were some things in his act that he refused to tone down. League officials had sent him notes saying that it didn't look good for him to light cigars on the bench.

Auerbach told the league he would stop his cigars when other coaches stopped their cigarettes, a response that angered some of his colleagues in the profession. A few coaches complained that Auerbach had an endorsement with Blackstone, a cigar company, and that he was putting on "an act."

"If this was an act, I'd be an actor," he replied. "I wouldn't be a coach."

Boy, could he coach. The Celtics broke their own record for regular season wins in 1964-65 with 62. And Auerbach finally got his coach-of-the-year award.

"He's getting the maximum out of me," Russell told reporters.

They added their eighth championship that year, but things in the Eastern Division became complicated at mid-season when San Francisco traded Wilt Chamberlain back to the new Philadelphia 76ers (the old Syracuse Nationals). Boston had finished well atop the standings but had to fight Philly in the playoffs through another seven-game series. Chamberlain's team wasn't vanquished until John Havlicek stole an in-bounds pass under Philadelphia's basket with five seconds remaining, which, of course, led to Johnny Most's famous line, "Havlicek stole the ball!!!"

For a matter of record, Havlicek deflected the ball to Sam Jones, who raced downcourt to celebrate.

With the momentum from that drama, the Celtics went on to meet the Lakers in the

Russell drives past Gene Wiley in Game Five victory.

Finals once again. Los Angeles, though, had been traumatized April 3 in the first game of the Western Division finals against the Baltimore Bullets when Baylor suffered a severe knee injury.

"I went up for a shot and my knee exploded," Baylor recalled. "I could hear a crack and a pop and everything else."

"That was really tragic," West said of the injury, "because he was a great, great player."

West and LaRusso were left alone to lead Los Angeles. They got help from their teammates, most of whom were new, but it was impossible to replace Baylor. Gone were Selvy and Hundley and Krebs (who was killed in

109

May 1965 in a freakish tree-cutting accident). The new people included Gene Wiley, a skinny 6'10" center out of Wichita, and LeRoy Ellis, another 6'10" player out of St. John's. The Lakers also got 14 points per game out of Dick Barnett, a 6'4" scorer who was underrated as a defensive player. Jim King, a second-year guard out of Tulsa, rounded out the backcourt. Also filling out the roster were Don Nelson, Darrell Imhoff and Walt Hazzard.

The Celtics, though, waltzed through Game 1 in Boston, 142-110, as K.C. Jones held West to 26 points. "K.C. Jones used to tackle West rather than let him get off a jump shot," Schaus said.

Reporters gathered around Jones in the locker room afterward and asked him about the defensive job he had done on West. Jones made the mistake of talking.

West got 45 in Game 2, but Boston still controlled the outcome, 129-123. Wounded as they were, the Lakers managed a home win in Game 3, 126-105, as West hit for 43 and Ellis 29. The Los Angeles crowd celebrated by pelting Auerbach with cigars. Game 4, though, was another Celtics win, 112-99, as Sam Jones scored 37. They went back to Boston to end it, 129-96, as the Celtics outscored the Lakers 72-48 in the second half. At the outset of the fourth period, Boston ran off 20 unanswered points, while the Lakers went scoreless for five minutes. At one stretch, West missed 14 out of 15 shots. They kept hitting the back of the rim. Russell played despite an eye injury and had 30 rebounds.

Auerbach had announced that he would coach one more season, then retire to the front office. He explained privately that coaching had become a burden, a drudgery. Perhaps more than any NBA coach ever, he loved winning, but success had taken its toll. He was nearing 50 and feeling 70. With Walter Brown's death the administrative load was heavier. Auerbach could no longer do both jobs.

Reporters asked Auerbach what the highlights of his coaching days had been. "After 1,500 games, who could remember?" he

Red Auerbach shows off his Earl of McIntosh award to broadcaster Johnny Most (center) and Boston Patriots coach Mike Holovak.

replied. "What you remember is how hard it was to get each individual win."

1966

The doctors told Elgin Baylor that his knee injury had ended his playing career, and for a time, he believed them. The main ligament in his knee had been severely damaged, and his knee cap had been split, practically in half. Immediately after the injury, he was worried about just being able to walk again.

But after a time, the pain subsided, and Baylor found he had some mobility. "The more I thought about it," he said, "the more determined I became to prove the doctors wrong."

"Afterward," West said, "to watch the slow, painful process of him getting better and improving and never really getting back to where he was, that was the thing that was difficult for the rest of us to accept.

"We wanted him back having all his greatness. He came back and played, and played incredibly well. But he wasn't the Elgin Baylor of old. After any major injury, no athlete is the same. I don't care what they say."

By training camp that next fall, Baylor was able to see limited action. Eventually he would return to full speed, but never to the dynamic player he had been.

"I wasn't the same player," Baylor said in 1990. "I was about 75 percent of the player I had been."

That, of course, was still better than the vast majority of players in the league. Before, Baylor had dazzled opponents with a fearless approach to driving and rebounding. After the injury, that part of his game diminished.

"It was very, very difficult," he said. "I would try to do a lot of things that I just couldn't do. It was frustrating. But it made me more determined, too. Before I was injured, I loved to penetrate and create, to pass off or take the

Baylor (left) wasn't the same after his knee injury, but Walt Hazzard was one of the newcomers who helped out.

shot. At times after I returned, I just couldn't do it. My knee wouldn't respond. I couldn't rebound as well. It just wasn't there. I just couldn't run the same.

"I had to rely more on perimeter shooting and posting up occasionally."

He played in 65 games the following season, 1965-66, and averaged 16.6 points. West, who was scoring at a 31.3 average, became the top option in the Lakers' offense. But Baylor's mere presence was enough to make them a stronger team. They won the Western with a 45-35 record and eliminated the Hawks in a seven-game conference final series. The team was further bolstered by the emergence of a pair of guards, Walt Hazzard and Gail Goodrich. Both had starred for John Wooden's national championship teams at UCLA.

The biggest boost perhaps came from the team's new owner. Jack Kent Cooke had bought the team for the then-incredible sum of $5.1 million. He immediately brought organization to the business operations and promotional flair to the marketing.

The Eastern Division, meanwhile, was a dogfight. Chamberlain led the 76ers back the following season, 1965-66, to take some of the steam out of the Boston dynasty. Heinsohn had retired at the end of the previous season, and Havlicek became a starter. Don Nelson, acquired after Los Angeles released him, inherited the role of sixth man. For the first time in a decade, the Celtics didn't win the Eastern Division title. The 76ers won 55 games and Boston 54. But Boston regrouped in the playoffs. Philly had received a first-round bye, while Boston fended off Cincinnati in a preliminary round. The layoff hurt Chamberlain and the Sixers. They were caught flat in the Eastern finals as Boston won, 4-1. Boston had lost six of 10 games to Philadelphia during the season, but again it was Russell's team that went on to play for the title.

The 1966 championship series quickly turned into another Celtics/Lakers scrap. The Celtics had a 38-20 lead in Game 1 in the Garden, but the Lakers fought back to tie it late.

With the score even in the final minute, Russell blocked a Baylor shot and was called for goaltending. Sam Jones scored for Boston to send it to overtime, where Baylor and West propelled the Lakers to a win, 133-129, for a 1-0 lead. Baylor had scored 36, West 41. But instead of the glory and the psychological edge falling to the Lakers, the attention abruptly shifted to Boston. Auerbach picked the postgame to announce that Russell would be his replacement as head coach. For months the speculation had been that Cousy, now the coach at Boston College, would get the job. Working as a player-coach, Boston's center would become the first black head coach in a major American sport. Auerbach had talked briefly with Cousy and Heinsohn about taking the job, but both men agreed no one could better motivate Russell than Russell himself.

Hazzard (left) gets past Jones, while Baylor lays in two points in action at the Boston Garden.

The announcement made headlines the next morning, while the Lakers' major victory was obscured.

With the future of the team settled, the Celtics bore down on the Lakers, winning the second game in the Garden, 129-109, then adding two more victories in Los Angeles for a 3-1 lead. The major problem for the Lakers was John Havlicek, who could swing between guard and forward. Schaus had tried to play LaRusso, a forward, on Havlicek, but it hadn't worked.

"No one in the league his size is even close to Havlicek in quickness," Schaus told reporters.

So the Lakers coach put LaRusso on the pine and played Goodrich on Havlicek. West moved to forward, and this three-guard lineup left Los Angeles weak on the boards. But it worked for a time. West, Baylor and Goodrich lashed back and won Games 5 and 6 to tie the series at three apiece.

Game 7 in the Garden was another in the series of classics. The Celtics took a big lead as Baylor and West were a combined 3 for 18 from the floor in the first half. But as usual, they came back, cutting the Boston lead to six with 20 seconds left. Still, it seemed time for Red to light another victory cigar. The Lakers took fire with that, cutting lead to two, 95-93, with four seconds left. The fans always rushed the floor to celebrate a Boston championship. The earlier the better, it seemed. The '66 celebration was premature and out-of-hand. Russell, who had played with a broken bone in his foot and had still gotten 32 rebounds, was knocked down. Orange juice containers on the Boston bench were spilled across the floor, and Satch Sanders lost his shirt to the crowd. Somehow, K.C. Jones got the inbounds pass to Havlicek,

Russell dominated again in his last year as a player only — then began his new role as a player/coach.

who dribbled out the clock for championship number nine, 95-93.

Schaus said later that he would love to have been able to shove the victory cigar down Auerbach's throat. "We came awfully close to putting that damn thing out," the Lakers coach said.

His players, though, had no one to blame but themselves. They had missed 11 free throws.

At Auerbach's retirement dinner, Russell addressed the gathering: "When I took this job, somebody said, 'What did you take it for? You have nothing to gain. You got to follow Red Auerbach.'

"I don't think I'm going to be another Red Auerbach," Russell continued. "Personally, I think you're the greatest basketball coach that ever lived. You know, over the years... I heard a lot of coaches and writers say the only thing that made you a great coach was Bill Russell. It helped. But that's not what did it.

"Now this is kind of embarrassing, but I'll go so far, Red, as to say this: I like you. And I'll admit there aren't very many men that I like. But you I do. For a number of reasons. First of all, I've always been able to respect you. I don't think you're a genius, just an extraordinarily intelligent man. We'll be friends until one of us dies. And I don't want too many friends, Red."

III.
Promise and Problems

Built at a cost of $32 million, the Houston Astrodome opened in 1967 — and just like that, the age of Supersport had dawned. The cavernous Los Angeles Sports Arena had seemed like a space-age wonder when it had opened seven years earlier, but the Astrodome was something else. It had 46,000 upholstered seats, and 53 private skyboxes that rented for $15,000 to $34,000 a season, incredible figures for 1967.

Basketball, of course, was caught in the first light of this new age. UCLA and Lew Alcindor met Elvin Hayes and the University of Houston in the Astrodome that January of 1968 in the first nationally televised college basketball game.

It was billed as the "game of the century." And it was, but not just because of what happened on the court (Houston upset UCLA). Within two decades, the NCAA would sell the annual television rights to its tournament games for nearly $100 million.

The NBA was an interested spectator to that game in Houston. The league had turned twenty with the 1966-67 season, and was still facing all the promise and problems of youth. The promise, as always, rested in the stars. Although their televisions appearances were infrequent in the 1960s, it was enough to get out the word about the great pro players. Tales of their prowess spread across America's playgrounds, where they were imitated and projected as teammates and opponents in a million imaginary games and an equal number of daydreams.

Each season, it seemed, the NBA's talent and enthusiasm thickened. About the only thing that could slow it down was the business itself. And therein lay the problems of youth. For the league, the challenges were money, marketing, and product. Turmoil had followed the NBA at every stage of its development. Those franchises in the major markets remained marginally secure, but those on the fringe faced mutation or failure. The Syracuse Nationals became the Philadelphia 76ers in 1963. The Chicago Packers were formed in '61, only to become the Chicago Zephyrs the next season, and then the Baltimore Bullets the following season (the old Bullets had failed in 1955).

The big development came in the fall of 1967, when the rival American Basketball Association began play with eleven teams. Whether it was ready or not, the NBA was forced into a sudden growth pattern. Pro basketball was being played everywhere, or so it seemed. The game became a geography lesson. Kentucky. Indiana. North Carolina. Colorado. Texas. Louisiana. Virginia. Even New Jersey.

The new league staked its identity on a red-white-and-blue game ball and the 3-point shot. To counter these bold moves by the upstart ABA, the NBA added eight new teams of its own. The Chicago Bulls in 1966. The San Diego Rockets and Seattle SuperSonics in 1967. The Phoenix Suns and Milwaukee Bucks in 1968. The Cleveland Cavaliers, Buffalo Braves and Portland Trail Blazers in 1970.

The competition immediately forced a new flair into the game. That, of course, suited the times, as the game tried to keep up with changing decade, but it was simply too much, too fast. The rival leagues bid for talent at a time when, frankly, the public had other distractions. Costs soared, but revenues didn't. The new league and the new teams created new interest in new markets. While that would prove to be a wonderful asset a decade later, it was a tremendous burden through most of the 1970s. The sport simply spread itself too thin. And because it did, pro basketball opened itself to the problems that infested society in general.

If the reality of those problems wasn't enough to turn off new fans, the image was. At times, it seemed to overshadow the very essence of pro basketball, what Bob Kurland called "the performing geniuses." The talent was growing, the game itself was improving, but that wasn't clear to the casual fan.

One by one, the big stars of yesteryear were retiring. Cousy. Russell. Baylor. Chamberlain. West. And pro basketball had a difficult time showcasing the new wave of talent coming behind them. The 1970s were not the best of times for the NBA.

The hardcore fans still hunkered down in their seat and saw some great hoops. But during much of the decade it seemed that the general public hardly noticed. That would correct itself in time. But in the interim, basketball experienced growing pains.

Wilt Chamberlain and Bill Russell

8.
Bill and Big Norman
The Greatest Matchup in Sports

His close friends called him "Big Norman." But to the basketball public, he was "Wilt the Stilt." He disliked that name, of course. He preferred being a person, as opposed to being a stilt. The name, as much as anything, defined his tenuous relationship with the fans and the writers. After all, he was a giant, and they expected giant things of him. That certainly was no more than he expected of himself. Unfortunately, the task was never up to him alone. Basketball is a five-man game. And that seemed to be the crux of the problem for Wilton Norman Chamberlain.

"It really bothered him with all the negative publicity he received, which was not justified," said Jerry West, who was once Chamberlain's teammate. "It was really pretty ugly at times. It really was."

The life of a professional basketball player is a search for context. He has to find the right team where his skills fit with those of his teammates. Only in such a context can athletes play their best. As big and talented as he was, Chamberlain's search took him along an uncertain path. His progress was often frustrated by the presence of Boston's Bill Russell. Where Chamberlain struggled most of his career out of context, Russell settled into his almost from the minute he entered the NBA. He had the right coach, the

Chamberlain often saw his progress frustrated in the presence of Russell.

On this play, Chamberlain drove to the hole; most of the time, Russell kept him farther from the basket.

Since his freshman year in high school in the early 1950s, Chamberlain had been the darling of eastern basketball. Scouts from college and pro teams followed his every move. As a 6'11" ninth grader in Philadelphia, he led his undefeated Overbrook High team to the finals of the city championship against a veteran team from West Catholic High.

The scenario that developed in the city finals would become miserably familiar to Chamberlain over the years. West Catholic packed four players around him inside, but his teammates couldn't make the open shots. Overbrook lost its only game of the season.

By Chamberlain's junior and senior years, he and Overbrook were dominant. He scored 90 points in one game. Over three years, his teams won 58 games and lost just three, while Chamberlain averaged 36.9 points. And Overbrook won consecutive city titles.

The basketball world was literally at his feet. Colleges across the country, even some in the segregated South, sent recruiting overtures. In those days of loose NCAA restrictions, the top athletes regularly received promises of money and cars. Being the best athlete in his time, Chamberlain fielded offers of big money, he later claimed in his book, "Wilt."

A friend in the NBA public relations offices got Chamberlain a job as a bell hop at Kutsher's Country Club in the Catskills. There, while still in high school, he played against the best talent pro and college basketball had to offer.

He humbled Philadelphia Warriors center Neil Johnston in one game. When he later did the same to All-America center B.H. Born from Kansas' 1953 NCAA finals team, Born told his coach, Dr. Phog Allen, just how good Chamberlain was. Phog Allen held an open contempt for big men. He called them "goons" and resented the fact that they had come to dominate the sport with size rather than athletic ability. But that didn't stop Allen from recruiting Chamberlain, who had grown to 7'1" by his senior season.

You see, Wilt was the kind of player to make a coach stop and reconsider his basic beliefs

right teammates, and they got the right results.

On the other hand, Chamberlain's career was a profound contradiction. For him, things were wonderfully easy and terribly difficult, all at the same time.

about the game. Unlike most of the giants who came before him, Chamberlain showed marvelous coordination and the athletic skills of men much shorter. Plus, his game already showed a sophistication, although he was only a high school student.

Allen promptly entered the recruiting fray. And where many of the college basketball coaches seemed to ooze ego and condescension, Allen was kind and considerate. He took the time to talk about academics and played up the Jayhawks' great basketball heritage running back to Dr. James Naismith. As might be expected, the Chamberlain family loved Dr. Allen.

In those days, Philadelphia featured great college basketball programs — St. Joe's, Penn, Villanova, Temple, LaSalle. But as a city kid, Chamberlain had always harbored a fascination with farming and decided he wanted to go to school in the Midwest. He narrowed his choices to Kansas, Indiana, Dayton and Michigan. Alumni from all of those schools made incredible financial offers, Chamberlain later claimed. And although the NCAA suspected this and grilled him repeatedly, Chamberlain later said he found ways around the questions.

He discounted Michigan because the school was dominated by football. And he chose Kansas because of Dr. Allen. Unfortunately, he never got to play for him.

In the spring of 1956, just months before Chamberlain moved up to the Kansas varsity as a sophomore, the University forced Allen to comply with the school's age 70 mandatory retirement rule. Like everyone else around the program, Chamberlain had known of Allen's retirement problem, but the player figured the coach would find some way around the rule. Allen did appeal the University's decision, but it held firm. So Dick Harp, Allen's long-time assistant who had started at guard on Kansas's 1940 NCAA finals team, took over the program. A man with many varied interests, including osteopathy, Allen immediately removed himself from the Kansas basketball scene.

And Harp, a head coach for the first time, assumed control of a team that was heavily favored to win the national championship. "I knew the situation would be difficult in terms of what people might do or think," Harp said. "But I wasn't overwhelmed with the pressure of it."

Neither, apparently, was Chamberlain. As a member of the freshman team, he had led the frosh to an 81-71 victory over the varsity

Billy Cunningham added double-figure scoring off the bench.

in which he scored 42 points with 19 rebounds. He participated in track, focusing on the shot put and triple jump. And he took a full academic load, including psychology, literature, algebra, statistics and government. Beyond that, Allen gave him a copy of Helen Keller's biography to read with the idea that it would further open his sensitivity and somehow improve his feel around the basket.

Unlike Lew Alcindor, who a decade later would enter a UCLA program brimming with talented players, Chamberlain had come to a Kansas team not quite complete enough to maximize his talents. The majority of the players were Kansas and Missouri boys, and most hadn't been highly recruited. Their offense, understandably, focused on Chamberlain inside. Which meant that opposing defenses did the same. "That was always the problem when Wilt was playing with us," Harp said. "The defense was always going to concentrate on him. Teams would rig zone defenses around him with three and four men, making it impossible for him to move, particularly around the basket.

"That, as you can imagine was quite frustrating, then as now, for big men."

And because Kansas couldn't shoot well from outside, the zones stayed packed around Chamberlain. And defenders became quite physical with him, beginning a tradition of rough play in the pivot that, as Harp and many traditional coaches see it, has become a curse on the modern game of basketball.

"It was difficult for the officials to be objective about Wilt," Harp said. "There were numerous opportunities for officials to call defensive fouls. But most of the time they didn't."

And even when officials did attempt to confront the problem, they found themselves constantly blowing the whistle, which can create another set of woes for a referee. Regardless of the circumstances, Chamberlain kept his composure, Harp said. And even with

the defenses he faced, he powered through opponents.

But, as Chamberlain himself noted, his frustrations led to errors in his method. When he rebounded, he liked to take the ball in one hand and slam it against the other, making a gunshot of a sound that startled the smaller players around him. What he should have been doing was whipping a quick outlet pass downcourt.

And when he blocked shots, he liked to smack the ball loudly and violently and usually out of play. As a result, opponents retained the ball and another chance to score. This habit would hurt him most in pro

Nate Thurmond of the Warriors and Chamberlain get mixed up under the basket.

Hal Greer took over the scoring chores for Philadelphia.

basketball when he faced Russell, who always brush-blocked the ball, creating a turnover and a real opportunity for his team.

Chamberlain later pointed out that none of his coaches ever changed these bad habits.

Harp, on the other hand, says he sought to take advantage of Chamberlain's full range of athleticism. The young center's unique ability to run and jump combined with his size made him an awesome factor in any game, regardless of the defenses.

"Wilt understood the game of basketball," Harp said. "He had an opinion about the game and was bright about it. He wanted to use his size in close proximity to the basket. But he didn't develop his skills beyond that. If he wanted to, he could have been a significant playmaker. Wilt had demonstrated he could have shot the ball and been an effective passer."

The Kansas coaches spent some time trying to broaden Chamberlain's game, Harp said. "But Wilt believed his most effective role was shooting the percentage shot. Wilt had strong opinions. He was a bright guy. But it's unfair to say he was difficult to work with. It wasn't easy for me. But from what he's written, it wasn't always easy for him to deal with me, either."

Chamberlain has written Harp was too nice a man to coach basketball, that he continued to play struggling players because he didn't want to hurt their feelings. The differences between player and coach have stood over the decades since. But even with that fundamental disagreement, the 1956-57 Jayhawks came within a pass of winning the national championship. And as a unit, they would still be supremely competitive today. Chamberlain, of course, was the major factor. Over his sophomore season, he averaged 30 points, 19 rebounds and nine blocked shots. And Kansas was clearly the best team in college basketball. But in the finals of the NCAA tournament, they lost a triple-overtime game to the University of North Carolina, an outcome that set the cornerstone of Chamberlain's frustrations. He returned to Kansas the next season, but the Jayhawks lost to cross-state rival, Kansas State, in postseason play.

Chamberlain was disgusted and decided to leave the University of Kansas. Because his class had not graduated, he was not eligible for the NBA draft under the rules of the day. So he played a barnstorming season with the Harlem Globetrotters, made a good sum of money and waited his turn.

That arrived the following season, 1959-60, when he made a heralded return to his hometown to play for the Warriors. His presence had an immediate impact on the league's statistical races. He led the NBA in scoring (37.6 points per game) and rebounding (27 per game). The next season, he continued that scoring and rebounding dominance and became the first player in league history to shoot better than 50 percent from the floor. For the 1961-62, Chamberlain maximized man's potential for 48 minutes of basketball by averaging 50.4 points per game. The next season, he scored a mere 44.8 points per game and won the league rebounding title for the fourth straight season.

Each season he achieved these wonderful things, and yet each season ended in bitter disappointment. The reason, of course, was the Boston Celtics. Quite often Chamberlain

Nate Thurman

would dominate Russell statistically, but he could never vanquish the Boston center and his teammates in the big games. Chamberlain was actually taller than his listed height of 7'1" and towered over the 6'9" Russell, which caused the public to marvel even more at the smaller man's success. To the basketball public's way of thinking, Russell had a winner's heart, while Chamberlain certainly had to be lacking in something.

In truth, the "something" was much more tangible than elusive things such as heart or desire. Russell was simply quicker than Chamberlain, said Bob Cousy, repeating a view that was held by insiders from the very first time the two met on a court.

"This is a tremendous advantage Russell had on Wilt," Cousy said. "He didn't give him the offensive position he wanted. Russell kept him from overpowering him and going to the basket. Russell had better speed and quickness, so he could always beat Wilt to the spot. He pushed Chamberlain out a little further from the basket, forcing him to put the ball on the floor once or twice. We always felt Russell could handle him one-on-one."

As a result, Chamberlain was forced to develop and shoot a fallaway jumper that was far less effective than his dunks and short bank shots. The public didn't pick up these developments. In their mind, it was simply a case of a giant failing to live up to his ability.

"It's interesting those things about him people would misinterpret," Jerry West said of Chamberlain. "They would say he was a selfish guy, that he didn't care, that he wasn't a team player. And that simply was not the truth. He's like all of us. No athlete wants to fail. Wilt Chamberlain certainly didn't want to."

The Warriors moved to San Francisco for 1963-64, and Chamberlain again led the league in scoring. He also broadened the scope of his game by finishing fifth in assists. It didn't matter. The Warriors lost in the NBA Finals that year to Russell and the Celtics.

Frustrated, San Francisco traded Chamberlain to the Philadelphia 76ers in the middle of the next season. "Chamberlain is not an easy man to love," Warriors owner Franklin Mieuli later said of the trade. "I don't mean that I personally dislike him. He's a good friend of mine. But the fans in San Francisco never learned to love him. I guess most fans are for the little man and the underdog, and Wilt is neither. He's easy to hate, and we were the best draw in the NBA on the road, when people came to see him lose."

He quickly made the 76ers into a title contender, but that spring they lost a seven-game series to the Celtics again. The following year, Philadelphia actually beat out Boston for the Eastern Division's regular-season crown, but they were caught flat-footed in the Eastern playoffs and lost to the Celtics, 4-1.

Chamberlain's frustration, of course, was no deeper than that felt by West, Baylor and the Lakers. Bill Russell had simply built a wall around the NBA title. He had made it his personal property, or so it seemed.

1967

The loss to Boston that previous spring cost 76ers coach Dolph Schayes his job. "Wilt and I never did see eye-to-eye," Schayes later explained. In his place, Philadelphia hired Alex Hannum, Chamberlain's former coach in San Francisco who had just been released by the Warriors.

Hannum and Chamberlain had come to an understanding three seasons earlier, in the fall of 1963, when both first joined the Warriors. The coach and his center almost came to blows during practice and had to be separated by players. Hannum, at 6'7", figured he was big enough to go outside and settle it. The players wanted none of that. Neither did Chamberlain, although he would have won easily. The incident, however, did get everybody on the same wavelength. They established a relationship and were eager to work together in Philadelphia.

With Hannum coaching, the season promised to be a battle in the Eastern. To reload, Auerbach had traded Mel Counts to the Baltimore Bullets to obtain Bailey Howell, a smooth-shooting veteran forward who had played his college ball at Mississippi State. In addition, Boston signed another veteran, 6'8", 255-pound Wayne Embry, as Russell's backup. Once again, Auerbach had found just the recycled talent that could boost the club through the next phase of its transition. The Celtics won 60 games in 1966-67, tying the second-highest total in their illustrious history. It didn't help much, though. Chamberlain and the 76ers won 68. They opened the season by winning 15 of their first 16, losing only a road game at Cincinnati. That was followed by an 11-game winning streak, then a loss to the Knicks, then another streak that brought their record to 37-3. After they won their next nine, their record stood at 46-4.

"That whole season was just magical, something where a team played almost perfect basketball," sharp-shooting guard Wali Jones said in a 1990 interview. "We played as a team/family concept."

If it was a family, it was a prolific one. They averaged 125.1 points per game. But for the first time in his career, Chamberlain wasn't the big daddy. He averaged a career-low 24.1 points per game. As he had in San Francisco, Hannum had persuaded Chamberlain to concentrate less on scoring and more on rebounding and defense. He again led the league in boards at 24.2 per game, plus he shot an unfathomable .683 from the floor, a league record. And he was third in the league in assists at 7.8 per game.

Another part of Hannum's coaching effort concerned luring Larry Costello out of retirement to help in the backcourt, where Jones and Hal Greer were the starters.

> **C**hamberlain's presence had an immediate impact on the league's statistical races. He led the NBA in scoring and rebounding. The next season, he continued that scoring and rebounding dominance and became the first player in league history to shoot better than 50 percent from the floor.

The Sixers took up Chamberlain's offensive slack with balance, with seven people scoring in double figures. Greer averaged 22.1 points a game, and Jones was good for 13. While the backcourt was merely excellent, the frontcourt was awesome. Chet Walker, the fifth-year forward out of Bradley, averaged 19.3. Reserve Billy Cunningham, in his second year out of North Carolina, scored at an 18.5 clip. And Lucious Jackson did the rest of the power work on the boards plus averaged 12 points a game. Jackson was 6'9", 240 pounds, and sported an almost shaven head. In other words, the picture of an intimidator.

"They all play me the same way," he said. "Keep me away from the boards."

Rookie Matt Guokas, Jr., son of Matt, Sr., the backup center of the old Philadelphia Warriors in '47, came on strong as the team's third guard at the close of the season.

They finished the year at a league-record 68-13, an overwhelming winning percentage of .840. But the real golden moment came when they blew past the Celtics 4-1 in the Eastern finals.

Across the league, fans marked the 1967 playoffs with a garbage-throwing spree. In Boston, the menu was eggs and tomatoes. In Philly, eggs, potatoes and coins. Boston lost the first game at Philadelphia. Then, when the Warriors took the second game in Boston, things turned nasty. The home crowd booed Russell, the man who had brought them nine championships. Writers questioned Russell's substitution patterns, or lack of. How, they asked, could he battle Chamberlain on the floor while matching wits with Hannum on the bench?

Russell juggled his lineup for the third game in Philadelphia, starting Havlicek and Siegfried in place of Sanders and K.C. Jones, who was retiring at the end of the season. Boston still lost, 115-104, as Chamberlain set a playoff record with 41 rebounds.

"I've never moved so much in my life," he told the writers afterward. "Not even the night I scored 100."

"They're playing the same game we've played for the last nine years," K.C. Jones said of the Sixers. "In other words, team ball."

In attendance for the game was Danny Biasone, who had come down from Syracuse to see the franchise that he had started with $1,000 blossomed into the most powerful team in basketball. With their 125-points per game, the 'Sixers were making the most of his shot clock.

The Celtics managed a win in Boston, but the fifth game in Philadelphia's smoke-filled Convention Hall brought a decisive end to Boston's string of championships, 140-116. At their garbage-throwing worst, the Philadelphia fans converged on the floor for a riotous celebration, as K.C. and Russell hugged and walked off.

In the Philadelphia locker room, the Warriors were about to break out the champagne when Chamberlain stopped them. The writers had expected Chamberlain to celebrate after years of frustration against

Russell. No matter how great this victory seemed, Chamberlain told his teammates, it would only be good if they won the championship.

Later, dressed in his customary black cape, Russell entered the Philadelphia locker room and went to Wilt.

"Great," he said softly, taking Chamberlain's hand.

"Right, baby," Chamberlain replied.

"Great," Russell said once more and left.

In the Western Division, the San Francisco Warriors had rebounded after firing Hannum and hiring Bill Sharman as coach. Sharman found a heavenly team to guide along. Five of his players were involved in church work. Sharman called them "my Sunday school team." The coach was astounded to make it through the season without having to fine a single player for a rules transgression. They won the regular season with a 44-37 record and dumped St. Louis in the Western finals, 4-2. It, too, was a garbage-strewn series, particularly in St. Louis, where the fans steadily rained eggs down on the floor. They also tweaked the Warriors' ears on the bench, forcing San Francisco management to hire two elderly security guards to stand behind the bench. For some reason, this move enraged Hawks owner Ben Kerner. At one point, the St. Louis fans pelted Warriors forward Rick Barry with Snickers bars. Barry had an endorsement contract for the candy.

"At least my sponsor will be happy," Barry said afterward.

When he sprained his ankle badly in the fourth game, the St. Louis fans booed loudly as he lay sprawled on the floor. He returned to the game, only to have his pants split with about two minutes to go and the score tied at 102. Barry snatched a towel and ran off to the locker room. He came back after a quick change, but the Warriors still lost.

Despite these trials and tribulations, the "Sunday school team" advanced to the Finals to meet Goliath. True to their image, they disdained alcohol and celebrated their Western title with soda pop. Unfortunately, all their goodness hadn't brought them any luck at playoff time. The team carried a variety of ailments into the championship series.

Nate Thurmond had recovered from a bad back to have a fine season at center. But he nursed a broken hand as the Finals began. Even so, he had evolved into a powerful center, capable of holding his own with Chamberlain.

Thurmond operated mostly out of a high post, and he had good enough depth to his shot to pull Chamberlain away from the hoop.

Barry, in his second year out of Miami, had stepped in as a superstar forward, averaging 35.6 points per game. He had just come off a rookie-of-the-year season in 1966 and was brimming with confidence. Maybe too much

Chamberlain goes for a rebound after Thurmond misses on the slam.

confidence, some observers thought, because the Warriors offense seemed to rely on him too often. That became trouble in the Finals, with his badly sprained ankle. To play, Barry required shots of Carbocaine, a local anesthetic.

Jim King, the former Laker who had a barber's license, did the playmaking chores and gave the team some outside shooting. He was healthy, but off guard Jeff Mullins, out of Duke, normally a smooth-moving player in the mold of West, was hobbled by leg bruises. Tom Meschery, the poetry-writing forward, still worked the corner, but he, too, had a broken hand. The other forward was Fred Hetzel, out of Davidson College, who contributed about 12 points and eight rebounds per game. Al Attles still played a tough defensive guard, and the Warriors got reliable shooting from Paul Neumann off the bench.

Thurmond countered Chamberlain's work on the boards with impressive rebounding for the Warriors.

It was a nice team, but they were hurting and no match for Chamberlain in his context. Convention Hall was strangely subdued for Game 1. In fact, it wasn't even a sellout. The Warriors used the lull in Philadelphia's emotions to force an overtime. Thurmond had 31 rebounds to match Chamberlain's 33. And Barry laced in 37 points. Philadelphia had led by 19 in the second quarter, but they slipped into the roundball ozone from there on out. The Warriors caught and tied them in the game's last minute on two free throws by Mullins. San Francisco almost won it with 10 seconds left in regulation. Barry had the ball against Walker and beat him by going right. Chamberlain moved in to stop the drive, and Barry neatly dished the ball to Thurmond. But somehow Chamberlain recovered and blocked the shot over Thurmond's left shoulder.

Thurmond wanted the call but didn't get it.

In overtime, Philly got the lead and kept it for a 141-135 win.

The scoresheet afterward read balance. Greer led them with 32, while Jones had 30, Cunningham 26 and Walker 23.

Chamberlain finished with 16.

"What really hurts is the way it happened," Sharman said, "coming back, getting into overtime, then losing. That's the worst way to lose. We not only get the loss, but we shake them up so that they'll really be ready for the next one."

Which is exactly what happened in Game 2. The Warriors shot 29 percent from the floor, and Philly blew 'em out, 126-95. Chamberlain had only 10 points this time, but 38 rebounds. Greer got another 30 and Cunningham 28.

The series then moved to the Cow Palace in San Francisco, where the Warriors needed something special to stay involved. They got it when Barry scored 55. Just as important, King jumped out of character and hit for 28. And once again Thurmond did the job on the board, with 27 rebounds. All together it was good enough for a Warriors win, 130-126, and they narrowed the series gap to 2-1.

Hannum, though, wasn't worried. The Warriors had worked to get 20- and 25-foot shots. He didn't think they could win the series that way.

And he was right. San Francisco got no closer. Greer provided the Warriors with their undoing in Game 4, scoring 38 points and giving the 76ers the killer road win, 122-108. Chet Walker pumped in 33, while Chamberlain resumed his low-key offensive game with 10. More important, though, he kept Thurmond off the boards.

After years of frustration, a Chamberlain-led team was heading home for Game 5 of the Finals with a 3-1 lead. So what happened? They lost. Barry scored 26 in the first half, but the 76ers still maintained control with a 96-84 lead heading into the fourth period. But on the verge of the title, they shot 3 for 17 in that final quarter. The Warriors, meanwhile, stayed hot and won going away, 117-109.

Suddenly the basketball public sensed another Chamberlain choke. Game Six, played on April 24 in the Cow Palace, was a sellout: 15,612. Another 4,400 paid to see the game on closed-circuit television.

The first quarter was an 84-point shootout that closed with Philly leading, 43-41. The Warriors owned a 102-96 lead at the end of three. The score was 106-102 when the rookie Guokas came in, hit a 20-footer, then followed it with a driving layup. There, he was knocked into the basket support and out of the game. But his two quick buckets had fired the turnaround.

"Gook! Gook!" Chamberlain would crow afterward in the locker room. "The rook showed us how."

From there, the fourth period turned into a defensive battle. Chamberlain and company held San Francisco to just 19 points, while Cunningham alone scored 13 of Philly's 29 to lead them to the championship, 125-122.

Barry led all scorers with 44 points, but Chamberlain had already learned the futility of individual stats. "Sometimes it's actually easier to play against a team that has one man doing most of the shooting," the 76ers center said. His scoring average was way down, but he had his trophy. In Game Six, he had 23 rebounds and six blocked shots (in the critical fourth quarter he had eight rebounds and six blocks). Hannum had convinced him to do it with defense, intimidation and boardwork.

At last, the 'Sixers got their champagne. They took turns pouring it over Hannum's bald head. Why not? The Philly coach had gotten his second championship. His first had come with St. Louis in 1958. He became the first and only coach to win it with two different teams. And he was the only coach not named Auerbach to win the title during Bill Russell's career.

The biggest angle, though, belonged to Chamberlain. No longer could the basketball public say the Stilt was a loser.

"Everyone who knows the game of basketball, knows who really is the greatest,"

said Jones, who had grown up in Philadelphia idolizing Chamberlain.

Maybe so.

1968

Many times in the years to come, John Havlicek would look back to that night in Philadelphia in 1967 when the 76ers beat the Celtics. "The Sixers' crowd kept yelling Boston was dead," he recalled in 1989, "and I kept reminding reporters we were dead only until October. I think I also expressed the feeling we'd had too many proud days to start hanging our heads that night."

There was no head hanging in Boston, but there wasn't any chest thumping, either. Even when the fall of 1967 arrived, the Boston players made no dramatic statements about their comeback intentions. The mood was a quiet confidence. They drew that from their player/coach. Russell had turned 34 and was making the then-substantial sum of $150,000 yearly. He offered no public pronouncements about the team, and he didn't waste time in private either. There were no pep talks behind closed locker room doors.

"Russell wasn't ever a holler guy," explained forward Bailey Howell. "He wasn't ever the rah-rah type. He just led the team with the way he played, and as you know, as far as pressure situations, he was at his best in crucial games, when it was on the line, when you had to have a great game for 48 minutes. Then you'd rather have Bill Russell on your side than anybody."

Russell did have one serious meeting. Before the season began, he called all the veterans together. Being both a player and a coach was a tough job, he told them. He said he would need their help and encouraged them to make suggestions freely. It wasn't that he hadn't been open to suggestions before. He had just never asked for them. Always a great player, Russell was learning the coaching lessons now. And he was determined to keep the jobs separate. At one point in the season, Russell, the coach, fined Russell, the player, $500 for getting snowbound and missing a game.

The Celtics again finished second in the divisional standings at 54-28, eight games behind Philly. The 76ers won 62 games, again the best in the league. And Chamberlain was named the regular-season MVP. That, of course, mattered little to the Boston regulars.

Butch Van Breda Kolff took over as the Lakers' new coach.

They were just eager to get into the playoffs, to get another shot at Philadelphia.

"We were very anxious, of course, for them to begin," recalled Howell, who averaged 19.8 points while starting at forward. "The season had been very long and very tiring. But we felt like we had a good shot at it. It was like a new season. We knew that the Philadelphia team was very strong, and if we could get by them, then we had a real shot at winning it."

K.C. Jones had retired to move into the college coaching ranks, and Larry Siegfried took his place in the backcourt. Satch Sanders, Russell and Howell started up front, with Don Nelson and Embry working as subs. Havlicek rotated between guard and forward.

Prompted by competition from the ABA, the NBA had added three new teams, the Chicago Bulls in 1967 and the San Diego Rockets and Seattle SuperSonics in 1968, so now the playoffs no longer required a first-round bye. The 76ers whipped New York in the first round, while Boston dumped Detroit. Suddenly they were back to the crunch time again, when Russell always seemed to come up with the answers.

Luck, always a major factor in sports, made its play early in the playoffs, when Chamberlain lost a $1,000 blackjack hand on the team bus, an omen if there ever was one. In the postseason battle, the Philly boys fell one at a time. Cunningham fractured his wrist and was out. Jackson had a badly pulled hamstring. And Wilt injured his big toe. None of which seemed to make a difference heading into the Boston series, but it would all add up afterward.

The Celtics, meanwhile, were reasonably healthy and ready. They needed no extra motivation going into the conference finals, Howell recalled. "Everywhere we went, especially in Philadelphia, they had a chant. 'Boston's Dead. Boston's Dead. The dynasty is over.' You'd hear it at the airport when you got off the plane in Philadelphia. The cab drivers would be on you, riding you a little. Everywhere you went, the fans were real vocal. So it just made you more determined, really. It just helped you to play. It's tough, playing as often as you do, to be emotionally ready every night. When you get some help like that from opposing fans, it's really a lift."

Emotions took another turn that Thursday, April 4, the day before the series was to open, when Dr. Martin Luther King, Jr., was assassinated. The first thought was to postpone the game. Chamberlain, a Republican, and Russell, something of a civil rights activist, met on the issue the afternoon of the game. And the 76ers even put it to a team vote, but only Chamberlain and Jones were for postponement. So the players reluctantly agreed to go on with it. The atmosphere was dead in Philadelphia because of it. In fact, the tragedy cast a pall over the whole series. In honor of King, the second game was delayed from Sunday to the following Wednesday.

Things turned particularly dark for Boston. The Celtics won the first game in Philadelphia, but then the 76ers won three straight and jumped out to a 3-1 lead in games. Things seemed hopeless for Russell and his players as they returned to Philadelphia for the fifth game. Even Auerbach sensed the inevitable. "There are some people who have already forgotten how great that man really was," he said sadly as he watched Russell warm up before the game.

But once it got going, they dug in. Sam Jones, then 34-years-old, scored 37. Havlicek, whom Russell had moved to starting guard during the playoffs, added 29, and they pulled to 3-2 with a 122-104 win.

"After that fifth game, we really felt like the pressure was on them, even though they still had a 3-2 series lead and they would be back home for the seventh game if they didn't beat us in Boston," Howell said. "When you play at home in the NBA, especially in the playoffs, you have a tendency to say, 'We have to win this game, because we have to win our home games.' So you put a little extra pressure on yourself, and then you're not quite as relaxed and don't play quite as good a basketball."

The Celtics won at home to even the series, then returned to Philadelphia on April 19 and miraculously claimed the seventh game in a final-second thriller. Down 98-96, the 76ers controlled a jump ball, and Chet Walker drove for a shot. Russell blocked it. Greer got the loose ball, shot it and missed. Russell rebounded, and Boston advanced, 100-96.

At the final buzzer, Russell raised both arms in exultation, his face a picture of exhilaration. "The Celtics are a way of life with me," he would declare afterward.

"When it came to crunch time, we made the plays and Philadelphia didn't," Howell said.

"If I were Russell, I'd have my defense take credit for it," Hannum said glumly.

The Philadelphia coach admitted that Boston had solid direction. "Russell did a fine job coaching this year," Hannum said. "He is more aware of situations. Some things he did last year, well, I just had to scratch my head at them. There was none of that this season."

In Los Angeles, the Lakers, having swept the Warriors in the Western finals, watched the game on television and pulled for Boston, figuring Russell would be easier to beat than Chamberlain. The Lakers still had no post strength, although they had a new coach. Butch Van Breda Kolff, the former Princeton boss, had been hired to replace Schaus. He brought a major change in style to the team. He came into camp stressing conditioning, and he wanted to get the rest of the team involved in the offense with West and Baylor.

But he had been a college coach, and he treated them like youngsters, going so far as to institute a bed check. The only problem was, Van Breda Kolff would make the check but wind up visiting with his players, sipping beer in their rooms and talking basketball for hours until they begged him to get some sleep. Eventually this college approach worked against him.

"There was a change in the attitude surrounding the team," Jerry West said in 1990. "There was a volatile person who pretty much said what he thought. He felt that was the way to do it. You simply cannot do that at the professional level. He was a purist and still is. But on the pro level it won't work."

The Lakers struggled at first, but in January, they acquired Irwin Mueller and

> The closer you get to the magic circle, the more enticing it becomes. I imagine in some ways, it's like a drug. It's seductive because it's always there, and the desire is always there to win one more game. I don't like to think I'm different, but I was obsessed with winning. And losing made it so much more difficult in the offseason.
>
> — Jerry West

Russell slaps away the ball as Archie Clark tries to score in Game Five.

Owner Jack Kent Cooke was immensely pleased when they battled their way to the Finals. The new success matched their new approach. Since he had purchased the team in 1965, Cooke had remade their look. No longer did the Lakers wear blue and white. Cooke outfitted them in purple and gold, only he hated the word purple and insisted that the team call it Lakers blue. They wore gold uniforms at home, the first time in league history that the home team didn't wear white. And no longer did they play in the Sports Arena. When Cooke had trouble working out a lease with local officials, he decided to build the Forum in Inglewood near Los Angeles International Airport. The Lakers had moved into the palatial structure on New Year's Eve.

Cooke called it the Fabulous Forum. Brand new, the building was now hosting the Fabulous Finals. Never mind that the championship series was a match of runners-up.

The Lakers liked their chances going in. "If we can rebound, we can win," West told the writers. "We're little, but we match up well with Boston. We're quick, and we shoot well, and that can be enough in a seven-game series."

They alternated Mel Counts and Darrall Imhoff in the post, and Mueller's quickness helped out on the boards. Archie Clark joined West in the backcourt, with Goodrich and Crawford coming off the bench. Baylor was still the man in the corner, but Tommy Hawkins had returned to the team to provide depth at forward. At 31, he still had no range to his shot, but he was playing the best ball of his career.

The Lakers opened the series with a not-too-surprising split in Boston Garden. They lost the first when West shot 7 for 24 and Baylor 11 for 31. But they pulled their usual surprise and won the second. The Celtics returned the favor when the series switched to L.A., winning Game 3, 127-119. Then West scored 38 points, and Baylor added another 30 as Los Angeles evened the series with a 118-105 win in Game 4, after Van Breda Kolff had been ejected.

Fred Crawford, which gave them quickness off the bench, a quality the Lakers had lost whenever Baylor and West left the floor. From January on, they went 38-9 the rest of the way, good enough for a 52-30 finish, second place in the Western behind the Hawks.

That victory was dampened when West sprained his ankle in the closing minutes. It appeared serious enough to keep him out of Game 5 back in Boston. He played anyway and scored 35, but it wasn't enough to counter the Celtics, who jumped to a 19-point first quarter lead. By the third quarter, the lead was still 18, but L.A. came back after that, tying the score at 108 in the fourth. The Lakers were down four with less than a minute to play, when West stole the ball and found Baylor downcourt for a layup. The Lakers then tied it when Clark got another steal and West scored. In overtime, Russell blocked a Baylor shot and Nelson hit a late free throw to give Boston a 3-2 series lead, 120-117.

The Celtics had five players with big numbers. Havlicek, the team captain, led them with 31, while Nelson, the former Laker, scored 26.

Just as the series returned to Los Angeles for Game 6, just as the tension turned high, things went terribly awry for the Lakers. It began with the national anthem. Johny

Sam Jones was moved to forward, forcing the Lakers to go with a taller, slower lineup.

Mathis, the featured vocalist, began with God Bless America, then switched to The Star Spangled Banner.

The best switch of the day, though, was made by Coach Russell, who moved Sam Jones to forward, where he posted Goodrich up and forced Van Breda Kolff to go with a taller, slower lineup. That didn't work either. The Celtics ended it in a blowout. Havlicek scored 40, the Lakers trailed by 20 at the half and Boston had its tenth title. To go with Havlicek's 40, Bailey Howell had scored 30.

"We weren't a dominant team," Howell said. "Unless everyone was playing well and together, we couldn't win. And so we wouldn't have won without every guy on that team."

For Russell and his boys, it was an exhilaratingly sweet victory. Old men appreciate things so much more. The sweetest thing about it was the silence. The chanting had died, and the taxi drivers had stopped talking their trash.

"He is an unbelievable man," West said of Russell afterward. "To be frank, we gave them the championship. We gave them the first game, and we gave them the fifth. But I take nothing from them. There is something there, something special. For instance, twice tonight the ball went on the floor and Siegfried dove for it. He didn't just go for it hard, he dove for it. And they're all that way on the Celtics, and you can't teach it."

Throughout the final minutes on the bench, Russell and Havlicek hugged each other with glee. Afterward, Russell, dressed in a black suit, turned to face reporters. They asked him what he had left to accomplish.

"Well, I don't know," he replied after a moment, "because I never had a goal. To tell you the truth, it's been a long time since I tried to prove anything to anybody. I know who I am."

1969

Championship number eleven was a bit tougher for Boston. The 1968-69 season found Russell struggling with leg injuries that forced his hospitalization briefly. With Sam Jones also hurting, Boston came to rely on Havlicek and Howell again.

"His knees really bothered him," Howell said of Russell, then 35. "So he didn't even practice. He just played the games. But once he got his knees warm, he was all right until the game was over. Then they were stiff and sore again."

In a blockbuster move, Philadelphia had traded Chamberlain to the Lakers, but the Celtics still struggled in the Eastern Division, finishing fourth with a 48-34 record. Then, once in the playoffs, they drew on their pride and chased off the upstarts one final time. First Philadelphia, then New York fell.

The Lakers, meanwhile, moved through the Western competition and advanced to the most disappointing of their Finals meetings with the Celtics. As hurt as the losses had left him, Jerry West justified them each year by remembering that Boston had the better team. But that was no longer the case in 1969. Los Angeles had taken the top seeding in the Western with a 55-27 record, and thus had home-court advantage for the Finals with Boston.

"Most of the years we played they were better than we were," West said of the Celtics. "But in '69 they were not better. Period. I don't care how many times we played it, they weren't better. We were better. Period. And we didn't win. And that was the toughest one."

For the first time in their meetings, the Lakers had a real center to use against the Celtics. Baylor, Chamberlain and West were the heart of the lineup. But there was more. There was Keith Erickson out of UCLA, recently acquired from Chicago. There were John Egan, the veteran guard, to boost the backcourt, and Mel Counts, the 7-footer and former Celtic, to do the same up front.

Havlicek was the thrust of the offense for Boston, at 21.6 points per game. Howell followed him at 19.7. Sam Jones, Siegfried, Nelson and Sanders all worked in double figures.

The 35-year-old Russell, meanwhile, managed to appear in 77 games and averaged 9.9 points.

The only new face who got much playing time was veteran Emmette Bryant, whom Auerbach had acquired as a backup at guard. His beard and spectacles gave him a deceiving countenance. Bryant was a defensive whiz, who played for the Knicks when Auerbach first came to admire him. For some reason, the Knicks had let him go in the expansion draft to the new Phoenix Suns. Auerbach got him for a second-round draft pick.

"You change the spokes, but the wheels keep rolling," Russell said gleefully.

But some spokes carried more weight than others. Sam Jones had announced it would be his last season. "Finis. End. Through. This is it," he would say when writers asked him about his decision.

On a team with an overpowering defensive mindset, his bank shot had been the important offensive element for years. Jones was irritating to Boston's competition for another reason — he was another piece of Auerbach's luck. In 1957, Auerbach wasn't sure what to do with his first-round pick, the last of the round. He needed a guard, so he called his old friend and former player, Bones McKinney, who recommended Jones out of little North Carolina Central.

"It was worth a shot," Auerbach said, "so I took him."

Jones came to the NBA as a ready-made player, Auerbach said. The only problem was, he had to wait for playing time behind Bill Sharman. But his teammates soon learned how well he could shoot and came to expect that of him. In fact, Jones was playing early in his career when he heard Cousy dribble by the bench and scream at Auerbach, "Get him out!"

What was the matter? Jones asked during a timeout moments later. He wasn't shooting enough, Cousy explained. The team was working to set up his shot, and he wasn't taking it.

That ceased to be a problem with Jones. He waited patiently behind Sharman for four seasons, making the most of his opportunities and taking his shots when they came. "He knew it was just a matter of time," Auerbach said. When Sharman retired after the 1961 season, Jones stepped in and gave the Celtics the steady offense they needed, averaging between 18 and 25 points over the next seven seasons.

For 1968-69, his scoring average dipped to 16.3, and Jones struggled during the playoffs. But he maintained his shooter's confidence and kept taking his open shots. Eventually, it would pay off for Boston.

But in the interim, the old talk about the Celtics' senior citizenship seemed to increase with each game. The average age of the team was 31, and over the last half of the regular season they showed it. They failed to play .500 ball.

Havlicek had just turned 29, and as one of the youngsters on the team, sought to turn down the debate. "I remember they were calling us old when I came in, and that was six years ago," he said. "We were fighting that then."

As the playoffs neared, it translated into an urgency for the team, particularly Russell, who had private thoughts about ending his career. "He didn't tell us," Howell said. "But he knew he was gonna retire, so he had an extra incentive to go out as a champion."

The season was wearing on him because Embry had moved on to a job as commissioner of recreation for the city of Boston. Russell didn't care for the play of his new backup, Jim "Bad News" Barnes. So Russell played more minutes, and grew weary. As he did, his defensive rebounding suffered. Without it, the Celtics famed fastbreak slowed to a jog.

A week before the season ended, Los Angeles beat them, 108-73, on national television. It was a humiliation and prompted Russell into one of his rare speeches.

"It was more a harangue than a speech," he told the writers. "You could not call anything with so many four-letter words a speech." As a final coaching move, he put Bryant in the starting lineup ahead of Siegfried for more defensive quickness.

The Lakers, meanwhile, entered the Finals with their own humiliations to contemplate. They had lost six previous finals to the Celtics (once in Minneapolis), and while that would seem to add pressure, West said that wasn't the case in 1969. "I never looked at it as pressure," he said. "You always had your goals and aspirations of winning a championship. We were always pretty concentrated in getting there."

The title held an almost mesmerizing effect on him, West said. "The closer you get to the

For Jerry West, losing in the Finals made for a difficult off-season.

magic circle, the more enticing it becomes. I imagine in some ways, it's like a drug. It's seductive because it's always there, and the desire is always there to win one more game. I don't like to think I'm different, but I was obsessed with winning. And losing made it so much more difficult in the offseason."

His West Virginia team had lost by a point in the NCAA finals in 1959. "I had my hands on the ball about midcourt with no time left on the clock," he recalled, "and I said, 'If I could have just gotten one more shot...' It wasn't to be. Those are the things frankly that stay with you more than the wins. Those are the things that really are wearing."

With Chamberlain, the Lakers now had a center and a real shot at winning. In fact, they were favored. But things weren't perfect with them, either. Baylor had struggled to adjust to Chamberlains' presence. Age was beginning to show on the Lakers' great forward. "I don't have to take his fakes as I always did before," Howell would brazenly tell the writers. "And he is not as quick on the drive or following the shot." Clearly, to be successful, Los Angeles needed its triumverate playing well.

Determined not to face another championship loss, West came out smoking in the 1969 NBA Finals. He scored 53, while

Chamberlain and Russell engaged in an old-men's struggle underneath. Havlicek scored 39 for Boston, but the Lakers nudged an advantage and won, 120-118.

Afterward, West was so tired he iced down his arms. Russell called West's show "the greatest clutch performance ever against the Celtics."

"It wasn't his 53 points that beat us," Russell said. "It was his 10 assists." Boston began with Bryant covering West, but he was too short to stop his outside shot. When the Celtics tried to play West close on the perimeter, he drove right past them for a variety of layups.

Wilt's presence meant that Russell couldn't drop off easily to stop the drives, West said. "I know he scares a lot of people, but if you're looking for Russell, you're not playing your game."

West cooled down to 41 points in Game 2, while Havlicek upped his total to 43. Very quickly, the series became a shootout between these two. Chamberlain scored only 4, but he countered Russell on the boards. Even better, Baylor, who had been sluggish, came alive to score the Lakers' last 12 points for another Los Angeles win, 118-112.

Up 2-0, the Lakers had private thoughts of a sweep as it returned to Boston. The Celtics took an early lead, but then Los Angeles owned the third period, when Keith Erickson poked a finger in Havlicek's left eye. The Lakers tied the game heading into the fourth and seemed poised to break the old men's backs and go up 3-0. But the Garden crowd helped pump the Celtics up for one final offensive surge. Havlicek, with his left eye shut, hit the late free throws to keep Boston alive, 111-105. He finished with 34.

Russell had helped the battered Havlicek off the court at one point. "I was thinking that he might be hurt badly," Russell explained later. "You see first these men are my friends. Above all, we are our friends."

Even though they had gotten close in Game 3, Game 4 provided the real opportunity for the Lakers to strike the death blow. It was what some might call one of those old-fashioned furious defensive struggles that Russell loved to wage. Others would call it just plain ugly. The two teams combined for 50 turnovers and enough bad shots and passes to last them a month. After Game 1, the Celtics had taken to double-teaming West, forcing him to make the pass rather than take the shot. That slowed the Lakers' scoring. Over the final four minutes, the two teams had one basket between them. But with 15 seconds left, the Lakers had an 88-87 lead and the ball. All they had to do was get the pass in safely and run out the clock. Instead Bryant stole it and the Celtics raced the other way. Sam Jones missed the jumper, but Boston controlled the rebound and called time at 0:07. On the inbounds, Bryant threw the ball to Havlicek, then set a pick to his left. Nelson and Howell followed in line to make it a triple pick. At the last instant, Havlicek passed to Jones, cutting to his right. Jones stumbled to a halt behind Howell, who cut off West. There, at the 0:03 mark, Jones lofted an 18-footer. He slipped as he took the off-balance shot, and it just cleared Chamberlain's outstretched hand. Jones knew it was going to miss and even tried to pull it back, he explained afterward. The ball went up anyway, hit on the rim, rose up, hit the back of the rim and fell in. Chamberlain leaped up and lorded over the basket, his face a picture of anguish as the ball came through the net.

Boston had tied the series, 89-88, and a dagger in West's heart wouldn't have felt any worse. "The Lord's will," he said later.

"I thought to shoot it with a high arc and plenty of backspin," Jones told the writers. "So if it didn't go in, Russell would have a chance for the rebound."

Russell wasn't even in the game, one scribe pointed out.

"What the hell," Siegfried said. "You hit a shot like that, you're entitled to blow a little smoke about arc and backspin and things like that."

The Lakers regrouped and headed home for Game 5. The Celtics just didn't have it. Russell scored two points with 13 rebounds. Chamberlain owned the inside, with 31 rebounds and 13 points, while West and Egan

Van Breda Kolff gives instruction to Baylor (right) as Chamberlain looks on.

rained down from the perimeter with 39 and 23 points respectively. Boston fell, 117-104, and trailed 3-2.

West, though, had injured his hamstring and was hobbled. He played in Game 6 and scored 26. But the Lakers needed more from him. And certainly more from Chamberlain, who made a measly two points. Boston won, 99-90, and tied the series at 3.

Once again a Celtics/Lakers series had come down to a seventh game. Only this time, Game 7 was in Los Angeles, this time there wouldn't be a Garden jinx. Or would there? West's hamstring had worsened. It was wrapped, and he declared himself ready to go. But everyone wondered. Everyone except Lakers owner Jack Kent Cooke.

As the series returned to California, Cooke began planning his victory celebration. He visualized the perfect finale for a championship season. He ordered thousands of balloons suspended in the Forum rafters.

According to Cooke's plan, they would be released as the Lakers claimed their championship. As the balloons rained down on the jubilant Lakers and their fans, the band would strike up "Happy Days Are Here Again." Cooke could see it clearly.

And so could Red Auerbach. The Celtics General Manager walked into the Forum that May 5 and gazed up into the cloud of balloons in the rafters. "Those things are going to stay up there a hell of a long time," he said.

No one was more infuriated by the balloons than Jerry West. The thought of them made him sick with anger. The Celtics, always looking for that extra little boost of emotion, found it in the Forum rafters. They hit eight of their first 10 shots on the way to a quick 24-12 lead. The Lakers charged back to pull within 28-25 at the end of the first. At the half, it was 59-56. Celtics. Em Bryant and Havlicek had carried the scoring load for Boston. Russell had done the boardwork.

The Lakers tied the score in the third before going strangely cold for five minutes. West, playing brilliantly despite his heavily bandaged leg, finally hit a shot to slow down the Celtics, who led 71-62 with about five minutes to go in the third. Then with 3:39 left, Russell took the ball inside against Wilt, scored, and drew Chamberlain's fifth foul to round out a three-point play. 79-66, Boston. Chamberlain had played his entire NBA career, 885 games, and never fouled out. Van Breda Kolff decided to leave him in. With him playing tentatively, Boston moved inside and took a 91-76 lead into the fourth. The balloons in the rafters weighed heavily on Cooke's team.

The lead went to 17 early in the fourth, but both Russell and Jones picked up their fifth fouls. The atmosphere then became tentative for everyone, and in the void, West went to work. A bucket. A free throw. Another bucket. The lead dropped to 12. They traded free throws. Then Havlicek got his fifth, and moments later, Sam Jones closed his career with a sixth foul. He had scored 24 on the day. After a Baylor bucket, and three more points by West, the Celtics answered only with a Havlicek jumper and the lead dropped to nine, 103-94, with a little more than six to play.

At the 5:45 mark, Chamberlain went up for a defensive rebound and come down wincing. His knee. He asked to be taken out. Van Breda Kolff sent in Counts. West hit two free throws, and the lead was seven. Russell and his boys were out of gas, hoping to coast. Another West jumper. And moments later, two more free throws from West. The lead was three, 103-100.

Three minutes to go, and Counts surprised everyone by popping a jumper, 103-102. Chamberlain was ready to come back in.

"We're doing well enough without you," the coach told his center. West, at the time, was unaware of this exchange, and when he later learned of it, was incredulous.

Boston and Los Angeles traded missed free throws. With a little more than a minute left, West knocked the ball loose on defense. Nelson picked it up at the free throw line and threw it up. It hit the rim, rose up a few feet and

Chamberlain grimaces as Jones' game-winning shot goes through the basket in Game 4.

dropped back through. The balloons were all but burst. The Lakers missed twice, the Celtics committed an offensive foul, all of which an angry Chamberlain watched from the bench. After a few meaningless buckets it ended. The Celtics had hung on to win their eleventh, 108-106.

The debate began immediately afterward. Chamberlain vs. Van Breda Kolff. And for the first time in his career, Russell expressed an opinion. Although they had been friendly through their careers, Russell criticized Chamberlain for leaving the game. Perhaps a broken leg should have taken Chamberlain out, Russell said, but nothing else.

The comments caused a rift between the superstars and ruined their friendship. Some observers later commented that perhaps Russell had only feigned friendship during their playing days to prevent Chamberlain from becoming angry and playing well against the Celtics. Like Auerbach, Russell had looked for an edge wherever he could find one. For years, opponents had claimed Auerbach turned up the heat in Boston Garden, that fire alarms unexplainably disturbed their sleep at hotels on the nights before key games.

All of this mattered little to Jerry West. He was merely disgusted with another loss. He had finished with 42 points, 13 rebounds and 12 assists. The Celtics went to the Los Angeles locker room immediately after the game. Russell took West's hand and held it silently.

"Jerry," Havlicek professed, "I love you."

"He is the master," Siegfried said of West. "They can talk about the others, build them up, but he is the one. He is the only guard."

West was named the MVP, the first and only time in NBA Finals history that the Most Valuable Player award has gone to a member of a losing team. The gestures were nice, West said, but they didn't address his agony.

"I didn't think it was fair," he said in 1990, "that you could give so much and maybe play until there was nothing left in your body to give, and you couldn't win. I don't think people really understand the trauma associated with losing. I don't think people realize how miserable you can be, and me in particular. I was terrible. It got to the point with me that I wanted to quit basketball. It was like a slap in the face, like, 'We're not gonna let you win. We don't care how well you play.' I always thought it was personal."

The Lakers, however, had no one but themselves to blame. They had made only 28 of 47 free-throw attempts. Always poor from the line, Chamberlain had made only 4 of 13.

West, who missed four free throws himself, said that free-throw shooting is one of the elements of winning, but the fault didn't belong solely to Chamberlain, who had hit seven of eight shots from the field and pulled down 27 rebounds (Russell, who played five more minutes, had 21).

Yet it was all the excuse the Chamberlain bashers needed. He was criticized roundly by sports editors around the country. That was totally unjustified, West said. "He was never seen to be really relaxed. I think after he got out of basketball, that has changed. I think he's much more relaxed and much more fun today than he was then. Maybe some of it had to do with the fact that he was Wilt Chamberlain. No one pulled for him. I think those things have always bothered him in his life. No question it's tough to be a giant. He always thought he was the best at everything he did. And it simply was not the case. If that was the case, he would have been an 80 percent free-throw shooter."

Cooke, meanwhile, was left with the task of figuring out what to do with all the balloons. He finally decided to send them to a children's hospital.

Three months after the season, Russell officially announced his retirement. The Boston dynasty was over, at least the Russell edition of it. They had won 11 titles in 13 years, a string unmatched by any team in any major sport. Auerbach, of course, continued to ply his trade, looking for talent, searching the horizon for that edge.

In 1985, the Celtics honored him with a celebration of his 35 years building the team. Dozens of old Celtics returned, stars and role players alike, long-termers and short-timers, all to honor Red. The occasion prompted Russell to reflect on exactly what set Auerbach apart. "He never made any pretensions about treating players the same," Russell recalled. "In fact, he treated everybody very differently. Basically, Red treats people as they perceive themselves. What he did best was to create a forum, but one where individuals wouldn't be confined by the system. And he understood the chemistry of a team. People tend to think teamwork is some mysterious force. It can really be manufactured, and he knew how to do that, to serve each player's needs."

The secret was to find players whose primary need was winning. The tricky part came in making sure they never got enough of it. To some around the league, this hunger in the Celtics was a piggishness.

Elgin Baylor, who joined West in suffering, didn't quite see it that way. "It was a challenge to play against Russell and the Celtics," he said. "It was fun. It was disappointing to lose. But it was the ultimate challenge. They were a proud team, and they had reason to be. Some people thought they were proud and arrogant. But I enjoyed playing against them. They were the best."

9.
The New Breed
Knicks, Bucks, and Finally the Lakers

Willis Reed earned the nickname "Wolf" when he played college basketball at Grambling University because he would hang around the boards gobbling up rebounds like a starved canine going after red meat.

At 6'9" and 235 pounds, he was a big man but not quite big enough to dominate the NBA with his size. Instead, he used his hunger, that red-meat factor. He was so serious and driven that he walked into New York Knicks training camp as a rookie in 1964 and immediately requested a copy of the NBA rule book.

"I just wanted to understand the game," he said.

Reed was a leader, not an overwhelming individual talent, although he could be overwhelming enough at times. He was the solid center of a great team, and that's how his playing career is remembered.

Which isn't bad at all. For Reed or the Knicks. The team and the player came to an understanding of each other at just the right time, the 1969-70 season. After years of being the personal banquet of Bill Russell and the Boston Celtics, the pro basketball championship had reverted to open invitation in 1970. Russell had retired, and Boston's fortunes fell with his leaving. As a result, a lot of old NBA hands rushed for the open seat.

Being the hungriest, Reed and the Knicks got there first, giving that franchise the title that owner Ned Irish had waited years for. Then came Oscar Robertson and the upstart Milwaukee Bucks, who won it in 1971. After that, Jerry West and the Lakers finally brought a trophy home to Los Angeles. All of them had been shut out while Russell played, and they all pursued the championship with a singleness of purpose seldom seen in professional sports. In 1970, the Knicks set a league record with 18 consecutive regular-season wins. The next season, the Bucks broke it by winning 20. Driven by more than a decade of frustrations, the Lakers then blasted to a new level, winning 33 straight games over the 1971-72 season.

Each team was success-starved. When a spot at the championship table opened, they all gulped the meal down hungrily. The Willis Reed way.

1970

The 1970 New York Knicks were pro basketball at its best. They didn't have one big star. Just a bunch of guys with guts and a coach who taught them to believe in defense.

If you don't know much about them, then you probably don't know much about basketball. They set some sort of record for books spawned by a championship season. Two decades later, publishers were still pumping out tomes on this team. After all, this was New York, which for years had been the money and mind of pro basketball, and this was the city's first NBA title. You can say what you want about New Yorkers, but when they get a championship team, they savor it. The 1970 story has been elevated to nearly mythical status in the Big Apple. Which makes you wonder, as Red Auerbach often has, what would have happened if his Celtics had been located in New York, in the media center of the universe. Such a thought approaches

sacrilege in New York. They love the Knicks, although many times over the suffering seasons they've wondered why.

The Knicks had sunk deeply into mediocrity through much of the 1960s, but that began to change in 1967-68 when they moved Red Holzman, who was working as their scout, to replace Dick McGuire as coach. Where McGuire had been nice, Holzman was tough and preached defense. In a quick turnaround, the Knicks made the playoffs.

Then that next December, 29 games into the 1968-69 season, they traded center Walt

Willis Reed goes up against Wilt Chamberlain. Reed had to use more than size against other NBA big men.

Bellamy and guard Howard Komives to Detroit for forward Dave DeBusschere. At first, the Knicks players were skeptical. If the Pistons didn't want DeBusschere, a local hero out of the University of Detroit, what good would he be in New York?

As it turned out, lots of good. He was one of basketball's early lessons in "chemistry," a somewhat overworked term today. But back in 1970, the idea was relatively fresh. Chemistry, of course, is the human element, how a group of five players mix. It is the wonderful thing about basketball, because it can't be measured by statistics, and it isn't always a function of talent. In fact, chemistry quite often flies in the face of logic. You take five good players, put them together, and find they aren't as successful as three good and two average players. Coaches can rarely identify just what makes it work. They only know that it does.

Really, though, DeBusschere's contributions to the New York Knicks weren't all that mysterious. Although he wasn't much of a leaper, he was a fine athlete. The first four years of his pro basketball career, he also worked as a pitcher in the Chicago White Sox organization. But in 1964, just months after DeBusschere's 24th birthday, the Pistons named him their player/coach, the youngest ever in the NBA. He threw baseballs one more season, then devoted his career solely to basketball.

Four seasons later he arrived in New York as a complete forward. Few people were better than the 6'6" DeBusschere at the subtleties of rebounding, of getting position and boxing out. He passed the ball as well as any frontcourt player in the game. And he had a smooth shot with great range. Even more important, he brought his mind to the Knicks. In coaching, Red Holzman focused almost completely on defense. "On offense, you guys can do what you want," he would jokingly tell his players. "But on defense you do what I want." Holzman was the perfect coach for a veteran pro team. He was tough and stressed discipline, but he was willing to listen. He let DeBusschere

install several key offensive plays that freed forward Bill Bradley to shoot, a development that would be critical to the team's success.

The most important thing about the DeBusschere deal was the shifting of team roles that it brought. Komives had started with Dick Barnett in the Knicks' backcourt, but his departure meant that the third guard, Walt

Coach Red Holzman preached defense and the Knicks responded.

"Clyde" Frazier, moved in as a starter. Perhaps the best defensive guard in the league, the left-handed Frazier unmasked his offense once he got more playing time. His development as a scoring threat pushed the Knicks to the next level.

But most of all, the DeBusschere trade benefited Reed, who had been playing out of position at power forward. With Bellamy gone, Reed moved to center, which set the team's identity.

"A lot of the pieces fell together at the right time," Reed said.

Like Bill Russell before him, Reed was quick and very intelligent. Unlike Russell, Reed had a smooth shot with plenty of range. Beyond all that, Reed had a presence. Boy, did he have a presence. It began with his overwhelming physical power. He wasn't a great leaper, but he was strong and determined that no one would out-hustle him.

"As a player and a man, he was always on fire," Frazier said of Reed.

As the story goes, Reed took on the entire Los Angeles Lakers team in a brawl during the first game of the 1966-67 season and whipped 'em all.

By himself.

"He just took over," recalled Sam Goldaper, the veteran writer for the New York Times. "The most unbelievable fight I ever saw in basketball."

It was a rough game, Reed recalled. "Rudy LaRusso threw a punch at me going up the floor, and the fight was on. I ended up hitting some people but I never did get a shot at Rudy. It was a wild fight."

Yet for all his power, Reed was no Bad Boy. He didn't pick fights, and he didn't look for trouble. He didn't back down from it either. But his presence put opponents

Dave DeBusschere, at 6'6", was a master at getting position for rebounds.

around the league on notice to leave him and his teammates alone. After five years in the NBA, Reed's hour had come round in 1969-70. First, he was named the MVP of the All-Star game, then later that spring, he was voted the league MVP. He capped that by picking up the MVP award in the Finals, the only player to capture all three in a single season.

As captain of the Knicks, he was a natural and imposing leader. He was the link that seemed to keep everyone — rookies, veterans, coaches, even management — together and headed in the right direction.

They had finished the 1969 season with a 54-28 record but lost to Boston in the Eastern Conference finals. "DeBusschere said in the locker room after the Boston series that next year was going to be our year," Reed recalled in 1990. "We really believed it. Everybody went home eager for next year. We couldn't wait for the season to start. Everybody came back in good shape and ready to go."

After a great training camp, they opened the season by winning five, losing one, then taking the next 18, a league record for consecutive wins. The Knicks rarely looked back from there, loping off to a league-best 60-22 finish. In so doing, they transformed the Garden crowd into a loud, silly horde. The upper deck screamed "dee-fense," and the city-hardened fans allowed themselves to believe. Like the Lakers, the Knicks, also had their courtside

attractions. Woody Allen, Dustin Hoffman, Dianne Keaton, Elliot Gould and Peter Falk were regulars. So was Soupy Sales. And author William Goldman. Suddenly it seemed that all of Manhattan wanted a seat in the Garden.

The Knicks had found their "chemistry," and it had taken them to the top. Guard Dick Barnett, known as "Skull" (because of his partially shaven head) during his college days at Tennessee State, was the bedrock of their offensive confidence. A veteran, he had played alongside West in the early '60s version of the Lakers backcourt. He had been known as a gun then, but playing for Holtzman required that he focus more of his considerable talent on defense. He was a veteran, but he made the adjustment without complaining.

Barnett also brought a looseness to the club, although you'd never know it at game time, when he was expressionless. Or at interview time, when he spurned the writers. "If you didn't know him," Frazier said of Barnett, "you saw him as a moody, unassuming person, because that was the image he projected to the press. But with the team, he was different. He was always an instigator, always had something going. He kept you laughing."

With Barnett and Frazier, the Knicks had the most stylish backcourt in the league. Frazier was "Clyde" from the movie "Bonnie and Clyde" because of his passion for a gangsterish hat and fancy suits. Barnett had the Carnaby Street look, complete with a cane, a cape and spats. He spent many of his off-court hours engrossed in postcard chess, trading moves with other players around the country, often engaging in several games at once. In his book, "One Magic Season And A Basketball Life," Frazier called Barnett the funniest man in basketball. He was the team's graybeard, and he had a million tales to tell. He delivered them deadpan, with his considerable storytelling abilities (he would later earn a Ph. D. in education at Fordham).

For the Knicks, Barnett was a complete pro. He called his shot the "fall-back, baby," meaning that when he shot it, there was no need to think rebound. Just fall back on defense.

The one glitch in the team's harmony came with the jockeying between Cazzie Russell and Bill Bradley at small forward. The two had competed against each other in college, but Russell had gone right to the pros after the University of Michigan, while Bradley had left Princeton to become a Rhodes Scholar at Oxford for two years. He had struggled after coming to the Knicks with much heraldry and a fat contract. Russell had a fat contract, too, and an offensive game to match it. He was a finely tuned athlete, brimming with confidence as a young pro. Bradley, on the other hand, returned to basketball in a swirl of publicity, and immediately struggled while attempting to convert from forward to guard. He didn't become comfortable until he returned to his natural position, forward, which, of course, was Russell's spot, too.

The situation could have had explosive consequences for a New York team, a white guy and a black guy, both high-profile types, competing for the starting job. It was a story made for the New York press, and the writers had a go at it. The rest of the Knicks, though, left it alone.

"We stayed out of that," Frazier said of the controversy in a 1990 interview. "It was always remedied by some freak, uncanny circumstances."

Russell was starting in 1969 when he broke his leg, and Bradley took over. Bradley kept the job when Russell returned the next season. The team played well with Russell filling a big role off the bench. An incredible offensive talent, he obviously wasn't happy about the circumstances, but he wasn't loud about it either. Then, in the spring of 1970, Bradley was injured, and Russell moved back into the starting lineup, only the team didn't fare as well. They suffered some losses, and it became obvious they were better with Bradley as the starter.

"Cazzie had his chance," Frazier said. "But he was better coming off the bench when we needed something. He could come in and get us points when we needed them."

Russell had great moves and could create opportunities to get himself open for the shot. There wasn't much need for him to pass the ball. Bradley, on the other hand, didn't move nearly as well and couldn't always get his shot. The team had to set picks to get him free. If the play didn't work, he passed the ball and seldom forced a shot. That helped, Frazier said, because it created movement in the offense and kept everybody involved.

Holzman went deeper into the bench than Russell. Mike Riordan was the third guard, while Nate Bowman and Dave "The Rave" Stallworth got good minutes in the frontcourt. The thing that held them together was Holzman's passion — defense. It drove them and bolstered them and defined them, particularly the press, which could create turnovers and easy points in bunches. "Any game we're down even 10 points going into the fourth quarter we can still win," Reed told the writers. They felt that good about it.

They clashed with Baltimore in the first round in a seven-game series. The Bullets had Earl "The Pearl" Monroe at guard, Gus Johnson at forward and Wes Unseld at center. It was a brutal series, with

Reed moved to center when DeBusschere came to the Knicks.

Unseld and Reed laboring mightily in the post. The Knicks finally closed them out in the seventh game in the Garden, 127-114.

In the Eastern finals, they met Milwaukee with rookie Lew Alcindor, who had learned plenty in his first year. But the Bucks were a year away and fell to the Knicks, 4-1. New York stepped up to face the Lakers in the Finals.

It had been an up-and-down year in Los Angeles. Van Breda Kolff was out as coach, replaced by Joe Mullaney, the veteran coach from Providence College. Chamberlain, now 33, had suffered a knee injury nine games into

Bill Bradley took over as the starter at small forward.

Dick Barnett drives for two vs. LA's Mel Counts.

the season and appeared to be lost for the year. But as the playoffs neared, he announced his intention to return, a move that surprised even his doctors. He played the final three games of the regular season and was force enough to help the Lakers thrive in the Western playoffs. They had finished second in the regular-season behind the Atlanta Hawks and Sweet Lou Hudson, but with Chamberlain the Lakers swept Atlanta in the divisional finals.

Despite that win and the Lakers' overwhelming edge in playoff experience, the Knicks were favored by the oddsmakers. Game

1 showed why. Although Reed had been worn down by battling first Unseld, then Alcindor and now Chamberlain, he quickly ran circles around Wilt. Barnett also was eager to match up with West, who had gotten the ball and the publicity when the two played together in Los Angeles. New York opened a quick lead, pumped it up to 50-30, with Reed popping from the perimeter while Chamberlain stayed down low. In the backcourt, Barnett harassed West. But the Knicks coasted a little too much with the lead in the second half and lost it late. Barnett got into foul trouble, and West found

his range, scoring 16 in the third period. Baylor, too, came alive, and between them they gave the Lakers a 98-95 lead early in the fourth.

First the Knicks turned up their defense with Riordan in the game. Then they added Russell's scoring and blew by Los Angeles rather easily over the last eight minutes to win, 124-112. Reed finished with 37 points, 16 rebounds and five assists.

Chamberlain, meanwhile, missed 9 of 10 free throws, but had 24 rebounds to go with his 17 points. The big scorer was West with 33, and Baylor hit for 21 with 20 rebounds.

"They just raise up and shoot," West told the writers afterward. "They're such a very, very intelligent team. Reed is so active, and they recognize this and use him so well in their offense. And they all can hit. They just work for an open 15-foot shot."

Asked why he had left Reed open outside, Chamberlain replied, "I just didn't come out after him. Next time I will."

For Game 2, the scenario was somewhat reversed. It was the Lakers who got the early lead, then struggled to keep it at the end. As promised, Chamberlain was much more active on defense. He hounded Reed into missing 17 shots. With a minute left, Frazier scored to tie it at 103. Then Riordan fouled West, who made two free throws at the 0:46 mark. Trailing 105-103, the Knicks got one last possession with 22 seconds left, but Chamberlain blocked Reed's shot. The Knicks retrieved it, but DeBusschere missed. Stallworth got the rebound for yet another try but was called for three seconds. The Lakers held on to even the series. Wilt had only scored 19 to Reed's 29, but his defense had made the difference. West led Los Angeles with 34.

Back home for Game 3 on April 29, the Lakers rolled out to a 56-42 halftime lead. Long-haired forward Keith Erickson, a beach-and-volleyball type from nearby El Segundo, helped West push the Lakers' offense along, while Chamberlain and Baylor ruled the inside. The Knicks couldn't seem to find a rebound. Erickson presaged a wild ending by hitting a 40-foot shot to close the first half.

The Knicks abruptly reversed the momentum in the third period. DeBusschere and Barnett started dropping shots in from the perimeter, setting off a run that allowed New York to tie it at 96 with two minutes left. Reed hit a free throw a minute later to give them the lead, 98-97. West put down a jumper from 19 feet at the 38-second mark to boost the Lakers back up. Barnett returned the favor at 18 seconds. Los Angeles called time to set up a play, but when the action resumed, Barnett did the smart thing — he fouled Wilt. Chamberlain managed to make the second of two, and the score was tied at 100 with 13 to go. Knicks' turn. The set play called for DeBusschere to set the pick and Bradley to hit the open jumper. "Dollar Bill" Bradley couldn't get open, so DeBusschere took a pass from Frazier, gave a head fake and dropped in a neat little jumper. 102-100, Knicks. Three seconds left. The Lakers were out of timeouts.

Chamberlain half-heartedly tossed the ball to West, who dribbled three times as Reed dogged him. Two feet beyond the key, just to

> **T**hat was the championship, the one great moment we had all played for since 1969. I didn't want to have to look at myself in the mirror 20 years later and say that I wished I had tried to play.
>
> — Willis Reed

the left of the lane, West let fly. 55 to 60 feet. Good. DeBusschere, underneath the basket, threw out his arms in disgust and collapsed. Wilt laughed and ran off to the locker room, thinking the shot had won it. But only the ABA had a three-point rule back then. The officials brought Wilt back out for overtime, 102-102.

In the New York huddle, Barnett frowned at the downcast faces around him. "What's the matter with you guys?" he groused. "This game's not over. It's just starting."

They went back to the seesaw, while West missed all five of his shots. With a little over a minute left, the score was tied at 108 when Reed hit a foul shot. Then Barnett, the former Laker, clinched it with a bucket at the 0:04 mark. West had no more miracles. It ended 111-108.

The scoreboard may have been bad for the Lakers, but the stat sheet looked sweet. Baylor had a triple double (13 points, 12, rebounds and 11 assists). West had another 34, and Chamberlain had scored 21 with 26 rebounds.

And Reed was continuing to run up MVP numbers, 38 points and 17 rebounds, while DeBusschere had 21 and 15, respectively. Most important, though, the Knicks had the big stat, a 2-1 lead in games.

A flow had been established to the series. Each side had an advantage, the Lakers their inside strength, the Knicks their running and quickness. One side would use its advantage to get a lead, the other would then come back. Injuries were beginning to be a factor as well. West had jammed his thumb, and both Chamberlain and Reed had aching knees.

Game 4 was another nail-biter. Barnett hit six of seven from the field in the first quarter as the Knicks opened up hot. West was the answer for the Lakers. Despite a badly sprained thumb, he played 52 minutes and scored 37, with 18 assists and five rebounds. Still the game would come to overtime and the hands of a Laker reserve forward, John Tresvant, who would go absolutely wild and lead Los Angeles to a 121-115 win. Baylor did his part, too, with 30 points.

Game 5 back in the Garden rang in as one of those golden moments in pro basketball history. At least it did if you were a New Yorker. Out on the left coast, it's a game they've gladly forgotten. Wilt came out strong and determined to cover Reed all over the floor. With a little more than eight minutes gone in the first quarter, Los Angeles had raced to a 25-15 lead. Then Reed caught a pass at the foul line, and Chamberlain was there to meet him. Reed went to his left around Wilt but tripped over his foot and fell forward, tearing a muscle in his thigh, a main muscle running from his hip to his thigh. The New York center lay writhing in pain as the action raced the other way and Holzman screamed for the refs to stop the game.

At the other end, DeBusschere halted the action by getting ahold of Chamberlain. "Oh my God," the Knick forward said as he looked back up the court at Reed on the floor.

"I drove past Wilt and I just fell," Reed recalled later. "I was having problems with my knee, and I tore a muscle in my right thigh. I was on a roll, too."

Reed was out, and the Lakers had a hot hand. The Garden crowd grew quiet. Holzman tried to prop up his players' spirits during the timeout. He inserted Nate Bowman to play Chamberlain, and that worked for a time. Then Holzman went with reserve forward Bill Hoskett, all of 6'7", who hadn't seen a minute of playing time in the entire playoffs. Hoskett hounded Chamberlain effectively enough, but it really wasn't getting the Knicks anywhere. By the half, they were down 13.

In the locker room, Bradley suggested they go to a 3-2 zone offense, which would either force Chamberlain to come out from the basket, or it would give them open shots. Holzman was happy to have the idea. He sent Russell, Bradley, Barnett, Frazier and DeBusschere out to answer the horn for the second half.

"Outside we had two wings with a point man," Bradley later explained. "Inside, we had one guy on the baseline and a roamer. When we saw Wilt not playing a man, it was like attacking a zone. Just hit the open spaces in a zone."

148

It began working in the third. The Lakers seemed almost possessed by the notion of taking advantage of the mismatch in the post. Time after time, they attempted to force the ball into Chamberlain, and the Knicks got bunches of steals and turnovers. The fourth period opened with the Lakers holding an 82-75 lead and a troubled hand. They were in obvious disarray. And the Knickerbockers were surging, cheered on by the awakened Garden crowd. "Let's go Knicks. Let's go Knicks," all 19,500 spectators chanted over and over. At just under eight minutes, Bradley hit a jumper to tie it at 87. Then at 5:19, Dollar Bill dropped in another jumper to give the Knicks the lead, 93-91. Then Stallworth scored. Then Russell with one of his acrobatic, off-balance shots. Then Russell again on a follow, and it was 99-93. Bradley did the final damage with about a minute to go, pushing it to 103-98.

Chamberlain passes off during Game Three action as Cazzie Russell (center) and DeBusschere go on defense.

After a brief flurry, the Knicks took the 3-2 edge, 107-100. Los Angeles had been forced into 30 turnovers for the game. In the second half, West didn't have a field goal, and Chamberlain scored only four points.

"The fifth game," DeBusschere said proudly 20 years later, "was one of the greatest basketball games ever played."

The Lakers returned home and corrected their mistakes in Game 6. With Reed out, Wilt scored 45 with 27 rebounds. The Lakers rolled, 135-113, to tie the series at three each.

The stage was set in New York for the seventh game drama. Would Reed play? The Knicks left the locker room for warmups not knowing. Before he had left, Bradley and DeBusschere had asked Reed to give the team just one half. About 20 minutes would do it, they figured. In the training room, Reed was set to receive injections of carbocaine and cortisone through a large needle. There were problems, though, because the skin on his thighs was so thick. The doctor had trouble getting the needle in.

"It was a big needle, a big needle," Reed recalled. "I saw that needle and I said, 'Holy sh--.' And I just held on. I think I suffered more from the needle than the injury."

The doctors had to place the injections at various places and various depths across his thigh in an effort to numb the tear. "I wanted to play," he recalled. "That was the championship, the one great moment we had all played for since 1969. I didn't want to have to look at myself in the mirror 20 years later and say that I wished I had tried to play."

In the Laker locker room, West faced a

similar situation — injections in both injured hands. "I don't even like to think about it," Mullaney told the writers. "A shooter getting needles in his shooting hand."

Reed appeared on the Garden floor just before game time that Friday, May 8, bringing an overwhelming roar from the crowd. "The scene is indelibly etched in my mind," Frazier said, "because if that did not happen, I know we would not have won the game." The Knicks watched him hobble out, and each of them soaked in the emotion from the noise.

Barnetts's late basket gives New York the 111-108 win in Game 5.

The Lakers watched, too, and made no attempt at furtive glances. Reed took a few awkward warmup shots. "I can't go to my right all that well," he jokingly told Chamberlain before the start. Reed couldn't go right when he was healthy.

He stepped into the circle against Wilt for the tipoff but remained immobile. That changed once play began. Reed scored New York's first points, a semi-jumper from the key, and he played incredibly active defense. Seventeen times the Lakers jammed the ball into Chamberlain in the post. Reed harassed him into shooting two for nine. And Reed hit another shot (he would finish 2 for 5 with four fouls and three rebounds). But it was enough. The emotional charge sent the rest of the Knicks zipping through their paces. They simply ran away from the Lakers. New York led 9-2, then 15-6, then 30-17. When Reed left

Bradley helped take up the slack when Reed went out in Game 5.

the game, having delivered the half that Bradley had asked for, New York led, 61-37. From there, they rolled on to Mr. Irish's first title, 113-99. Frazier hit 12 of 17 from the field and 12 of 12 from the line to finish with 36 points and 19 assists. Barnett had scored 21, and DeBusschere had 17 rebounds. But their efforts were second to Reed's appearance.

"He gave us a tremendous lift just going out there," Holzman said. "He couldn't play his normal game, but he did a lot of things out there. And he means a lot to the spirit of the other players."

In the locker room, Stallworth was soaked with champagne and beaming. "There was no way Reed could play," he told a writer. "He was limping so bad. The guy is beautiful, just beautiful."

"It's like getting your left arm sewed back on," Russell said. "Everybody puts his in the pot. We're like one big beef stew."

The outcome was yet another item in the Lakers' craw, yet another defeat after years of losing to Boston. "They played well together, were well-coached and played good team defense," Baylor said of the Knicks in a 1990 interview. "They were exciting to watch. But that was disgusting, frustrating, because I felt we were the better team. Willis played hurt and gave them a tremendous lift. Willis was a great player and a great competitor. Just his mere presence did so much for the team."

Chamberlain was gracious afterward, almost upbeat. "Willis has played better basketball against me than any center I've ever faced in playoff competition," he said, taking an obvious jab at Bill Russell.

"We fell into a faster tempo," Mullaney said afterward, "instead of trying to get back two points at a time. We just can't play that kind of pace against a team like the Knicks."

"There's not one other guy in the league that gives the 100 percent that Reed does every night, every game of the season, at both ends of the court," Bill Bridges of the Atlanta Hawks had said earlier in the season. It was true.

Reed, for sure, was the darling of pro basketball at that moment. And it was a feeling that would last for years. "There isn't a day in my life that people don't remind me of that game," he said in 1990.

"It was," DeBusschere said, "a warm, wonderful time."

1971

Over the years, the language of basketball has settled on the term "complete," as in "the complete player," to describe the ultimate, the best. It means the guy who can do everything. Shoot. Dribble. Pass. Rebound. Play defense. Win.

In other words, Oscar Robertson.

At least that's what UCLA's legendary coach, John Wooden, has said of Robertson many times. Innumerable players and coaches alike have agreed.

"In his time, he was the greatest," said Ed Jucker, a former coach at the University of Cincinnati. "No one was the equal to him. I always called him a complete ball player, and there are not many truly complete players. But he could play any position."

Not only was Robertson complete, but he was almost nonchalant about it, former Kansas coach Dick Harp said. "He had unbelievable control of a basketball game, and many times he looked like he was taking a walk in the country when he did it. He was so much in control of things. He had the size, the quickness, everything. He had all those great blessings, but among them he had great judgment about what to do with the ball."

Some observers like to compare Robertson to the big-name modern players, Magic Johnson or Michael Jordan. But Pete Newell, the former pro and college coach, says Robertson actually has more in common with Larry Bird. Most people think of Robertson as a guard, Newell said, because he played guard as a professional. But in college at the University of Cincinnati, Robertson was a forward.

"Oscar played forward more like Larry Bird plays forward," Newell said. "He was such a great passer. He brought the ball up even though he was playing forward. He was so tough when he got the ball. Oscar would go down and get it. Then they'd clear for him, and he'd just take it on his own. There was no way you could stop Oscar one-on-one from penetrating and getting his shot."

Robertson led the nation in scoring three straight years as a collegian at the University of Cincinnati, setting in the process the NCAA career-scoring record. He did this while averaging 15.2 rebounds and setting Cincinnati's single-season assist record.

Ultimately, however, the question for players like Jordan, Bird and Robertson is not how complete they make themselves, but how complete they make their teams.

Robertson attempted to answer that question everywhere he played, every time he played. As a prep star, Robertson had carried Crispus Attucks High School in Indianapolis to back-to-back state championships in 1955 and '56, the first time an all-black team had ever won an Indiana state title. But throughout his college years and a dozen pro seasons, that special championship magic had eluded him. In a three-year varsity career at the University of Cincinnati, he had motored the Bearcats to the top ranking in college basketball. Twice he took them to the Final Four. Of his three varsity teams, the 1959-60 squad was the best. It lorded over college basketball with a 27-1 record before losing to the University of California in the national semifinals.

The top pick of the 1960 NBA draft, Robertson was the heart and soul of the Cincinnati Royals for the first 10 years of his pro career. But they were frustrating years. Despite making the playoffs several times, the Royals never advanced to the Finals.

Then in 1970, Robertson was traded to the Milwaukee Bucks, a three-year-old team with a future. The future was one Lew Alcindor, the 7'2" center who was about to change his name to Kareem Abdul-Jabbar after converting to Islam. The name had a regal ring to it, suggesting power and dominance. Just what you would expect a giant to be named.

His career stood in direct contrast to Robertson's. Alcindor's UCLA teams had won three straight NCAA titles. In fact, his biggest adjustment as a Bucks rookie during the 1969-70 season had been learning how to lose.

"Now I think I'm a pro," Alcindor told writers after failing to win the NBA title in his first season. "In my last three years of amateur basketball, my team lost three games. That was unreality."

Wooden often said Alcindor was the most valuable college player ever. The UCLA coach emphasized that most valuable didn't necessarily mean most talented. It simply meant that Alcindor was the kind of gifted, versatile player who could take a team beyond the sum of its players. Without doubt, he was the best college-age center in history, the kind of player to whom all the adjectives apply. Well-schooled. Intelligent. Dominating. He was the single player around which a championship could be built.

Larry Costello was hired when the Milwaukee Bucks were formed.

His basketball life had been that way since early high school, when Alcindor began leading Power Memorial to a series of New York City championships. An only child, he had been quiet and bookwormish. His mother, Cora, was a singer, and his father studied at the Julliard School of Music while working at a variety of jobs to support the family.

But Alcindor's success quickly boosted him past the quiet world of his family life. College coaches all over the country wanted him, and the pros did, too. "I'll trade two first round draft picks for him right now," quipped Gene Shue, coach of the Baltimore Bullets, when Alcindor was a high school junior.

By the time he arrived at the Bucks, winning was almost the non-chalant by-product of Alcindor's businesslike approach to the game.

That made him a perfect match for Robertson. Playing in an exhibition game that fall of 1970, Robertson was driving for the basket when the young center cut the wrong way. Robertson yelled at Alcindor, just as he had corrected teammates throughout his career. Alcindor listened quietly. The next time Robertson drove, the center cut the right way.

"He wants that championship," Alcindor explained to reporters later. "Me, I've got some time, but Oscar wants it right now. Right this year. And he's got us all feeling that way."

In a 1990 interview, Robertson stipulated that he wasn't frustrated by not winning a title during his years with the Royals. "I had done all that I could," he said. "What else could I do? I made All-Pro every year. I played as hard as I could. It wasn't up to me at that point."

In Milwaukee, the situation was entirely different. It was up to Robertson. Alcindor was the centerpiece, but it was Oscar's team to run.

His reputation around the league was Oscar the Grouch, the guy who'd blister you right out on the court if you weren't hustling. He respected those who could perform, but if you didn't keep up, watch out. That attitude worked well in Milwaukee, where the Bucks had set a record for rapidly assembling a team. With General Manager Ray Patterson, it was trade city. "We got Lucius Allen in a trade," Robertson said. "We got Bob Boozer in a trade. I went there in a trade."

And just about all of those who hadn't come in a trade were brand new. Bobby Dandridge, a 6'6" forward out of Norfolk State, had been selected in the fourth round of the 1969 draft. He and Alcindor had earned all-rookie first-team honors for the '69-70 season. Allen was a second-year player, too, having been obtained from Seattle. Greg Smith, the other starting forward, was only in his third year out of Western Kentucky.

The veterans were solid. Jon McGlocklin, a fifth-year player out of Indiana, started alongside Robertson in the backcourt, where he averaged 15.8 points per game while shooting .535 from the floor. Boozer, also obtained from Seattle, was the major frontcourt substitute. Both Boozer and McGlocklin had played with Robertson in Cincinnati.

While the assembly was rapid, the chemistry took a little while to develop. "It was a gradual thing," Robertson said. "It just evolved. It was more what I had to do than anybody else, because I was the senior person playing. I made the biggest adjustment. I didn't try to score any more. I tried to get other people involved in each game to make us a stronger team. And I did. I needed Greg Smith to be a player who had confidence in himself. I needed Bobby Dandridge to be better. When Lucius came in the game and Bob Boozer, they needed to have a role. And that was my job, to help them all find their places."

The team came out of a strong training camp and went undefeated through a 10-game exhibition schedule, Robertson said. "We played some very good teams, and that helped us more than anything."

With 17 teams, the NBA was now organized into four divisions, and Milwaukee dominated all four with a league-best 66-16 record. At one point, they won 20 straight, breaking the Knicks' year-old record for consecutive wins.

Robertson's scoring average, usually above 30 during his years in Cincinnati, dipped to 19.4, as he spent his time running the team and sending the ball down low to the big man. That worked. Alcindor led the league in scoring at 31.7 points and was named MVP.

By season's end, the Bucks had become machinelike in their efficiency, which was exactly what coach Larry Costello had sought. A 12-year pro himself, Costello had been hired three seasons earlier when the team formed. Yet by 1971, he was still running the Bucks like a college program. He set up hard, well-organized practices packed with drills and repetition. And he and assistant Tom Nissalke spent hours watching game films. With Costello, Robertson and Alcindor, the atmosphere was all business. Some observers thought it was almost cold, but it matched the personnel.

"Larry, Oscar and I have the same ways about us," Alcindor told reporters as the season came to a close. "We agree that being as efficient as possible cuts down on our chances for errors."

This emphasis on execution made Milwaukee one of the greatest offensive teams in league history. They led the league in scoring, yet were only twelfth in field goals attempted. And they were the first team in league history to average better than 50 percent from the field.

"There's no nonsense," Alcindor said of Costello, "because he's a man dedicated wholly to basketball."

Some observers wondered why Costello allowed Alcindor to return to Los Angeles during a brief lull at the end of the regular season. But the coach knew his center had been worn down by the schedule, and he figured the rest and time away would be good.

It was. The Bucks reassembled for the playoffs and promptly dusted San Francisco in the first round, 4-1. They lost their only game to the Warriors when sub Joe Ellis hit a 43-foot buzzer beater. Chicago with Bob Love, Chet Walker and Jerry Sloan provided some trouble at the next level but eventually fell 4-3.

The Bucks advanced to meet the Lakers in the Western finals, but it wasn't the same Los Angeles team of a year earlier. West and Baylor were out with injuries, and with Chamberlain as the focal point, Los Angeles had become a plodding halfcourt team. Milwaukee pushed them aside, 4-1.

Joe McGlocklin was a veteran who had played with Robertson in Cincinnati.

All along, the Bucks had their eyes on the Eastern, where the Knicks were embroiled in a tight final with the Baltimore Bullets. With Reed bullying Alcindor, the Knicks had taken a 4-1 edge in their regular-season series with Milwaukee. "I'm not interested in tag-team wrestling," Alcindor told reporters who asked about his lack of success with the power game.

The writers figured Reed would handle Alcindor easily in the championship series. "We're just gonna have to count on me and Oscar doing more than our usual," Alcindor said of the Bucks' chances against the Knicks. "We've got to spread a little anarchy out there, shake 'em up, move 'em around."

But the match-up was not to be. Baltimore outlasted New York in a seven-game Eastern final, a development that deeply disappointed the Bucks. "I'm wearing a New York jersey out there tonight," Baltimore forward Jack Marin joked as the Finals were set to begin. "I don't want to disappoint these people."

The Bullets, though, were no match for Milwaukee. Baltimore center Wes Unseld had badly sprained his ankle as the season ended and was supposed to be out six weeks. Somehow he hobbled back for the playoffs. From there, the seven-game battle with New York had further thinned the ranks. Forward Gus Johnson had sore knees and would miss two games against Milwaukee. So did Earl "The Pearl" Monroe, who had pulled muscles to go with his chronically sore knees.

With the Bullets' offense hurting, the Bucks squeezed a defensive noose around the games. Baltimore would shoot better than 40 percent in only one game in the Finals series. And in only two quarters did they score more than 30 points.

"They stopped us from getting the layup," Marin said of the Bucks.

"You've got to give Lew all the credit," Baltimore guard Kevin Loughery agreed. "He may just block one shot here or there, but guys have to change their shots because of him."

The result was only the second sweep in Finals history, the other being the Celtics over Minneapolis in 1959.

If not for the injuries, the series might have offered great potential. Unseld was seven inches shorter but 13 pounds heavier than Alcindor. And Robertson versus a healthy Monroe could have been a matchup for the ages. Monroe did score 26 in Game 1. But Alcindor had 31, and the rest of the Bucks were dominant in a 98-88 win. Alcindor had gotten in early foul trouble, but came back to have a big second half.

Reporters immediately began asking Robertson if he was eager to win the title. "If it comes, it comes," he replied with a frown.

In Game 2, held in Baltimore, Unseld used his muscle to shove Alcindor farther out, but it didn't help the outcome. Robertson held Monroe to 11 while scoring 22 himself. The ABC broadcast crew was desperate for something to jazz up the game. They focused their cameras on Marvin Cooper, a free-form rock dancer who was performing. He attempted to put a hex on the Bucks during a timeout, but that didn't work either. Milwaukee won, 102-83.

Back in Milwaukee for Game 3, the ABC crew had only Steve Swedish's Polish band as the entertainment, which was about as thrilling as the series. Milwaukee went up 3-0 with a 107-99 win, as Dandridge had 29 points.

Robertson did the major damage with 30 points in Game 4 in Baltimore, as the Bucks closed it out, 118-106.

"It was almost like pure basketball," Robertson said years later.

At the time, the writers and fans thought they were witnessing the birth of another dynasty. Instead, Milwaukee management broke up the team.

"After the championship, they did something which was really foolish," Robertson said. "They traded Greg Smith, Bob Boozer and Dick Cunningham. You had people who really did not understand what a team concept means. You win a championship and make a trade of any key ballplayer, and it's the kiss of death."

1972

The Milwaukee Bucks didn't die an instant death the next season. They won the Midwest Division with a 63-19 record. But the year belonged to somebody else, somebody who had been there before and had come away wanting.

With their failure in the 1971 playoffs, it became clear that time was running out for owner Jack Kent Cooke's collection of talented Lakers. Bill Russell had been out of basketball for two years, and they still hadn't won a championship. Heading into the 1971-72 season, Elgin Baylor was struggling to come back from yet another injury. Chamberlain had turned 35, and West was 33. If this wasn't their last shot, it was close.

The answer, in Cooke's mind, was to try yet another coach. Having worked his way through Fred Schaus, Butch van Breda Kolff and Joe Mullaney, the owner made overtures to UCLA coach John Wooden, who discussed the job over a cup of tea in the library of Cooke's Bel Air mansion. "John turned it down," Cooke recalled. "He had had his time. He said he was too old to start into professional basketball."

Fred Schaus then asked Cooke to consider 45-year-old Bill Sharman, the former Celtic guard who had just coached the Utah Stars to the 1971 ABA title. Sharman's 1967 San Francisco Warriors had lost the NBA championship series to Wilt's 76ers. Before that, Sharman had made a winner of the miserable program at Cal State Los Angeles. He'd even coached the Cleveland Pipers to the old American Basketball League title in 1962 (the Pipers were owned by a young shipping magnate named George Steinbrenner, so it was established that he could get along in difficult circumstances).

Cooke was intrigued by Sharman. "He had that inner intensity," the owner recalled, adding that he later saw the same quality in Joe Gibbs, who coached Cooke's Washington Redskins to three Super Bowl championships. "They were both seemingly quiet, almost shy. But I saw this quality after I talked to them five or 10 minutes."

Sharman's friends said he was crazy to consider the offer. They pointed out that the ideal situation would be a young team on the way up. Never get involved with an old team

on the way down, they told him. After all, who needed the pressure of dealing with old superstars and a demanding owner? "Everybody told me, 'You don't want that job,'" he recalled.

He took it anyway, which left his Celtics buddies shaking their heads. The Lakers announced his hiring that July of 1971, after working out the legal details with the Stars, who claimed they still had Sharman under contract. Asked his goal, Sharman declared "the world championship." That plot line, of course, was all too familiar to the reporters covering the team. They wondered what made Sharman think he could write a different ending this time.

The 1971-72 Laker roster presented a mishmash of gnarly egos. "Egads, they were prima donnas," Cooke recalled. The owner, of course, was the granddaddy of them all. His demanding style set the tone for what was a substantial cult of personality. Chamberlain had his giant pride. West was sullen with frustration, and "Motormouth" Baylor struggled with his declining skills and influence. To go with them were forward Happy Hairston, an irascible lockerroom lawyer who chattered incessantly; Gail Goodrich, a determined scorer who liked to control the ball; and Jim McMillian, a chunky Ivy Leaguer pushing for a starting role.

Among the bit players were Pat Riley, Keith Erickson and Flynn Robinson, all of whom sported healthy self-concepts. "On that one team you probably had more diverse, strong personalities than you had on any championship team in the history of the game," Bill Bertka observed.

The egos had tugged the Lakers in different directions for a few seasons now, and at times they had seemed on the verge of pulling the team apart. "We had a lot of players who'd had personal success but hadn't enjoyed team success," West said, "a lot of very frustrated people. It had been frustrating to lose each year. It was terrible."

"But," Bertka said, "you had the strongest personality in Bill Sharman. He was on fire right at that time. He was at the peak of his career with his personal intensity as a coach. He was a great communicator. No frills. No bullsh--. With Bill, it was all down to productivity."

Intensity had always been Sharman's trademark as a player. "I was always kind of aggressive," Sharman admitted. "When we played in the '50s, pro basketball was still growing. It was kind of like hockey. The owners didn't say go out and fight. But they didn't discourage it. Back then they didn't throw you out of games for fighting. They kind of let it go. If you backed off and didn't hold your own, they kind of took advantage of you. I always feel I never started a fight, but I never backed away from one. If you did, they just kept pushing and grabbing at you. I saw a lot of good basketball players in those days get pushed right out of the league because they wouldn't push back."

Beneath this tough exterior was a neat freak who always folded and put away his clothes on road trips, even for a 12-hour stay in a hotel room. On a Celtics roster bristling with partiers, he was the guy who filled 3x5 notecards with reminders on shooting technique and opponents' defensive tendencies and studied them in the lockerroom before games. He was the diet and exercise nerd, eating and working out at exact times during the day. Forget the usual beer and steak, Sharman wanted honey, toast and tea as his pre-game meal. Then in the lockerroom, he would stretch and do warm-ups. Nobody did that stuff in the fifties. And they didn't jog either. But Sharman did. Strangest of all, he insisted on going to the gym each morning before a game for shooting exercise, running through exactly the shots he planned to take that night.

As a coach, he would insist that his players go through these same routines. They often grumbled, but Sharman's game-day shootaround soon became a staple of NBA preparation. As would his notions on diet and exercise. Beyond that, he required his players to become students of the game. His Lakers were the first NBA team to break down game film and study it as football coaches did. In that age before videotape, scout Bill Bertka would spend hours cutting and splicing film. When the players seemed a little bored with the idea, Bertka spliced in occasional shots of Playboy Bunnies.

"It kinda got their attention," Sharman recalled with a chuckle.

An eight-time All-Star, Sharman would later author an instructional book on shooting. As a coach, he used his understanding of the mechanics to improve his players' touch. In

K.C. Jones joined Bill Sharman on the Lakers' coaching staff.

Los Angeles, however, he soon met his match. Chamberlain's foul shooting presented an unconquerable mountain. After years of trying everything, Wilt admitted he was befuddled at the line. Crowds at the Forum took to cheering wildly when he made one. Dolph Schayes and previous coaches had become obsessed with improving Chamberlain's free throws, thinking that practice would make perfect. Chamberlain did, in fact, become a good practice shooter only to resume his impotence during games.

"I never could figure out how to help him with free throws," Sharman said.

At first, Lakers weren't quite sure what to make of Sharman. They found him to be a strange mix of fight and quiet innovation. He was a Southern California boy, but he was also a Celtic. "It was difficult for us to relate to him in the beginning, because he was covered with Boston green," recalled Pat Riley, a Laker sub at the time. "But in time we came around. He was a low-key guy, but very competitive, very feisty."

It didn't help that Sharman gave them another dose of green when he added K.C. Jones, his Boston teammate, as the first assistant coach in Laker history. "We've never had an assistant coach before," Cooke grumbled, "except, of course, Chick Hearn." The two former Celtic guards had seen Red Auerbach's running game work wonders with Bill Russell snatching rebounds and firing outlet passes on the fastbreak. They understandably wanted to perpetuate Red's revolution in Los Angeles.

Sharman's announcement that he planned to make the Lakers a running team brought a lot of laughs around the league. Use Chamberlain, the NBA's resident dinosaur, in a running game? Absolutely loony. Chamberlain was the premier post-up weapon.

Sharman knew he would have to sell the key players on the idea.

First he invited Chamberlain to a pricey LA restaurant for lunch. Once there, they discussed the need for Wilt, the greatest scorer in the history of the game, to focus on defense and rebounding. The big center had heard this line from other coaches. But Sharman was different. He listened to Chamberlain's opinions on the issue. Sharman had played the running game and he knew exactly what it took. Chamberlain had his doubts but said he would cooperate fully.

"When they got up to go, Sharman had forgotten his billfold," Schaus recalled. "Wilt had to pay for the meal."

Chamberlain grinned and reached for his cash. He was used to it by now. Wherever he played, the tabs were left to him. Some observers believed he wouldn't have it any other way.

Next, Sharman asked Happy Hairston to shelve his funky offensive game to concentrate on rebounding. Dominating the defensive boards was a two-man job. Every great center needs a tough power forward to help out. Hairston's sacrifice would be a key to winning the title, Sharman said. A muscular 6-foot-7, 225-pounder, Hairston agreed. (It helped that Cooke had just awarded him with a new contract. "Management has been very generous to me," Hairston explained.) The new emphasis would cause his scoring to dip from

18.6 in 1971 to 13.1 in '72. But he would average 15 boards over the last half of the season and become the first forward to pull down 1,000 rebounds while playing alongside Chamberlain.

With Hairston and Wilt controlling the defensive boards, the Lakers had West and Gail Goodrich to run the fast break. But Goodrich, who had started his career in LA, then gone to Phoenix, liked to control the ball. Now that he had returned to the Lakers, Sharman wanted him to give up the ball and use his great ability to move without it, working to get open for a pass from West. "Gail always had the ball in Phoenix," Bertka recalled. "People said we were going to need two balls with West and Goodrich in the backcourt, but Gail began taking great pride in playing without it."

He and West would both average 25 points per game over the season as they hauled in pass after pass from Chamberlain. West, who was working his way back from knee surgery, would run the break from the center with Goodrich finishing from the wing. "Jerry was a great player and I think we complemented each other," Goodrich said. "We blended and didn't hurt each other's games."

The last remaining problem was the other forward, where Baylor was a painful question mark. The team's captain, he had been the Lakers' dominant figure for most of 13-year career. But he had missed all but two games of the previous season with injury. In the offseason, he had worked hard to come back and was now able to play again, only Sharman's new running system required a very active small forward. Baylor just didn't have the mobility. At first, Sharman wasn't sure exactly how to handle it. So he waited. The answer would come soon enough.

Bill Bertka was ill the first time he scouted Jim McMillian at a college holiday tournament. Maybe it was because he had the flu, or because he had ridden cross country with Red Auerbach and they ate candy bars the whole way. Whatever, Bertka was so sick he couldn't sit up. So he climbed to the nosebleed section, lay on his side and watched McMillian, a senior at Columbia. Ill as he was, he still liked what he saw. Columbia was playing Villanova with Howard Porter. "I was surprised by McMillian's ability to play Porter in the post," Bertka said. "The thing I saw about him was how smart he was."

With Bertka's recommendation, the Lakers made McMillian the thirteenth pick of the first round of the 1970 draft. Soon afterward, Fred Schaus endured a tongue lashing from Cooke. Knicks owner Ned Irish had phoned Cooke and told him, "I can't believe you guys drafted Jim McMillian. Why he's an overweight small forward."

Schaus, one of Cooke's favorite shouting targets, was worried. "I can't believe we drafted this guy," he told Bertka.

"Look, you have to wait and find out," the scout said. "He's got character. He's gonna play in this league."

McMillian did have a tendency to gain weight. Baylor thought he looked like a chubby Floyd Patterson and dubbed him "Floyd Butterball," or "Butter" for short. But he slimmed down on a grapefruit diet and steadily improved over his rookie season. "He came to epitomize what you wanted in a small forward," Bertka said. "He could run the floor. He could post up. He could pass the ball. He had a nice medium-range jumper. He had a quick release on his shot. And he was smart."

By the opening of the 1971-92 season, McMillian was pushing Baylor for the starting role at small forward. The Lakers broke out to a 6-3 record that first month. "But Bill wasn't happy with the results," Bertka said.

"Elgin started every game," Sharman said. "But Jim McMillian was coming on strong."

He hustled and ran the floor just like Sharman wanted, which put him in position to run the break with West and Goodrich. After those first nine games, Sharman decided McMillian should start. The coach knew he had to approach Baylor carefully about a reserve role. Before practice one morning at

Loyola University, Sharman informed his captain that McMillian would start. "He just wasn't the Elgin Baylor of old," Sharman said. "I knew he felt bad, and I wanted him to keep playing. But he said if he couldn't play up to his standards he would retire."

Baylor announced his retirement the next day, and their 33-game win streak began that night. The 1971-72 Lakers would win more games than any team in NBA history with a 69-13 record. "One of the happiest times of my life was when the Lakers were on that 33-game winning streak," Cooke said, "a record I dare say will never be broken in the history of professional sports. It's as good as my Washington Redskins winning three Super Bowls. Each time they'd play, we'd wait for the win with bated breath."

"All the pieces just fit," Sharman said.

Especially the big one, the Big Dipper.

With Baylor's retirement, Sharman had asked West and Chamberlain to become team captains. West declined, but Wilt relished the leadership role. In the past, he had infuriated Laker coaches, sometimes snacking on hot dogs or fried chicken on the bench before a game. But now he was all business. He had 25 rebounds, six assists and a dozen points in the first victory of the streak, at home over Baltimore. Next came Oakland and a 19-rebound effort, followed by 22 rebounds and seven assists against New York in the Forum. In Chicago two nights later it was 20 rebounds and eight assists. Most of the assists came from his pulling defensive rebounds and hitting the streaking Goodrich, West and McMillian for fastbreak buckets. Yet even those statistics said little about the blocks and changed shots he forced on defense. Instead of smacking the ball out of bounds as he had in years past, he began brush-blocking shots and starting a fastbreak the other way.

Their twenty-fifth straight came in Wilt's hometown of Philadelphia, where he celebrated with 32 points, 34 rebounds and 12 blocks.

"Sharman has Wilt playing like Russell," Joe Mullaney said after watching the Lakers on television.

"Baylor should be the MVP in the league this season," Baylor told one writer, a sentiment echoed by Philadelphia's Billy Cunningham.

Many observers rushed to credit Sharman for the "new" Wilt. "I don't think I should get the credit," the coach quickly pointed out. "He's always had a bad rap. Whatever they ask of him, he's done. He's just doing more things better now that he is not mainly a scorer. He must block a zillion shots a game. And he scares guys out of other shots or makes them take bad shots."

The secret to the entire running game, Sharman added, "has been Wilt's rebounding and fast passes."

"I really like the man," Wilt said. "I've never had a coach as conscientious as Bill."

Still, Chamberlain, always a stat freak, admitted feeling a twinge every time he looked at his drooping scoring average, down to 14.8 for the season. "I'm happy about it," he said of the streak, "but here I am the greatest scorer in the game of basketball and I've been asked by many coaches not to score. Now where else in a sport can you ask a guy to stop something he's the best in the world doing? It's like telling Babe Ruth not to hit home runs, just bunt."

Each win brought more notoriety for Sharman's shootaround. Soon just about every coach in the league had instituted a game-day practice. Which was bad news for Wilt. A night person and late sleeper, he had reluctantly agreed in his preseason meeting with Sharman to give the shootaround a try. "I'm still not for those 11 o'clock practices," he said as the streak rolled on. "I don't think they've done anything personally for Wilt Chamberlain except to make him lose some sleep. But we're winning and I'm not going to do anything to knock the winning way."

"After we started out 6 and 3, Wilt started to vacillate on the shootaround," Sharman said. "But after we won 33 straight, it was hard for him to say anything. Wilt only missed two morning practices all season, and he called ahead both times."

The streak ran through January 9, 1972, when they lost a road game to rival Milwaukee and Kareem, 120-114. Bucks coach Larry Costello had scouted the Lakers thirty-third consecutive win, a road victory over Atlanta, and quickly devised a defense to cut off their fast break.

"We knew it had to end sometime," Sharman said.

Through each game, he'd been a fiend on the bench, shouting incessantly. "I was always a yeller," he said. "When I got back from Milwaukee my throat was sore that whole week. It got to where I couldn't even be heard. I went to the doctor and he told me I really had a bad case, not to even talk for a week or 10 days. I couldn't do that. We were in the middle of a season, a championship season.

Gail Goodrich got ABC to remove some extra lights — but it didn't help in the 92-73 loss.

"So I tried using one of those battery-operated megaphones. But in a game I couldn't use it. So I just kept hollering. The doctors said I shouldn't do it. But I thought after the season it would come back. But the damage had been done. My voice never came back."

The voice damage suffered during the streak was permanent and would eventually force Sharman from coaching.

They went 30-10 over the last half of the season. Each win brought them a little closer to that unreachable goal. But as the playoffs neared, the team sensed that old Laker luck hovering somewhere nearby. "We were waiting for something to happen, something bad to happen again," Riley said. "But it didn't."

By the end of the season, McMillian was averaging 18.8 points and 6.5 rebounds and had become a Forum favorite, with the crowd erupting over his long jumpers from the corner. "I really can't tell you how I fit into this team," he told reporters. "I'm just the fat little dude wearing No. 5."

Chicago, their first-round opponent, had won 57 games, but the Bulls had no center and were forced to play a control game. They fell in four. The Lakers' big challenge came in the Western finals, against the Bucks and Kareem. In Game 1 at the Forum, the Milwaukee defense overplayed and double-teamed the Lakers, forcing them out of their favorite shooting spots and into a 27-percent performance from the floor. Los Angeles scored a mere eight points in the pivotal third period, and the Bucks took away the home-court advantage, 92-73.

In practice before the start of the series, Goodrich had complained about the ABC television lights that had been added for broadcasts. Cooke asked the network to remove some of the lights, which it did. Cooke wanted even more removed, and ABC again complied. After Game 1, the Los Angeles owner wanted even more adjustments.

It wasn't the lights, Sharman finally said. "It was that our good shooters were all way off."

The Lakers did manage a win in the second game, 135-134, but they were obviously shaky. West had shot 10 for 30 from the field. "I know what I'm doing wrong," he said afterward. "I'm turning my hand too much. But I can't get it stopped. It's got to go away by itself."

Somehow they overcame 61-percent shooting from the Bucks in Game 3 in Milwaukee. The Lakers drove frequently, drawing fouls and shooting free throws. On defense, Wilt overplayed Kareem to stop his sky hook, forcing him instead into short jumpers and layups. At one point, Chamberlain blocked five shots. In the critical fourth period, Wilt held Kareem scoreless for the last 11 minutes. Abdul-Jabbar still finished with 33, but Chamberlain had done the job. The Lakers won, 108-105, and regained the homecourt advantage. Goodrich had scored 30 and McMillian 27 to lead Los Angeles.

The Bucks lashed back in the fourth game, taking a 75-43 rebounding advantage and tying the series at two-all with a 114-88 blowout. Abdul-Jabbar celebrated his 25th birthday with 31 points. West, on the other hand, was only 9 of 23 from the field, and afterward he complained that Cooke was requiring him to play too many minutes.

The Lakers headed back to the Forum where they ran away with the fifth game, 115-90, despite West's continued slump. They returned to Milwaukee for the sixth game, and in practice West kicked at a press table after missing an open jumper. In the past, he told the writers, nobody seemed to notice when he had great scoring games because the Lakers always lost in the Finals. Now that they were winning, he said, all that people seemed to be interested in was his slump. As usual, Sharman said, people had failed to notice that West could virtually rule the floor with his defense alone.

It helped some that they vanquished the Bucks in Milwaukee, 104-100, to take the series, 4-2. Their opponent in the 1972 Finals would be the New York Knicks, who had beaten a resurgent Boston club in the Eastern finals, 4-1.

The Knicks, however, were not the team of old. They had lost Nate Bowman, Donnie May, Bill Hoskett and John Warren in the 1970-71 expansion draft. Cazzie Russell had been traded away after the '71 season to get Jerry Lucas from the Warriors. And Mike Riordan and Dave Stallworth were shipped to Baltimore in exchange for Earl Monroe.

Reed was out of action with his nagging knee injuries, and Dick Barnett was also out. Lucas, who had starred with John Havlicek and Larry Siegfried at Ohio State, filled in for Reed at center. Dean Meminger and Phil Jackson were the chief subs. Monroe was still troubled by his knees but able to work as a third guard.

But it was the absence of Reed that changed the entire nature of the team. "We operate on such a small margin of error," Bill Bradley told the writers. "We don't have Willis there to take care of our mistakes."

With his smooth outside shooting, Lucas did quite a bit to help them forget that in Game 1 in the Forum. He scored 26 points but was only one of several Knicks who were red hot.

Bradley hit 11 of 12 shots from the field as New York shot 53 percent as a team for the game. They used a nearly perfect first half to jump to a good lead and won much too easily, 114-92. Early in the second half, the Forum crowd began filing out dejectedly. It looked like another Los Angeles fold in the Finals.

Just like that, the Lakers had lost their homecourt advantage again. Then, in Game 2, they got another piece of luck. DeBusschere hurt his side and didn't play after the first half. With no one to hold him down, Happy Hairston scored 12 points in the second half, and Los Angeles evened the series with a 106-92 win.

Luck had always been such a big factor for the Lakers. Each of the previous Finals, they were overcome with a sense that fortune had turned against them. But that all changed after Game 2 in 1972. That night West lay awake wondering how he would act if they actually had a championship to celebrate. He wasn't a drinker or a whoop-it-up type. How would he act?

At the Garden for Game 3, DeBusschere attempted to play in the first half and missed all six of his field-goal attempts. He was hurting and elected not to play in the second. "I didn't feel I was helping the team," he explained later. The Lakers danced out to a 22-point lead and regained the homecourt advantage with a 107-96 win. The Lakers' luck seemed stronger than ever, although they felt a tremor in the first quarter of Game 4, when Chamberlain fell and sprained his wrist. Obviously in pain, he decided to stay in. It was a crucial decision. The game went to overtime, but at the end of regulation the Los Angeles center picked up in his fifth foul. In 13 NBA seasons, he had never fouled out of a game, a statistic of which he was immensely proud. Immediately speculation started along press row that he would play soft in the overtime. Instead, he came out in a shot-blocking fury that propelled the Lakers to a 116-111 win. At 3-1, their lead now seemed insurmountable.

"The patient is critical and about to die," Frazier said afterward.

There did seem to be some hope, however, when the early word on Chamberlain was that he would be unable to play Game 5 at the Forum. But as game time neared, Chamberlain received a shot of an anti-inflammatory drug and took the floor.

Almost single-handedly he was the Knicks' demise. He scored 24 points and pulled down 29 rebounds as Los Angeles finally broke the jinx, 114-100. The effort earned Chamberlain his second Finals MVP award. Afterward, the Lakers sipped champagne from wine glasses. There was no shaking and spewing. No riotous behavior. And certainly no rain of balloons from the Forum rafters.

West even found it in himself to offer a toast or two. He toasted Sharman and then Chamberlain. "As for Wilt," he said, "he was simply the guy who got us here."

For West, the finish was rife with irony. After years of losing, his emotions were nearly empty, and when the Lakers got it, the championship seemed anti-climatic. "I played terrible basketball in the Finals," he said in 1990. "And we won. And that didn't seem to be justice for me personally, because I had contributed so much in other years when we lost. And now, when we won, I was just another piece of the machinery. It was particularly frustrating because I was playing so poorly that the team overcame me.

"Maybe," he said after a moment's thought, "that's what the team is all about."

1973

The 1973 Finals had a feeling of familiarity. The Knicks met the Lakers there for the third time in four years.

The Boston Celtics had run off the league's best regular-season record, an incredible 68-14. But New York dumped 'em in a seven-game Eastern finals series. The Knicks particularly enjoyed taking the seventh game in Boston Garden, where Walt Frazier scored 25 to push his team to a 93-78 win.

"It will be nice to see Jerry," Frazier said afterward, referring to West and his Lakers.

Walt Frazier (top) called Game 1 his worst playoff game, as Goodrich and the Lakers won, 115-112.

"Between us it will be a battle of pride."

Not to mention age.

Chamberlain was 36. West was turning 35 and was philosophical about it. "There's no question that are a lot of things I can't do that I once could, particularly on offense," he said. He was no longer among the scoring and assist leaders in the league. Neither was Chamberlain. Although he led the league in rebounding and shot an incredible .727 from the floor, critics complained that Chamberlain seemed increasingly lethargic.

Goodrich still led the team from the backcourt, and Keith Erickson and Jim McMillian still worked from the corners. But Happy Hairston spent much of the season injured, and to bolster the frontcourt the team picked up veteran forward Bill Bridges.

This group won the Pacific Division with a 60-22 record and prospered in the playoffs, defeating Chicago in a seven-game series then brushing aside the surprise Golden State Warriors, who had upset Milwaukee.

The Knicks were also a team aware of its age. Barnett was 36 and no longer a starter. DeBusschere was 32, Reed near 31 and Bradley 30. Jerry Lucas was 33, but coach Red Holzman had traded for him because of his hunger. Lucas had played on a national championship team at Ohio State, but his pro career hadn't allowed him to play for a contender until he came to the Knicks.

The same was true for Earl "The Pearl" Monroe, who had come to the Knicks the previous season. Both Monroe and Lucas made much of their desire to play on an NBA championship team, and Holzman liked that. The team needed it.

Reed had returned from knee surgery, but the going was slow. So he and Lucas split time at center, averaging 20 points between them, which Holzman figured was good production from the post. "I had to accept it," Reed said of splitting time with Lucas. "Red said, 'Some nights you'll start. Some you won't.' I was struggling back from my injury. And we were good for the team. We were different kinds of players. We presented different problems for different teams."

Reed liked to take a good 10- to 15-foot shot from the perimeter, but Lucas was a smooth shooter who liked to blast from 20 or farther. "He shot it with that high arc," Reed said of Lucas. "It took forever for them to get to the basket. But he didn't miss many."

The starting guards were Frazier and Monroe. The previous season, Monroe had worked as the third guard, which surprised the people who thought he wouldn't adjust after being a star. "They said he'd never work, and he came in and took the back seat," Reed said. "It was Walt's team, and Earl didn't try to change that."

By 1972-73, the Knicks needed Monroe to start, and he was ready with his array of playground moves and fakes and his unorthodox shots. He had incredible balance and some nights seemed capable of magic.

When they needed backcourt defense, they brought Dean Meminger off the bench. And when they needed quickness, they went for Henry Bibby, the former mighty mite from UCLA. Phil Jackson was still the main sub at forward, where Bradley and DeBusschere were the starters.

This group won 57 games and finished 11 back of Boston. But they got better as the season went along and closed strong. Where the '70 Knicks traveled on emotion, the '73 edition moved along on execution.

"The '73 team was a better playoff team," Reed said. "It was a good team to watch in terms of the style of basketball. Good shooting. Good passing. Good technique."

They were so efficient that 20 years later Walt Frazier said he couldn't recall much about him. While the emotional '70 team was etched in his memory, Frazier said he recalled the '73 Knicks won the title, but that was about it.

Their playoff triumph over the Celtics had been emotional, though. They had arrived in Boston and were ushered into a smaller dressing room than usual, where no whirlpool was available. For Frazier, the immediate goal respect. The Celtics don't respect us, he told his teammates.

They used that theme to upset the Celtics in the seventh game in Boston on Sunday April 29. Then they had to scramble to Los Angeles for a Tuesday night meeting with the Lakers. The Knicks phoned to ask if the Lakers would consider delaying the start of the championship series until Wednesday.

No way, the Lakers said.

The Knicks arrived tired and promptly met a rested monster. Chamberlain blocked seven shots and intimidated five others. Met Counts, the Lakers' other seven-footer, had nine rebounds. Los Angeles owned the interior, while the Knicks shot from the perimeter and rebounded poorly. The Lakers jumped out to a 20-point lead with 26 fastbreak points.

The Knicks did make a good run in the second half. West, who had 24 points, fouled out with three minutes to go. And Bradley found a seam where he was able to sneak along the baseline for open shots. New York cut it to 115-112, but Erickson got a defensive rebound at the end and whipped the ball out to Bridges to preserve the win.

"My worst playoff game that I can remember," Frazier said afterward.

But the momentum abruptly shifted to Knicks once they got a little rest. "After that, we took names on them and won the next four games in a row," Reed said.

In Game 2, New York slowed the Lakers' fastbreak with a get-back effort on defense. The Knicks took a 10-point lead into the fourth quarter, but Los Angeles charged in the final minutes. Only when McMillian missed a pair of free throws with 24 seconds to go was the victory assured. The Knicks evened it at 99-95. The Lakers had 19

turnovers and missed 13 free throws. Chamberlain himself missed eight of nine attempts and drew quick fouls just about every time he looked to score, as Reed and Lucas alternated doing the hatchet work. New York's big lift came from Jackson off the bench. He finished with 17 points and seven rebounds.

Jerry Lucas hadn't played for a contender until he joined the Knicks.

Game 3 in New York appeared to be a debacle for the Knicks as both Bradley and DeBusschere struggled for a combined 8 of 27 from the floor. Chamberlain took only three shots, and West suffered from two strained hamstrings. Still, the Lakers managed to come back. The Knicks survived on Reed's jumpers and nine fourth-quarter points from Monroe, who finished with 21. New York won, 87-83, to move the lead to 2-1.

West, Chamberlain and McMillian all struggled against the Knicks' defense. Chamberlain, in fact, would make only 22 field goals in the series and miss 24 of 38 free throws. "I don't feel either team has done badly on offense," West told the writers. "They've done just about as well as the defenses will let them."

DeBusschere opened Game 3 with an offensive outburst, hitting 11 of 15 from the floor in the first half. Still it was tight down to the end. At 0:48 with the Knicks up by two, Bradley missed. Chamberlain and Reed went for the rebound and deflected it. DeBusschere picked it up and laid it in as Wilt fouled him. The free throw gave New York a 3-1 lead in games, 103-98.

Game 5 in the Forum was another tight one, but the Knicks got the lead down the stretch. Then DeBusschere went out in the fourth period with a sprained ankle, and things seemed in doubt until Monroe scored eight points over the last two minutes to ice it, 102-93.

The Knicks had their second championship, but Lucas and Monroe did most of the celebrating in the locker room. The Lakers were again losers, and Chamberlain again practiced diplomacy.

"The Knicks are so well-balanced," he told the writers, "and have tremendous passing and so many good shooters that you can't concentrate on one man. The key to the series was that their defense stopped our running game."

10.
Rebirth and Revolution
Boston's Redheaded Revival, and the Golden State Surprise

After a couple of lean seasons, the Boston Celtics pushed their way back to the top of the NBA power structure in the 1970s. For opponents around the league, it wasn't a welcome sight. There was Auerbach again with that annoying cigar.

Red had rebuilt his Celtics much the same way he had constructed the team's original dynasty — employing the unorthodox. And he found most of what he wanted right in the college draft. When he couldn't get it there, Auerbach fell back on the old standby — he outfoxed his opponents in a trade.

The Celtics drafted defensive standout Donald "Duck" Chaney out of the University of Houston in 1968. The next year they got JoJo White from the University of Kansas. They would require a little seasoning, but before long the pair would make a splendid backcourt.

Red's real coup, though, was at center.

As the story goes, Auerbach saw Dave Cowens play only one college game. The more the Celtics' general manager watched the Florida State center, the more he liked him. Cowens played so well that Auerbach began hoping he would mess up. There were other pro scouts at the game, and Auerbach didn't want them to get too excited about what they saw. Finally, after about five minutes,

Auerbach got up and left the game with a disgusted look on his face. He was hoping the other scouts would think Cowens didn't have it.

As it turned out, Auerbach didn't have to conceal his delight. The Celtics picked fourth in the 1970 draft. Detroit took Bob Lanier of St. Bonaventure with the first pick. The San Diego Rockets selected Rudy Tomjanovich second, and the Atlanta Hawks went with Pete Maravich third.

Auerbach got Cowens, but the Celtics' GM still wasn't sure what to do with him. He feared that at 6'8" Cowens might be too short to be an NBA center. But in training camp later that summer, Cowens resisted being moved to forward. He wanted to stay in the post.

Auerbach struggled with the problem, then decided to phone Bill Russell for a bit of advice.

Let him play where he wants, Russell told Auerbach. "No one's going to intimidate that kid."

It didn't take Auerbach long to see what Russell was talking about. Playing against Wilt Chamberlain, Cowens scored 33 points and had 22 rebounds in his first pro exhibition game.

That and his performance in several summer — league games convinced the Celtic brass that he could be a center. Given the chance, Cowens played the position the way no one ever had before. He was too small to try to ban around in the low post with his larger opponents. So he used his other asset. He was a fine leaper and he had great speed and long arms. More importantly, he showed the aggressiveness a linebacker.

"I don't worry about injuries," he said cockily. "I'm the one going a little bit nutty out there. I don't get hit because I'm the one doing the hitting.

His speed and agility allowed him play corner-to-corner. It also meant that the Celtics had the best switching defense in the league, because Cowens could switch to a smaller man and not lose a step.

"He adds a different dimension to Boston's game," said Chicago guard Norm Van Lier not long after Cowens came into the league. "He has a great defensive range on a horizontal rather than a vertical plane. He'll meet me at the top of the key, spread those long arms and make it almost impossible to pass off."

Over time, Cowens proved he could neutralize the giants of his era — Abdul-Jabbar, Chamberlain, Lanier, and Thurmond — with his quickness. "He's so quick he's like a 6'9" Jerry West," said Jerry Lucas of the Knicks. "One minute he's standing in front of you and the next he's gone, rolling in toward the basket or straight up in the air shooting his jumper. It's like he disappears."

"He's the toughest I've ever played against," Thurmond allowed.

Off the court, Cowens was a man of the times. He displayed a heavy streak of zaniness. He invested in a catfish farm in British Honduras, and during his second season in Boston he became so involved in an auto mechanics course that Auerbach asked him to drop it. He was given to wearing beat-up corduroy trousers and plaid shirts, and his musical tastes ran from blue-grass to Beethoven. Even for a red-head, he was high-strung. By game time each night he was a ball of nervous energy, ready to explode with the opening jump. He would dash here and

there with reckless abandon, diving for loose balls, giving hard fouls, shooting his nifty left-handed hook, and rebounding like a demon.

He celebrated good plays by butting heads with his teammates. "Dave's got one hard head," confided Don Nelson to the press. That was true in more ways than one.

As a young pro, Cowens was hesitant to shoot from outside, until his teammates finally convinced him that the team needed it. With a little work, he added a shot with some decent range to it, although he never did develop his right-handed shooting touch. Still his game was enough to take the Celtics where they needed to go.

Tommy Heinsohn, the erstwhile gunner, had followed Russell as the Celtics' coach. Heinsohn's goal was to make them a running team again, and his young center was perfect for it.

Tommy Heinsohn took over from Bill Russell as the head coach.

Cowens figured he was faster in the 100-yard dash than any player in the league.

Eventually, the Boston newcomers would mix well with the holdovers from the Russell years — John Havlicek, Nelson, and Satch Sanders. But it wasn't automatic. Heinsohn's major developmental work involved the guards. White was a gazelle, but it took him a while to become accustomed to Heinsohn's running game. Thinking of the future, Heinsohn decided to bench starting guards Em Bryant and Larry Siegfried during the 1969-70 season and replace them with second-year man Chaney and rookie White. It wasn't a popular move in Boston at the time, but the younger guards had the speed and skills to run, and Heinsohn knew he had to get them the necessary experience. The move would become even less popular when Heinsohn gave up Siegfried, Havlicek's good friend and teammate from Ohio State, in the expansion draft that spring. But the Celtics had just been through a 34-48 season, and the coach knew something drastic was called for.

Yet even with playing time White presented a particular problem for Heinsohn. He had immense talent and the confidence to go with it, but he had played in a controlled, walk-it-up offense at Kansas and had little experience with the running game. Particularly the version Heinsohn wanted to use, which was based on the philosophy of overloading players to one side. It required complicated decision-making running the break.

Because he was so talented and proud, White at first rejected Heinsohn's attempts to teach him the intricacies of playing the point in the Celtics' running game. Heinsohn backed off and tried another direction.

Instead of overwhelming White with dramatic change, Heinsohn worked in the new approach a bit at a time. Eventually, player and coach came to an understanding, and when they did, the team moved to a new level.

The 6'5" Chaney was the other backcourt ingredient, a superb defender. He had been a high-school All-American at McKinley High in Baton Rouge, Louisiana, before going to Houston to play for Guy Lewis. There he performed in the shadow of Elvin Hayes but was a critical element in the Cougars' pressing defense. "Chaney had long arms and great anticipation for a pass," said Lewis. "We didn't keep steals in those days, and there's no telling how many he had. But it would have been some kind of record."

He started at guard during his junior and senior years and averaged double-figure scoring both seasons, although most of his points came on layups, off steals, and turnovers. He didn't have an outside shot, but he had all the mental skills to be a great defensive guard. "Chaney was a super leader, a quiet leader but a super one all the same," Lewis said. "He knew the game of basketball in and out."

At first, that didn't appear to be enough to allow him to make it in the NBA. He played little his first season and shot a woeful .319 from the floor. But Heinsohn made Chaney one of his pet projects, and the two spent hours working on Chaney's shot. After a time, Chaney became a decent shooter, adding yet another block to Boston's rebuilding job.

Don Chaney moved into the starting lineup in the 1970s.

This new edition of the Celtics wasn't pretty, but it was a winner. They nailed down 44 games in 1971 and 56 in 1972, clear indications of their progress. Still, the team's veterans, particularly Havlicek, were frustrated by the imprecision of this younger group. Havlicek was used to the crisp ballhandling and overall dominance of the Celtics teams of Cousy and K.C. Jones and Russell, and with each transitional season his patience wore a bit thinner.

Fortunately, the final ingredient in their chemistry arrived before the 1972-73 season. Auerbach knew he needed a power forward, someone to help Cowens with the rebounding. The Boston boss finally was able to obtain Paul Silas from Phoenix for the NBA rights to Charlie Scott, who was playing in the ABA and about to jump to the senior league.

An eight-year pro, Silas had always been on the chunky side. But the season before coming to the Celtics he had trimmed to a svelte 6'7" 230 pounder an was ready to join Heinsohn's version of the Boston marathon. He came in and played like a charm, albeit a bullish one that first season. Silas pulled down 1,039 rebounds (13 per game), while Cowens got 1,329, making Boston the leading rebounding team in the league.

All that defensive rebounding, of course, was just what the doctor ordered for Heinsohn's running game. The Celtics ran off to a 68-14 record, the best in the club's distinguished history. They were a terror to face. But then an unprecedented thing happened in Boston. The two best teams in basketball, the Celtics and the Knicks, met in the Eastern Conference finals, and in the decisive seventh game, in Boston Garden no less, the Celtics stumbled. They lost, and watched New York go on to trample Los Angeles for the world championship.

It was a bitter ending to a bright beginning.

As Boston fans hoped, the Celtics returned with a vengeance to open the 1973-74 season, racing out to a 30-7 start. From there, though, they grew strangely complacent and barely played .500 ball over the remainder of the schedule.

Fortunately, they had the luck of the Irish with them. The Eastern Conference was a bit weak with the champion Knicks suddenly aging and injured. Boston finished 56-26, good enough for the best record in the conference, but short of Milwaukee's 59-33 mark in the West. The Buffalo Braves with Bob McAdoo created problems for the Celtics in the first round of the playoffs, but Havlicek played well enough to help them advance, 4-2. The Knicks, with Reed and DeBusschere injured, fell easily, 4-1, and Boston advanced to the Finals for the first time ever without Bill Russell.

Milwaukee had held serve in the West, dropping Los Angeles 4-1 and Chicago 4-0. The outcomes provided something of a prize for pure basketball fans because the two best teams in the pro game were meeting in the championship round. Their matchup was an invigorating clash of styles. With Kareem Abdul-Jabbar and his famed sky hook, the Bucks were the consummate half-court team and nearly unstoppable when the big center got the ball in the low post. For this to happen, Bucks coach Larry Costello and his assistant, Hubie Brown, had devised myriad schemes, all encased in a massive playbook which detailed options upon options.

The Celtics, on the other hand, were a small, quick, pressing and running team that approached things simplistically. Their starting front line measured 6'7", 6'8", and 6'5". Heinsohn knew if his troops were going to win, the press would have to do it for them. They'd

have to take the ball away before the Bucks ever got it upcourt to the big guy.

This, of course, highlighted the crucial glitch for the Bucks. Lucius Allen the guard who shared the ballhandling chores with Oscar Robertson, had torn up his knee slipping on a warmup jersey at the close of the season and was lost for the playoffs. Robertson was thirty-five and in the last season of his career. He faced the vaunted Boston press virtually alone. The Bucks still had Bobby Dandridge at forward and Jon McGlocklin at off guard, but their test would be to get the ball up the floor against Chaney.

Basketball purists also relished the idea of the small, quick Cowens meeting the giant, athletic Abdul-jabbar in the Finals. Under the Celtics' scheme, they would leave their center to fend for himself man-to-man. Fear, it seemed, was a good motivator for the redhead. As a rookie, Cowens once had watched helplessly as Kareem had scored 53 against him. He knew it could happen anytime. "No one wants to look used and foolish out on the court," said Cowens. "Our style doesn't give me much help because the other guys are off pressing, so I have to try and stop him by myself and remember that if he has a big game I won't be the first guy it's happened to. But I have a couple of things going for me. When the guys are off pressing, they're really helping me. The better they press, the less often Kareem's going to get the ball. And on offense I can score from the outside, which puts him at a disadvantage."

That, in short, became the blueprint for the series. It quickly developed into one of the more engrossing championship rounds in league history, one in which the home-court advantage meant almost nothing.

The Celtics wasted little time in playing their hand. In the first quarter of Game One in Milwaukee, they harassed Robertson and Allen's replacement, Ron "Fritz" Williams, into frequent turnovers and ran off to a 35-19 lead. The Bucks never solved their ballhandling problems and watched the Celtics dance off to a 98-83 shocker. Kareem had scored 35, but the offense remained in disarray.

"If we could just get the damn ball out of the backcourt, our problems would be solved," Costello lamented.

The Bucks coach shifted strategy a bit for Game 2, pushing all the help upcourt and leaving Robertson to face Chaney alone. The new plan meant that Milwaukee conceded 22 turnovers, but it worked. Kareem scored 36 points, but more importantly, the big center was able to set up and run the Bucks' offense in the halfcourt. He set picks, and he passed, which was a factor in Dandridge scoring 24. On the defensive end, Kareem forced Cowens into shooting 3 of 13 from the floor. With the game tied and down to one final shot, and Cowens open for a running hook in the lane, Abdul-Jabbar swooped down and blocked it. In overtime, the Bucks took it, 105-96, to even the series at 1-1 as it headed to Boston.

Cowens responded in Game 3 with a determination to concentrate on his outside shot. Despite foul trouble that reduced him to 32 minutes of playing time, he scored 30 points. The Celtics press also turned up the heat, forcing 11 first-quarter turnovers and helping Boston to a 21-point lead. With Cowens in foul trouble, Henry Finkel, Boston's seldom-used seven-footer, did an admirable job of spot defense on Kareem, who finished with 26.

At game's end, the Bucks had turned the ball over 27 times, enough for a 95-83 Boston win.

Costello knew his team was in real trouble. McGlocklin had sprained an ankle early on and was unable to help. The Boston full-court press had destroyed Williams' confidence. The Bucks needed somebody to step forward at

> **B**asketball purists relished the idea of the small, quick Cowens meeting the giant athletic Abdul-Jabbar in the Finals.

guard. So Costello called on 6'7" Mickey Davis, a substitute forward who had played little guard over his three-year career. Davis, though, was tall enough to present major problems for White. When Davis began scoring in Game 4, Heinsohn was forced to shift the taller Chaney to cover him, thus cutting the heart out of Boston's press. Robertson brought the ball upcourt relatively unmolested. Davis scored 15, and Kareem got the ball in their halfcourt offense, where he shredded the Celtics for 34 points and 6 assists. Milwaukee got the lead and kept it down the stretch for a 97-89 win. That quickly, the teams' fortunes seemed to have reversed themselves. The Bucks headed back to Milwaukee with the homecourt advantage restored and a series now reduced to three games. But, good as it looked at the time, the homecourt advantage proved worthless.

The Bucks had concentrated most of their defensive efforts on stopping thirty-five-year-old John Havlicek, the silent but deadly part of Boston's operation. "When things are swinging easy, we all get in the flow of it," Paul Silas told the press. "And sometimes then it almost looks like we ignore John. But when things don't go well, we look to him all the time to make the tough play. We probably do it too much. Sometimes I'll have an open shot and still pass to him even though he's farther out and two guys are on him. We do this instinctively because he has usually been the guy who's turned bad moments into good ones for us."

Havlicek successfully stepped through and fought past the double teams over the balance of the series. An incredibly conditioned athlete, he was able to keep running on offense and moving and crouching on defense after opponents many years his junior were winded.

It was a natural gift, Havlicek often explained, and he used it to the fullest. He and the Celtics wore down the Bucks with their constant motion in Game 5, regaining the series edge, 3-2, with a 96-77 win that set up a classic Game Six back in Boston.

The situation produced Kareem at his best, although that wasn't exactly what the packed house at the Garden had in mind on May 10. Cowens got into foul trouble early and watched from the bench as Milwaukee took a 12-point lead in the first half. The Celtics were down 6 late in the game, but they came back to force overtime. With a little over a minute left in regulation, Havlicek hit a long jumper to tie it at 86, then Robertson was caught in a 24-second violation as time expired. In the first extra period, Milwaukee led 90-88 when Chaney got a steal and zipped the ball to Havlicek. Kareem was back on defense and forced him to take a pull-up jumper. Havlicek missed but got the long rebound and scored to send the game to a second overtime.

There Havlicek scored 9 of Boston's 11 points. With 7 seconds left, he had the ball on the right baseline, and the Boston bench screamed for a timeout. Instead, Havlicek lofted a rainbow over Kareem's outstretched hand. Good, for a 101-100 lead. It looked like champagne time.

But the Bucks called for a timeout, and for some strange reason they decided that Kareem shouldn't take the shot. Instead, he was to set a pick for McGlocklin, who had been hampered by the sprained ankle. When McGlocklin couldn't get free, Abdul-Jabbar, with the ball, moved to the right of the lane. He looked for the open man, but Boston had all options covered. So he dribbled to the baseline, turned, and put up the skyhook from 17 feet. Swish. 102-101, Milwaukee.

The Celtics put up a failed desperation heave, but that was it. Kareem had made a shot that left him lying awake in bed that night, still tingling with excitement. The series was tied 3-3 and going back to Milwaukee.

The circumstances called for special efforts,

so on the eve of the game, Auerbach called together the entire Boston brain trust, Cousy included. They decided that for this final game, they would abandon their single-man coverage of Kareem and go for the double- and triple-teams.

With less of a defensive load, Cowens turned his thoughts to offense. He had shot a miserable 5 of 16 from the floor in Game 6. He remedied that in the first half of the seventh game, making 8 of 13 as Boston loped out to a lead and coasted down the stretch for a 102-87 win and Boston's twelfth title. Cowens finished with 28 points and 14 rebounds.

Havlicek had scored 16 while continuing to draw the Bucks' defensive attention. Soaked in pink champagne, he grinned broadly in the Celtics locker room afterward and accepted the MVP award. This young team had finally lived up to his standards and Bill Russell's tradition. Back in Boston, they were making room in the Garden rafters for title banner number twelve.

The Eastern Conference came down to one of those good old-fashioned scraps in 1975. Washington and Boston were the combatants, and they drew all the attention. Boston got 60 wins to rule the Atlantic Division, and the Bullets had the same number to win the Central. But the homecourt edge went to the Celtics late in the year, when they won the final meeting between the two teams, 95-94.

That single point could determine the league championship, several writers predicted. At the time, that observation seemed reasonable enough. But there was this little overlooked factor of the Western Conference, where the Golden State Warriors had trudged along to an undistinguished 48 wins and the regular season crown. Their progress wasn't exactly silent. It just seemed that way back east.

"I guess no one took us very seriously," Warriors coach Al Attles would say several weeks later as the playoffs wound to a close.

Even in years to come, Golden State alumni would continue to take umbrage at the snub they received that spring of 1975. "I don't think there's ever been a team so looked-down upon that wound up winning the championship," Rick Barry said with more than a trace of satisfaction during a 1990 interview.

The reasons for the oversight were simple enough. Golden State had undergone several key personnel changes, and adjustments had to be made. At the start of the season, many writers hadn't even picked the Warriors to make the playoffs. The franchise had needed cash, so before the season management had traded veteran center Nate Thurmond to Chicago for center Clifford Ray, a first-round draft pick, and $500,000. The deal wasn't exactly considered a blockbuster for Golden State. Ray was viewed as a journeyman, and he had undergone major knee surgery just two seasons earlier. Thurmond himself was hobbled by age and in the twilight of his career. Besides, success in pro basketball required that a team have a major talent at center. Yet by the end of the season the trade would loom as the seeding of a championship.

"Our key change was getting Clifford Ray for Nate Thurmond," Barry said. "Ray was one of the best defensive centers in the game."

"Clifford gave us that presence," agreed Attles. "He could close off the middle on defense and set screens on offense."

The Warriors also got help in the post from George Johnson, a 6'11" stringbean out of little Dillard College who provided solid backup minutes for Ray at center. "We got two different looks from our two centers," Barry said. "Ray was the physical presence, and Johnson brought us shotblocking." Mainly a finesse player, Johnson knew how to rebound. Together, they gave the Warriors nearly 18 rebounds and 14 points per game.

The 6'9" Ray offered many qualities important to a team — a physical style; an unselfish nature; a solid leadership quotient; and a friendly and unassuming manner. "Clifford was sort of like everyone's big brother," recalled Jamaal Wilkes, then a rookie. "He was very critical in my career in terms of breaking the game down into very simple fundamentals, in terms of keeping me

loose and helping me to keep it all in perspective."

Besides his own play, Ray's influence on Wilkes' development was critical in helping the young player win the Rookie of the Year award. Before the season opened, Golden State watched two forwards — Cazzie Russell and Clyde Lee — head to other clubs. Then another, Derrek Dickey, was hampered by injury. As a result, Wilkes found himself the starting power forward, an unlikely development. A willowy 6'6", 190-pounder, Wilkes had been a controversial first-round selection, eliciting questions and complaints from fans and Bay-area writers. At best, Wilkes was forecast as a backup to Barry at small forward, and the team had other critical needs.

"There were a lot of questions about whether I could survive the rigors of the NBA," Wilkes conceded.

"The biggest surprise of the season was Wilkes," recalled Golden State guard Butch Beard. "I didn't think he'd be able to play a lot of forwards in the league, but he wound up doing a hell of a job."

Al Attles coached the Warriors to 48 regular-season wins.

Because of his smooth shot from the corner, Wilkes would come to be known as "Silk," but that name didn't begin to address his toughness and defensive abilities. He had played for John Wooden at UCLA and was a well-schooled player. Beyond that, Wilkes was mature and unselfish for a twenty-one-year-old rookie. The son of a Baptist minister, he had the presence of mind to focus on the game while paying little attention to the controversy swirling about him.

"He's a very fine but very unspectacular player," Attles said of Wilkes as the season progressed. "He's played under a lot of pressure, and I think he's proved he has great talent. And he has done it playing out of position at power forward."

Wilkes averaged better than 14 points and 8 rebounds over the course of the season. He could have done even better at small forward, but he wasn't the type of player to create dissension. "Playing with Rick isn't all that bad," Wilkes told the writers. "I get a lot of open shots because of him. He's so great one-on-one, they all sag on him, leaving me open. And you learn a lot from Barry just watching him."

Without question, it was Barry's team. His confidence had a quality that didn't endear him to opponents around the league. His every step seemed a swagger. His game was steeped in an air of hauteur. Even on a bad night, he knew he would hit for 20, and on a good night 35 to 40. Yet beneath all these superficial irritants, Barry was a real gamer. "I didn't have any problem with him," Attles said. "He was like most players. They have their own ideas about things. But he came to play."

"I was never the most popular player," conceded Barry, "because I never went out to make friends. I went out to win games."

Barry was always complaining to the refs or talking back to the fans, said Beard. "He complained about every call or claimed he got fouled every time he missed a shot. Rick's demeanor on the court probably turned a lot of people off, but it seemed to be a part of who he was."

Quite often Barry would use the real or imagined slights as motivation for his scoring outbursts, Beard said.

Barry had begun his career with the Warriors in 1964. In a highly publicized move, he had sat out a year to gain control of his contract, then jumped to the ABA, where he led Oakland to the 1969 league title. He finally bounced back to Golden State and the NBA in 1972. By 1974-75, he had a decade of pro basketball under his belt, and most of that time his scoring average had hovered around 30 points per game. The time hadn't made Barry particularly humble, but it had left him wiser. He knew that his scoring alone wasn't

going to win championships. So when Attles preached defense, Barry was willing to listen. "He was the most gifted player on the team," Attles said. "We needed him to play a lot of minutes."

It also helped that Barry was enjoying one of his best seasons in 1974-75. As the focus of the Warriors' offense, he averaged 30.6 points per game. "It all kind of fell together," he said. "I had as good a season as I'd ever had." Many observers thought Barry was the league MVP, although the award went to Bob McAdoo of the Buffalo Braves. Barry didn't expect the award because he knew he wasn't popular with the players around the league.

In retrospect, although Barry's offense was important to the team, the most important element was the Warriors' dedication to defense. That, of course, was due largely to Attles. The team mirrored the coach's personality. The Philadelphia Warriors had made Attles a fifth-round draft pick out of North Carolina A&T in 1960. He was a six-footer with a brickbat of a shot. But he survived in the NBA on his guile and tenacity.

"He was the toughest single fighter I ever saw in the league," his former teammate, Tom Meschery, once said.

For all his spunk, Attles was destined to be under-appreciated and overlooked. One of his biggest games-the night he went 8 for 8 from

Rick Barry had stepped in as a superstar forward, averaging 35.6 points per game.

the floor and hit his only free throw also happened to be the night that Wilt Chamberlain, his teammate, scored 100 points. Attles' performance went unnoticed, a fact he would frequently work into his speeches in later years when he became the Warriors' general manager. Attles liked to tell dinner crowds about the night he and Wilt scored 117 between them.

He was blessed with that special combination

of toughness and modesty necessary for an NBA coach. Yet those properties would have been wasted had he not been a solid technical strategist with a nose for defense. And if Attles wanted anything from his teams, it was defense.

As an added special touch that fall of 1975, he brought into training camp the veteran coach, Bud Pressley, of little Menlo College, to talk about defense.

"He really got us thinking defense, and that was a big reason for our success," Barry said of Pressley.

Pressley was one of the true defensive innovators, Attles said. "He really had us ready to play."

The Warriors used a high-pressure style that would presage the tough college game of the 1980s. "We pressured the ball the full 48 minutes," Attles explained. "It was almost like a platoon system. We played all 12 people. In fact, it was one of the first times in pro sports that the first 10 people all averaged better than 10 minutes a game. We just wore people down."

Attles and assistant coach Joe Roberts deserved credit because they persisted in playing 10 people through the tough spots of the regular season, said Beard. "We had the one constant in Rick, because he was our superstar. The rest of us played well as complimentary players."

With their press, the Warriors found they could come back on opponents. In fact, it became such a pattern that they began joking about it in the locker room at halftime. "We're down a dozen," they would say. "We got 'em where we want 'em." As the season progressed, that became increasingly true.

The veteran factor in the backcourt was Beard. Although Attles disdained the idea of separate roles for guards, the 6'4" Beard did most of the ballhandling/point-guard chores. And Charles Johnson, a six-footer, played more of a scoring role. The Warriors would trade Beard the year after their championship, a development that Attles often has described as a mistake.

"He really was a player who didn't get the credit he deserved," Attles said of Beard. "He was the glue. Butch had been a first-round draft pick out of Louisville. He had bounced around the league with a couple of teams. Of all the guards we had, he was more the classic point guard. He ran the break and took care of the ball."

"Butch was our leader who made sure we ran things in the right fashion," claimed Barry. "He wasn't flashy. He didn't have big numbers. But he played very, very smart basketball. Without Butch Beard, we wouldn't have won the title."

The backcourt reserves were also vital to Attles' approach. Charles Dudley, a free agent, and Phil Smith, a rookie from the University of San Francisco, were the fresh legs off the bench needed to keep the defensive pressure high. "Those four just got after you," Attles said of his guard rotation. "They played like a pack of wild dogs."

Dudley, in particular, was such a wild defensive player that Beard took to calling him "Grasshopper" because of his Kung-Fu style. "He'd irritate the hell out of you," Beard said of Dudley.

Veteran Jeff Mullins was troubled by leg problems and had planned on retiring after the previous season. But Attles said he talked Mullins into coming back to play another year of off guard. But Mullins suffered a collapsed lung before the season opened, which meant the inexperienced Charles Johnson had to start in his place. Eventually, Mullins returned to provide a steadying influence on a team with many rookies and new faces. "He was the old pro who knew the game," Attles explained. "He was good in the locker room, and he could play guard and forward."

Dickey, after coming back from his injury, filled in nicely in the frontcourt, giving the team about 7 points and 7 rebounds off the bench. But then rebounding was a team strength. They led the league in that category, a fact that escaped many observers.

"We don't have that one big rebounder," Attles reminded the writers at one point in the season. "What we have is eight guys getting 8 each. Everybody is involved. Sometimes I think when you have that one big rebounder, everyone else has a tendency to stand around."

Not long after the season opened, Western teams began noticing that Attles had a competitive club. "You could see that Al was putting their team together," said Lakers assistant John Barnhill. "They were going to go out and hustle a team to death. He just seemed to lift them right up and make them go, and that's a tribute to Attles the coach."

Bill Sharman, Barnhill's boss, agreed. "Early in the season, I thought they were playing over their heads," he said during the 1975 playoffs. "But they aren't. They are very quick. They rebound well. They move the ball fast. If they can stay healthy, they have a shot at the title."

What was a strong rotation became even stronger just before the trading deadline, when Warriors General Manager Dick Vertlieb acquired 13year veteran Bill Bridges from the Lakers for the express purpose of playing defense against Chicago's Bob Love in the playoffs. Such foresight would pay dividends.

The Warriors vanquished Seattle in the Western semifinals, 4-2, but had to fight their way through a riotous crowd after the last game to survive. At the time, it was widely reported that an angry Seattle fan hit Barry with a pocketbook, setting off the melee. But Beard claimed she actually threw a beer on Barry as the Warriors were walking to the visitors' locker room. Barry turned to the woman, and her boyfriend intervened, said Beard. "Rick clocked him. Then I clocked the guy next to him because he was getting ready to hit Rick."

Immediately it was a matter of twelve Warriors against thousands, or so it seemed. They fought their way to the locker room only to discover that six of them were still out in the crowd.

Hal Childs, the assistant general manager, told the six players to stay put, and went out to retrieve the other six. When Childs didn't return after a few minutes, the other six went back out after their teammates. Somehow they survived with no major injuries and no lawsuits.

Then they found themselves in another type of scrap, this one on the court, a seven-game battle with the Bulls in the Western finals. There, Bridges filled just the role he'd been acquired for. Even so, the Chicago series became tougher than it should have been. Barry complicated the situation when he became confused over the 24-second clock and blew a critical game early in Chicago. Then the situation was further aggravated when the Warriors lost the fifth game at home and had to go into Chicago Stadium trailing the Bulls, 3-2. There, the Bulls forwards, Love and Chet Walker, were having a field day until Attles sent Bridges into the game to slow them down. He did, and the Warriors won to tie the series at three apiece.

Barry had rebounded by playing well in the sixth game, but he struggled in the seventh game, hitting only one of a dozen shots. Finally, Attles pulled him. Barry sat on the bench praying for his teammates to bail him out, which they did down the stretch. The Golden State defense forced the Bulls into a cold streak with about seven minutes to go, and the Warriors pulled even. Then Barry returned to the game and hit several key shots near the end to send his team on to the championship round.

It was their first trip to the Finals since 1967, when they had lost to Chamberlain and the Sixers. Most observers were hardly impressed, though. Washington seemed far superior. In their last regular-season meeting with Golden State, the Bullets had won in a blowout. They had dominated the Eastern Conference by virtue of their running game and their depth of talent. Despite struggling through an exhausting seven-game series with Buffalo and McAdoo in the first round, they had handled Boston in six games in the Eastern finals.

They were a swift, strong team, coached by former Celtic K.C. Jones. Little Kevin Porter

Attles used all 12 players throughout the season.

spearheaded the offense by driving and dishing with an array of dazzling fakes and moves. He led the league in assists by penetrating and then dropping the ball off to Elvin Hayes, Phil Chenier, or Wes Unseld. At 6'9", Hayes displayed a full repertoire of shots, from snazzy post moves to bombs from the deep corners. He and jump shooter Chenier were among the top scorers in the league. The backcourt also featured Mike Riordan, the former Knick defensive specialist who had developed into a solid offensive player. He, too, fit nicely into the Washington running game with his endless energy and superior conditioning.

As Jones had seen the Celtics do during his playing days, he set up his team to feed the fastbreak with powerful defensive rebounding. Unseld, the league's top rebounder, and Hayes controlled the boards against most opponents, while Kevin Grevey, Riordan, and Porter raced upcourt on the break.

On paper and in the papers, the Warriors didn't seem like much of a match for this group. "I think they were a bit overconfident," Barry said. "People were talking about how they would sweep us in four, how Mike Riordan

would shut me down."

There was no better example of this confidence than the Bullets' evaluation of a glitch in the playoff schedule. Originally, the schedule set the first two games in Washington, the next two in Oakland, with the remaining games to be alternated. But the Ice Follies show created a conflict for the Oakland Coliseum Arena for Game 3, and if the Warriors shifted the site to the Cow Palace in San Francisco, Game 4 conflicted with a karate championship.

Thus, K.C. Jones and his staff faced two options. The Bullets could play the first game on the road, then three straight at home. Or they could play the first at home, then two on the road. Jones didn't like the idea of losing the first game and getting behind, so he chose to play one at home, then two on the road. It was a tough choice. "Three straight at home sounded good," he would say later. "But I didn't want them to win that first game."

"I guess they felt they had beaten us so badly during the year that it didn't matter where they played us," said Attles.

So the 29th NBA Finals series opened in Washington with an array of interesting matchups, not the least of which was the fact that for the first time in a major American sports championship, the head coaches of the opposing teams were black. Oddly enough, this seemed of no overwhelming interest to the media. "It wasn't something we thought about," said Attles. "I know it wasn't on K.C.'s mind, because we never mentioned it, and we talked a good bit. The only thing we were concerned about was trying to beat each other."

Jet lag left the Warriors strangely out of synch in Game One, yet by the half they had somehow managed to build a 14-point lead. When they began flagging in the third period, the bench rescued them, particularly Phil Smith, Dudley, and Dickey. Smith scored 20 points in 31 minutes of playing time as K.C. Jones saw his worst nightmare realized. Golden State took a 1-0 lead, 101-95.

"Our guards just came out and literally beat on and did a job on Kevin Porter," Barry said.

175

"Jamaal Wilkes was playing tough on Elvin Hayes. We were sending people at him, and he didn't do a good job of passing out of the double team."

The Bullets now faced two games on the West Coast. Still, their confidence seemed only slightly shaken. "Things will be different," Unseld promised.

And they were. First of all, the Warriors had their choice of playing in their regular building in Oakland or moving to the Cow Palace in San Francisco. Barry talked his teammates into choosing the Palace because its rims favored shooters. Even better, none of the Bullets had ever played there.

Washington jumped on Golden State from the start of Game 2 and established a 13-point lead. But with the home crowd behind them, the Warriors refused to disappear. Behind Barry's 36 points, they battled back to take a 92-91 lead in the closing seconds. The nervous Bullets got the ball back with 6 seconds left but missed two shots.

"We came back and won that ball game," Barry said, "and that was like the handwriting on the wall. They never recovered."

With a 2-0 lead and more confidence than ever, Golden State established its superiority in Game 3. The Bullets, meanwhile, were under intense pressure. No team had ever come back from a 3-0 deficit in the Finals. They had to win.

It was Barry, though, who responded to the pressure with 38 points. George Johnson, subbing for Ray, was another major factor. His 10 points and 9 rebounds helped take the heart out of Washington's game. Toward the end, the Bullets appeared disorganized and dazed.

"Now they were down 3-0 and they just couldn't believe what was happening," remembered Barry.

"I think they might have been a little shocked," agreed Attles. "They were such a great team in their thinking."

The major factor in their undoing was the Warrior defense, particularly Wilkes, who had held Elvin Hayes to a total of 29 points over three games. The secret was making Hayes

work for his points, Wilkes told the writers. "Pushing him out, fronting him, making him play defense and tiring him out. Then what happens, happens." Meanwhile, the Golden State bench had flourished, outscoring the Bullet bench 115-53 over the same span.

"They're plain out-hustling us," said a dejected Riordan. "They're getting to the loose balls, to the rebounds, cutting off the easy baskets."

Abruptly, the once-confident Bullets stopped talking of winning and began speaking of saving face. "It's very important that we get a couple of victories," said Unseld. "Even if we lose the series, we need it for the future. For next year, for our state of mind. If we don't there's so much humiliation over the summer."

But Attles' fire had built with his team's momentum. In a series ripe with implied insults, every development seemed to offer him a new angle for motivation. As stunned as the Bullets were the writers, who began speaking of the Warriors as a team of fate. "I see they are calling us a team of destiny," Attles replied testily. "I guess that means they're trying to say that we're not a very good team. We play hard, we're tough and that's why we win. No one likes us. No one thought we should be here. But I'm not saying prayers. There aren't any old ladies going to churches making novenas for us to win. This team is good. That's why we are winning."

Yet even he didn't speak directly of winning the championship with his players. That realization was just as surprising to the Warriors as it was to everyone else. Even on the plane, as his team headed across the country to face Washington for Game 4, Attles discussed the possibilities in cloaked terms. "If we win one more game," he told his players, "we'll have done something that no one ever expected us to do."

He didn't dare say more. Attles feared that a big loss in Washington could completely shift the momentum, because after that, two of the next three games would be played there. A sixth game back in California would bring unbearable pressure on his team.

On Sunday, May 25, things immediately got off to a bad start for Golden State in Game 4. Attles was ejected following a fracas in the first quarter, and the Warriors fell behind by 14 points. But their pressure defense carried them back, and Beard scored the last seven points. He delivered the coup de grace with a pair of free throws that assured the win, 96-95.

The Warriors had won four games by a total margin of 16 points. "It wasn't like we blew them out," Attles said. "Each game was close. And we were getting much better all the time."

"Like the Phoenix, we have risen from the ashes," exulted Golden State owner Franklin Mieuli.

The Warriors returned to Oakland afterward and found a throng waiting at the airport. "I remember this incredible crush of people," Barry said. "We got really scared because they caved in the roof of the cab we were in."

Among the congratulatory telegrams for the coach was one from Eddie Gottlieb, the little man back in Philadelphia who had started and built the Warriors, the man who had given Attles, the fourth-round draft pick, a chance to play in the NBA.

"He used to call me Little Al," Attles said of Gottlieb. "He just wanted to let me know he was proud of me, proud of what we had accomplished."

Yet even before the champagne had warmed the bad news struck. Beard got a call from a reporter informing him he was on the trading block. He was gone to Cleveland in a matter of days. "It was painful the way it was done," Beard said of the trade. "It was done so quickly, I really didn't get to enjoy the championship the way I should have."

The full impact of his departure wouldn't be felt until the 1976 playoffs. In the meantime, the loss of Beard was almost overlooked in the Bay area's joy.

Barry wears his championship ring proudly and still watches videotapes of the games from time to time. Beard, a former NBA assistant coach and now the head coach at Howard University, shares that pride. He also has tapes that he enjoys watching with his children. Mostly, though, the kids get a laugh out of the large Afro he sported then.

Which is typical. No one ever has taken the 1975 Warriors seriously.

"It has to be the greatest upset in the history of the NBA Finals," claims Barry. "But few people paid any attention to it. *Sports Illustrated* didn't even do a cover story on us. They hadn't expected us to win it. It was like a fairy-tale season. Everything just fell into place. It's something I'll treasure for the rest of my life."

The Warriors ground out the best regular-season record in the league for 1975-76, a respectable 59 wins. No longer were they the Cinderellas of the West. That role belonged to another upstart, the Phoenix Suns, an eight-year-old franchise that started two rookies. They had finished the regular schedule at 42-40 but had gotten better with each game, and by the playoffs the Suns had arrived.

First Phoenix tripped Seattle and the Suns followed that by upsetting Golden State in a seven-game showdown. The Suns took the seventh game in Oakland, 94-86, by holding Rick Barry scoreless for nearly 30 minutes.

Barry, for his part, maintained that the Warriors could have been the first back-to-back champions since the '69 Celtics had they not traded away Butch Beard after the '75 playoffs.

The Suns, however, were no slouch replacements in the Finals. They had traded Charlie Scott to the Celtics for sharpshooter Paul Westphal, and their phenomenal season grew out of that deal.

The Celtics filled in the other side of the bracket, although they weren't the same team that had won in 1974. Don Chaney had moved on to the ABA. And Westphal, the third guard, now played for the Suns. Scott, a slight but wonderfully gifted guard at 6'5", 175 pounds, joined JoJo White in the Boston backcourt, which led to immediate speculation that one basketball wouldn't be enough for the two of them. That did prove to be a consideration but not a problem. Boston adjusted and finished atop the East with a 54-28 record. Then in the playoffs, they brushed aside Buffalo and Cleveland in a pair of six-game series.

The Celtics were still coached by Heinsohn and still played that tough old brand of ball. In a display of team defense never equalled before or since, Havlicek, Cowens, and Silas — the starting frontcourt — were named to the league's All-Defensive team. That and their tradition made them big favorites against the Suns. There was even talk of a sweep.

After all Phoenix was a young team with a young coach, John MacLeod, who had a reputation as a motivator and a flashy dresser.

But he was much more than just another guy sporting a silk necktie. MacLeod had solid ideas about tough defense and team offense. Best of all, his youth was peppered by his idealism. The whole package spelled enthusiasm.

"MacLeod would have made a fantastic preacher," Westphal said of his new coach. "He sees a crippled guy and he comes in and uses it in his pregame talk."

Heinsohn, on the other hand, had once used 72 "bleeps" during his halftime talk for a Christmas Day game, claimed Westphal. How did he know? "I sat in the back and counted them," he explained.

All of MacLeod's goodness didn't count for much at the start of the season. His Suns were picked to finish last. After all, they started two rookies, Alvan Adams at center and Ricky Sobers at guard, and two well-traveled veterans, Garfield Heard and Curtis Perry, at forward.

Wherever Phoenix hoped to go, Westphal was the designated driver. A fourth-year player out of Southern Cal, he was 6'4" and a whiz at moving with or without the ball. That made him all the more important to Phoenix because he could get his shots without a lot of help. He also displayed acrobatic movies that thrilled the fans. A backup at Boston, he became better with each game he started in Phoenix. Over the last half of the season, his average soared to better than 23 points per game. Plus, he wasn't a bad defensive player and showed a knack for slipping into the passing lanes unnoticed to snatch the ball.

Sobers, out of Nevada-Las Vegas, hadn't been billed as a big-time player but joined Westphal in the backcourt when thirty-three-year-old veteran Dick Van Arsdale fractured his left arm. He was a surprisingly sound ballhandler for a rookie and showed a feisty streak that allowed him to play older than his years.

Adams was nearly as unsung as Sobers, although he wound up winning the Rookie Of The Year award by averaging 19 points and 9 rebounds as the Suns starting center. He had planned to be a doctor but had given up his senior year at Oklahoma to earn an NBA salary. The young center had matured over the season with the rest of the team. "Before he'd explode for big scoring games, but now he's more consistent," said Westphal near the end of the year. "He's the backbone of the team. We wouldn't be anywhere near the playoffs without him."

When MacLeod needed more experience in the game he went to former Laker Keith Erickson off the bench. The Suns also got decent minutes out of 6'10" Dennis Awtrey in the frontcourt and mid-sized Nate Hawthorne. Once healthy, Van Arsdale helped in the backcourt. All told, they played with a conviction that impressed all their opponents.

"Phoenix is ambitious, hungry and has great energy," said Phil Smith of the Warriors after the Western finals. "They've had a coming together that reminds me of us."

Age, again, was the dominant theme with the Celtics. Havlicek had torn a muscle in his left foot during the playoffs and was hobbling. Don Nelson was another graybeard off the bench. Like the Boston teams of the '60s, they were frank in discussing it. "One of these nights," warned Silas, we re going to reach back and nothing's going to be there."

The series at first appeared headed toward the predicted sweep. After all, the Suns hadn't beaten the Celtics since December 1974.

Boston won the first game at home, 98-87, a surprisingly flat affair in which the Suns shot only 38% from the floor. "If felt more like January than May," Silas said afterward. "It didn't seem like a playoff game."

Then the Celtics took the second in a rout, 105-90, after Boston went on a 202 run in the third quarter. "This team is like a Swiss watch, a bunch of different parts working together," White said afterward. Scott, always thought of as an offensive prima donna, hounded Sobers like a madman. So much so, in fact, that Scott fouled out of the first two games. Whenever he went to the bench, backup Kevin Stacom took up where he left off, harassing Sobers to the point of explosion. In the frontcourt, Cowens was doing a similar number on Adams. And when Cowens took a breather, backup center Jim Ard was there in Adams' face.

Afterward, the Phoenix papers ran a story suggesting that the Beantown boys were controlling the series because Cowens, Ard, and Silas were being allowed to play rough. The Boston coaches countered by saying the Suns coaching staff had "planted" the stories.

"Every team cries about the same thing," White told reporters. "Look, if you let a team do all they want to do, they're going to crush you. But stop them, and they get mad."

White himself squared off against Westphal, which was a rematch of their battle for the starting job in Boston. "I know his moves from the knock-down, drag-out practices we had," said White. He had used that knowledge to stifle the Suns' scoring leader in Game 1. Westphal had responded with 17 points in the first half of Game 2, but then White shut him down again in the second half.

The Suns stepped up their intensity for Game 3, played at Veterans Memorial Coliseum on Sunday morning to accommodate television. (Suns general manager Jerry Colangelo would later apologize to local clergy for the early tipoff time.) Boston didn't score for nearly five minutes at the outset of the second period and trailed 33-17 at one point. Then Sobers and Stacom got into a fistfight,

Paul Westphal came to the Suns from the Celtics for Charlie Scott.

and both were ejected.

"We can't let them bully us," Sobers explained afterward.

Boston began to charge back in the third and cut a lead that had once been 23 points down to 2 with three minutes left in the game. At that point, Adams came alive. He drove for two buckets, hit Westphal going to the hoop for another, then tipped in a Westphal miss moments later.

That was enough to get Phoenix a win, 105-98. Adams finished with 33 points and 14 rebounds. Both Scott and Cowens had fouled out, Scott for the third straight game, which left the Boston coaching staff fussing that the officials had been influenced by the media. The Celtics also picked up two technicals during the course of the game.

"The newspapers beat us," Heinsohn lamented. "I didn't know the power of the press was that big. We were lucky to run up and down the floor. That was hometown cooking. That's what it was."

"We're still 2-1," said Cowens confidently. "I ain't worried. We'll get 'er. If we don't get'er today, we'll get 'er tomorrow."

As expected, the officials made their statement in Game 4. Refs Don Murphy and Manny Sokol whistled 21 fouls in the first 10 minutes. Heinsohn responded by raging and stomping on the sideline and claimed later that the affair was pure "high school."

Havlicek and Cowens, though, called it straight up and said the Celtics had persisted in committing stupid fouls. Even so, the game was anybody's to steal. When Sobers took the ball down the middle and hit a bank shot that put the Suns up by 4 points with 90 seconds left, Boston still had a chance to tie. They lost 109-107 when White's late jumper was off.

Tied at 2-2, the series returned to Boston on Friday night, June 4, for a nationally televised game that treated the country to all the best the NBA had to offer in one three-overtime package.

"That was the most exciting basketball game I've ever seen," said Rick Barry, who worked the event as part of the CBS broadcast crew. "They just had one great play after another. I'll never forget the end. JoJo White was so exhausted, he just sat down on the court. It was such an emotional and physical game for everybody involved."

It didn't exactly begin as a classic, though. After nine minutes, Boston was up, 32-12. The Celtics went on to score 38 points in the first quarter and seemed on the verge of breaking the Suns. They stayed in it somehow, cutting the deficit to 15 by the half. Then the Suns stepped up their defense and held Boston to a mere 34 points over the last two quarters of regulation. The two teams battled to a tight finish. Perry missed two free throws for Phoenix, and Havlicek did the same for Boston. Regulation ended with the score 95-95.

The first overtime brought 6 more points for each team and a controversy for the ages. With time running off the clock, Silas signalled to official Richie Powers that he wanted a Boston timeout. The Celtics had none left, and according to the rules, Powers was supposed to call a technical on Silas for calling a timeout the team didn't have.

But the signal went unacknowledged, and time ran out. The Suns' coaches were incensed. If the technical had been whistled, the officials would have awarded Phoenix a free throw and a chance to win.

"It could have been over right there," said Barry. Instead, with midnight nearing, the marathon game went into a second overtime. Angry and drained as they were, the Suns stashed their complaints and went back to the fray.

The controversy only grew with the second overtime. With 15 seconds left, the Celtics owned a 3-point lead, and the Garden was rocking with chants of "We're Number One." But at that point, the teams took turns

matching miracles. First, Van Arsdale scored for Phoenix. Then Westphal got a steal, but Perry missed with a 14-foot jumper. He rebounded and scored on the second effort to put the Suns up, 110-109. With four seconds left, the Celtics raced back upcourt, where Havlicek motored along the left side, cut toward the hoop, stopped, and shoved up a 15-foot bank shot. When it fell through, the Garden erupted. The Celtics celebrated as hundreds of fans poured onto the floor, overwhelming the Garden's elderly and understaffed security force. A table was overturned and general mayhem prevailed, while Powers tried to get both coaches' attention.

The officials ruled that one second remained on the clock. It took some time for the public address announcer to communicate that to the crowd. Eventually, the security staff got the floor cleared, and play was set to resume. Phoenix would have to go the length of the floor to score with only a second remaining.

But during the delay Westphal had come up with an idea. Why not call a timeout, which the Suns didn't have? The officials would have to call a technical. The Celtics would get a free throw, but then the Suns would get the ball at halfcourt with a better shot to tie.

MacLeod agreed, and this time the officials called the technical. White hit the free throw, giving the Celtics a 112-110 lead.

Then, as the hour neared midnight, the Suns went to Gar Heard on the inbounds pass. Standing several feet beyond the top of the key, he arched a high turnaround shot that swished through the net, flooring the Celtics. With the score tied at 112, the game headed into a third overtime.

With most of his prime-timers on the bench with six fouls, Heinsohn went rummaging among his troops to find someone to play. He settled on little used Glenn McDonald, a 6'6" forward who had been the team's number-one draft pick out of Long Beach State in 1974. His NBA career would last just nine more games after the 1976 Finals, and he would be released in the 1976-77 season by Milwaukee.

But for five minutes of the third overtime, McDonald had the basketball world's attention. He scored 6 points, the last 2 on a short jumper, to give Boston a 128-126 win.

The Suns had gotten nothing for their effort except bruises. Afterward, they were more defiant than ever. "We know we're going to beat them," Heard declared. "It's going to take seven now, but we know we're going to beat them. We showed we came to play."

Trailing 3-2, they headed home for Game Six. There, they traded hand checks with the Celtics in a defensive struggle. Each team scored 20 in the first, then Boston scored 18 in the second while holding the Suns to 13. Erickson had attempted to play at the start of the second, but he re-injured his sprained ankle and never returned. After falling behind by 11, Phoenix moved even again in the third and actually took a 67-66 lead on a Sobers free throw with 7:25 left in the game.

But Cowens, Havlicek, and Scott took control from there. Havlicek hit two free throws, then Cowens stole the ball, drove, scored, drew the foul, and made the extra shot for a 3-point play. Then Cowens scored two baskets and Havlicek another to put it away.

During the run, Phoenix's only response was 4 free throws. The Celtics rode their surge to an 87-80 win and their thirteenth championship.

"We had to gut it out all the way," Heinsohn told the gathering of writers after the game. "Phoenix has a fine team with a great shooter. When the game was up for grabs, it was a question of pure guts. Everyone was tired, but our guys have been there before and did it."

Much of the Boston run had been fueled by Charlie Scott's 3 steals. He also scored 9 points in the fourth period, finishing the game with 25 points and 11 rebounds. The outburst shoved

Paul Silas came to Boston from Phoenix and played like a charm.

him out of an 11-for-44 shooting slump through the first five games of the series. In all five he had fouled out.

White had scored 15 on the afternoon and led Boston throughout the series with 130 points in six games. For that performance, he was named the series MVP. "Our offense really wasn't that great," he admitted later. "But defense will do it for you every time, and our defense did it."

Adams had scored 20 and Sobers 19 for the Suns. At the time it seemed a promise of championships to come, but that promise ultimately went unfulfilled. "Our players felt they would win today," said an obviously disappointed MacLeod. "But Boston drove us out of our patterns. But certainly nobody has to be embarrassed about being associated with the Phoenix Suns anymore."

"We were no fairy tale," Perry said. "We were for real."

The Celtics weren't about to argue.

"They earned their respect," said Silas.

For the eighth time in his career, Havlicek had some championship champagne. "You get yourself so worked up psychologically and physically that you wonder at times if it's really worth it," he said. "But after it's over, it feels like 15,000 years lifted off your shoulders."

He was asked if winning ever got old. He took another sip.

"It never gets old," he replied. "It gets old only if you lose."

11.
The Northwest Connection
Sonics, Bullets, and Blazers

1977

For pro basketball it was the year of the blender. The NBA was beginning its 31st season in the fall of 1976. Just months earlier, the ABA had ended its ninth and last. The combining of the two leagues, long fought by the players, finally happened.

Of the seven ABA teams, the four strongest — Denver, New York, San Antonio, and Indiana — survived and joined the NBA. The other three — Kentucky, St. Louis, and Virginia — agreed to take a cash settlement and close up shop. Immediately, their players were dispersed across the new 22-team league.

In a special $6 million deal, the Nets sold Julius Erving, the ABA's leading scorer, to the Philadelphia 76ers for $3 million. The other $3 million went to Erving himself, by way of a new contract. In Philly, he joined another scoring machine, George McGinnis, who had come over earlier from Indiana. This accumulation of talent brought talk of an immediate championship.

Other big names went elsewhere, some in moves within the NBA, others in the dispersal of ABA talent. Former Kentucky power forward Maurice Lucas to Portland. Moses Malone went to Houston after brief stops in Portland and Buffalo. Paul Silas went to Denver, Artis Gilmore to Chicago, Gail Goodrich to New Orleans, Sidney Wicks to Boston, and Nate Archibald to the Nets.

Nearly every team got deeper in talent, or more difficult to manage, depending on the perspective. There were only so many minutes of playing time to accommodate 25 teams compressed into 22, and this created some conflicts.

Bill Walton had trouble living up to expectations — except for one bright season

The pro game suddenly became a trial of quick assimilation. And that very first merged season offered yet another lesson in the value of team over talent.

Denny Crum was an assistant to UCLA coach John Wooden when he first saw Bill Walton play in 1968. Crum had gotten a tip about Walton, then a high school sophomore in San Diego. The coach was dubious, but he scouted him anyway.

"I came back and told Coach Wooden that this Walton kid was the best high school player I'd ever seen," Crum recalled. "We were sitting in Coach Wooden's office, and he got up and

Maurice Lucas (left) and Dave Twardzik, who came over from the ABA, played big roles for Portland.

closed his door and said, 'Denny, don't you ever make that stupid statement again. It makes you look like an idiot to say that some redhaired, freckled-faced kid from San Diego is the best high school player you've ever seen. First of all, there's never, ever been, since I've been here, a major college prospect from San Diego, let alone the best player you've ever seen.'"

Crum replied that maybe he sounded like an idiot, but this Walton kid was something to behold.

Time, of course, proved Denny Crum a pretty good judge of talent. He went on to coach his own national championship teams at Louisville. And the redhaired, freckle-faced kid from San Diego wound up setting a new standard of excellence for center play.

In three years of varsity competition, Walton led UCLA to two NCAA championships and 88 consecutive wins, smashing the 60-game streak set by Bill Russell's teams at the University of San Francisco. Walton also set UCLA's career assist record, which left observers declaring him the best passing center in the history of the game.

His college performance led to projections that Bill Walton would be pro basketball's next great dominating player. Yet those dreams would go largely unfulfilled due to a series of foot injuries that hampered and frustrated him and eventually ended his career. But for one bright shining season, he passed and played the Portland Trail Blazers to a storybook NBA championship. In the 1977 playoffs, Walton and his teammates found a chemistry that enabled them to confuse and humiliate one of the most talented pro teams ever assembled.

"Bill Walton is the best player, best competitor, best person I have ever coached," Blazers coach Jack Ramsay would declare moments after Walton delivered Portland the title.

That moment would prove to be the height of Walton's career, although he would come back from injury in 1986 to help the Celtics win a world championship as a backup center. But for the most part, his full pro potential was realized just that once.

By just about any standard, he was an intriguing figure. The son of a San Diego social worker, he championed causes that often seemed radical, even for the 1970s. Off the court, he held suspect rules and tradition. But as a player, his every move suggested the orthodox. He was the picture of precision, schooled and polished in every phase of the game.

"He's another one of those who make all the players around him better," Wooden said of Walton.

Broadcaster Curt Gowdy recalled seeing Walton play at the beginning of his college career. "I wrote a story for a magazine, and it came out in December 1971 predicting the All-America team," Gowdy said. "UCLA was playing their first game of the season that night, and I went out to watch them play. Some guy from the team comes to me and asks, 'You know Bill Walton?' I said, 'Yes, he's a new center.' The guy said, 'He wants to see you.' Well, I talked to Walton, and he tore into me for not picking him for the All-America team. He was a sophomore and he was going to play his first varsity game that night. He pointed out that his freshman team had beaten the varsity by 20 points.

"I said, 'No, I didn't pick you. I didn't know much about you.' He said, 'Well, you should have done better research.' He really jumped all over me. I watched him play that night, and I could tell he was going to be great. He was a very emotional type. Every time he'd come down the court he'd look over at Wooden to see if he'd done all right, and Wooden would shake his head at him."

Walton's emotional approach infused his off-court activities as well. "He always ran around campus with cut-off Levis and T-shirts and thongs, or whatever you call them on his feet," said Crum. "He rode a motor scooter and was a champion of all the minority classes on campus. He had a different philosophy and he and Coach Wooden clashed a number of times, not about basketball, but other things."

"Bill was a rebel," Wooden recalled with a smile. "Of course, during Bill's playing days,

it was probably a little more rebellious time. He was fighting to end the Vietnam war and had various other causes. In between practices, I was always concerned about him."

After four years of keeping his hair short to meet Wooden's team rules, Walton took his fiery game to Portland, where he grew his hair long and added a scraggly auburn beard. Suddenly opposing centers around the league found themselves facing a seven-foot hippy with a toothy grin. Walton epitomized the "alternative lifestyle," at least the NBA version of it. He pedaled a bike, crunched health food, and subscribed to High Times magazine. The times were uncertain and full of questions, and he was a man of the times. The idealism of the '60s had faded somewhat, and people were searching for answers. On the other coast, Dave Cowens went so far as to take a 30-game leave of absence from the Celtics and even briefly drove a cab.

For Walton, it wasn't a question of wanting to play but of being able to. Injuries repeatedly interrupted his progress as a pro player, which didn't exactly endear him to the Portland fans. On the court, when he was healthy, he was the ultimate team player. He missed 17 games over the 1976-77 season. The Blazers lost 12 of them. With him in the lineup, they were 44-21, their .677 winning percentage during those games the best in the league. No team's record was overwhelming; the redistribution of talent had resulted in greater parity, with six clubs getting at least 48 wins and another nine winning 40.

The dispersal of players had been a particularly beefy one for Portland. Lucas was simply the most dominating power forward in the game, and his arrival only boosted Walton's effectiveness in the frontcourt. But his role was far from merely complimentary. Lucas led the team in scoring at 20.2 points per game and averaged better than 11 rebounds.

His intimidation factor was even bigger than his numbers. At 6'9" and a muscular 215 pounds, he wasn't the bulkiest player in the league — but he was almost the strongest. Lucas had first established his reputation as an enforcer at Schenley High in Pittsburgh, then at Marquette where he'd played for feisty Al McGuire. The result of this schooling was a burnished menace. He was the perfect steeltown alum.

"Lucas treats George McGinnis like a little boy," Philadelphia 76ers guard Fred Carter observed after Portland and Philly met early in the season. Carter would be shipped to the Milwaukee Bucks not long after that. But by playoff time, that truth would be firmly established.

Because he played in Portland, the national media overlooked Lucas through much of the season. By April, though, his antics were in full view. Against the Chicago Bulls in a brutal first-round playoff series, Lucas threw a strong jab at a team trainer and even jerked an official's whistle lariat, then later attempted to explain his behavior. "I'm no boxing madman," he said, "but I just want them to know Luke is out busting chops. If I had this kind of year in New York, I'd be governor."

Or at least the chief of police.

Coming over with Lucas from the ABA was lead guard Dave Twardzik, with four, pro seasons with Virginia under his belt — schooling enough to make him a starter in Ramsay's system. The off guard was 6'3" Lionel Hollins, a second-year player out of Arizona State who averaged nearly 15 points a game.

Ramsay believed in using his roster — eleven players averaged better than 10 minutes per game over the season, and the twelfth player got 9 minutes an outing. That depth would prove vital late in the season when Twardzik suffered a badly sprained ankle.

Veteran Herm Gilliam was the third guard, and rookie Johnny Davis played well, particularly in Twardzik's absence. Bob Gross, 6'6", in his second season out of Long Beach State, was the starting small forward and role player. He gave Ramsay 11 points and solid defense each game. And 6'5" Larry Steele added 10 points in 20 minutes a game off the bench.

Ramsay wrapped this crew into a rebounding and running package that sent jolts through the Portland crowds. He was, after all, Dr. Jack Ramsay, the thinking man's coach. In his past life, he had been the most respected of college coaches, molding wonderful teams at St. Joe's with a record of 23-47-2 in eleven seasons. His 1962 group went to the Final Four, but some of his players were later implicated in the widespread point-shaving scandal that enveloped college basketball that season. The revelation left Ramsay abjectly disillusioned. He resigned and moved to the pro game, first at Buffalo, then Portland. In more than twenty seasons as an NBA coach, he would pile up 864 regular-season wins.

But the 1976-77 season wasn't about regular-season wins. Because of the losses during Walton's absences, the Blazers finished 49-33, four games back of the Lakers in the Pacific Division. In the first round, Walton battled Artis Gilmore and the Chicago Bulls before winning a tough series, 2-1. The next round brought a 4-2 dismissal of Denver, coached by Larry Brown. Portland simply offered too much running and too much rebounding for the Nuggets. But the victory cost the Blazers Twardzik, who went down with a severely sprained ankle.

The Western finals pitted the Blazers

Bill Walton's dreams would go largely unfulfilled due to a series of foot injuries that hampered and frustrated him and eventually ended his career.

against the Lakers, which created a classic one-on-one matchup between Walton and his predecessor at UCLA, Kareem Abdul-Jabbar. Their meeting left the writers yodeling about future battles of Russell/Chamberlain proportions. The team contest, however, left a lot to be desired. Portland swept, 4-0. With an inferior team around him, Kareem got the statistical edge but lost the real numbers game. Walton, meanwhile, contented himself with a few thunder dunks in his elder's face.

Still, few in attendance tried to pretend that Walton had dominated. Kareem outscored (121-77), out-rebounded, and out-blocked Walton, but remained stoic about the situation. "I know Bill is enjoying this," he said. "It's not Amsterdam Avenue back on the playgrounds. But if he jams a couple, I've got to get the baskets back, so I dunk. I like the way the Blazers play. They should be national champs."

The Blazers, in turn, were sincere in their respect for the Lakers center. "Kareem would never give up," Lucas said as the series ended. "He's the most respected player in the league because he never bows his head. Such great inner strength. You may beat his team but you never beat him."

All this respect did not, however, prevent the Blazers from squealing with glee. The franchise was a mere seven seasons old and headed to the NBA Finals.

Their opponents would be the mercurial but awesomely talented Philadelphia 76ers, who had posted the best record in the Eastern Conference, 50-32.

Gene Shue was the coach. Erving (the esteemed Dr. J), McGinnis, and 6'6" shooting guard Doug Collins were the big guns. The quarterback on the floor was point guard Henry Bibby. World B. Free rained long-range jumpers off the bench. And Caldwell Jones started at center with 21-year-old Darryl Dawkins, the self-proclaimed "Chocolate Thunder," in a backup role. As reserve forwards they had Steve Mix, Harvey Catchings and Joe Bryant.

On the whole, though, they were perceived

as an undisciplined lot, beginning with the chainsmoking McGinnis and ending somewhere off in Lovetron, Dawkins' imaginary home planet. Shue admitted as much. "We have the best of one world — the playground," he deadpanned.

In the last few months of the season, Erving and McGinnis had averaged 50 points per game together. Still, most observers thought they

World B. Free gave the 76ers scoring punch off the bench.

couldn't manufacture a championship chemistry in one short season. "I've never seen it happen," said Boston's John Havlicek. "Everyone thought West and Wilt and Baylor were going to do that right away, but they didn't. There can always be a first, but I've never seen it."

The team started strongly as they downed Boston and Houston on the way to the Eastern Conference championship. Yet as the Finals opened in the Spectrum on Sunday May 22, few observers were convinced of the Sixers' resolve.

Philadelphia General Manager Pat Williams acknowledged that the club was unpredictable. "But," he added, "we could win it all going away with our manes blowing in the wind."

That seemed to be just what was going to happen after the first two games. Erving opened Game 1 with a stupendous dunk off the opening tip. He finished with 33 points, and Collins had 30, as Philly won 107-101. The big factor, though, was Bibby's unheralded defense on Hollins. The Blazers were rattled enough to commit 34 turnovers.

Walton finished with 28 points and 20 rebounds, but when the media came calling after the game, Erving didn't want to engage in hero worship. "I'll challenge anybody," he said.

And in Game 2 four nights later, the Sixers did an even better job, winning handily, 107-

89. Jones and Dawkins handled Walton easily, and the Sixers ran off with the second quarter, scoring 14 points in one three minute stretch on their way to a 61-43 halftime lead.

The game turned sour with about five minutes left. First Portland's Lloyd Neal and McGinnis squared off. Then Lucas and Erving traded elbows. Finally, Dawkins and Gross went at it. After a tug-of-war over a rebound, Gross screamed at Dawkins, who responded with a roundhouse. Gross ducked at the last instant and the blow caught Dawkins' own teammate, Collins, who had been holding Gross. Lucas then nailed the 6'11", 260-pound Dawkins with a shot from behind, and both benches jumped into the fray along with coaches, spectators, security guards, and officials.

George McGinnis joined Erving in leading the 76ers' scoring parade.

Even Ramsay and his assistant, Jack McKinney, took on a few fans before Ramsay turned his ire on Dawkins, only to be shoved out of the way. When the floor was finally cleared, Lucas and Dawkins were ejected. They would later be fined $2,500 each, and Collins would need four stitches.

Dawkins then trashed Philly's locker room, turning over lockers, breaking a toilet, and smashing a chalkboard. He stormed out in a rage, saying he was angry that his teammates had let Lucas jump him from behind. Professional wrestling couldn't have claimed a gaudier main event.

"I'm too professional to let this carry over," Lucas said afterward. "But this dude gets built up like a gorilla, then thinks he can gorilla everybody. I'll see Dawkins Sunday."

"Lucas is a fighter, but I can box," Dawkins later replied. "My uncle, Candy McDaniels, fought Joe Louis. He taught me. I usually stand 'em up with a left and take 'em out with

a right."

Lucas seemed ready to settle the matter right off the bat that Sunday, May 29. He strode directly to the Philly bench, then startled everybody, including Dawkins, by sticking out his paw for a shake. That matter settled, he and the Blazers proceeded to take out the Sixers with offense. Lucas himself contributed 27 points and 12 rebounds. Walton had a mere 9 assists, 20 points, and 18 rebounds. Twardzik, too, had returned to speed, driving the Portland offense along to a 42-point fourth quarter. They won in a blaze, 129-107, closing the gap in the series to 2-1.

"We seem to get energy and sustenance from the response at home," Ramsay said.

The Philadelphia coaches decided they were relying on Collins' perimeter shooter too much, so they changed strategy for Game 4, attempting to send the ball inside to McGinnis and Jones. Walton responded with a shotblocking fury at one end, while Lucas did the offensive damage at the other. Portland opened up a quick 17-point lead, then spread the shellac thickly onto a 130-98 win. Even when Walton went to the bench with five fouls in the third, the Blazers didn't miss a beat.

"We've got to challenge the other team," Erving said afterward. "Be aggressive. Get some axes and chop some arms and legs."

What Erving really could have used was some offensive help. McGinnis had shot 16 for 48 in the first four games. "I feel like a blind man searching for the men's room," he told the press.

The Blazers, meanwhile, were more confident than ever. Walton popped the Grateful Dead into his tape deck as his team headed back across the continent to confront Philly in the Spectrum on Friday night.

The first half of Game 5 was just what the Doctor ordered — plenty of hacking that led to a halftime score in the 40s. But the Blazers got their running game going in the third, feeding it off steals and zooming to another 40-point quarter, their third of the series. With a little more than eight minutes left in the game, Portland led 91-69, and the crowd was headed home.

The Doctor rallied the Sixers to make it respectable at the end, 110-104, but the naysayers had been confirmed. Gross scored 25 to lead the Blazers, while Lucas had 20 with 13 rebounds. Walton finished with 24 rebounds and 14 points.

Erving, who scored 37, was distraught afterward. "I had a good feeling about tonight," he said. "It all backfired. It's a bad scene."

Commanding a 3-2 series lead, the Blazers arrived home at 4:30 a.m. to find 5,000 crazy fans waiting to greet them. The official word for the mayhem was Blazermania. Always an emotional player, Walton rode to new heights on the crest of this wave. The next afternoon, a glorious, sunny Sunday, he had 20 points, 23 rebounds, 8 blocks, and 7 assists.

"He's an inspiration," Erving would say afterward.

The Doctor himself wasn't bad in that department. His Sixers kept even through the first period, then fell behind by 15 in the second. The Portland lead was still 12 with just half of the fourth quarter left when Erving led his teammates on one final run. At the four-minute mark, the lead was cut to four, 102-98. Portland upped it back to 8 moments later, but Free hit a free throw and Erving canned a 20-footer and two foul shots to trim it to three. Lucas answered with a free throw for Portland. Then McGinnis came through with a jumper, and the lead was only 2 with 18 seconds left.

The Sixers needed a turnover, and finally got it from McGinnis, who forced a jump ball with Gross. Philly controlled and headed upcourt. At 0:08, Erving put up a jumper in the lane. No good. Free got the ball and lofted a baseline shot. Again no good. With a second left, McGinnis got a final shot. It drew iron, and that was it.

Walton knocked the loose ball away just to be sure, then turned, ripped off his drenched jersey, and hurled it into the delirious crowd. "If I had caught the shirt, I would have eaten it," Lucas allowed later. "Bill's my hero."

Somewhere, Denny Crum was smiling. And John Wooden was no longer wondering about the redhaired, freckle-faced kid from San Diego.

1978

The Washington Bullets presented a head-on clash of styles in the late 1970s. There was new coach Dick Motta, a little guy with a lot of intensity. Perhaps too much intensity, some said. Then there was Elvin Hayes, the 6'9" power forward who did what he wanted, when he wanted.

When Motta was named the Bullets coach before the 1976-77 season, Hayes announced that he'd rather give up the game than play for such a man. But when training camp opened, Hayes was there, and he immediately encountered the raging Motta, true to reputation. Do it my way, or get out, the new coach told his players.

The Big "E" was known for his special spot to the left of the key. He wanted the ball there, and that was where he'd wait until he got it. Usually when he got it, if the defense wasn't too strong, he could find a way to score. But whatever happened, Elvin Hayes wanted to call the shots.

Motta had been a fine college coach at Weber State in Idaho. His ideas about the game were chiseled in marble. His teams played spiritbreaking defense, and at the other end of the floor, they took their time moving through Motta's patterns, until a score was the logical conclusion.

For a while, it looked as if neither side would budge in this test of wills. But eventually both men gave in a bit and did something neither had done very often in their careers.

They compromised.

The results were back-to-back trips to the NBA Finals in 1978 and 1979, and sweet memories for years to come. Hayes smiled broadly in 1990 when asked to reminisce about Motta. "Dick demanded a lot of his players," he said. "He demanded a lot of himself. He gave us a direction, and we followed it."

It helped, of course, that despite being successful both men harbored their insecurities. Throughout his career, Hayes had been a statistics machine, always scoring and rebounding but never seeming to find the necessary range in the big games, and never winning a championship.

Motta, meanwhile, had never even been to a pro game when he was hired to coach the Chicago Bulls in 1968. He eventually directed the young franchise to four straight 50-win seasons, but his teams never made it to the Finals. Fortunately, there were moderating factors, the most substantial of which was 6'7", 245-pound Westley Sissel Unseld. A granite block of a man, Unseld was entering the twilight of his career with a set of bad knees. When it came to shooting, he looked to pass. Nevertheless, he was the ultimate team player. Solid at setting picks and rebounding, selfless and fierce, he was just the foundation upon which Motta could build.

"What we needed was an iron hand," Unseld would say later when asked about Motta.

Indeed they did. For ten straight years they had made the playoffs without ever really accomplishing anything. Motta set out to change that. He had traded away Truck Robinson and Nick Weatherspoon, then moved perennial All Star guard Dave Bing out of a starting spot.

The Bullets, meanwhile, finished with 48 wins in Motta's first campaign and again lost in the playoffs. The Washington crowd had booed the coach from the very first game, and his insecurities deepened. Still, he could joke about it. He liked to tell people that he had gotten a standing ovation in his first game in Washington — all booing.

Motta entered his second season with some reason for optimism. He had forged a compromise with Hayes. And the Bullets had picked up free agent Bobby Dandridge, formerly of the Bucks, to play small forward. In many ways, Dandridge was the most complete small forward in the business. Which in turn meant that Kevin Grevey, average as a small forward, could move to his natural position of off guard, where he played smartly.

The final ingredient came in January with the acquisition of backup guard Charles Johnson. Hayes remembered the day clearly. "We were playing on a Sunday afternoon when Charles Johnson came to the Bullets," Hayes said. "He flew in that afternoon in a helicopter, and we won the game. That was the beginning of the coming together of the Washington Bullets. I knew then that we had a championship-caliber team. We had been struggling along, and all of a sudden, boom. It all came together."

Johnson, a six-foot guard out of the University of California, had come to the Bullets from Golden State, where he had started on the 1975 championship team. For somebody who wasn't a name player, he possessed an amazing confidence in his outside shot, and he became the immediate glue man for Washington's impressive bench.

"We had such diverse talent on that team," said Hayes. "We had Mitch Kupchak, Larry Wright, Charles Johnson, and Greg Ballard-all of them coming off the bench. Any one of those guys would have been a great starter on another team. For starters, we had Unseld, Grevey, Tommy Henderson, Bobby Dandridge, and myself. From the bench to the starters, we had great balance."

Flayes and Dandridge led the scoring with better than 19 points per game apiece. Hayes was used to scoring more than that, but he sacrificed his higher average for the team, and as a result had perhaps his best all-around season. Although he didn't start, Kupchak scored at a 15.9 clip as the backup center to Unseld. Grevey was good for another 15.5 points a game, and Henderson, the starting point guard, also scored in double figures. Motta gave regular playing time to ten men, although jump shooter Phil Chenier missed 46 games with back problems.

Even with all this generosity from the coach, Washington finished the regular season with a 44-38 mark, only third best in the Eastern Conference. The experts weren't optimistic about their chances in the playoffs, but the Bullets had circumstance in their favor. It was a year of opportunity in the NBA. After jumping off to a 50-10 record, the defending champion Portland Trail Blazers were struck by a series of critical injuries. Walton went down first with a bad left foot. Then it was Lloyd Neal, followed by Lucas, Gross, Steele, and Twardzik. Once the strongest team in the league, they lost 14 of their last 22 games and died in the playoffs.

In their place rose the Seattle SuperSonics, whose season had followed a reverse course.

The Sonics were terrible at first, losing 17 of their first 22 games. Then coach Bob Hopkins was fired and Lenny Wilkens, who two seasons earlier had been fired as Portland's boss, was hired. Wilkens stressed defense, and the Sonics turned their fortunes around, winning 42 of their last 60 games.

They were a good mix of rooks and veterans, and their ways continued to be winning in the playoffs. Dennis Johnson and Gus Williams started in the backcourt, with Fred "Downtown" Brown standing in as a third guard/designated bomber. The frontcourt had

Unseld splits the defense on the way to Finals MVP honors.

greybeard Paul Silas, who had just moved over from Denver, and 7'1" shotblocker Marvin Webster (the Human Eraser) at center. Rookie Jack Sikma, a freshfaced, blonde giant, held down the other forward spot. With the addition of backup forward John Johnson, the fans and media took to calling them "Goldilocks and the Three Bears."

When they were good, they played as if they had just come out of hibernation. Which is sort of what the Sonics did that spring. They whipped the Lakers in the first round, then jumped on Portland before trimming Denver in the conference finals.

Back east, the Bullets were undergoing a similar emergence. After whipping Atlanta and San Antonio in the early going, Washington met favored Philadelphia in the Eastern finals and used tremendous injections of enthusiasm to boost their tired bones toward an upset. Along the way, Motta took to reciting a favorite phrase of his: "The opera isn't over 'til the fat lady sings." Each time things got tight and the writers brought out their doom questions, Motta told them to wait for the fat lady.

She showed in Philly in the first game of that series but did her number for the Sixers. From there on out, Erving and his mates were faced with fighting back. They never quite made it.

Motta and his team advanced, claiming the series 4-2. At the end, long after the players had run off to the locker room, Motta stood in the wild throng at the Capital Centre and raised his arms in his own private exultation.

Suddenly the Finals had the most unexpected of participants. The Bullets, who had finished third in their conference, against the Sonics, who had finished fourth in theirs. It was a series that seemed to offer little to fans across the country, but in the respective cities, the enthusiasm was tremendous. Seattle embraced the Sonics as their first winning big-league team. And even stately Washington came alive, from Georgetown and the neighborhoods of the northwest to Capitol Hill and the suburbs in Virginia. The city

hadn't had a championship team since the Redskins won the NFL title way back in 1942. As the politicians took turns pointing out, the place needed something positive.

It didn't happen right away. Seattle took Game 1 at home, 106-102, when the 34-year-old Silas did a solid defensive number on Hayes. The Bullets actually led by 19 at one point. But then Brown got untracked with a 16-point binge in the last nine minutes of the fourth period.

Under the playoff schedule that had been adjusted due to building conflicts in Seattle, the Bullets returned home for the next two games, where they had to face a cynical Washington media brimming with reminders about their 1975 Finals foldup.

Hayes again hadn't been evident in the fourth period of the first game, and the press started in on him. He, in turn, took a shot at Unseld, who shot so infrequently that the Sonics left him alone to double-team elsewhere. Hayes complained that Motta should give more minutes to Kupchak, who could score.

This time, however, the Bullets answered the questions before they got started by winning Game 2 106-98. Unseld did his best blue-collar bit, with 15 rebounds, 5 assists, and extra body work on Marvin Webster. His boneshattering picks in the lane on Silas freed Hayes and Dandridge for open shots on offense. They opened hot and moved the Bullets out to a 16-point lead. The Sonics cut it to 4 by the half, and then pulled even tighter in the third with Hayes in foul trouble. But Unseld just kept setting those wallsized picks of his, and in the end Goldilocks and the Three Bears looked like they needed their porridge. Dandridge got loose for 34 points and Hayes for 25. Henderson added 20, mostly on drives.

Motta was understandably pleased afterward. "That's our game," he said. "Hayes and Dandridge going off tackle. People know where we're going. They're just going to have to stop us."

That pretty much summed up the series. There was no way the Sonics could avoid such

192

a direct challenge, so they answered in Game 3, again in the Cap Centre. The intensity, already high, increased noticeably. Dennis Johnson and Silas led the Seattle charge. Silas closed down the holes in the Bullets' offensive line. Dandridge and Hayes still had decent games, but they weren't able to break loose down the stretch with the game on the line. Meanwhile, the 23-year-old Johnson was a force on the perimeter. He blocked 7 shots and had Grevey talking to himself with a 1-for-14 shooting day.

Even with this effort, the Sonics almost blew it in the last 10 seconds. They were leading 93-90 and had the ball, but Johnson sent the inbounds pass to Henderson, who happily popped in a layup to bring it to 93-92 with 5 seconds on the clock. Then it was Silas' turn to goof. He stepped on the line trying to make the inbounds pass, turning the ball over to the Bullets. The Sonics fell back on defense, though, and forced Dandridge into lofting a long shot from the side. It rimmed out, and Seattle was homeward bound with a 2-1 lead.

In the Northwest, it was recordsetting time. Game 4 was held in the Kingdome because the Seattle Coliseum, where the Sonics usually played, was tied up with a mobile home show. Thus, 39,457 Sonics worshippers helped fill the vast domed stadium, a record for an NBA Finals. Which made their disappointment only larger that afternoon and has some Seattle fans still wondering if that mobile home show didn't cost them a championship. The Sonics began well enough and even had a 15-point lead in their grasp with about two minutes left in the third quarter. It was about then that the much-maligned Washington guards began to earn their respect. They had been outscored 43-15 in the first half, not to mention similar difficulties earlier in the series.

The Sonics' problems began when Dennis Johnson took an elbow to the ribs that sent him to the bench for nearly six minutes. With Charles Johnson, Wright, Kupchak, and Dandridge in the lineup, the Bullets reversed the momentum and took the lead, 103-101,

with about 3/2minutes left in the game. Dennis Johnson had returned by then and was well on his way-to 33 points, 7 rebounds, and 3 blocks. He went crazy in those final three minutes, scoring first to tie the game, then picking up loose balls, blocking a Dandridge shot, getting an offensive rebound, and pushing the Sonics to a 104-103 lead with a foul shot.

Dandridge answered this outburst with a 3-point play that returned the lead to Washington, 106-104. Seattle got the ball back and tied it with one of Brown's custom-made downtowners. With two seconds left, Dandridge got a good shot in the lane, only to have Dennis Johnson block it, thus treating the record crowd to an extra period.

The treats ended there, though. Charles Johnson hit three quick shots in overtime to give the Bullets a 120-116 win. As improbable as it had seemed considering the record Seattle crowd, the Bullets had tied the series at two wins each.

"We could have lain down like puppy dogs with our stomachs in the air," Charles Johnson allowed afterward, "but we're made of more than that."

They had to wait a few days for the next test. For Game 5, the Sonics were allowed to return to their familiar Coliseum, and there they got the job done, although the Bullets didn't make it easy. Brown had 26 and D.J. 24 to carry Seattle to a 98-94 win and a 3-2 series lead. The Bullets lost it at the line, making only 9 of 20 free throws in the second half. Even so, they cut Seattle's 11-point lead to two with less than two minutes to go before Sikma hit 3 free throws down the stretch.

Then it was back to Washington for Game 6 on Sunday. There, it was all Bullets, 117-82. At first, the game had the opposite tenor. Grevey was injured, and the Washington backcourt was struggling. So Motta moved Dandridge to guard (he had little experience at the position) and inserted Greg Ballard at forward. They produced a run that gave the Bullets a 12-point lead at the half. Washington scored 70 points in the second half, and the

Sonics weren't up to that pace. It was something to see, these old men of basketball doing repeated weave drills down the floor. The young Bullets didn't do badly, either. Kupchak finished with 19, and Ballard had 12 points and 12 rebounds.

"I saw a lot of smiling and laughing over there," D.J. said of the Washington bench. "But we've got the seventh game at home."

More than a decade later, the memory of that flight back to Seattle still rested sweetly in Hayes' memory. "I remember flying out to Seattle," he said, "thinking about all the things that had gone through all the years that I had played in the NBA. All of that was coming down to one game, a championship game, and after that game, I remember feeling a joy over the next 48 hours, just a spring of joy, a feeling of great accomplishment. Out of my 16 years of playing, I had waited for that moment, and that moment came, and it was just tremendous."

For the Sonics, it was a drop into bottomless anguish, particularly for Dennis Johnson, who missed each and every one of his 14 shots from the floor. Gus Williams was a bit more accurate, shooting 4 for 12. But the Sonics' frontcourt came through as Webster scored 27 and Sikma 21, and that kept it close. With 90 seconds left, Seattle whittled the lead from 11 down to 4, but Kupchak came up with a 3-point play. Brown, who finished with 21, wasn't through, however. He hit a short jumper, then Silas got a tip-in to cut it to 101-99. Silas then fouled Unseld, a 55% free-throw shooter during the playoffs. He hit 2, and moments later Washington sealed it, winning 105-99.

The Bullets became only the third team ever to win the title in a seventh game on the road. They did it with everybody contributing. Charles Johnson and Dandridge each scored 19, while Kupchak, Unseld, and Henderson all played well. Hayes fouled out with 12 points, a development that brought a couple of needling questions from the writers. "They can say whatever they want," Hayes replied with a smile. "But they gotta say one thing — E's a world champion. He wears the ring."

Motta, too, was a world champion, wearing his "The Opera Isn't Over 'Til The Fat Lady Sings" T-shirt, which his players soaked in beer. This time, she had belted out a sweet one for the Bullets, especially the older players. Unseld was voted the MVP, a vote for the work ethic if there ever was one.

"What I feel is relief," he told the writers afterward.

They all did, and it was one agreement that didn't require a compromise.

1979

When he was a young pro, Dennis Johnson was considered a leaper, an athletic defensive guard who could block shots and rebound. That view of him changed after more than a decade in the league. In his later years with the Boston Celtics, he would amble upcourt with a stiff gait, seemingly locked in a perpetual state of chafe. He came to be viewed as a crafty vet who survived on pride, guile, and experience.

Lenny Wilkens had to make several changes for the 1978-79 season...

Despite his transformation over the years, two constants remained in his game. First, his shooting percentage seldom emerged from the low 40s, yet he was always deadly at hitting the big shot with the game on the line. Thus, he developed a reputation as a money player.

The second constant was his outstanding defensive effort. He always had quick hands and quick feet and knew how to use them, as well as his long arms.

...But Silas was still "Papa Bear" to the younger players.

Understandably, Johnson's defensive emphasis changed with age. As a veteran, he approached the task with subtlety. He would delight in the crafty steals, the brush blocks, the changed shots, the denials, and all the other facets of a solid defensive game.

But as a younger player, Johnson was one of those demonstrative souls who play defense as if every point an opponent scores is a personal affront to their humanity. These types are driven by a territorial urge, challenging for every inch of playing space. They tend to have "attitudes" and find great pleasure in getting in an opponent's face.

It was the great misfortune of the Washington Bullets that they faced the younger version of Dennis Johnson in the 1979 NBA Finals.

"I really believe defense is an art," Johnson would say later in his career.

But in 1979, his outlook wasn't quite so effete. Back then, he wielded his defense like a knife.

Of course, he had just turned 24, and there was reason for his desperation. He had come up hard by most standards, raised as one of sixteen children in Compton, California, where he had a relatively anonymous career at Dominguez High. His jumping ability did, however, earn him the nickname "Airplane." It didn't get him any scholarship offers, though. So Johnson began working as a forklift operator, and shortly thereafter enrolled at Harbor Junior College. It was there that he began to find prominence as a player. Still, he was a 6'4" forward, sometimes a center, and his prospects seemed limited. Somehow he managed to catch the attention of the coaches at Pepperdine. He played forward there for one season and in the process established some of his defensive reputation. But then Johnson took a very big, very abrupt gamble. He decided to turn pro.

He entered the draft in the spring of 1976 after his junior season, but few in the NBA paid much notice except for Bill Russell, then the coach at Seattle, who drafted him in the second round. As it turned out, that was all the chance Johnson needed.

Sikma moved to the post after Webster left and Tommy LaGarde went out with an injury.

Two years later, he had the attention of the entire league as he led the Sonics in a seven-game battle with the Washington Bullets for the NBA title. Through the first six games, his play bordered on brilliant. Then, in that seventh game, he experienced the ultimate nightmare for a basketball player. His offensive game folded completely. He missed each of the 14 shots he took from the floor that day. Jumpers. Layups. Nothing fell. Except for Johnson's confidence.

It was a tough performance for a spirited type like Johnson. He wasn't the kind to crawl away. So he didn't. He survived the nightmare and brought the Sonics back the next season. For all of them, it became a matter of pride.

"We weren't respected last season," Johnson told the media as the 1979 playoffs neared. "But our adrenaline flowed into momentum,

Johnson drives the lane...

...plays defense...

a piece stuck in everybody, and it's all still with us."

Certainly respect was no longer an issue. In 1978, both the Bullets and Sonics were surprise teams in the Finals. But that had all changed by 1979. Now they were expected to win.

"Don't be fooling yourself," Seattle's Fred Brown said when asked his projections for the playoffs. "You know it all boils down to us against Washington one more time. Both teams have great people all the way through the lineup. They're deeper, but we make up

196

...and powers for two points in his MVP series.

After all, they clearly had the best and deepest frontcourt in basketball, with Hayes and Dandridge at forwards, Unseld and Kupchak at center, and Greg Ballard off the bench. Their backcourt, too, had become deeper, with Phil Chenier returning from injury.

However, in the midst of their strength and success, they faced the same old harmony problems.

Dandridge made it known that he was upset Hayes made $200,000 more per year than he, and the discontent became something of a wrench in Motta's machine.

Even so, Washington charged to a league-best 54-28 record for the regular season, and by playoff time most observers figured the Bullets were ready to roll.

The Sonics had also kept their prestige, but not without a struggle. They finished at 52-30, best in the West, and did it despite substantial turnover in the frontcourt. First, center Marvin Webster, the Human Eraser, went off to New York as a free agent. Then his replacement, Tommy LaGarde, got injured. So Lenny Wilkens moved Jack Sikma from forward to the post and brought in Lonnie Shelton, who had come from New York, at forward. Of course, the Sonics still had John Johnson and Paul Silas, the infamous Papa Bear of the previous sea-

for that with our backcourt...I think it will be wild and picturesque all over again."

There was some excitement generated over the idea that Washington had a clear shot at being the first NBA team to repeat as champions since the Celtics had last done it in 1969.

197

son. Now 35, he was more respected than ever, which was exactly what the young Sonics needed.

"Look anywhere on our team, and you'll see Paul's influence," explained Wilkens, who had played with Silas in St. Louis and encouraged him to join Seattle.

Silas had earned two championship rings with Boston and was eager for a third. The Sonics banished the Lakers, 4-1, in the Western semifinals, then held onto their hats against the supercharged Phoenix Suns in a seven-game series. Seattle actually lost the key fifth game at home to the Suns and had to win the sixth in Phoenix to stay alive. They did so by one scary point, then returned home and iced another trip to the Finals with a four-point win. More than talent, they seemed to be playing on chutzpah.

"The Sonics will win because they believe they will win," declared Rick Barry, who was now playing with Houston and broadcasting for CBS on the side.

Wilkens agreed. "The difference from last year is maturity," he said. "Last year we were so young, we played on emotion. There were questions. Now we run strictly on confidence."

The Bullets, meanwhile, were stepping through what they believed to be their own destined paces, only they found the going a bit rougher. In the Eastern semifinals, they met the Atlanta Hawks, coached by Hubie Brown. The Bullets gained a 3-1 edge on the Hawks, then fell asleep at the wheel, only to awaken and find themselves in a seven-game tussle for control. They survived at home by six points but were no sooner out of that mess than they found themselves in another. The San Antonio Spurs, coached by Doug Moe and iced by George Gervin, insisted on playing seven games, too. They jumped out to a two-game lead on the Bullets in the Eastern finals. Washington finally resolved that one with a come-from behind two-point win at home on Friday night, May 18.

"I about passed out," Motta said afterward. "Now I know what Vince Lombardi meant. To get there is tough. To stay there is tougher."

"It's all so different from last season, when we were relaxed," said Hayes. "The pressure. The mental part. Everyone's after us. Defending this is the hardest thing I've ever done in my life."

Little did Hayes know then that it would only get harder.

About 36 hours after they finished off the Spurs, the Bullets found themselves entertaining the Sonics in Game One of the NBA Finals. No problem, the Bullets told themselves, and promptly secured a 99-97 win. They led by 18 points in the third quarter but attempted to get some much needed rest before the fat lady got around to her singing. Given a chance, the Sonics jumped back in the game. The score was tied in the last seconds of regulation when D.J. attempted to block Larry Wright's jumper. Whistles sounded, and Wright was awarded two free throws with no time on the clock.

He made both, but the Bullets had used up their quotient of luck and wins. It was about to become Dennis Johnson's series. Wilkens just knew it. "You know when I thought we had them?" he would say later. "When we came back from 18 points down in the third quarter in Game 1 in Washington. I never really worried after that."

The Sonics promptly shut down Dandridge and Hayes in the second half of Game 2 and seized the home-court advantage with a 92-82 win.

Game 3 was in the Kingdome, where 35,928 fans deafened the Bullets. The Sonics opened by double teaming the ball and ushered Washington into 30% shooting for the first quarter. At the other end, Seattle was red hot and opened a 13-point lead.

Things got even worse for the Bullets in the second period-they shot 20%. Seattle coasted to a 105-95 win and a 2-1 series lead as Gus Williams had 31 points. D.J. had 17 with 9 rebounds and 2 blocks. Inside, Sikma scored 21 and added 17 rebounds to the total.

With Washington's guards struggling, Motta had again tried moving Dandridge to the backcourt, just as he had during the 1978

Finals. But this time the move only left his players complaining. Grevey wanted plays run to get the guards open. Dandridge just wanted to get back to the frontcourt. "I can do whatever I want from the forward position," he said. "But out there I'm hampered."

Even in their disarray, the Bullets almost turned it around in Game 4. It was a night of whistles. In all, 59 fouls were called. The game went to overtime, and Washington eventually lost Hayes, Dandridge, and Unseld. Sikma sat down, too, after hitting the clutch free throws that sealed the win.

In the fourth quarter, the Bullets were down 7 when Charles Johnson finally found his range. Then Unseld, who would finish with 16 points and 16 rebounds, hit a final layup to send the game into overtime at 104-104. But the extra period belonged to the Sonics, specifically their guards. Gus Williams finished with 36 points and D.J. 32, while Sikma scored 20 with 17 rebounds and 5 blocks.

Grevey had one last chance to send it to a second overtime with three seconds left, but D.J. notched his fourth block of the night and it ended, 114-112, Seattle.

"I think the knockout punch was delivered tonight," Brown said afterward.

But the Bullets didn't seem to be reeling as Game 5 opened in Washington. Hayes scored a quick 20 points, and the Sonics trailed by 8 at the half. Washington maintained that lead through most of the third quarter, but as the period drew to a close the Sonics took off on a 12-0 run that put them up 72-69. Fred Brown took over down the stretch, hitting 4 of 5 shots in the final 13 minutes and Seattle clinched its first title, 97-93.

Johnson — who had played end-to-end the entire series-scoring, blocking shots, clogging the passing lanes, getting back on defense — was named the Finals MVP. He reacted by saying that he was just a "funny-looking black kid with red hair and freckles," that he was just doing what needed to be done. His teammates had worked just as hard as he had, Johnson said, and they looked just as funny.

Then he and running mate Gus Williams — the two of them had scored more than half of Seattle's points in the series — celebrated in the best Auerbachian tradition. They lit cigars and puffed proudly.

IV.
Prosperity

Ever since the NBA was formed in 1946, it had been trying to combine the most skilled competition in the world with the youthful charm and spirited exuberance of the college game. After more than three decades of failed attempts, the NBA finally succeeded in the fall of 1979.

That, of course, is when Bird and Magic arrived upon the scene. And in a sense, so did all of pro basketball. The entire sport soared to unimagined heights of popularity on the wings of their highflying personal competition.

Their college teams had met for the first time that spring in the 1979 NCAA championship game. Bird and Indiana State against Johnson and Michigan State. The resulting battle attracted the highest television ratings in the history of the Final Four.

They were merely college athletes, each of them relatively unknown before that season, yet their excitement was so strong it attracted the casual observer as well as the serious fan. Although major television networks have spent millions since then hyping and promoting the NCAA championship, the audience has never equalled that for the 1979 game.

"It was as if this massive national television audience had a sixth sense for history," TV

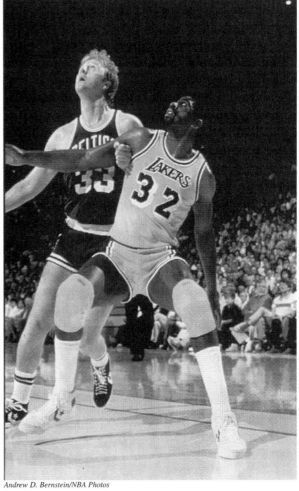

Andrew D. Bernstein/NBA Photos

Larry Bird and Magic Johnson took pro basketball to unimagined heights of popularity.

commentator Billy Packer said in amazement a decade afterward.

Within months of their college clash, these two dynamic players had moved on to the NBA as rookies and assumed leadership of two of the league's most storied franchises. In one short season, Larry and Magic virtually transformed the NBA into their personal one-on-one match, while millions of new fans followed the proceedings with fascination.

The pro game proved to be the superior showcase for the special talents of the two young superstars. Each and every facet of their competition and their personal abilities could be examined and analyzed. The chances for a fluke outcome were reduced over an 82-game schedule and the many best-of-seven playoff series.

The decade itself seemed to be one big series. Who could win the most championships? Magic's Lakers first won the title in 1980. Bird's Celtics followed in '81. Then Magic's Lakers again in '82 for a 2-1 lead. Larry and the boys in green came back in '84 to even it at 2-all. Then Magic and Los Angeles jumped up 3-2 with their stupendous victory over Boston in '85. Bird and company answered in '86 to make it 3-all. But Magic and Showtime stepped up and claimed the next two league titles to take that particular race of the 1980s, 5-3.

Of course, the real winners were the NBA and its fans. Larry and Magic lifted the league out of its 1970s doldrums. They helped renew interest in veteran stars such as Kareem and Dr. J. Even better, the Magic-Bird phenomenon spread the spotlight to a generation of dynamic young stars close on their heels. Isiah Thomas. Dominique Wilkins. James Worthy. Patrick Ewing. Charles Barkley. And most of all, Michael Jordan.

In 1984 David Stern became the NBA's commissioner and provided just the right mix of forwardlooking leadership and savvy marketing sense needed for the times. Under Stern's supervision, the NBA came up with an innovative labor agreement that sent the majority of the league's profits to the people who made it all possible-the players-while providing owners with a cap on escalating salaries. An effective, first-rate antidrug policy also was established, and record television contracts were negotiated. Those developments paved the way for expansion. Dallas had joined the NBA in 1980, making it a 23-team league. Under Stern's guidance, franchises were added in Charlotte and Miami for 1988, and in Minnesota and Orlando for 1989, spreading the competition among 27 healthy clubs.

This harmony and growth resulted in healthy profits for pro basketball, which in turn fueled speculation about future growth. The dawning of the 1990s brought an infusion of European talent into the league and the official clearing for NBA players to compete in the Olympic Games.

12.
Young Bucks
Rookies in Name Only

Almost from the start of their relationship, Larry Bird and Earvin "Magic" Johnson were basketball's Odd Couple. Although the media tended to describe them as "inextricably linked," Larry and Magic didn't cross paths that often or get to know each other very well back in the early days of their rivalry.

Magic was a precocious sophomore at Michigan State in 1979, an easygoing kid with dancing eyes and a quick smile. He got along with just about everybody and was open with reporters and fans alike.

Larry Bird rested somewhere toward the other end of the spectrum. He moved through his final year at Indiana State with a grim silence. He didn't trust reporters and seldom spoke with them or anyone else who was outside his immediate circle. The burden of carrying the Sycamores seemed to leave him sullen.

Only when his team reached the NCAA championship game in Salt Lake City did Bird loosen up a bit. "To me, it's a serious game," he said when asked about the difference between Magic and himself. "Now you wouldn't expect me to be havin' all kinds of fun when the score's tied, two seconds are left on the clock and the other guys have the ball. It's nice that Magic laughs a lot. I just hope he won't be laughing in my face after he makes a big play."

Actually, Magic was pretty good about keeping his game face affixed. Only after the Spartans had defeated Indiana State for the national championship did he allow himself a smile. Then he went home, got some rest, and began pondering his future. Should he turn professional? It was a big decision. His coaches and fans at Michigan State — even Jay Vincent, his childhood friend and college teammate-said he should stay in school.

Bird, on the other hand, already had his future set out for him. The Celtics had drafted him with the sixth pick of the first round the previous spring of 1978. As a fifth-year college player, Bird had been eligible for the draft, and Boston was willing to wait a year for his services. Red Auerbach and Bob Woolf, Bird's agent, dickered over the contract until finally agreeing on a $650,000-per-year deal, then the highest salary ever paid an NBA rookie.

"Now, I don't think I'm worth as much as Bird," Magic said facetiously that spring as he waited to make his decision. "But think of me in the NBA. One thing I'm always going to do is have fun. There is time for business, time for school and time for fun. You know, things can be happening at a party before I get there, but when I show up they just happen more."

Johnson decided to join Bird at the NBA party that fall of 1979, and just as he had predicted, things started happening. He made the rounds of the summer all-star games and rookie leagues, and everywhere he went, large crowds gathered. People were impressed with what they saw.

Still, both young players faced numerous questions about their abilities. In a sense, they both shattered stereotypes every time they played.

Larry Bird was white and raised in near poverty in a family torn apart by alcohol abuse. Earvin Johnson was black, the product of a stable middle-class home where both parents worked to provide their children with the advantages. As a player, Johnson was considered a fleet, supremely talented blue-chipper. In reality, he wasn't much of a jumper, possessed less than lightning speed, and had virtually no outside shot. But he had honed his skills with endless hours on the playgrounds. The product of his effort was a truly unique player, big enough to post low in the pivot but fluid enough to play point guard brilliantly.

Bird was considered slow and leadfooted, unable to jump. He even played that angle up a bit that fall of 1979. "I've never considered myself a super athlete," he told reporters. "I admit I'm not the quickest guy in the world. In fact, I'm slow. But I've always tried to make up for that in other ways. I block out and I follow up shots for rebounds. And if there's a loose ball on the floor, I'll be down there bumping heads."

In reality, Bird was a marvelously gifted athlete who had worked constantly to improve his natural ability.

However, he was not entirely healthy as he embarked on his pro career. Bird had shattered his right index finger catching a line drive in a softball game the spring of his senior year, which led to even more questions about his adjustment to the pros. He answered them by altering his shot to compensate for the injury, and although the injured digit was taped to his middle finger, he established a strong presence in training camp that fall.

His first real pro test came in Boston's opening 1979-80 exhibition game against the Philadelphia 76ers and Julius Erving. Shooting 7 of 15 from the field, Bird scored 18 points, but the Sixers won easily, 115-90. "I guess the best thing to say is that he can play," Erving commented afterward. "You can feel the intensity he has, the moves. He can create his own offense; he was talking all the time out there. I have a very favorable opinion of him as a player."

The same things, of course, were being said about Magic. Over the coming years, their careers would unfold with an almost eerie symmetry. They would continue to mirror each other's experiences and successes and failures. Eventually they would even come to be friends, mainly because they shared one very important trait — an incredible, sometimes overbearing drive to succeed.

To that end, both players used any and every possible edge they could find. Rather than be hindered by the stereotypes they faced, both had the smarts to turn them into powerful weapons and motivational tools.

"We're both the same," Johnson would later admit. "We'll do anything to win. You can list all the great players you want, but there are only a couple of winners."

That's how they defined themselves in the 1980s — as winners. Which isn't a bad bond for an odd couple.

1980

A sportswriter in high school first gave him the nickname.

Magic because of his beauty of a smile. Magic because of his uncanny ability with a basketball. But mostly he was Magic because he somehow transformed good teams into great ones.

He did that everywhere he played. At Everett High School in East Lansing, Michigan. At Michigan State. And finally with the Los Angeles Lakers.

"I'm asked a lot what was the greatest thing Earvin did," his coach at Michigan State, Jud Heathcote, said later. "Many say passing the ball, his great court sense, the fact that he could rebound. I say the greatest things

Earvin did were intangible. He always made the guys he played with better. In summer pickup games, Earvin would take three or four non-players, and he'd make those guys look so much better and they would win, not because he was making the baskets all by himself, but because he just made other players play better."

A 6'8", 220-pounder, Johnson came to Michigan State after leading Everett High to the state title in the spring of 1977.

"I'd heard about Magic at Everett High School," recalled Terry Donnelly, teammate at Michigan State, "and I'd even seen him play. But it didn't really hit me until I got in the backcourt with him, on the first day of practice. You're running down the floor and you're open and most people can't get the ball to you through two or three people, but all of a sudden the ball's in your hands and you've got a layup."

To his credit, Heathcote immediately recognized Magic's unique talent. Although the Michigan State program was short on big men, the coach didn't hesitate to run Johnson at the point. "I still remember the first game that Earvin played," Heathcote said. "We were playing Central Michigan. I think he had 7 points and about 8 turnovers, and everyone said, 'Heathcoate's crazy. He's got Earvin handling the ball, he's got him playing guard out there on offense, he's got him running the break, he's got him doing so many different things. Nobody can do all those things.' It's just that Earvin was nervous playing that first game and he didn't play like he played in practice. Actually, he was very comfortable in all those areas. When he went to the pros and right away they had him playing forward, I said sooner or later they'll realize that Earvin can play anywhere on defense and he has to have the ball on offense."

The Los Angeles Lakers needed many things in the fall of 1979. They needed rebounding help for Kareem in the frontcourt, and, as Heathcote projected, Magic filled in nicely as a power forward on the defensive end. The Lakers also needed help for Norm Nixon in the backcourt. And although Nixon was already a young, promising point guard, the Lakers eventually moved him to shooting guard, and — as Heathcote also projected — they gave Magic the ball at the point.

Perhaps the team's biggest need as it opened the 1980s was enthusiasm. No one player needed it more than Kareem, who had carried the Lakers for half a decade. During that time, the team had never reached the Finals, which meant the giant center was blamed for this shortcoming. The criticism had particularly stung when the Lakers were thumped by

Bird was drafted the previous spring by the Celtics

Seattle in the second round of the 1979 playoffs. "Is it fair?" Kareem replied when reporters asked about the situation. "Of course not. But I'm a target. Always have been. Too big to miss."

Abdul-Jabbar's response to the circumstances was to pull even deeper within his shell. His already cool approach to the game — and the hoopla surrounding it — became even cooler.

Magic, of course, changed all that.

"His enthusiasm was something out of this

Johnson decided to come out early and give the NBA a try.

world," said Jamaal Wilkes, then the Lakers' small forward, "something I had never seen prior to him and something I haven't seen since. It just kind of gave everyone a shot in the arm."

For the 20-year-old Magic, life was one big disco, a joyous journey from one party to another. All he had to do was pop on the

Norm Nixon moved to shooting guard when Magic took the point.

aplenty. But they couldn't dent Magic's boundless optimism.

First, there was the new coach. The Lakers had hired Jack Ramsay's veteran assistant Jack McKinney, a man enamored of the running game, to run the team. McKinney promptly set up an offense geared to Magic's abilities, and he acquired Jim Chones, the veteran forward, to help Kareem up front. It worked beautifully. They opened the season 9-4 and were primed to take off.

But then tragedy struck. McKinney suffered a serious head injury in a bicycle accident. He had been headed to a tennis match with his best friend and assistant coach, Paul Westhead. For a time, it appeared McKinney might not make it. At the very least, he was faced with months of convalescence. So Westhead, a Shakespearean scholar, served as interim coach, and the Lakers moved on.

They won, but they weren't entirely happy. Nixon made the adjustment to shooting guard well enough, but the veterans complained that Magic was controlling the ball too much, keeping it to himself. The coaches cautioned him as well, and eventually Magic changed.

"Magic had to learn to keep everybody in the game," said Nixon at the time. "He was losing 'em. He had to make an effort, and he did. I like playing with him much more now. We complement one another."

His presence certainly was good for Kareem. The Lakers center won the league's MVP Award for an unprecedented sixth time. (Russell had won five.) "When you paint a picture," Westhead said of Abdul-Jabbar, "the sunshine goes in first, then you fill in the trees

headphones, snap his fingers, and smile. The team eventually took to calling him "Young Buck" (later shortened to Buck) for his contagious zeal. When Kareem won their opening game at San Diego with a last-minute skyhook, Magic smothered him in a youthful celebratory hug. The big center was visibly startled. Take it easy, kid, he said. We've got 81 more of these to play.

"Everybody was shocked," Magic recalled, "but I was used to showing my emotions."

Reality did set in for the Lakers shortly thereafter. In fact, there were problems

206

and the flowers." Abdul-Jabbar was shining more than ever in the Lakers' universe, the coach said. As a result, Los Angeles finished as the top team in the Western Conference with a 60-22 record.

Only Bird's Celtics bettered that with a 61-21 finish. The young forward had averaged 21.5 points in leading his team to what was then the best turnaround in league history. The year before Bird arrived, Boston had finished 29-53. That upswing of 32 games resulted in Bird being named Rookie of the Year.

That, in turn, injected high octane into Magic's competitive carburetor. During the regular season he had averaged 17.6 points, 7.7 rebounds, and 7.3 assists while shooting 52% from the floor. Eager to prove his superiority as a player, he upped those numbers during his 16 playoff games that spring of 1980 to 18.3 points, 10.5 rebounds, and 9.4 assists.

With the team in synch and Kareem playing his best ball in years, the Lakers ditched Phoenix and defending champion Seattle on their way to the Western Conference championship and the Finals.

Bird's Celtics, meanwhile, had run aground against Julius Erving and the Philadelphia 76ers in the Eastern Conference finals and lost 4-1. The much-anticipated matchup between Bird and Johnson in an NBA Finals would have to wait.

The Sixers, now coached by Billy Cunningham, had finished 59-23, just two games behind Boston during the regular season. They brought a strong, veteran lineup to face the Lakers for the 1980 title, with Erving still near the top of his high-flying game. "I don't think about my dunk shots," he said during the Boston series. "I just make sure I have a place to land."

The 6'11" Darryl Dawkins joined 7'1" Caldwell Jones in the frontcourt, and both players had matured since their 1977 Finals debacle against Portland. The sixth man was Bobby Jones, who besides being the defensive forward in basketball was an extraordinary leaper and excellent at filling the lane on the fastbreak. He gave them 13 points per game off the bench. If that wasn't enough in the frontcourt, the Sixers also got good minutes and 11.6 points from veteran Steve Mix.

Running the break for Philly was an excellent young point guard, Maurice Cheeks, and they still had Henry Bibby as a third guard. In February, the Sixers had acquired shooter extraordinaire Lionel Hollins from Portland in exchange for a draft pick. Hollins filled in nicely for veteran Doug Collins, who had suffered a knee injury.

Bird and Magic continued to mirror each other's experiences and successes and failures. Eventually they would even come to be friends, mainly because they shared one very important trait — an incredible, sometimes overbearing drive to succeed.

The matchup at center pitting Caldwell Jones and Dawkins against Abdul-Jabbar was particularly intriguing. The Lakers' center claimed the first round for himself and his team with 33 points, 14 rebounds, 6 blocks, and 5 assists on the way to a 109-102 win in the Forum. For the first time in years, though, Kareem didn't have to go it alone for Los Angeles. Nixon had 23 points and Wilkes finished with 20 while the Lakers did an excellent double-teaming job on Erving. "Every time I caught the ball I had two people on me." the Philly star said afterward.

Magic, too, lived up to his game with 16 points, 9 assists, and 10 rebounds. More and more in the playoffs, Westhead went to Magic as the power forward on offense, while Nixon and sixth man Michael Cooper ran the backcourt.

"That's our best lineup," the coach had said earlier in the playoffs.

Dawkins had opened the game with a tremendous Chocolate Thunder dunk, but the Sixers center finished with only 12 points, 3 rebounds, and a passel of offensive fouls and turnovers.

"I ain't afraid to go to the hoop on Kareem," Dawkins allowed afterward. "But when the refs are callin' 'em that way, it's a waste of time. I lost my funk."

He regained it nicely for Game 2 after Cunningham decided Dawkins didn't need the assignment of guarding Kareem. That went to Caldwell Jones, the team's frontcourt defensive specialist.

Nothing seemed to work for Los Angeles in Game 2. Even with Jones's defense, Kareem still got 38 points. But Philly's team effort was impressive. They virtually shut down the vaunted Laker fast break and did it without fouling.

Erving scored 12 points in the first quarter, beginning the game with a dunk over Kareem. Dawkins stepped outside to hit several jumpers on his way to 25 points. And Cheeks matched Erving's game total of 23 while Bobby Jones provided his usual 13 off the bench.

Philly had led by as much as 20 in the fourth period, but the Lakers roared back, trimming the lead to 105-104 late in the game. Then Bobby Jones popped in a jumper with 7 seconds left, and that was enough for 107-104 Philly win that tied the series at 1-all.

Los Angeles quickly relieved the Sixers of the home-court advantage. For Game Three, it was the Lakers with the defensive switch, moving Chones to cover Dawkins. With only the nonshooting Caldwell Jones to worry about, Kareem parked his big frame in the lane and dared the Sixers to drive in. Meanwhile, Westhead switched Magic to

covering Hollins on the perimeter, which stifled Philly's outside game. The result of this double shutdown was a 15-point Laker lead in the first quarter.

Erving, however, took charge in the second period with an array of shots that included a dunk, a scoop, and a finger roll. The Lakers called time, talked things over, and finished the period by surrendering only one more dunk to the Doctor. Over the last 2 minutes of the period, Los Angeles went on a 9-0 run that upped their lead back up to 14 at the half.

From there, Kareem and Company powered to a 111-101 win and a 2-1 lead in the series. The Lakers' big guy had again put up big numbers: 33 points, 14 rebounds, 4 blocks, and 3 assists. And once again he got plenty of help from Nixon, Johnson, and Wilkes.

As expected, Philly lashed back for Game 4, aided by the officials. In the game's first minute, Los Angeles was hit with an illegal defense warning.

The lead switched back and forth throughout the first three periods, but the Sixers took control in the fourth. That was when the Doctor unleashed one of his fines highlight moves. Off the dribble, he scooted

Paul Westhead took over as the Laker's head coach.

around Laker reserve Mark Landsberger on the right baseline to launch himself toward the basket. In midair, Erving encountered Abdul-Jabbar. Somehow, the Doctor moved behind the backboard and wrapped his right arm behind Kareem to flip it in. It was pure magic, the Philly variety, and the Sixers went on to even the series with a 105-102 win. Dawkins led them with 26 points, and Erving had 23.

That was enough to buy time for Adbul-Jabbar, who limped back into the game early in the fourth period. His appearance aroused the Forum regulars, and, despite the bad ankle, he acknowledged their support by scoring 14 points down the stretch. With the game tied at 103 and only 33 seconds left, Kareem scored, drew the foul, and finished Philly by completing the three-point play. Los Angeles won, 108-103, and took a 3-2 series lead.

The next morning the Lakers arrived at Los Angeles International Airport for their flight to Philly and learned that Kareem wouldn't be making the trip. His ankle was so bad that doctors had advised him to stay home and try to get ready for Game 7.

Westhead was worried about the effect the news would have on the team. In a private meeting, the coach told Magic he would have to move to center. No problem, the young guard replied. He had played center in high school and loved challenges such as the one he was about to face.

When the team boarded its flight to Philadelphia, Magic plopped himself down in the first-class seat always set aside for Abdul-Jabbar. Then he went through Kareem's normal routine, stretching out in the seat and pulling a blanket over his head. This done, Magic looked back at his coach and winked.

"Never fear," he told his teammates. "E.J. is here."

Somehow the folks in Philly never really believed the Lakers would head into the game without their captain. Radio stations reported regular sightings of Kareem at the airport. One taxi driver even claimed to have taken the L.A. center to his hotel.

Cunningham was just as distrusting as the man on the street. "I'll believe he's not coming when the game ends and I haven't seen him," the coach told the writers.

The Lakers, meanwhile, were almost too loose, Westhead feared. Magic was unchanged — about the only thing that punctured his mood were reporters' questions about his thoughts for Game 7. It was perfect, he told his teammates later. Nobody expects us to win here. In reality, most of the Lakers figured they didn't have a chance.

Jim Chones moved over to cover Dawkins for Game 3.

But when they arrived at the Spectrum that Friday, May 16, they were greeted by the sounds of carpenters hammering out an awards presentation platform. The NBA required that Philadelphia provide some facility to present the trophy, just in case Los Angeles happened to win.

"It should be interesting," Westhead told his players before the game. "Pure democracy. We'll go with the slim line." Which meant Magic, Chones, and Wilkes in the frontcourt while Nixon and Cooper took care of things up top. Kareem, who was sprawled on his bed back at his Bel-Air home, sent a last-minute message.

Go for it.

With that last blast of confidence pushing them sky high, the Lakers took the floor. Magic grinned broadly as he stepped up to jump center against Dawkins. The Sixers seemed hesitant. Los Angeles went up 7-0, then 11-4. Finally Philly broke back in the second quarter and took a 52-44 lead. Westhead stopped play and told his men to collapse more in the middle, because Nix had come off the bench to knife inside for 16 points. The Lakers listened and closed to a 60-60 at the half.

They opened the third period with a 14-0 run, keyed by Wilkes, who had 16 points in the quarter. But the Sixers drew close again in the fourth period.

Back home in Bel-Air, Kareem was twisting and turning and going crazy as he watched the televised game from his bed. Finally, late in the last period, he got up and hobbled out to his back yard to let out a scream.

With a little over 5 minutes left, it was 103-101 Lakers. Westhead called time again and made one last attempt to charge up his tired players. They responded with a furious run over the next 76 seconds to go up by 7. Then Magic scored 9 points down the stretch to end it. Final score: 123-107, Lakers.

Throughout the roster, the Lakers had something to celebrate. Wilkes had a career-best outing, scoring 37 points with 10 rebounds. And Chones lived up to his vow to shut down the middle. He finished with 11 points and 10 rebounds, and held Dawkins to another Chocolate Blunder game — 14 points and 4 rebounds. Cooper scored 16 points, and Landsberger contributed 10 rebounds.

But the big news, of course, was Magic, who simply was that. He scored 42 points, including all 14 of his freethrow attempts. He had 15 rebounds, 7 assists, 3 steals, and a block.

"It was amazing, just amazing," said Erving, who led Philly with 27.

"Magic was outstanding. Unreal," agreed the injured Collins, who had watched from the sideline. "I knew he was good, but I never realized he was great."

He was the hands-down choice as series MVP. "What position did I play?" Magic responded to reporters afterward. "Well, I played center, a little forward, some guard. I tried to think up a name for it, but the best I could come up with was CFG-Rover."

How had they done it without their center? Magic was asked. "Without Kareem," he said, "we couldn't play the halfcourt and think defensively. We had to play the full court and take our chances."

Then, in the post-game interview on national television, Magic turned to the camera and addressed Kareem back home. "We know you're hurtin', Big Fella," he said. "But we want you to get up and do a little dancin' tonight."

The Lakers celebrated all the way back to Los Angeles, where Kareem and a cast of thousands greeted them at the airport. There were hugs and cheers and high fives all around.

E.J. the deejay had delivered. He and the Lakers had just gone one-up on Bird and the Celtics in the race for the rings. The competition, though, was just getting started.

1981

The loss to Philadelphia in the 1980 playoffs had taught the Boston Celtics one clear lesson — they had to get bigger. They couldn't battle the Sixers' twin towers of Darryl Dawkins and Caldwell Jones with a front line that ran no taller than 6'9".

So Red Auerbach went shopping in the spring of 1980. Which meant it was time for the rest of the league's franchises to secure their billfolds and make sure they avoided public places. Pro basketball's biggest pickpocket was afoot. Actually, Red had already pulled a smooth one on the Detroit

Kevin McHale joined the Celtics in 1980.

Pistons and their coach, Dick Vitale. In 1979 Auerbach had been eager to get rid of Bob McAdoo, the prolific scorer who hadn't fit into the Celtics system. Vitale was just as eager to get such a player, so the Pistons agreed to make a deal.

Earlier, the Celtics had signed Detroit's M.L. Carr as a restricted free agent, and as a result they owed the Pistons compensation. Accordingly, Auerbach offered to "give up" McAdoo for Detroit's two first-round draft picks in 1980. For some reason Detroit agreed.

Then the Pistons sweetened the deal by finishing a dreadful last in the NBA for 1980, meaning the Celtics had the number-one pick to go with the 13th selection. Auerbach wanted Kevin McHale, a smooth power forward out of the University of Minnesota, but he and Coach Bill Fitch also wanted veteran center Robert Parish, whom the Golden State Warriors were shopping around the league.

The Warriors, who picked third, wanted to draft Joe Barry Carroll out of Purdue and figured they would need the top pick to get him. So Auerbach traded Boston's two picks to Golden State for Parish and the number-three pick in the draft. As a result, Auerbach and Fitch got the frontcourt of the '80s-Parish at center and McHale at power forward joining Bird at the other forward spot. The Warriors, meanwhile, drafted Carroll first and Rickey Brown thirteenth. The deal was branded the most lopsided trade ever by 19 NBA general managers in a 1989 poll by *The Sporting News.*

"Red has done it again," Fitch declared during a draft-day press conference.

That he had. But Auerbach's wheeling and dealing didn't leave the team trouble-free. McHale couldn't come to terms on his contract and threatened to play in Italy. Veteran point guard Nate "Tiny" Archibald also was disgruntled and held out until a week before the season began. That, in effect, may have saved his career. Fitch ran a brutal conditioning regimen in his training camps, and his 1980 version thinned the Celtics' ranks considerably. First, veteran Pete Maravich packed up without notice and left camp. Starting center Dave Cowens finished the camp but decided he had little enthusiasm left to take into the season. He stepped on the team bus during an exhibition road trip to Indiana and announced his retirement.

The camp had been nearly as rough on the 7'1" Parish. "We had always played our way into shape at Golden State," he told the press that fall. "I don't know if I'll make it." He made it, but not without an abiding dislike for the autocratic Fitch. The coach held a master's

Robert Parish came to Boston from Golden State.

degree in educational psychology and was sometimes accused of overcomplicating his relationships with players. With backup center Rick Robey troubled by injuries and Cowens fading fast, Fitch had pushed Parish hard.

As these factors developed, the Boston season appeared headed toward a personnel disaster. Also disgruntled over his contract was Cedric "Cornbread" Maxwell, the team's first-round pick in 1977. He had developed into a powerful frontcourt player, with defensive ability to match his post moves on offense. He had adjusted well to Bird's presence, and the two liked playing together. But Maxwell also got a late start that fall while waiting for the team to come up with more money.

Even after Archibald and Maxwell began playing, McHale stayed out until the Celtics finally worked out an agreement with his agent. As it was, all three key players came in late, and the team got off to a slow start.

Fitch decided to start backup point guard Gerald Henderson, a minor-league refugee,

M.L. Carr was another new addition to the Celtics' roster.

and M.L. Carr in the backcourt to open the season. The starting guards from the previous year, Archibald and Chris Ford, came off the bench. This helped build Henderson's confidence, but the arrangement only lasted a few games. With the team struggling, Fitch switched back to Archibald and Ford.

The 6'1" Archibald, in particular, was important to the team. A New Yorker, his instincts had been honed on a Bronx playground. He had attended Texas-El Paso, and after that was drafted by the Kansas City Kings, where he was groomed and coached by Bob Cousy. He adopted much of the former Boston great's freewheeling approach to the game. In 1972-73, Archibald had led the league in scoring (34 points per game) and assists (11 per game). But that was followed by a season with a broken foot, another season with a ruptured Achilles tendon, and then time with the Nets and Buffalo Braves. His career

was on the skids by the time he arrived in Boston, and he wasn't a favorite of then player/coach Cowens. To get through the hard times, he talked frequently with Cousy, recalled Archibald. "Cooz would tell me, 'Don't get down, Tiny. These are the Celtics. Things will get better.' Well, the man was right."

Archibald pulled his game together and pleased Fitch with his play. For 1979-80, he had averaged roughly 14 points and 8 assists on a club that badly needed help in the backcourt. When he was finally offered a contract that confirmed how highly the team thought of him, no one was happier than Bird.

"There is nobody better than Tiny," he told the writers.

Ford filled in nicely enough at off guard. The league had just adopted the three-point shot, and Ford acquired the distinction of making the first trey in league history. He, like Carr, had come from Detroit, where he had been described as smart and a hard worker-another way of saying he didn't have much talent. But he fit in well in Boston.

For Fitch, ideal basketball was a motion offense that wound its way toward setting up an inside bucket. He stressed passing and disciplined patterns of play. Having been an excellent college coach at North Dakota, he liked hard workers who accepted their roles. Which is exactly how Ford approached the game.

So did Henderson. And Carr was another in the same mold. In fact, he more than any player came to epitomize the Celtic ideal of team first, strong defense, and heady play. With Cowens' departure, Bird assumed the silent leadership of the team, but it was Carr who supplied the spirit.

The frontcourt, in time, came together. Maxwell was at the height of his career, and

McHale quickly showed an ability to score and block shots. He was happy enough to come off the bench, at least for the time being. Parish, too, survived training camp and began to do all the things that had caught Fitch's attention in the first place. He played with pride and grace. He ran the floor and shot his startlingly accurate rainbow jumper, which he had acquired in high school in Shreveport, Louisiana, when his coach made him shoot over an extended broom.

Out of the gate, this group struggled to a 7-5 record, and Bird placed the blame on himself. "Max isn't scoring enough," he said, "and it's my fault, because I should be getting the ball to him. I know how to do it, and I haven't been doing it."

Like Magic with the Lakers, Bird's passing sustained the Celtics. And Bird, too, had to learn to keep his teammates involved. That facet of his game improved greatly as the season progressed, and the Celtics grew into an inspiring example of precise ball movement. From their fast breaks to their half-court game, they developed a knack for finding the open man.

Their main competition in the Eastern Conference again was the Philadelphia 76ers, who had added an impressive rookie in Andrew Toney, an off guard who could go on torrid shooting streaks. The regular-season crown came down to a final meeting between the two teams at Boston Garden, which the Celtics won, 98-94, behind Bird's 24 points. Archibald hit two free throws at the end to get the win, which tied Boston and Philly at 62 wins apiece. The teams had split their series, 3-3, but Boston got the homecourt advantage in the playoffs with a better conference record.

After a first-round bye, Boston blew past Chicago in the second round, setting up another meeting with Philadelphia in the Eastern finals. The Celtics felt confident and ready. They lost their first game at home, captured the second, and lost two more in Philadelphia. Suddenly, they had fallen behind 3-1 and were facing a repeat of 1980, when the Sixers had easily moved them aside

4-1.

Fitch told them he had been associated with only one team that had ever come back from a 3-1 deficit, but he felt this team could do it. "I'm telling you, it was the most rewarding experience a group of guys can have in this sport," he said. "We can do it."

Nevertheless, they trailed 59-49 at halftime of the fifth game in the Garden. In the locker room, Fitch made one more appeal, this time a shouting one. He said he didn't mind losing but he did mind seeing them play passively. They worked hard over the next two quarters but made little progress.

With 1:51 to go, the Sixers led by 6 and Boston's season seemed over. Fitch called a timeout and set up a shot for Parish, but Darryl Dawkins stole Bird's inbounds pass, further darkening the future. But Maxwell blocked Andrew Toney's shot and Archibald took the loose ball to the other end, where he

Larry Bird

scored and drew the foul for a 3-point play. Like that, the lead was cut to 109-106.

The Sixers tried to inbound the ball, but Boston's swarming defense was so thick they were forced to call two timeouts. When they finally did make the pass, Bird stole it and scored, cutting the lead to one. Then Carr got another steal and drew a foul. He hit both shots to give Boston the lead, 110-109. Bobby Jones put up a shot for Philly, but Parish hampered it. Carr rebounded and was fouled again. On Fitch's instructions, he made the first and missed the next two (the league rule of three free throw attempts to make two was still in effect) on the notion that time would run out and Philly wouldn't be able to score.

However, one second remained, and Philly had one last chance. Fortunately, the pass was off and Boston survived, 111-109. Auerbach, however, was infuriated. He and Fitch exchanged heated words afterward in the locker room, and Auerbach stormed out. The Celtics didn't have much reason to celebrate anyway. They trailed 3-2 and were headed to the Spectrum for Game 6. Boston hadn't won in Philly in the 11 games they had played there during Bird's pro career.

Their failure seemed a sure bet in the first half, as the Sixers went up by 12. In the second half, Maxwell got involved in a brouhaha with the Philly fans under one of the baskets. The Boston bench came to his aid, and when play was resumed Maxwell went wild, playing like a man possessed. Late

in the game, Boston had the ball and the lead, 96-95, when Bird took a 20-footer as the shot clock ran down. The ball hit the rim, rose up, and fell back through to make it 98-95. Toney raced back upcourt with the ball and stopped in the lane, but McHale blocked his jumper. Moments later, Maxwell hit two free throws to keep Boston alive for yet another game, 100-98.

There was no way the Celtics figured to lose Game 7 back in the Garden, only somebody forgot to notify the Sixers. Philly led by 11 in the second half and was still up, 89-83, with 4:34 on the game clock. The Celtics scrambled back to tie it at 89, and seconds later Bird came up with a loose ball. He rushed upcourt, looked off to his right, then fired up an 18-foot bank shot. Good. That was enough. Philly added a

Top row standing from L to R: Asst. Coach K.C. Jones, Wayne Kreklow, M.L. Carr, Rick Robey, Robert Parish, Kevin McHale, Eric Fernsten, Gerald Henderson, Asst. Coach Jimmy Rodgers, Trainer Ray Melchiorre.
Bottom row from L to R: Chris Ford, Cedric Maxwell, President and General Manager Red Auerbach, Head Coach Bill Fitch, Chairman of the Board Harry Mangurian, Larry Bird, Nate Archibald.

free throw, but the boys in green held on, 91-90, for another tremendous comeback.

"There was no one else in the world I wanted to have the ball but me," Bird said of his last shot. With it, he had sent his team to the Finals.

Out west, Magic and the Lakers had fallen on hard times. He had suffered a cartilage tear in his knee during the season, then struggled back from surgery to rejoin his team late in the schedule. But they never had time to jell. Instead, they lost 2-1 to Moses Malone and the Houston Rockets in the opening round. Houston had finished a mediocre 40-42 in the regular season after spending most of the year trying to be a running team. But a late-season loss to Boston convinced coach Del Harris that he needed to slow it down and cater to Malone's pace. After dumping the Lakers, the Rockets battled San Antonio through a seven-game semifinal series. From there, they trashed Kansas City in the Western finals, 4-1.

The Rockets' backcourt featured Mike Dunleavy, Calvin Murphy, and Allen Leavell. Robert Reid was a smooth swing player, while Rudy Tomjanovich and Billy Paultz helped Malone up front.

No one figured it to be much of a Finals. Houston, in fact, had lost their previous dozen games to the Celtics. But Malone, who had averaged nearly 28 points and 15 rebounds over the season, would have none of it. He came into the series fired up. The Celtics were chumps, he informed the press.

Game One in the Garden was surprisingly tight. Houston led 57-51 at the half and kept that intensity through the game. Late in the fourth period, with Boston struggling, Bird came upcourt and put up an 18-footer from the right side. As soon as he turned it loose, he knew it was bad and immediately rushed in for the rebound. He caught the ball in mid-air as his momentum was carrying him out beyond the baseline. In an instant, he switched the ball to his left hand (a right-handed shot would have hit the side of the backboard) and swished a 12-footer. The crowd went nuts, with Auerbach leading the cheers. Bill Russell, who was broadcasting the game for CBS, looked on in disbelief. "Larry was able to make the play," said Russell, "because he not only knew where the ball was going to land-he knew that he knew."

The shot carried Boston to a 98-95 win and left Auerbach puffing another cigar. "It was the one best shot I've ever seen a player make," he claimed.

Danny Ainge (pictured) and Dennis Johnson gave Boston a strong backcourt.

"Bird sort of flipped it," said Houston's Robert Reid. "What can you say about a play like that?"

After playing on emotion for four straight games, Boston came out flat for Game 2. Fitch was so infuriated he put his fist through a blackboard in the locker room at halftime. That did little good, though. Houston's precision and Malone's inside play. and rebounding kept the game close. Then the Rockets stole it at the end, 91-90.

"Sometimes a slap in the face wakes you up," said Carr.

They responded with a stifling defense and a 94-71 blowout of the Rockets in the Summit. Maxwell did much of the work for Boston, as Bird was held to just 8 points. Late in the game, he and Reid got into a little fracas, which seemed to be more a result of Bird's frustrations than anything else.

Harris tightened things up in Game 4 by using just six players. Bird was again held to just eight points, while Malone ruled the inside. Houston got a lead, then held on for a 91-86 win that evened the series. Afterward, Malone had plenty to say. He told the media he could get four guys off the streets of Petersburg, Virginia, his hometown, and beat the Celtics. "I don't think they're all that good," he said. "I don't think they can stop us from doing what we want to do."

It seemed to be just the emotional spark the Celtics were looking for. "The man threw down a challenge," Maxwell replied, "and this is a team that responds well to challenges."

In Game 5, Robert Reid continued his defensive domination of Bird, holding him to 12 points. The Boston forward was averaging nearly 16 rebounds and 8 assists during the series, but his shooting was nothing short of frosty. Not to worry; the rest of the Celtics, particularly Maxwell, took care of business. They won at home, 109-80, to take a 3-2 lead.

"The Celtics are still chumps," insisted Malone afterward.

The series returned to Houston that Thursday night, May 14, and Bird broke out of his slump. Boston had a 6-point lead at the half and kept it down the stretch. When Houston pulled close late in the fourth, Bird came downcourt and laced in his only 3-pointer of the series, which sent Boston on to a 102-91 win and the team's fourteenth championship.

Afterward, in the locker room, Bird stole Auerbach's lit cigar and puffed impishly.

"We're the champions," he said as he broke into a coughing spell.

"He's just one of a kind," said Fitch.

Or maybe one of a pair. The other half of the odd couple was waiting in Los Angeles for another chance at the ring.

13.
The Stylish Show

Sixers vs. Showtime

When the Los Angeles Lakers met the Philadelphia 76ers in the NBA Finals in 1982 and 1983, it wasn't so much a clash as it was a mixing of styles.

These were two elegant basketball teams that shared several common properties, most prominent the sense of embarrassment they had suffered in the 1981 playoffs. The Lakers had fallen to Houston in the first round, and the Sixers had collapsed in the Eastern finals after leading the Boston Celtics 3-1.

Coach Pat Riley of the Lakers acknowledged this common embarrassment as the 1982 Finals opened. "When I looked at the entire playoff picture," he said, "I thought the two teams most committed to winning this year would be the two teams that were stung and humiliated last year. Philadelphia, I felt, was the best team last year, but they gave it away. That was the ultimate slap in the face. Then there was our humiliating loss, and our players remember that pain. Maturity makes the veterans ask, 'How many more times are we going to have the chance to win it with Kareem or with Doc?' I see that with this team, and it could be a tremendous motivating force. They talk about it constantly."

The next two years proved Riley's intuition correct. Los Angeles broke loose in the '82 playoffs, sweeping 9 straight playoff games before finally closing out the championship with a record-tying 12 wins against only 2 losses. The next season, Philly bettered that, ripping off 12 wins while suffering only a single loss on their way to the title.

Each team wanted badly to dominate. After all, time was running down on their opportunity for immortality. For Philly, there was the Doctor, Julius Erving, a poetic player if there ever was one, with his acrobatic moves to the basket his twirling dunks, and his eloquent, diplomatic manner. But he was thirty-two as the 1982 playoffs opened, and he was making his third trip to the Finals since coming to the NBA in 1976. Each time the Sixers failed, they had to fight the public perception that they were wasting Erving's bountiful talent.

Kareem, too, was thinking about age. He had turned thirty-five during the season, and with each successive year speculation had increased about his impending retirement. It helped, of course, that he now played with the twenty-two-year-old Magic — if not a fountain of youth, certainly a spring of enthusiasm. In 1982, no one would have believed that Magic's presence could keep the great Laker center playing another seven years. By no means would those seasons be easy or uncomplicated. Still, they would be fruitful, bringing the

Lakers three more titles. And if that didn't keep Abdul-Jabbar young, it at least made him ageless.

1982

Maybe there has been an NBA team that has survived as much controversy as the 1982 Los Angeles Lakers and then gone on to win an NBA championship.

But it's doubtful.

The list of their troubles is long and substantial:

• During the 1981 playoffs, Magic and Norm Nixon had engaged in a much-publicized debate through the media, thus damaging their once-close relationship;

• Just weeks before training camp opened, forward Jamaal Wilkes lost a second infant daughter, this time to crib death (his first daughter had died of heart disease);

• In mid November, Magic, who felt Coach Paul Westhead's offense was stifling the team's creativity, asked to be traded;

• The text day, team owner Jerry Buss fired Westhead, who had just directed the team through a five-game winning streak;

• The team was then caught in confusion over the Westhead's successor. Buss had badly wanted Jerry West, then a personnel consultant to the team, to return to the bench. West vehemently declined and instead offered to help thirty-six-year-old assistant coach Pat Riley adjust as head coach;

• In the Lakers' next home game, Magic was stung by a chorus of boos from the Forum crowd. For months afterward, he would hear extensive booing on road trips;

• The ensuing weeks brought round after round of condemnation from editorialists across the country who labeled Buss a meddlesome owner and Magic a spoiled, overpaid crybaby (Magic's new $25-million, 25-year contract was cited as part of the problem);

• In December, power forward Mitch Kupchak, whom the Lakers had acquired as a free agent for a bundle of cash, blew out his knee in a game at San Diego and was lost for the season;

• Just days after Kupchak went down, Abdul-Jabbar suffered a severe ankle sprain.

The injuries left the Lakers undermanned in the frontcourt. Faced with this adversity, the team responded by going on a short winning streak, much of it the result of gutty performances from Earvin Johnson. But it was clear that emotion could only carry them so far. Even when Kareem returned they would face the same dearth of rebounding.

But then help arrived in two very unexpected forms. First came the acquisition of thirty-year-old free agent Bob McAdoo, the same McAdoo who was disdained in Boston and considered a selfish problem in Detroit despite a league MVP award and three scoring titles under his belt. Few people figured he would fit in with the Lakers, but he showed a remarkable willingness to play off the bench. Even better, he was good at it, giving the team just the scoring punch it needed at key times.

The other unexpected assist came with the emergence of power forward Kurt Rambis, the Clark Kent look alike and free agent who reluctantly signed with the Lakers only after management assured him he had a solid shot at making the team. Not long after Kupchak went down, Rambis got an unexpected start and responded with 14 rebounds. True, he couldn't shoot and displayed a noticeable lack of athletic grace. But the Lakers had enough of those properties. They needed his hustle, his defense, his rebounding, and his physical play. Combined with the other Showtime elements and Kareem's return, McAdoo and Rambis would became major factors in the team's playoff success.

But before that happened, there was more rough terrain to cross. The Lakers struggled through a couple of short losing streaks in January, and Riley seemed a bit lost. The son of a minor-league baseball manager, he had starred in football, basketball, and baseball in high school in Schenectady, New York. Bear Bryant had wanted him as a quarterback for the University of Alabama, but Riley decided to play basketball for Adolph Rupp at the University of Kentucky. There, he had been an All-American forward in the 1960s and had starred on Rupp's last Final Four team in 1965. He was a first round draft pick of the San Diego Rockets, but in the pros, his transition to guard was difficult. He spent most of his seven-year career as a reserve, although he was a solid contributor on the Lakers 1972 championship team. After his playing days he wound up serving as the color analyst on Laker radio broadcasts with Chick Hearn. Riley was working that spot in the fall of 1979 when Westhead asked him to be an assistant coach. Riley had jumped at the chance and remained loyal to Westhead, even after the firing.

"I was numb," Riley said. "I thought the firing was horrible."

Although confused, he agreed to take the head job, and he agreed to make the wide-open, full-speed game the team's top option, which meant that Magic was happy again. But that still didn't translate into immediate success. Between January and March, the Lakers barely played .500 ball.

"Don't be afraid to coach the team," Buss finally told Riley in one meeting. Riley listened and took the advice to heart. He began to assert himself. When the team lost at home to Chicago on March 12, he flashed his anger. "I got fed up," he said. "I didn't know what I wanted to do when I took the job. I gave them too much trust. I said, 'This is their team.' It was their team, but they needed direction. That's my job. It took me three months to realize it, but I have certain responsibilities to push and demand. They have to play. I have to coach. They were waiting for me to put my foot down. That's my nature, anyhow."

He put his foot down, and no one shouted. In fact, the players seemed relieved. Despite their struggles, they finished the regular season with a best-in-the-West 57-25 record. More importantly, they were peaking as the playoffs opened. After March 31, they won 21 of their final 24 games. Suddenly Buss raised his eyebrows. The coach he hadn't particularly wanted was getting the job done.

Dawkins was a force in the middle.

Much of the success, of course, was due to Magic, who fought through the distracting boos by concentrating on his game. "The crowds still get me going," Magic said toward the end of the regular schedule. "They still jack me up. And I still love the game. I don't think I'll ever lose that."

219

"Magic has become a great player," said West. "I've watched him go from one level to another, higher level this year. He's become solid, that's the big thing. He's in control out there. He knows what he's doing every minute he's on the floor. He's had a great, great season, especially under the circumstances."

The Eastern Conference, meanwhile, had evolved into another Philadelphia Boston battle. Once again the Celtics led the league with a 63-19 record, and once again they fell behind to the Sixers 3-1 in the Eastern finals. And once again they came back to tie it at 3-all with a gutty win in Philadelphia. As with the previous year, the seventh game was in Boston, so Philadelphia's fans were prepared for other latespring entertainment.

This time, though, there was no folding act. In the Garden, Doc and Company overwhelmed the Celtics, 120-106, the Boston fans sending them off to the Finals with chants of "Beat L.A.! Beat L.A.!"

The Lakers watched this drama on the tube, having dispatched Phoenix and San Antonio by identical 4-0 scores. Their last game against the Spurs ended a full twelve days before Philly finished off Boston. Rather than get rusty, they had worked two-a-day practices and battled each other to pass the time.

"That's the best thing about this team," said Riley, "the work ethic."

The second-best was their nifty zone trap. They produced it at just the right time in the Finals opener at the Spectrum on Thursday, May 27. Fresh from the battle of Boston, the Sixers worked their offense to precision until midway through the third period. At the time, Philadelphia led by 15. Then, over the next 11 minutes or so, the Lakers ripped through a 40-9 blitz. The bewildered Sixers fell, 124-117, and just that quickly the Lakers had snatched away the home-court advantage.

In the post-game autopsies, Sixers coach Billy Cunningham called it both ways. He said the zone trap wasn't hurting his team all that much. Then he called it an obviously illegal zone.

So Riley decided to back off the trap a bit. "The officials read the papers, too," he explained. Instead, he switched Magic to cover Erving on defense.

"Magic on Doc seemed like an ideal matchup to me," offered Riley. "Dr. J is a great offensive rebounder. He'd hurt us real bad. Defensive rebounding is Magic's strength. So we put him in the position we wanted him to be in. It was great to watch. No pushing, no shoving, no hammering. They played with their talents. Magic played him as honestly as he could play him. Two great players going against each other."

"I've always been his fan," Johnson said of the Doctor. "I respect him. I'm in awe of him. But when you've got a job to do, you do it the best you can."

In Game 2, that wasn't quite enough, as Erving brought the Sixers back with 24 points and 16 rebounds. Cunningham ran all three of his centers — Caldwell Jones, Darryl Dawkins, and Earl Cureton — at Kareem. "The second game they got 38 second chances and converted that into 50 points," said Riley later. "We got 6 for 25."

The Sixers used that advantage to take a 110-94 win that evened the series. Their balance was impressive. Maurice Cheeks had 19 points and 8 assists, Caldwell Jones had 12 points and 11 rebounds, and Bobby Jones and Clint Richardson each scored 10.

All season long Philadelphia had lacked consistency, so much so that in the playoffs columnist Bill Lyon of The Philadelphia Inquirer began referring to them as "Team Schizo." The players conceded the name was accurate.

> # H
> e is in control out there. He knows what he's doing every minute he's on the floor.
> — Jerry West on Magic

"It's not like we're trying to give everybody ulcers," Caldwell Jones said. "It just goes that way."

"The personality of this team is basically casual, loose," explained Bobby Jones, "especially when things are going well." But the resulting looseness often cost them.

It did the next two games in the Forum, where the Lakers dominated completely. Norm Nixon led the parade in Game 3 with 29 points as the Lakers marched to a 129-108 victory. Again the zone trap was Philly's undoing. But the Sixers did their share, too, with incredibly flat play. Andrew Toney scored 36 and Erving 21, but no one else came through.

"Tonight was just a bad game for us," Caldwell Jones offered lamely.

So was the next night, Thursday, June 3. The Lakers controlled the tempo by ditching Showtime and going to their half-court power game with Kareem. On the other end, they kept up the pressure with their zone trap. Altogether, it was enough for a first-half run that put the contest away. The Lakers went up, 3-1, with a 111-101 win. Wilkes and Magic had 24 points each, while Kareem added 22 and McAdoo 19. Rambis thumped his way to 11 rebounds.

"We haven't won it yet, but we're starting to smell the aroma," said Riley.

But in Philly the Sixers reverted to their old personality-the good one for Game Five. In a shocker, they held Kareem to just 6 points. He hadn't scored that few since being tossed out of a game for punching out Kent Benson several years earlier. "They pushed and shoved a lot," Abdul-Jabbar contended.

Playing one of the better defensive games of his career, Dawkins had been the prime pusher/shover. "I tried working hard," Chocolate Thunder said. "I tried stopping him from getting position. It's hard. He's strong, and if you let him get position he gets the skyhook. You can't block that. Wilt Chamberlain couldn't block it, so how do you expect me to block it?"

Dawkins also contributed 20 points and 9 rebounds to the effort.

Their strong showing gave the Sixers hope as they headed cross country for Game Six in the Forum. But again the team changed faces. Erving scored 30 and Toney 29, but Dawkins got 6 fouls, 1 rebound, and 10 points in only 20 minutes of play, and everyone else struggled as well.

The Lakers got the early lead and were up, 66-57, at the half. Finally, in the third period, the Sixers found some defensive toughness. They held Los Angeles to 20 points for the quarter and several times cut the lead to one point. "I had a few butterflies about then," said Wilkes, whose 27 points led six Lakers in double figures.

Newcomer Andrew Toney helped out with the scoring.

The Lakers surged early in the fourth period to boost their lead to 11. Toney and the Doctor responded, and with a little under four minutes to go they trimmed the edge to 103-100.

That was about as far as the pair could take Philadelphia, however. Kareem scored and was fouled on the next play. He made the free throw to put Los Angeles up by 6. Moments later, Wilkes got a breakaway layup to close it out, 114-104.

The Lakers had won yet another title with yet another rookie coach. Riley and Buss smiled broadly as the Lakers' owner accepted the trophy afterward. "It seems like a millennium since I took over," Riley said of his seven months as a head coach. "Yeah, a millennium. I've got brain drain right now, mush brain. I dug down for everything I could find. I need four months to rest up.

Johnson, with 13 points, 13 rebounds, and 13 assists in Game 6, was named the series MVP, a choice deemed questionable by some members of the media who thought there were other Lakers just as deserving.

The Lakers, though, had had about all the controversy they could stand for one season.

"There were times earlier in the year when I didn't think this would be possible," Wilkes said as champagne cascaded over his face. "We had so many unhappy people around here you wouldn't believe it."

None was happier than McAdoo, who had 16 points, 9 rebounds, and 3 blocks in Game 6. Throughout the series, he had provided consistent scoring and rebounding off the bench. "This is the happiest moment of my life," he said. "People have said bad things about me during my career, but this makes up for it. I always said I would trade my scoring titles to be on a championship team, but I guess that wasn't necessary."

In the Philadelphia locker room, the Sixers again were answering the tough questions. Erving had yet another opportunity to be eloquent. "A lot of good things have come out of this season," he said. "Hopefully the organization will maintain a positive posture, and we can carry on next season. Nobody really expected us to get this far."

After three trips to the Finals, Erving still had no NBA title ring. "My heart really goes out to him," said Wilkes. "He's a basketball genius and a complete gentleman, and I love him. I would have loved for him to get a championship ring-but not at our expense."

They were prophetic words for Erving would get his championship, and the Lakers would pick up the tab.

1983

During his basketball life, Julius Winfield Erving 11 came to enjoy a splendid array of nicknames. As a kid in the Long Island, New York community of Roosevelt, he was known as "Jewel." Then, as he established his prowess on Roosevelt's playgrounds, the name shifted to "Little Hawk," because he had massive hands that allowed him to control the ball off the dribble in a manner reminiscent of Connie Hawkins, the original "Hawk."

Finally, of course, Erving came to be known as "Dr. J." As "the Doctor," he set his own style, operating on the court as no one ever had

before. His manner and ability had made him one of the highest-paid stars in the NBA. It had brought him fame and respect. It had even gotten him close to an NBA title.

But for Harold Katz, the new owner of the Philadelphia 76ers, close wasn't good enough. As the team struggled in the 1982 playoffs, Katz began implying that he wouldn't be shy about making big changes after the season ended.

True to his word, Katz made some big changes in the off-season. He sent Darryl Dawkins to the New Jersey Nets, and he acquired Moses Malone, the scoring/rebounding machine, from the Houston Rockets. For compensation, be sent Caldwell Jones to Houston.

From the very start of the schedule, the season had a championship feel to it. "Everybody had a sense that this was our opportunity," recalled forward Bobby Jones, who won the league's first Sixth Man Award in 1983. "The motivation was there, and we were healthy, too. We got off to a good start, got some confidence and didn't get cocky-we kept that good work ethic. I think Moses really established a lot of that. Julius had always had it. But then a big guy comes in and does that, and it helps."

Malone had always been underestimated both as a person and a player. Raised an only child in the hard-core neighborhoods of Petersburg, Virginia, he found a familiar escape in the playgrounds, only his efforts went far beyond the typical basketball hardwork stories. He would shoot alone long into the nights, by streetlight. Dick Vitale, then a college coach, recalled seeing Malone as a highschool star at a summer camp. While the other campers were off at lunch, Malone stayed in the gym practicing his offensive rebounding. Time after time, he would tip the ball up and go after it. Fascinated, Vitale watched this effort and finally went over and asked Malone why he was doing it.

"Coach," he said, "you got to get the ball before you can shoot it."

That tremendous drive to improve his rebounding made him a sensational star at

Petersburg High, and scores of college coaches recruited furiously in hopes of signing Malone to a scholarship. After he and his assistants spent long hours camped out in a Petersburg motel room, Maryland coach Lefty Driesell finally landed Malone. But at the last moment, the 6'11" center decided to sign a pro contract with the ABA's Utah Stars right out of high school.

Critics contended that Malone wasn't mature enough for the rigors of pro basketball. A year later, Dawkins would sign with Philadelphia and Bill Willoughby with Atlanta right out of high school, and in those cases the critics would be right. Because they entered the NBA too early, neither ever achieved the stardom that had been predicted for them. But the same couldn't be said about Moses Malone. He had turned twenty the spring of his senior year in high school and was very much a man.

Especially on the offensive boards. "When you get an offensive rebound, you're right there to shoot it back up," Malone once explained.

He wasn't much of a leaper, but he had a technique of powering back from the baseline to create position for himself. Time after time, he would snatch the offensive rebound and draw the foul on the putback. Then he was deadly from the line.

Katz knew his team needed just such power and dedication in the frontcourt. So the owner signed Malone to a multi-year contract worth more than $2 million per year.

Some observers were surprised by the move. Malone wasn't exactly considered selfish, but his style demanded that he get the ball in the halfcourt. And he wasn't very good about passing out of the numerous double teams that came his way.

Those same observers wondered about Moses teaming with Julius Erving. In many ways they were opposites. Malone was far from communicative, while Erving was perhaps the most urbane, articulate athlete in the game. And while Erving could leave earth at the foul line and float to the basket

Erving provided the 76ers with "high-brow" leadership.

for a jam, the 6'10", 265-pound Malone sat like a tank trap underneath. Erving had often commented that his one concern about flying was looking for a place to land.

Won't Malone clog the runways? observers asked.

The answer, of course, was sometimes.

But they had one tremendous thing in common during the Sixers' 1982-83 season—each wanted a championship ring in the worst kind of way.

"His intensity was very high," Bobby Jones said of the Doctor that season. Erving provided the team with high-brow leadership.

On the other side was the blue-collar Malone, solid as a block of concrete. "His was silent leadership," said Jones. "He always had confidence, and so you always had confidence because he was always so dominant at his position. Even if things weren't going right for you, you always knew, 'Well, we can depend on Moses. Because every night he's gonna get the rebounds. Every night he's gonna put it back in and get to the free throw line.' That was reassuring."

Actually, this confidence ran the course of the organization, said Jones. "The talent was there. There was a realization that the owner of the franchise had taken the extra steps to get players and to bring a team together. Then it was up to the players and the coaches to step back from what our individual talents were and to play as a team and help each other to win."

The Sixers ripped through the regular-season schedule with a 65-17 record. When writers asked Malone how the Sixers would fare in the playoffs, he uttered his famous "Fo, fo, and fo" prediction, meaning that Philly would sweep to the title in 12 straight games. It was quite a brassy comment, yet Jones said it didn't stun or anger the rest of the team. "Again, it was that Malone confidence," Jones explained. "It was confidence that he had backed up before with his actions."

Moses Malone joined the 76ers after the 1982 Finals loss.

Sure enough, they swept the Knicks in the Eastern semifinals and then confronted the Milwaukee Bucks in the conference finals. The Sixers took the first three, then stumbled in a 100-94 loss in the fourth game. They quickly corrected themselves, 115-103, in the fifth game to move on to the NBA Finals for the third time in four years.

There they met a hobbling and wearied Lakers team that had finished the regular season 58-24. Los Angeles had added forward James Worthy, the top pick in the previous NBA draft. Having led North Carolina to the NCAA championship the previous spring, Worthy fit nicely into the Showtime revue. His quickness to the basket was almost startling. But all of that came to an abrupt halt a week before the playoffs opened when Worthy jumped for a tip-in and landed unevenly on his left foot, causing a fracture of his leg just below the knee that finished him for the season.

Even without Worthy, the Lakers were deep enough to overcome Portland and San Antonio in the Western playoffs. But their injury troubles continued into the Finals. Bob McAdoo and Norm Nixon would miss all or part of the series. Without help, Kareem Abdul-Jabbar found himself in a situation similar to the one that frustrated him so during the late '70s. Malone dominated the boards, out-rebounding Abdul-Jabbar 72-30 over the course of the series.

The Lakers fell in line with Philadelphia's other victims. Los Angeles would lead each game at the half, yet each time the Sixers would power ahead. Philadelphia took Game 1 at home, 113-107. Even worse, Nixon suffered a partially separated shoulder. He continued to play, but the injuries mounted. The Sixers also took Game 2, 103-93. In the Forum, the Sixers sensed their opportunity. Game 3 was a 111-94 blowout that left Nixon with a wrenched left knee and four stitches in his chin. He sat out Game 4. Without him the Lakers battled furiously, and even held a 106-104 lead late in the game. To sort things out, Philly called a timeout. Having been burned by comebacks in the past, Coach Billy Cunningham and his players wanted to close out the series before anything got started.

"I'm taking over," the Doctor said in the huddle.

He immediately stole the ball and dunked it to tie the game. Next he chalked up a 3-point play, then followed it moments later with another score, a one-hander in Magic's face from the perimeter. The momentum from those 7 late points pushed the Sixers beyond reach as they won, 115-108.

Erving had finally nailed down an NBA title to go with the two ABA rings he had gotten with the New Jersey Nets. His pain hadn't been nearly as protracted as that of Jerry West or Elgin Baylor. Still, it was substantial. As a champion, he displayed the same grace in winning that he had in losing. "I've always tried to tell myself that the work itself is the thing, that win, lose, or draw, the work is really what counts," he said. "As hard as it was to make myself believe that sometimes, it was the only thing I had to cling to each year — that every game, every night, I did the best I could."

He more than anyone knew that wasn't enough, that no one player's effort is enough to win an NBA title.

"Let's not make believe," Cunningham said. "The difference from last year was Moses. He gave us the consistency inside that the Lakers had always gotten from Abdul-Jabbar. We got that and more from Moses."

For the first time, the Sixers could put away their loser's talk and answer the winner's questions. "Being behind at the half of every game and coming back and winning those games was very special," Jones said, "very much a team effort."

To remedy years of anguish and disappointment, it was just what the Doctor ordered.

14.
Head to Head

The Bird and Magic Show

For four seasons, they had danced around each other in the NBA, meeting only twice each year in regular-season games. But Larry Bird and Magic Johnson were always aware of each other. In a sense, their competition was carried on in that part of the sports pages called the "agate" — the box scores, league standings, category leader lists, and other statistics that make up much of the inside sports pages in every daily newspaper. That, of course, was no way for two great players and two great teams to decide who was best.

"Championship rings — I live for them," Bird would say.

Magic did, too.

A showdown seemed inevitable and it was. On three glorious occasions in the mid-1980s, Magic and the Lakers met Bird and the Celtics in the Finals. Each battle was portrayed as a clash of many opposites. East vs. West. Tradition vs. New Wave. Hollywood vs. Beantown. Showtime vs. Shamrocks. Celtic Pride vs. L.A. Cool.

Andrew D. Bernstein/NBA Photos

Bird and Magic engage in a splendid struggle for dominance.

227

"It's like the opening of a great play," said Lakers General Manager Jerry West just before the 1984 Finals. "Everyone's waiting to see it."

The media hype was tremendous. But beneath all the symbols and media, at the heart of everything, were two guys with three things in common: immense confidence, supreme talent, and an overwhelming desire to dominate.

"With Magic, it's a macho thing," explained West. "He wants to be better than everybody else."

The same was true of Bird. "The number one thing is desire," he said, "the ability to do the things you have to do to become a basketball player. I don't think you can teach anyone desire. I think it's a gift. I don't know why I have it, but I do." It was a gift Magic shared, and it made their competition that much more wonderful to watch.

In retrospect, the league should be ever so thankful. The Boston/Los Angeles fling in the Finals provided the juice for the NBA's resurgence. Over Larry and Magic's first dozen years in the league, television-rights money alone zoomed from roughly $14 million per year to more than $200 million.

Across America, the competition between Bird and Johnson spawned a running debate as to who was the greatest. Boston claimed a brassy win in 1984, and Bird followed that up with two more years of superior regular season play, resulting in his being named the league MVP for three consecutive seasons, 1984-86. On the heels of that, Auerbach went so far as to declare him the greatest basketball player ever, greater even than Bill Russell, the cornerstone of the Celtics's dynasty.

"All I know," Bird said in reply, "is that people tend to forget how great the older great players were. It'll happen that way with me, too."

Yet even as Bird claimed his awards, plenty of observers, including Chamberlain, thought Johnson was being shortchanged. "I don't know if there's ever been a better player than Magic," said Wilt.

Bird himself readily agreed. "He's the perfect player," he said of Magic.

The debate rolled on. Magic took his team to three championships in four years from 1985 to 1988, including the first back-to-back titles (in '87 and '88) since Russell and the Celtics had last done it in 1968 and 1969.

The Lakers' success resulted in Magic winning three league MVP awards. Which only renewed the question: who was better?

1984

Things had gone awry for the Boston Celtics after their 1981 title. They kept adding quality players and kept looking better and better on paper. But on court they still lacked something. In the fall of 1981 they had obtained Danny Ainge, the former Brigham Young guard who played pro baseball with the Toronto Blue Jays. Then the Celtics had traded for backup point guard Quinn Buckner and a smooth-shooting former All-Star forward, Scott Wedman. The only problem with these acquisitions was the ensuing traffic jam. Where and when would they all play? It wasn't an easy question to answer. When Milwaukee swept Boston in the 1983 playoffs, Red Auerbach decided it was time for even more changes. Big ones. Just weeks after the season ended,

Coach Bill Fitch resigned and was promptly replaced by assistant K.C. Jones. The two coaches had had their tiffs during Fitch's four-year tenure in Boston. Fitch's autocratic approach didn't allow much input from K.C., leaving the assistant openly frustrated at times.

Jones approached the job from a completely different perspective. Jones was a players' coach. He had been one of them. He understood them. He treated them as adults and welcomed their opinions. Where Fitch was a practice monster who spent hours reviewing videotape and expected his players to do the same, K.C. was a bit more laid back, a bit less insistent. Practices were important with Jones, but he favored a relaxed setting. Most of all, he wanted the complete effort from his players at game time — and he usually got it.

"I think everyone is more at ease," Cedric Maxwell said about Jones. "We have older players on this team. We know what we can do without being chastised or scolded."

Jones's promotion roughly paralleled another major development in Boston. In August 1983, Celtics owner Harry Mangurian sold the team for $15 million to Donald Gaston, Alan Cohen, and Paul Dupee. It was the twelfth ownership change that Red Auerbach had witnessed in three and a half decades with the team, yet he remained in firm control of the basketball operations.

Auerbach made another big change heading into the 1983-84 season: the acquisition of guard Dennis Johnson from Phoenix for center Rick Robey. The Celtics needed a big defensive guard to match up against Sidney Moncrief in Milwaukee and Andrew Toney in Philadelphia, and the 6'4" Johnson fit the bill.

The move surprised observers because Johnson had been branded as a troublemaker both in Seattle, where he had helped lead the Sonics to the '79 championship, and in Phoenix, where he had helped lift the Suns to the next level of competitiveness.

Auerbach, though, figured Johnson would fit in well on Boston's veteran club. Ultimately he was right, although there were some problems. "It was tough at the beginning," Gerald Henderson, a guard on the '84 Celtics, said of Johnson's adjustment. "We didn't know at first how it was going to work out, how he and K.C. were going to get along. Or how he and Danny (Ainge) were going to get along.

"D.J. just had to learn his teammates, and we had to learn him. And then everything was fine," Henderson said. "I really liked playing with D.J. He could play both guard positions, and I could play both positions. When we had

The 1986 Celtics were considered by many to be the greatest team ever.

a big guard to defend, he could defend that guy. And when we had a little guard to defend, I could defend him. That backcourt was very versatile, and we played good, tough defense."

With Ainge, Buckner, and M.L. Carr coming off the bench, the Celtics had a deep, solid backcourt rotation. But Boston's real strength was its frontcourt. Cedric Maxwell started at power forward with Parish at center and Bird at the other corner. Off the bench came McHale, Wedman, and backup center Greg Kite. There were no thin spots.

For Bird, the effort was always there.

Carr and Maxwell provided megadoses of spirit and banter. "Cedric was real funny," remembered Henderson. "Our whole team was cocky. But he was our team comedian. We had a good time kidding around. But when the time came to get serious and win basketball games, we got serious."

It was the perfect atmosphere for Bird. With Carr and Maxwell around, Bird didn't have to be the spirited leader. Bird wasn't an outgoing person, but Maxwell and Carr drew him out and kept the proceedings loose. "He was just kind of to himself," said Henderson. "But he communicated on the floor, and that's where we needed him most."

The 1983-84 season would see a rise in the level of Bird's play. The loss to Milwaukee the previous spring had provided him with a new surge of motivation. He had taken the setback personally. "It's the toughest thing that ever happened in Celtic history," he had said. "I'll tell you one thing, I'm going to play more basketball than ever this summer. People say, 'As Larry Bird goes, so go the Celtics.' So okay, next season I'll take on that pressure. I'll come back with more desire than ever. If it's got to start somewhere, it might as well start here."

And so it did. After an offseason of nonstop work, several elements of his game showed noticeable improvement. The one move that came closest to emerging as his signature was the step back, a quick movement away from the defender just before the shot to create shooting or driving room. He became just as well known for his improved ambidexterity and passing. Increasingly prominent was a capacity for making unusual plays that somehow worked. He produced them almost nightly, giving the definite impression that he had an aura, and if not a halo around his head, at least an ethereal horse shoe.

Despite his oft-mentioned lack of leaping ability, Bird's positioning, timing, and strong hands made him a solid rebounder. And his offense had a lethal character to it, particularly when he made a play at a crucial moment to kill the spirit of an opponent. Around the league, Bird became known for his heartlessness.

"Look in his eyes," Atlanta's Dominique Wilkins said, "and you see a killer."

"I guess I try to carry myself in a certain way on the court," Bird said of his hauteur. "It's funny because nobody else in my family is like that. It's not that I don't have respect for my opponents. When you lose that, you've got nothing. But tradition is important here acting like a Celtic."

"There are so many factors involved with him," K.C. Jones said of Bird. "People don't see everything he does. He's such a hard-nosed competitor and very determined. His effort is always there."

While other forwards could score, none could match Bird as a passer. In the negotiations for Bird's rookie contract, agent Bob Woolf had argued that as a dominant player Bird was worth $1 million per year. Auerbach attempted to counter that centers, occasionally guards, dominated NBA play, but never forwards, never from the corner of the floor. But as his game developed Bird's passing came to demoralize opponents as much as his three-point shot. "I grew up all of a sudden," he once said of his adolescence. "I was a guard as a sophomore and junior in high school, before I grew up. And we had some great shooters. I tried to get the ball to the great shooters. Passing is so much part of basketball it's unbelievable. It doesn't matter who scores the points. It's who gets the ball to the scorer."

From top to bottom, the Celtics displayed a fierce arrogance. When an October 1983 exhibition game between the Sixers and Celtics erupted into a melee, Red Auerbach charged onto the court, took off his glasses, and taunted Moses Malone. "I'm not big, hit me," said the sixty-six-year-old Auerbach. The Boston boss was fined $2,500 for his actions, but the mood had been set for the Celtics' season, and it was decidedly aggressive.

As a player, Jones had always been a defensive standout, and that carried over to his coaching approach. He studied opposing players endlessly and had a knack for identifying weaknesses. While the rest of the league was thinking of defense in terms of individual flashy plays, Jones was building a team mentality.

"We used to just flat-out stop people," said Henderson.

They would shut opponents down at one end and burn them at the other, then snicker while running back downcourt. They posted a league-best 62 wins over the course of the regular season, and with each victory, their confidence increased. That was fortunate, because they would need it in the playoffs.

The Celtics brushed by Washington in the first round only to run into major problems

> T he number one thing is desire, the ability to do the things you have to do to become a basketball player. I don't think you can teach anyone desire. I think it's a gift. I don't know why I have it, but I do.
>
> —Larry Bird

with Bernard King and the Knicks in the Eastern semifinals.

They finally vanquished New York in seven games and pasted Milwaukee 41 in the conference finals.

Two nights later Los Angeles finished off the Phoenix Suns and took the Western Conference title. Like the Celtics, the Lakers been through some changes. The sweep by Philadelphia in the 1983 NBA Finals had left Jerry West figuring ways for a quick reshuffle. During the 1983-84 preseason he sent popular starting guard Norm Nixon and reserve Eddie Jordan to the San Diego Clippers for backup center Swen Nater and the draft rights to rookie guard Byron Scott of Arizona State. In short time, the 6'4" Scott would work right into the Laker backcourt, and Showtime would be off and running again.

Despite injuries and the adjustment to the Nixon-Scott switch, they had finished the regular season at 54-28. Magic missed 13 games early in the schedule with an injured finger. Then in February, Jamaal Wilkes contracted an intestinal infection that hampered him the remainder of the season. Still, the year had some special moments. Kareem had first broken Chamberlain's record for career field goals, then for career scoring when he sank a skyhook against the Utah Jazz for his 36,420th point. Although he was no longer as dominant as he had once been, Abdul-Jabbar still gave the Lakers a formidable half-court game when they needed it.

And James Worthy had quietly come into his own as a forward. He had amazing quickness — the fastest first step in the game for a big man and when Magic got him the ball in the low post, the result was usually a score. Worthy took delight in faking one way, then exploding another. And he continued to add range to his shot, building consistency from fifteen feet out.

The Lakers also continued to get good frontcourt minutes and scoring from reserve Bob McAdoo. In the backcourt, Michael Cooper had found his niche as a defensive stopper and a three-point specialist, while third-year guard Mike McGee contributed 9.8 points per game.

Once Magic put his finger injury behind him, they won 41 of their last 56 games, including a nice 11-3 roll through the first three rounds of the playoffs. As the Finals opened, there was a sense that Los Angeles was the better team. Even K.C. Jones said as much — at least to anyone within earshot. "The Lakers are more talented than we are," he admitted.

There were two factors in Boston's favor — the rest factor and the homecourt advantage. The Celtics had ended their conference final on May 23, while the Lakers didn't wrap things up until Friday night, May 25. With the first game of the Finals set for that Sunday in Boston Garden, the Celtics' four days rest looked to be a major factor. From the Lakers' perspective, the situation was laced with tension. It had been fifteen years since Los Angeles had last faced Boston in the Finals, yet the numbers were on everyone's mind. Seven times the Lakers had met the Celtics for the championship, and seven times the Lakers had lost.

Just hours before Game 1, Kareem was wracked by one of the migraine headaches that had troubled him throughout his career. Team trainer Jack Curran worked the center's neck and back an hour before game time, at one point popping a vertebra into place. That seemed to do the trick on the thirty-seven-year-old captain. He walked out and treated the Garden crowd to 32 points, 8 rebounds, 5 assists, 2 blocks, and a steal. He made 12 of his 17 shots from the floor and 8 of 9 free throws. He did all of that only when the Lakers slowed down. They spent most of the time running their break to a 115-109 win.

Game 2 was a James Worthy showcase, at least for the first 47 minutes or so. He hit 11 of 12 shots from the floor and scored 29 points. The Lakers had come from behind to take a 115-113 lead with 18 seconds left when McHale went to the free throw line for two shots but missed both. With the series about to shift to Los Angeles, thoughts of a sweep were beginning to cross Boston minds. But the Lakers picked that particular moment for a snooze. Pat Riley had told Magic to call timeout if McHale made the shots. But Magic misunderstood and called timeout after the misses, which gave Boston time to set up its defense. Inbounding at midcourt, Magic tossed the ball to Worthy, who spied Byron Scott across the court and attempted to get the ball to him. Lurking in the background praying for just such an opportunity was Henderson. He stepped in, snatched the pass, and loped downcourt for an easy layup. The game was tied, and Magic allowed the clock to run out without getting off a final shot.

"The other players never did anything to help him," Riley would say later in defense of Magic. "They stood out on the perimeter and didn't get open. Kareem moved with 12 seconds left, which meant he was open too early. Magic got blamed."

Late in overtime, Henderson found Wedman on the baseline and got him the ball. The reserve forward knocked down the key jumper to give Boston a 124-121 win and a 1-1 tie in the series.

"I guess what I'll be remembered for in my career is that steal," Henderson said recently. "People mention it to me all the time. But in that same game, in overtime, I like the play where I set up Scott Wedman for the winning jumper. That goes unnoticed, but I appreciate that play more than the steal. Those were the two points that won the game."

Henderson may have treasured the assist, but Pat Riley's attention was fixed on the steal. "What will I remember most from that series?

Simple. Game 2. Worthy's pass to Scott. I could see the seams of the ball, like it was spinning in slow motion, but I couldn't do anything about it."

The Lakers quickly recovered back home in the Forum. Magic had a Finals-record 21 assists, and Showtime rolled to a 137-104 win. Bird was outraged at Boston's flat performance. "We played like a bunch of sissies," he said afterward. "I know the heart and soul of this team, and today the heart wasn't there, that's for sure. I can't believe a team like this would let L.A. come out and push us around like they did. Today I didn't feel we played hard. We got beat bad, and it's very embarrassing."

The next day the Los Angeles papers began touting Worthy as the series MVP, a development that infuriated the Boston players. None was angrier than Dennis Johnson, who had scored only four points in Game 3. "I thought I was into the game," he said, "but Game 3 convinced me I wasn't. Even K.C. had to come over and ask what was wrong. I told him whatever it was, it wouldn't be there again. It was a case of getting mentally and physically aggressive."

The same was true for the entire team. Jones adjusted the team's defense, switching D.J. to cover Magic in Game Four. The Lakers took an early lead and seemed ready to run off with another victory. From the bench, Carr screamed at his teammates to become more physical. McHale complied in the second quarter when he clotheslined Kurt Rambis on a breakaway layup, causing a ruckus under the basket. The incident awakened the Celtics and gave the Lakers reason to pause.

Later Riley would call the Celtics "a bunch of thugs."

Maxwell, on the other hand, was overjoyed with the development. "Before Kevin McHale hit Kurt Rambis, the Lakers were just running across the street whenever they wanted," he said. "Now they stop at the corner, push the button, wait for the light, and look both ways."

Los Angeles held a five-point lead with less than a minute to play. But Parish stole a bad pass from Magic, and the Laker point guard later missed two key free throws, allowing the Celtics to force an overtime. Late in the extra period Worthy faced a key free throw. Carr hooted loudly from the bench that he would miss and Worthy did; Maxwell stepped up and greeted him with the choke sign. The Celtics vaulted to a 129-125 win to tie the series again and regain the homecourt edge.

The free throw misses and the turnover would trouble Magic for a long time. "I thought the free throws more than the pass were mistakes," he said. "Those were things I — not the team — should have taken care of. When you miss the shots you go home and sit in the dark."

The Celtics realized they were onto something. The Lakers could be intimidated. "We had to go out and make some things happen," Henderson recalled. "If being physical was gonna do it, then we had to do it. The fourth game, that was the turnaround. We had to have that game or we were gonna be down 3-1."

Dennis Johnson helped them get it. After struggling early in the series, he would score 22, 22, 20, and 22 points in the last four games. Bird, too, came through in the clutch, particularly in Game Five back in Boston.

Dennis Johnson was an athletic defensive guard who could rebound and block shots.

Boston Globe sportswriter Bob Ryan had seen Bird perform in many tight situations but listed the fifth game of that '84 series as his favorite. "The so-called 'heat game' in 1984," he said. "The fifth game with Los Angeles. It was 97 degrees in the Boston Garden, and the one player that you could have predicted to turn this heat into a positive was Larry Bird. The Lakers were sitting there sucking on oxygen and Bird is saying, 'Hey, we've all played outdoors in the summer. We've all played on asphalt. We've all done this. Why should this be different? It's just because we have uniforms on and it's a national television audience.' That game and that performance summed up Bird to me as much as anything else he's ever done."

In that crucial match, Bird shot 15 for 20 from the floor for 34 points as Boston won, 121-103. Thirty-seven-year-old Abdul-Jabbar, meanwhile, showed his age in the sweltering heat. How hot was it? a reporter asked.

"I suggest," Kareem replied, "that you go to a local steam bath, do 100 pushups with all your clothes on, then try to run back and forth for 48 minutes. The game was in slow motion. It was like we were running in mud."

"I love to play in the heat," Bird said, smiling. "I just run faster, create my own wind."

But it wasn't just Bird. The Celtics were a full-blown team. "This is probably the best game we ever played," said D.J.

The Lakers answered the Celtics' aggressiveness in Game Six back in the air-conditioned Forum. In the first period, Worthy shoved Maxwell into a basket support. From there, the Lakers rode their new-found toughness and an old standby: Abdul-Jabbar scored 30, and Los Angeles pulled away down the stretch for a 119-108 win to tie the series 3-3.

The entire city of Boston was juiced up for the next game. The Lakers needed a police escort to get from their hotel to the Garden. Carr came out wearing goggles to mock Kareem and told the Lakers they weren't going to win. Not in the Garden.

Maxwell, meanwhile, told his teammates to put the load on his back because he was ready to carry them. And he did. He presented a high-action, low-post puzzle that the Lakers never solved. He demoralized them on the offensive boards. He drew fouls. By halftime, he had made 11 of 13 free throws. When they tried to doubleteam him, he passed them silly. He finished with 24 points, 8 assists, and 8 rebounds. Bird had 20 points and 12 rebounds, Parish had 14 points and 16 rebounds, and D.J. had 22 points.

Even against that barrage, the Lakers fought back from a 14-point deficit to trail by just three with little more than a minute left. Magic had the ball, but D.J. knocked it loose. Michael Cooper recovered it for L.A. Magic again went to work and spied Worthy open under the basket. But before he could make the pass, Maxwell knocked the ball away yet again, and the Celtics recovered. At the other end, D.J. drew a foul and made both shots, cementing the Celtics' 111-102 win and their fifteenth championship. Bird was named the Finals MVP after averaging 27.4 points, 14 rebounds, 3.2 assists, and 2 steals, but Maxwell's seventh-game performance had been incredible, and once again Dennis Johnson had delivered down the stretch.

"We worked hard for this," Bird said in the din of the locker room. "Anybody gonna say we didn't earn it?"

Auerbach enjoyed yet another of his very fat, very special cigars as Commissioner David Stern presented the championship trophy. The Celtics' president clutched it with satisfaction and asked, "What ever happened to that Laker dynasty I've been hearing so much about?"

1985

The Lakers couldn't get out of town immediately after the 1984 Finals. They had to spend one more night in their hotel, saddled with the Celtic blues again. Needless to say, it was a sleepless night. Owner Jerry Buss chain-smoked. Michael Cooper spent the time in deep and miserable mourning sequestered in his room with his wife Wanda. Pat Riley just wished he had a reason to diagram tomorrow's plays, anything to fight the insomnia.

Magic Johnson was joined by his two close friends, Isiah Thomas of the Detroit Pistons and Mark Aguirre of the Dallas Mavericks. They talked the night away. About music. Cars. Old times. Anything but the Finals. Occasionally the conversation would drift that way, but they'd steer it away. It was too tender a subject.

"We talked until the morning came," Thomas said, "but we never talked about the game much. For that one night I think I was his escape from reality."

The pain would remain for months. Magic returned to California, where he was set to move into his new Bel-Air mansion, only the furniture hadn't arrived. So he hid out for three days in his Culver City apartment. His mother phoned to see how he was doing. He told her he just couldn't talk about it.

Yet everywhere he turned, there seemed to be something to read about it. The Celtics were having fun with their victory. McHale

Andrew D. Bernstein/NBA Photos

Kareem lashed back to take charge in the 1985 Finals

even dubbed him "Tragic Johnson." Asked about the 1984-85 season, Bird said of the Lakers, "I'd like to give them the opportunity to redeem themselves. I'm sure they have guys who feel they didn't play up to their capabilities." Everyone knew who he meant.

Even worse than the Celtic cockiness was the trashing Johnson took from the Los Angeles newspapers. "I sat back when it was over," he said, "and I thought, 'Man, did we just lose one of the great playoff series of all time, or didn't we? This was one of the greatest in history. Yet all you read was how bad I was."

Despite the sauciness between Bird and Magic, their relationship warmed that summer when they made a sneaker commercial together. They became friends, but their competition remained as intense as ever. At 28, Bird flexed his talent during the regular season, averaging 28.7 points, 10.5 rebounds, and 6.6 assists per game. As a team, the Celtics were not as strong. Henderson had held out for more money over the summer, so Boston had traded him to Seattle. The Celtics' brass figured Danny Ainge had progressed enough to carry the starting load. Yet there was no doubt the trade left the Celtics thin in the backcourt. Additionally, Maxwell was troubled by chronic knee problems that eventually required exploratory surgery. In his absence, McHale moved from sixth man to starter. Observers noted that the Celtic starters — Bird, McHale, Johnson, Ainge, and Parish

Andrew D. Bernstein/NBA Photos

Michael Cooper's defense was a key Laker weapon against Boston.

— had each averaged better than 21,500 minutes of playing time over the season, more than any other team in the league.

The Lakers, on the other hand, bounced back with a vengeance, and were once again a deep, talented team. By playoff time, the frontcourt was bolstered by the return of Mitch Kupchak and Jamaal Wilkes to go with Abdul-Jabbar, Worthy, Rambis, McAdoo, and Larry Spriggs. In the backcourt were Magic, Scott, Cooper, and McGee. As a group, the Lakers were driven by their '84 defeat.

"Those wounds from last June stayed open all summer," Riley said as the playoffs neared. "Now the misery has subsided, but it never leaves your mind completely. Magic is very sensitive to what people think about him, and in his own mind I think he heard those questions over and over again to the point where he began to rationalize and say, 'Maybe I do have to concentrate more.' I think the whole experience has made him grow up in a lot of ways."

After all, Johnson was a mere 25, and already owned two championship rings. Throughout the season he played like a man intent on adding to his jewelry collection. The Celtics, however, were conceding nothing. With a 63-19 regular-season record — one win more than the Lakers— they had again claimed the homecourt advantage. And neither team dallied in the playoffs. Boston dismissed Cleveland, Detroit, and Philadelphia in quick succession, while the Lakers rolled past Phoenix, Portland, and Denver, setting up the rematch.

For the first time in years, the Finals returned to a 2-3-2 format, with the first two games in Boston, the middle three in Los Angeles, and the last two, if necessary, back in Boston. The situation set up an opportunity for the Lakers to steal one in the Garden, then pressure the Celtics back in Los Angeles. In whatever fashion, Magic, Kareem, and Company figured on rectifying their humiliation from 1984.

Little did they know they would have to suffer one final, profound embarrassment.

Game 1 fell on Memorial Day, May 27, with both teams cruising on five days' rest. The Lakers, however, quickly took on the appearance of guys who had just come off two weeks on the graveyard shift. The thirty-eight-year-old Abdul-Jabbar, in particular, slogged up and down the court, while his counterpart in the pivot, Robert Parish, seemed to motor effortlessly from one baseline to another. Kareem seemed to be not one but many steps behind. He finished the day with 12 points and 3 rebounds, while Magic pulled down only one board. The famed Showtime running game had been slowed to a belly crawl.

And the Celtics?

They raised a huge red welt on the Lakers' scar from the previous year with an overwhelming 148-114 win that became known as the Memorial Day Massacre. Scott Wedman hit 11 for 11 shots from the floor, including four 3-pointers. But it was Ainge who lashed the whip hardest, lacing in six straight buckets at the end of the first quarter to finish the period with 15 points. "It was one of those days," K.C. Jones said, "where if you turn around and close your eyes, the ball's gonna go in."

Despite their domination, the Celtics uncharacteristically eased back on their braggadocio, as if they sensed that they had gone too far. They hadn't expected it to be this easy. And the last thing they wanted to do was rile the Lakers. "It's definitely time to back off," Maxwell said. "It's not like backgammon or cribbage, where if you beat someone bad enough you get two wins."

But it was too late. The teams didn't play again until Thursday, and there was an uneasy air in Boston despite the big win.

In the Lakers' film sessions the next morning, Kareem moved to the front row, rather than recline near the back as he usually did. He didn't blink when Riley ran and reran the gruesome evidence of his terrible performance. In fact, the captain later went to each of his teammates and personally apologized for his effort.

"He made a contract with us that it would never happen again — ever," Riley said. "That game was a blessing in disguise. It strengthened the fiber of this team. After that, Kareem had this look, this air about him."

As the second game approached, the Lakers knew exactly what they had to do. "Our break starts with good tough defense," Rambis said. "That forces teams out of their offense. Then we must control the boards. That's where the work comes in. If we do those two things, the fast break is the easiest part."

It was time, Riley said in his pregame talk, to make a stand.

And they did. Kareem, in particular, reasserted himself with 30 points, 17 rebounds, 8 assists, and 3 blocks. Cooper hit 8 of 9 shots from the floor to finish with 22 points. Like that, the Lakers evened the series, 109-102. Best of all, they had stolen a game in the Garden and now returned to the Forum for three straight.

"They expected us to crawl into a hole," said Lakers assistant Dave Wohl of the Celtics. "It's like the bully on the block who keeps taking your lunch money every day. Finally you get tired of it and you whack him."

They hosted the Celtics on Sunday afternoon and whacked them again with a 136-111 blowout. Worthy was the man of the hour with 29 points. But Kareem's presence was felt again with 26 points and 14 rebounds.

At one point, Boston had led 48-38, but Worthy dominated the second quarter and led Los Angeles to a 65-59 edge at intermission. The Lakers ran away in the second half, during which Kareem became the league's all-time leading playoff scorer.

Bird, meanwhile, had extended his shooting slump to two games, going 17 for 42 from the field. He had been troubled by a chronically sore right elbow and bad back, although some speculated his real trouble was Cooper's defense. Bird offered no excuses.

As in '84, the series was marked by physical play, although this time around it seemed to be the Lakers who were determined to gain an intimidation edge. "We're not out to physically harm them," explained Kareem. "But I wouldn't mind hurting their feelings." Before Game 4, the NBA's vice president of operations, Scotty Stirling, warned each coach that fighting and extra rough play would be met with fines and suspensions. Riley told his players of Stirling's warning, but K.C. Jones chose not to.

The close game came down to one final Celtic possession. With only seconds left and the game tied, Bird had the ball but faced a double-team, so he dumped it off to D.J. above the foul line. Johnson drilled the winning basket with two seconds left, and Boston's 107-105 win had evened the series.

Boston always seemed to win the one- and two-point games, Cooper said afterward. "Those are the games where you see the heart of a good ball team. We've just gotta buckle down and win one of these."

Game 5 two nights later in the Forum was the critical showdown. McHale answered the call for Boston, scoring 16 early points and forcing Riley to make a defensive switch in the second period. The L.A. coach put Kareem on McHale and left the shorter Rambis to contend with Parish. It worked immediately. The Lakers went on a 14-3 run at the close of the half to take a 64-51 lead. They stretched it to 89-72 after intermission, but the Celtics closed to within four at 101-97 with six minutes left. Then Magic hit three shots and Kareem added four more, giving him 36 points on the day, as the Lakers walked away with a 3-2 lead, 120-111.

Jerry West, the Lakers' GM, elected not to make the trip back to Boston for fear of spooking the proceedings. Across the country old Lakers held their breath and watched the tube. After eight painful losses, this seemed to be their best chance yet to end Boston's domination. The Celtics would have to win the final two games. With a mere 38 hours rest between games, that just didn't seem possible for the boys from Beantown. Especially when Kareem showed up to play again, this time with 29 points 18 of them in the second half of Game Six, when it mattered.

The score was tied at 55 at intermission. Kareem had sat out much of the second period in foul trouble while Kupchak did admirable work at backup. The Celtics had played only seven people in the first half, and Magic could see that they were tired. It was written on their faces. Riley told him to keep pushing it at them, not to worry about turnovers. Just keep up the pressure. Keep pushing.

He did.

And the Celtics did something they had never ever done before. They gave up a championship on their home floor, on the hallowed parquet, 111-100. McHale kept them alive with 36 points, but he fouled out with more than five minutes left. And, thanks in part to Cooper's defense, Bird was closing out a 12-for-29 afternoon.

In the end, the Lakers' victory was signaled by the squeaking of sneakers in the deathly quiet Garden as the crowd slipped away. It was the same crowd that had riotously jostled the Lakers the year before.

"We made 'em lose it," Magic said with satisfaction.

Kareem was named the MVP. "He defies logic," Riley said of the ageless Laker center. "He's the most unique and durable athlete of our time, the best you'll ever see. You better enjoy him while he's here."

Magic's trophy was sweet redemption, although he had said earlier that he didn't need any. "You wait so long to get back," he admitted. "A whole year. That's the hard part. But that's what makes this game interesting. It's made me stronger."

1986

Kevin McHale and Robert Parish owned distinctions beyond those of other NBA big men. McHale had the coat-hanger shoulders and those telescoping arms that held the ball beyond a normal seven-footer's reach. And the Chief, well, he had the face, that unchanging Rushmorelike expression of dignity. Come to think of it, McHale had a face, too, the kind that led Mychal Thompson, then his University of Minnesota teammate, to label him "Herman Munster" upon their first meeting.

Certainly, McHale frightened people around the league, but it was his game, not his visage, that did the damage. "You can't have somebody guard me one-on-one when I get position," he once remarked. "I make two or three fakes and that guy is going to move. I'll either get a basket or get fouled, and that can hurt a team. You have to double team in that situation."

Parish showed an offensive flair himself, and that, not their faces, was the reason they stood out in the Boston Celtics' frontcourt. Both men possessed excellent 8- to 10-foot shots and loved to use them. In Parish's case, the weapon of choice was an arching, rainbow jumper, an ungainly but accurate shot. He also showed a nifty spin move where he would whirl around an opponent, dropping one short dribble before powering up for the jam. Or, if Parish was facing the defender, he would flash a pump fake, watch the defender go airborne, then stride to the hole.

For McHale, the turnaround fadeaway shot from over his head became nearly unstoppable. "I learned to arch my back in a semi-fadeaway and that way I could always get it off," McHale said of his college days at Minnesota. Over his first five years in the league, his arms seemed to grow, at least to those playing against him. As the Celtics sixth man, he became known as a shotblocking irritant at one end of the floor and a half-court nightmare at the other. Long arms are fine, McHale said when asked about them, but by themselves they don't make an inside game. Moves do. And by the time he became a Celtic starter during the 1985 season, he had his moves down pat. He would fake one way. If the defender took it, McHale went the other. If the defender didn't take the fake, McHale kept powering up. If a defender got an early start on blocking his fadeaway, McHale would simply step inside and take the easy layup. Many times he drew fouls as the defender attempted to recover.

Parish was never as flashy as McHale, but he was just as efficient at earning the same

Andrew D. Bernstein/NBA Photos

The Celtics took on the Houston Rockets for the 1986 championship

kind of respect from opponents. When Parish joined the Celtics in 1980-81, Cedric Maxwell took one look at his stonelike face and remarked that he looked like Chief Bromden in the movie One Flew Over The Cuckoo's Nest. "The Chief just seemed to stick with me," said Parish.

But his lack of expression often left his emotions open to misinterpretation, first in his four years with Golden State, then on occasion in Boston. He came to the Celtics in the same move that allowed Boston to acquire the draft pick used to select McHale. Coach Bill Fitch wanted a bigger front line and had viewed Parish as an undeveloped talent at Golden State. While Parish seemed a dispassionate young player, he had made roughly 50% of the field goals he attempted as a Warrior. He also ran the floor well and showed flashes of shot-blocking brilliance. That first season he became Boston's starter in the post, a position he would play with excellence for more than a decade. Over the years, K.C. Jones repeatedly referred to Parish as "the backbone of the ball club." Jones often spoke appreciatively of watching Parish fill the lanes on the break, not getting the ball, yet continuing to run, playing his role, even as a decoy.

"He does get overshadowed by Larry and Kevin," said Jones, "but he does get the job done and is so strong in the hard areas-rebounding, blocking shots, defense. He has done it all."

For Bird, this team-oriented style of play was critical. In their years of playing together, he and Parish victimized opponents on countless pick-and-roll plays. The opponent almost always knew what was coming. Seldom did it matter. "The thing about Robert is if he sets a pick, he's always going to roll," said Bird. "He's got good hands, and if he's not all the way to the basket, then he can pull up and hit that 8- to 10-footer. Robert sets a thousand picks for me in a game. That's my reward to him, to give him the ball like that. He's so big, he has a potential three-point play almost every time."

Far beyond even what Fitch had imagined, McHale and Parish had given Boston perhaps the most imposing frontcourt in the league. Teamed with Maxwell, Bird, and Wedman in 1984, they could present problems in every area of the game. As a group, they were brilliant and consistent scorers and superior defenders. But Maxwell's knee problems changed this special working combination in 1985. Parish and McHale put in extra minutes, and it became obvious that the team needed more depth.

It was particularly obvious to Bill Walton. The former Portland center had traveled basketball's hard road since the Trail Blazers won the 1977 title. Foot injuries and reconstructive operations had virtually taken him out of the game, leaving his career a frustrating chain of stops and starts. He had left the Trail Blazers in 1978 and eventually dropped out of basketball to attend law school at Stanford. He later discovered that he had healed enough to play part-time for the San Diego Clippers. His feet didn't feel too bad in 1985, and he got the notion that perhaps he could help the Celtics, a team he had always admired. As a backup to Parish, Walton figured he could play just enough to give the team quality center play while Parish or McHale rested. Walton contacted Red Auerbach, who consulted Bird, who thought it was a great idea. Shortly thereafter, the Celtics traded Maxwell to the Clippers for Walton.

It was the kind of deal that brought immediate scrutiny. Why would the Celtics want to gamble on Walton when every season brought a recurrence of the injuries? The answer became apparent just a matter of games into the 1985-86 schedule Boston had combined the greatest passing center with the

Andrew D. Bernstein/NBA Photos
Boston's Kevin McHale discovered the difficulty of launching a shot against Olajuwon.

greatest passing forward in the game. The result was an exhibition of ball movement and team play that left the rest of the NBA in another class. In December, the Celtics lost a game to Portland in Boston Garden. It would be their only home loss of the year.

They roared out on a winning tear that converted doubters at every stop. "Right now, there's no doubt that Boston is a much better team," Magic Johnson said in February 1986 after the Celtics beat the Lakers in the Forum to extend their record to 41-9. On their way to a club-record 67-15 season, the Celtics would claim a winning record against every team in the league.

Few people foresaw this amazing turnaround, including Bird, who had contemplated sitting out the '86 season because of back pain. But the acquisition of Walton and guard Jerry Sichting from Indiana had convinced him it would be wise to hang around and see how things turned out. His reward was the kind of season that even superstars dream about. He averaged 25.8 points and nearly 7 assists, 2 steals, and 10 rebounds per game. He shot .423 from three-point range and finished first in the league in free-throw percentage. For the second consecutive season, Bird broke the 2,000-point mark. And he finished the year with 10 triple doubles.

At the All-Star game in Dallas in February, Bird had 23 points, 7 steals, 8 rebounds, and 5 assists. The day before, on All-Star Saturday, he had won the long-range shootout, and afterward raised his arms in triumph, shouting "I'm the three-point king!"

Later, midway through the NBA Finals, he would pick up his third league MVP award. "I just felt there was no one in the league who could stop me if I was playing hard," Bird said in accepting the award. "What makes me tough to guard is that once I'm near the three-point line, I can score from anywhere on the court. It's kind of hard to stop a guy who has unlimited range."

His personal confidence was at an all-time high, and it infused the team and coursed through the roster. Despite a sore Achilles tendon that forced him to miss 14 games in the middle of the season, McHale responded to his first year as a full-time starter by averaging 21.3 points. His .574 fieldgoal percentage was fifth best in the league. He blocked 134 shots during the regular season and another 43 during the playoffs. The former two-time Sixth Man award winner was named to the All-Star team and to the NBA All-Defensive first team.

Walton, meanwhile, jumped into McHale's vacancy and claimed the Sixth Man award. He played 80 regular-season games for the Celtics (a career high for Walton) and gave them 20 minutes per outing. He shot .562 from the floor and had 162 assists. The team's other acquisition, Sichting, shot an impressive .570 from the floor as a backcourt sub.

Playing fewer minutes, Parish averaged 9.5 rebounds and 16.1 points per game while shooting .549 from the floor. On occasion, he and Walton played side-by-side in a "twin towers" setup. The towers became triplets when McHale joined them in the lineup. And if K.C. Jones didn't need size, he could go to a smaller, quicker group with Bird, Wedman, and McHale. The backcourt had similar depth with Ainge, Dennis Johnson, Sichting, David Thirdkill, and Rick Carlisle, all of whom contributed valuable minutes, scoring, and defense.

The season took an unexpected turn when Houston eliminated the Lakers in the Western Conference Finals, 4-1. Los Angeles had reshuffled its lineup, releasing Bob McAdoo and Jamaal Wilkes and picking up veteran power forward Maurice Lucas in a trade and rookie A.C. Green through the draft. The Lakers got off to a good start on their way to a 62-20 record, but the chemistry wasn't there in the spring.

The Rockets, on the other hand, played with confidence and enthusiasm. With Bill Fitch as coach, they sported the original twin towers, 7'4" Ralph Sampson at forward and 6'11" Akeem Olajuwon at center. Jim Petersen was the backup power forward, while Robert Reid and Rodney McCray shared time at the other corner. The guards included Mitch Wiggins, Allen Leavell, and Lewis Lloyd. Veteran John Lucas had played most of the season in the backcourt but fell by the wayside with a recurrence of his drug problem. The Rockets adjusted to this setback and claimed the Midwest Division title with a 51-31 record. They ousted Sacramento and Denver quickly before losing the first game against the Lakers in the Forum, then coming back to sweep four straight. Their fourth victory against Los Angeles came on a buzzer-beating, turnaround jumper by Sampson in the Forum. Houston had set up the final play with a mere second on the clock. Sampson caught the inbounds pass, whirled, and released. The ball hit the rim, bounced high, and fell right to the bottom of Laker hearts.

Boston, meanwhile, scorched Chicago (3-0), Atlanta (4-1), and Milwaukee (4-0) in a searing playoff drive, then had to wait eight days for the Finals to begin on Monday, May 26. The Celtics were highly favored, and for good reason. For the Rockets to win, Sampson had to play well, which didn't always happen. A solid defensive rebounder with a soft shooting touch and excellent mobility and quickness for a big man, Sampson had been plagued by inconsistency since becoming the top pick in the 1983 draft. He was also prone to foul trouble at times.

In Game 1, both of those plagues returned. He picked up his third foul just five minutes into the first period and spent the rest of the half on the bench, and when he did return in the second half, he missed 12 of his first 13 shots. Olajuwon, always a fierce competitor, tried to compensate for Sampson's absence with 33 points and 12 rebounds. But McHale and Parish powered around the frontcourt at will, while Bird displayed all-around brilliance with 21 points, 13 assists, 8 rebounds, and 4 steals. His double-teaming on Olajuwon helped frustrate the Rockets further.

The Celtics shot 66% from the floor for the game. Ainge and Johnson had a big third quarter, and the whole team floated on a high-octane confidence. They won 112-100 and privately wondered if they weren't headed for another sweep.

That mentality carried right through Game 2, in which Bird failed to pick up a single foul despite double-teaming Olajuwon much of the game. He did, however, collect 31 points, 8 rebounds, 7 assists, 4 steals, and 2 blocks. He worked McCray over on offense, backing in for an assortment of shots and working the pick and roll with Parish. Sampson played better and finished with 18 points and 8 rebounds, but he still seemed intimidated by Boston Garden. The Celtics ran away with the third quarter, 34-19, and won easily, 117-95.

Bird's performance left Olajuwon awestruck. "He's the greatest player I've ever seen," the Houston center said after the game. But he stated that once the Rockets got back to Houston for the next three games, he didn't see how the Celtics could beat them in the Summit.

While the series was in Boston, Bird had received his MVP award. And once in the Summit, he again rang up big numbers — 25 points, 15 rebounds, 11 assists, and 4 steals. Running their break smoothly, the Celtics seemed in control in the third period with a 76-65 lead. But then Fitch switched Reid to cover Bird, and the Boston forward shot 3 for 12 in the second half. On offense, Sampson found his comfort zone and powered Houston into the lead in the fourth period. He finished with 24 points and 22 rebounds. In the closing minutes, the Rockets ripped through a 9-0 run and took a 103-102 lead with 67 seconds to go. Boston regained the lead on an Ainge jumper, but Wiggins answered with a tap-in and then the Houston defense forced Boston into a bad shot. Later Parish stepped on the sideline as Boston was inbounding the ball, and Houston survived, 106-104.

Game 4 was the test. Parish faced down Houston's big men to lead Boston with 22 points and 10 rebounds. Then Bird took over in prime time. With the score tied at 101 and a little over two minutes left, he threw in a three-pointer. Then, on a last-minute Boston possession, Walton rammed home an offensive rebound. The Celtics had a 106-103 win and a 3-1 lead in the series.

Game 5 was marred by a fight between Sampson and Sichting. With a little more than three minutes gone in the second period, the Houston forward and Boston guard got tangled up over the ball. They exchanged words, which led to Sampson throwing punches, one of which struck Dennis Johnson in the left eye when he attempted to break things up. The outburst resulted in Sampson's ejection. But rather than fold, the Rockets found motivation in the incident. They got inspired backup play from Petersen, and Olajuwon put on a grand show with 32 points, 14 rebounds, and 8 blocks. The Rockets won 111-96, and the series stood at 3-2. Fortunately for the Celtics, it was headed back to Boston Garden, where their combined record for the regular and postseason was 49-1.

As expected, the Beantown crowd was ready for Sampson for Game 6. Every time the Houston forward touched the ball, the Garden regulars booed to their hearts' delight. "Sampson Is A Sissy" read one poster. "Sampson you fight like Delilah" read another. The atmosphere made for a tough time for Ralph. He missed his first seven shots before punctuating his frustration with a dunk in the second period. For the day, he would total only 8 points.

"I just played badly," a dejected Sampson said later when asked if the crowd had affected him.

Bird, meanwhile, was afire, yelling at his teammates and diving for loose balls. He finished the first half with 16 points, 8 rebounds, and 8 assists to give Boston a 55-38 lead. His teammates knew he wanted the ball.

Andrew D. Bernstein/NBA Photos

Andrew D. Bernstein/NBA Photos

Boston's Danny Ainge (above) penatrated and dished while Houston's Ralph Sampson (below) went inside against McHale.

"Just by getting mad and storming around, I got everybody's attention," he said later. "I didn't want this day to slip away from me."

In the third period he buried several 3-point

Andrew D. Bernstein/NBA Photos

Boston had a front court to match Houston's Twin Towers

shots. That and Boston's swarming defense sent the Rockets down hard. The Celtics led by 30 in the fourth period and went on to claim their 16th championship with a 114-97 thrashing. Bird rang up 29 points, 11 rebounds, 12 assists, and 3 steals. The player that Bill Fitch had initiated into the league had disassembled his old coach's new team. Nobody appreciated his performance more than Fitch himself.

"Once the lights go out and play starts, the crowd has more effect on Larry than anyone I've ever seen," said the Houston coach. "I've never seen him more intense than he was today."

"He is undoubtedly, in my mind at least, the best basketball player playing the game today,"

said Dennis Johnson afterward. Despite the praise, Bird played the perfectionist. "I've got some things to work on," he said. "I'm not real comfortable with my moves to the basket. By next fall, I want four or five moves I can go to. If I do that, I think I'll be unstoppable."

As a team, Boston had concluded its most impressive season. Throughout the regular season and the playoffs, the Celtics had run up a 50-1 homecourt record. The Bird-led offense usually grabbed the headlines, but it was their defense that had befuddled the Rockets. "I don't remember the last time I was hounded by a team more than I was today," said Sampson. "Every time I touched the ball, there were two and three guys around me. And that went for Akeem, too."

None of the defense was accidental, claimed K.C. Jones proudly. "Our defensive intensity was phenomenal. We contested every pass and every dribble. They were under constant pressure every time they touched the ball."

With their third championship, Bird and his Celtics had evened the ring count with Magic and his Lakers.

1987

Over the summer of 1986, Pat Riley heard the question often. What did he think of Ralph Sampson's shot that had killed the Lakers in the playoffs? Pretty soon, Riley fashioned a standard reply.

It was stimulation, he told his questioners.

Stimulation for change. Kareem was almost forty heading into the 1986-87 season. As long as anyone could remember, he had been the focus of the Lakers offense. But Riley wanted to change that. Kareem's retirement was inevitable, and Riley wanted to begin shifting the burden to other players. He wanted Magic Johnson, and to a lesser degree James Worthy, to become the focus of the offense. So Riley and his staff began formulating their ideas of how this transition should work and took their notions into training camp that fall.

Within days, the players became comfortable with the new system. Kareem personally reassured Riley that everything was working fine. Then Magic sealed it in gold by turning in a stellar season, one that would make him the first guard since Oscar Robertson to win the league MVP award. His scoring zoomed to a career-high 23.9 points per game, and he topped the league in assists at 12.2 per game.

He didn't do it alone, of course. Kareem. Worthy. Byron Scott. Michael Cooper. A.C. Green. They all wanted to establish their superiority. They constituted one of the greatest teams in basketball history, yet they had just barely survived a fracture. Just days after the Lakers' 1986 playoffs loss to Houston, owner Jerry Buss had wanted to trade Worthy to Dallas for Mark Aguirre. But Jerry West talked him out of that deal. Bird and his Celtics had held their breath, hoping that Buss would break up the Lakers. But Worthy stayed, and the Lakers went about the business of proving that West's decision was a wise one.

Their big boost arrived February 13, when the front office acquired Mychal Thompson from San Antonio. Larry Bird was heartsick at the news. The 6'10" Thompson gave the Lakers just what they needed up front. He could play backup to Kareem at center, and he was a solid power forward. Better yet, he was an excellent low-post defender, and having played with McHale on the college level, he knew better than anyone how to defend Boston's long-armed forward. With Thompson, the Lakers surged to a 65 win regular season, the best in the NBA.

All the while, Boston's fortunes were headed in the other direction.

It had been eighteen seasons since a team had won back-to-back championships in the NBA. The 1986-87 Celtics had hopes of being the first modern team to repeat. But one by one things fell apart for them. Tragedy struck the day after the draft when Len Bias, the second player chosen behind Brad Daugherty, collapsed and died from cocaine-induced heart failure. From what investigators could determine, the incident was either the first time, or among the first times, Bias had used

Andrew D. Bernstein/NBA Photos

The addition of Mychal Thompson gave the Lakers an edge in '87.

the drug. Yet it cost him his life and destroyed the Celtics' plans. From there, the team's troubles came in waves.

The Boston bench, which seemed so deep in 1986, rapidly disintegrated. After an early-season accident on a stationary bike, Bill Walton was sidelined with the foot injuries that had plagued him throughout his career. Scott Wedman was struck down by a heel injury and never played for Boston again, and Jerry Sichting was slowed by a persistent virus. To bolster the frontcourt, the Celtics picked up Darren Daye and Fred Roberts, but they needed time to build confidence. Without a strong bench, the Boston starters were forced to play Herculean minutes. As a result, Ainge, Bird, and Parish were all troubled by nagging injuries. Then, late in the season, McHale broke a navicular bone in his right foot and tore ligaments as well. The doctors were worried that continued play might cause McHale permanent damage, but because the Celtics seemed to have a good chance in the playoffs, he decided to play hurt.

The Celtics finished the regular schedule at 59-23, the best in the Eastern Conference, but they quickly found themselves in one brutal playoff struggle after another.

Walton had returned in March, but his effort was almost painful to watch. He helped in the first round as Boston eliminated Chicago, 3-0. After that, he never regained his touch and never performed well enough to contribute. Boston survived Milwaukee in a seven game Eastern semifinal, then bashed heads with Detroit in the Eastern finals. Again the series went to seven games, and Boston escaped, but only by virtue of Bird's last-second steal of an Isiah Thomas pass in Game 5. Bird quickly fed Dennis Johnson for the winning layup to complete a play for the ages if there ever was one.

The Lakers, meanwhile, were scorching. Detroit assistant Dick Versace scouted them during the playoffs and came away shaking his head. "They're cosmic," he said. "They're playing better than any team I've ever seen."

First, Denver (3-0), then Golden State (4-1), and finally Seattle (4-0) fell to the Lakers machine. They concluded their conference work on May 25, while the Detroit-Boston series was just getting interesting. Faced with a week off, Riley set up a mini-camp in Santa Barbara to keep his players focused.

On Saturday, May 25, they had a pancakes-and-strawberries breakfast buffet and watched the Celtics advance with a 117-114 win over Detroit.

Three days later the Finals opened in the Forum before a crowd peppered with even more celebrities than usual. Their presence only seemed to inflame Pat Riley more. He had begun stewing with the end of the Eastern Finals, when the press began describing the injured Celtics as a blood-and-guts brigade. Riley threw this up to his troops as inspiration. The Celtics get all the respect

Andrew D. Bernstein/NBA Photos

Bird was anguished by nagging injuries in '87, but losing hurt worse.

for being hard-working, while the Lakers are packaged as a bunch of glitzy, super-talented guys who glide through Show-time without much character or thought, Riley told his players. "A bunch of glitter-group, super-ficial laid-backs," he spat. "This is the hardest-working team I've ever had, but regardless of what we do, we're minimized...We're empty people... and most of us aren't even from California."

The Celtics came in weary from two straight seven-game battles. Their tired legs dragging, they could do little more than watch the Lakers blow past them up and down the floor. "The Celtics looked to me like they were keeping up pretty good," Mychal Thompson would quip later, "just at a different pace."

Magic led the rout with 29 points, 13 assists, 8 rebounds, and zero turnovers. Worthy, on the receiving end of many of Johnson's passes, had 33 points and 9 rebounds. The Lakers ran thirty-five fast breaks in the first two quarters and led by 21 at intermission. They settled into a canter thereafter, finally ending it 126-113.

The Celtics knew they were reeling, and to catch themselves they had to stop Magic. They accomplished that in Game 2, but in the process they allowed Michael Cooper to switch specialties, from defense to offense. K.C. Jones put Danny Ainge on Magic and that seemed to work for a while. But Boston trailed by seven in the second quarter as Cooper pushed the Lakers through a 20-10 outburst, scoring or assisting on all 20 points. When it was over, he had laced in six of seven 3-point attempts, a playoff record.

And the Celtics had spent another day in feeble pursuit of the Laker break. "One of the Laker girls could've scored a layup on us," backup center Greg Kite said later. Kareem flicked in 10 of 14 shots for 23 points, while Magic posted 20 assists and 22 points. In Coop's big second quarter, he racked up 8 assists, tying a Finals record.

It all added up to a 141-122 rout, Boston's sixth straight road loss in the playoffs, and left them eager to get back home. Bird expressed doubts about teammates who only played well in front of their families. Maybe, he said, it was time to get people who would play hard every night. The L.A. papers enjoyed these developments thoroughly and took to calling the Celtics "Gang Green."

Before doubt crept too far into Celtic minds, they righted themselves in Game 3. McHale had limped off the floor in Game 2 after further exacerbating his injury by stepping on Parish's foot. But the Boston forward bounced back in Boston to score 21 points with 10 rebounds while letting the air out of Worthy's game, limiting the Laker forward to only 13 points and 3 rebounds. Byron Scott hit 2 of 9 shots from the field to finish with 4 points. The Laker load fell on Magic and Kareem. The former scored a game-high 32, but Kareem was left to contend with much-maligned Celtic backup center Greg Kite. K.C. Jones loved the way Kite worked before and after practice to improve his game, calling him an inspiration to the team.

That Sunday, June 7, he was more than inspiration. He played 20 minutes and while he failed to score, he grabbed 9 rebounds, blocked a Magic layup, and did solid body work on Kareem. The defensive minutes Kite gave Boston were just enough from the bench, as Bird scored 30 points and D.J. hit 11 of 22 attempts from the field to finish with 26. The Celtics' big effort came in the second quarter, when they hit 17 of 21 from the field.

"I hope that's as well as they can play," said Kareem after the 109-103 Boston victory.

"Maybe we were just due for a game like that," said Magic. "I know we won't play that way again."

For a brief moment the pressure was off the Celtics. No longer did they have to worry about the big embarrassment.

"We're just too good a team to be swept," Bird said. "This was the most important game of the series for us. If we lost, it might've been tough to get up for Game 4. Now it's going to be easy."

He was right. For more than three quarters, Game 4 would be easy. And the pressure would shift to the Lakers, which made Riley's mood even blacker. During a closed Los Angeles practice in the Garden, Riley had requested

Andrew D. Bernstein/NBA Photos

L.A.'s Kurt Rambis got past Walton to score on this stickback.

that the cleaning staff leave the building. "Maybe he thought they had VCRs in their brooms," the Garden security director quipped.

Boston went up by 16 after halftime, but L.A. cut the lead to 8 with three and a half minutes to go in the game. The game's conclusion-the series, actually-came down to one Magic sequence.

With half a minute left, the Lakers called a timeout to set up a pick for Kareem. But Magic told Kareem to fake it as his defender, Parish, attempted to fight through the pick, and then roll to the basket. He did. The pass was there, and the Lakers took a 104-103 lead. But Bird's 3-pointer with 12 seconds left put Boston up 106-104. On the next possession, Kareem was fouled and went to the line, where he made the first and missed the second. McHale grabbed the rebound, but Mychal Thompson gave him a gentle push and the ball went out of bounds. McHale signaled a Boston ball, but the officials saw it the other way, giving possession to the Lakers.

What followed was another play for the ages. Magic took the inbounds pass to the left of the key and at first contemplated a 20-footer, but McHale came out to change his mind. So Magic motored into the key, where Bird and Parish joined McHale in a trio of extended arms. Nevertheless, Magic lofted a hook which just cleared Parish's fingertips and then gently settled into the basket with a swish. K.C. Jones, watching from a twisted stance from the Celtics bench just feet away, felt his heart sink into an abyss.

The Celtics got a timeout with two seconds left, and the Lakers even left Bird open for a shot. But the ball rattled in and then out and Magic ran off happily, having stolen Game 4 107-106. In the locker room, he dubbed the shot "my junior, junior, junior sky hook."

"You expect to lose on a sky hook," Bird said with a pained smile. "You don't expect it to be from Magic."

The Celtics made the mistakes down the stretch, he continued. "We turned the ball over twice. We missed a rebound after a free throw. We really can't blame anybody but ourselves."

Would the game be remembered just for its last minutes? Bird was asked. "It should," he replied. "A lot happened in the last minute-and-a-half. Robert gets the ball taken away from him. I throw the ball at Kevin's feet. They miss a free throw, and we don't get the rebound. How many chances do you need to win a game?"

Then someone asked how he liked the Celtics chances for the rest of the series. "How would you like it?" he replied. "I know when we're up 3-1, I always say it's over. It's not a good position. There's no question we're in trouble. We're not a good road team. I don't know if we can beat them twice out there. But we'll give it a try."

First they had to win Game 5 in the Garden. Fortunately, the Lakers were compliant enough. And Danny Ainge had his outside shot

Andrew D. Bernstein/NBA Photos

Byron Scott slashed to the hole through the Boston Defense.

going. The Celtics got the lead and kept it. Ainge missed a trey early in the second half, bringing the Celtic bench to shout that they didn't need threes. But Ainge must have had plugs in his ears. He kept throwing them up, hitting four in the period. For the game, he made 5 of 6 from 3-point range.

Magic countered for Los Angeles with 29 points, 12 assists, 8 rebounds, and 4 steals, but there wasn't much help. Before the game, Bird had told his teammates, "If they want to celebrate, let's not let them do it on the parquet." At one point during the contest, the Laker staff even iced down several cases of champagne. But the Celtics had incentive enough. They got their second win, 123-108, and the series jetted back across the continent.

Kareem arrived for Game 6 with a shave job on his balding head. And for a time, it seemed Los Angeles was intent on cutting the game just as close. Magic had only 4 points by the half, and the Celtics led, 56-51. But like Kareem's pate, the Lakers glistened after intermission. Worthy finished with 22, and Kareem had 32 points, 6 rebounds, and 4 blocks. Mychal Thompson had 15 points and 9 rebounds. And Magic led them with another display of all-around brilliance. On top of his previous efforts, his 16-point, 19-assist, 8-rebound showing brought him the Finals MVP award as Los Angeles claimed its fourth title of the decade, 106-93.

"Magic is a great, great basketball player," Bird stated flatly, settling the issue for the moment. "The best I've ever seen."

"He's the best in the game," agreed Riley. "He proved it in the regular season and the playoffs. We wouldn't be anywhere without him. We wouldn't be a championship contender without him."

Magic saw his special talents reflected in his team. "This is a super team, the best team I've played on," he said. "It's fast, they can shoot, rebound, we've got inside people, everything. I've never played on a team that had everything before. We've always had to

Andrew D. Bernstein/NBA Photos

Kareem's passing helped keep the options open for L.A.

play around something, but this team has it all."

Bird had to agree. "I guess this is the best team I've ever played against," he said. "In '85, they were good. In '84, I really thought they should have beaten us ... I don't know if this team's better than they were, but I guess they are. Their fast break is better. They're deeper."

Then Bird added, "I would have loved to play them with a Bill Walton and a Scotty Wedman ...We would have given them a hell of a try."

The Lakers and Celtics had established a standard for pro basketball, and by 1987 they had begun to assume that the championship round was theirs to share. On his way to the shower after Game 6, Dennis

Johnson looked in on Michael Cooper in the Lakers training room.

"Same time, same place, next year," said Johnson.

Cooper nodded in agreement.

But there was a newcomer on the block, one eager to join the elite. Before long, both teams would realize that Isiah Thomas and the Detroit Pistons were up to the challenge.

15.
Back to Back

Lakers and Bad Boys

To repeat.

That was Pat Riley's obsession.

Soon after the Lakers had wrapped up their 1987 title, someone got around to asking the Laker coach if his team could repeat as champions.

"I guarantee it," he said flatly.

Nineteen seasons had passed since the Celtics had won consecutive championships in 1968 and '69. Obviously, the feat had become difficult to accomplish in the modern NBA, but Riley rejected the notion that it was impossible. He believed that winning and winning again was a test of will, that greatness was available to the team that had the mental toughness to fight for it. He knew that the Lakers were a team of mentally strong individuals. They just needed someone to drive them to greatness. And he was that person.

Beginning with training camp and throughout the season, he pushed them like a man obsessed. He was Captain Ahab, and the repeat championship was the elusive great whale. On occasion the crew came close to mutiny, but somehow Riley knew when to lighten up just enough to keep them going.

The Lakers' Showtime image — Magic's smile and the electraglide fast break, the run and gun and fun — was a bit misleading. All

Andrew D. Bernstein/NBA Photos

Laker coach Pat Riley watched Isiah Thomas work against Byron Scott in the '88 Finals.

251

in all they were a serious lot. Kareem and Worthy and A.C. Green were as businesslike as accountants. Magic, too, had his fun face, but he had hardly been frivolous in his pursuit of basketball excellence over his career. As a team, they practiced as hard as a Marine drill team. Detail mattered. Distraction wasn't tolerated. They had to be tough. They had to work. And they didn't slip often, but when they did, Riley was there to remind them, to irritate them with his professorial tone and his mind games. In retrospect, Riley probably burned out his relationships with his players during the 1987-88 season, which led to his leaving the Lakers after the 1990 playoffs. But the coach knew that was the price he might have to pay to get that consecutive title, and he was willing to pay it.

In the end, the Lakers' intensity became a way of life, one the Boston Celtics couldn't match.

But there was a team in the Eastern Conference that could. The Detroit Pistons were driven by obsessions of their own. They, too, were a collection of mentally strong individuals who, like the Lakers, were led by a point guard with a beaming smile. But where Magic Johnson was 6'9", the Pistons' Isiah Lord Thomas II was a mere 6'1", a little man capable of dominating a big man's game. He was quick, he could leap, he could handle the ball like a showman, and he had taught himself to shoot quite well. But it was his mental approach to the game, not his physical talents, that set Isiah Thomas apart.

The other Pistons wanted an NBA championship, but Thomas was obsessed by the notion. He had spent his NBA career studying the people who won championships. He wanted to know what they knew, and he had turned this study into a mystical quest. He revered winners, particularly his good friend Magic Johnson.

He would pick Magic's brain in late-night phone calls to the West Coast. They would spend hours talking about what it took to win a championship. "I hate that I taught him," Magic would say later. "That's the only thing. I should go back and kick myself."

For the most part, it was only knowledge. The real wisdom Isiah would have to earn himself, the hard way. Which he gladly did, pushing himself and his teammates, night in and night out.

Why did Isiah Thomas want a championship so badly? Some observers have concluded that his drive came from his meager beginnings in a Chicago ghetto. But while many youngsters have come out of the inner city playing basketball, few have driven themselves to the point of exhaustion to win a championship. Thomas had first shown this singular desire at the University of Indiana, where as a sophomore he had led the Hoosiers to the NCAA title.

After that championship season he entered the 1981 NBA draft, and the Pistons made him the second overall pick in the field. He really didn't have to prove anything. He was a bright young guard who showed offensive brilliance. But he was only 6'1", and Detroit was a terrible team. Nobody really expected him to be dominant. He could have had a lot of fun and made great money just being Isiah, the kid with the million-dollar smile. But he wanted to be more than that. He wanted to be bathed in that ineffable light of joy reserved for champions.

So he did what Pat Riley and Magic Johnson and Larry Bird and Bill Russell had done.

He played the mind game.

1988

It is important to note that he liked to be called James Worthy. Not Jim Worthy, or Air Worthy, or even Wings Worthy. Just James. In every facet of his life and his game, he seemed to opt for quiet dignity and grace rather than for flash and fame. It wasn't that he disliked the Hollywood aspect of playing for the Los Angeles Lakers. He just didn't immerse himself in it. Rather than own a mansion, he lived quietly with his wife Angela in a middle-class neighborhood in Westchester, not far from the Forum. If he wanted, he could ride his bike to work. Other folks could take the limos.

Even so, he was the Lamborghini in the Laker motorcade. At 6'9", James Worthy was incredibly quick and swift. No man his size in the league could stay with him. Without a doubt, Magic was the guard who drove the Showtime machine, but Worthy was the forward who made it go.

"Earvin can push the ball upcourt at an incredible tempo," Riley explained. "But he needs someone even faster than himself to break for the wing and fly upcourt. James is the fastest man of his size in the NBA. In terms of finishing the fast break creatively and swiftly and deceptively, no one else compares."

And when the game slowed down a bit, Magic particularly enjoyed getting the ball to Worthy in the low post. Then, Magic said with a smile, it would be over in a matter of seconds.

"His first step is awesome," admitted longtime NBA forward Maurice Lucas.

Worthy developed an array of moves, a repertoire of head fakes and twitches and shifts that he used to reduce his defenders to nervous wrecks. "He'll give a guy two or three fakes, step through, then throw up the turnaround," Riley said. "It's not planned. It's all just happening."

Worthy had begun compiling this arsenal as a youngster in Gastonia, North Carolina. He would go to nearby Charlotte or Greensboro to catch occasional Carolina Cougar games in the ABA. His favorite was Julius Erving, but Worthy studied them all. He was especially good at picking up their moves, then emulating what he had seen, practicing the steps and fakes over and over again before a mirror at home. He grew and became adept enough with the moves to attract scholarship offers from colleges across the country. He flirted with the idea of joining Magic at Michigan State, but his heart was true Carolina blue. He opted to play at Chapel Hill for Dean Smith. Some observers have pointed out that Smith's controlled system kept Worthy's offensive potential tightly leashed, but James had no complaints. Smith turned the force loose just enough to allow Worthy to lead the Tar Heels to the 1982

NCAA championship. He was named the tournament's Most Outstanding Player, and from there it just got better.

He entered the draft as a junior that summer, and the Lakers snatched him up with the top pick. To the pro game, Worthy brought the same strong sense of security that had served him well at UNC. He was coachable and patient and eager to learn. His physical skills and serious approach to the game made him an immediate fit in Los Angeles. He soon established a reputation for raising his level of play in the big games. Over his first five

The Detroit defense collapsed on Magic Johnson.

Andrew D. Bernstein/NBA Photos

years in the league, he came to be known for his quiet excellence.

"I've always been the type of person who just wanted to play my own game," he explained.

It was a storybook tale, but not without complications. In January of his freshman year at UNC, he shattered his ankle on a drive to the basket, and the injury required several operations and a determined rehabilitation. Then a similar injury sidetracked him as a rookie, when he broke his leg just before the 1983 playoffs. He returned with a strong season in 1984 only to throw the bad pass in Game Two of the Finals that allowed the Celtics to avert disaster. But the worst turn came against Houston in the 1986 playoffs when his subpar performance left Lakers owner Jerry Buss pondering a trade that would have sent Worthy to Dallas for Mark Aguirre.

Jerry West interceded and talked Buss out of that deal. Worthy was simply too good to trade, said West. The Lakers' 1987 championship season only confirmed that. As time passed, it became more apparent that the Lakers would need Worthy's low-post game if Riley's obsession with repeating was to be realized. During the 1987-88 season, Kareem would be 41, and while he was still a presence in the Lakers' halfcourt game, he simply couldn't carry the load that he once had. Much of that burden would fall on the shoulders of James Ager Worthy.

Other people stepped forward to do their parts as well. Byron Scott began to realize his potential at shooting guard. He hadn't played well during the 1987 Finals, but the 1987-88 season brought new confidence. He led Los Angeles in scoring, averaging 21.7 points over the regular season while shooting .527 from the field. Also vital was the development of A.C. Green at power forward. He didn't shoot much, but his shot selection and accuracy were outstanding. He rebounded well and continued to learn the intricacies of low-post defense.

Magic once again played brilliantly, although he missed ten games at midseason due to a groin injury. If there was a problem for the Lakers, it was Kareem's age. His decline was apparent throughout the season, yet Mychal Thompson's presence off the bench provided just enough patchwork to keep the Lakers effective in the post.

They started the schedule with an 80 run, the finest opening in their history, and despite a series of ups and downs, they claimed the league's best regular-season record at 62-20. "Guaranteeing a championship was the best thing Pat ever did," Scott said as the schedule

> # I guarantee it.
> — Pat Riley on whether the Lakers would repeat as champions.

drew to a close. "It set the stage in our mind. Work harder, be better. That's the only way we could repeat. We came into camp with the idea we were going to win it again, and that's the idea we have now."

The Celtics groaned their way to the best record in the Eastern Conference at 57-25, but they ran into trouble in the playoffs. After a first-round dismissal of New York, they got ensnarled in a wooly seven-game series with Atlanta and Dominique Wilkins. Boston barely survived, only to face their annual test by Thomas and his persistent band of Pistons. Detroit had claimed the Central Division title with a club-record 54 wins.

The Pistons had been the Isiah Thomas show for most of the past seven years, but slowly but surely General Manager Jack McCloskey had worked the additional pieces into place. Thomas had been the singular talent around which the other components were added.

"It's much easier now because we have an array of talent, people who can go out and do other things," Thomas explained. "I'm not the guy who always has to deliver the basketball, and it takes a lot of pressure off me."

The team came together under the guidance of coach Chuck Daly. A Pennsylvania native, Daly had spent years working his way through the coaching ranks, from high school to college assistant to college head coach. From there, he moved to the pros as an assistant to Philadelphia coach Billy Cunningham. After that came a brief midseason stint as the coach of the woeful Cleveland Cavaliers. He was fired there and wound up back in Philadelphia broadcasting 76ers games. It was there in 1983 that McCloskey approached Daly, who jumped at the chance to help turn Detroit around. By the spring of 1988, Daly was 57 and every bit as hungry as Riley for a championship. But where Riley was intense and professorial, Daly

Andrew D. Bernstein/NBA Photos

Adrian Dantley found many ways to score against the Lakers.

was subdued and fatherly. He flashed his anger when necessary, but he also gave his players, particularly Thomas, plenty of room to breathe.

The same couldn't be said for the Pistons themselves. They gave opponents no room for anything. Their signature was their defense. Daly liked it physical and aggressive, which brought a lot of attention from the officials. The league took to fining them frequently for altercations, and before long the Pistons had acquired the nickname "Bad Boys." They fancied themselves the "Raiders of the NBA," which pleased Al Davis, managing general partner of the Los Angeles Raiders. During the season, he sent sweaters and various gifts displaying the Raiders' silver and black logo.

This style suited the Pistons' personnel, particularly Bill Laimbeer, a role-playing center from Notre Dame often described as the most disliked man in the league. A tough-minded rebounder who wasn't opposed to giving hard fouls on defense, the 6'11" Laimbeer had arrived in a 1982 trade with Cleveland. In Detroit he had worked to

expand his skills and became an excellent defensive rebounder and a fine perimeter shooter, which made him a difficult matchup for opposing centers.

The other major role in the Bad Boys routine was played by power forward Rick Mahorn. He had been acquired from Washington, where he was known as a physical player. In Detroit he expanded that reputation, but he also lost weight and developed his overall game. As Detroit gained momentum, Mahorn's style became increasingly controversial. Some saw him as one of the game's best low-post defenders. Others considered him a thug. Regardless, he was immensely popular with Detroit fans.

To go with this muscle, the Pistons developed one of the best backcourts in the history of the game. Joe Dumars, an unselfish, well-rounded player drafted out of McNeese State in 1985, gave them the best big defensive guard in pro basketball. In time, he would also come to be known for his offensive brilliance, although the team already had plenty of that. The Pistons' firepower began with Thomas, and when he grew weary of scoring, there was always Vinnie "The Microwave" Johnson, the veteran shootist so nicknamed by Boston's Danny Ainge because he heated up so quickly off the bench.

The team's leading scorer was another veteran, forward Adrian Dantley, a legitimate superstar brought in from Utah during the 1986-87 season. He was well-traveled, with stops in Los Angeles, Buffalo, and Utah, and although there were reports of conflicts with Thomas and Daly, he gave Detroit the one thing it didn't have low-post scoring. Although barely 6'5" and hardly a leaper, Dantley had refined a unique ability to score inside. He had a scorer's ego and wanted the ball. While he wasn't exactly negligent on defense, the task didn't make his heart throb.

When Daly needed a stopper in the frontcourt he often went to his bench, which was young and enthusiastic. The '86 draft had brought John Salley out of Georgia Tech and Dennis Rodman, from Southeastern

Oklahoma. After playing through rough spots as rookies, both developed into floor-running forwards, remarkable in their flexibility and utility. Together, the eight-man rotation allowed Daly to deploy a variety of looks. Mostly he went for patient offense and brutally stifling defense. It proved to be a winning formula.

As if this lineup wasn't strong enough, the Pistons then got a midseason gift from Phoenix — seven-foot center-forward James Edwards — in a trade for Ron Moore and a 1991 second-round draft choice. A veteran with dependable offensive ability, Edwards gave Daly yet another option, a big man who could score down low.

Across the league, opponents realized that a force was building in Detroit. In the first round of the playoffs, the Pistons struggled through a best-of-five series with the Washington Bullets before winning the fifth game 99-78. Next came the Chicago Bulls with league MVP Michael Jordan, but Detroit snuffed that threat with defense, 4-1.

At last the Pistons came to the Eastern Finals and their much-awaited showdown with Boston. Bird and the Celtics had escaped the Hawks in a classic Boston Garden showdown, and three days later the Pistons were in town with a week's rest and an issue or two to settle. Much of the pre-game hype centered on the fact that Detroit hadn't beaten the Celtics in the Garden in 21 straight games dating back to December 19, 1982, Thomas's first season in the league. Beyond that, there were the memories of the painful 1987 playoff loss to Boston. Much was made of the Celtic mystique, but the Pistons were determined not to be sidetracked.

"I don't care if we have to play the Little Sisters of the Poor to get to the Finals," said Thomas. "That's what it's all about."

In reality, the Bad Boys wanted Boston in the worst kind of way. That became evident when they promptly won the first game in the Garden and nearly took the second. The Celtics, though, fought for a win in Detroit and tied the series at 2-2. With Game Five in Boston, it appeared that the Celtics had again escaped. But the Pistons worked a big second-half comeback and then finished off Boston back in the Silverdome, 4-2. In the hours leading up to Game Six, Daly had said that the Celtics were like a snake — you had to sever their heads to make sure they were dead. To emphasize that line, Laimbeer showed up for the Friday night practice before the Saturday game with a sickle. The next day, the Bad Boys issued the final cut, 95-90, to advance to the Finals.

Despite their newfound toughness, the Pistons weren't projected as much of a problem for the Lakers. Magic and the boys were a bit winded, having wrestled first Utah then Dallas through a seven-game series. But their determination was convincing. Maybe the series would go six games, figured the experts. Maybe it wouldn't.

As the Finals opened at the Forum on June 7, Magic again made known his determination to win consecutive titles. Isiah allowed that he, too, was determined to win a championship. Yet all this was tempered a bit by the sight of Magic and Isiah kissing before the tipoff of Game One. It was a display of brotherly love, they explained, one which wore a bit thin as the series intensified.

Detroit wasted little time casting doubt on L.A.'s repeat plans. Dantley went to work, making 14 of 16 shots from the floor. Despite his best defensive efforts, Green watched helplessly as Dantley worked his peculiar offense. "It's so slow, you almost fall asleep," Green said of Dantley's shot. "He's got a slow release on it. You don't expect him to shoot it because of the timing, he's out of rhythm. You expect him to pass. And he has it back far enough, so it's difficult to reach."

Dantley's confidence was enough to lead the Pistons to a shocking 105-93 win and a 1-0 lead in the series. Suddenly, the Los Angeles press noticed that the Lakers bore a remarkably striking resemblance to the Celtics: i.e. old and tired. Riley agreed with the writers that it would be difficult to stop Dantley through the rest of the series. "Adrian seems so committed," Riley said, "so dedicated to a mission. That's the beauty of players who have been on struggling teams. When they see a chance to be a champion, they get that special commitment."

Dantley took immediate offense at that notion. Just because he had played for weaker teams before coming to the Pistons didn't mean that he hadn't given 100%, he replied. "Everybody talks about the playoffs being the time to turn it up a notch. Not me. I'm already full-force."

As the shock of the loss wore off, the Lakers felt humiliation. Like the Bulls and Celtics before them, the Lakers had gotten a taste of Detroit's defense. Much of the credit belonged to assistant coach Ron Rothstein, who would leave the Pistons after the season to become head coach of the Miami Heat. But the last thing he wanted to do was start crowing. "To say I am the architect of the defense...is a misnomer," Rothstein said. "There is nothing tricky about it, absolutely nothing. We have not written the book on it. It's been done before and it'll be done again. Good defense requires that you defend off the dribble, defend low-post people and help each other, and what nobody talks about is we are an excellent defensive rebounding team. But you're only as good as your people, and you're only as good as your people want to work at it."

The Detroit staff immediately sensed the danger of false security. "The onslaught will be unbelievable," Daly said before Game Two. "They'll attack in every way. Usually, when something like this happens, Pat comes up with some big move or

something unusual. So we spent all night trying to figure it out. Nothing came to mind."

Actually, things looked bad for the Lakers. They were tired and down 1-0. They faced a confident, eager opponent. To make things worse, Magic came down with the flu. He played anyway and scored 23 points in Game Two. Worthy scored 26 and Scott had 24, and as Daly had feared, the Lakers charged back and evened the series with a 108-96 win. "I don't think there's any doubt Earvin Johnson showed the heart of a champion," Riley said.

Andrew D. Bernstein/NBA Photos

Isiah had eyes for the title.

"He was weak, very weak. But this is what I call a hope game you hope you get through it-and we got through it."

Dantley had led the Pistons with just 19 points, and Thomas finished with 13 after spending much of the game on the bench in foul trouble. "I'd like to say I'm satisfied with a split," said Daly, "but I'm not really. We had a chance to win the basketball game. Now we've got three at home. It'll be interesting to see if we can hold serve in our home territory."

It was interesting. Game Three would bring the Finals to the Pontiac Silverdome, where crowds of 40,000 or more were expected. On Sunday, June 12, the Lakers returned a high, hard one past the Pistons to win 99-86. The main damage was done in the third period when Los Angeles shot 64% and outscored Detroit 31-14 to break open a one-point game.

The Pistons realized that they had finally met the real Lakers, the defending champions. "Today's the first time in a long time that we felt we were beaten," Laimbeer said. "In all the Boston series, we felt we won all six games. And we felt we outplayed the Lakers in the first two games of the series even though we lost Game Two.

This is the first time since Game Two against Chicago we felt someone beat us rather than us just blowing it."

Once again, Magic had shone despite his illness. His 18 points, 14 assists, and 6 rebounds had pushed the Lakers right along. They also got a solid inside game from Green, who pulled down 8 rebounds and scored 21 points by hitting 9 of 11 from the field. He also held Dantley to only 14 points, including just 2 in the second half.

"They just whipped us," Dantley said. "They were just better than us today. I know one thing: I got hammered today, and I only went to the free-throw line once."

The Pistons, though, had more to worry about than free throws. Isiah had sustained a lower back bruise trying to block a Mychal Thompson shot. He spent the hours before Game Four in bed or in a hot tub. "He wasn't going to miss a championship game," Salley

Andrew D. Bernstein/NBA Photos

Kareem's skyhook remained a weapon.

said later. "I kept whispering in his ear, 'You've never felt better, you've never felt better,' and he said, 'You're right.'"

He made the lineup, and the Pistons came right back to take the game 111-86, as the love affair between Isiah and Magic turned into a scrap. Daly had been concerned that Johnson's smiling demeanor was stripping his players of some of their intensity. Those worries departed as the Pistons focused their efforts on shutting down the Laker guard. The main assignment went to Rodman, whose annoying defense wore Johnson down and erased his perpetual smile.

"Magic is tough because he likes to penetrate," explained Rodman. "But I try to distract him, and hopefully he won't be able to look up the court and make one of those great passes."

Of the added defensive attention, Magic would only say, "[Rodman] doesn't frustrate me. I don't get frustrated. He creates some problems for me, but not a lot."

Yet anyone who witnessed the runaway fourth quarter had to disagree with Magic. At one point, he knocked Isiah to the floor with an elbow, and Thomas leaped back up in his face. Afterward, the press wanted to know if the friendship was off.

"It was nothing personal — just business," Thomas replied.

"That's all it is," agreed Magic. "It's business."

Would it be forgotten?

"It's forgotten until Thursday," Magic said.

The Pistons also aimed their offense at Magic and drove him to the bench early in the second half with foul trouble. "We looked to go inside very strong and try to get fouled," Salley explained. "It put Magic on the bench."

With him out of the game, the Pistons built a substantial lead. During the timeouts, Laimbeer was almost frantic. He kept saying, "No letup! We don't let up!"

They didn't, and blew out the defending NBA champions by 25 points.

Although Isiah scored only 10 points on 2-of-7 shooting from the floor, he ignored the back pain and turned in an excellent performance with 12 assists and a game-high 9 rebounds. "I think my presence, just my being out on the court, was really all we needed," he said. "I think I was a threat. The Lakers always had to be conscious of me."

If anything, his injury disrupted the Lakers by shifting his focus from scoring to passing. He had 6 assists in the first quarter alone. "I was at home the last two nights and I was looking at the tapes, seeing the kind of defense the Lakers were playing," he said. "I knew we could take advantage of a lot of traps they were using. It was a matter of us handling the ball and getting it in the right position."

Dantley was the major beneficiary of this development. Left open by the trapping Laker defense, he led the team with 27 points. Vinnie Johnson came off the bench to add 16 while Edwards had 14 points and 5 rebounds.

Daly was probably as pleased as he'd ever been with a Pistons effort. "It's not just the talent on this team we've got a lot of pride and determination," he said. "Our guys gave us a big effort. They've been doing it all year when we've had our backs to the wall. Now my only concern is they don't go back to prosperity in the next game."

Opponents could always expect a friendly greeting from Bill Laimbeer.

Andrew D. Bernstein/NBA Photos

Detroit played well despite a round of distractions. Game Five would be the Pistons' last in the Silverdome. After a decade in the indoor football stadium, they would move to their new home, the Palace of Auburn Hills, for the 1988-89 season. As a result, there was plenty of reminiscing about the good old days when Piston teams struggled in the giant arena before tiny crowds. The building had seen the club's transformation from a cellar dweller into a championship contender.

The Lakers opened Game Five with a fury of physical intimidation, scoring the game's first 12 points. But that approach soon backfired.

"It seemed to me [the Lakers] were trying to be physical," Dantley said later. "They made fouls they didn't have to make. It seemed they were trying to say, 'Hey, we can play physical.' Then they had all their big guys on the bench."

Dantley played a major role in this turnabout, scoring 25 points, 19 of them in the first half to rally the Pistons to a 59-50 halftime lead. "A.C. and the guys played him hard, as hard as they could," Magic said of Dantley. "Give him credit...he made the fallaway jumpers."

Daly turned the full heat of the Pistons' bench on the Lakers early. Vinnie Johnson scored 12 of his 16 points in the first half to keep Detroit moving.

It was just another example of Detroit relying upon its "D's" — defense, depth, Dantley, Dumars (19 points on 9 of 13 from the floor), and of course, Daly. The depth received extra emphasis. "They [the Lakers] played great in spots," Vinnie said, "but we had fresher guys: myself, Salley, Rodman, and Edwards. When you're playing against fresh guys, it's tough to hang in there."

The Lakers had gotten away from what they did best-rebounding and running. "We couldn't contain anyone on the boards," Riley said. "We had 2 defensive boards in the fourth quarter and they had 10 offensive boards. You're not going to beat anyone with that."

The Pistons' 104-94 victory was a perfect farewell to the Silverdome. "I told Joe Dumars

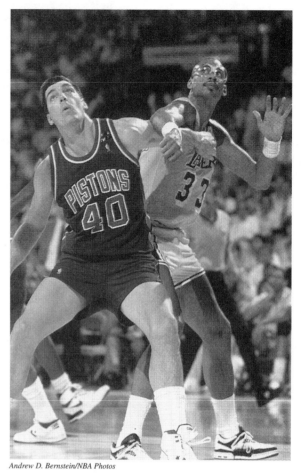

Andrew D. Bernstein/NBA Photos

Abdul-Jabbar's age made the tussle in the post a struggle.

with a minute left in the game to look around and enjoy this because you'll never see anything like it again," Laimbeer said. "Forty-one thousand people waving towels and standing...it was awesome."

Detroit held a 3-2 lead, but the Pistons would have to claim the championship in the Forum, and that wouldn't be a cakewalk. The series had come down to a classic confrontation, and both sides responded appropriately.

The Pistons trailed 56-48 early in the third quarter of Game Six, when Thomas scored the next 14 points in trancelike fashion — two free throws after a drive in the lane, then a five-footer off an offensive rebound, followed by four jumpers, a bank shot, and a layup.

Then, with a little more than four minutes to go in the period, Isiah landed on Michael

Cooper's foot and had to be helped from the floor. Despite a severely sprained ankle, Thomas returned 35 seconds later and continued the offensive assault. By the end of the quarter, he had hit 11 of 13 shots from the floor for 25 points, setting an NBA Finals record for points in a quarter. Better yet, he had single-handedly given his team an 81-79 lead.

That momentum stayed with them, and with a minute left in the game, they held a 102-99 edge. They were a mere 60 seconds from an NBA title, the franchise's first ever. The league trophy was wheeled into the Pistons' locker room. Iced champagne was brought in. CBS requested the presence of team owner Bill Davidson to receive the trophy. Moments later, those plans would be rapidly disassembled, the trophy taken away before Davidson could feel it.

"A minute is a long time," Magic would say later. "A long time. It's just two scores and two stops and you're ahead."

The first Laker score came with 52 seconds left on Byron Scott's 14-foot jumper, which brought L.A. within one at 102-101. Detroit struggled for the right shot on its possession and failed when Isiah Thomas missed an 18-footer. With 14 seconds left, Abdul-Jabbar set up for his skyhook from the baseline, and Laimbeer was whistled for a foul. The Lakers captain made both free throws, giving L.A. a 103-102 lead.

Although they had lost their lead, the Pistons couldn't have asked for a better position. They had the ball and a chance to win it. At 0:08, Joe Dumars took the shot for Detroit, a double pump from six feet away. The shot missed, and the rebound slipped through Dennis Rodman's frantic hands. Byron Scott controlled the loose ball, the series was tied, and the Lakers were smug again.

The dream ending had quickly become a nightmare for Detroit. They faced Game Seven in enemy territory with Isiah's status in deep doubt.

"His ankle is pretty swollen," said Daly. "We got a miraculous game from Isiah, as hurt as

he was. He got us back in the game. On offense, we didn't give him as much support as I would like. We were 45 seconds away from an NBA championship. What can I say?"

Thomas had finished the game with a jammed left pinkie, a poked eye, a scratched face, a ballooned ankle, 43 points, 8 assists, 6 steals, and enough respect to last a lifetime.

"What Isiah Thomas did in the second half was just incredible," said Riley.

Magic added: "I think he was just unconscious. I think he said, 'Okay, I'm going to take this game over.' I've seen him do that before. He was in his rhythm. When he starts skipping and hopping, that means he's in his rhythm. That means he's ready."

"No one said it would be easy," said Thomas. "I'm not devastated. I want to win this championship. I'm willing to pay whatever it

Magic still found ways to get to the basket through the Bad Boys' defense.

Andrew D. Bernstein/NBA Photos

takes. My ankle's hurting, but this game and this series means too much not to be playing. I'm playing — period."

The team trainers had 48 hours to try to work a miracle. But nature needed more time. The ankle took Thomas to the third quarter but no further. Despite limping badly in warmups, he scored 10 points in the first half on the way to leading the Pistons to a 52-47 lead at intermission. But the time between halves brought on stiffness, and he was no longer effective.

The Lakers, meanwhile, got going behind Worthy's low-post scoring and raced to a seemingly insurmountable 90-75 lead in the fourth quarter. Yet just when Riley could taste the reality of his repeat fantasy, the Lakers let up. Somehow the Pistons found a way back. Daly went with a pressure lineup of Johnson, Dumars, Salley, Rodman, and Laimbeer, and they ate up the Lakers' lead in big gulps. At 3:52 Salley knocked in two free throws to close to 98-92, and the Lakers were in obvious panic. At 1:17, Dumars, who led the Pistons with 25 points, hit a jumper to make it 102-100. But Magic scored a free throw off a Rodman foul, stretching it to 103-100. Detroit then had its best opportunity, but Rodman took an ill-advised jumper at 39 seconds. Scott rebounded and was fouled. His two free throws pushed the lead to 105-100. After Dumars made a layup, Worthy hit a free throw and Laimbeer canned a trey, pushing the score to 106-105 with six seconds showing. Green completed the scoring with a layup, making it 108-105, and although the Pistons got the ball to Isiah at midcourt with a second remaining, he fell without getting off a shot.

The furious rally made it hard for Daly, even in all his disappointment, not to feel good. "I love the way we fought back," he said. "Storm back from 15 down against the world champions? You have to love it. You have to love them. I can't say enough about my club. I had doubts, but this team just wouldn't quit. And they had every reason to quit."

Rodman was despondent about taking and missing the jump shot with 39 seconds left. "I don't know why," he said. "I'm not a jump shooter. I don't know what clicked in me. Why couldn't I have just taken it to the rim and torn it down?"

Riley could only give thanks. "It was a nightmare to the very end," he said. "I kept saying, 'Please don't let this end in a nightmare.' We were a great team trying to hold on. Hey, they just put on one of the greatest comebacks in the history of this game and they have nothing to be ashamed of. We're a great team and they had us hanging on at the end. We were able to do

it because of who we are, but they gave us all we could handle."

Worthy had racked up 36 points, 16 rebounds, and 10 assists, a monster triple double if there ever was one. For that and his earlier efforts in the series, he was named the Finals MVP. Self-effacing as usual, Worthy said he would have voted for Magic.

The league had a repeat champion at last. The Lakers had realized their greatness. They were all relieved. And to make sure Riley had no more wise ideas about the future, Kareem kept his eye on the coach during the post-game interviews. It did little good, though. Riley already was working on a name for the next chapter of the Laker adventure.

He planned to call it "Three-peat."

1989

The Pistons opened their training camp in the fall of 1988 with an air of impatience. As Isiah explained, they didn't want to fool with the 1988-89 regular season; they just wanted to go directly to the Finals again where they could correct their mistakes.

But there were distractions. A rift had begun to develop on the team during the 1988 Finals. Before Game Six, when the Pistons held a 3-2 lead, Thomas and Laimbeer had agreed that if either won the MVP award, the winner would split the $35,000 prize money among his teammates. Dantley, however, had said he would do no such thing. The irritation at this attitude worsened when they ultimately lost, and no Piston won the award.

Also, Dantley had sat on the bench during the Game Seven comeback against the Lakers and was sulking about it. Although he admitted to wondering about it privately, he said he had never questioned Daly about keeping him on the bench in the last minutes while Rodman played. For his part, Daly said he didn't care what Dantley thought of Game Seven. Daly said he had gone with a quick lineup that had almost wiped out the Lakers' big lead and pulled off a miracle.

Although the Pistons were winning their way through the regular season, it soon became obvious that they weren't playing all that well together. Thomas speculated that the team was struggling offensively because it was playing so well defensively. He wanted to pick up the tempo, an obvious solution to the doldrums, but that would take the team further away from Dantley's halfcourt post game. The team split on this issue, headed in two different directions.

It seemed that one event after another added to the turmoil. First, assistant coach Dick Versace, who communicated well with Dantley, left to become head coach of the Indiana Pacers. Then, on January 11, Dumars broke a bone in his left hand during a 100-93 loss to the Knicks in the Palace. The injury sidelined him a month and added to Detroit's offensive woes. Over the first 27 days of January, the Pistons went 6-6.

Finally, Dantley was traded to Dallas for Mark Aguirre, a childhood friend of Thomas's. The night before the trade, the Pistons took it to the champion Lakers in the Forum, 111-103. Dumars had returned from injury, and the team's spirits had buoyed.

Which explains why Dantley was caught off-guard by the news. He balked, and at first refused to report to Dallas. Aguirre, for his part, was elated. The number-one pick ahead of Thomas in the 1981 draft, he had played well for Dallas for seven seasons yet had acquired a tarnished image at the same time. Some of his teammates said he was selfish, that he didn't always play hard. The expectations in Dallas had been unrealistic, claimed Aguirre.

"The offense is not as much concentrated on me," he said of his new team, "but I am able to contribute to a better team and that makes me happy."

Dantley was anything but happy, and neither was Dumars, his closest friend on the team. Like Dumars, Dantley was a quiet man, with a modest, conservative approach to life. With a dozen pro seasons under his belt, Dantley's nickname of "Teacher" was apt. There was much he had taught the younger Dumars about coping with the pro lifestyle.

Andrew D. Bernstein/NBA Photos

The acquisition of Mark Aguirre was one factor that helped swing the balance to Detroit in '89.

Throughout his career, Dumars, the youngest of seven children of a Louisiana trucker, had quietly amazed the sportswriters covering the Pistons. But never more so than in the aftermath of the trade.

Although deeply hurt by his friend's trade, Dumars never allowed so much as a ripple to enter his businesslike approach to the game.

Detroit had given the 33-year-old Dantley plus the next year's first-round draft pick for the 29-year-old Aguirre. Was the trade good or bad? The players were very similar, both post-up small forwards, both used to getting the ball. Would Aguirre show the spoiled act that had turned off some fans in Dallas? Would he agree to share playing time with the incredible rebounding, defensive machine, Dennis Rodman?

The answer was yes. Aguirre wanted to fit in, and Detroit was deep enough to allow him to be introduced slowly. Besides, they were winning. As tumultuous as February had been, the Pistons finished the month 8-3. By mid-March, Daly was witnessing the transformation. "I see more signs of unselfishness," the coach said. "We're definitely more cohesive offensively. We're moving the ball more quickly, making that extra pass."

Aguirre had speeded up the offense, and it was something the players noticed almost immediately. Thomas, who had never played organized basketball with Aguirre before, was as surprised as the rest. Rather than waiting for Dantley to work his unique offensive style, the Pistons found themselves benefitting from Aguirre's passing. Eager to fit in, the 6'6" forward was the offensive threat Detroit needed inside to force the double-team. As soon as the second defender arrived, Aguirre dumped off the ball and the Pistons' perimeter game did the rest.

"We're going in as a unit," Aguirre said proudly as the playoffs began, "and to go in as a unit, you're a lot stronger." NBA beat writers began exchanging puzzled glances. Is this the same Mark Aguirre they knew from Dallas?

"Yes," Aguirre said, smiling. "I just shoot less."

The Pistons closed out March at 16-1, and Daly was named Coach of the Month. At the end of February, they had languished five games behind Cleveland in the Central Division standings. But two weeks later, the Pistons had taken the lead. They closed out the schedule with the league's best record, 63-19, which gave them the homecourt advantage throughout the playoffs.

The finish had been particularly satisfying to Laimbeer, who with Thomas had been with the team through most of the '80s. Asked the difference between this team and its competition, the center replied, "We have an unusually large number of mentally strong players on this ball club. Make no mistake, we did learn from Boston the last few years about how far mental toughness can carry you. They were the champions of that department every year."

The Pistons had never before entered the playoffs as the dominant team in basketball.

Then again, no other team had been in the league so long without winning a title. Fred Zollner had founded the club in 1941 to play in the old National League in Fort Wayne, Indiana, naming the team for his product. The Fort Wayne Pistons won a series of titles in the old league in the early 1940s, then joined the NBA for 1947-48. In 1955 and again in 1956 the Pistons went to the NBA Finals, but lost both times. They moved to Detroit in '57 but showed little torque. For the next twenty-five years, the Pistons didn't even make the playoffs.

But by 1987, that had changed. The rivalry with the Boston Celtics, for example, had grown to the point that 61,983 fans filled the Silverdome for a regular-season meeting in 1987-88. The Pistons set an NBA attendance record that season, and gained the distinction of being the first team in NBA history to draw one million fans in a season.

Thomas and Dantley didn't always agree.

But even with all those people in the Silverdome, it simply wasn't a basketball facility. So owner William Davidson and a group of partners acquired land in Auburn Hills, north of Detroit and just beyond the Silverdome, and built the Palace, a state-of-the-art sports facility.

Hopes were high heading into the playoffs that the Pistons could do something they had never done before.

The Lakers, of course, had even bigger dreams. They had finished the regular season at 57-25, and Riley had gone so far as to patent his "Threepeat" slogan in hopes of cashing in on the souvenir market. His prospects for big royalties seemed to improve with each round of the playoffs.

264

In the NBA Playoffs, 1989 was the Year of the Broom. The Knicks swept the Philadelphia 76ers in three close first-round games, and in a fit of youthful excess, some New York players grabbed brooms from the custodial staff in Philadelphia and began doing the floor. Unfortunately, the Chicago Bulls, led by the amazing Michael Jordan, upset New York in the next round in a hard-fought six-game series.

For better or worse, the tone had been set for the playoffs. Detroit made a sweep of its first two rounds. In Boston, Larry Bird had spent virtually the entire season on the sidelines after undergoing heel surgery in November. As a result, the Pistons easily pushed aside the Celtics 3-0 in the first round. The same fate befell the Milwaukee Bucks in the second round, 4-0. Only Michael Jordan and the Chicago Bulls interrupted this trend. They won a pair of games before falling 4-2 to the determined Pistons. The Lakers had taken the sweep concept to even greater lengths, going on an unprecedented 11-0 run to the Finals. Portland, Seattle, and Phoenix — each had gone out with the dustpan. The wins meant that Riley needed only one more victory to become the winningest coach in playoff history. It seemed like a lock.

The Detroit papers had fun with the Pistons/Lakers rematch in the Finals, calling it "The Sequel." As things turned out, it certainly had the properties of one. Big on staging, hype, and promotion, and plenty of talent.

"In training camp," Laimbeer said, "we knew that we wanted to get back to the Finals. We wanted to win a championship. And we set about a game plan where we had to do A, B, C, and D to get back there. We've done A, B, C, and D. Now comes the E part."

The E didn't stand for easy. After all, the Pistons were facing Magic, who had a real shot at staking out a plot of basketball history by claiming three consecutive titles. To a man, the Pistons knew Magic and Company would be dangerous.

"I understand the Lakers as a basketball team," said Isiah. "But more importantly, I understand them as people. In order to beat the opponent you've got to understand the people that you're playing against. Because in a playoff, plays don't beat you, passing and all that. What beats you in the playoffs is people, individual people digging deep down within themselves and deciding that they're going to win a basketball game. That's what beats you.

"L.A. has our rings from last year and we want our own ring," Laimbeer said. "That's enough incentive right there."

At the outset, the potential for drama seemed high. The 42-year-old Kareem Abdul-Jabbar had announced his retirement effective at the close of the season. The Lakers hoped to send him out with another ring. It wasn't hard to imagine Los Angeles stealing a third title and the Bad Boys condemned to the life of a bridesmaid. But just before Game One in Detroit, Byron Scott suffered a severe hamstring injury in practice. He would miss at least the first two games.

What did the loss of Scott mean to the Lakers? a writer asked Isiah. "I don't know what it means to them and I don't care," Thomas said quickly. "They didn't care about me last year when I was hurt."

The Pistons further emphasized this by absolutely smoking the Lakers in Game One, with the guards popping from every place on the floor. Thomas had 24 points, Dumars 22, and Johnson 19. Daly was ecstatic; during the Chicago series, the backcourt had shot less than 40% from the field. With six minutes left, Detroit led 97-79 and the final score was 109-97. "We played probably our best playoff game," Daly said afterward. "We were aggressive offensively and defensively, particularly on offense."

"It's nice," agreed Thomas, "but we know from experience that it takes four. We have one win and there are six games left."

Once bitten, twice shy, the Pistons weren't about to let their spirits soar just because of an opening homecourt win, no matter how much the Lakers offense had struggled. The big effort had come from Mahorn, who harassed James Worthy into 6-for-18 shooting.

265

As Daly expected, the Lakers snapped right back in Game Two, pounding the boards and taking a strong first-quarter lead. But Dumars got hot with 24 points in the first half (he would finish with 33) to keep Detroit close. L.A. held a 62-56 lead at intermission; Michael Cooper, Scott's backup, was hitting, and Magic had that look in his eye. But events turned in the third quarter. With about four minutes left, a Salley block of a Mychal Thompson shot started a Detroit fast break. Magic dropped back to play defense, and in so doing, pulled his hamstring. He sensed immediately that the injury was serious and flailed at the air in frustration. He hobbled off the court, never to return.

The Pistons had made the bucket on the break to tie the game at 75, but the Lakers charged to a 90-81 lead late in the third quarter. But Detroit had owned the fourth through most of the playoffs, and Game Two was no different. The Lakers opened the period with three missed baskets and an offensive foul as Detroit first tied the game, then went up 102-95.

Next it was the Pistons' turn to miss and mess up, as Thompson led a Los Angeles comeback. The final snafu came with a 24-second violation by Detroit, giving the Lakers the ball with 8 seconds left. Down 106-104, they had a chance to tie or win it. The tie seemed a cinch when Worthy was fouled and went to the line.

There, the exhaustion caught up with the MVP of the previous year's Finals. He missed the first and made the second, leaving the Lakers short at 106-105. Thomas then hit two free throws with a second remaining for the final 108-105 score.

Things looked good for the Pistons with a 2-0 lead, only nobody was saying that as the series headed to L.A. But the immediate speculation centered on Magic. Could he play?

He tried, but he had to leave Game Three after just five minutes of the first quarter with the Lakers leading 11-8. "I wanted to play so bad, but I just could not," Johnson said later. "I could not make the cuts, defensively, that I had to make."

"He made a heck of an effort," Dumars observed, "but it just wasn't there. You could tell by his motion. One time, the ball was right there a couple feet away, and he just couldn't get it."

Without him, the Lakers still played like a championship contender. Worthy scored 26 points, and Kareem played like a much younger man, scoring 24 points with 13 rebounds. The only veteran in the backcourt, Cooper had 13 assists and 15 points.

But it wasn't enough.

For starters, there was Dennis Rodman. Wracked by painful back spasms, he ripped down 19 rebounds between gasps — going to the sideline for rubdowns, then coming back in to worm his way inside the Lakers' interior defense for offensive boards.

That was the supporting work. The marquee effort came from the guards. Once again, the Detroit backcourt lit it up. Dumars hit for 31, including a blind, unconscious third quarter in which he scored 17 consecutive-points (21 in all for the period). The Lakers had trouble switching on defense and left him open repeatedly, and Dumars was obliged to do the damage. And when he went to his seat for a rest, Vinnie Johnson picked up the slack, scoring 13 points in the crucial fourth period (he finished with 17).

Thomas pitched in with 26 points and 8 assists. Much of his best work came in the clutch — 6 key points and 3 assists. The only problem was, so did his only real mistakes of the afternoon, including a bad pass with the Pistons leading 103-102. Still, things seemed pretty secure with 2:06 left when the Microwave hit one of his big-time jumpers to give Detroit a 109-104 lead.

The Pistons maintained that 5-point margin until 15 seconds remained, when Thomas allowed A.C. Green to tie him up and steal the ball. Thomas then fouled the Lakers' rookie point guard, David Rivers, who made both, pulling L.A. to 113-110 with 13 seconds left.

Dumars came back in the game then, and with 9 seconds left he tipped the ball out of bounds, giving the Lakers a shot at the tie.

Prior to this game, Rivers had played only eight minutes in the playoffs, none of it in the clutch. But with the injuries to Johnson and Scott, the rookie suddenly found himself with lots of prime time. Now, he was the number-one option on a last-second three-pointer.

"He got away from me," Dumars said of Rivers. "I let up a little because when he broke, I let him go. I thought, 'He can't be the first option, so I am going to take a look and see where the ball is going.' I turned back and the ball was going right to him. Then I knew I had to react. I knew he wouldn't be going to the goal because they needed three. I can't even think of the last time I blocked a shot. It was just instinct. I was a good ways from him. It's amazing what you do in pressure situations."

From about eight feet to Rivers' right, Dumars wheeled about and lunged at the shot. Not only did he block it, he then landed and saved it from going out of bounds.

"That was a first team All-Defensive play right there," Laimbeer said afterward. "To block the shot...yeah, everybody blocks shots, but to block the shot and save the ball to your teammate — that's a big play. That's a play you win championships with."

Not to mention MVP awards. The writers began asking the quiet, reserved Dumars if he had thought about taking the Finals MVP honors. "It would be great," he admitted. "I don't want to downplay it, but championship rings —that's what you play for."

The defensive play seemed to seal the award for Dumars, especially when combined with his offensive outburst. "I just happened to get into one of those zones where a couple of shots went down and I wanted to touch the ball every time it came down the floor," he said of his third-quarter scoring.

"Was it a case where you would talk to Isiah and say, 'I'm hot'?" a writer asked. "Or does he just know that?"

"He knows it," said Dumars. "At one point he asked me, 'What do you want?', meaning what play did I want. I said, 'Just the ball.' That's about how it was, 'Just give me the ball.'"

Andrew D. Bernstein/NBA Photos

The 1989 Finals brought Kareem's last game.

Down 3-0, the Lakers still talked of making history — specifically, becoming the first team ever to overcome a three-game deficit. Tony Campbell, the reserve guard who had filled in admirably for Scott, asserted that such a comeback was in the works.

Wiser voices weren't quite so optimistic.

"It's like you have a real nice sports car and a great driver," Kareem said of the circumstances, "and then all of a sudden you have to find somebody who has been driving a bus to be a driver. That's a learning experience."

The Lakers knew things would be tough. Riley told Worthy he would have to up his game a few notches and get them a win. Riley reminded Worthy how his efforts had paid off in '88. And Worthy responded with a championship effort — 40 points on 17 of 26 shots from the floor, and that with Mahorn in his face every step of the way. But he couldn't do it alone.

The crowd had come expecting an event — Kareem's final game. The big center had conducted his final warmup, his bald pate glistening under the Forum lights. He was composed, spending much of the session standing silently in a half slouch, his hand on his hip. He dropped in one final finger roll and headed over to the bench. With that signal, the team had followed, igniting a round of applause that spread across the Forum crowd.

Once the game started, the pattern was familiar. Mahorn and Cooper mixed it up in the first period, drawing a double technical. With Worthy playing out of his mind, the Lakers took a 35-23 lead at the end of the first. Detroit missed free throws like they were dental appointments, 11 in all in the first half. But Vinnie made one to close out the first-half scoring with L.A. leading 55-49 at intermission.

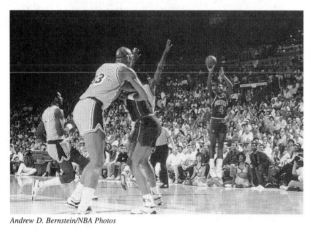

Andrew D. Bernstein/NBA Photos

The Pistons often relied on Dumars' perimeter game.

The Pistons started fast in the third quarter, beginning with an opening trey by Laimbeer. Mahorn then scored 4 quick points and the Pistons took a 59-58 lead moments later when Dumars hit a driving bank shot, drew the foul, and made the free throw, giving him 19 points on the evening. Mahorn followed that with another bucket, and suddenly it was timeout L.A.

When Worthy blasted them back into the lead later in the quarter, the crowd chanted "Three-peat." It was a Hollywood dream that would never see the light of reality. The Lakers held a 78-76 lead at the end of the third, but they knew the Pistons were coming on Everyone in the building knew it. The Pistons turned the chores over to James Edwards, who slammed and picked his way along, giving Detroit the lead in the process. As their momentum increased, the Lakers appeared drained.

When Detroit got the ball back with 3:23 left and a 100-94 lead, the crowd rose to a standing ovation — more a note of thanks than a plea for a miracle Kareem came back in the game, but neither team was playing well. The next two minutes were an exchange of missed shots and turnovers.

At 1:37, Kareem broke the chill with a spin move and bank shot, his last two NBA points, bringing the Lakers to 100-96. The Big Guy went out at 0:47. Then Laimbeer hit a jumper at 0:28, and the Pistons figured it was safe to start hugging during the ensuing timeout. Mahorn stood in the midst of this outbreak, a towel draped over his shoulders, and slowly rotated, looking up into the crowd. Then he raised his arms in triumph. Laimbeer was shouting it-ain't-over-'til-it's-over kinds of things. Dumars just sat quietly, his face pressed into a towel.

Riley sent Kareem back in after the timeout, but Cooper missed a three-pointer and Isiah got fouled. Riley sent Orlando Woolridge in for the Cap. It was hug time for the Lakers. Magic came out to meet Kareem. The crowd's applause was both large and warm, and the Pistons all stepped onto the floor, faced the Laker bench, and joined in.

Then Aguirre suddenly grabbed Thomas and began squeezing his head. Somehow Isiah escaped. Then he turned, hugged Daly, and cried openly for the cameras. Daly later said he forced a tear or two himself, but it looked like a little more than that.

"Free throws. Let's go," Daly said, breaking the spell. Isiah went back to the line. Soon it was over, 105-97. "Kareem. Kareem. Kareem," the crowd intoned again and again.

Just before the fans rushed the floor, Riley strode down the sideline to shake Daly's hand.

It was the only sign Isiah needed. As the final seconds ticked off the clock he sent the ball zipping into the Forum rafters.

As expected, Dumars was named the Finals MVP. Prior to the '89 playoffs, the 6'3" guard was considered one of the best-kept secrets in basketball, primarily because he played in Isiah's shadow. But in the aftermath of the championship, Dumars was swept away in a tide of celebrity. Normally a controlled, measured man, he struggled to keep his emotions in check amid the din of celebration in the Pistons' locker room.

After all, his teammates were the Bad Boys, and Dumars was their resident Good Guy. He played steady defense, provided outbursts of scoring when necessary, and otherwise blended into the background. On a roster bristling with personalities, Dumars was inordinately plain. "I can understand," he said, "that people want to see the fancy stuff. But, believe me, we've got enough fancy stuff on the Detroit Pistons where I don't have to be fancy."

Dumars said he looked to his father, Joe Dumars II, a hard-working Louisiana trucker, for help in maintaining his equilibrium. "I compare myself here to the way he was on his job," he explained. "A lot of truckers are some rough guys. For him at his work, it was almost like it is here for me — he was one of the good guys with the bad guys, the Bad Boys. Because those truckers are some bad boys. He was one of the good guys. He drove the speed limit and didn't hog the road."

The jubilation of the championship did little to alter Dumars' modus operandi. While his teammates celebrated loudly, he quietly retreated to the back of the locker room to answer a few questions. His answers were as steady and unfancy as his play.

Before Dumars could acknowledge a request for an on-the-spot TV interview, Vinnie Johnson yelled from across the room, "Broadway Joe! Yo, yo, yo!"

Broadway Joe? Dumars said he wanted to be recognized for his ability, yet when the media came in waves, he met the onslaught with a fluttering smile and retreated a little further into the background. The challenge, he said in an aside during the locker room celebration, is to keep your emotions from blasting through the ceiling and going skyward, taking your ego with them.

It seemed that Dumars had met that challenge.

1990

For the Detroit Pistons, pursuing the 1989 championship had been a do-or-die kind of proposition. If they hadn't won the title, it wouldn't have been too hard to imagine Isiah Thomas and Bill Laimbeer doing weave drills in the loony bin.

They had wanted the trophy that badly. And when the Pistons finally got their golden prize, they embraced it, kissed it, sweet-talked it, and danced with it, beginning an orgy of celebration that eventually spanned the continent.

But they barely had time to come down to earth when they heard the news: General Manager Jack McCloskey had been forced to leave four players from the roster unprotected in the expansion draft, and among the four was Mahorn, the team's starting power forward. The 6'10", 255-pound Mahorn had been so much a part of the Pistons mindset, no one had really considered him a candidate. Besides, the coaches loved him. McCloskey and the Pistons staff had guided him through a weight problem when he first came to the team in 1985. They had been positive and encouraging in his development as a player. In return, Mahorn was fiercely loyal to the organization. He had often said publicly that he would run through a wall for Chuck Daly.

McCloskey had tried without luck to make a deal that would keep him in Detroit. When the expansion Minnesota Timberwolves made Mahorn their pick, all of Detroit was stunned.

Mahorn was devastated, but he maintained his composure. He spoke briefly with his teammates, told them he had enjoyed playing with them, and wished them luck.

"It's a sad, sad day," said McCloskey. "We feel like we're being penalized for having depth. It's heartbreaking."

Deep as his disappointment was, Mahorn joined the team for their visit with President Bush at the White House. The President laughed with them and spoke of a kinder, gentler Pistons, and Thomas declared that with Mahorn's departure the Bad Boys would be laid to rest.

But Daly wasn't so sure that the Bad Boys label could be dismissed that easily. "I think it will be difficult to put aside," he said just before training camp opened. "I don't know if we'll want to."

The Pistons had patented their aggressive style of play, though it would change a bit with Mahorn's departure. Edwards and Rodman would become starters, and Aguirre would move to the bench as sixth man. Edwards gave the team a post-up feature, but the Pistons would still rely on aggressive defense and a strong perimeter game.

Some observers thought Mahorn's leadership would be Detroit's biggest loss. Daly wasn't so sure. "His leadership was an abstract thing," the coach said of Mahorn. "He was a very physical, intimidating player. We're going to miss those attributes."

Understandably bitter, Mahorn refused to report to the Timberwolves until his contract was renegotiated, so Minnesota traded him to Philadelphia, which only increased the Pistons' anguish. Not only had they lost an intimidating player, but he would now make one of their Eastern Conference opponents much tougher. In Philly, Mahorn teamed with Charles Barkley to give the 76ers a surprisingly strong and intimidating frontcourt. They were labeled "Thump and Bump," which was both accurate and catchy. The Sixers gained power as the season progressed, and that only increased speculation over whether Detroit had given up the wrong player.

The Pistons got off to a so-so start, going 18-11 through November and December, but their wins included a victory over the Lakers at the Forum. By January, they had made their adjustments and were playing with the confidence of defending world champions. For Isiah and his teammates, years of questions and doubts had been abruptly answered with the 1989 NBA title. Yet they also found that success merely meant that the old questions had been replaced by new ones. Was their title a fluke, made possible by Magic's hamstring injury? Would one ring be enough for the Pistons? Did they have the toughness to repeat?

An indication that they had grown a bit complacent came in January when the Lakers whipped them soundly in Auburn Hills. It wasn't the loss itself so much as it was the way the Pistons lost. They were outfought by the Lakers, who pushed and shoved and banged the Pistons out of the low post and out of the game.

"Aggressiveness is defined as the disposition to dominate, and they had dominated us in the aggressiveness department," Pat Riley said. "They're used to playing that game." What the Lakers did to the Pistons was merely turn their own rough game upon them. Edwards had given the Pistons a new look, the kind of low-post scoring Detroit hadn't seen in years. But the Lakers simply shoved him out beyond his range and shut down the Pistons' halfcourt offense.

The loss illuminated the need to cut a new groove, and they did. "We are a different team," Daly said. "We're physical, but not as physical." Surprisingly, they played better defense. In 1989, they gave up 101 points per game on the average. For 1990, they allowed opponents only 98.3 per outing. The explanation was simple, Daly said. Their success in the 1989 playoffs had made the Pistons real believers in defense. And with Mahorn gone, Rodman, the defensive whiz, was seeing more playing time.

Just as surprisingly, the Pistons were scoring less in 1990, 102 points per game as opposed to 106 for 1989. But that could partly be explained in the efficiency of their halfcourt game. With Edwards scoring down low, the offense was controlling the clock more. "We've changed up front," Daly said. "Jimmy is playing very, very well in the low post, scoring great, because he's getting a lot more minutes." Bolstering all of this was a newfound

Andrew D. Bernstein/NBA Photos

With Johnson and Scott out, Kareem's swan song was a sweep.

confidence, which the Pistons toted everywhere they went around the league.

They responded to the Laker loss by going on a 25-1 win streak, the third strongest in league history, stretching from January to March. Each successive win became more of a battle. Every team they met seemed ready to match the Pistons blow for blow.

"That takes a lot out of you," said John Salley, "because everybody else is playing real tough against us. Everybody else is trying to prove how tough they can be, how strong they can be."

There were times when even their mental toughness wasn't enough to get a win. "It's only so much that your body can take," Thomas said. "Sometimes you can say it's a matter of mind over matter. Sometimes your mind can be as strong as you want it to be,

and your body will say, 'Hey, I got to stop and rest.' It's like a built-in clock that tells you your body can only take so much. And then you hit the wall. The key is if you can regroup as a team and go back at it again."

They hit the wall March 21. A loss in Houston ended their streak, and in a way the Pistons seemed almost relieved. They had made their statement. "To have a streak like that today, with all the great scorers in the game today, is a tremendous achievement," Houston coach Don Chaney said. "They convinced everybody that a team doesn't need a big man in the middle to win if they're committed to playing team ball and working hard on defense."

That sounded fine, said Joe Dumars, "but the streak will be insignificant if we don't wind up as champions."

Vinnie Johnson speculated that they would get right back on track. But the next night against San Antonio, Dumars broke his left hand. Over the next few days, there were reports that he could be lost for the remainder of the regular season. Two nights later, the Pistons lost again, in Dallas. Their magic spell had been broken, and suddenly they seemed vulnerable.

For a time during the win streak, Detroit had owned the best record in the league. But the Lakers were red hot as well and eventually passed them on their way to a league-best 63-19 finish. To replace Kareem Abdul-Jabbar at center, Los Angeles used a combination of Mychal Thompson and rookie Vlade Divac of Yugoslavia, and it had worked well. As the season closed, the Lakers seemed assured of another trip to the Finals.

Detroit seemed in real peril. Dumars returned early from his injury, but the Pistons put forth an average showing in April to finish 59-23. Although their record was still enough to give them top billing in the Eastern Conference, some observers thought their lukewarm finish was a sign that they didn't have the drive to repeat. In 1989, they had focused their entire mindset on claiming the home-court advantage in the playoffs. Midway through the 1990 season, Thomas had foreseen that the Pistons probably wouldn't have the home-court advantage against the Lakers and would instead have to rely on their ability to win on the road.

Detroit promptly swept Indiana in the first round of the playoffs, then dropped the Knicks 4-1 in the second round. The news got even better for the Pistons when Chicago eliminated Philadelphia. For the second year in a row, Detroit would have to contend with Michael Jordan in the conference finals, but that appeared preferable to battling the physical Sixers.

As the Pistons were finding new life, the Lakers stumbled in the Western playoffs. They beat Houston in the first round but then came apart in the second round against a young and inspired Phoenix team. The Suns won, 4-1, and in the aftermath Pat Riley decided to leave coaching to become a broadcaster for NBC. Just like that, the team of the '80s had come unraveled.

The Lakers' demise opened the way for the Portland Trail Blazers in the Western Conference. The Blazers had always been considered a talented, dangerous team in the West. But for four straight years they had lost in the first round of the playoffs, and the subsequent frustrations led to team conflicts, particularly between Coach Mike Schuler and 6'7" shooting guard Clyde Drexler. In the middle of the 1988-89 season, the team released Schuler and promoted his assistant, Rick Adelman, himself a former Portland guard.

The turnover didn't change things immediately, though. The Blazers still lost to the Lakers in the first round of the '89 playoffs. But in the offseason, they acquired veteran power forward Buck Williams from the New Jersey Nets. Drexler was so impressed by this acquisition that he flew to New York to have dinner with Williams right after the trade.

"I think we have a championship caliber team, and we're going to get there," said Drexler.

Having spent the first eight years of his career with the perennially woeful New Jersey

Nets, Williams was more than a bit skeptical of any talk about a championship. But he hadn't been in Portland too long before he, too, realized the potential was there. They had a quality starter at every position. Drexler, the high-flying scoring guard, led them with a 24.3 scoring average, while Terry Porter, at 6'3" and 190 pounds, gave them a big point guard with quickness. Jerome Kersey was a 6'7" leaper at small forward who averaged 16 points a game and put out an inspired defensive effort just about every night. At center, 7-foot, 270 pound Kevin Duckworth was the ultimate wide body, but one with a deft shooting touch and, according to Salley, "the biggest rear end on Earth," which was useful in boxing out. Williams at power forward was the final piece of the puzzle. On the bench Adelman had options of 6'9", 245-pound Mark Bryant or 6'10" scorer Cliff Robinson. Danny Young and Yugoslavian rookie Drazen Petrovic were the backcourt subs. Veteran Wayne Cooper worked behind Duckworth in the post.

In some respects, they resembled the Pistons, with their depth and belief in fundamentals. "Our guys really believe that when times get tough, if they rebound and defend, they'll win," said Adelman.

In fact, they fancied themselves the "Pistons of the West," but the two clubs really weren't all that similar. The Blazers were aggressive defensively, but they pressed and went for the steal and liked to use their defense to drive their ferocious fast break. They frequently scored off turnovers.

And while the Blazers were physical, they weren't as stifling as the Pistons. Portland gave up 107.9 points per game, which wouldn't have been acceptable in Detroit. On the other hand, the Blazers' rammin', jammin' offense averaged 114.2 points per game, which indicated a tempo that the Pistons would never want to match. The Blazers ran up big scores despite a .473 team shooting percentage (18th in the league) because Williams, a veteran strong on leadership, infused the entire roster with a rebounding fury.

They finished the regular season at 59-23, the same record as Detroit, then fended off Dallas, San Antonio, and Phoenix in the playoffs to make their first trip to the Finals in thirteen seasons. The success brought a return of the "Rip City" mania that had gripped Portland when the Blazers won the '77 championship with Bill Walton. Even through their playoff frustrations of the previous four years, their fans had stayed loyal to the Blazers, giving the team 569 consecutive sellouts in Memorial Coliseum, the longest such streak in pro sports. With only 12,884 seats, the compact Coliseum created a dread in visiting teams. The Pistons, in particular, didn't like the place. They hadn't won in Portland since 1974.

Once the Lakers had been ousted, observers began penciling in the Pistons as champions. Jordan and the Bulls pushed them to seven games in the Eastern finals, but Detroit won big in Game Seven. Even so, the Pistons weren't about to get overconfident. They were banged up and sluggish. Rodman had a badly sprained left ankle, Dumars was slowed by a pulled groin muscle, and Vinnie Johnson was in a mild shooting slump.

"Portland is going to be very tough," Thomas said as the Finals opened. "The matchups are what makes this series so interesting. It'll be me and Terry Porter, and that's a draw. It'll be Dumars and Clyde, which is a lot like Joe going against Jordan. It'll be Rodman on Kersey, Buck on Edwards, and Bill and Duckworth. Interesting matchups."

But Magic Johnson, who had followed the Pistons through the playoffs, looked beyond those obvious pairings. Portland's bench wouldn't be able to match Detroit's, he said. "When Salley, Mark, and Vinnie are out there, that's Detroit's best lineup. I think that's where the Pistons get the edge."

Another factor would be Magic's little buddy, Isiah. Once considered a superstar, Thomas's reputation had dipped despite Detroit's success. For his third, fourth, and fifth seasons in the league, he had been paired with Magic on the All-NBA First Team. But Thomas fell

to Honorable Mention status during the three seasons, 1988-90, when he led the Pistons to the Finals. The reason? He had sacrificed his personal statistics to make the team better, placing a priority on winning, not personal stats. Rather than worry about honors and awards, he focused his energy on improving. Bird and Magic had always done something during the summer to boost their games for the upcoming year, so at the end of the '89 season, Isiah decided he wanted to add something to his game. He wasn't a big man, so he couldn't develop a junior skyhook or some power move. Instead, he focused on the three-point shot, spending hours each night in the gym at his home shooting hundreds of jumpers. Often, his shooting sessions would run well past midnight.

Andrew D. Bernstein/NBA Photos

Aguirre could score in a variety of ways.

When the opportunity for another championship came, Isiah wanted to be ready.

That opportunity arrived with Game One in the Palace on June 5. The Pistons, though, were anything but ready. For 41 minutes, the Blazers used their intensity to control the tempo. They rebounded. They played defense. They scored on offensive rebounds. Whenever the Pistons made a run, Portland found an answer. As the game went on, Detroit's difficulties deepened. With seven minutes left, the Blazers led, 90-80.

Then, during a timeout, Isiah realized that he had to do something. Throughout the year he had worked on his 3-point shot, but he hadn't quite developed the confidence to make it his main offensive weapon. Now he knew it was time. Detroit needed some answers in a hurry. He had to make things happen.

What followed was an amazing turn of events.

The Pistons turned up their defense, and it worked. Strong and confident throughout the early going, Drexler and Porter abruptly began making mistakes. They took bad shots and committed turnovers and fouls.

At the same time, Isiah got the Pistons going with a layup and a jumper. Then Dumars completed a three-point play and Aguirre scored on an offensive rebound. In less than three minutes, Detroit had tightened the game to 92-89.

Williams gave Portland a little room with a jumper to move it to 94-89, but Isiah reeled off seven straight points. At 4:18 he stripped Porter of the ball, and when Porter tried to steal the ball back he drew a whistle. Thomas made both free throws, then hit a three-pointer moments later to tie the game at 94. On Portland's possession, Drexler was whistled for an offensive foul, the Blazers' sixth turnover of the period. Thomas exploited it with an 18-footer that gave Detroit the lead, 96-94.

The Pistons then got another stop on defense and began searching for a way to expand their lead. Thomas worked the ball into three-point range, and Porter laid back, waiting for him to make his move.

At 1:49, Isiah stunned the packed house and a nationwide television audience by sticking the open three-pointer for a 99-94 lead.

"He was just tremendous," Adelman said. "He made all the plays. That three-point shot he made was just a huge play. He wanted the ball. He wanted to take control. And he did it."

Andrew D. Bernstein/NBA Photos

The 1990 Finals brought the best from Isiah Thomas.

"It just kind of happened," Thomas said. "This was a battle of wills, not a battle of skills."

Isiah's outburst made the difference. The Pistons escaped, 105-99.

"We were dead in the water — belly up," said Daly. "It was just a special player making great shots."

Thomas finished with 33 points, including 10 in a row at crunch time that propelled the Pistons to a 23-4 run. They had won despite shooting 37.4 percent from the floor. The big reason, besides Thomas, was their 19 offensive rebounds, eight of which belonged to Salley.

Both teams got balanced scoring from their starters. Dumars had 20 points. Laimbeer had 11 with 15 rebounds. But as Magic had predicted, Detroit's bench was the other big difference. Led by Aguirre's 18 points, the Pistons subs outscored Portland's, 26-7.

The win was nice, but the Pistons wouldn't be that lucky again, Daly said. "We've got to find our offense."

The Blazers were more concerned about stopping Thomas. "We're going to throw a blanket over him, tackle him, and pull him over to the sideline," Drexler quipped.

That seemed to be a fitting strategy for Game Two. Whatever the Blazers did, it kept them close enough to win it in the end. Detroit came out strong and took a 31-19 lead, but then the Pistons fell into a rash of turnovers, committing 13 in the first half. That was enough to open the way for the Blazers, who charged back to take a 53-48 lead at intermission.

The Pistons made a strong rush in the third quarter, but by then their problem was excessive fouling. Their hacking and aggressive defense sent the Blazers to the line for 41 attempts, of which they made 31.

The game tightened in the fourth, and it seemed the Pistons were on the verge of another outburst, this time from Laimbeer. He had scored only seven points over the first three periods, then went wild in the fourth, hitting 19 points over the last 17 minutes. For the game, he laced in six three-pointers, tying a Finals record set by Michael Cooper in 1987. It was a Laimbeer trey at the 2:59 mark that gave Detroit an 89-86 lead.

But Drexler, on his way to a 33-point evening, quickly answered that with a trey of his own to tie it. The two teams grappled from there until 49.3 seconds were left, when Salley soared to score on a tip-in and drew Duckworth's sixth foul. Salley missed the free throw, but his acrobatics gave Detroit a 94-91 edge.

Five seconds later, Drexler made a free throw. Then at 0:23, Isiah proved his mortality by missing a layup. With 10 seconds left, Porter tied the game at 94 with a pair of free throws, and it went to overtime when Isiah missed an 18-footer at the buzzer.

The Pistons again surged in the extra period, first on a hook from Edwards, then on a pair of three-pointers from Laimbeer, the second of which gave Detroit a 102-98 lead

with 1:30 left. Porter hit another set of freebies to trim the lead to two, then Drexler tied it at the one-minute mark with a 17-footer.

Portland finally took the lead at 104-102, and the Pistons faced a final possession without Isiah, who had fouled out with 1:10 left in overtime. But Laimbeer promptly bailed them out at 4.1 seconds by hitting a 25-footer for a 105-104 margin. Aguirre came rushing across the court to embrace Laimbeer, who shooed him away.

"After I hit the shot, I looked at the clock and saw there were four seconds," Laimbeer said later. "And in the NBA, four seconds is an eternity."

If not an eternity, it was at least enough time for the Blazers to work their offense. Portland got the ball to Drexler, and Rodman, who was playing on his bum ankle, promptly handchecked him. The foul was called with two seconds left, and Drexler swished both of them for a 106-105 lead.

The Pistons showed that they, too, could set up and shoot on time. Edwards got a good shot from the left of the paint, but rookie Cliff Robinson came over and blocked it at the last second.

Like that, the Blazers had taken away the homecourt advantage. "At times we played stupidly, unemotionally," said Laimbeer, who finished with 26 points and 11 rebounds.

Porter had 21 points and 10 assists. He made 15 of 15 free throws for the game, setting a Finals record for the most without a miss. But it was Drexler's last two that made the difference. "It was a sweet win for us," Clyde said with a grin. "All I wanted to do was make it. Total concentration."

The Pistons were upset but not entirely surprised by their blunder. "I guess we have to put on our raincoats and win some games there," said Laimbeer. The Pistons could probably get a win in Portland, most observers suspected.

At that point the series took an unexpected emotional turn. Dumars' father, Joe Dumars II, died of congestive heart failure an hour and a half before the tipoff of Game Three on

Andrew D. Bernstein/NBA Photos

Vinnie Johnson was Detroit's "Microwave" in the clutch.

Sunday, June 10. He had suffered from a severe diabetes that had forced the amputation of both of his legs in 1985. To instill the work ethic in his six sons, the elder Dumars had taken each of them on his grocery truck route. "I was fortunate enough to take all my sons out there with me and teach them how to work," he said in a 1989 interview. "I think that helped shape their lives. Out of the six, every one of them, they don't mind tackling work."

It was this work ethic that made Joe III so valuable to the Pistons. As his father's conditioned worsened, Dumars realized that the news of his father's death might come before or during an important game. So he asked Debbie, his new wife, not to inform him of any news until after the game had ended.

His father had instilled such professionalism in Dumars, and his wife kept his wish.

Daly, his assistants, and Thomas were informed of the news prior to Game Three. Joe and the rest of the team weren't told until afterward.

It was a special afternoon for the Pistons. They had faced a crossroads headed to Portland with the series tied. They had to play without Rodman, whose ankle injury had worsened and who was replaced by Aguirre. The real test came from the venue. In a building where they hadn't won in seventeen years, they needed to take at least one of the three games scheduled. True to their style, they wasted little time getting the job done. For the first time in the series, Vinnie found his range, making 9 of 13 shots for 21 points. But Dumars was the most potent, leading Detroit with 33 points on an array of shots. At one point in the third period, Portland cut a sizeable Piston lead to 68-60, but Dumars answered with a trey that killed the Blazers' momentum.

Later, Isiah recalled watching Dumars and thinking that moments after he was through, his world would be devastated by word of his father's death. "It was hard to look at him at times," Isiah said. Moments after Detroit won, 121-106, Debbie Dumars used a courtside phone to inform Joe of his father's death.

Dumars decided he would play the next game but declined press interviews. Faced with demanding schedules and the realities of a business atmosphere, pro basketball teams often attempt to draw emotion from any available source. But there was no attempt to exploit the situation for those purposes. Instead, the Pistons seemed to become charged with a quiet determination, adopting an attitude that the job of winning the championship needed to be completed as swiftly and efficiently as possible.

At first, the Pistons had been elated at taking a 2-1 lead in the series, but the news abruptly subdued them. "Death is strange," said Detroit reserve Scott Hastings. "Even if you expect it, it still hits you like a bolt of lightning. But if there's anybody who can handle this, it's Joe Dumars. He's what every father wants their son to be. He's the personification of class and dignity."

There had been much to cheer in their performance. The once-struggling offense had hit better than 53% from the floor, and beyond Dumars and Johnson, the scoring had been balanced, with Aguirre, Edwards, and Laimbeer hitting for 11 points apiece inside. Salley scored another 10 off the bench, and Thomas had yet another strong game, scoring 21 with 8 assists and 5 rebounds.

The Blazers, on the other hand, complained about the officiating. Williams, Kersey, and Duckworth each got into foul trouble in the first quarter. "They take your starting lineup out of the game in the first six minutes — what can you do?" Adelman asked afterward.

"Laimbeer flopped the whole game," Duckworth said of the way the Detroit center drew offensive fouls. "He's done it all along, and they know how he plays. It's a crying shame."

Laimbeer played up the part by donning a black hat he borrowed from Aguirre. But far more than his flopping, it was his rebounding that hurt Portland. He had another 12 for Game Three. As for the flopping charges, Laimbeer replied, "You gotta do what you gotta do."

Some thought the Blazers had become sidetracked and lost their concentration on this issue. Williams, for one, said his teammates should keep their minds on the game. "I'm not going to cry about it," he said. "That's the easy way out."

The Blazers desperately needed to play some defense. Giving up 121 points in their first home game wasn't going to win them any championships. Portland had responded to the foul trouble by playing three guards, which forced Daly to go to a three-guard lineup. Detroit's backcourt met the challenge, outscoring Portland's trio, 76-49.

The Pistons had shot well, said Drexler, but he added that he didn't think they could keep it up.

The first quarter of Game Four made Drexler's assessment seem sound. The Pistons' shooting dipped below 40% while the Blazers raced off to a 32-22 lead at the end of the period. The outlook worsened for Detroit just minutes into the second quarter when Thomas picked up his third foul. But Vinnie and Dumars took over from there, leading a 9-0 run that pulled the Pistons to 32-31 with 7:49 left in the half. The Blazers tried to answer with ill-timed one-on-one basketball and poor shots. With Dumars running the point and Vinnie blazing away from shooting guard, Detroit kept charging and took a 51-46 lead at intermission.

Portland had scored only 14 points in the second period, and things grew worse right after the half. Isiah returned with a fire to score 22 points in the third. His three-pointer at the 2:15 mark pushed the Pistons to an 81-65 lead that quieted the Coliseum. The Blazer fans turned their thoughts to the parking lot, and Detroit seemed to settle in for a comfy ride.

But it was a game of strange twists and turns. Over the next eight minutes, the Blazers suddenly remembered the pressure defense and running game that had gotten them to the NBA Finals. They turned on the gas and ran off a 28-11 run of their own. Porter drove for a layup to give them a 93-92 lead with 5:20 left in the game.

They exchanged the lead twice until Detroit gained a three-point edge with two minutes to go. The Pistons expanded that to 106-102 on a jumper by Dumars at 1:16, but the Blazers fought back and had a chance to tie it with 35 seconds left. But Buck Williams missed one of two free throws and Portland trailed 106-105.

Four seconds later, in a scramble under the Pistons basket, Laimbeer drew his sixth foul, and Drexler made both free throws to give Portland the lead, 107-106 with 31.8 seconds left. But Thomas responded by sinking a 22-footer that returned the edge to Detroit, 108-107.

With nine seconds left, Porter attempted to drive on Dumars, but Joe blocked his path.

The ball came loose, and Isiah scooped it up and headed the other way. Danny Young quickly fouled him, and an instant later Thomas let fly a 55-footer that went in. The officials quickly ruled it no good, but Thomas made the free throws for a 110-107 lead with 8.4 seconds showing.

Aguirre then fouled Porter with 6.5 seconds left, and he made both, drawing Portland to 110-109. On the ensuing play, Edwards got the ball downcourt to a wide-open Gerald Henderson, whom Daly had put in the game seconds earlier. Henderson took the ball in for an easy layup, and although he scored to put the Pistons up 112-109, his play gave Portland the ball and 1.8 seconds to get a shot.

The Blazers whipped the ball upcourt to Young, who promptly knocked down a 35-footer from the right sideline. Immediately players from both benches came onto the floor.

Good! Good! screamed the Blazers.

No good! answered the Pistons.

It would be the final game called by veteran referee Earl Strom, and it ended in bedlam. Strom huddled the officials amid the din and signaled that the shot was too late. Videotaped replays later confirmed the accuracy of the call. The Blazers were down 3-1, and no team in Finals history had ever been that far down and made it back to win the championship.

For much of Game Five it appeared they would at least send the series back to Detroit. While the Blazers played like their necks were on the line, the Pistons opened the fifth game slowly, missing 7 of their first 11 shots, but still led 26-22 after one quarter. They held the same edge at the half, 46-42, but the Blazers rallied in the third period, and with 10 minutes to play in the game, they led 77-69.

It was then that Vinnie Johnson went on the first of two scoring binges. After struggling earlier in the game, he scored all of Detroit's points in a 9-0 run to give his team a 77-76 edge with 6:35 to go. The Blazers stepped up their pressure and again built a lead. At the 2:05 mark, they pushed it to 90-83. It looked like there'd be at least one more game in Detroit. At just that point, Vinnie found his magic again. Johnson scored 7 points in Detroit's astounding 9-0 run to close the game and the series.

In the final seconds, with the score tied at 90-90, Isiah worked the ball up top, but he was covered. So he sent the ball to Vinnie, who had Kersey draped all over him. But, ball of muscle that he was, Johnson exploded into the air and launched a 15-footer from the right sideline with 0:00.7 showing on the clock. (His teammates would later take to calling him 007, the James Bond of Basketball.) One of his typical low-projectile missiles, it just cleared the rim, and punctuated Portland's nightmare with a gentle swish.

The Blazers had lost three straight at home. Because he was the primary culprit in their

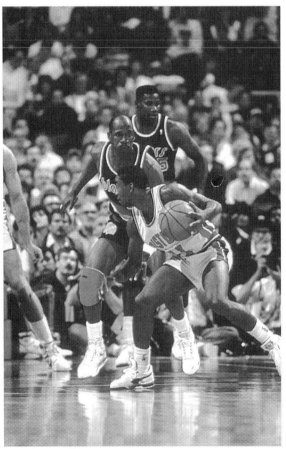

Andrew D. Bernstein/NBA Photos

Thomas could break the Blazers down off the dribble.

278

dismantling, Thomas was named the Finals MVP. He had scored 33, 23, 21, 32, and 29 points in the five games. From three-point range he had made 11 of 16 shots. For the series he had averaged 27.6 points, 8 assists, and 5.2 rebounds, a performance that caused him to unleash his full smile afterward.

"You can say what you want about me," he said, "but you can't say that I'm not a winner."

Vinnie, too, had plenty to smile about. He had scored 16 points in Game Five, 14 of them under a stinging pressure. One of the few players to average double figures in scoring over his career while never being a starter, his performance had finally brought him the spotlight.

"It's something you dream about," he said.

The Finals was something to dream about. But as sweet as this second championship was,

soon it was back to real life.

Joe Dumars made his father's funeral on that Saturday, having lived up to the family's tradition of hard work and professionalism. And Daly, after considering an offer to become a network commentator, opted at age sixty to remain in coaching.

After all, the Pistons had a chance to win three consecutive league titles. The lure of history was strong for Chuck Daly. But it was much more than history. At its simplest form, it was an opportunity to keep winning. Long before the NBA had ever thought of having a history, the shiny feeling of winning was what had kept everybody going.

Like Eddie Gottlieb after his Warriors won the league's first championship in 1947, Chuck Daly had taken the long drink.

And he wanted more.

16.
Air Show

Jordan Takes The Bulls Up Top

Michael Jordan left the University of North Carolina after his junior season in 1984 and entered the NBA draft. The Houston Rockets selected center Hakeem Olajuwon first. With the second pick, the Portland Trail Blazers took Kentucky center Sam Bowie, leaving many observers dumfounded. Waiting with the third pick were the Chicago Bulls, who grabbed Jordan.

Portland's mistake would go down as the greatest blunder in draft history.

Jordan led the U.S. to the Olympic gold medal in Los Angeles that summer, then exploded into an instant phenomenon that fall when he joined the NBA.

Bill Blair, who was then a Bulls' assistant coach, recalled that head coach Kevin Loughery decided to have a scrimmage on the second day of practice to see if Jordan was going to be as good as the team thought. "Michael took the ball off the rim at one end," Blair said, "and went to other end. From the top of the key, he soared in and dunked it, and Kevin says, 'We don't have to scrimmage anymore.' "

"When we started doing one on one drills," Loughery recalled, "we immediately saw that we had a star. I can't say that we knew we had the best player ever in basketball. But we always felt that Michael could shoot the ball.

A lot of people had questioned that. But Michael had played in a passing game system in college under Dean Smith and in the Olympics under Bobby Knight. So people never got the opportunity to see him handle the ball individually the way he could handle it.

"We saw his skills, but you've got to be around him every day to see the competitiveness of the guy. He was gonna try to take over every situation that was difficult. He was gonna put himself on the line. He enjoyed it. But as much as you talk about Michael's offensive ability, he's probably one of the best defensive players to play the game. His anticipation was so great, he could see the

Andrew D. Bernstein/NBA Photos

Magic vs. Michael was the matchup everyone wanted.

281

floor, his quickness, and then his strength. That's another thing that's overlooked, how strong Michael is. He really had the whole package."

His new teammates soon realized that Jordan was anything but a rookie. "I will never forget the first day he walked into camp right after the Olympics," said former Bull Sidney Green. "Everybody said that he would be tired, drained. I remember his first practice. He was jumping from the free throw line, dunking on drills. And everybody said, 'Aw, he's gonna cut that out by midseason.' At midseason, it seemed like he was jumping from the top of the key. We said, 'By the three-quarter mark of the season his legs are going to die out.' At the three quarter mark, he was still going strong, plus more. That's when I made my quote to the press, 'Michael Jordan is the truth, the whole truth and nothing but the truth, so help us God.' And that's what he is; he's the truth."

"Early in the year we went to Milwaukee," Blair recalled, "and Michael played against Sidney Moncrief. When he started abusing Sidney Moncrief, who we considered one of the top five defensive guards in the league, we knew that we had a special person. You knew you had somebody special because Michael was always there at practice 45 minutes early. He wanted to work on his shooting. And after practice he'd make you help him. He'd keep working on his shooting. He didn't care how long he was out there. The thing that I always loved about him, when you'd take him out in practice to give him a rest during a scrimmage, he was constantly back on you to get him back in. Michael loved to play the game."

Jordan scored 27 in an early loss to the Celtics in Chicago Stadium. "I've never seen one player turn a team around like that," Larry Bird, the league's reigning Most Valuable Player, said afterward. "All the Bulls have become better because of him. . . Pretty soon this place will be packed every night. . . They'll pay just to watch Jordan. He's the best. Even at this stage in his career, he's doing more than I ever did. I couldn't do what he

does as a rookie. Heck, there was one drive tonight. He had the ball up in his right hand, then he took it down. Then he brought it back up. I got a hand on it, fouled him, and he still scored. All the while, he's in the air.

"You have to play this game to know how difficult that is. You see that and say, 'Well, what the heck can you do?'

"I'd seen a little of him before and wasn't that impressed. I mean, I thought he'd be good, but not this good. Ain't nothing he can't do. That's good for this franchise, good for the league."

In just his ninth pro game, Jordan scored 45 points against San Antonio. Six weeks later he burned Cleveland for another 45. Then came a 42-point performance against New York. Another 45 against Atlanta, and his first triple-double (35 points, 15 assists and 14 rebounds) against Denver. Then, just before the All-Star break, he zipped in 41 against defending champion Boston.

Pippen found his confidence in the '91 playoffs.

Andrew D. Bernstein/NBA Photos

In one of his early appearances, he was greeted by a pack of screaming teen-age girls. "Michael Jackson eat your heart out," quipped teammate Orlando Woolridge.

But it wasn't just point totals that thrilled the crowds. His appeal began with his energy level. He played all-out, every minute. On defense, he was a roaming thief. On offense, he was simply a cornucopia. Jumpers. Elegant dunks. Reverses. Finger rolls. Short bank shots. All executed with a style that bordered on miraculous. When he couldn't get to the hoop by land, he traveled by air. Literally, he could fly. (The definition of flying, according to the Random House Dictionary of the English Language, is "to be carried through the air by the wind or any other force or agency.")

For the first time in their history, the "force" was with the Bulls, and it meant a profound transformation for both the team and its young superstar. Chicago had joined the NBA in 1966 as an expansion franchise and had suffered through two decades of frustration. The Bulls had fallen into deep misery in the half dozen seasons before Jordan's arrival, and crowds in Chicago Stadium had dwindled to a few thousand most nights.

The fans returned in droves to see Jordan, although he still didn't generate regular sellouts that first season. The Bulls would have to become winners to draw regular crowds. To build the team around Jordan, new Bulls chairman Jerry Reinsdorf brought in longtime scout Jerry Krause to run the basketball operations.

After two decades of upheaval and misfires in the team's front office, Bulls fans were openly leery of Krause's seemingly unorthodox approach. There were early missteps greeted by loud hisses from the media and fans. In retrospect, it seems obvious that a pattern of success was emerging. But at the time, the entire enterprise was a burgeoning gamble with careers on the line. The primary casualties were coaches. A line of them — Kevin Loughery, Stan Albeck and Doug Collins — fell by the wayside.

Meanwhile, Jordan himself was witnessing dramatic change in his own life. Seeing that the Bulls' young star was going places, Nike soon built a multimillion-dollar shoe and clothing deal around his image. Michael, the player, quickly became Air Jordan, the incredibly successful corporate entity. Before long, he was making far more money off the court than on it. Rather than dull his unique

drive, this off-court success seemed to shove it into a higher gear.

"He's as much as image as he is a symbol," agent David Falk had said late that October 1984 after revealing that Jordan had already signed promotional deals with Nike, Wilson Sporting Goods and the Chicagoland Chevrolet Dealerships Association. The Nike deal alone paid him $500,000 per year. "I know everybody's eyes are on me," Jordan said, "and some of the things I do even surprise myself. They aren't always planned. They just happen."

He led the lowly Bulls to the playoffs that first year, where they quickly lost to Milwaukee. The next season, 1986, he overcame a serious foot injury to carry them into the playoffs once more, where they were vanquished 3-0 by Boston, but not before Jordan scared the Celtics blue by scoring 63 points in one game, an NBA playoffs record.

He went on from there, shoving the Bulls a notch higher each year. And in the process, he claimed nearly every major individual achievement imaginable. By the 1991 playoffs, he had captured the league scoring title five times. He had been named the league's Most Valuable Player twice. He had been named to the All-NBA first team five times in seven years.

But, alas, the Bulls had won nothing. In 1987, the Celtics again swept them in the first round of the playoffs. In 1988, they beat Cleveland, then fell to the Detroit Pistons in the Eastern semifinals. In 1989, they advanced to the conference finals with wins over Cleveland and New York but again ran into the Pistons and lost, 4-2.

Krause responded to the loss by firing the popular Collins and promoting assistant Phil Jackson, whose first move was to adopt the triple-post offensive scheme of veteran Bulls assistant Tex Winter. Each of Jordan's first three coaches had ignored Winter's advice, but Jackson, who had won a championship ring as a member of the 1973 New York Knicks, had decided to have an offense that featured ball movement and a defense that offered opponents nothing but pressure.

"When Phil came in our first training camp was as difficult a camp as I'd ever had," recalled guard John Paxson. "It was defensive-oriented. Everything we did was, start from the defensive end and work to the offensive end. Phil basically made us into a pressure-type team. Defensively, he knew that was how we would win."

"We were gonna play full-court pressure defense," Jackson said. "We were gonna throw our hearts into it."

Key to the Bulls' pressure was the maturing of Scottie Pippen and Horace Grant, the two young players with enough athleticism to give the defense its bite. Assistant coach Johnny Bach called them the Dobermans. "He's on the cusp of greatness,' Bach said of Pippen. "He's starting to do the kinds of things only Michael does."

"It's just a matter of working hard," Pippen said. "I've worked to improve my defense and shooting off the dribble. I know I'm a better spot-up shooter, but I'm trying to pull up off the dribble when the lane is blocked."

"Jordan led them in scoring, but it was Pippen that gave opposing coaches nightmares. Few teams had a means of matching up with him, particularly when they also had to worry about Jordan.

The win streaks propelled them to a 55-27 finish in 1990, good for second place in the Central behind the 60-win Pistons, the defending World Champions. And Jordan harvested another batch of honors: All-NBA, All-Defense, and his fourth consecutive scoring title. Plus he led the league in steals.

The Bulls sailed into the playoffs with new confidence and Pippen playing like a veteran. First they dismissed the Milwaukee Bucks and followed that by humbling Charles Barkley and the Philadelphia 76ers. But Pippen's 70-year-old father, Lewis, died during the series, and the young forward rushed home to Arkansas for the funeral. He returned in time to help finish off Philly. Next up were the Pistons and the Eastern Finals. In essence, it was the big exam for Jackson's new style of play. The series was a gauntlet. The year before in the playoffs, Bill Laimbeer had

knocked Pippen out of Game 6 with an elbow to the head. The Detroit center claimed the shot was inadvertent, but that wasn't they way the Bulls saw it. To win a championship, they knew they had to stand up to the "Bad Boys."

"I thought they were thugs," Reinsdorf said of the Pistons, "and you know, you have to hold the ownership responsible for that. I mean, Billy Laimbeer was a thug. He would hit people from behind in the head during dead balls. He took cheap shots all the time. Mahorn and lunatic Rodman, I mean, they tried to hurt people.

"They called themselves the Bad Boys, and they marketed themselves under that name. I would never have allowed that. You know I blame the league and David Stern a little bit for that, too. It was terrible."

"There were times," Pippen said, "a few years before the flagrant foul rules, when guys would have a breakaway and [the Pistons] would cut their legs out from under them. Anything to win a game. that's not the way the game is supposed to be played. I remember once when Michael had a breakaway, and Laimbeer took him out. There was now way he could have blocked the shot. When you were out there playing them, that was always in the back of your mind, to kind of watch yourself."

The Bulls, however, thought they were ready to challenge Detroit in 1990. At first, their conference final series seemed to develop as a classic, with each team winning tight battles at home to tie it at 3-3 heading into Game 7 at the Palace of Auburn Hills. The Pistons had homecourt advantage, but the Bulls had worked for years to get to this point. But things went dreadfully wrong, beginning with Paxson limping from a badly sprained ankle and Pippen developing a migraine headache just before tipoff.

"Scottie had had migraines before," trainer Mark Pfeil explained. "He actually came to me before the game and said he couldn't see. I said, 'Can you play?' He started to tell me no, and Michael jumped in and said, 'Hell, yes, he can play. Start him. Let him play blind.'

Jordan showed his usual brilliance in Chicago Stadium.

Andrew D. Bernstein/NBA Photos

"Horace Grant kind of backed up a little bit that game, too," Pfeil added. "It was more a matter of maturity than wimpin' out. It took a certain period of time before they would stand up and say, 'Damn it, I've been pushed to the wall enough.' Scottie played with the headache, and as the game went on he got better."

Pippen played, but the entire roster seemed lost. They fell into a deep hole in the second quarter and never climbed out. With the Bad Boys flying their skull 'n' crossbones banners and their "Bad to the Bone" theme music playing, the Pistons advanced easily, 93-74.

"My worst moment as a Bull was trying to finish out the seventh game that we lost to the Pistons in the Palace," Jackson recalled. "There was Scottie Pippen with a migraine on the bench, and John Paxson had sprained his ankle in the game before. I just had to sit there and grit my teeth and go through a half in which we were struggling to get in the ball game. We had just gone through a second period that was an embarrassment to the organization. It was my most difficult moment as a coach."

Furious with his teammates, Jordan cursed them at halftime, then sobbed in the back of the team bus afterward. "I was crying and steaming," he recalled. "I was saying, 'Hey, I'm out here busting my butt and nobody else is doing the same thing. These guys are kicking our butt, taking our heart, taking our pride.' I made up my mind right then and there it would never happen again. That was the summer that I first started lifting weights. If I was going to take some of this beating, I was also going to start dishing out some of it. I got tired of them dominating me physically."

With each Chicago loss in the playoffs, observers grew more convinced that the Bulls were flawed because Jordan made them virtually a one-man team. Some pointed out that it had taken Wilt Chamberlain, Jerry West and Oscar Robertson many years to lead teams to the NBA title. Some critics said Jordan fit into the category with those players. Others wondered if he weren't headed for the same anguish as Elgin Baylor, Nate Thurmond, Pete Maravich and Dave Bing, all

285

great players who never played on a championship team.

Jordan was understandably angered by such speculation and by the criticism that he was a one-man team. He was also pained by the losses each year to Detroit. He and Pistons point guard Isiah Thomas weren't fond of each other, which made the losses all the more difficult.

In some ways, however, the burden of the loss fell on Pippen. Everyone, from the media to his own teammates, had interpreted the headache as a sign of faint-heartedness. Lost in the perspective was the fact that the third-year forward had recently buried his father.

"I'm flying back from the migraine game," recalled Chicago radio reporter Cheryl Ray, "and who should be sitting across from me but Juanita Jordan. And she says, 'What happened to Scottie?' I said, 'He had a headache.' She goes, 'He had a headache!?!?' And she just shook her head."

"It grabbed me and wouldn't let go," Pippen later said. "It's something the fans will never let die."

1991

Despite the outcome, Jackson and his assistants came away from the 1990 playoffs with tremendous optimism. They knew they would have to sell Jordan and his teammates on using the triple-post offense, and they would have to get tougher defensively.

The key to their defensive toughness was 7-foot-1 Bill Cartwright, whom the Bulls had acquired from the Knicks. His career had featured one frustrating battle after another with injuries, all played out before the merciless New York media. He went through foot surgery after foot surgery, until the newspapers dubbed him "Medical Bill." The Knicks' problem was that they didn't know how to play Cartwright with Patrick Ewing. They tried putting them in a Twin Towers alignment with modest success. Finally, they traded him to the Bulls, where Cartwright's reputation preceeded him. He had come into the league as a big-time low-post offensive threat.

But what the Bulls saw in him was the defensive intimidator they needed. Either way, Michael Jordan was not pleased to have him on the roster. Phil Jackson, however, had seen his value, not only as a defender but as a leader. The coach began calling Cartwright "Teacher," and the name stuck.

More than that, his teammates and opponents around the league knew Cartwright for his elbows. He held them high when he rebounded or boxed out. Cartwright's elbows weren't as notorious as the Pistons' style of play, but they were close. "You had to be cognizant of those elbows because they could hit you any time," recalled Bulls backup center Will Perdue. "I got hit constantly in practice. That's just the way Bill played. He was taught to play with his arms up and his elbows out."

Jordan, however, was irritated that Cartwright sometimes had trouble catching the ball, and often set up in the lane, in the way of Jordan's drives to the hoop.

"Michael really didn't know Bill Cartwright as a person," Jerry Krause said of the early troubles that developed between Jordan and Cartwright. "Michael made Bill prove himself. Michael did that with everybody. That was Michael's way. I knew what Bill was. Bill was gonna be fine with Michael. I told Bill, 'It's coming. He's gonna needle you. Michael's gonna drive you crazy.' Bill said, 'He ain't gonna do nothing to me.'"

"Michael and I had a comfort problem," Cartwright explained, "the fact that he wanted to do some things, and I was in the way. It took some getting used to. It took him getting used to me."

The relationship eased as Jordan realized that Cartwright could anchor the Bulls defense. "I'll never forget the battles Willis Reed had to fight against Kareem to get to the championship in 1970," Phil Jackson recalled, "the fight Willis had to wage against Wilt Chamberlain in both '70 and '73. We, the Knicks, had to have this guy who said, 'You're gonna have to come through my door, and you're gonna have to get over me to win a championship.' At some level, that sacrifice had to be made. That's what Bill Cartwright brought to the Bulls as a player. He was the one who said, 'You're gonna have to come through me.'

"Bill's an extremely stubborn person, and he believes you've got to work real hard to get what you want in life. He gave us that element, that 'I'm-gonna-work-real-hard-to-get-this-accomplished' attitude. He was dogged, dogged persistence. One of the things that got to us was that Detroit used to have a way of bringing up the level of animosity in a game. At some level, you were gonna have to contest them physically, if you were gonna stay in the game with them. If you didn't want to stay in the game with them, fine. They'd go ahead and beat you. But if you wanted to compete, you'd have to do something physically to play at their level. Bill stood up to the Pistons. Bill's statement was, 'This isn't the way we want to play. This isn't the way I want to play. But if it is the way we have to play to take care of these guys, I'm not afraid to do it. I'm gonna show these Detroit guys this is not acceptable. We won't accept you doing this to us.' You can't imagine how much that relieved guys like Scottie Pippen and Horace Grant, guys who were being besieged constantly and challenged constantly by more physical guys like Dennis Rodman and Rick Mahorn."

With Cartwright providing the necessary toughness, Jordan and his teammates matured into a determined unit over the 1990-91 season, although their progress was sometimes frustrating and difficult. Jordan again led the league in scoring at 31.5 points per game (to go with six rebounds and five assists per outing). Another key development came with the 6-foot-7 Pippen. He had been stung by criticism, most of it stemming from his migraine headache in Game 7 of the 1990 Eastern Conference finals. A gifted swing player, Pippen performed with determination over the 1990-91 campaign, playing 3,014 minutes, averaging nearly 18 points, seven rebounds and six assists.

"I thought about it all summer," he said of the migraine. "I failed to produce last season."

Pippen made the transition from being a wing into a point guard role, Jackson said. "He became a guy who now had the ball as much as Michael. He became a dominant force."

Other key factors were power forward Horace Grant (12.8 points, 8.4 rebounds); point guard John Paxson (8.7 points while jumpshooting .548 from the floor); and center Bill Cartwright (9.6 points and interior toughness on defense). Jackson also made great use of his bench with B.J. Armstrong, Craig Hodges, Will Perdue, Stacey King, Cliff Levingston, Scott Williams (a free agent rookie out of North Carolina), and Dennis Hopson, who had come over in a trade with New Jersey, all contributing.

John Paxson's shooting was the key to taking the pressure off Jordan.

Andrew D. Bernstein/NBA Photos

These efforts resulted in impressive displays of execution. In December, the Bulls' defense held the Cleveland Cavaliers to just five points in one quarter at Chicago Stadium. Crowds there presented an atmosphere that no opponent wanted to face. The Bulls lost to Boston there the third game of the season. They wouldn't lost at home again until Houston stopped them March 25, a run of 30 straight home wins.

The Bulls won the Eastern Conference with a 61-21 record, and Jordan claimed his fifth straight scoring title with a 31.5 average. During the playoffs, he was named the league's MVP for the second time. The Bulls, however, had seen all that window dressing before. The only awards they wanted came in the playoffs.

They opened against the Knicks and won the first game by a record 41 points, then went on to sweep them, 3-0. Next Charles Barkley and the 'Sixers fell, 4-1, setting up the only rematch the Bulls wanted: the Pistons in the Eastern Conference Finals.

The Bulls hammered the Pistons, who were reeling from injuries, in three straight games, and on the eve of Game 4 Jordan announced they were going to sweep. "That's not going to happen," responded an infuriated Isiah Thomas. But it did.

At the end of the Game 4 the next day in Detroit, Thomas and the Pistons stalked off the floor without congratulating the Bulls, a snub that angered Jordan and thousands of Chicago fans.

"I have nothing but contempt and disgust for the Pistons organization," Reinsdorf said. "Ultimately, David Stern felt the pressure and made rules changes to outlaw their style of play. It wasn't basketball. It was thuggerism, hoodlumism. . . That's one of the things that made us so popular. We were the white knights; we were the good guys. We beat the Bad Boys, 4-0, and they sulked off the court the way they did. I remember saying at the time that this was a triumph of good over evil. They were hated because they had used that style to vanquish first the Celtics and then the Lakers, who had been the NBA's most popular teams for years."

The Portland Trail Blazers had ruled the regular season in the Western with a 63-19 finish, but once again Magic Johnson and the Lakers survived in the playoffs, ousting Portland in the conference finals, 4-2.

For most observers, the Finals seemed a dream match-up: Jordan and the Bulls against Magic and the Lakers. In 1990, promoters had come up with an idea for a one-on-one game between Magic and Michael to be staged for pay-per-view television. But the NBA vetoed the idea — which would have paid big money to the participants — after Isiah Thomas, the president of the players' association, objected.

Jordan lashed out at Thomas' intervention, charging that the Detroit guard was jealous because no one would pay to see him play.

Thomas had no response to Jordan's comment. The dispute was yet another thorn in their relationship. Magic said he would love to play the game, but he declined to get involved in the scrap between the two. "That's their thing," he said.

Johnson did, however, have some fun speculating over the outcome. Jack Nicholson, the Laker superfan, said that if he were a betting man, he'd put his money on Jordan, the premier individual star in the game, as opposed to Johnson, pro basketball's ultimate team player.

Johnson, though, wouldn't concede a thing. "I've been playing one-on-one all my life," he said. "That's how I made my lunch money."

Asked his best one-on-one move, Johnson said, "I didn't have a best move. My best move was just to win, and that's it. I did what I had to do to win."

Basketball fans everywhere were disappointed that the one-on-one match wouldn't be held, Magic said. "A lot of people wanted to see it. Michael is really disappointed. His people are disappointed. We're all disappointed. It was something we were all looking forward to."

Although the 1991 Finals wouldn't be a one-on-one match-up of the superstars, it still provided a great opportunity to see them battle. Many observers, including former Laker coach Pat Riley, figured the Lakers' experience made them a sure bet. Los Angeles was making its ninth Finals appearance since 1980, and had five titles to show for it.

"The Lakers have experience on us," Pippen said as the series opened in Chicago Stadium, "but we have enough to win."

Just as important, the Lakers' James Worthy had a badly sprained ankle, which took away much of his mobility. Some insiders figured Worthy's injury would cost the Lakers the series. Others figured that without Abdul-Jabbar (who had retired after the 1989 season), Los Angeles just wasn't as potent as a playoff team. Game 1, however, seemed to confirm Riley's prediction. The Lakers won,

93-91, on a three-pointer by center Sam Perkins with 14 seconds left in the game. The Bulls got the ball to Jordan, but his 18-foot jumper with four seconds left went in the basket and spun out. It seemed that Jordan was human after all and that the Laker experience just might deliver them.

The Bulls, though, would have none of the conventional thinking. They blew out the Lakers in Game 2, 107-86. The Chicago starters shot better than 73 percent from the floor, with Paxson going eight for eight to score 16 points. "Does Paxson ever miss?" the Lakers' Perkins asked.

Paxson shrugged at reporters' questions and said his job was to hit open jumpers. "When I'm in my rhythm, I feel like I'm going to make them all."

Jordan himself had hit 15 of 18 to finish with 33.

Even with the loss, the Lakers were pleased. They had gotten a split in Chicago Stadium and were headed home for three straight games in the Forum. The pressure was on Chicago.

But the Bulls met the challenge in Game 3. Jordan hit a jumper with 3.4 seconds left to send the game into overtime. There, the Bulls ran off eight straight points for a 104-96 win and a 2-1 lead in the series. Jordan was elated, but he refused to dwell on the victory. The Lakers had plenty of experience in coming back, he said.

Yet experience proved no match for the Bulls' young legs and determination. For Game 4, Chicago's weapon was defense. The Bulls harried the Lakers into shooting 37 percent from the floor. Chicago won, 97-82. The

Andrew D. Bernstein/NBA Photos

After getting a win in Game 1, Magic never dreamed the Lakers would be swept at home.

Lakers' point total was their lowest since before the shot clock was adopted in 1954. They managed a total of 30 points over the second and third quarters. Perkins had made just one of his 15 shots.

"I didn't even dream this would happen," Magic said.

But the Bulls did. Suddenly, they were on the verge of the improbable.

Andrew D. Bernstein/NBA Photos

For Pippen the title erased a lot of bad memories.

"It's no surprise the way they've been defending," Laker coach Mike Dunleavy said of the Bulls. "They are very athletic and very smart."

And very hot.

On the eve of Game 5, Jordan publicly acknowledged the team's debt to Cartwright. "He has given us an edge in the middle," he said. "He has been solid for us. . . This guy has turned out to be one of the most important factors for this ball club, and he has surprised many who are standing here and who play with him."

Told of Jordan's comments, Carwright said, "That stuff really isn't important to me. I've always figured what goes around comes around. What's really important to me is winning a championship."

"We went up 3-1 and had a long wait, from Sunday to Wednesday, for Game 5," recalled Bulls equipment manager John Ligmanowski. "Those three days took forever. Before we had even won it, Michael would get on the bus and say, 'Hey, how does it feel world champs?' He knew. That was a pretty good feeling. We just couldn't wait to get it over with."

As Jordan predicted, the Bulls turned to their offense to claim the title in Game 5, 108-101. Pippen led the scoring parade with 32 points, and Paxson did the damage down the stretch, hitting five buckets in the final four minutes to score 20 points and seal the win. Time and again, Jordan penetrated, drawing the defense, then kicked the ball out to Paxson, who hit the open shots. In the bedlam on the Forum floor following the Bulls 108-101 victory, Laker superfan Jack Nicholson hugged Phil Jackson, and Magic Johnson tracked down Jordan to offer his congratulations. "I saw tears in his eyes," Johnson said. "I told him, 'You proved everyone wrong. You're a winner as well as a great individual basketball player.'"

By the time Jordan squeezed through the crowd to the locker room he was openly weeping. "I never lost hope," he said, his father James and wife Juanita nearby. "I'm so happy for my family and this team and this franchise. It's something I've worked seven years for, and I thank God for the talent and the opportunity that I've had."

It had been a long haul.

The tears flowed freely for Jordan. "I've never been this emotional publicly," he said.

"When I came here, we started from scratch," he said. "I vowed we'd make the playoffs every year, and each year we got closer. I always had faith I'd get this ring one day."

Jackson and Jordan agreed that the key to the game had been Paxson hitting the open shots. "That's why I've always wanted him on my team and why I wanted him to stay on my team," Jordan said.

"It was done and over, and it was dramatic, like a blitzkrieg," Jackson recalled. "Afterward, there was a lot of joy. There was Michael holding the trophy and weeping. For me, it was doubly special because the Forum was where I had won the championship as a player nearly 20 years earlier, in 1973. This was the same locker room where the Knicks had celebrated. With the Bulls, what made it extra special was the way we won it, to split our first two games at home and then to sweep three on the road. It was special."

Afterward, the Bulls quarters at the Ritz Carlton became party central. "I remember going up to Michael's room," equipment manager John Ligmanowski said. "He told me to order like a dozen bottles of Dom Perignon and enough hors d'oeuvres for 40 people. We're at the Ritz Carlton, and I call down to the concierge. I said, 'Yeah, send up a dozen bottles of Dom and hors d'oeuvres for 40 people.' So they were like, 'Wait a second.' They didn't want to send it up because they knew it wasn't Michael on the phone. So I handed the phone to him. He grabbed the phone and said, 'Send it up!'"

The Bulls returned to Chicago and celebrated their championship in Grant Park before a crowd estimated at between 500,000 and a million. "We started from the bottom," Jordan told the screaming masses, "and it was hard working our way to the top. But we did it."

Jordan and the Bulls had begun with a faithful coterie of about 6,000 in 1984. Along the way, they added millions of fans, all captivated by his Air Show. One hundred years earlier, James Naismith had set the height of the goal at 10 feet. A century later, it remained the same challenge. Yet there was little doubt in anyone's mind that Michael Jordan and the Chicago Bulls had elevated the possibilities.

1992

Perhaps the most amazing thing about the Bulls' second championship was the amount of discord and controversy they had to overcome to win it. Long-festering resentment surfaced during the 1991 championship celebration when Michael Jordan decided not to join the team in the traditional Rose Garden ceremony with President George Bush. Much

of the discord stemmed from the relationship between Horace Grant and Jordan.

"I think it was a situation," Phil Jackson later observed, "where Horace felt demeaned, felt that he was made light of, and he wanted to be a person of importance. There were some things about Horace that bothered Michael. Basically, Horace says whatever comes into his mind in front of the press. One of the situations that was exacerbating to Michael came after our first championship when Horace and his wife and Michael and his wife went to New York. They went to dinner and to see a play. While they were out, Michael basically told Horace that he wasn't going to see President Bush. Michael said, "It's not obligatory. It's on my time, and I have other things to do."

"Horace at the time had no problem with it," Jackson added. "He knew about this in a private situation and said nothing. Yet when the press came into the picture later, after the story became public, and asked Horace if it bothered him, he made a big issue of it. Basically, the press had put the words in his mouth, and he felt it was a good time to make this kind of statement. It was immediately team divisive and made Michael look bad and basically got that whole thing started. That bothered Michael about Horace, that he would do something personal like that. Horace had problems in that area, where a lot of times he said things that the press had put in his mind, or in his consciousness. I would call him in and remind him that he could be fined for making comments that were detrimental to the team. I'd say, 'Horace I have every reason to fine you, but I'm not going to because I know the press put words in your mouth.' He would say, 'I'm not ever gonna tell lies.' I told him, 'No one's saying you have to tell lies. You have to be conscious of what you're saying. You don't want to be divisive.'"

Grant also served as a major source for the book, The Jordan Rules by Chicago Tribune sportswriter Sam Smith. Marketed as the inside story of the Bulls' championship season, the book and its unflattering portraits of

Clyde Drexler vs. Jordan was one of the Finals' all-time great individual matchups.

Andrew D. Bernstein/NBA Photos

Jordan and Jerry Krause rocked the franchise just as the 1991-92 season opened.

"I went to the best libel lawyer in the country," Krause said. "He said I couldn't do a thing because I was a public figure. Sam Smith made some money on that book. I hope he chokes on every dollar."

"The Jordan Rules was very divisive to the team," Jackson said. "But the one great thing about this group of guys. They never let the external stuff bother the team's play on the floor."

Indeed it didn't. Krause set the roster with a November trade, sending disgruntled Dennis Hopson to Sacramento for reserve guard Bobby Hansen. The Bulls raced out to a 37-5 record including a 14-game winning streak, the longest in history. They slipped over late January and February, going only 11-8. By the first of March, the Bulls were back on track and closed out the schedule with a blistering 19-2 run to finish 67-15, the franchise's best record. Jordan claimed his sixth straight scoring crown and won his third league MVP award. He and Pippen were named to the All-Defense first team, and Pippen earned All-NBA second team honors.

"We really had an outrageous year," Jackson said. "We won 67 games, and basically I felt like I had to pull back on the reins, or they would have tried to win 70 or 75. The playoffs were an entirely different story from the regular season. We had injuries, and we had to face New York. And teams were coming at us with a lot of vim and vigor. We lost seven games in our championship run. It wasn't as easy this second time. There had been a challenge to our character as a team.

In the first round of the playoffs, the Bulls faced the Miami Heat, a 1989 expansion team making its first postseason appearance. Chicago quickly claimed the first two games in the best-of-five series, then headed to Miami for Game 3.

"In Miami's first playoff game ever, it was clacker night," recalled Bulls broadcaster Tom Dore. "What they said was, any time Michael gets the ball or shoots a free throw, go nuts with those clackers. Make all kinds of noise. Well, it worked in the first quarter. The Heat had a big lead. And in fact, we were wondering, can the Bulls come back from this? And Michael stopped by the broadcast table and looked at Johnny Kerr and me and said, 'Here we come.' That's all he said. Boy did he ever. He went absolutely beserk, scored 56 points, and the Bulls won, swept the series."

Next up were the New York Knicks, now coached by Pat Riley and employing a physical style strikingly similar to the Pistons. The

Knicks used their muscle to claim Game 1 in Chicago Stadium. B.J. Armstrong helped even the series at 1-1 by hitting big shots in the fourth quarter of Game 2. Then the Bulls regained the homecourt advantage in Game 3 in New York when Jordan finally broke free of New York's cloying defense for his first dunks of the series.

The Knicks, powered by Xavier McDaniel, fought back to even it with a win in Game 4.

In critical Game 5, Jordan took control by going to the basket. The Knicks kept fouling him, and he kept making the free throws, 15 in all to finish with 37 points as the Bulls won, 96-88. "Michael is Michael," Riley said afterward. "His game is to take it to the basket and challenge the defense. When you play against a guy like him, he tells you how much he wants to win by how hard he takes the ball to the basket."

The Knicks managed to tie it again with a Game 6 win in New York, but the Bulls were primed for Game 7 in the Stadium and walked to the win, 110-81. "We got back to playing Bulls basketball," Armstrong explained.

They resumed their struggle in the conference finals against the Cavaliers, who managed to tie the series at 2-2, but the Bulls had just enough to escape Cleveland, 4-2. "John Paxson turned to me in the locker room and said, 'What a long strange trip it's been,'" Jackson confided to reporters. "And he wasn't just quoting the Grateful Dead. It has been a long strange trip. Last year was the honeymoon. This year was an odyssey."

The Finals against the Portland Trailblazers brought more turbulence, which was intermittently calmed by Jordan's memorable performances. The Blazers — driven by Clyde Drexler, newly acquired Danny Ainge, Cliff Robinson, Terry Porter, and Buck Williams — answered with a few performances of their own. Ultimately, though, the glory was Jordan's. In Game 1, he scored 35 points in the first half, including a record six three-pointers, enough to bury the Blazers, 122-89.

"The only way you can stop Michael," said Portland's Cliff Robinson, "is to take him off the court."

"I was in a zone," said Jordan, who had focused on extra hours of practice shooting long range before Game 1. "My threes felt like free throws. I didn't know what I was doing, but they were going in."

In Game 2, the Blazers hopes dimmed when Drexler fouled out with about four minutes left. But they rallied with a 15-5 run to tie the game, then somehow won, 115-104, on the strength of Danny Ainge's nine points in overtime. "Momentum is a fickle thing," Ainge mused afterward.

"It was a gift in our hands and we just gave it away," Horace Grant said.

The Blazers had their split with the series headed to Portland for three games. But the Bulls' defense and a solid team effort — Pippen and Grant scored 18 each to go with Jordan's 26 — ended thoughts of an upset with a win

Andrew D. Bernstein/NBA Photos

Danny Ainge, now in Portland, helped even the series in overtime of Game 2.

in Game 3, 94-84. Later, Jackson would explain that the Blazers rushed to take a late flight home after Friday night's Game 2, which cost them important sleep, while the Bulls waited until Saturday to travel. "They controlled the tempo, we shot poorly and never got in the groove," Portland coach Rick Adelman admitted.

Having regained their rest, the Blazers struggled to stay close through most of Game 4, then moved in front with just over three minutes left and won it, 93-88, on a final surge. The outcome evened the series at 2-2.

But Game 5 was another Jordan showcase. Going to the hole repeatedly, he drew fouls and made 16 of 19 free throws to finish with 46 points, enough to give the Bulls a 119-106 win and a 3-2 lead. Again, the Blazers had stayed close, but Jordan's scoring had kept them at bay over the final minutes. His raised clenched fist and defiant grimace afterward served notice to Portland.

Game 6 back in the Stadium should have been a Chicago walk, but the Bulls fell into a deep hole, down 17 points late in the third quarter. Then Jackson pulled his regulars and played Bobby Hansen, B.J. Armstrong, Stacey King and Scott Williams with Pippen. Hansen stole the ball and hit a shot, and the rally was on. Strangely, Jordan was on the bench leading the cheering.

With about eight minutes to go, Jackson sent Jordan back in, and the Bulls powered their way to their second title, 97-93, bringing the Stadium to an unprecedented eruption.

"The final against Portland was a dramatic night for us and all Chicago fans," Phil Jackson recalled. "We came from 17 down at the end of the third quarter to win the championship. What followed was an incredible celebration."

"The team had gone down to the dressing room to be presented with the Larry O'Brien trophy by David Stern and Bob Costas," remembered Bulls vice president Steve Schanwald. "Jerry Reinsdorf and Jerry Krause and Phil Jackson and Michael and Scottie stood on a temporary stage and accepted the trophy. But we didn't have instant replay

Andrew D. Bernstein/NBA Photos

Bill Cartwright brought toughness to the Bull's front court.

capability, so the fans were not able to share in that moment. Up in the Stadium, we were playing Gary Glitter on the loudspeaker, and the crowd was just reveling in the championship. It had been a great comeback in the fourth quarter, really initiated by our bench. So the victory was a total team effort. I went down and asked Jerry Reinsdorf if we could bring the team back up. He said, 'It's all right with me, but ask Phil.' I said, 'Phil, the fans are upstairs. They're not leaving; they're dancing. We've got to bring the team back up and let them enjoy this thing.' Phil thought for a moment, and Bobby Hansen was standing nearby. Phil asked Bobby what he thought, and Bobby said, 'Let's do it!' Phil has the ability to whistle very loud. He put two fingers in his mouth and whistled over all that noise and champagne and everything. He got everything quieted down. He said, 'Grab that trophy. We're going back up to celebrate with our fans!' With that, Michael grabbed the trophy, and we went back upstairs. When we started emerging through the tunnel, we started to play the opening to our introduction music. It's very dramatic. It's "Eye in the Sky" by the Alan Parsons Project. So the crowd knew when the music started playing something was happening. The team came up through the tunnel, and all of the sudden the crowd just exploded. It was a 10,000-goose bump experience. All of a sudden some of the players Scottie and Horace and Hanson, those guys got up on the table so that everybody could see them in the crowd. Then Michael came up and joined them with the trophy, and they started dancing. It was just an electrifying experience, and I think for anybody that was there it was a moment that they will never forget as long as they live."

"They told me the fans were still celebrating up top," Jackson said. "Everybody said, 'Let's go up.' I heard that and went upstairs with the players into this scene of bedlam. But I got tripped up by some television people, from the cables on their equipment. It occurred to me that this was a little bit wilder than I wanted it to be. I got hit and got tripped. I thought, 'I guess this really isn't something I have to be a part of. This is a time for the fans and the players.' I stood and watched them for a while celebrating on the tables. Then I went back downstairs and collected myself and my thoughts. My family stayed up there and was a part of the celebration. But I went back downstairs and enjoyed some private thoughts. How the first championship had been more of a glory ride, and the second one was more of a journey. It had been a special time of nine months together. Things had been up and down, but we had had this one goal together, and despite our differences, we had focused on that one goal. I told the guys, 'A back-to-back championship is the mark of a

great team. We had passed the demarcation point. Winning that second title set us apart.'"

The team opted for another rally in Grant Park a few days later to rejoice with their fans. Again hundreds of thousands gathered to scream and celebrate. "We will be back," Bill Cartwright promised.

"let's go for a three-peat," Pippen suggested, and the crowd's roar in response made it clear that no one in Chicago doubted that it was possible.

1993

Jerry Krause had hoped that Scottie Pippen and Michael Jordan would decline their invitations to play for the United States on the Dream Team in the Olympic games in Barcelona over the summer of 1992. Krause wasn't being unpatriotic. He just wanted the Bulls' superstars to rest. They both agreed to the honor, however, and despite the United States' easy breeze to the gold medal that August, both players came home thoroughly tired by the experience.

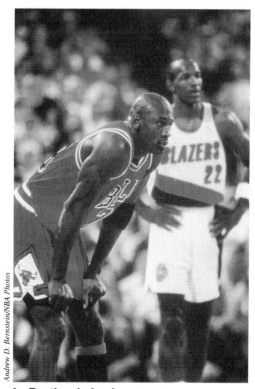

Andrew D. Bernstein/NBA Photos

In Portland, Jordan was as masterful as he needed to be.

Horace Grant, who had said many times that no one understood his importance to the Bulls, seemed jilted by the attention showered on Jordan and Pippen. And when Jackson allowed the two stars to take a casual approach to training camp in early October, Grant complained to the media about "double standards" and "preferential treatment."

Later in the season, he would accuse Pippen of arrogance. Ultimately, this sniping would prove to be a minor rift between the two friends, but both agreed that they weren't as close as they had been.

Besides the divisiveness that Jackson loathed, the Bulls encountered a rash of physical ailments. Cartwright, 35, and Paxson, 32, had offseason surgery on their creaky knees, and Pippen would be troubled by a bad ankle for most of the season. For Jordan, the pains were first his arch and then his wrist.

B.J. Armstrong, who had long struggled with the Bulls' triple post offense, finally found enough of a comfort level to replace Paxson in the starting lineup. Finding his playing rhythm coming off the bench clearly stumped Paxson, and the media kept steady track of the difficulties brought on by the shift. But no rift developed between the two guards. The 25-year-old Armstrong was simply better equipped to play in the Bulls' pressure defense, and that would make the difference in the playoffs. Plus, he would lead the league in three-point shooting, hitting better than 45 percent.

For the regular season, however, Jackson backed off from the pressure defense, thinking that he needed to conserve their energies and health. But the other problem for this veteran club was boredom, and the slowed pace worked against them to the point that at one point during the season Jordan called an oncourt conference and told his teammates to resume the pressure. Later, Jordan debated Jackson's strategy with reporters. "Maybe we gamble and we lose our legs," Jordan said. "I still don't think we get conservative now. When we try

Andrew D. Bernstein/NBA Photos
Charles Barkley led the Phoenix Suns to 62 wins in 92-93.

to slow down, things get too deliberate."

All of these wrinkles ultimately proved no hindrance. Their only real opponent was the sameness. Jordan called it "monotony." For most teams, that might have meant 38 wins. For the Bulls, it meant another divisional championship, 57 wins (their fourth straight

50-win season) and a seventh straight scoring crown for Jordan, tying him with Wilt Chamberlain.

On January 8th, Michael scored his 20,000 career point, having reached that total in just 620 games. The only man to do it faster was Wilt Chamberlain, who reached the milestone in 499 games. "It looks like I fell short of Wilt again, which is a privilege," Jordan said. "I won't evaluate this until I'm away from the game. I'm happy about it, but we still have a long season to go. I'm sure as I get older, I'll cherish it more."

In another game, an overtime loss to Orlando, Jordan scored 64 points, although Pippen complained afterward that Jordan had taken too many shots.

Jordan would be named All NBA first team again, and both he and Pippen would make the All-Defense first team. In the Finals, Jordan would collect an unprecedented third straight MVP award

For Jackson, December would bring his 200th win, reaching the mark faster than any coach in league history. Even with the accomplishments, it was not a regular season to treasure.

"Guys were hurt," Jackson explained. "Pippen with his ankle, Jordan with his plantar fascia. All of those things prevented us from getting a rhythm. We weren't in great condition. So when practices were done hard and precise, we ended up suffering in our game effort.

"I have always liked practice," Jordan said, "and I hate to miss it. It's like taking a math class. When you miss that one day, you feel like you missed a lot. You take extra work to make up for that one day. I've always been a practice player. I believe in it."

"They were tired," recalled Bulls trainer Chip Schaefer. "No question. Michael and Scottie were tired in the fall of '92. That was just a tough long year and really a tough year for Michael. It seemed like one thing after another. The press was picking on him, things just happening all year long. As soon as one thing would let up, it seemed like another

came into play. There was one book or one incident constantly. It got to be not about basketball but personal things that really shouldn't have been part of it at all. You could just see it starting to wear on him a little bit. In some private moments, he expressed that. It was really evident that he was getting tired. Tired physically, tired mentally of the whole thing."

Jackson's answer was a series of psychological ploys to motivate his players. "Phil played a lot of mind games," Jordan recalled. "He waged psychological warfare to make you realize the things you have to do to be a winner."

"It's a funny thing to look at the history of the NBA and the way teams kind of rise and

Nathaniel S. Butler/NBA Photos

The Sun's Kevin Johnson challenged Chicago's defense and played a Finals record 62 minutes in Game 3.

fall," Schaefer noted. "For all intents and purposes, it looked like it was going to be New York's year. They paid their dues. The Knicks absolutely destroyed us, beat us by 37 points in late November that year. They played like it was Game 7 in the playoffs. We went in kind of yawning. No big deal. Michael sprained his foot early in the game, and they just crushed us. We still won 57 games that year, but we just kind of foundered."

For two years, the New York Knicks had seen their championship hopes end in seven-game playoff battles with the Bulls. With good reason, they figured they needed the homecourt advantage to dethrone Jordan and his teammates. So coach Pat Riley turned the full force of his considerable intensity to driving New York to 60 wins and the homecourt advantage in the Eastern Conference.

Nathaniel S. Butler/NBA Photos

Jordan wowed even his good friend Barkley.

The Bulls, meanwhile, slipped quietly into second place and seemed almost distracted heading into the playoffs. But they quickly picked up the pace, sweeping three from Atlanta in the first round, then devastating the Cleveland Cavaliers again by winning four straight. Jordan capped the series with a last-second game winner in Cleveland that closed the chapter on his domination of the Cavs.

"Once the playoffs rolled around," Schaefer recalled, "and Michael managed to turn it on again. But we faced New York again. We didn't have home court so there really wasn't much reason to be optimistic about it."

Jordan loathed the Knicks' brutish style. "They play like the Pistons," he said testily. Perhaps New York's frustration made them worse. Plus Jackson and Riley made no great effort to hide their dislike for one another. In Game 1 in Madison Square Garden, the Knicks banged Jordan into a 10-for-27 shooting performance and won, 98-90. "I told the team I let them down," Jordan said afterward.

The acknowledgment did little good because the same thing happened in Game 2. Jordan missed 20 of 32 shots, and the Knicks won again, 96-91. Afterward, the smugness in New York was tangible. "Now the Bulls are down two games and have to beat the Knicks four games out of five games if they are going to have a chance at three titles in a row," crowed New York Daily News columnist Mike Lupica.

A media firestorm then erupted after a New York Times report that Jordan had been seen at an Atlantic City casino in the wee hours before Game 2, suggesting that perhaps he wasn't properly rested for competition. The headlines brought Jackson and Krause quickly to his defense. "There is no problem with Michael Jordan," Krause told reporters. "He cares about winning and is one of the great winners of all time."

"We don't need a curfew," Jackson added. "These are adults. . . You have to have other things in your life or the pressure becomes too great."

With this issue hovering over the events, the series moved to Chicago.

"The Bulls came back for practice at the Berto Center," recalled veteran Chicago radio reporter Cheryl Ray. "I've never seen as much media gathered for an event. Michael stepped out of the training room, and I said, 'Michael would you just go over the chain of events for us? Would you tell us what happened and where this story is coming from?' He did, and then a television newsperson from a local Chicago station started grilling him as though he were an alderman being convicted of a crime. Chuck Gowdy from Channel 7 was saying things like, 'Do you do this before every game? Do you have a gambling problem?" He kept hammering and hammering away, and eventually Michael just shut up and walked away. He didn't talk until the first game against Phoenix."

Jordan ceased speaking with the media, and his teammates followed suit. With Pippen taking charge, the Bulls won big in Game 3 in the Stadium, 103-83.

"The moment I knew we were going to win that series was after Game 3," Schaefer recalled. "After we'd beat them pretty soundly and brought the series back to 2-1, Patrick Ewing made a comment that, 'We don't have to win here in Chicago.' As soon as I heard him say that, I knew we were going to win the series. If you have that attitude, you may lose a game and lose your edge. You can't assume you're going to win all of your home games. As soon as he said that, it told me he was counting on winning all their home games, which wasn't going to happen. It was Scottie who got us that series. He always seemed to have a knack when Michael might have been having a tough time, to step up and do what needed to be done."

Jordan scored 54 points to drive Chicago to a win in Game 4, 105-95, and it was Jordan's triple double (29 points, 10 rebounds, and 14 assists) that dominated the statistics column in Game 5, when Chicago took the series lead, 3-2. But it was Pippen's successive blocks of putback attempts by New York's Charles Smith late in Game 5 in New York that closed off the Knicks' hopes. Then, when the Bulls completed their comeback in Game 6 in Chicago, it was Pippen again doing the final damage, a corner jumper and a trey, in a 96-88 victory.

The Bulls had persevered to return to their third straight NBA Finals. This time, Charles Barkley, now with the Phoenix Suns, was the opponent. After several frustrating and troubled years in Philadelphia, Barkley had been traded to the Suns before the 1992-93 season, and like that he was reborn, earning league MVP honors and leading the Suns to 62 wins and a trip to the Finals.

Andrew D. Bernstein/NBA Photos

B.J. Armstrong had given Chicago backcourt quickness since moving into the lineup.

It was a memorable series, not so much for the basketball, but because of the extracurricular activities, which included sightings between games of Barkley and Madonna at a Phoenix restaurant. In the championship matchup with Jordan, Barkley was a fitting opponent. It was Charles vs. Michael. Mano y mano. Shaved pate vs. shaved pate. Nike commercial vs. Nike commercial. In his shoe advertisement, Jordan pondered, "What if I were just a basketball player?" while Barkley in his spot declared, "I am not a role model."

That stance only added to the controversy of Sir Charles' public image. Some critics saw him as another highly paid performer shirking his responsibility. Others, though, understood that Barkley's statement was intended as a reminder that pro athletes are merely media images and that the real responsibility for instilling values in young people belongs in the home. Barkley explained as much, but that did little to deter his critics.

As it turned out, both he and Jordan were players, both role models, their determination showing the 1993 NBA Finals' worldwide audience real confidence, real energy. Having come into the league together in the fall of 1984, the two superstars had formed a solid friendship over the years. While Barkley had shown no forethought, no hesitation in trashing his own public image during his early NBA seasons, the more circumspect Jordan had proceeded cautiously, always saying and doing the correct corporate things while persistently building Chicago into a winner. At times, when Barkley's occasional barfights or misguided public statements boiled over into controversy, Jordan had even taken on the task of trying to explain his friend to writers and reporters, the primary message being that Charles may tend to run his mouth before thinking, but he's an honest, genuine person and a tough competitor.

For these defenses and for Jordan's friendship, Barkley was quite grateful. In fact, some said too grateful to be successful in the 1993 championship series. Later, Scottie Pippen, Jordan's teammate, would berate Barkley for "kissin' Michael's ass," an accusation that left Sir Charles bristling. Yet it would remain one of the great unanswered questions of his career. The Lakers' Magic Johnson and the Pistons' Isiah Thomas had formed a similar friendship in the 1980s, but that relationship fell apart when their teams met in the 1988 and 1989 Finals. There was no way, Johnson later admitted, that their intense competition could not get in the way of their friendship.

Faced with the same tough choice of building and nurturing an intense dislike for his championship competition, Barkley had chosen to remain a good guy and Jordan's friend. The Suns had won 62 games and had the homecourt advantage for their brand new

America West Arena. The Bulls, though, had plenty of confidence. They had always done well against Barkley's Philadelphia teams. Pippen's and Grant's defense would shackle him again, and B.J. Armstrong had the quickness to stay with Phoenix point guard Kevin Johnson.

Those plans eventually worked out, but in the short term there was more turbulence ahead. No sooner had Jordan's Atlantic City casino jaunt slipped out of the news than Richard Esquinas, a San Diego businessman, stepped forward with a book claiming that Jordan owed him $1.2 million from high-stakes losses from betting on golf games.

In a taped interview on NBA at halftime of Game 1 of the Finals, Jordan answered, admitting that he had lost substantial sums to Esquinas but nowhere near the figure claimed. Questions about whether this distraction would hinder the Bulls were quickly put aside when Chicago claimed the first game, 100-92. Jordan hit for 31, Pippen for 27, while the Bulls' defense harassed Barkley into shooting 9 for 25.

"I don't think anybody was scared or had the jitters," said Phoenix guard Kevin Johnson, a statement that met was with no Amens. Frankly, the Suns seemed quite nervous. And they sank deeper into trouble in Game 2. Barkley and Jordan both scored 42 points, but the Bulls defense clamped down on Kevin Johnson and Phoenix guard Dan Majerle to take a 2-0 series lead, 111-108. Bulls assistant Johnny Bach had devised a defensive scheme, deployed by Armstrong, that had Johnson talking to himself and sitting much of the fourth quarter.

Suddenly Phoenix faced three games in Chicago and the prospects of a sweep. The Suns answered by scratching out a 129-121, triple-overtime win in Game 3. This time KJ had played an NBA Finals record 62 minutes and scored 25 points with seven rebounds and nine assists. Majerle had scored 28 and Barkley 24.

"I thought it was never going to end," Phil Jackson said afterward.

Sensing a vulnerability in his team, Jordan came on strong in Game 4, scoring 55 points and driving the Bulls to a 108-98 win and a 3-1 series lead. The Suns had allowed Jordan time and again to glide inside for handsome little dunks and bank shots. Phoenix was only down two at the end, but Armstrong's pressure and a key late steal. Jordan's point total tied Golden State's Rick Barry for second place on the all-time single-game list. The record was held by Elgin Bayor, who had scored 61 in a game against Boston in 1962.

The Bulls were up 3-1 with Game 5 on their home floor. However, they strangely teetered at the brink of their accomplishment. Jordan swore to his teammates that he wouldn't accompany them back to Phoenix if they failed to deliver the championship in the Stadium. Regardless, the Bulls stumbled, and the Suns busied themselves with defense. Jordan's easy baskets disappeared as Phoenix congregated in the lane. Suns rookie Richard Dumas scored 25 points. "It was just a matter of slipping into the open spots," he explained. "There were a lot of them."

Jordan shook off the pressure to lead the Bulls to their third straight title in '93.

With Johnson scoring 25 and Sir Charles 24, the Suns got the win they needed, 108-98, to return the series back to their home court. Afterward, Barkley forecast a Suns title. "It's just that I believe in destiny," he said.

There had been speculation that if the Bulls won Game 5 in Chicago, the city would be racked by the riotous celebration that had marred the team's previous championships. In fear of that, many merchants had boarded up their stores.

"We did the city a favor," Barkley said as he left town. "You can take all those boards down now. We're going to Phoenix."

So was Jordan, contrary to his vow, and the Bulls were fighting feelings that they had let their best opportunity slip away.

"Michael seems to sense what a team needs," recalled Bulls broadcaster Tom Dore. "They had just lost. But Michael walked on the plane going to Phoenix and said, "Hello, World Champs." He's got a foot-long cigar, and he's celebrating already because he knows the series is over. He knew, going to Phoenix, that they were going to win. It wasn't a question with him, and I think that's what the team had. They just had this arrogance. They weren't mean about it. They just felt like they were going to win."

Barkley had claimed that "destiny" belonged to the Suns, but over the first three quarters of Game 6 it seemed the Phoenix players were feeling pressure more than anything else. Meanwhile, the Bulls phalanx of guards, Jordan, Armstrong, Paxson and seldom-used reserve Trent Tucker fired in nine three-pointers over the first three periods to stake Chicago to a 87-79 lead.

From there, however, it was the Bulls' turn to succumb to the pressure. They missed nine shots and had two turnovers the first 11 times they got the ball in the fourth quarter. The Suns closed within a point, then surged to take a 98-94 lead with 90 seconds left. Then Jordan pulled down a defensive rebound and wound his way through traffic to the other end for a short bank shot. It was 98-96 with 38 seconds to go. Majerle's shooting had helped Phoenix back into the series, but on their next-to-last possession he shot an air ball.

The Bulls had another chance with 14.1 seconds to go. After a timeout, Jordan inbounded the ball to Armstrong, then got it back and passed ahead to Pippen. The ball was supposed to go back to Chicago's Superman, but Pippen saw that Jordan was covered and motored into the lane, where he was greeted by Suns center Mark West.

Alone on the near baseline was Grant, who had scored a single point in the game, who had had a stickback opportunity moments earlier and almost threw the ball over the backboard. Pippen whipped him the ball, and scrambling out of his personal terror, Grant passed up the shot to send the ball out to John Paxson, all alone in three-point land to the right of the key.

"I knew it was in as soon as Pax shot it," Jordan said.

Paxson's trey and a key Grant block of Johnson's last shot moments later delivered the Bulls' third championship.

"That's instinct," Paxon said of the shot afterward. "You catch and you shoot. I've done it hundreds of thousands of times in my life. Horace gave me a good pass."

Reporters converged upon Jordan afterward to ask if he planned to retire. "No," he assured them. "My love for this game is strong."

Yet time would reveal it was more than a matter of love. Still the effects of Paxson's big shot and three straight championships would linger sweetly in Chicago.

"It was like a dream come true," Paxson recalled in 1995. "You're a kid out in your driveway shooting shots to win championships. When you get down to it, it's still just a shot in a basketball game. But I think it allowed a lot of people to relate to that experience, because there are a lot of kids and adults who lived out their own fantasies in their back yards. It made the third of the three championships special. It's a real nice way of defining a Threepeat, by making a three-point shot.

"I'm not sure what winning did for us outwardly, but inwardly it justified all the effort and hard work that we put into it. It confirmed our belief that we could win, and with that comes a confidence that carries over into your personal life as well as your professional life. I saw that in a lot of my teammates after we won the first one and we continued to win. It was like, outside of Michael and Scottie, who were already established stars, the other guys kinds of blossomed. It was recognition. We all became a little more noticed as players. For so long, it was Michael Jordan. Can these other guys hold up their end and help him win? We proved to the basketball world that we could.

"That's the greatest part about winning, is how you feel as a group. You're happy for one another. You look at small plays that happen in a game, the people who come off the bench and provide something that the group needs. In our first championship run, Cliff Levingston provided some key minutes in the games out in Los Angeles. Craig Hodges did the same thing. You understand how important each individual is to your success. It's not just the best player. It's from one to twelve, the coaches included, and your appreciation for each is very high."

17.
The Dream Rises to the Top

At the close of the 1993 playoffs, Michael Jordan sat atop the NBA mountain. During the Finals, he had averaged 41 points per game, breaking the championship series record of 40.8 points per game set by San Francisco's Rick Barry in 1967.

Yet there was little question among Jordan's close associates that he had grown weary of the grind, of the lack of privacy. In his public comments during the 1993 season, he had made oblique references to his retirement. Yet in the locker room victory celebration, Jordan had said he would be back for another campaign come fall.

However, late that July, a dreadful turn of events hastened his departure from the game. Jordan's popular father, James Jordan, was found murdered in South Carolina, ostensibly the victim of a random roadside killing. Yet the news of Mr. Jordan's death was followed quickly by wild speculation that somehow Jordan's golf wagering might be a factor. That, as much as anything, seemed to be the final insult for Jordan. On October 6, 1993, he abruptly announced his retirement from the Bulls.

"That's what killed us about Norm Van Lier, who works as a broadcaster here in Chicago," said Bulls coach Phil Jackson. "He was broadcasting theories about Michael's father's death and gambling and the NBA and all this stuff. Michael had to go talk to Van Lier and say, 'Norm. Cool this stuff about gambling and the NBA and the grand scheme and all this other stuff about my father's death. There's no conspiracy going on here.' That's the paranoia that builds in people's minds and sometimes drives you crazy."

The situation was clearly too much for Jordan to handle, so he came to a quick decision to leave the game, so quick in fact that he didn't have time to notify his mother. "I was in Kenya with Michael's mom and a group of school kids," recalled Bulls vice president Steve Schanwald. "It had been so peaceful out there. We were on safari in a remote portion of Kenya, living in tents. No newspapers, no radio, no TV, no nothing. I told the people that the world could be coming to an end, and we wouldn't know. Two days later we flew back to Nairobi, back to civilization for the first time in about 10 days. I got off the plane and got on the bus that was going to take us to have lunch. The bus driver was reading a newspaper, a tabloid called the *Daily Nation*, Kenya's national newspaper. On the back page, there was a picture of Michael, and the headline said, 'Michael Jordan Retires.' I thought it was somebody's idea of a bad joke. But two days earlier, Michael had announced his retirement. Apparently, Michael's mom didn't know. I went up to her and thanked her for lending us her son for nine great years. She said, 'What are you talking about?' I said, 'Mrs. Jordan, your son retired two days ago.' She said, 'He did! I don't believe it.' So I went and got the newspaper and showed her. That was how we found out about Michael retiring.

"That night at dinner I bought some champagne for everybody, and we toasted Michael on his great career. But by the time I got back to Chicago, the festive mood was gone. People were definitely depressed. It happened with such suddeness, it was so out of the blue that it kind of took the wind out of people's sails."

Perhaps the greatest emptiness was felt in the NBA's administrative offices, where staff members began trying to figure out how to replace the greatest attraction in basketball history.

Jordan soon announced that he would try his hand at minor league baseball in the Chicago White Sox farm system with the hopes that he might someday make it to the big leagues.

"It was really his father's dream that he play baseball," Phil Jackson pointed out. "His

Hakeem Olajuwon and Patrick Ewing both hungered for a title.

Nathaniel S. Butler/NBA Photos

father wanted to play pro ball and did play semi-pro. When his father passed away, I think Michael was kind of living out his father's dream. That's one of the things I thought when I heard it. 'Geez, this guy wants to go play baseball in the major leagues!?!?' But then I realized basketball players are always fantasizing that they could play baseball. Looking back on it, it was a beautiful thing Michael did. What a risk he took trying to play baseball. The whole idea that he's going to go out and give up everything to try that at his age. That's the wonderful thing about it. Michael is such a special person."

It was that risk-taking competitive nature that had helped make Jordan a fan favorite. And it was that same nature that it impossible for the NBA to replace him.

1994

Jordan's departure had suddenly left the field open for a variety of superstars whose teams had never won an NBA title. Clyde Drexler in Portland, Charles Barkley in Phoenix, Karl Malone and John Stockton in Utah, Patrick Ewing in New York, all of them had hopes of leading their teams to the 1994 NBA championship.

Yet none, perhaps, was more eager or more prepared than Houston's Hakeem Olajuwon. For eight consecutive seasons, he has finished with at least 100 steals and 200 blocks, a string unmatched in NBA history. For his first nine seasons in the league, Olajuwon had averaged better than 11 rebounds per game. Only Wilt Chamberlain (14 seasons), Bill Russell (13), Elvin Hayes (12), and Bob Pettit (11) had longer streaks, but that's because they played longer.

"Now that Michael has left, Hakeem is the most complete player in the game — there's no doubt in my mind," observed Cleveland center Brad Daugherty during the 1993-94 season. "He's 31 years old, an age when you're considered to be on the downside of your career, but he's just exploded into the greatest player in the league."

Olajuwon's journey to the highest levels of the game had begun in Lagos, Nigeria, in 1978, when at age 15, he played hoops for the first time. The son of a businessman, Olajuwon thought he had found his calling as a soccer goalie. But Richard Mills, an American coaching Nigeria's national team, began campaigning for the young seven-footer to switch sports, saying he was too tall for soccer.

Olajuwon was swayed but almost got sidetracked in his first big game because he had no offensive skills. "I didn't know how to dunk," he explained. "And I didn't know how to lay it up either. I didn't know how to use the glass."

Frustrated, he almost quit, but his coaches kept talking up his potential. Then in 1980 he saw an Ebony magazine story on Kareem Abdul-Jabbar and Magic Johnson, who had just led the Lakers to the NBA title. The young African liked the sound of their names and was amazed by the star-quality of their status. That opened his eyes to basketball's promise.

"My coaches in Nigeria thought I could play competitively at the college level," he recalled. "So that was the ultimate goal, to go to school for free. I just wanted to get my degree and either work here in the United States or go back to Nigeria."

According to an old story, he nearly enrolled at N.C. State or several other schools, but Olajuwon says his only choice was the University of Houston. On his first flight to this country in 1981, he landed for a brief stay in New York but quickly came to detest the traffic and cold weather and moved on to Texas.

After some mixed-up directions that almost took him to the University of Texas in Austin, Olajuwon's taxi dropped him on the steps of Houston's gym, where the African center would begin his stormy but productive relationship with legendary Cougars coach Guy Lewis. His coaching style seemed caustic and overly critical to the sensitive young Olajuwon, but no college coach in America was a better teacher of post play. And no coach better loved watching his players dunk.

In the young African, Lewis found the ultimate post student, although it didn't seem

The careers of Olajuwon and Ewing had paralleled one another.

Andrew D. Bernstein/NBA Photos

that way at first.

Fortunately, Olajuwon's parents owned a concrete business, and from that affluence, he had been able to gain a good education. He spoke French, English and four Nigerian dialects, which meant a relatively smooth off-court adjustment. On court was another matter.

"Olajuwon had played exactly four months of basketball when he came here," Lewis recalled. "That's not even equal to one full season of junior high ball. . . I don't mind telling you, when I first saw him play, I wasn't sure he could do it. He was 6'11". He could run and he could jump. But he knew absolutely nothing about basketball. And he couldn't shoot."

Olajuwon started only six games as a freshman and averaged 8.3 points, but he remained an unpolished sub who got most of his playing time in practice. "I go in, I get my five fouls and I go back to the bench," he said of that first year at Houston. "Coach Lewis keeps yelling at me, 'Akeem, stay on the floor.' Basketball wasn't fun."

He entered Houston's starting lineup for the 1982-83 season as a full-fledged member of the school's dunking fraternity, Phi Slama Jama, but in many game situations he was still unsure of what to do. "We really spent time working with all our post people," Lewis said. "I played the post myself and have always emphasized its importance. But after a year of working with Olajuwon, it still wasn't there yet."

Lewis remembered laughing early in the year, when reviewing a game videotape, he heard a TV announcer say that Olajuwon had learned his post moves by playing soccer in Africa. Soccer certainly provided Olajuwon the opportunity to develop excellent footwork, but the intricacies of playing the post were another matter. On raw talent alone, the center had some big offensive games early in his sophomore season, including 30 points against the University of Utah and 22 rebounds against SMU. But the tougher competition easily found ways of neutralizing him.

The breakthrough for Olajuwon didn't come until February. Houston had gone to Fort Worth to meet a tough Texas Christian team, and Olajuwon's picture was prominent in the local papers. The publicity irritated Lewis because Olajuwon was struggling while the rest of the team, led by Clyde Drexler, was playing well.

The center seemed lost against TCU, and late in the game, he had failed to score and had only one rebound. "Olajuwon was fouled and went to the line for two shots with a little time left and we were protecting a two-point lead," Lewis recalled. "The first shot hit the backboard like a rifle shot but somehow banked through. He missed the next one, but we held on and ended up winning. Olajuwon ended up with two points and one rebound, and I sarcastically told him he won the game for us.

"Then I told him he had gotten more publicity and done less than any player in the history of Houston basketball," Lewis said. "From that point, he seemed determined to show me. He just became dominating in practice."

His game performances weren't bad either. Houston became the first school to keep stats for dunks, and Olajuwon led Phi Slama Jama that season with 68 slams. Yet it was on the

Andrew D. Bernstein/NBA Photos

Robert Horry was an athletic addition to the Rockets' front court.

defensive end that he set himself apart with a school-record 175 blocks (5.1 per game). His intimidating presence allowed his Cougar teammates to gamble for steals (they averaged 11.4 per game).

Olajuwon's surge pushed Houston to the top of the college game, and that spring of 1983 the Cougars dominated the field in the NCAA tournament. Yet all of his personal progress seemed lost in the hoopla when N.C. State pulled one of the greatest upsets in tournament history, defeating Houston with Lorenzo Charles' last-second dunk, which left Lewis fuming to reporters that Olajuwon had failed to box out Charles.

Even with the defeat, Olajuwon was named the Final Four's Most Outstanding Player with 41 points, 40 rebounds and 19 blocks in two games.

Drexler turned pro after that season, but Olajuwon returned to take the Cougars back to the NCAA championship game yet again, this time for a loss to Patrick Ewing and the Georgetown Hoyas. Yet the Houston program's success and the high-profile losses established Olajuwon as the central figure in the city's complicated sports persona.

That spring of 1984, the Houston Rockets held the top pick in the NBA draft, and hoping that he would be their selection, Olajuwon decided to forego his senior year in college. Although the Rockets already had a Rookie-of-the-Year center in Ralph Sampson and Michael Jordan was also in the draft, the Rockets took Olajuwon and announced formation of the Twin Towers.

The move paid almost immediate dividends. With Sampson and Olajuwon presenting matchup problems for opponents around the league, the Rockets upset the Lakers and earned a spot against the Celtics in the 1986 NBA Finals. They lost in six games, a defeat that Olajuwon considered the most painful in his career, but hope for the future loomed large. Olajuwon figured he was part of a team that would come to rule over the NBA.

Instead, things fell apart. Sampson's knees went bad, and the Rockets traded him. Coach Bill Fitch was eventually fired, and the Rockets' front office never could seem to find a supporting cast of guards and forwards to play with Olajuwon. Four seasons of promise passed with no dividends.

Still, by 1991, things seemed on the upswing. Olajuwon had long established himself as the best center in the game. Otis Thorpe, obtained in a trade with Sacramento, had fit in nicely at power forward. And Don Chaney had replaced Fitch to drive the Rockets to a franchise-best 52 wins.

But fortunes swiftly plummeted in 1992. Olajuwon wanted a pay raise to bring his salary in line with the league's other superstars and soon found himself in a standoff with the front office. Then he injured his hamstring and missed several games. The team's doctor cleared him to play, but Olajuwon listened to a second medical opinion that said the injury needed more time to heal. The front office responded by accusing him of malingering to spur contract talks. Furious, Olajuwon demanded to be traded. The ensuing blowup cost the team its progress and Chaney his job.

Assistant Rudy Tomjanovich was promoted to replace Chaney, but the 1992-93 season opened under a cloud. On media day, Olajuwon told the press that the Rockets were being run by fools, that then-owner Charlie Thomas was a coward hiding behind then-General Manager Steve Patterson.

Non-plussed, Thomas told reporters that his wife had called him worse things "and I still live with her."

Fortunately, the Rockets faced a 14-hour plane ride for a game in Tokyo. On the trip, Olajuwon and Thomas talked out their differences. "When you are on a plane, you can run but you can't hide," Olajuwon said upon deplaning in Japan. "You can't get off, and 14 hours is too long to spend locked in a bathroom."

The offshoot was a four-year, $25.4-million contract extension that paid Olajuwon on a level with the league's other centers. "It's a great day in Rockets history," Tomjanovich said with a huge smile. From there, the coach went to work convincing his center to pass out of the double- and triple-teams he faced.

In Olajuwon's defense, passing the ball hadn't always been his best option, considering the Rockets poor perimeter game. But Tomjanovich had remedied that by setting up an armada of three-point specialists around Olajuwon to make opponents pay for their double teams. "When the Rockets are hitting their threes, you might as well pack it up and go home," explained Phoenix forward Charles Barkley, "because you can't double-team Hakeem."

Houston made a nice run in the 1993 playoffs. Then they opened the next season by winning 18 of 19 games, which established Olajuwon and his Rockets as the primary contenders. Alongside him in the frontcourt were power forward Thorpe and a host of utility forwards including Robert Horry, Chucky Brown, Mario Elie, Carl Herrera and Matt Bullard. The backcourt consisted of starters Vernon Maxwell and Kenny Smith and rookie backup Sam Cassell.

Despite hitting some turbulence along the way after their big start, this group had managed to fight their way to a 58-24 finish, second in the league only to Seattle's 63 wins.

With Jordan out of the NBA, the national press suddenly turned its focus on Olajuwon, prompting Houston Chronicle columnist Fran Blinebury to observe that Hakeem was "the elephant who has been standing smack in the middle of the living room for the past 10 seasons and is just beginning to get noticed by the experts sitting on the sofa."

For the fourth time in his decade-old career, Olajuwon ranked among the top 10 in four statistical categories. He finished second in blocked shots (3.71); third in scoring (a career-high 27.3 points per game); fourth in rebounding (11.9); and tenth in field goal percentage (.528).

His season began to look even better when the Denver Nuggets upset Seattle in the first round of the playoffs. Houston's path to the championship, however, was by no means clear. The Rockets promptly lost their first two second-round home games to Phoenix, bringing the Chronicle to declare CHOKE CITY in its next morning's headlines, a reference to the city's long-suffering anguish over its sports teams' failure to produce in the clutch.

Earlier in the week, Olajuwon and guard Vernon Maxwell had lashed out at Houston fans for their lackluster support during a Sunday afternoon playoff game. This time, though, Olajuwon only commented that you can't tell about the character of a team when it's winning. You have to wait until times get tough.

Only one other team in NBA history, the 1969 Lakers, had come back after losing its first two games at home in a seven-game series. But with Olajuwon ruling the lane the

Rockets caught the Suns and escaped with a seventh game victory in Houston.

From there, they nixed Utah 4-1 in the Western Finals and came face-to-face with Ewing and Knicks, who had survived a pair of seven-game series with the Jordanless Bulls and the Indiana Pacers in the Eastern Conference. A decade earlier, Ewing's Georgetown Hoyas had defeated Olajuwon's Houston Cougars for the 1984 NCAA title. Now the rematch would be a seven-game format, with the Rockets holding homecourt advantage.

"They're true warriors who should be here," said Knicks coach Pat Riley as the Finals opened, "not only for what they've accomplished but for how they've carried themselves."

Riley was referring to Olajuwon's maturing as a player and a person, much of which had been attributed to his rekindled faith as a Muslim. Since becoming more serious about his religion, Olajuwon had discovered the peace of a moral, contemplative lifestyle. He spent Fridays at the Mosque praying. Despite his millions, he lived simply, studying the Koran and falling five times each day to face Mecca, seeking absolution and harmony and a deeper relationship with Allah.

When he chided an NBA official for a bad call, he never used profanity. When he answered reporters' questions, he proceeded thoughtfully, producing insights at nearly every turn in the conversation.

Of course his life hadn't always flowed so transcendently. The old Olajuwon, then known as Akeem the Dream, was sometimes considered selfish and petulant, just like so many other rich, talented, young NBA stars. He seemed determined not to pass the ball away from the double- and triple-teaming defenses that neutralized him. Even worse, he seemed destined to waste the best years of his career bickering with the Houston Rockets front office.

But that had all changed over the past two seasons, as witnessed by the throng in the Summit. Each night during warmups, with a jazz band blaring nearby, Olajuwon would choreograph his spinning post moves. Like a dancer, he would whirl with the ball cradled in his arm, pivoting first right, then left. He'd pause, facing the goal, to execute a jab step. Up and back. Leaning in with the ball pulled into his waist, waiting to launch his fallaway jumper over an imaginary opponent.

Then he would resume whirling and pivoting, facing the basket then moving away, pausing to send his head fake flying before spinning suddenly into a 360. Without a doubt, Olajuwon was the most graceful big man to ever play the game.

But grace alone wasn't going to beat the rough, tough Knicks. Charles Oakley, Anthony

Andrew D. Bernstein/NBA Photos

Olajuwon did much of his damage through double teams.

Mason and Ewing would meet his mastery with forearm shivers. To overcome them, Tomjanovich knew he was going to have to keep the floor spread and use his three-point shooters to make New York pay for double-teaming Olajuwon.

The Knicks, though, were able to slow the action to a sludge-like pace with their physical defense. Fortunately, the Rockets got a lead in the first half of Game 1 because the second was perhaps the ugliest in league championship history. With New York outpacing Houston 32-31, it was certainly the lowest scoring.

But the Rockets had a 77-65 lead with about nine minutes left, and although the Knicks cut it to three with two minutes remaining, they just didn't have enough offense. Houston won 85-78, with Olajuwon scoring 28. Otis Thorpe had 16 rebounds, while Ewing finished with 23.

"That's a step in the right direction," Olajuwon said.

What came next, then, was a trip. Knicks shooting guard John Starks had made just three of 18 shots in Game 1. His answer to that misery was a bit of locker room meditation that allowed him to turn in a solid 19-point performance in Game 2. That, plus balanced scoring from his teammates and their usual stevedore defense allowed New York to tie the series with a 91-83 win. Houston had taken a 79-78 lead, but the Knicks' Derek Harper hit a pair of late threes to open the margin.

"We're still confident," Houston's Vernon Maxwell allowed.

But the Rockets had lost home-court advantage and were headed to Madison Square Garden for three straight games. There, amid the noise and mania, Houston lost a 14-point lead in the third quarter of Game 3, only to see the situation saved by rookie guard Sam Cassell in the fourth quarter. He scored nine of his 15 points in the last period, including seven in the final 33 seconds to give Houston a 93-89 win and a 2-1 lead.

"He's fearless," Tomjanovich said, smiling.

The Knicks answered by rushing out to a 17-2 start in Game 4, then watched it slip away. Down six in the third period, they came back behind Harper's and Starks' three-point shooting and Oakley's 19 rebounds (despite being hobbled by a sore left foot) to win 91-82, pushing the series to 2-2.

"We have to get back to the things we do best," Riley said.

"You want to take advantage of the situation," said the 32-year-old Harper, who was making his first trip to the Finals. "You don't know if that chance will present itself again." He had spent his entire career in Dallas until coming to New York in a midseason trade. Besides his usual defensive toughness, Harper hit five threes to finish with 21 points.

Olajuwon had outscored Ewing, 32-16, but that didn't seem to bother the Knicks' center. "I don't care what I shoot," he said, "as long as we win."

Despite the competitiveness,

Ray Amati/NBA Photos

Kenny Smith went to the hole against the Knicks' muscular defense.

many media critics expressed disappointment with the proceedings, particularly the absence of show and finesse with the Rockets and Knicks hammering away at each other. Never mind that Jordan himself often had to stoop to conquer the brutish Knicks, the chorus of complaints about a boring Finals obscured Olajuwon's superb performance. The championship series, critics said, was butt ugly, particularly the physical defense and unimaginative offense provided by Riley's Knicks.

Not to be deterrred, Riley's guys turned again to their defense to win Game 5, 91-84, holding the Rockets to 40 percent shooting and

fewer than 90 points for the fourth time in five games. Ewing had scored 25 to drive New York to a 3-2 series lead, which left fans in the Garden chanting, "Knicks in six! Knicks in six!"

They had a good shot at that late in Game 6 back in the Summit. The Rockets had a lead, but Starks blasted 16 of his 27 points in the fourth quarter, including a three-pointer with just over a minute left to pull New York within two at 84-82. Then he had a turnover with 30 seconds left, but the Knicks got the ball back late. With two seconds left, Starks took a trey to win it. But Olajuwon stretched out to brush it.

"I got a piece of it," he said. "That's all you need."

For the first time since the Pistons and Lakers had battled in '88, the Finals would be decided by a seventh game. To the Rockets' advantage, the previous 19 times that a playoff series had gone to seven games in the NBA, the home team had won. And 11 of the 14 previous NBA Finals to go to a seventh game had been claimed by the home club.

"We don't even think about that," Ewing said.

Just about all parties agreed that a showdown between these two great centers should come to a seventh game. Olajuwon, the first pick in the '84 draft, and Ewing, the first pick in '85, had faced each other 22 times previously in their careers. The Rockets had won 13 of those games.

Both were asked if their place in history would be decided by the outcome. "I don't think my career will be defined by it," Ewing said. "I'll be disappointed if we don't win. That's it."

"I'm not playing for my place in history," Olajuwon said. "I just don't know any other way to play than to play to win."

With this background, Game 7 unfolded much like the six others that preceded it. The Knicks challenged, and the Rockets looked for room to work. Ultimately, they found it. Olajuwon scored 25, Maxwell 21, and Starks found himself mired in another nightmare, 2 for 18 shooting, with Maxwell harassing him at every turn. Cassell, too, played another huge game, scoring eight of his 13 points in the fourth as the Rockets claimed their first title, 90-84.

"You go with your players," Riley said of Starks' troubles. "You go up with them, you go down with them."

"It hurts," admitted Ewing, who finished with 17 points and 10 rebounds. "I am extremely disappointed with the fact that we didn't win the championship. But I'm still proud of my teammates."

In the other locker room, the Rockets were launching high fives and showering in bubbly. "If you write a book, you can't write it any better," said Olajuwon, the series MVP. "I'm so happy to bring a championship to this city."

For Olajuwon, the main motivation had come after Game 5, when NBA officials had flown the trophy to Houston in anticipation of the presentation. "I thought, 'How can they bring this trophy to Houston -- we want it more than any other city -- and then fly it out of Houston . . . to New York?' It would have been a disaster. I can't even picture that.

"I was more concerned about that than the championship itself. At that point, it wasn't about the championship. It was about pride."

1995

Despite the Rockets' joy over the 1994 title, Olajuwon and his teammates would later complain that they didn't receive all of the "respect" that they deserved. They complained that both the media and the fans seemed to consider their championship an anomalie, almost as if the Rockets had snuck in and stolen it when the rest of the basketball world was snoozing. Actually, though, most coaches and players around the league had long viewed Olajuwon as a slumbering giant, one that just about everybody hoped would stay asleep. Now, however, he had awakened to his prime.

He became the first player in NBA history to be named the Most Valuable Player of both the regular-season and the Finals and to claim the league Defensive Player of the Year award

(although Bill Russell certainly should have garnered those honors several times over). But those feats didn't seem to have people convinced.

Then the Rockets opened the 1994-95 season with a struggle, and their irritation deepened. By February, they had slipped into a funk of mediocrity and seemed to have little hope of repeating as champions. That's when the franchise made one of the most daring, unusual moves in league history.

After spending his entire career in Portland and twice leading the Blazers to the league championship series, Clyde Drexler found himself in a drawn-out feud with the team's management in 1995, which led to a request to be traded. The longer the disagreement dragged on, the wider his split became with the team. Then, in early February, the Rockets came to town and were routed by Drexler and his teammates. Afterward, Olajuwon and Drexler had a quiet dinner at the Marriott. They had been teammates together at the University of Houston. Drexler had grown up in Houston. The Rockets were badly in need of a revived running game, and at 6-7, Drexler was the kind of big, strong, athletic guard to deliver the big finish. Bringing him to Houston seemed like an ideal solution. But who would the Rockets have to give up?

The answer was power forward Otis Thorpe, and the trade the Rockets worked later that month prompted critics to charge that Houston had foolishly given away a component vital to their success. "When they traded Otis, it killed Houston," Charles Barkley told reporters.

The move understandingly created tension on the Houston roster. There was no way, Mario Elie observed, that the Rockets could win another championship without a special power forward like Thorpe. And feiry guard Vernon Maxwell seethed, knowing that Drexler would take his place in the starting lineup and huge chunks of his playing time. Rarely in league history had two starters in a championship team been discarded.

Drexler, though, was understandably elated. "If I had stayed in Portland, my plans were to play out my contract in 1995-96 and then probably retire," he said. "I loved the fans in Portland, but it wasn't much fun for me toward the end of my stay there. The team was getting older and going down. But with this trade, I really feel like I want to play another two or three years. As a kid growing up in Houston, I watched Rudy T. play ball with the Rockets. I played college ball with Hakeem. It all just feels so right to be back here."

The rightness of the move, however, would take some time to establish. Drexler had told Tomjanovich that he didn't have to start, but the Rockets were soon hit with so many injuries that that wasn't an issue. Already missing Thorpe, Houston lost both Horry and Herrera for long stretches. Then Olajuwon himself missed two weeks with an iron-deficiency anemia. Soon the big trade began to look like the big flop. Drexler stepped in and powered the offense with big games (41 points and 18 rebounds against the Clippers and another 41 against Sacramento), but the Rockets struggled to a 17-18 record over the last 35 games to finish just 47-35, which netted them just the sixth seed in the difficult Western Conference playoffs.

Yet even as the disappointments mounted, Tomjanovich refused to doubt the trade. "I had the king of Houston, and then somebody offered me the prince," the coach said. "Was I going to turn that down? With all the injuries we had, I question whether we could have even made the playoffs if we hadn't had Clyde."

Fortunately, much of the proceedings had gone unnoticed by the media covering the NBA. In mid March, Michael Jordan announced his abrupt return to the game after nearly two seasons of "retirement." Jordan had been irritated that the baseball strike was threatening to get in the way of his attempt to make the Chicago White Sox roster. Then he got into a parking dispute with the team manager during spring training and decided to abandon his baseball efforts. "I'm back," he said in announcing his return to basketball.

The story created intense media speculation about his reappearance in a Bulls uniform for the final 17 games of the regular season. Could he reappear and magically lead Chicago to another title? Although the Bulls had struggled to stay above .500 through most of the season before his return, no one seemed willing to bet against him. His presence provided an obvious lift for Chicago, but no amount of magic could give the Bulls anything better than a fifth seed in the Eastern playoffs, which meant they had no homecourt advantage.

Somehow, despite all the late-season turmoil, the Rockets came together during the playoffs, although guard Vernon Maxwell grew dissatisfied and left the team after they lost the first game of their first-round series with Utah. The Jazz, in fact, took a 2-1 lead in the five-game series, but Houston managed to tie it with a key home win with Drexler scoring 41 and Olajuwon 40. Utah even had a solid lead late in the fourth quarter of Game 5 in Salt Lake City, but the Rockets closed in a swirl and won the series on a critical late shot. Once again the big numbers had come from Olajuwon with 33 and Drexler with 31.

"Does that end the controversy over the trade?" Olajuwon asked afterward. "In Clyde, we got experience and talent. He knows what to do in the big game. He's a franchise player in his own right."

From their win over Utah, the Rockets moved on to the semifinals to dispatch Barkley and the Suns in similar wrenching fashion. Barkley and Kevin Johnson had both struggled with injuries, but the Suns had taken a 3-1 series lead over Hakeem and the Rockets. The morning of Game 5, Drexler woke up with the flu and was not expected to play, but he showed up at the arena 35 minutes before the game and wound up playing 38 minutes as the Rockets turned the series around. From there, they went on to take the final two games of the series, including a 95-94 win in Game 7 that left Barkley and his teammates stunned and Olajuwon claiming, "This is a team of destiny."

Later, Barkley would tell reporters that for once he'd like to be healthy for a Game 7. "A championship is not that important to me," he said. "I keep hearing how important it is to me. If we win it, all right. If we don't, I'll be all right. I'm not gonna kill myself. . . The sun will still come up tomorrow."

Led by Nick Van Exel, the Los Angeles Lakers had upset the Seattle Super Sonics in the first round, then faced the Spurs in the Western semifinals. It proved to be a nice run for coach Del Harris' first Los Angeles team, but they were outmatched by the Spurs and fell in six games.

With the win, David Robinson's Spurs advanced to the Conference Finals for the first time in club history. Robinson had turned in an outstanding season and was rewarded by being voted the league MVP. Yet just when they seemed strongest, the Spurs fell apart in the face of a strong challenge from Houston.

"Going into the playoffs we had won 62 games," Spurs reserve Jack Haley said, "and we had an extreme air of confidence. We went in and crushed Denver in the first round. The LA series was good for us. Then we went up against Houston and we ran into a situation where good teams expect to win, and Hakeem came out and killed us that first game. But we weren't real concerned because we had won so many games. But when we lost the second game at home we had a complete and total chemistry meltdown. Every single guy started pointing fingers at each other and yelling."

Miraculously, the Spurs lashed back to claim two games in Houston after losing two at home. But with the series knotted at two-all, Spurs management decided to suspend Dennis Rodman for the critical fifth game for violations of team rules, i.e., removing his shoes while on the bench, being late to practice, etc.

The Spurs' season and their hopes for a championship ended with a Game 6 loss in Houston. Olajuwon had averaged 35.3 points over the series, and reporters noted that he was obviously motivated by Robinson's MVP award. Drexler, too, had created matchup headaches for the Spurs.

Orlando's Shaquille O'Neal and Houston's Hakeem Olajuwon figured to be the treat of the '95 Finals.

Nathaniel S. Butler/NBA Photos

Nathaniel S. Butler/NBA Photos

"One more series," Drexler said afterward. He was returning to the league Finals. Having lost there twice before, he was determined this time to come away a champion.

Meanwhile, in the Eastern Conference the Bulls had managed to oust the fourth-seeded Charlotte Hornets in six games in the first round. But it became increasingly obvious that Jordan still lacked the stamina and timing to deliver a miracle.

In the second round, against the Orlando Magic with Shaquille O'Neal, Anfernee

Houston's newly acquired Clyde Drexler proved unstoppable.

up a meeting between Shaq and Company and the Rockets for the league championship. The Magic were talented but young (Shaq was 23, Hardaway 21). The Rockets were defending champions yet strangely unsatisfied. "To win it the first time is a very unique feeling," Olajuwon said. "You don't know what it's going to be like until it happens. But to win it a second time is a different kind of thrill. You know the reward, and that makes you want it even more."

Orlando, though, had homecourt advantage, the benefit of their 57 regular season wins. If the Rockets won, they would be the only team in history to overcome the homecourt advantages of four different teams. It was their opportunity to get the respect they felt they had been denied.

"I defy anyone to say we backed into this one," said Houston vice president Bob Weinhauer.

Judging from the first half of Game 1, there seemed to be reasonable doubt that they would get there at all. With Orlando Arena crowd rumbling, the Magic bullied their way to a 57-37 second quarter lead. Then Houston's Kenny Smith found his three-point range. With the floor opened up, Olajuwon had some room to move, and by midway through the second half, the Rockets had moved ahead by nine. The Magic answered in the finals minutes and held a three-point edge with just under two seconds left.

Smith then tied it with his seventh three-pointer, a Finals record, and sent the game to overtime.

The Magic, however, were already shaken, with Nick Anderson missing four free throws in the finals seconds of regulation that could have iced the win. Still, they managed to tie it again on a trey late in overtime by marksman Dennis Scott. But Olajuwon, who finished with 31

Hardaway and Horace Grant, the Bulls and Jordan found themselves out of sync, particularly in Game 1 in Orlando when Jordan committed two late turnovers that cost the Bulls the game. From there, Jordan missed shots, made miscues and watched Grant's play shift the balance in the series. At one point, Jordan donned his old jersey number 23 to get a second win, but the Magic took over from there to claim a 4-2 series victory.

Orlando then eliminated the Indiana Pacers in seven games in the Eastern Finals, setting points, tipped in a Drexler miss with .3 seconds left for a 120-118 win and a 1-0 series lead.

"It was so quiet that I didn't realize the basket was in," Olajuwon said of the stunned arena.

"I'd be a hypocrite if I said I thought it was a fluke," Tomjanovich said. "Not with the way this team has played."

Smith had scored 23 points, including 20 in the second half, and Horry finished with 19.

In an interview session a day later, a reporter referred to Anderson's missing his free throws as "tragic."

"I've been in worse situations than this," Anderson said quickly. "My high school teammate [Ben Wilson], I watched him die. He got shot twice in the stomach, and I saw it. I was right there, no more than 25 feet away. . . You grow up on the streets of Chicago, you can see anything. Wednesday night was not a tragedy. It's just something that happens. This was just basketball."

And Game 2 was Sam Cassell's turn to shine. The backup point guard repeatedly penetrated the Orlando defense, and when he wasn't doing the damage, Drexler was taking Anderson off the dribble. Cassell finished with 31 points, while Horry had a Finals record seven steals to go with his 11 points and 10 rebounds.

And Olajuwon offered what was becoming his routine playoff brilliance: 34 points and 11 rebounds. It all added up to a 117-106 Houston win. Having lost their first two at

home, Orlando was now headed to the Summit.

"You could tell they became frustrated," Horry observed.

To their credit, the young Magic fought hard throughout Game 3. But Houston held a one-point lead with about 30 seconds left, and Horry's late three-pointer settled it, 106-103.

What had looked to be a competitive series heading into the event now was clearly headed toward a sweep. "This is our first time," said O'Neal, who averaged 28 points, 12.5 rebounds and six assists for the series. "This is a learning experience. I'm going to get here again before I retire. I'm going to get here many times."

The secondary players continued to play big for Houston in Game 4. Mario Elie had 22 points and Horry finished with 21 and 13 rebounds. The Rockets used a run in the fourth period to put away their second consecutive title, 113-101.

"How sweet it is," Drexler said.

"I'm proud of my 12 seasons in basketball," he said later. "Now, I'll have a ring to show for it. I always tried my best, and finally I was on a team good enough to win it all."

"This Rockets team is all about class," Elie pointed out. "Hakeem and Clyde give us that image. First and foremost, they are both gentlemen. They don't talk trash. They just play hard and carry themselves with great dignity. The city of Houston is very fortunate to have two stars who carry themselves like Hakeem and Clyde."

18.
The Bulls Run To History

Magic Johnson, the great Los Angeles Lakers point guard, was once asked to describe how it felt to lose in the postseason. "It's a hurtin' thing," he replied.

That was exactly how the Chicago Bulls felt following their loss to the Orlando Magic in the 1995 NBA Playoffs.

It was a hurtin' thing.

For many reasons.

First, it hurt because the loss rather rudely punctured the city of Chicago's euphoria over the unexpected return of Michael Jordan to pro basketball. After all, His Airness was king of the city, the man who had led the Bulls to three straight NBA championships between 1991 and 1993. Surely Michael would resume his miraculous, high-flying style and lift the Bulls to yet another championship despite the fact that he had played only 17 regular-season games and had been away from the sport for nearly two years.

Jordan did treat the fans to some rather stunning performances over the spring of 1995, but he also faltered with uncharacteristically clumsy moves in key moments against the Magic in the Eastern Conference semifinals. Who could forget his last-minute turnover that cost the Bulls Game 1 of the series? A similar collection of gaffes in the final minutes of Game 6 helped seal the

Orlando victory and left Bulls fans stung by disappointment.

What made the loss worse was that the Bulls' primary executioner was Horace Grant, who had played power forward on Chicago's three championship teams, the same Horace Grant who had frequently clashed with Jordan and later departed the Bulls to join Orlando as a free agent after a nasty public exchange of accusations and insults with Bulls chairman Jerry Reinsdorf.

In preparing to defend Orlando center Shaquille O'Neal, Bulls coach Phil Jackson had decided to double-team Shaq while leaving Grant unguarded. It was a logical move. The rest of Orlando's starters were deadly three-point shooters. Jackson figured that leaving Grant open would mean that if he made shots, they would only be two-pointers. Logical as it seemed, Jackson's move backfired. Grant, who always felt that he had been disrespected during his playing days in Chicago, took umbrage and answered Jackson's strategy by scoring early and often, a performance that further emphasized Chicago's weakness at power forward. The final insult came when the Magic closed out the series on the Bulls' home floor, then the young Orlando players hoisted Grant to their shoulders and carried him off in celebration.

317

Bad as all this seemed, the loss hurt most because the Bulls' coaching staff studied the tape of the series in the aftermath and came away with the firm conclusion that Chicago could have, should have, won the series and possibly even swept it.

"We should have won all six games," assistant Jim Cleamons said of the 4-2 outcome. "The reality of it was we didn't win, but we weren't that far from winning. . . We lost games at the end of the clock, on last-second shots and turnovers, matters of execution. Good teams close the doors; they end the case. The teams that are trying to become good teams have those straggling situations, those dangling participles, if you will. They just don't quite get the job done."

Strange as it seemed, the Orlando loss left the Bulls realizing that they now resided in the latter category: a team trying to become good. It wasn't a status they wanted to inhabit very long, "The day after we were out of it we started planning for next year," team chairman Jerry Reinsdorf said.

The only acceptable goal would be winning the team's fourth NBA championship.

One critical aspect of that would be re-establishing a homecourt advantage in Chicago. For years, that had been a foregone conclusion when they played in the creaky old Chicago Stadium, the "Madhouse on Madison," whose thundering crowds and intimidating acoustics had hammered many an opponent into submission. But the Stadium was now headed toward life as a parking lot, having been razed to make way for the United Center, the fancy new $175 million building just across Madison Street.

Brand new when the 1994-95 season opened, the United Center seemed awkward and foreign to Jordan, who had once vowed never to play there. He relented, of course, but didn't like it and quipped that he'd like to "blow it up." The remark was something of a setback to the Bulls administrative staff, who had hoped to establish the United Center as the "New Madhouse on Madison," a snazzier, high-tech version of the old barn. But then the

Magic had won two playoff games in Chicago, and those hopes dimmed.

In the aftermath of the 1994-95 season, Chicago's sports radio talk show airwaves were filled with anguished calls for changes, particularly for ditching the triple-post offense, the Bulls' offensive scheme pioneered by veteran assistant coach Tex Winter. The offense had played a large role in the team's three championship seasons, but now even the 73-year-old Winter expressed doubt. In all their years of working together, Michael Jordan had never told Winter what he thought of the offense. In the wake of the Orlando loss, Winter wanted to know, so he pushed Phil Jackson to discuss the issue with Jordan in the season-ending conference Jackson held privately with each player.

"With his impulsiveness, Tex said, 'Phil, I'd like you to ask him, does he think we need to change the offense,'" Jackson recalled. "Is it something we should plan on using next year? I want you to ask him just for me.' So I did, and Michael said, 'The triple-post offense is the backbone of this team. It's our system, something that everybody can hang their hat on, so that they can know where to go and how to operate.'"

For others, the concern wasn't the offense or the United Center but rather Jordan himself.

It seemed pretty clear that Michael's time as the game's dominant player had passed, which meant that the Bulls' fortunes were declining as well. There was even speculation among some Bulls administrative staff members that Jordan might retire again rather than deal with the hassles of NBA life. This speculation intensified over the summer as Jordan became involved in the battle over the collective bargaining agreement between the NBA and its players.

In years past, Jordan had failed to show the slightest interest in league labor issues, and he held a particular determination that he would never seek to renegotiate his contract with the Bulls. Yet, now, here Jordan was, at the urging of his agent, David Falk, taking a leadership role in a renegade effort to decertify the players union and force the league into giving its players a better deal that allowed them more freedom to negotiate contracts.

Despite the great public anguish over Jordan and the team's future, the Bulls coaching staff remained quietly but remarkably upbeat about the their prospects. It was obvious that Orlando's talented young team would be the main contender in the Eastern Conference, and if the Bulls hoped to win another championship they would have to rebuild their team with one purpose in mind: improving their matchups with the Magic. Specifically, the Bulls would have to find a power forward and strengthen their post play. Plus, they would have to find bigger guards to counter Orlando's trio of Anfernee Hardaway, Nick Anderson and Brain Shaw.

With this in mind, the Bulls decided to leave veteran B.J. Armstrong, a fan favorite from the championship years, unprotected in the upcoming expansion draft. Moving quickly, the Toronto Raptors picked up Armstrong with the first pick in the draft and traded him to the Golden State Warriors in a multi-player deal.

The coaching staff didn't have to look far to find a bigger guard to replace Armstrong. Already on the roster was former All-Star Ron Harper, whom Bulls vice president Jerry Krause had originally signed in 1994 to help fill the void created by Jordan's retirement. Harper's bountiful athleticism had declined with a series of knee injuries since his days as a young superstar with the Cleveland Cavaliers, but the Bulls figured he still had promise.

"When we brought Harper in initially, we felt that if he could regain some of his old skills, his old abilities after the knee injuries he'd had, he could be an ideal player for us because of his size," Tex Winter said.

The problem was, Harper had struggled most of the 1994-95 season to get the hang of the complicated triple-post offense, and just when he had started to come around, Jordan returned, taking most of his playing time. Soon the whisper circuit around the NBA had

Nathaniel S. Butler/NBA Photos

Jordan came back with determination in the fall of '95

Harper pegged as finished, his legs gone, his game headed for moth balls. The circumstances had left Harper understandably despondent, struggling through the lowest point in his 9-year career. "Suicide was an option," he would say later, only half jokingly.

"Last season was something I learned from. It was frustrating, but my friend had a frustrating year, too," he said, referring to Scottie Pippen, who had spent much of the '95 season fighting with management, "and we both grew."

Out of that growth came Harper's motivation to show everybody just how wrong they were about the status of his career.

In the wake of the Orlando loss, Jackson realized that Harper could be part of the answer and told him so in their season-ending conference — if Harper would dedicate himself to offseason conditioning. "Phil let Ron know that we very definitely were counting on him to be a big part of the team," Winter said. "I think that helped Ron no end. Phil put it to him in no uncertain terms: 'You gotta go out and get yourself ready to play.' And Ron did that, he really prepared himself."

"Phil asked me what my role was going to be on this team," Harper recalled, "and I told him, 'When Michael returns, I'll be a player who plays defense and fills the spot. If there's a chance to score, I'll score.' I think that we felt as a team that we had something to prove. And on my own I had something to prove. I figured this was going to be a very good ball club. . . I trained hard. I felt that last year I definitely didn't have the legs to play the style here. I had to learn that, too."

Jordan faced the same task, rebuilding his conditioning and mindset from the months of basketball inactivity, losing what Reinsdorf called his baseball body for a leaner basketball body. Jordan was scheduled to spend the summer months in Hollywood making an animated Bugs Bunny film with Warner Brothers. On another team, with another player, the coaches might have been concerned about a major summer conflict taking away from the intensity of the star player's offseason work. But this was not an issue with the Bulls coaches.

"We didn't worry about Michael," Winter said. "We figured Michael could take care of himself."

"Michael's just a hell of a competitor," Cleamons agreed. "I don't think the way he went out last year after our loss to Orlando is indicative of the way he wanted to be remembered as a player. He didn't want people to think that his skills were diminished. The man has a tremendous amount of pride. We knew he was gonna come back in the best shape he could possibly be in and dedicated to the idea of another championship."

Failing his team against Orlando had been a tremendous setback for Jordan, one that bruised his giant pride. For years he had thrived on taking the Bulls' fortunes on his shoulders and lifting them with brilliant performances in front of millions of witnesses. Now the public phenomenon was his fall. "We

agonized for him when he went through the postseason trauma," Jackson explained later that summer. "But knowing Michael so well, I put my arm around him after that first game in Orlando when he lost the ball and said, 'As many times as we've won behind you, I never expected to see this happen. Let's use it for our tool. Let's use it to build a positive. You're our guy, and don't ever forget that."

"Michael's not the same player," Jackson added. "He's aged like everybody else has aged. But he's still Michael Jordan. He'll go back and shoot 50 percent this year, you can bet your bottom dollar on that. Will he break through all the defenses that people bring at him, the double teams and triple teams? No. But he'll probably start knowing where to pass the ball better. Michael lost perspective of where the passing would have to come from a lot of times."

Missing out on the teamwork of an 82-game season had hurt Jordan, Jackson said. "But we see Michael returning to form. . . He saw and heard the criticism that went on in the postseason. There was a lot of the blame game going on in Chicago, a lot of people whining and gnashing teeth. Michael's going to use that for this strength."

Indeed, Jordan made it clear that the situation was his source of motivation. "The game taught me a lesson in the disappointing series I had last year," Jordan would later say. "It pushed me back into the gym to learn the game all over again."

For the most part, his "gym" would be a temporary floor in the Hollywood studio he occupied while making his film. There, Jordan could work on his game yet be within reach of the film crew when he was needed to shoot a scene. "I've never seen anybody work harder than Michael Jordan," trainer Tim Grover would later say. "He fulfilled his normal summer obligations — shooting commercials, making some personal appearances — and he shot a movie. But his conditioning program always remained his primary objective."

For Jordan, the torturous offseason program was just the beginning to a year-long effort to regain the dominance he had enjoyed in the NBA as a younger man. Now, he was nearing his 33rd birthday, trying to prepare himself to face not only the game's talented young players but the specter of his own legendary youth. No matter what he did as an aging comeback player, he would have trouble measuring up to the standard he had set from 1986 to 1993, when he lorded over the league, leading the NBA in scoring for seven straight seasons and driving the Bulls to three straight world championships. Now, the older Michael Jordan was taking on the younger, magical version.

"I'm the kind of person who thrives on challenges," Jordan explained, "and I took pride in people saying I was the best player in the game.

"But when I left the game I fell down in the ratings. Down, I feel, below people like Shaquille O'Neal, Hakeem Olajuwon, Scottie Pippen, David Robinson and Charles Barkley. That's why I committed myself to going through a whole training camp, playing every exhibition game and playing every regular-season game. At my age, I have to work harder. I can't afford to cut corners. So this time, I plan to go into the playoffs with a whole season of conditioning under my belt."

Heading into the 1995 playoffs, it had been General Manager Jerry Krause's concern that the Bulls lacked the meanness and nastiness in the frontcourt necessary to win another championship. In their three title years, center Bill Cartwright had anchored the defense with ferocity.

Now that Cartwright had retired, the Bulls had come to rely on a trio of centers, Will Perdue, Luc Longley and Bill Wennington, to get the job done in the post. Perdue could block shots, Wennington had a feathery offensive touch and Longley had the huge body necessary to struggle against giant forces like Shaq. None of the three Chicago centers was a complete force on his own, but collectively they formed what the press had taken to calling a "three-headed monster," a patchwork solution assembled by the coaches.

Ideally, the Bulls would get a complete center to match Orlando for 1995-96. The only problem was, there just weren't any around. The answer for the Bulls had been to try to develop a solid center. In this effort, Longley was their leading candidate, primarily because he was young (26), and at 7-2, 290 pounds, he had the big body to fit the specifications. "The kid's a solid worker," Jackson said in assessing Longley's upside in June 1995. "He's got a great desire to play the game. He's very intelligent. He doesn't have fear. But he's not mean, that's one of the things that we know about him. He's not rugged mean like that. Some people think that you have to have a center that's ferocious, that threatening type of defender.

"We've found that chemistry-wise, you can build that back up. We may have to get another position player, a power forward that does have that meanness. But with Michael and Scottie, you know we have those kinds of defenders out there already. An added person is what this team needs to get back to that level of being resilient, not being bullies, not being threatening, but being resiliently tough."

The Bulls coaches figured that with Jordan back full time and committed to winning a championship, with Pippen, Longley and Toni Kukoc maturing, with Ron Harper refurbishing his game, they had just about all of the major pieces in place, except for what was perhaps the most important one.

> **I**'m the kind of person who thrives on challenges, and I took pride in people saying I was the best player in the game.
>
> — Michael Jordan

"We still needed a rebounder," Jimmy Cleamons said.

Someone to give the roster a nasty factor, someone to play defense and buck up the Bulls' courage, someone to go get the ball when the team needed a tough rebound. In other words, someone like Dennis Rodman, the NBA's resident weird dude.

Dennis Rodman had been one of the NBA's great mysteries since the Detroit Pistons first selected him in the second round of the 1986 draft. Although some people in the Pistons organization would later claim that Rodman was fundamentally troubled, many in Detroit simply saw him as a fun-loving, immature guy who could be surprisingly sweet. One of his favorite pastimes was hanging out with teenagers in mall game rooms (growing up in Dallas he had gotten the nickname "Worm" from his antsiness playing pinball.) He was unlike many other NBA players in that he had not come up through the ranks of the great American basketball machine. He had not been on scholarship his entire life, wearing the best shoes and equipment and staying in fancy hotels where the meal checks were always paid. Rodman had missed all of that.

Although his two younger sisters were hoops stars in high school and college, Rodman was only 5-foot-9 when he graduated from South Oak Cliff High School in Dallas, where he grew up. Shy and insecure, he hadn't even played high school basketball. His only prospects after high school were a series of menial jobs. But, miraculously, Rodman's life was rescued by his pituitary. He grew 11 inches in one amazing year, yet even that only increased his isolation. By age 20, he was 6-8 and had outgrown his clothes, leaving his only attire the oversized coveralls from his job washing cars. About the only place he didn't feel like a geek was the playgrounds. Pickup basketball became his refuge, and his height was one of his first real advantages in life.

It was one of his sisters' friends who got him a tryout at Cooke County Junior College in nearby Gainesville, Texas. He played there briefly, dropped out, then wound up at Southeastern Oklahoma State, where he used his size and quickness to become something of a force in NAIA basketball, averaging nearly 26 points and 16 rebounds over the next three seasons. He led the Southeastern Oklahoma State Savages to a district title and into contention for the NAIA national title, all of which prompted the Pistons to select Dennis with the 27th pick in the 1986 draft, the next giant step in his amazing transformation.

Former Pistons coach Chuck Daly recalled that Rodman's first efforts in training camp were rather disappointing, but he recovered and soon found a place in the league by focusing on playing defense and rebounding. He performed these chores so well that most observers considered him a key factor in the

Andrew D. Bernstein/NBA Photos

For 1995-96, Jackson gave up his old frowing ways and grew a beard.

Pistons claiming back-to-back league titles in 1989 and '90.

To accomplish goals as a player, Rodman had come to rely on a natural hyperactivity that supercharged his frenetic playing style. "My friends knew I was hyper. Real hyper," he once said of his days growing up in Dallas. "They knew I wouldn't settle down, I wouldn't sleep. I'd just keep going. And now I just focus my energy in something I love to do. Now, I just play basketball, go out there and have a lot of fun and enjoy."

This joy was obvious in his gait. In warmups, he would run erect, proudly springing off each toe, then kicking his heels up behind him almost daintily. There was something almost Victorian in his posture as he jogged, something old-fashioned, something prim, smacking of Casey at the Bat and barbershop quartets, or some other cockiness from a long-lost era. Rodman, in that way, was a throwback. . . Until you saw him fill the lane on a fastbreak, when he threw off all the pretensions. Then, he was just a blur. He liked to finish from the right. The ensuing slam would be executed with an impressive enthusiasm. Rodman would land with a jet skid, a tight angle, fall back a bit, catch himself with his left hand and right himself with rocketlike quickness, rising straight up in the air for the crowd, jutting the index finger. He was number one, or somebody was number one. Anyway, before you could blink, the hyperactivity had refilled his tanks as he circled and headed back upcourt where he could have some real fun and play defense, making somebody's night very miserable.

At these times, it seemed that Dennis Rodman was the past and the present all rolled into one.

Back in the netherworld of Dallas, he had worked briefly pounding fenders in an auto body shop. You could still see some of that in his game. Like any smart player with unrefined offensive skills, Rodman made his living on the offensive boards. When his team had the ball, he would often back away from the lane, his hands on his hips, his eyes always on the guards working the ball on the perimeter. He watched intently, waiting to make his move, waiting to get that special little piece of position for an offensive rebound. That was his primary study, his soul's joy of joys. Sometimes, after he had snuck in and stolen an offensive rebound, he would dribble out to the perimeter, stand there with the ball in one palm and punch the air with his other fist while the crowds bathed him in warm applause, and he would stand there, soaking in the glow of limelight.

After watching him in the 1989 Finals, Lakers broadcaster Chick Hearn declared that Rodman was the NBA's best rebounder. Hearing that, Rodman was stunned. "The best rebounder?" he asked. "In the game? You mean they put me in front of Oakley, Barkley, all those guys? I wouldn't say that. I think I'm one of the best ones, one of the top 10. But I can't be the best rebounder. I'm just in a situation where they need my rebounding here. I rebound with the best of them even though I'm not as bulky as some guys. I use my ability to jump and my quickness to get around guys."

Daly had persuaded him to use these advantages to become a superb rebounding specialist and defender. Rodman bought into the plan and worked to make himself a marvelously versatile sub. Quick enough to stay with a big guard/small forward. Motivated enough to play power forward. Even tough enough to survive at center against much bigger bodies.

Rodman began studying videotape of his opponents to discover their tendencies and pet moves. He described his approach as "focusing in on the guys that I have to play and bearing down on what I need to do to stop this guy. Just having the hunger and desire to want to do the job. Because not many guys in this league want to play defense. Not many guys want to do that. If you can kind of put it in your mind and say, 'Hey, I know I got to play defense because I know I'm not going to score as much; I know I'm not going to get the ball on offense.' So why would I exert myself on offense when I can exert myself on defense?"

Daly, of course, couldn't have been more pleased if he had asked the question himself. Rodman moved into the starting lineup for 1989-90 and helped the Pistons to yet another championship. It was during this period, as the Pistons shoved aside Jordan and the Bulls in the playoffs for three straight seasons, that fans in Chicago came to absolutely despise Dennis Rodman, Bill Laimbeer and all the other Piston Bad Boys.

Eventually, however, Detroit's guard-oriented offense declined. The Pistons were swept by Chicago in the 1991 playoffs, and although Detroit made a playoff run in 1992, Daly moved on to coach the New Jersey Nets, leaving Dennis without the fatherly coaching connection he badly wanted. Besieged by personal and off-court problems, Rodman's frustrations built, leading to clashes with Pistons coaches and management.

That October of 1993, the Pistons traded Rodman to the Spurs, thus igniting the next amazing stage in the transformation of Dennis Rodman. From all accounts, he came to San Antonio a changed man. As Rodman explained it, "I woke up one day and said to myself, 'Hey, my life has been a big cycle. One month I'm bleeding to death, one month I'm in a psycho zone.' Then all of a sudden the cycles were in balance."

This new "balance" left him searching through a series of tattoo shops, piercing pagodas, alternative bars and hair salons to find the new Dennis, the one with the electric hair. The old Dennis, however, still played basketball like a wild man.

Jack Haley, a free agent signed as the Spurs' 12th man, was assigned a locker next to Rodman. "I walked in," Haley recalled of that first day, "and said, 'Hey, howyadoin? I'm Jack Haley.' He wouldn't even acknowledge I was in the room or shake my hand. We sat next to each other for almost three months and never spoke a word. I would try occasionally. I'd say, 'Hey, howyadoin?' I'd get no response. Just like the rest of the team."

Haley watched in amazement that winter of 1994 as Rodman moved in and silently took control of the power forward spot in San Antonio, giving Spurs center David Robinson the kind of help that he'd never enjoyed before. Soon Rodman was regularly pulling down 20 rebounds a game, an astounding feat.

"I figured they were padding his stats," Haley said. "I figured no one could get 20 rebounds a night. So I started counting his rebounds. I'd come to him in a game and say, 'You got 17. You need three more.' Or, 'You need two more.' Or, 'You're having an off night. You only got five.' One game, he said to me, 'How many rebounds do I have?' From there, we developed a slow dialogue."

Perhaps it was the fact that Haley is one of the least threatening people in the NBA. Perhaps, it was the fact that he was patient, that he made a low-key effort. Whatever it was, this casual acceptance somehow accelerated into a full-blown friendship about midway through the season.

Indeed, Haley found he could hang rather easily on Rodman's zany planet, among his offbeat circle of friends, including a growing number of celebrities, models, hairdressers, coin dealers and whoever else happened to nudge their way into Rodman's presence. Almost overnight, the pair became inseparable, tooling around in Rodman's pink-and-white custom Ford monster truck, watching television at Rodman's house amid the clatter of his 15 exotic birds and two German shepherds, jetting back and forth to Vegas for gambling junkets.

Still, to observers, they seemed like an odd couple. Here was Jack Haley. Nice guy. Clean cut. All-American. And there was Dennis Rodman. Obviously on the highway to hell. And honking his horn to get into a passing lane.

Before long, though, their relationship became apparent to those around them. Haley and Rodman had the simplest yet strongest of bonds. They needed each other.

Haley needed Rodman to legitimize his NBA existence, and Rodman needed Haley to interpret his actions and communicate his feelings and intentions to the people he didn't want to deal with, mostly the players and management of the San Antonio Spurs.

The main problem, it seemed, was that Rodman had almost nothing to say to his teammates, particularly David Robinson. They stood in stark contrast to Rodman, with his constantly changing hair colors, his body piercings and the cornucopia of new age symbols etched into his well-muscled arms, shoulders and back.

Asked how it felt to have Rodman for a teammate, Spur Terry Cummings, a power forward and ordained minister, replied, "For the most part, Dennis is not an unusual experience to me. I grew up with Dennises all over Chicago, a lot of people who were different, had their own flair and their own mentality about things. It didn't make it right; it didn't make it wrong. It's just the way they were. The only difference is, is that on a team level, a lot of that stuff just isn't acceptable as when you're out in the streets playing ball."

Rodman seemed intent on living by his own rules, being late to practices and games, wearing bizarre clothing and jewelry in practices and generally violating much of the protocol that had been established for pro basketball teams over the decades. Spurs coach John Lucas had decided the best way to keep Rodman happy and motivated was to allow him to live by a different set of rules than the rest of the Spurs, which is to say almost no rules at all.

"He gave Dennis way too much leeway," Haley would later say of Lucas. "Dennis did not have to come to practice if he didn't want

Croatian Toni Kukoc gave the Bulls scoring off the bench.

Andy Hayt/NBA Photos

to. Dennis did not have to ride the team bus if he didn't want to. Dennis would not have to come to a game until 20 or 30 minutes before tipoff. And that causes team dissension. How can a guy walk in 15 minutes before the buzzer and still start? And have the coach basically say, 'So what?'"

When Rodman acted up in the 1994 playoffs, and the Spurs lost to the Utah Jazz, the policy of appeasement cost Lucas and general manager Bob Bass their jobs. Next San Antonio brought in general manager Gregg Popovich, who had a military background, and coach Bob Hill with the idea that they would provide a more structured, disciplined system to keep Rodman in check.

Dennis, however, rebelled against these tighter regulations. Mainly, though, he was angry because he believed the team had promised to rework his contract because it paid him less than many of the substitutes on the team. When Rodman balked at playing under his old contract, the team suspended him to start the 1994-95 season. Finally, after missing six weeks' pay, Rodman agreed to give the team his best effort, an immense relief to coach Bob Hill.

"Defensively, if you just take a tape and watch him, his instincts for knowing where the ball is all the time are incredible," Hill said shortly after Rodman rejoined the team.

The Spurs won plenty of games over the winter and spring of 1995, but Rodman's differences with management dogged the team like a running skirmish. The Spurs had their rules, and Rodman answered with an insurrection that cost him tens of thousands of dollars in fines.

"They were fining him $500 and they were fining him every single game," Haley would later confide. "I'm talking about every single day, $500 a day. Because Dennis made a concentrated effort to be late. It was his way of sticking it in their side.

"I pulled up one day to practice. He's sitting there 15 minutes early for practice. I said, 'C'mon, let's go.' He said, 'I'm listening to some Pearl Jam.' He walks into practice 25 minutes

Pippen found a new comfort zone with Jordan back.

1995, an age when most hoop stars are looking at limited futures. It was clear that the Spurs wanted to trade him, rather than deal with another year of headaches. But they were having trouble finding takers. Rodman's ideal scenario was to get with another team for the last year of his contract, perform well and sign a new two- or three-year deal in the neighborhood of $15 million. "I'll put $5 million in the bank, live off the interest and party my a — off," Rodman told reporters, just the kind of talk that made NBA general managers very nervous.

"Everybody in the league was scared to death of Dennis," said Toronto Raptors coach Brendan Malone.

Yet, Rodman did have a small group of supporters. For example, former Boston Celtic guard and Hall of Famer K.C. Jones remarked that in some ways Rodman reminded him of Boston's great center Bill Russell. Quickness to the ball, selfless defensive mentality and an eccentric streak were characteristics that the two men share, Jones said.

Jerry Krause said he remained interested in Rodman only because of Bulls scout Jim Stack. "Jim Stack came to me early in the summer and asked me to look at Rodman," Krause said. "When I put him off, he finally pleaded with me. He talked me into finding out if all the bad things we had heard were true. Without Jim's persistence, we wouldn't have looked behind all the rumors to see what the truth was."

Bulls chairman Jerry Reinsdorf wasn't surprised when Krause came to him about the possibility of getting Rodman because the Bulls had looked at Rodman a year earlier. "I thought it was a great idea as long as he didn't play dirty," Reinsdorf said, "and Jerry and Phil could satisfy themselves that he was a good bet to not self-destruct. I didn't know Dennis. I only knew about the stories, like sitting in a parking lot with a gun in Detroit and the problems he had with other teams. I told Jerry that if you can satisfy yourselves that it's a good risk, then I'm all for it, because we need to rebound the ball better. But I wanted he

late. It was almost his way of saying, 'You're not going to control me. I'm gonna be one minute, two minutes late, every single day.'"

Rodman's disruptions continued right through the 1995 playoffs, where the Spurs advanced to the Western Conference finals against Houston. But, enraged by behavior it called detrimental to the team, Spurs management suspended Rodman for the pivotal fifth game in the series. San Antonio lost that game and the next to fall 4-2 to the Rockets. Immediately afterward, Spurs management began looking around to see if someone would take their Dennis the Menace in a trade.

Rodman's contract with the Spurs held only one more season of guaranteed money. But Rodman indicated that he wanted the Spurs to give him $15 million to play another season there. He had no options for imposing that demand other than some type of work disruption, and Spurs had had enough disruptions. He had turned 34 on May 13, and Phil to be sure that the odds were with us, so that's why they spent a great deal of time talking to Dennis."

Friends, enemies, former coaches, former teammates, the Bulls contacted a whole group of people in their investigation of Rodman. Chuck Daly told them that Rodman would come to play and play hard.

Encouraged by what he heard, Krause invited Rodman to come to Chicago for an interview. Rodman was immediately skeptical, but agreed to come. They met at Krause's house for what turned out to be a long, frank discussion about Rodman's past. He told Krause he removed his shoes on the bench because of a sweating problem with his feet. Rodman talked about his problems with Spurs management, how he felt the team had made him specific promises then failed to follow through. As they talked, Krause came to the realization that he liked Dennis Rodman. Krause was confident in his ability to judge people, and he thought Rodman was a good person. Krause also knew that Rodman had the potential to be a problem, but he believed that Jackson could take care of that.

"Anyway," Krause told Sports Illustrated. "Phil's no virgin. He's had his confrontations. He came from the CBA, so I guess he knows about problem children."

Satisfied, Krause sent Rodman to speak with Jackson, who spent hours talking to the forward, trying to read his attitude about the team system. It was obvious that Rodman wanted to come to the windy city to play with Jordan. He even allowed the Bulls to talk to a psychiatrist he had been seeing.

"Phil told me I was not going to average the 15 to 16 rebounds I was used to averaging," Rodman recalled. "He told me the figure would be more like 10 or 11."

Rodman said, "No problem."

"Phil and I thought very carefully about this," Krause would explain later. "It's been under consideration for quite some time. We certainly did an awful lot of homework and were satisfied with the results we got."

Yet even after Krause's investigation turned up good news, he and Jackson hesitated before moving forward. After all, Jordan and Pippen had loathed Rodman as a Piston. In fact, you could say that just about every player in the league despised his tactics. "When he played in San Antonio, I used to absolutely hate Dennis Rodman," said Bulls guard Steve Kerr. Pippen, in particular, held a dislike for Rodman, who had shoved him into a basket support during the 1991 playoffs, opening a gash on Pippen's chin that required stitches. Pippen still had a scar from the incident.

"If he's ready and willing to play, it will be great for our team," Pippen said. "But if he's going to be a negative to us, I don't think we need that. We could be taking a huge step backwards."

Jackson admitted as much. "There are no assurances with anything," he said. "We're just talking about trying to take some good chances with the basketball club to put them in a championship state."

Jordan and Pippen thought about it, then told Krause to go for the deal, which sent Bulls longtime backup center Will Perdue to San Antonio for Rodman in early October, just days before training camp opened. That news elated Rodman, who badly wanted to find a basketball home. "I had no choice," he said. "I feel like that I had a lot of negative energy going on in my life, and that was the best way to get rid of it."

Jackson, who was himself a bit of a rebel as a member of the New York Knicks back in the '70s, grew confident that he could coach Rodman. So the move was made, and as extra insurance for communicating with Rodman, the Bulls signed Haley to a $300,000 contract. Haley would be placed on injured reserve and kept there all season, which allowed him to practice and travel with the team.

Rodman appeared at the press conference announcing the deal with his hair dyed Bulls red with a black Bull in the crown and his nails done in a nifty layered Bulls motif. "I understand that they're a little leery and a little cautious of having someone like me in here," he said. "They wonder how I will respond to the team. I guess they'll find out in training camp and during the preseason. I think Michael knows he can pretty much count on me doing a good job. I hope Scottie feels the same way."

The announcement of the trade set off the expected firestorm of media and fan interest in Chicago. But just days into training camp, Bulls insiders began to have doubts that the situation was going to work. It seemed Rodman still hadn't spoken to any of his Chicago teammates, and his silence was getting stranger with each passing day.

"It was a tough training camp because everybody was guarded," Haley offered. "Again, you're Michael Jordan. You're Scottie Pippen. Why would you have to go over to Dennis? Michael Jordan made $50 million last year. Why would he have to go over and basically kiss up to some guy to get him to talk? They came over and shook his hand and welcomed him to the team, and this and that. But other than that, it was a slow process."

"I think everybody was skeptical of what might happen," recalled assistant coach John Paxson. "But we were also optimistic as to what could happen. The optimism stemmed from Phil's personality. We felt that if there was anyone around the league who could get along with Dennis and get Dennis to respect him as a coach it would be Phil."

Sports Illustrated came into town the first week of the preseason and wanted to pose one of the Bulls star players with Rodman for a cover shot. Jordan, who had a running feud with SI since the magazine had ridiculed his attempt to play professional baseball, refused to pose. The previous spring, Rodman had appeared on the cover of the magazine in a dog collar and a bustier, one of the strangest posings in *SI*'s history. Apparently this time, Rodman wasn't going to wear a strange getup, but Pippen also declined, saying privately that he didn't want to make a fool of himself.

Finally, the magazine got Jackson to do the shot, (which was never used).

It was just one of an avalanche of media requests for interviews set off by Rodman's

becoming a Bull. In fact, several gay magazines approached the team about securing an interview with Dennis because of his racy comments. Haley, however, chalked much of that interest up to Rodman's having learned to manipulate the media while dating Madonna two years earlier. He had discovered he could generate substantial news coverage by projecting a conflicted sexuality.

"He spent time with Madonna, and when he was with Madonna that increased his time in the public eye and made him more of a star," Haley explained. "So now all of the things he does are because of the shock value. He talks about, 'Oh, yeah, I hang in the gay community and I hang out with gay people in gay bars.' That's all shock value. We're best friends; we're together every single night. In the two years I've known him, we've been to one gay bar. But he talks about it all the time, because it's part of his aura and his stigma."

"Have you ever played on a team where one of your teammates lives with his male hair dresser?" one Chicago reporter asked Michael Jordan during the preseason.

Jordan said he couldn't think of any.

Yet the interest in Rodman's sexuality wasn't the reason his presence seemed a threat to team chemistry. More central to the uneasiness was the relationship between Rodman and Pippen.

"No, I have not had a conversation with Dennis," Pippen acknowledged early in the year. "I've never had a conversation with Dennis in my life, so I don't think it's anything new now."

Fortunately, things seemed to take a sudden turn for the better with the Bulls' first two exhibition games. They opened play in Peoria, of all places, against the Cleveland Cavaliers, whom the Bulls defeated easily with Jordan scoring 18 points and Rodman getting 10 rebounds.

"Once he gets a little more familiar with everybody out on the floor and there's more continuity, he's going to start to shine," Jordan predicted.

Team chemistry got another boost in the second preseason game when Rodman rushed to Pippen's aid after Indiana's Reggie Miller made some threatening moves. It was clear that Dennis was going to be the kind of rebounder, defender and intimidator that Krause wanted. "I'm looking forward to a lot of brawling around here," he told reporters. "We need brawling on this team."

While Rodman was a surprise early fit, the other factors would take time. Jordan wasn't so sure that his pairing with Harper in the backcourt was going to work, but Jackson advised patience. Harper's presence meant that Jordan was handling the ball more. With his offseason work he had regained his basketball conditioning. Michael seemed like his former self on the floor. The confidence was tangible. Pippen, too, seemed more at ease with Michael back. Pippen's private life had gone through some changes, and Jackson noticed that he seemed more focused than ever.

At center Luc Longley seemed eager to face the challenge of the coming season as a starter, and veteran Bill Wennington was comfortable in his role as a backup. For additional insurance in the post, Krause signed 39-year-old James Edwards, himself a former Piston and a friend of Rodman's, in late October, thus assuring that the Bulls would have post depth and the oldest roster in the league. Krause had also brought in guard Randy Brown to work with Steve Kerr as backcourt reserves. Also coming off the bench were Jud Buechler, Dickey Simpkins and first-round draft pick Jason Caffey out of the University of Alabama.

The other bubble in the mixture was Toni Kukoc's reluctance to play the sixth man, or third forward. He wanted to start, instead of coming off the bench, but his role in the lineup had gone to Rodman. Jackson talked to Kukoc about the success that Celtic greats Kevin McHale and John Havlicek had enjoyed as sixth men, but it was not a concept that Kukoc embraced immediately.

Changing Kukoc's mind would take patience, Jackson reasoned, but there was a whole season ahead and there would be plenty of time.

Andrew D. Bernstein/NBA Photos

Dennis Rodman's rebounding was unequaled.

The only remaining question was Rodman. Early on, his behavior had been strange but acceptable. But how long would it last? Would he take his act too far? Could he destroy this team despite the strong will and leadership of Michael Jordan and Scottie Pippen?

Rodman was obviously thrilled to be a Bull. "People have to realize that this team is going to be like a circus on the road," he said. "Without me, it would be a circus. But Michael, Scottie and me, it's more of a circus. A lot of people want to see the Bulls again."

Indeed, Rodman's presence made the Bulls even more of a magnetic attraction, if that was possible. Yet, where Jordan and Pippen had always taken a businesslike approach to winning, Rodman brought a fan-friendly, interactive, fun-filled style to the game that always seemed to set any arena on edge. What was he going to do next? was the question in everyone's mind.

Rodman admitted that even he didn't know sometimes.

"The very first preseason game of the year," Haley said, "Dennis goes in the game, Dennis throws the ball up in the stands and gets a delay-of-game foul and yells at the official, gets a technical foul. The first thing I do is I look down the bench at Phil Jackson to watch his reaction. Phil Jackson chuckles, leans over to Jimmy Cleamons, our assistant coach, and says, 'God, he reminds me of me.' Whereas last year in San Antonio, any tirade Dennis threw, it was 'Get him out of the game! Sit him down! Teach him a lesson! We can't stand for that here!' Here in Chicago, it's more, 'Get it out of your system. Let's go win a game.'"

Rodman had discovered that rather than fine him $500 for being late to practices, as the Spurs had, Jackson handled the matter with a light hand. Fines were only five bucks. "Here, the first couple of days, he walked in one or two minutes late," Haley said. "Nobody said anything. So once Dennis realized it wasn't a big deal, he was on time."

Reporters and observers began noting that Jackson, who was sporting a beard grown during the offseason, seemed to be taking a more relaxed approach to the game.

"Somewhere about the middle of training camp I realized I was having a lot of fun coaching this team," Jackson later explained, "and Dennis Rodman to me brings a lot of levity to the game. I mean I get a kick out of watching him play. . . He's such a remarkable athlete and has ability out there. There are some things about his individuality that remind me of myself. He's a maverick in his own way."

Even before he became the coach of the Chicago Bulls in 1989, Jackson had a well-earned reputation around the NBA as an eccentric. Yet once he took over the high-profile position, the public began learning just how unusual Jackson really was. He had a past in

Sixties counterculture, but rather than put it behind him like any other self-respecting yuppie, Jackson gloried in it. He burned incense in his coaching office, practiced meditation, rode a motorcycle, mixed Zen and Native American philosophy with proverbs from his fundamentalist Christian upbringing, and clung to the Greatful Dead, Timothy Leary and other icons of the period, all to the great amusement of the media, the fans and even his players.

Yet it would be a mistake to assume that Jackson's eccentricities were merely something he did for effect. They lay at the heart of philosophical beliefs he held dearly. Just as important, they were his means of self preservation, of protecting himself from the rigors and stresses of his job.

If anything, the passage of his time with the Bulls had reinforced his approach. Even though he had taken care to "rethink the treadmill," the seasons had been exhausting and Jackson had found himself in 1995 heading into his fiftieth birthday with a depleted store of energy for the task of rebuilding the Bulls and coaching them back to a championship level.

For rejuvenation, he decided that he needed to step back even further from the game. That began with the process of finishing his book, Sacred Hoops, during which he spent time reflecting what his seasons coaching the Bulls had meant to him. Putting that in writing, interpreting his unique approach for the fans, helped him better understand it himself.

Then, in the fall, he got an unexpected jolt of energy with the opening of the season. "Somewhere about the middle of training camp I realized I was having a lot of fun coaching this team, and Dennis Rodman to me brings a lot of levity to the game," Jackson explained. "I mean I get a kick out of watching him play."

Most important, though, Jackson did a dipstick check on his own intensity levels. The season had opened with the NBA's regular officials on strike, which meant that the league had put together two-man replacement crews from the Continental Basketball Association.

Jackson had always expended a good deal of energy each game riding the refs, but dealing with the replacements' unorthodox calls brought him to a new revelation. "I realized that it didn't matter what referees do out there, there's not much you can do walking up and down the court and yelling," he said. "I decided I was going to have to sit down and shut up and enjoy the game and coach at the timeouts and coach at the practices rather than on the floor, and practice what I preached a little bit."

The unspoken truth here was that the coaches couldn't expect Rodman to behave better if they weren't doing the same. Jackson still had his moments of animation — especially when Toni Kukoc took an ill-advised three — but he turned his demeanor down yet another notch, much to the delight of his players.

Asked about Jackson early in the year, Rodman said, "Well, he's laid back. He's a Deadhead." Rodman laughed hard at this assessment, and when a reporter asked, "Is he your kind of coach?" he replied, "Oh yeah. He's fancy free, don't give a damn. With him it's just, 'Go out there and do the job, and let's go home and have a cold one.'"

Later in the season, when John Salley came to the roster, he gained an immediate appreciation for Jackson's style. "A lot of coaches on other teams get mad that Phil just sits there," he said. "It makes them look bad. But he sits there because that's his seat. He prepares us enough in practice, trust me, that he doesn't have to do all that whooping and hollering, all those sideline antics. A lot of coaches get into that yelling and whooping and hollering, carrying on and trying to demean a guy. They say, 'Well I'm trying to get them to play harder.' Well, no, some coaches are just angry, frustrated fans."

The results, perhaps, provide the greatest testimonial. The 1995-96 season marked his seventh consecutive campaign coaching the Bulls, the longest tenure in one job among the NBA's 29 coaches, and during that time he had guided his club to what now appeared to be four championships. He had accomplished those things by overcoming the elements that had made casualties of many of his peers — the exhausting grind of the 82-game schedule, the daily practices, the shuffling and reshuffling of priorities, and always the pressure to win. Jackson's simple answer had been to find his sense of self elsewhere. "Sometimes," he explained, "I think you have to jump off the treadmill, step back a little ways from it, relook it and rethink it."

If that meant preaching to his players about the great white buffalo or giving them obscure books to read or having them pause amid the looniness of the NBA for a meditation session, so be it. On more than one occasion, Jackson's approach has left his players shaking their

Barry Gossage/NBA Photos

Although he could still fly to the basket on occasion, it was Ron Harper's defense that was crucial to the Bulls.

heads in amusement. "He's our guru," Michael Jordan quipped when asked about Jackson's quirkiness in early 1996. "He's got that yen, that Zen stuff, working in our favor."

But make no mistake, Jackson is so compelling a figure that, while his players may not accept each and every of his unconventional remedies, they have an utter and complete faith in him. And they understand when Jackson talks of the spiritual connection to the game. Jordan credited just that connection with showing him how to relate with less-talented teammates. "I think Phil really has given me a chance to be patient and taught me how to understand the supporting cast of teammates and give them a chance to improve," Jordan said.

"He's an interesting guy," Steve Kerr said of Jackson. "He keeps things very refreshing for

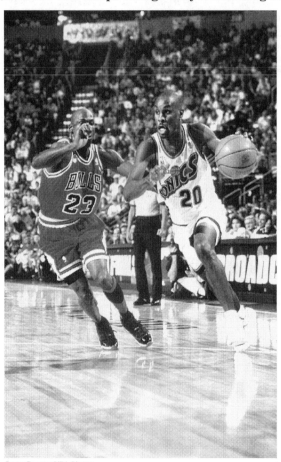

Barry Gossage/NBA Photos

The Bulls feared that the Sonics' Gary Payton could hurt them in the open court.

us all season. He keeps things fun. He never loses sight of the fact that basketball is a game. It's supposed to be fun. He doesn't let us forget about that. But at the same time, this is our job, too, and he doesn't let us forget about that either. The amount of work involved and what it takes to win, and finally the feeling of success when you do win. He's constantly reminding us of all that."

"That's not to say that Jackson would hesitate to get in a player's face," Kerr added. "But when he does it you know it's not personal. That's his strength. He always maintains authority without being a dictator. And he always maintains his friendship without kissing up. He just finds that perfect balance, and because of that he always has everybody's respect. And ultimately that's the hardest part of being a coach in the NBA, I think, is having every player's respect."

"Phil understands the game better than most people," observed Salley, who has played for a variety of coaches. "And he expects certain things that he knows his guys can give him. He gets the utmost respect from his players. A lot of people say Michael really runs the Bulls. But Phil runs this team. He runs the squad. He runs practice. He runs the film sessions. He splices the film. He organizes practice. He dissects the other team we're playing against. He knows his stuff.

"He understands the players' bodies. He understands when not to overuse them. He understands when he can rest you. He knows when to watch enough film. He knows when to push his players, when not to push 'em. He knows who to yell at, who not to yell at. He knows who can take it. And he treats you like a man, as opposed to downplaying you, or talking to you like you're less than him because of his position. He's a great coach. He laughs and smiles at life."

It was during the preseason, that veteran Sun Times columnist Lacy J. Banks predicted that the Bulls would win 70 games, which brought hoots of derision. But the seed had been planted.

As if Jordan needed any more motivation.

Over the past six seasons, he had often used his fierce competitiveness to drive his teammates as well. Now, in the process of trying to revive his game, he had turned again to that motivation. He had returned in the spring of 1995 to find a Bulls roster of new faces. And that had proved to be almost as much of an adjustment as his conditioning. He seemed closer to Pippen, but his relationships with his newer teammates seemed strained. Some of them thought he was aloof, unless they happened to elicit his competitive anger. Then they felt a singe.

"He knows he intimidates people," Jackson said of Jordan. "I had to pull him in last year when he first came back. He was comfortable playing with Will Perdue. . . He was tough on Longley. He would throw passes that, at times, I don't think anybody could catch, then glare at him and give him that look. And I let him know that Luc wasn't Will Perdue, and it was all right if he tested him out to see what his mettle was, but I wanted him to play with him because he had a big body, he wasn't afraid, he'd throw it around, and if we were going to get by Orlando, we were going to have to have somebody to stand up to Shaquille O'Neal."

Jordan tempered the fire directed at his new teammates without banking his competitiveness. Instead, he refocused it to drive his offseason conditioning fervor and weightlifting. He knew that he would need the added strength during the 1995-96 season to overcome the nagging injuries that accompany age. Yet even there, he had an edge. "Between games, Jordan can bounce back from injuries that would sideline other players for weeks," Bulls trainer Chip Schaefer pointed out. "He has a remarkable body."

His potent capacity for recovery, his restraint with teammates, and his unique commitment would amaze the many witnesses to his 1995-96 performances, beginning with the very first tipoff. He scored 42 points on opening night in a victory over the Charlotte Hornets at the United Center, setting in motion a momentum that would carry his team to five straight wins, the best start in Bulls' history. Now, in retrospect, it seems almost ludicrous to say that. It was a season of incredible starts, with the Bulls seemingly setting a new record each week. Yet the opening night outburst was a message: I'm all the way back.

Sensing he had latched on to a whirlwind, Rodman told reporters, "We're mean here. In San Antonio we had guys who liked to go home and be breast-fed by their wives."

Yet no sooner had Rodman started to settle in with the Bulls than a calf muscle injury sidelined him for a month.

Even with Rodman out of the lineup, Jordan continued on his tear, scoring big numbers to drive Chicago to five quick wins. If the five quick wins did anything to dull Jordan's sense of purpose, the Orlando Magic were there with a reminder in the sixth game, just as the Bulls were breaking in their new black with red pinstripe road uniforms. Penny Hardaway outplayed Michael, giving the Magic a key home victory. The Bulls responded with two quick wins back in Chicago before scorching through a western road trip winning six of seven games. The trip opened in Dallas, where Chicago needed overtime and 36 from Jordan (including six of the Bulls' final 14 points) to win, 108-102. "As far as I'm concerned, he's still one of the best in the game," the Mavericks' Jason Kidd said of Jordan. "He still finds a way to win."

"This is a very aggressive basketball club and very confident," Jackson said afterward. "I think people are surprised who we are, or are surprised how we are playing, or they're not comfortable with our big guard rotation. It is giving us some easy offensive opportunities so we are getting going early."

On December 2, they closed out the trip at a sizzling 6-1 with Jordan scoring 37 in a win over the Los Angeles Clippers. "I feel I'm pretty much all the way back now as a player," Jordan said, reflecting on the first month of the season. "My skills are there. So is my confidence. Now it's just a matter of me going out and playing the way I'm capable every night."

Indeed, his shooting percentage, a stellar .511 prior to his return, had dipped to just .411 during his 17-game run over the spring of 1995. Now, it had jumped to .493. His scoring, too, was headed back up to a 30-point average from the nine-year low of 26.9 in 1995.

Having witnessed the display, Sun Times columnist Lacy J. Banks put together a comparison that showed if Jordan played through the 1998 season, he would rest third on the all-time scoring list with almost 29,000 points, behind only Wilt Chamberlain's 31,419, and Kareem Abdul-Jabbar's 38,397.

"Forget Jabbar," Jordan said when Banks asked about his staying in the game long enough to eclipse the great Laker center. "No way do I plan to play anywhere close to 20 years."

For Jordan, it was the present, not the future, that held supreme importance.

"He's right where I knew he'd be about now," Ron Harper told the writers covering the team. "And that's leading the league in scoring and pulling away from the pack. He's removing every shadow of a doubt that he's the greatest player of all time."

And it was that player — not Kareem, not Wilt, not the young guns — who provided Jordan his greatest competition. "I'm old," he admitted. "Agewise, I think I'm old. But skillwise, I think I'm still capable of playing the type of basketball I know I can play. . . The question [people] end up asking me the most is, how do I compare the two players, the one before baseball and the one after.

"Quite frankly, I think they are the same. It's just a matter of putting out the stats to show that they are the same. And I think by the end of the year, hopefully, you will see that it's basically the same player with two years in between.

"Right now, I'm still being compared to Michael Jordan," he said, "and according to some people, I'm even failing to live up to Michael Jordan. But I have the best chance of being him because I am him. In the meantime, I'm improving and evolving. . .And I'm pretty sure that I'm turning some of you guys into believers."

The Bulls finished November with 12-2 record. Then December passed at 13-1. With each victory, speculation mounted as to whether Chicago could win 70 games, breaking the all-time record for wins in a season, set by the 1972 Los Angeles Lakers with a 69-13 finish.

Jerry West, the Lakers vice president for basketball operations who was a star guard on that '72 Los Angeles club, pegged the Bulls as dead ringers to win at least 70 games — unless injuries set them back.

The success also prompted reporters to ask Jordan to compare this Bulls team to other great NBA clubs. "I look at the Celtics back in '86 back when they had Bill Walton and Kevin McHale coming off the bench," Jordan said. "Those guys were tough to deal with. Those guys played together for a long time. We're starting to learn how to play together, but those guys were together for a period of time. They knew arms, legs, and fingers and everything about each other. We're just learning fingers."

It was pointed out to Jordan that most great NBA teams had a dominant low-post defender, someone to stop other teams in the paint. "We don't have that kind of animal," he admitted. "But I think Pippen compensates for that. I don't think any of those teams, other than maybe the '86 Boston Celtics, had a small forward that was as versatile on offense and defense as Scottie Pippen is."

Even without a dominant center, the Bulls seemed to have power to spare. During their big start, they had toyed with opponents through the first two or three quarters before flexing their might and finishing strong.

Observers began pointing out that with expansion, the NBA had grown to 29 teams, which had thinned the talent base, making it easier for the Bulls to win. Those same observers had conveniently forgotten that the 90s talent base had been broadened by the drafting of European players and that in 1972, when the Lakers won, the American Basketball Association was in operation, meaning there were exactly 28 teams fielded in pro hoops between the two leagues. Not only that, the NBA had just expanded dramatically before 1972, adding six teams in five years.

When the Bulls burned their way through January at 14-0, Jackson began talking openly of resting players just to lose a

Pippen moved past Seattle's Hersey Hawkins.

few games and slow things down. In other words, he was worried that his team would get so drunk with winning during the regular season that they wouldn't play sharp ball in the playoffs. If necessary, Jackson planned to slow them down.

"You can actually take them out of their rhythm by resting guys in a different rotation off the bench," he explained. "I have considered that."

Such talk by the coach only seemed to drive the Bulls harder to keep winning.

"What amazes me most about our team," said Jack Haley, "is that we probably have the league's greatest player ever in Michael Jordan, we have the league's greatest rebounder in Dennis Rodman, and we have what is probably this year's MVP in Scottie Pippen, and what amazes me most is the work ethic and leadership that these three guys bring to the floor night in and night out. With all of the accolades, with all of the money, with all of the championships, everything that they have, what motivates them besides winning another championship? How many months away is that? And these guys are focused now."

Particularly Rodman, who, with his constantly changing hair colors, his raving style, diving for rebounds, challenging opponents, piping off outbursts of emotion, was creating one funny circumstance after another. Each night he would cap off his performance by ripping off his jersey and presenting it to someone in the home crowd.

"I think they like me," Rodman said of the fans in the United Center. "People gotta realize this business here is very powerful. They can love you or they can hate you, but . . . Chicago fans they hated my guts, and now all of a sudden, I'm like the biggest thing since Michael Jordan."

Not everybody, however, was completely taken with the circumstances. As the team's designated worrier, assistant coach Tex Winter had concerns that Rodman was so intent on getting rebounds and winning another rebounding title that he was neglecting to play his role in the Bulls' triple-post offense. Beyond that, Winter wondered if Rodman really had a handle on his emotions.

Still the juggernaut pushed on, cruising through February at 11-3, and although March was interrupted by a Rodman outburst after which he was suspended for six games for head-butting an official, the Bulls still finished the month at 12-2. The 70-win season became an increasing reality, bringing with it constantly mounting pressure, which the Bulls answered with more wins.

About the only unanswered question as the Bulls headed to Milwaukee seeking win number 70 on Tuesday April 16 was the color of Rodman's hair. A few days into his return, he had reverted to blond, but with a swirling red streak. Then, headed into the team's historic week, he had opted for a Flamingo pink, as if the fans needed a reminder that the Bulls were sitting pretty.

They closed the regular season with a road win in Washington for a 72-10 finish. From there, Jackson refired the engines for an astounding playoff push. The Miami Heat fell in the first round in three quick games. Then came a grunting rematch with the Knicks, who managed an overtime win at home before stepping aside, 4-1. Next was the rematch the

335

Bulls had waited a whole year for — the Orlando Magic in the conference finals.

To prepare his team, Jackson spliced shots of "Pulp Fiction," the story of two hired assassins, into the scouting tapes of Orlando. The message was clear. He wanted the Bulls playing like killers, which they did. Rodman held Horace Grant scoreless for 28 minutes of Game 1, until the Orlando forward injured his shoulder in the third quarter and was lost for the year, What followed was a series of injuries, and the Magic went poof in four straight games.

"He's the baddest dude to ever lace up a pair of sneakers," Orlando's Nick Anderson said of Jordan after he scored 45 points in Game 4 of the Eastern Conference finals to complete the Bulls' playoff sweep of the Magic.

1996

After battling all season to be crowned NBA champions, the Chicago Bulls climbed close enough to see their glittering prize, only to discover they'd have to sit back a while and twiddle their thumbs.

The matter of winning their fourth title developed into a humongous waiting game over late May and early June. Their sweep of Orlando in the Eastern Finals set up the problem. The Seattle SuperSonics had taken a 3-1 lead over the Utah Jazz in the Western Finals, only to watch the Jazz fight back and tie the series. The net result for the Bulls was a nine-day layoff waiting for Seattle to claim the seventh game so that the championship round could begin. At last, the 1996 NBA Finals opened on Wednesday, June 5, but even that didn't mean the Bulls' waiting was over. What lay ahead were several unexpected delays in Seattle.

The Bulls were 10-1 favorites to defeat the Sonics, who had won an impressive 64 games during the regular season, which meant that the Finals carried the anticipation of an unfolding coronation. As if that needed any further emphasis, England's Princess Di visited Chicago for a medical fundraiser as Game 1 was set to begin, leaving the city stuck with divided royalties.

Should the well-connected locals go the Field Museum of Natural History for a candlelit evening of dinner and dancing with Her Royal Highness? Or should they truck over to the United Center to watch the fallaway jumpers and slick reverses of His Royal Airness?

Even Deloris Jordan, Michael's mom and a serious Di fan, was confounded by the conflicting events. The Bulls or the ball? She decided to slip into an evening gown and catch dinner with the Princess, then change clothes and dash across town to watch Her Son Who Would Be King Again.

"I know Michael expects me to be there," she explained.

Others decided to break away from the ball for quick updates on radio and TV. Regardless, there were no extra seats at the United Center. The NBA had credentialed approximately 1,600 journalists from around the globe to cover the event. The whole world would be watching, which had become standard procedure for just about all of Jordan's performances, particularly since the Bulls had added Rodman as a court jester. The team's resident rebounder did his part by showing up with a wildly spray-painted hairdo, a sort of graffiti in flames, with various red, green, blue hieroglyphics and symbols scrambled on his skull.

As usual, he had made a major contribution to the off-court news of the day. An Idaho company announced it was marketing a Worm lollipop, a "bloated worm with Rodman's head on it," that sold for 99 cents in cherry, strawberry-banana, strawberry creme, root beer, grape and tutti fruiti flavors. And just recently his lawyers had secured a court ban against a company distributing a T-shirt with a tattoo pattern remarkably similar to Rodman's own skin.

But if Rodman gave the championship proceedings an MTV feel, there were plenty of golden oldies on hand as a reminder of The Finals' 50-year tradition. In particular, Commissioner David Stern had invited hoary-faced Bill Russell, the ultimate pro basketball champion, as his guest. And new Charlotte coach Dave Cowens, himself an old Finals hand, stood courtside chatting up another championship series veteran, Maurice Lucas. Just 20 years earlier, Cowens and his Boston Celtics had taken on the upstart Phoenix Suns in a memorable Finals series, one that included the first triple-overtime game in NBA championship history.

The Sonics, too, held a place in that lore, with back-to-back trips in 1978 and '79. Coached then by Lenny Wilkens, they had claimed the championship the second of those efforts. This latest edition from Seattle hoped to follow that tradition, and some observers thought they had the athletic talent and defensive pressure to turn back the Bulls. Luc Longley, however, mostly approached the series with relief. After contending with Alonzo Mourning, Patrick Ewing and Shaq in the Eastern playoffs, he no longer faced brute force in the low post. The Sonics started spindly Ervin Johnson at center, let him play a few minutes, then turned the game over to 6-9 veteran Sam Perkins, who got most of his offense from the perimeter.

As with every other Bulls' opponent, Seattle's big concern was holding back Jordan, who was asked by reporters if he could still launch the Air raids that made him famous. "Can I still take off? I don't know," he said. "I haven't been able to try it because defenses don't guard me one-on-one anymore. But honestly, I probably can't do it. . . I like not knowing whether I can do it because that way, I still think I can. As long as I believe I can do something, that's all that matters."

As an added measure, Seattle coach George Karl had hired recently fired Toronto coach Brendan Malone to scout the Bulls during the playoffs. Malone, during his days as a Pistons assistant, had helped devise the infamous "Jordan Rules" to help defeat Chicago. The Sonics hoped that his perspective might help them find a deployment to slow down Jordan, who had averaged 32.1 points during the playoffs.

"You have to try to match their intensity," Malone advised. "Forget Xs and Os. They are

Barry Gossage/NBA Photos

The Sonics' Shawn Kemp could score with authority.

going to try and cut your heart out right away, right from the first quarter."

For Game 1, the United Center crowd greeted the Sonics with a muffled, impolite boo that seemed to imply a lack of respect. In keeping with this mood, Rodman ignored Seattle forward Shawn Kemp as they brushed past each other heading toward center court for the opening tip.

The Sonics opened the series with 6-10 Detlef Schrempf playing Jordan, but when Michael posted up, guard Hersey Hawkins went immediately to the double team. Seldom one to force up a dumb shot, Jordan found Harper for an open three, and the 1996 Finals was off and running. The surprise move by the Bulls was having Longley cover the athletic Kemp, who responded by dropping in a pair of early jumpers. Longley used his size to power in 12 first-half points with the Sonics obviously intent on forcing Jordan to pass. Pippen and Harper both found their offense, leading to Chicago opening an 11-point lead by the third quarter.

The Sonics had seemed to drag a bit, the obvious after-effects of their seven-game series with Utah, but they found their legs and pulled to 69-67 as the fourth quarter opened. It was then that Toni Kukoc, injured and in a slump for much of the playoffs, regained his form. The layoff, he explained later, had given him time to heal. Indeed, he scored 10 straight points in the first five minutes of the quarter. The outburst included a pair of treys. He was fouled on the second three-pointer and made the free throw, one of only three four-point plays in Finals history.

"I was waiting for just one good game to come," he said. "I thought I had to go out and post up some guys instead of hoping that my three-point shot would go in. So I did that, and after that happened, I took a couple of three-point shots, made them, and that opened up the game."

To go with his scoring, the Bulls turned on their pressure, forcing seven turnovers in the fourth quarter alone, and won big, 107-90. The Sonics had been especially hurt by the loss of big third guard Nate McMillan, which left point guard Gary Payton shouldering most of the ballhandling duties alone.

Jordan topped the Bulls with 28 points, but Seattle's defensive effort had meant that his teammates got off to a good championship start. Pippen scored 21, Kukoc 18, Harper 15 and Longley 14.

Rodman finished with 13 rebounds and watched as the officials ejected Seattle reserve Frank Brickowski for a dubious attempt to engage him in a scuffle, a silly little ploy played out before the network cameras.

The circumstances left Karl furious. "Dennis Rodman is laughing at basketball," the Seattle coach said before Game 2. "It's silly to give him any credibility for what he does out there."

"A lot of people don't give me enough credit for being an adult," Rodman replied.

"Yesterday was a perfect example that I can be under control."

In retrospect, Karl probably should have held back in provoking Rodman, because the Worm was ready with an answer in Game 2, a 20-rebound performance, including a record-tying 11 offensive rebounds that helped Chicago overcome 39 percent shooting. Rodman's total tied a Finals record set by Washington's Elvin Hayes in 1979.

Time and again, Rodman's rebounding helped the Bulls get through their all too frequent offensive lulls. Others played a factor, as well. Although he struggled, Jordan willed 29 points into the baskets. And the defense forced another 20 Sonics turnovers, including a batch during a three minute stretch of the third period, when Chicago pushed the margin from 66-64 to 76-65. Once again, it was Kukoc off the bench contributing the key offense. He hit two three-pointers. Then Pippen got a

Nathaniel S. Butler/NBA Photos

Dennis Rodman battled Seattle's Detlef Schrempf for a rebound.

breakaway jam after a steal, which was followed by a Kukoc slam on a pass from Jordan, whose anger had prompted the outburst in the first place.

"Are you scared?" he had asked Kukoc. "If you are, then sit down. If you're out here to shoot, then shoot."

Kukoc did, and the run provided enough margin for the Bulls to withstand a fourth-quarter Sonics surge. The Bulls opened an 81-68 lead, but fell into a stupor after Kukoc scored on a stickback with six minutes left. They would not get another field goal and were forced to hang on with free throws. The Sonics pulled to 87-81, but missed on four straight possessions. In the last minute, they closed the gap to 91-88, but Rodman got a rebound on a Kerr miss and later hit a big free throw after Pippen had missed a pair.

The Bulls knew they had escaped with a 92-88 margin but would take whatever they could get. Harper, the key to their pressure defense, had reinjured his creaky knees, requiring that fluid be drawn off one of them just before the game. That allowed him to play and contribute 12 points and key defense, but it also meant that he would miss all or most of the next three games.

Karl found himself having to acknowledge just how important Rodman was to Chicago. "He's an amazing rebounder," the Sonics coach said. "He was probably their MVP tonight."

"The second opportunities, the little things he does," Jackson said appreciatively. "He finds a way to help the team out."

With Harper's knee hurting, the Bulls figured they were in for a fight with the next three games in Seattle's Key Arena. But the Sonics were strangely subdued for Game 3. With Kukoc starting for the injured Harper, the Bulls were vulnerable defensively. But Chicago forced the issue on offense from the opening tip. With Jordan scoring 12 points, the Bulls leaped to a 34-12 lead by the end of the first quarter. For all intents and purposes, the game was over. By halftime, Chicago had stretched the lead to 62-38, and although Seattle pulled within a dozen twice in the

third, the margin was just too large to overcome. The second half was marked by Rodman's smirking antics that once again brought the Sonics' frustrations to the boiling point. Brickowski was ejected for a flagrant foul with six minutes left, and the Key Arena fans, so rowdy in earlier rounds of the playoffs, witnessed the display in numbed silence.

Jordan finished with 36, but the big surprise was 19 from Longley, who had struggled in Game 2. Asked what had turned the big center's game around, Jackson replied, "Verbal bashing by everybody on the club. I don't think anybody's ever been attacked by as many people as Luc after Friday's game. Tex gave him an earful, and Michael did, too. I tried the last few days to build his confidence back up."

Apparently it worked because Longley's size was one of several elements of the Bulls attack that troubled the Sonics. Both Pippen and Kukoc responded with solid floor games. Pippen had 12 points, nine assists and eight rebounds, while Kukoc finished with 14 points, seven rebounds and seven assists.

"I saw Chicago with killer eyes," Karl lamented.

"These guys, once they get the grasp on a team seem, to be able to keep turning the screws down more and more," Jackson agreed and later advanced the notion that Seattle might have been tired from taking a flight immediately after Friday night's game. "They might be learning that you don't take a Friday night flight on a situation where you have a day off and a game on Sunday afternoon," Jackson said. "You get in at 4:30 or 5:00 in the morning, and it changes up things. We've always made the statement that when you get here you better be prepared for it. It's a tough experience. The lack of sleep, the duress of travel. The energy that the games take. . . . The critiquing and the over critiquing. Sometimes a team comes apart, or joins together, in those kind of activities. Fortunately for our team, it has bonded them and helped them out, and they've become stronger because of it."

Jackson said his team reminded him of the 1973 New York Knicks team he played on. The Knicks had been built from players drafted in the 60s who grew up together, but in the wake of the team's 1970 title, a host of new players was brought in. "We made some trades after we won the first championship, and Earl Monroe and Jerry Lucas came in," he recalled. "All of a sudden we had people going in different directions, with different interests. They didn't personally like each other as friends, but they liked to play ball together. This group reminds me of that group; they like each other on the court just fine. Personally, they're probably not gonna go out to dinner together. Some of them are. We tell them that's fine; that's good. Before the season started, we told them, "As long as you keep your professional life together, the rest of the things don't matter." I get them in the same room a lot of times. I believe in bringing them together so that they have to hear the same message, breathe the same air, so to speak.

"They're not that close, and they're not that distant. They respect each other, and that's the most important thing, especially at this level, when guys are working in this type of business, an entertainment business, where they're vying for glory and fame and commercial success. Guys understand and respect each other's game and territory. Michael and Scottie have given credence to Dennis' commercial avenue that he runs down, and they've all sort of paid homage to Michael and his icon that he carries. And Scottie's been able to take this team and do things as a leader that are very important for us. And there's plenty of room for guys who have an international appeal like Toni Kukoc and Luc Longley. Those things have all worked very well together."

With the victory, the Bulls were up 3-0, on the verge of a sweep that would give them a 15-1 run through the playoffs, the most successful postseason record in NBA history.

With Game 4 set for Wednesday, the next two days of practice took on the air of a coronation, with the media hustling to find comparisons between the Bulls and pro basketball's other great teams from the past. ESPN analyst Jack Ramsay, who had coached the '77 Trail Blazers to an NBA title and served as general manager of Philadelphia's great 1967 team, said the Bulls just might be the greatest defensive team of all time. "The best defenders in the game are Pippen and Jordan," he said. "They're just so tough. In each playoff series, they take away one more thing from the opponent, and then you're left standing out there naked, without a stitch of clothes. It's embarrassing."

The key to the Bulls' drive was Jordan, Ramsay added. "He is such a fierce competitor that he brings everybody beyond their individual levels. I watched Steve Kerr, who had the reputation of being a no-defense guy, a good spot-up shooter. Now you watch him, he's out there playing defense, challenging everybody that he plays, he's right in their face. He may get beaten, but he's not going to back down from the chore. He now puts the ball on the floor and creates his own shot. That's something he never did before. Michael's influence on all those players is tremendous.

"They play as a team, and there appears to be no selfishness. There's no evidence of ego. The guys from the bench, they go in the game, and when they come out, you don't see any of them look up at the clock and look at the coach. They go over and sit down. When they come in, the guys on the floor bring them right into the game and get shots for them. They all know their roles, and they all can fill their roles."

Arriving for the interview session Tuesday just as the Bulls were leaving, the Sonics' Kemp wasted little time blasting his team for giving up in Game 3. Any member of the team who failed to show up for Game 4 would be a coward, Kemp said.

The reporters gathered around him listened politely and took notes. But it seemed pretty clear that the series was over.

Tex Winter was worried that the Bulls were being seduced by all the talk about the greatest team ever, and later he would kick himself for not complaining louder about it. But it wasn't just the talk that did them in. Ron Harper had been unable to practice for more than a week, and his availability for Game 4 was in doubt. The Sonics, on the other hand, were optimistic that Nate McMillan would be able to go.

Three hours before game time, NBA officials gathered in Key Arena to practice the awards ceremony in the event that the Bulls won. This was standard procedure, but the Sonics players arrived during the practice, and it added to the sting of their umbrage.

In their locker room, the Bulls tried to put off the nervousness. Jordan, his blue suit jacket removed, perched in the corner, intently filling out ticket voucher envelopes. In the opposite corner, Rodman sat in his usual pajamas turned inside-out, his headphones half mast, doing his best to ignore the furtive questions of NBC reporter Jim Gray. Stretched out on the floor a few feet away, a shirtless Scottie Pippen screwed his focus on a video replay of Game 3, trying to look past the two international TV crews that hovered over him.

Finally, 45 minutes before game time, the media were ushered out of the locker room, where the Bulls remained sequestered even beyond the National Anthem.

Harry Connick, Jr., opened the game by singing what was perhaps the most restrained rendition in Finals history. He implored the Key Arena crowd to sing along with him, but the best the gathering of 17,000 could produce was a light murmur. If the Sonics played the same way, the Bulls seemed set to win their fourth.

Harper had vowed he would be able to play, and sure enough, he was in the starting lineup. But his knees allowed him no more than token minutes, which left a huge gap in the Bulls' pressure.

It took the Sonics a few minutes to discover this. They missed their first four shots, but a Kemp slam at 9:26 finally pulled the crowd all the way out of bed. The Sonics felt a glimmer of confidence. Midway through the period, they got their first home lead of the series and

never looked back.

The outcome was really settled by a second quarter blitz from which Chicago never recovered. Actually the burst of momentum began with 1:28 left in the first when Nate McMillian appeared, and the arena crowd pounded out a prolonged thunder, bringing to mind New York

Kukoc hit some big shots in Game 6.

Knicks' center Willis Reed's limping appearance in the 1970 Finals against Los Angeles. When McMillan dished Payton an assist for a 25-19 Seattle lead, the building thundered again, touching off a run that would take them to a 36-21 lead. Kukoc scored to stop the flow, but then the Sonics zoomed off again while the Bulls racked up misses and turnovers. On the bench, Winter scribbled furiously trying to keep up with the mistakes on his chart.

When Perkins hit a jumper as the shot clock expired, the lead had stretched to 53-32.

In a series sorely lacking in drama, the Bulls had finally managed to produce some — by falling behind by 21 points. They had covered worse spreads during the regular season, so the circumstances begged the question. Could they come back?

In a word, no.

Against Orlando, when the Bulls had fallen behind by 18, Jackson had quipped in the locker room at half time that "we got 'em where we want 'em." There was none of that this time.

The Bulls pushed as Jordan furiously berated both his teammates and the officials, but without Harper, the defense offered no real pressure, because there was no one to free Jordan and Pippen to do their damage.

With four minutes left in the period, the arena operators played a scoreboard lookalike game during a time out, flashing first a photo of Madonna, then Rodman in drag with his feather boa. The arena roared in delight as the PA system blared the Aerosmith classic "Dude Looks Like A Lady."

The fourth period offered more of the same, which Jackson witnessed morosely, chin in palm. Midway through the quarter, Jordan was called for a double dribble. Furious, he stomped his foot, obviously rattled.

He left the game minutes later, having hit just six of 19, barked furiously from the bench in the closing minutes, with Pippen laughing, squeezing his shoulder. Easy, Mike. We'll get 'em the next one.

That, for sure, was their intent. At the next day's practice, Jackson was asked if he feared that the Sonics had gotten their confidence. No, he replied, at this level it was a matter of more than confidence.

Funny, but it sure seemed that way in Game 5.

Branford Marsalis blew the National Anthem, but again the Bulls were nowhere to be seen.

When they showed up moments after the anthem had been concluded, the Key Arena public address announcer, said derisively, "Ladies and Gentlemen, a warm welcome to the visiting Chicago Bulls," which brought a shower of boos.

Once again, Harper was unable to go, which put Kukoc in the lineup. The Bulls struggled to play well, but again had no pressure in their defense. The Sonics had only two unforced turnovers at halftime. Still, the game stayed tight. The Bulls trailed 62-60 at the end of the third and pulled even tighter in the fourth.

With eight minutes to go, Pippen put home a Randy Brown miss to pull to 71-69, but the Sonics answered with an 11-0 run that the Bulls couldn't answer. Up 80-69, the Sonics crowd pushed the decibel level above 117. On the floor, a fan held up a sign that said, "Dennis" Departure Will Leave Us Sleazeless in Seattle."

Pippen and Kerr hit treys that made it 84-77 with two minutes to go, but the effort took

them no further. Rodman showed his anger when Jackson replaced him with Brown; Haley tried to calm him, but Rodman knocked his hand away. Jordan and Pippen, too, had shown flashes of anger, and the media that had been ready to crown them just two days earlier began noting that the Bulls seemed fragmented and tired.

Finally, it ended, 89-78, and for the second straight game, the arena air glittered with golden confetti. The series, miraculously, was returning to Chicago. "The Joy of Six," the Seattle newspapers declared the next day in a headline.

The Bulls had shot 37 percent from the floor and only 3 for 26 from three point land, 11.5 percent. Tex Winter looked very worried.

"It's all on them now," Payton said.

Nathaniel S. Butler/NBA Photos

Kemp had a tendency to play out of control sometimes.

They kept their game faces at Saturday's practice, but the Bulls would admit it later. They were rattled. Now, however, they were back home, with a 3-2 series lead. Now the Sonics had to face the task of winning in the United Center. So much hinged on whether Harper could play. In the locker room before the game, he vowed he would. He had never taken so much as an anti-inflammatory, saying he didn't believe in putting drugs of any kind in his body. But he said he would play with pain. And that was all his teammates needed to know.

Game 6 was played on Father's Day, June 16th, and Jordan felt the rush of emotion, much of it stemming from thoughts of James Jordan, his friend and advisor. "He's always on my mind," Jordan said. His answer was to dedicate the game to his father's memory. Would it be too much to handle? Even Jordan didn't know that answer.

For the third straight time, league officials had spent the pre-game hours practicing the trophy presentation. Would they finally get it right?

Once again the Bulls stayed in the locker room during the anthem, but no sooner had Jesse Campbell started singing than the United Center crowd launched into a large noise. Across the arena they were calling for the Bulls to come out and end this matter.

As introductions were set to begin, another loud prolonged applause, drowning out anything electronic, spread across the building, bringing the fans to their feet to pound out the noise. The very mention of the Sonics brought a deep and troublesome boo.

"Anhhnnnd Nooww," announcer Ray Clay began the introductions, but you could hear no more after the 24,000 saw that Ron Harper was in the lineup.

Taking all this in, the Sonics stood courtside, chomping their gum and setting their jaws. At tipoff, the audience sent forth another blast of noise, just in case the Bulls didn't get the message the first time. Then yet another explosion followed moments later when Pippen went to the hoop with a sweet underhand scoop to open the scoring.

With Harper back, the Bulls' pressure returned, and they picked the Sonics clean time and again. On the day, Harper would play 38 minutes, and when he paused, an assistant trainer would coat his knee with a spray anesthetic. Spurred by his presence, Pippen pushed the Bulls out of the gate in the first period with seven points and two steals, giving Chicago a 16-12 lead.

The Bulls used more of the same to extend the lead in the second, as Jackson leaned back in his seat with his arms folded. Fifty feet away, Karl strolled the baseline, downcast, his hands jammed in his pockets. The lead moved

to 27-18 on another Pippen steal and dish to Jordan, but the Sonics pushed right back, moving to 31-27 on a Kemp jam.

Another run by the Bulls punched it back up to 41-29, then Seattle answered again, pulling to 45-38 at the half.

The Bulls, though, saved their killer run for the third, a 19-9 spurt capped by Pippen dishing to Rodman on the break, with the Worm flipping in a little reverse shot, jutting his fists skyward, bringing yet another outburst from the building, which got louder yet when Rodman made the free throw for a 62-47 lead.

Just when it seemed they would be run out of the building, the Sonics responded with a 9-0 run. To turn Seattle back, Kerr launched a long three over Perkins, and the Bulls ended the third period up nine, 67-58.

Jackson had left Jordan on the bench for a long stretch at the end of the third, so that he would be fresh for the kill in the fourth. But with Jordan facing double teams and his own rush of emotions, at least some of the momentum would come from Kukoc, who canned a three from the corner to push it to 70-58.

Later, Kukoc would knock down another trey, for a 75-61 lead. Rodman, meanwhile, was on his way to grabbing 19 rebounds, including another 11 offensive to tie the record that he had just tied in Game 2. Then Luc tried to slam, drew Kemp's sixth foul, and made two free throws to jack the score to 79-65. Pippen followed that with a deep trey, and the party atmosphere rumbled. Kerr hit a jumper to drive it to 84-68 at 2:44, and the whole building was dancing to Whoop, There It Is! Yes, there it was, in game number 100, the sweet conclusion to this Great Bull Run, with the Luvabulls wiggling during a timeout, the building hopping, the scoreboard flashing. . . In the middle of this delirium, the standing ovations came one after another. The dagger, Pippen's final trey on a kick out from Jordan came at 57 seconds, and moments later, the last possession of this very historic season, Jordan dribbling near midcourt, then relinquishing to Pippen for one last delirious airball.

As soon as it was over, Jackson stepped out to hug Pippen and Jordan, who broke lose to grab the game ball and tumble to the floor with Randy Brown. Pippen gave Kukoc a big squeeze, then grabbed Harper, his old buddy, to tell him, "Believe it! Dreams really do come true." Nearby, Jackson shared a quiet hug with Rodman, and Longley there taking it all in with a big Aussie grin. Then Jordan was gone, the game ball clutched behind his head, disappearing into the locker room, trying to escape those damn NBC cameras, searching for haven in the trainer's room, weeping on the floor in joy and pain over his memories on Father's Day.

"I'm sorry I was away for 18 months," he would say later after being named Finals MVP. "I'm happy I'm back, and I'm happy to bring a championship back to Chicago."

In a nod to 1992, the last time the Bulls won a championship at home, the players jumped up on the courtside press table for a victory jig to acknowledge the fans. With them was Rodman, already shirtless, living the vision just as he knew it would be.

"I think we can consider ourselves the greatest team of all time," Pippen said with satisfaction.

Strangely, it was Karl who put the whole show in perspective. "This Bulls team is like the Pistons or Celtics, or some team from the '80s," he said. "This is the 90s, but they play with a learned mentality from an earlier time. This an old-time package.

"I don't know about the Bird Era or the Magic Era. They were great teams, but this Bulls team has that same basic mentality. I like their heart and I like their philosophy."

Which had Jordan already gazing into the future. "Five is the next number," he said with that smile.

Statistics

NBA Finals Results

Year Dates	Winner (coach)	Loser (coach)	Games
1947-Apr. 16-Apr. 22	Philadelpia (Ed Gottlieb)	Chicago (Harold Olsen)	4-1
1948-Apr. 10-Apr. 21	Baltimore (Buddy Jeannette)	Philadelphia (Ed Gottlieb)	4-2
1949-Apr. 4-Apr. 13	Minneapolis (John Kundla)	Washington (Red Auerbach)	4-2
1950-Apr. 8-Apr. 23	Minneapolis (John Kundla)	*Syracuse (Al Cervi)	4-2
1951-Apr. 7-Apr. 21	Rochester (Les Harrison)	New York (Joe Lapchick)	4-3
1952-Apr. 12-Apr. 25	Minneapolis (John Kundla)	New York (Joe Lapchick)	4-3
1953-Apr. 4-Apr. 10	*Minneapolis (John Kundla)	New York (Joe Lapchick)	4-1
1954-Mar. 31-Apr. 12	*Minneapolis (John Kundla)	Syracuse (Al Cervi)	4-3
1955-Mar. 31-Apr. 10	*Syracuse (Al Cervi)	*Fort Wayne (Charles Eckman)	4-3
1956-Mar. 31-Apr. 7	*Philadelphia (George Senesky)	Fort Wayne (Charles Eckman)	4-1
1957-Mar. 30-Apr. 13	*Boston (Red Auerbach)	St. Louis (Alex Hannum)	4-3
1958-Mar. 29-Apr. 12	St. Louis (Alex Hannum)	*Boston (Red Auerbach)	4-2
1959-Apr. 4-Apr. 9	*Boston (Red Auerbach)	Minneapolis (John Kundla)	4-0
1960-Mar. 27-Apr. 9	*Boston (Red Auerbach)	St. Louis (Ed Macauley)	4-3
1961-Apr. 2-Apr. 11	*Boston (Red Auerbach)	St. Louis (Paul Seymour)	4-1
1962-Apr. 7-Apr. 18	*Boston (Red Auerbach)	Los Angeles (Fred Schaus)	4-3
1963-Apr. 14-Apr. 24	*Boston (Red Auerbach)	Los Angeles (Fred Schaus)	4-2
1964-Apr. 18-Apr. 26	*Boston (Red Auerbach)	San Francisco (Alex Hannum)	4-1
1965-Apr. 18-Apr. 25	*Boston (Red Auerbach)	Los Angeles (Fred Schaus)	4-1
1966-Apr. 17-Apr. 28	Boston (Red Auerbach)	Los Angeles (Fred Schaus)	4-3
1967-Apr. 14-Apr. 24	*Philadelphia (Alex Hannum)	San Francisco (Bill Sharman)	4-2
1968-Apr. 21-May 2	Boston (Bill Russell)	Los Angeles (Butch van Breda Kolff)	4-2
1969-Apr. 23-May 5	Boston (Bill Russell)	Los Angeles (Butch van Breda Kolff)	4-3
1970-Apr. 24-May 8	*New York (Red Hozman)	Los Angeles (Joe Mullaney)	4-3
1971-Apr. 21-Apr. 30	*Milwaukee (Larry Costello)	Baltimore (Gene Shue)	4-0
1972-Apr. 26-May 7	*Los Angeles (Bill Sharman)	New York (Red Holzman)	4-1
1973-May 1-May 10	New York (Red Holzman)	Los Angeles (Bill Sharman)	4-1
1974-Apr. 28-May 12	Boston (Tom Heinsohn)	*Milwaukee (Larry Costello)	4-3
1975-May 18-May 25	Golden State (Al Attles)	*Washington (K.C. Jones)	4-0
1976-May 23-June 6	Boston (Tom Heinsohn)	Phoenix (John MacLeod)	4-2
1977-May 22-June 5	Portland (Jack Ramsay)	Philadelphia (Gene Shue)	4-2
1978-May 21-June 7	Washington (Dick Motta)	Seattle (Lenny Wilkens)	4-3
1979-May 20-June 1	Seattle (Lenny Wilkens)	*Washington (Dick Motta)	4-1
1980-May 4-May 16	Los Angeles (Paul Westhead)	Philadelphia (Billy Cunnigham)	4-2
1981-May 5-May 14	*Boston (Bill Fitch)	Houston (Del Harris)	4-2
1982-May 27-June 8	*Los Angeles (Pat Riley)	Philadelphia (Billy Cunningham)	4-2
1983-May 22-May 31	*Philadelphia (Billy Cunningham)	Los Angeles (Pat Riley)	4-0
1984-May 27-June 12	*Boston (K.C. Jones)	Los Angeles (Pat Riley)	4-3
1985-May 27-June 9	Los Angeles Lakers (Pat Riley)	*Boston (K.C. Jones)	4-2
1986-May 26-June 8	*Boston (K.C. Jones)	Houston (Bill Fitch)	4-2
1987-June 2-June 14	*Los Angeles Lakers (Pat Riley)	Boston (K.C. Jones)	4-2
1988-June 7-June 21	*Los Angeles Lakers (Pat Riley)	Detroit (Chuck Daly)	4-3
1989-June 6-June 13	*Detroit (Chuck Daly)	Los Angeles Lakers (Pat Riley)	4-0
1990-June 5-June 14	Detroit (Chuck Daly)	Portland (Rick Adelman)	4-1
1991-June 2-June 12	Chicago (Phil Jackson)	Los Angeles Lakers (Mike Dunleavy)	4-1
1992-June 3-June 14	*Chicago (Phil Jackson)	Portland (Rick Adelman)	4-2
1993-June 9-June 20	Chicago (Phil Jackson)	*Phoenix (Paul Westphal)	4-2
1994-June 8-June 22	Houston (Rudy Tomjanovich)	New York (Pat Riley)	4-3
1995-June 7-June 14	Houston (Rudy Tomjanovich)	Orlando (Brian Hill)	4-0
1996-June 6-June 16	*Chicago (Phil Jackson)	Seattle (George Karl)	4-2

*Had best record (or tied for best record) during regular season.

345

Statistics

NBA FINALS MOST VALUABLE PLAYER

1969-Jerry West, Los Angeles
1970-Willis Reed, New York
1971-Kareem Adbul-Jabbar, Milwaukee
1972-Wilt Chamberlain, Los Angeles
1973-Willis Reed, New York
1974-John Havlicek, Boston
1975-Rick Barry, Golden State
1976-JoJo White, Boston
1977-Bill Walton, Portland
1978-Wes Unseld, Washington
1979-Dennis Johnson, Seattle
1980-Magic Johnson, Los Angeles
1981-Cedric Maxwell, Boston
1982-Magic Johnson, Los Angeles

1983-Moses Malone, Philadelphia
1984-Larry Bird, Boston
1985-Kareem Adbul-Jabbar, L.A. Lakers
1986-Larry Bird, Boston
1987-Magic Johnson, L.A. Lakers
1988-James Worthy, L.A. Lakers
1989-Joe Dumars, Detroit
1990-Isiah Thomas, Detroit
1991-Michael Jordan, Chicago
1992-Michael Jordan, Chicago
1993-Micael Jordan, Chicago
1994-Hakeem Olajuwon, Houston
1995-Hakeem Olajuwon, Houston
1996-Michael Jordan, Chicago

NBA CHAMPIONSHIPS BY FRANCHISE

Team	Number	Last	Coach
Boston Celtics	16	1985-86	K.C. Jones
Minneapolis-Los Angeles Lakers	11	1987-88	Pat Riley
Chicago Bulls	4	1995-96	Phil Jackson
Philadelphia-Golden State Warriors	3	1974-75	Al Attles
Syracuse Nats-Philadelphia 76ers	3	1982-83	Billy Cunningham
Detroit Pistons	2	1989-90	Chuck Daly
New York Knickerbockers	2	1972-73	Red Holzman
Baltimore Bullets*	1	1947-48	Buddy Jeannette
Houston Rockets	2	1994-95	Rudy Tomjanovich
Milwaukee Bucks	1	1970-71	Larry Costello
Portland Trail Blazers	1	1976-77	Jack Ramsay
Rochester Royals-Sacramento Kings	1	1950-51	Lester Harrison
St. Louis-Atlanta Hawks	1	1957-58	Alex Hannum
Seattle SuperSonics	1	1978-79	Lenny Wilkens
Washington Bullets	1	1977-78	Dick Motta

*Defunct

NBA PLAYOFF COMEBACK KINGS

No team in NBA history has ever come back from a 3-0 deficit to win a playoff series. In fact, only five teams have been able to wipe out 3-1 deficits and just 12 have come back to win after being behind 2-0. Following are those comeback teams (all series best-of-7 unless indicated):

DOWN 3-1
Boston vs. Philadelphia, 1968 Eastern Division Finals
Los Angeles vs. Phoenix, 1970 Western Division Semifinals
Washington vs. San Antonio, 1979 Eastern Conference Finals
Boston vs. Philadelphia, 1981 Eastern Conference Finals
Houston vs. Phoenix, 1995 Western Conference Semifinals

DOWN 2-0
Fort Wayne vs. St. Louis, 1956 Western Division Finals (best-of-5)
Boston vs. Los Angeles, 1969 NBA Finals
Los Angeles vs. San Francisco, 1969 Western Division Semifinals
Baltimore vs. New York, 1971 Eastern Conference Finals
Portland vs. Philadelphia, 1977 NBA Finals
Golden State vs. Utah, 1987 Western Conference First Round (best-of-5)
New York vs. Boston, 1990 Eastern Conference First Round (best-of-5)
Phoenix vs. L.A. Lakers, 1993 Western Conference First Round (best-of-5)
Chicago vs. New York, 1993 Eastern Conference Finals
Denver vs. Seattle, 1994 Western Conference First Round (best-of-5)
Houston vs. Phoenix, 1994 Western Conference Semifinals
Houston vs. Phoenix, 1995 Western Conference Semifinals

Of the above teams, Boston in 1968, 1969 and 1981, Portland in 1977, Chicago in 1993 and Houston in 1994 and 1995 won the NBA Championship that year.

FINALS STATISTICAL LEADERS
SINGLE-GAME BESTS
*Denotes number of overtime peiods
POINTS

	FG	FT	Pts.
Elgin Baylor, Los Angeles at Boston, April 14, 1962	22	17	61
Rick Barry, San Francisco vs Philadelphia, April 18, 1967	22	11	55
Michael Jordan, Chicago vs. Phoenix, June 16, 1993	21	13	55
Jerry West, Los Angeles vs. Boston, April 23, 1969	21	11	53
Bob Pettit, St. Louis vs Boston, April 12, 1958	19	12	50
Michael Jordan, Chicago at Portland, June 12, 1992	14	16	46
Jerry West, Los Angeles at Boston, April 19, 1965	17	11	45
Jerry West, Los Angeles vs. Boston, April 22, 1966*	19	7	45
Wilt Chamberlain, Los Angeles vs. New York, May 6, 1970	20	5	45
Rick Barry, San Francisco vs. Philadelphia, April 24, 1967	16	12	44
Michael Jordan, Chicago vs. Phoenix, June 13, 1993* * *	19	3	44
Elgin Baylor, Los Angeles at Boston, April 21, 1963	15	13	43
Jerry West, Los Angeles vs. Boston, April 21, 1965	13	17	43
Rick Barry, San Francisco vs. Philadelphia, April 20, 1967	17	9	43
John Havlicek, Boston at Los Angeles, April 25, 1969	15	13	43
Isiah Thomas, Detroit at L.A. Lakers, June 19, 1988	18	5	43
George Mikan, Minneapolis vs. Washington, April 4, 1949	14	14	42
Jerry West, Los Angeles vs. Boston, April 17, 1963	14	14	42
Jerry West, Los Angeles vs. Boston, May 5, 1969	14	14	42
Magic Johnson, Los Angeles at Philadelphia, May 16, 1980	14	14	42
Charles Barkley, Phoenix vs. Chicago, June 11, 1993	16	10	42
Michael Jordan, Chicago at Phoenix, June 11, 1993	18	4	42
Elgin Baylor, Los Angeles at Boston, April18, 1962	13	15	41
Jerry West, Los Angeles at Boston, April 17, 1966	15	11	41
Elgin Baylor, Los Angeles at Boston, April 24, 1966	13	15	41
Jerry West, Los Angeles vs. Boston, April 25, 1969	12	17	41
Michael Jordan, Chicago vs. Phoenix, June 18, 1993	16	7	41
George Mikan, Minneapolis vs. Syracuse, April 23, 1950	13	14	40
Cliff Hagan, St. Louis at Boston, April 5, 1961	16	8	40
Bob Petit, St. Louis vs. Boston, April 9, 1961	14	12	40
Jerry West, Los Angeles at Boston, April 8, 1962	13	14	40
John Havlicek, Boston at Los Angeles, May 2, 1968	14	12	40

Jerry West, Los Angeles at Boston, April 29, 1969	15	10	40
Julius Erving, Philadelphia at Portland, June 5, 1977	17	6	40
Kareem Abdul-Jabbar, Los Angeles vs. Philadelphia	16	8	40
James Worthy, L.A. Lakers vs. Detroit, June 13, 1989	17	4	40

FIELD GOALS

	FMG	FGA
Elgin Baylor, Los Angeles at Boston, April 14, 1962	22	46
Rick Barry, San Francisco vs. Philadelphia, April 18, 1967	22	48
Jerry West, Los Angeles vs. Boston, April 23, 1969	21	41
Michael Jordan, Chicago vs. Phoenix, June 16, 1993	21	37
Wilt Chamberlain, Los Angeles vs. New York, May 6, 1970	20	27
Bob Petit, St. Louis vs. Boston, April 12, 1958	19	34
Jerry West, Los Angeles vs. Boston, April 22, 1966	19	31
Kareem Abdul-Jabbar, L.A. vs. Philadelphia, May 7, 1980	19	31
Michael Jordan, Chicago vs. Phoenix, June 13, 1993 ***	19	43
Isiah Thomas, Detroit at L.A. Lakers, June 19, 1988	18	32
Michael Jordan, Chicago at Phoenix, June 11, 1993	18	36
Tom Heinsohn, Boston vs. St. Louis, April 13, 1957**	17	33
Sam Jones, Boston at Los Angeles, April 16, 1962	17	27
Jerry West, Los Angeles vs. Boston, April 17, 1963	17	30
Jerry West, Los Angeles at Boston, April 19, 1965	17	38
Rick Barry, San Francisco vs. Philadelphia, April 20, 1967	17	41
Willis Reed, New York at Los Angeles, April 29, 1970	17	30
Julius Erving, Philadelphia at Portland, June 5, 1977	17	29
James Worthy, L.A. Lakers vs. Detroit, June 13, 1989	17	26
Cliff Hagan, St. Louis at Boston, April 5, 1961	16	28
Sam Jones, Boston at Los Angeles, April 23, 1965	16	27
Rick Barry, San Francisco vs. Philadelphia, April 24, 1967	16	38
Jerry West, Los Angeles vs. Boston, May 1 1969	16	31
Willis Reed, New York vs. Los Angeles, April 24, 1970	16	30
Kareem Abdul-Jabbar, Milwaukee vs. Boston, May 7, 1974	16	31
Kareem Abdul-Jabbar, Milwaukee at Boston May 10, 1974**	16	26
Kareem Abdul-Jabbar, L.A. vs. Philadelphia, May 14, 1980	16	24
Jamaal Wilkes, Los Angeles at Philadelphia, May 16, 1980	16	30
Kareem Abdul-Jabbar, L.A. Lakers vs. Boston, June 7, 1985	16	28
James Worthy, L.A. Lakers vs. Boston, June 2, 1987	16	23
Michael Jordan, Chicago vs. Portland, June 3, 1992	16	27
Michael Jordan, Chicago vs. Portland, June 5, 1992*	16	32
Charles Barkley, Phoenix vs. Chicago, June 11, 1993	16	26
Michael Jordan, Chicago vs. Phoenix, June 18, 1993	16	29

FREE THROWS

	FTM	FTA
Bob Pettit, St. Louis at Boston, April 9, 1958	19	24
Cliff Hagan, St. Louis at Boston, March 30, 1958	17	18
Elgin Baylor, Los Angeles at Boston, April 14, 1962	17	19
Jerry West, Los Angeles vs. Boston, April 21, 1965	17	20
Jerry West, Los Angeles vs. Boston, April 25, 1969	17	20
Bob Petit, St. Louis vs. Boston, April 11, 1957	16	22
Michael Jordan, Chicago at Portland, June 12, 1992	16	19
Bob Petit, St. Louis at Boston, March 30, 1957 **	15	20
Frank Ramsey, Boston vs. Los Angeles, April 18, 1962*	15	16
Elgin Baylor, Los Angeles at Boston, April 18, 1962*	15	21
Elgin Baylor, Los Angeles at Boston, April 24, 1966	15	17
Jerry West, Los Angeles at New York, April 24, 1970	15	17
Terry Porter, Portland at Detroit, June 7, 1990*	15	15

Joe Fulks, Philadelphia vs. Chicago, April 22, 1947   14   17
George Mikan, Minneapolis vs. Washington, April 4, 1949   14   16
George Mikan, Minneapolis vs. Syracuse, April 23, 1950   14   17
Dolph Schayes, Syracuse vs. Fort Wayne, April 9, 1955   14   17
Jerry West, Los Angeles at Boston, April 8, 1962   14   15
Jerry West, Los Angeles at Boston, April 10, 1962   14   16
Bill Russell, Boston vs. Los Angeles, April 18, 1962*   14   17
Jerry West, Los Angeles vs. Boston, May 5, 1969   14   18
Rick Barry, Golden State vs. Washington, May 23, 1975   14   16
Magic Johnson, Los Angeles at Philadelphia, May 16, 1980   14   14
Cedric Maxwell, Boston vs. Los Angeles, June 12, 1984   14   17

REBOUNDS

	No.
Bill Russell, Boston vs. St. Louis, March 29, 1960	40
Bill Russell, Boston vs. Los Angeles, April 18, 1962*	40
Bill Russell, Boston vs. St. Louis, April 11, 1961	38
Bill Russell, Boston vs. Los Angeles, April 16, 1963	38
Wilt Chamberlain, San Francisco vs. Boston, April 24, 1964	38
Wilt Chamberlain, Philadelphia vs. San Francisco, April 16, 1967	38
Bill Russell, Boston vs. St. Louis, April 9, 1960	35
Wilt Chamberlain, Philadelphia vs. San Francisco, April 14, 1967*	33
Bill Russell, Boston vs. St. Louis, April 13, 1957**	32
Bill Russell, Boston at San Francisco, April 22, 1964	32
Bill Russell, Boston vs. Los Angeles, April 28, 1966	32
Bill Russell, Boston vs. St. Louis, April 2, 1961	31
Nate Thurmond, San Francisco at Philadelphia, April 14, 1967*	31
Wilt Chamberlain, Los Angeles at Boston, April 29, 1969	31
Wilt Chamberlain, Los Angeles vs. Boston, May 1, 1969	31
Bill Russell, Boston vs. Minneapolis, April 5, 1959	30
Bill Russell, Boston at Minneapolis, April 7, 1959	30
Bill Russell, Boston at Mineapolis, April 9, 1959	30
Bill Russell, Boston vs. Los Angeles, April 25, 1965	30

ASSISTS

	No.
Magic Johnson, Los Angeles vs. Boston, June 3, 1984	21
Magic Johnson, L.A. Lakers vs. Boston, June 4, 1987	20
Magic Johnson, L.A. Lakers vs. Chicago, June 12,1991	20
Bob Cousy, Boston vs. St. Louis, April 9, 1957	19
Bob Cousy, Boston at Minneapolis, April 7, 1959	19
Walt Frazier, New York vs. Los Angeles, May 8, 1970	19
Magic Johnson, L.A. Lakers vs. Boston, June 14, 1987	19
Magic Johson, L.A. Lakers vs. Detroit, June 19, 1988	19
Jerry West, Los Angeles vs. New York, May 1, 1970*	18
Magic Johnson, Los Angeles vs. Boston, June 6, 1984*	17
Dennis Johnson, Boston at L.A. Lakers, June 7, 1985	17
Magic Johnson, L.A. Lakers vs. Boston, June 7, 1985	17
Robert Reid, Houston vs. Boston, June 5, 1986	17
Magic Johnson, L.A. Lakers at Detroit, June 16, 1988	17
Magic Johnson, L.A. Lakers vs. Boston, June 2, 1985	16
Bob Cousy, Boston vs. Minneapolis, April 5, 1959	15
Magic Johnson, Los Angeles at Boston, June 12, 1984	15
Bob Cousy, Boston vs. St. Louis, April 9, 1960	14
Bob Cousy, Boston vs. St. Louis, April 5, 1961	14
Bob Cousy, Boston vs. Los Angeles, April 21, 1963	14
Norm Nixon, Los Angeles vs. Philadelphia, June 3, 1982	14
Dennis Johnson, Boston at Los Angeles, June 6, 1984*	14

Magic Johnson, L.A. Lakers at Boston, June 9, 1985	14
Dennis Johnson, Boston vs. L.A. Lakers, June 9, 1987	14
Magic Johnson, L.A. Lakers at Detroit, June 12, 1988	14
Magic Johnson, L.A. Lakers vs. Detroit, June 21, 1988	14
Magic Johnson, L.A. Lakers at Detroit, June 6, 1989	14
Anfernee Hardaway, Orlando at Houston, June 11, 1995	14

STEALS

	No.
Robert Horry, Houston at Orlando, June 9, 1995	7
John Havlicek, Boston vs. Milwaukee, May 3, 1974	6
Steve Mix, Philadelphia vs. Portland, May 22, 1977	6
Maurice Cheeks, Philadelphia at Los Angeles, May 7, 1980	6
Isiah Thomas, Detroit at L.A. Lakers, June 19, 1988	6
Rick Barry, Golden State vs. Washington, May 23, 1975	5
Phil Chenier, Washington vs. Golden State, May 25, 1975	5
Charlie Scott, Boston at Phoenix, June 6, 1976	5
Julius Erving, Philadelphia vs. Portland, May 26, 1977	5
Gus Williams, Seattle at Washington, June 4, 1978	5
Lionel Hollins, Philadelphia at Los Angeles, May 4, 1980	5
Norm Nixon, Los Angeles at Philadelphia, May 11, 1980	5
Larry Bird, Boston vs. Houston, May 7, 1981	5
Larry Bird, Boston at Houston, May 9, 1981	5
Robert Reid, Houston vs. Boston, May 10, 1981	5
Julius Erving, Philadelphia at Los Angeles, June 8, 1982	5
Michael Cooper, Los Angeles at Boston, May 31, 1984*	5
Robert Parish, Boston vs. Los Angeles, May 31, 1984*	5
Danny Ainge, Boston vs. L.A. Lakers, June 9, 1985	5
Scottie Pippen, Chicago at L.A. Lakers, June 12, 1991	5
Michael Jordan, Chicago at L.A. Lakers, June 12, 1991	5
Michael Jordan, Chicago at Phoenix, June 9, 1993	5

BLOCKED SHOTS

	No.
Bill Walton, Portland vs. Philadelphia, June 5, 1977	8
Hakeem Olajuwon, Houston vs. Boston, June 5, 1986	8
Patrick Ewing, New York vs. Houston, June 17, 1994	8
Dennis Johnson, Seattle at Washington, May 28, 1978	7
Patrick Ewing, New York vs. Houston, June 12, 1994	7
Hakeem Olajuwon, Houston at New York, June 12, 1994	7
Kareem Abdul-Jabbar, Los Angeles vs. Philadelphia, May 4, 1980	6
Patrick Ewing, New York at Houston, June 10, 1994	6
Darryl Dawkins, Philadelphia vs. Portland, May 26, 1977	5
Elvin Hayes, Washington vs. Seattle, June 4, 1978	5
Marvin Webster, Seattle at Washington, June 4, 1978	5
Jack Sikma, Seattle vs. Washington, May 29, 1979*	5
Caldwell Jones, Philadelphia at Los Angeles, May 4, 1980	5
Kareem Abdul-Jabbar, Los Angeles vs. Philadelphia, May 7, 1980	5
Julius Erving, Philadelphia at Los Angeles, May 7, 1980	5
Robert Parish, Boston at Houston, May 10, 1981	5
Bob McAdoo, Los Angeles at Philadelphia, June 6, 1982	5
Kareem Abdul-Jabbar, Los Angeles vs. Philadelphia, June 8, 1982	5
Julius Erving, Philadelphia vs. Los Angeles, May 22, 1983	5
John Salley, Detroit vs. L.A. Lakers, June 6, 1989	5
Sam Perkins, L.A. Lakers vs. Chicago, June 7, 1991*	5
Horace Grant, Chicago vs. Portland, June 5, 1992*	5
Dan Majerle, Phoenix vs. Chicago, June 11, 1993	5
Hakeem Olajuwon, Houston at New York, June 15, 1994	5
Robert Horry, Houston at Orlando, June 7, 1995*	5

CAREER

(Active players in CAPS)

SCORING AVERAGE

(minimum 10 games)

	G	FGM	FTM	Pts.	Avg.
Rick Barry	10	138	87	363	36.30
MICHAEL JORDAN	17	245	103	617	36.29
Jerry West	55	612	455	1,679	30.5
Bob Pettit	25	241	227	709	28.4
HAKEEM OLAJUWON	17	187	91	467	27.5
Elgin Baylor	44	442	277	1,161	26.4
Julius Erving	22	216	128	561	25.5
CLYDE DREXLER	11	99	78	281	25.5
Joe Fulks	11	84	104	272	24.7
Andrew Toney	10	94	53	244	24.4

FIELD-GOAL PERCENTAGE

(minmum 50 made)

	FGM	FGA	Pct.
John Paxson	71	120	.592
Bill Walton	74	130	.569
HORACE GRANT	108	192	.563
Wilt Chamberlain	264	472	.559
Kevin McHale	210	386	.544
Bobby Jones	77	143	.538
Walt Frazier	129	240	.538
James Worthy	314	589	.533
KURT RAMBIS	78	147	.531
Darryl Dawkins	96	182	.527

FREE-THROW PERCENTAGE

(minimum 40 made)

	FTM	FTA	Pct.
Bill Sharman	126	136	.926
JOE DUMARS	79	99	.888
SAM CASSELL	45	51	.882
Magic Johnson	284	325	.874
Larry Bird	177	203	.872
Paul Seymour	79	91	.868
TERRY PORTER	68	79	.861
Adrian Dantley	55	64	.859
Andrew Toney	53	62	.855
John Havlicek	240	283	.848

THREE-POINT FIELD GOAL PERCENTAGE

(minimum 10 made)

	FGM	FGA	Pct.
Scott Wedman	10	17	.588
MARIO ELIE	10	19	.526
John Paxson	17	36	.472
Isiah Thomas	18	39	.462
B.J. ARMSTRONG	11	24	.458
ANFERNEE HARDAWAY	11	24	.458
SAM CASSELL	14	31	.452
DEREK HARPER	17	39	.436
DAN MAJERLE	17	39	.436
Larry Bird	19	45	.422

GAMES

Bill Russell	70
Sam Jones	64
Kareem Abdul-Jabbar	56
Jerry West	55
Tom Heinsohn	52
Magic Johnson	50
John Halicek	47
Frank Ramsey	47
Michael Cooper	46
Elgin Baylor	44
K.C. Jones	44

MINUTES

Bill Russell	3,185
Jerry West	2,375
Kareem Abdul-Jabbar	2,082
Magic Johnson	2,044
John Havlicek	1,872
Sam Jones	1,871
Elgin Baylor	1,850
Wilt Chamberlain	1,657
Bob Cousy	1,639
Tom Heinsohn	1,602

POINTS

Jerry West	1,679
Kareem Abdul-Jabbar	1,317
Elgin Baylor	1,161
Bill Russell	1,151
Sam Jones	1,143
Tom Heinsohn	1,035
John Havlicek	1,020
Magic Johnson	971
James Worthy	754
George Mikan	741

POINTS

Jerry West	1,679
Kareem Abdul-Jabbar	1,317
Elgin Baylor	1,161
Bill Russell	1,151
Sam Jones	1,143
Tom Heinsohn	1,035
John Havlicek	1,020
Magic Johnson	971
James Worthy	754
George Mikan	741

FIELD GOALS MADE

Jerry West	612
Kareem Abdul-Jabbar	544
Sam Jones	458
Elgin Baylor	442
Bill Russell	415
Tom Heinsohn	407
John Havlicek	390
Magic Johnson	339
James Worthy	314
Wilt Chamberlain	264

FIELD GOALS ATTEMPTED

Jerry West	1,333
Kareem Abdul-Javvar	1,040
Elgin Baylor	1,034
Tom Heinsohn	1,016
Sam Jones	994
John Havlicek	926
Bill Russell	910
Bob Cousy	766
Magic Johnson	657
Dennis Johnson	602

FREE THROWS MADE

Jerry West	455
Bill Russell	321
Magic Johnson	284
Elgin Baylor	277
George Mikan	259
John Havlicek	240
Kareem Abdul-Jabbar	229
Sam Jones	227
Bob Petit	227
Tom Heinsohn	221

FREE THROWS ATTEMPTED

Jerry West	551
Bill Russell	524
Elgin Baylor	367
Wilt Chamberlain	329
Kareem Abdul-Jabbar	327
George Mikan	326
Magic Johnson	325
Bob Petit	301
Tom Heinsohn	298
John Havlicek	283

3-POINT FIELD GOALS MADE

Michael Cooper	35
Danny Ainge	27
MICHAEL JORDAN	24
ROBERT HORRY	22
Larry Bird	19
Isiah Thomas	18
DEREK HARPER	17
DAN MAJERLE	17
John Paxson	17
JOHN STARKS	16

3-POINT FIELD GOALS ATTEMPTED

Michael Cooper	92
Danny Ainge	65
ROBERT HORRY	65
MICHAEL JORDAN	57
JOHN STARKS	50
Larry Bird	45
CLYDE DREXLER	45
VERNON MAXWELL	40
BYRON SCOTT	40
DEREK HARPER	39
DAN MAJERLE	39
Isiah Thomas	39

REBOUNDS

Bill Russell	1,718
Wilt Chamberlain	862
Elgin Baylor	593
Kareem Abdul-Jabbar	507
Tom Heinsohn	473
Bob Petit	416
Magic Johnson	397
Larry Bird	361
John Havlicek	350
Sam Jones	313

ASSISTS

Magic Johnson	584
Bob Cousy	400
Bill Russell	315
Jerry West	306
Dennis Johnson	228
John Havlicek	195
Larry Bird	187
Kareem Abdul-Jabbar	181
Michael Cooper	178
Elgin Baylor	167

PERSONAL FOULS

Bill Russell	225
Tom Heinsohn	209
Kareem Abdul-Jabbar	196
Satch Sanders	179
Frank Ramsey	178
Michael Cooper	159
Jerry West	159
John Havlicek	154
Sam Jones	151
Slater Martin	148

STEALS

Magic Johnson	102
Larry Bird	63
Michael Cooper	59
Dennis Johnson	48
Danny Ainge	46
Kareem Abdul-Jabbar	45
Julius Erving	45
Maurice Cheeks	38
BYRON SCOTT	35
MICHAEL JORDAN	34
Isiah Thomas	34
James Worthy	34

BLOCKED SHOTS

Kareem Abdul-Jabbar	116
HAKEEM OLAJUWON	54
ROBERT PARISH	54
Kevin McHale	44
Caldwell Jones	42
Julius Erving	40
Dennis Johnson	39
Darryl Dawkins	35
JOHN SALLEY	32

DISQUALIFICATIONS

Satch Sanders	12
Tom Heinsohn	9
George Mikan	7
Frank Ramsey	7
Arnie Risen	7
Vern Mikkelsen	6
Cliff Hagan	5
Art Hillhouse	5
Slater Martin	5
Charlie Scott	5

ALL-TIME TEAM STANDINGS

OVERALL

Team	W	L	Pct.
Chicago Bulls	16	7	.706
Baltimore Bullets*	4	2	.667
Milwaukee Bucks	7	4	.636
Boston Celtics	70	46	.603
Seattle SuperSonics	7	5	.583
Sacramento Kings	4	3	.571
Golden State Warriors	17	14	.548
Detroit Pistons	15	13	.536
Houston Rockets	12	11	.522
Philadelphia 76ers	23	25	.479
Los Angeles Lakers	66	75	.468
New York Knickerbockers	19	24	.442
Atlanta Hawks	11	14	.440
Portland Trail Blazers	7	10	.412
Phoenix Suns	4	8	.333
Washington Capitols*	2	4	.333
Washington Bullets	5	15	.250
Chicago Stags*	1	4	.200
Orlando Magic	0	4	.000
Totals	.290	288	.502

*Defunct

HOME

Team	W	L	Pct.
Baltimore Bullets*	3	0	1.000
Detroit Pistons	9	3	.750
Golden State Warriors	12	4	.750
Sacramento Kings	3	1	.750
Boston Celtics	44	17	.721
Houston Rockets	8	4	.667
Philadelphia 76ers	16	8	.667
Seattle SuperSonics	4	2	.667
Washington Capitols*	2	1	.667
Atlanta Hawks	7	4	.636
Los Angeles Lakers	40	31	.563
New York Knickerbockers	11	9	.550
Chicago Bulls	7	4	.500
Chicago Stags*	1	1	.500
Milwaukee Bucks	3	3	.500
Portland Trail Blazers	4	5	.444
Phoenix Suns	2	4	.333
Washington Bullets	3	7	.300
Orlando Magic	0	2	.000
Totals	179	110	.619

*Defunct

SERIES WON-LOST

Team	W	L	Pct.
Chicago Bulls	4	0	1.000
Baltimore Bullets*	1	0	1.000
Sacramento Kings	1	0	1.000
Boston Celtics	16	3	.842
Golden State Warriors	3	3	.500
Houston Rockets	2	2	.500
Milwaukee Bucks	1	1	.500
Seattle SuperSonics	1	1	.500
Los Angeles Lakers	11	13	.458
Detroit Pistons	2	3	.400
Philadelphia 76ers	3	5	.375
Portland Trail Blazers	1	2	.333
New York Knickerbockers	2	5	.286
Atlanta Hawks	1	3	.250
Washington Bullets	1	3	.250
Chicago Stags*	0	1	.000
Orlando Magic	0	1	.000
Washington Capitols*	0	1	.000
Phoenix Suns	0	2	.000
Totals	50	49	.505

*Defunct

ROAD

Team	W	L	Pct.
Chicago Bulls	9	3	.889
Milwaukee Bucks	4	1	.800
Seattle SuperSonics	3	3	.500
Boston Celtics	26	29	.473
Detroit Piston	6	10	.375
Portland Trail Blazers	3	5	.375
Los Angeles Lakers	26	44	.371
Houston Rockets	4	7	.364
New York Knickerbockers	8	15	.348
Baltimore Bullets	1	2	.333
Golden State Warriors	5	10	.333
Phoenix Suns	2	4	.333
Sacramento Kings	1	2	.333
Philadelphia 76ers	7	17	.292
Atlanta Hawks	4	10	.286
Washington Bullets	2	8	.200
Orlando Magic	0	2	.000
Chicago Stags*	0	3	.000
Washington Capitols*	0	3	.000
Totals	111	178	.384

*Defunct

NBA FINALS
INDIVIDUAL, SERIES

MOST POINTS

4-game series
131-Hakeem Olajuwon, Houston 1995
118-Rick Barry, Golden State 1975

5-game series
169-Jerry West, Los Angeles 1965
156-Michael Jordan, Chicago 1991

6-game series
246-Michael Jordan, Chicago 1993
245-Rick Barry, San Francisco 1967

7-game series
284-Elgin Baylor, Los Angeles 1962
265-Jerry West, Los Angeles 1969

MOST MINUTES PLAYED

4-game series
187-Robert Horry, Houston 1995
186-Bob Cousy, Boston 1959
     Bill Russell, Boston 1959

5-game series
240-Wilt Chamberlain, Los Angeles 1973
236-Wilt Chamberlain, Los Angeles 1972

6-game series
292-Bill Russell, Boston 1968
291-John Havlicek, Boston 1968

7-game series
345-Kareem Abdul-Jabbar, Milwaukee 1974
338-Bill Russell, Boston 1962

HIGHEST FIELD-GOAL PERCENTAGE
(minimum 4 made per game)
4-game series
.739-Derrek Dickey, Golden State 1975
.649-Mario Elie, Houston 1995

5-game series
.702-Bill Russell, Boston 1965
.653-John Paxson, Chicago 1991

6-game series
.667-Bob Gross, Portland 1977
.622-Bill Walton, Boston 1986

7-game series
.638-James Worthy, Los Angeles 1984
.625-Wilt Chamberlain, Los Angeles 1970

MOST FIELD GOALS

4-game series
56-Hakeem Olajuwon, Houston 1995
46- Kareem Abdul Jabbar, Milwaukee 1971

5-game series
63-Michael Jordan, Chicago 1991
62-Wilt Chamberlain, San Francisco 1964

6-game series
101-Michael Jordan, Chicago 1993
94-Rick Barry, San Francisco 1967

7-game series
101-Elgin Baylor, Los Angeles 1962
97-Kareem Abdul-Jabbar, Milwaukee 1974

MOST FIELD-GOAL ATTEMPTS

4-game series
116-Hakeem Olajuwon, Houston 1995
102-Elgin Baylor, Minneapolis 1959

5-game series
139-Jerry West, Los Angeles 1965
129-Paul Arizin, Philadelphia 1956

6-game series
235-Rick Barry, San Francisco 1967
199-Michael Jordan, Chicago 1993

7-game series
235-Elgin Baylor, Los Angeles 1962
196-Jerry West, Los Angeles 1969

MOST THREE-POINT FIELD GOALS MADE

4-game series
11-Anfernee Hardaway, Orlando 1995
    Robert Horry, Houston 1995
10-Nick Anderson, Orlando 1995
    Brian Shaw, Orlando 1995

5-game series
11-Isiah Thomas, Detroit 1990
8-Bill Laimbeer, Detroit 1990

6-game series
17-Dan Majerle, Phoenix 1993
14-Michael Cooper, L.A Lakers 1987

7-game series
17- Derek Harper, New York 1994
16-John Starks, New York 1994

MOST THREE-POINT
FIELD-GOAL ATTEMPTS
4-game series
31-Nick Anderson, Orlando 1995
29-Robert Horry, Houston 1995
    Dennis Scott, Orlando 1995

5-game series
25-Terry Porter, Portland 1990
22-Bill Laimbeer, Detroit 1990

6-game series
39-Dan Majerle, Phoenix 1993
28-Michael Jordan, Chicago 1992

7-game series
50-John Starks, New York 1994
40-Vernon Maxwell, Houston 1994

HIGHEST FREE-THROW PERCENTAGE
(minimum 2 made per game)
4-game series
1.000-Dennis Scott, Orlando 1 995
.944-Phil Chenier, Washington 1975

5-game series
1.000-Bill Laimbeer, Detroit 1990
        Vlade Divac, L.A Lakers 1991
.957-Jim McMillian, Los Angeles 1972

6-game series
.968-Bill Sharman, Boston 1958
.960-Magic Johnson, L.A. Lakers 1987

7-game series
.959-Bill Sharman, Boston 1957
.947-Don Meineke, Fort Wayne 1955

MOST FREE THROWS MADE
4-game series
34-Phil Chenier, Washington 1975
33-Joe Dumars, Detroit 1989

5-game series
51-Jerry West, Los Angeles 1965
48-Bob Pettit, St. Louis 1 961

6-game series
67-George Mikan, Minneapolis 1950
61-Joe Fulks, Philadelphia 1948

7-game series
82-Elgin Baylor, Los Angeles 1962
75-Jerry West, Los Angeles 1970

MOST FREE-THROW ATTEMPTS
4-game series
47-Moses Malone, Philadelphia 1983
42-Shaquille O'Neal, Orlando 1995

5-game series
60-Bob Pettit, St. Louis 1 961
59-Jerry West, Los Angeles 1965

6-game series
86-George Mikan, Minneapolis 1950
79-Bob Pettit, St. Louis 1958

7-game series
99- Elgin Baylor, Los Angeles 1962
97-Bob Pettit, St Louis 1957

MOST REBOUNDS
4-game series
118-Bill Russell, Boston 1959
76-Wes Unseld, Baltimore 1971

5-game series
144-Bill Russell, Boston 1961
138-Wilt Chamberlain, San Francisco 1964

6-game series
171-Wilt Chamberlain, Philadelphia 1967
160-Nate Thurmond, San Francisco 1967

7-game series
189- Bill Russell, Boston 1962
175- Wilt Chamberlain, Los Angeles 1969

MOST OFFENSIVE REBOUNDS
4-game series
27-Moses Malone, Philadelphia 1983
19-Horace Grant, Orlando 1995

5-game series
21-Elvin Hayes, Washington 1979
20-Wes Unseld, Washington 1979

6-game series
46-Moses Malone, Houston 1981
34-Cedric Maxwell, Boston 1981

7-game series
33-Elvin Hayes, Washington 1978
    Marvin Webster, Seattle 1978
32-Patrick Ewing, New York 1994

MOST DEFENSIVE REBOUNDS
4-game series
53-Wes Unseld, Washington 1975
45-Moses Malone, Philadelphia 1983

5-game series
62-Jack Sikma, Seattle 1979
55-Bill Laimbeer, Detroit 1990

6-game series
91-Bill Walton, Portland 1977
76-Larry Bird, Boston 1981

7-game series
72-Larry Bird, Boston 1984
64-Marvin Webster, Seattle 1978

MOST ASSISTS

4-game series
51-Bob Cousy. Boston 1959
50-Magic Johnson, Los Angeles 1983

5-game series
62- Magic Johnson, L.A. Lakers 1991
57- Michael Jordan, Chicago 1991

6-game series
84- Magic Johnson, L.A. Lakers 1985
78- Magic Johnson, L.A. Lakers 1987

7-game series
95- Magic Johnson, Los Angeles 1984
91-Magic Johnson, L.A. Lakers 1988

MOST PERSONAL FOULS

4-game series
20-Michael Cooper, Los Angeles 1983
19-Kevin Porter, Washington 1975
    Tony Campbell, L.A. Lakers 1989

5-game series
27-George Mikan, Minneapolis 1953
25-Art Hillhouse, Philadelphia 1947
    Lonnie Shelton, Seattle 1979
    Bill Laimbeer, Detroit 1990

6-game series
35-Charlie Scott, Boston 1 976
33-Tom Heinsohn, Boston 1958
    Tom Meschery, San Francisco 1967

7-game series
37-Arnie Risen, Boston 1957
36-Vern Mikkelsen, Minneapolis 1952
Jack McMahon, St. Louis 1957

MOST DISQUALIFICATIONS

4-game series
1-John Tresvant, Baltimore 1 971
  Elvin Hayes, Washington 1975
  George Johnson, Golden State 1975
  Kevin Porter, Washington 1975
  Marc Iavaroni, Philadelphia 1983
  Michael Cooper, Los Angeles 1983
  Tony Campbell, L.A. Lakers 1989
  A.C. Green, L A. Lakers 1989
  Rick Mahorn, Detroit 1989

5-game series
5-Art Hillhouse, Philadelphia 1947
4- Chuck Gilmur, Chicago 1947

6-game series
5-Charlie Scott, Boston 1976

7-game series
5-Arnie Risen, Boston 1957
3-Mel Hutchins, Fort Wayne 1955
Jack McMahon, St. Louis 1957

MOST STEALS

4-game series
14-Rick Barry, Golden State 1975
2-Robert Horry, Houston 1 995

5-game series
14-Michael Jordan. Chicago 1991
12-Scottie Pippen, Chicago 1991

6-game series
16-Julius Erving, Philadelphia 1977
    Magic Johnson, Los Angeles 1980
    Larry Bird, Boston 1986
15- Maurice Cheeks, Philadelphia 1980
    Magic Johnson, Los Angeles 1982
    Byron Scott, L.A. Lakers 1985
    Danny Ainge, Boston 1986

7-game series
20- Isiah Thomas, Detroit 1988
17- Derek Harper, New York 1994

MOST BLOCKED SHOTS

4-game series
11-Elvin Hayes, Washington 1975
    George Johnson, Golden State   1975
    Julius Erving, Philadelphia 1983
    John Salley, Detroit 1989
10- Shaquille O'Neal, Orlando 1995

5-game series
16-Jack Sikma, Seattle 1979
12-John Salley, Detroit 1990
Vlade Divac, L.A. Lakers 1991

6-game series
23-Kareem Abdul-Jabbar, Los Angeles 1980
22-Bill Walton, Portland 1977

7-game series
30-Patrick Ewing
27-Hakeem Olajuwon, Houston 1994

MOST TURNOVERS

4-game series
24-Magic Johnson, Los Angeles 1983
21-Shaquille O'Neal, Orlando 1995

5-game series
25-Isiah Thomas, Detroit 1990
22-Terry Porter, Portland 1990
    Magic Johnson, L.A. Lakers 1991

6-game series
30-Magic Johnson, Los Angeles 1980
26-Magic Johnson, Los Angeles 1982
　　Kevin Johnson, Phoenix 1993
　　Scottie Pippen, Chicago 1993

7-game series
31-Magic Johnson, Los Angeles 1984
26-Gus Williams, Seattle 1978
　　Isiah Thomas, Detroit 1988

TEAM, SERIES

MOST POINTS

4-game series
487-Boston vs. Minneapolis 1959
456-Houston vs. Orlando 1995

5-game series
617-Boston vs. Los Angeles 1965
605-Boston vs. St. Louis 1961

6-game series
747-Philadelphia vs. San Francisco 1967
707-San Francisco vs. Philadelphia 1967

7-game series
827-Boston vs. Los Angeles 1966
824-Boston vs. Los Angeles 1962

FEWEST POINTS

4-game series
376-Baltimore vs. Milwaukee 1971
382-Washington vs. Golden State 1975

5-game series
458-L.A. Lakers vs. Chicago 1991
467-Fort Wayne vs. Philadelphia 1956

6-game series
520-Houston vs. Boston 1981
579-Boston vs. Houston 1981

7-game series
603-Houston vs. New York 1994
608-New York vs. Houston 1994

HIGHEST FIELD-GOAL PERCENTAGE

4-game series
.527-Detroit vs. L.A. Lakers 1989
.504-Milwaukee vs. Baltimore 1971

5-game series
.527-Chicago vs. L.A. Lakers 1991
.470-New York vs. Los Angeles 1972

6-game series
.515-L.A. Lakers vs. Boston 1987
.512-L.A. Lakers vs. Boston 1985

7-game series
.515-Los Angeles vs. Boston 1984
.494-Los Angeles vs. New York 1970

LOWEST FIELD GOAL PERCENTAGE

4-game series
.384-Baltimore vs. Milwaukee 1971
.388-Minneapolis vs. Boston 1959

5-game series
.365-Fort Wayne vs. Philadelphia 1956
.372-St. Louis vs. Boston 1961

6-game series
.355-Boston vs. St. Louis 1958
.379-Houston vs. Boston 1981

7-game series
.339-Syracuse vs. Fort Wayne 1955
.396-Boston vs. St. Louis 1957

MOST FIELD GOALS

4-game series
188-Boston vs. Minneapolis 1959
180-Minneapolis vs. Boston 1959

5-game series
243-Boston vs. Los Angeles 1965
238-Boston vs. St. Louis 1961

6-game series
287-Philadelphia vs. San Francisco 1967
　　San Francisco vs. Philadelphia 1967
280-L.A. Lakers vs. Boston 1987

7-game series
332-New York vs. Los Angeles 1970
327-Los Angeles vs. Boston 1984

FEWEST FIELD GOALS

4-game series
144-L.A. Lakers vs. Detroit 1989
147-Washington vs. Golden State 1975

5-game series
163-Fort Wayne vs. Philadelphia 1956
167-L.A. Lakers vs. Chicago 1991

6-game series
203-Houston vs. Boston 1981
211-St. Louis vs. Boston 1958

7-game series
207-Syracuse vs. Fort Wayne 1955
217-Fort Wayne vs. Syracuse 1955

MOST FIELD-GOAL ATTEMPTS

4-game series
464-Minneapolis vs. Boston 1959
463-Boston vs. Minneapolis 1959

5-game series
568-Boston vs. Los Angeles 1965
555-Boston vs. St. Louis 1961

6-game series
743-San Francisco vs. Philadelphia 1967
640-Boston vs. Los Angeles 1963

7-game series
799-Boston vs. St. Louis 1957
769-Boston vs. St. Louis 1960

FEWEST FIELD-GOAL ATTEMPTS

4-game series
310-L.A. Lakers vs. Detroit 1989
317-Detroit vs. L.A. Lakers 1989

5-game series
374-L.A. Lakers vs. Chicago 1991
404-Chicago vs. L.A. Lakers 1991

6-game series
478-Chicago vs. Portland 1992
479-Portland vs. Chicago 1992

7-game series
523-Houston vs. New York 1994
531-L.A. Lakers vs. Detroit 1988

MOST THREE-POINT FIELD GOALS MADE

4-game series
41-Orlando vs. Houston 1995
37-Houston vs. Orlando 1995

5-game series
25-Detroit vs. Portland 1990
13-L.A. Lakers vs. Chicago 1991

6-game series
32-Chicago vs. Phoenix 1993
27-Phoenix vs. Chicago 1993

7-game series
37-Houston vs. New York 1994
36-New York vs. Houston 1994

MOST THREE-POINT FIELD-GOAL ATTEMPTS

4-game series
118-Orlando vs. Houston 1995
92-Houston vs. Orlando 1995

5-game series
56-Detroit vs. Portland 1990
47-Portland vs. Detroit 1990

6-game series
69-Chicago vs. Phoenix 1993
65-Chicago vs. Portland 1992

7-game series
121-Houston vs. New York 1994
105-New York vs. Houston 1994

HIGHEST FREE-THROW PERCENTAGE

4-game series
.785-Los Angeles vs. Philadelphia 1983
.776-Detroit vs. L.A. Lakers 1989

5-game series
.826-Chicago vs. L.A. Lakers 1991
.810-L.A. Lakers vs. Chicago 1991

6-game series
.821-Boston vs. Phoenix 1976
.813-Los Angeles vs. Philadelphia 1980

7-game series
.827-Boston vs. Los Angeles 1966
.805-Los Angeles vs. Boston 1962

LOWEST FREE-THROWW PERCENTAGE

4-games series
.675-Baltimore vs. Milwaukee 1971
.685-Orlando vs. Houston 1995

5-game series
.616-San Francisco vs. Boston 1964
.647-Los Angeles vs. New York 1973

6-game series
.613-Philadelphia vs. San Francisco 1967
.631-Chicago vs. Phoenix 1993

7-game series
.641-Los Angeles vs. Boston 1969
.688-Los Angeles vs. New York 1970

MOST FREE THROWS MADE

4-game series
111-Boston vs. Minneapolis 1959
108-L.A. Lakers vs. Detroit 1989

5-game series
146-Los Angeles vs. Boston 1965
145-New York vs. Minneapolis 1953

6-game series
232-Boston vs. St. Louis 1958
215-St. Louis vs. Boston 1958

7-game series
244-St. Louis vs. Boston 1957
239-Los Angeles vs. Boston 1962

FEWEST FREE THROWS MADE
4-game series
52-Baltimore vs. Milwaukee 1971
61-Orlando vs. Houston 1995

5-game series
73-New York vs. Los Angeles 1973
76-Chicago vs. L.A. Lakers 1991

6-game series
82-Chicago vs. Phoenix 1993
94-Boston vs. Houston 19891

7-game series
100-Milwaukee vs. Boston 1974
108-New York vs. Houston 1994

MOST FREE-THROW ATTEMPTS
4-game series
159-Boston vs. Minneapolis 1959
144-L.A. Lakers vs. Detroit 1989

5-game series
211-San Francisco vs. Boston 1964
199-New York vs. Minneapolis 1953
     Los Angeles vs. Boston 1965

6-games series
298-Boston vs. St. Louis 1958
292-St. Louis vs. Boston 1958

7-game series
341-St. Louis vs. Boston 1957
299-Boston vs. St. Louis 1957

FEWEST FREE-THROW ATTEMPTS
4-game series
77-Baltimore vs. Milwaukee 1971
89-Orlando vs. Houston 1995

5-games series
92-Chicago vs. L.A. Lakers 1991
96-New York vs. Los Angeles 1973

6-game series
129-Boston vs. Houston 1981
130-Chicago vs. Phoenix 1993

7-game series
137-Milwaukee vs. Boston 1974
148-New York vs. Houston 1994

HIGHEST REBOUND PERCENTAGE
4-game series
.557-Golden State vs. Washington 1975
.533-Milwaukee vs. Baltimore 1971

5-game series
.548-Boston vs. St. Louis 1961
.542-Los Angeles vs. New York 1972

6-game series
.580-Los Angeles vs. Philadelphia 1980
.570-Boston vs. New York 1972

7-game series
.541-Rochester vs. New York 1951
.538-Boston vs. Los Angeles 1966

MOST REBOUNDS
4-game series
295-Boston vs. Minneapolis 1959
268-Minneapolis vs. Boston 1959

5-game series
369-Boston vs. St. Louis 1961
316-Boston vs. Los Angeles 1965

6-game series
435-San Francisco vs. Philadelphia 1967
425- Philadelphia vs. San Francisco 1967

7-game series
487-Boston vs. St. Louis 1957
448-Boston vs. St. Louis 1960

FEWEST REBOUNDS
4-game series
145-L.A. Lakers vs. Detroit 1989
160-Detroit vs. L.A. Lakers 1989

5-game series
178-L.A. Lakers vs. Chicago 1991
196-Chicago vs. L.A. Lakers 1991

6-game series
223-Philadelphia vs. Los Angeles 1980
225-Chicago vs. Portland 1992

7-game series
263-L.A. Lakers vs. Detroit 1988
280-Houston vs. New York 1994

HIGHEST OFFENSIVE REBOUND PERCENTAGE
4-game series
.396-Philadelphia vs. Los Angeles 1983
.375-Golden State vs. Washington 1975

5-game series
.336-Washington vs. Seattle 1979
.332-Detroit vs. Portland 1990

6-game series
.410-Boston vs. Houston 1981
.407-Philadelphia vs. Los Angeles 1982

7-game series
.384-Boston vs Los Angeles 1984
.366-Seattle vs. Washington 1978

MOST OFFENSIVE REBOUNDS
4-game series
72-Golden State vs. Washington 1975
Philadelphia vs. Los Angeles 1983

5-game series
82-Washington vs. Seattle 1979
72-Detroit vs. Portland 1990

6-game series
112-Houston vs. Boston 1981
111-Houston vs. Boston 1986

7-game series
131 Boston vs. Los Angeles 1984
127-Seattle vs. Washington 1978

FEWEST OFFENSIVE REBOUNDS
4-game series
44-Houston vs. Orlando 1995
45-Detroit vs. L.A. Lakers 1989

5-game series
55-Chicago vs. L.A. Lakers 1991
57-Portland vs. Detroit 1990

6-games series
57-Philadelphia vs. Los Angeles 1980
61-Chicago vs. Portland 1992

7-game series
72-L.A. Lakers vs. Detroit 1988
73-Houston vs. New York 1994

HIGHEST DEFENSIVE REBOUND PERCENTAGE
4-game series
.756-Orlando vs. Houston 1995
.737-Washington vs. Golden State 1975

5-game series
.718-Detroit vs. Portland 1990
.705-Chicago vs. L.A. Lakers 1991

6-game series
.782-Los Angeles vs. Philadelphia 1980
.796-Boston vs. Phoenix 1976

7-game series
.745-Detroit vs. L.A. Lakers 1988
.735-Portland vs. Chicago 1992

MOST DEFENSIVE REBOUNDS
4-game series
143-Golden Sate vs. Washington 1975

136-Orlando vs. Houston 1995

5-game series
162-Seattle vs. Washington 1979
151-Washington vs. Seattle 1979

6-game series
240-Boston vs. Phoenix 1976
228-Portland vs. Philadelphia 1977

7-game series
223-Seattle vs. Washington 1978
220-Milwaukee vs. Boston 1974
Washington vs. Seattle 1978

FEWEST DEFENSIVE REBOUNDS
4-game series
98-L.A. Lakers vs. Detroit 1989
110-Los Angeles vs. Philadelphia 1983

5-game series
119-L.A. Lakers vs. Chicago 1991
141-Chicago vs. L.A. Lakers 1991

6-game series
144-Houston vs. Boston 1981
160-Philadelphia vs. Los Angeles 1982

7-game series
191-L.A. Lakers vs. Detroit 1988
196-New York vs. Houston 1994

MOST ASSISTS
4-game series
114-Boston vs. Minneapols 1959
110-Orlando vs. Houston 1995

5-game series
139-Chicago vs. L.A. Lakers 1991
130-Boston vs. St. Louis 1961

6-game series
192-L.A. Lakers vs. Boston 1985
188-Los Angeles vs. Philadelphia 1982

7-game series
198-Los Angeles vs. Boston 1984
192-New York vs. Los Angeles 1970

FEWEST ASSISTS
4-game series
78-Baltimore vs. Milwaukee 1971
82-Golden State vs. Washington 1975

5-game series
88-San Francisco vs. Boston 1964
     Los Angeles vs. New York 1973
94-Detroit vs. Portland 1990

6-game series
105-Los Angeles vs. Boston 1963
108-Houston vs. Boston 1981

7-game series
121-Seattle vs. Washington 1978
135-Los Angeles vs. Boston 1962
Boston vs. Los Angeles 1969

MOST PERSONAL FOULS
4-game series
120-Los Angeles vs. Philadelphia 1983
116-Golden State vs. Washington 1975

5-game series
149-Portland vs. Detroit 1990
146-Boston vs. San Francisco 1964

6-game series
194-Boston vs. St. Louis 1958
    St. Louis vs. Boston 1958
182-San Francisco vs. Philadelphia 1967
    Portland vs. Philadelphia 1977

7-game series
221-Boston vs. St. Louis 1957
210-Boston vs. Los Angeles 1962

FEWEST PERSONAL FOULS
4-game series
83-Houston vs. Orlando 1995
84-Milwaukee vs. Baltimore 1971

5-game series
96-L.A. Lakers vs. Chicago 1991
106-Los Angeles vs. New York 1972

6-game series
121-Houston vs. Boston 1981
124-Boston vs. Houston 1986

7-game series
149-Houston vs. New York 1994
150-Los Angeles vs. New York 1970

MOST DISQUALIFICATIONS
4-game series
2-Washington vs. Golden State 1975
    L.A. Lakers vs. Detroit 1989
1-Baltimore vs. Milwaukee 1971
    Golden State vs. Washington 1975
    Los Angeles vs. Philadelphia 1983
    Philadelphia vs. Los Angeles 1983
    Detroit vs. L.A. Lakers 1989

5-game series
9-Chicago vs. Philadelphia 1947
8-Philadelphia vs. Chicago 1947

6-game series
11-Boston vs. St. Louis 1958
9-Minneapolis vs. Syracuse 1950

7-game series
10-Boston vs. St. Louis 1957
9-Minneapolis vs. New York 1952
    St. Louis vs. Boston 1957
    Boston vs. Los Angeles 1962

FEWEST DISQUALIFICATIONS
4-game series
0-Boston vs. Minneapolis 1959
    Minneapolis vs. Boston 1959
    Milwaukee vs. Baltimore 1971
    Houston vs. Orlando 1995
    Orlando vs. Houston 1995

5-game series
0-Los Angeles vs. Ne York 1972
1-New York vs. Los Angeles 1972
    Chicago vs. L.A. Lakers 1991

6-game series
0-Los Angeles vs. Philadelphia 1980
    Boston vs. Houston 1986
    Houston vs. Boston 1986
1-By seven teams

7-game series
0-St. Louis vs. Boston 1960
    L.A. Lakers vs. Detroit 1988
1-Los Angeles vs. Boston 1969
    Los Angeles vs. New York 1970
    Houston vs. New York 1994

MOST STEALS
4-game series
55-Golden State vs. Washington 1975
45-Washington vs. Golden State 1975

5-game series
49-Chicago vs. L.A. Lakers 1991
38-Seattle vs. Washington 1979

6-game series
71-Philadelphia vs. Portland 1977
64-Portland vs. Philadelphia 1977
Los Angeles vs. Philadelphia 1982

7-game series
65-Boston vs. Los Angeles 1984
59-Los Angeles vs. Boston 1984

FEWEST STEALS
4-game series
16-Detroit vs. L.A. Lakers 1989
21-Orlando vs. Houston 1995

Statistics

5-game series
28-Detroit vs. Portland 1990
29-Washington vs. Seattle 1979

6-game series
30-Boston vs. L.A. Lakers 1987
40-Boston vs. Houston 1981

7-game series
21-Milwaukee vs. Boston 1974
40-Seattle vs. Washington 1978

MOST BLOCKED SHOTS

4-game series
32-Golden State vs. Washington 1975
   Philadelphia vs. Los Angeles 1983
29-Los Angeles vs. Philadelphia 1983

5-game series
39-Seattle vs. Washington 1979
25-Detroit vs. Portland 1990
   Chicago vs. L.A. Lakers 1991

6-game series
60-Philadelphia vs. Los Angeles 1980
51-Philadelphia vs. Los Angeles 1982

7-game series
49-Seattle vs. Washington 1978
43-New York vs. Houston 1994

FEWEST BLOCK SHOTS

4-game series
16-L.A. Lakers vs. Detroit 1989
20-Washington vs. Golden State 1975
   Houston vs. Orlando 1995
   Orlando vs. Houston 1995

5-game series
17-Portland vs. Detroit 1990
22-L.A. Lakers vs. Chicago 1991

6-game series
10-Boston vs. Phoenix 1976
21-L.A. Lakers vs. Chicago 1991

7-game series
5-Boston vs. Milwaukee 1974
21-L.A. Lakers vs. Detroit 1988

MOST TURNOVERS

4-game series
94-Golden State vs. Washington 1975
92-Milwaukee vs. Baltimore 1971

5-game series
104-Los Angeles vs. New York 1973
88-New York vs. Los Angele 1972

6-game series
149-Portland vs. Philadelphia 1977
144-Boston vs. Phoenix 1976

7-game series
142-Milwaukee vs. Boston 1974
126-Seattle vs. Washington 1978

FEWEST TURNOVERS

4-game series
41-Houston vs. Orlando 1995
46-Detroit vs. L.A. Lakers 1989

5-games series
66-Chicago vs. L.A. Lakers 1991
74-New York vs. Los Angeles 1973

6-game series
68-L.A. Lakers vs. Boston 1987
76-L.A. Lakers vs. Boston 1985

7-game series
87-Detroit vs. L.A. Lakers 1988
92-New York vs. Houston 1994

INDIVIDUAL

MINUTES

Most minutes, game
62-Kevin Johnson, Phoenix at Chicago, June 13, 1993 (3OT)
61-Garffield Heard, Phoenix at Boston, June 4, 1976 (3OT)
60-Jo Jo White, Boston vs. Phoenix, June 4, 1976 (3 OT)

Most minutes, one championship series
49.3-Kareem Abdul-Jabbar, Milwaukee vs. Boston, 1974 (345/7)
48.7-Bill Russell, Boston vs. Los Angeles, 1968 (292/6)
48.5- John Halvicek, Boston vs. Los Angeles, 1968 (291/6)

SCORING

Most points, game
61-Elgin Baylor, Los Angeles at Boston, April 14, 1962
55-Rick Barry, San Francisco vs. Philadelphia, April 18, 1967
   Michael Jordan, Chicago vs. Phoenix, June 16, 1993
53-Jerry West, Los Angeles vs. Boston, April 23, 1969

Most points, rookie, game
42-Magic Johnson, Los Angeles at Philadelphia, May 16, 1980
37-Joe Fulks, Philadelphia vs. Chicago, April 16, 1947
   Tom Heinsohn, Boston vs. St. Louis, April 13, 1957 (2OT)

34-Joe Fulks, Philadelphia vs. Chicago, April 22, 1947
Elgin Baylor, Minneapolis at Boston, April 4, 1959

Highest scoring average, one championship series
41.0-Michael Jordan, Chicago vs. Phoenix, 1993 (246/6)
40.8-Rick Barry, San Francisco vs. Philadelphia, 1967 (245/6)
40.6-Elgin Baylor, Los Angeles vs. Boston, 1962 (284/7)

Highest scoring average, rookie, one championship series
26.2-Joe Fulks, Philadelphia vs. Chicago, 1947 (131/5)
24.0-Tom Heinsohn, Boston vs. St. Louis, 1957 (168/7)
23.0-Alvan Adams, Phoenix vs. Boston, 1976 (138/6)

Most consecutive games, 10 or more points
25-Jerry West, Los Angeles, April 20, 1966-May 8, 1970
19-Julius Erving, Philadelphia, May 22, 1977-May 22, 1983
18-Kareem Abdul-Jabbar, Milwaukee-Los Angeles, April 21, 1971-May 30, 1982

Most consecutive games, 30 or more points
13-Elgin Baylor, Minneapolis-Los Angeles, April 9, 1959-April 21, 1963
9-Michael Jordan, June 10, 1992-June 20, 1993
6-Rick Barry, San Francisco, April 14, 1967-April 24, 1967

Most consecutive games, 40 or more points
4-Michael Jordan, June 11, 1993-June 18, 1993
2-Jerry West, Los Angeles, April 19-21, 1965
Rick Barry, San Francisco, April 18-20, 1967
Jerry West, Los Angeles, April 23-25, 1969

Scoring 30 or more points in all games in championship series
Elgin Baylor, Los Angeles vs. Boston, 1962 (7-game series)
Rick Barry, San Francisco vs. Philadelphia, 1967 (6-game series)
Michael Jordan, Chicago vs. Phoenix, 1993 (6-game series)
Hakeem Olajuwon, Houston vs. Orlando, 1995 (4-game series)

Scoring 20 or more points in all games of 7-game championship series
Bob Pettit, St. Louis vs. Boston, 1960
Elgin Baylor, Los Angeles vs. Boston, 1962
Jerry West, Los Angeles vs. Boston, 1962
Jerry West, Los Angeles vs. New York, 1970
Kareem Abdul-Jabbar, Milwaukee vs. Boston, 1974
Larry Bird, Boston vs. Los Angeles, 1984
Hakeem Olajuwon, Houston vs. New York, 1994

Most points, one half
35-Michael Jordan, Chicago vs. Portland, June 3, 1992

Most points, one quarter
25-Isiah Thomas, Detroit at L.A. Lakers, June 19, 1988

Most points, overtime period
9-John Havlicek, Boston vs. Milwaukee, May 10, 1974
Bill Laimbeer, Detroit vs. Portland, June 7, 1990
Danny Ainge, Portland at Chicago, June 5, 1992

FIELD GOALS
Highest field-goal percentage, game (minimum 8 made)
1.000-Scott Wedman, Boston vs. L.A. Lakers, May 27, 1985 (11/11)
John Paxson, Chicago vs. L.A. Lakers, June 5, 1991 (8/8)
.917-Bill Bradley, New York at Los Angeles, April 26, 1972 (11/12)
James Worthy, Los Angeles at Boston, May 31, 1984 (11/12) (OT)

Most field-goals, game
22-Elgin Baylor, Los Angeles at Boston, April 14, 1962
Rick Barry, San Francisco vs. Philadelphia, April 18, 1967
21-Michael Jordan, Chicago vs. Phoenix, June 16, 1993

Most field-goals, one half
14-Isiah Thomas, Detroit at L.A. Lakers, June 19, 1988
Michael Jordan, Chicago vs. Portland, June 3, 1992
Michael Jordan, Chicago vs. Phoenix, June 16, 1993

Most field-goals, one quarter
11-Isiah Thomas, Detroit at L.A. Lakers, June 19, 1988

Most field-goal attempts, games
48-Rick Barry, San Francisco vs. Philadelphia, April 18, 1967
46-Elgin Baylor, Los Angeles at Boston, April 14, 1967
43-Rick Barry, San Francisco at Philadelphia, April 14, 1967 (OT)
Michael Jordan, Chicago vs. Phoenix, June 13, 1993 (3OT)

Most field-goal attempts, one half
25-Elgin Baylor, Los Angeles at Boston, April 14, 1962

Most field-goal attempts, one quarter
17-Rick Barry, San Francisco at Philadelphia, April 14, 1967

THREE-POINT FIELD GOAL
Most three-point field goals, none missed, game
4-Scott Wedman, Boston vs. L.A. Lakers, May 27, 1985
3-Danny Ainge, Boston at L.A. Lakers, June 2, 1987
Isiah Thomas, Detroit at Portland, June 14, 1990
Sam Cassell, Houston at New York, June 12, 1994

Most three-point field goals, game
7-Kenny Smith, Houston at Orlando, June 7, 1995 (OT)
6-Michael Cooper, L.A. Lakers vs. Boston, June 4, 1987
Bill Laimbeer, Detroit vs. Portland, June 7, 1990 (OT)
Michael Jordan, Chicago vs. Portland, June 3, 1992
Dan Majerle, Phoenix at Chicago, June 13, 1993 (3OT)

Most three-point field goals, one half
6-Michael Jordan, Chicago vs. Portland, June 3 1992
  Kenny Smith, Houston at Orlando, June 7, 1995

Most three-point field-goal attempts, one quarter
5-Kenny Smith, Houston at Orlando, June 7, 1995

Most three-point field-goal attempts, game
12-Nick Anderson, Orlando at Houston, June 11, 1995
11-John Starks, New York at Houston, June 22, 1994
  Kenny Smith, Houston at Orlando, June 7, 1995 (OT)
  Brian Shaw, Orlando at Houston, June 14, 1995

Most three-point field-goal attempts, one half
10-John Starks, New York at Houston, June 22, 1994

FREE THROWS
Most free throws made, none missed, game
15-Terry Porter, Portland at Detroit, June 7, 1990 (OT)
14-Magic Johnson, Los Angeles at Philadelphia, May 16, 1980

Most free throws made, game
19-Bob Petit, St. Louis at Boston, April 9, 1958
17-Cliff Hagan, St. Louis at Boston, March 30, 1958
  Elgin Baylor, Los Angeles at Boston, April 14, 1962
  Jerry West, Los Angeles vs. Boston, April 21, 1965
  Jerry West, Los Angeles vs. Boston, April 25, 1969

Most free throws made, one half
12-Rick Barry, San Francisco vs. Philadelphia, April 24, 1967
  Dennis Johnson, Boston vs. Los Angeles, June 12, 1984

Most free throws made, one quarter
9-Frank Ramsey, Boston vs. Minneapolis, April 4, 1959

Most free-throw attempts, game
24-Bob Petit, St. Louis at Boston, April 9, 1958
22-Bob Petit, St. Louis vs. Boston, April 11, 1957
21-Elgin Baylor, Los Angeles at Boston, April 18, 1962 (OT)

Most free-throw attempts, one half
15-Bill Russell, Boston vs. St. Louis, April 11, 1961

Most free-throw attempts, one quarter
11-Bob Pettit, St. Louis at Boston, April 9, 1958
  Wilt Chamberlain, Philadelphia vs. San Francisco, April 16, 1967

REBOUNDS
Most rebounds, game
40-Bill Russell, Boston vs. St. Louis, March 28, 1960
  Bill Russell, Boston vs. Los Angeles, April 18, 1962 (OT)
38-Bill Russell, Boston vs. St. Louis, April 11, 1961
  Bill Russell, Boston vs. Los Angeles, April 16, 1963
  Wilt Chamberlain, San Francisco vs. Boston April 24, 1964

  Wilt Chamberlain, Philadelphia vs. San Francisco, April 16, 1967

Most rebounds, rookie, game
32-Bill Russell, Boston vs. St. Louis, April 13, 1957 (2OT)
25-Bill Russell, Boston vs. St. Louis, March 31, 1957
23-Bill Russell, Boston vs. St. Louis, April 9, 1957
  Bill Russell, Boston at St. Louis, April 11, 1957
  Tom Heinsohn, Boston vs. St. Louis, April 13, 1957 (2OT)

Highest average, rebounds per game, one championship series
29.5-Bill Russell, Boston vs. Minneapolis, 1959 (118/4)
28.8-Bill Russell, Boston vs. St. Louis, 1961 (118/4)
28.5-Wilt Chamberlain, Philadelphia vs. San Francisco, 1967 (171/6)

Highest average, rebounds per game, rookie, one championship series
22.9-Bill Russell, Boston vs. St. Louis, 1957 (160/7)
13.0-Nate Thurmond, San Francisco vs. Boston, 1964 (65/5)
12.6-Tom Heinsohn, Boston vs. St. Louis, 1957 (88/7)

Most consecutive games 20 or more rebounds
15-Bill Russell, Boston, April 9, 1960-April 16, 1963
12-Wilt Chamberlain, San Francisco, Philadelphia, Los Angeles, April 18-April 23, 1969

Most consecutive games, 30 or more rebounds
3-Bill Russell, Boston, April 5, 1959-April 9, 1959
2-Bill Russell, Boston, April 9, 1960-April 2, 1961
  Wilt Chamberlain, Philadelphia, April 14, 1967-April 16, 1967
  Wilt Chamberlain, Los Angeles, April 29, 1969-May 1, 1969

20 or more rebounds in all championship series games
Bill Russell, Boston vs. Minneapolis, 1959 (4-game series)
Bill Russell, Boston vs. St. Louis, 1961 (5-game series)
Bill Russell, Boston vs. Los Angeles, 1962 (7-game series)
Wilt Chamberlain, San Francisco vs. Boston, 1964 (5-game series)
Wilt Chamberlain, Philadelphia vs. San Francisco, 1967 (6-game series)
Nate Thurmond, San Francisco vs. Philadelphia, 1967 (6-game series)

Most rebounds, one half
26-Wilt Chamberlain, Philadelphia vs. San Francisco, April 16, 1967

Most rebounds, one quarter
19-Bill Russell, Boston vs. Los Angeles, April 18, 1962

Most offensive rebounds, game
11-Elvin Hayes, Washington at Seattle, May 27, 1979
10-Marvin Webster, Seattle vs. Washington, June 7, 1978
  Robert Reid, Houston vs. Boston, May 10 1981
  Moses Malone, Houston vs. Boston, May 14, 1981

Most defensive rebounds, game

20-Bill Walton, Portland at Philadelphia, June 3, 1977
  Bill Walton, Portland vs. Philadelphia, June 5, 1977
18-Dave Cowens, Boston vs. Phoenix, May 23, 1976

ASSISTS

Most assists, game

21-Magic Johnson, Los Angeles vs. Boston, June 3, 1984
20-Magic Johnson, L.A. Lakers vs. Boston, June 4, 1987
  Magic Johnson, L.A. Lakers vs. Chicago, June 12, 1991

Highest average, assists per game, one championship series

14.0-Magic Johnson, L.A. Lakers vs. Boston, 1985 (84/6)
13.6-Magic Johsnon, Los Angeles vs. Boston, 1984 (95/7)

Most assists, rookie, game

11-Magic Johnson, Los Angeles vs. Philadelphia, May 7, 1980
10-Tom Gola, Philadelphia vs. Fort Wayne, March 31, 1956
  Walt Hazzard, Los Angeles at Boston, April 25, 1965
  Magic Johnson, Los Angeles vs. Philadelphia, May 4, 1980
  Magic Johnson, Los Angeles vs. Philadelphia, May 14, 1980

Highest average, assists per game, rookie one championship series

8.7-Magic Johnson, Los Angeles vs. Philadelphia, 1980 (52/6)
6.0-Tom Gola, Philadelphia vs. Fort Wayne, 1956 (30/5)
5.2-Walt Hazzard, Los Angeles vs. Boston, 1965 (26/5)

Most consecutive games, 10 or more assists

13-Magic Johnson, L.A. Lakers, June 3, 1984-June 4, 1987
6-Magic Johnson, Los Angeles, June 8, 1982-May 27, 1984

Most assists, one half

14-Magic Johnson, L.A. Lakers vs. Detroit, June 19, 1988
13-Robert Reid, Houston vs. Boston, June 5, 1986
  Magic Johnson, L.A. Lakers vs. Boston, June 4, 1987

Most assist, one quarter

8-Bob Cousy, Boston vs. St. Louis, April 9, 1957
  Magic Johnson, Los Angeles vs. Boston, June 3, 1984
  Robert Reid, Houston vs. Boston, June 5, 1986
  Michael Cooper, L.A. Lakers vs. Boston, June 4, 1987
  Magic Johnson, L.A. Lakers vs. Boston, June 4, 1987
  Magic Johnson, L.A. Lakers at Detroit, June 16, 1988
  Magic Johnson, L.A. Lakers vs. Detroit, June 19, 1988

PERSONAL FOULS

Most minutes played, no personal fouls, game

59-Dan Majerle, Phoenix at Chicago, June 13, 1993 (3OT)
50-Jo Jo White, Boston at Milwaukee, April 30, 1974 (OT)
  Nick Anderson, Orlando vs. Houston, June 7, 1995 (OT)

DISQUALIFICATIONS

Most consecutive games disqualified

5-Art Hillhouse, Philadelphia, 1947
  Charlie Scott, Boston, 1976
4-Arnie Risen, Boston, 1957

Fewest minutes played, disqualified player, game

9-Bob Harrison, Minneapolis vs. New York, April 13, 1952
10-Bob Harrison, Minneapolis vs. New York, April 4, 1953

STEALS

Most steals, game

7-Robert Horry, Houston at Orlando, June 9, 1995
6-John Havlicek, Boston vs. Milwaukee, May 3, 1974
  Steve Mix, Philadelphia vs. Portland, May 22, 1977
  Maurice Cheeks, Philadelphia at Los Angeles, May 7, 1980
  Isiah Thomas, Detroit at L.A. Lakers, June 19, 1988

BLOCKED SHOTS

Most blocked shots, game

8-Bill Walton, Portland vs. Philadelphia, June 5, 1977
  Hakeem Olajuwon, Houston vs. Boston, June 5, 1986
  Patrick Ewing, New York vs. Houston, June 17, 1994
7-Dennis Johnson, Seattle at Washington, May 28, 1978
  Patrick Ewing, New York vs. Houston, June 12, 1994
  Hakeem Olajuwon, Houston at New York, June 12, 1994

TURNOVERS

Most turnovers, game

10-Magic Johnson, Los Angeles vs. Philadelphia, May 14, 1980
9-Magic Johnson, Los Angeles vs. Philadelphia, May 31, 1983

Most minutes played, no turnovers, game

59-Dan Majerle, Phoenix at Chicago, June 13, 1993 (3OT)
48-Rodney McCray, Houston vs. Boston, June 5, 1986
47-Wes Unseld, Washington at Seattle, May 27, 1979
  Michael Cooper, Los Angeles vs. Boston, June 6, 1984 (OT)
  Robert Horry, Houston at Orlando, June 7, 1995 (OT)

TEAM

WON-LOST
Most consecutive games won, all championship series
6-Houston, 1994-95 (current)
5-Minneapolis, 1953-54
   Boston, 1959-60
   Los Angeles, 1972-73
   Detroit, 1989-90
   Chicago, 1991-92

Most consecutive games won, one championship series
4-Minneapolis vs. New York, 1953 (5-game series)
   Boston vs. Minneapolis, 1959 (4-game series)
   Milwaukee vs. Baltimore, 1971 (4-game series)
   Los Angeles vs. New York, 1972 (5-game series)
   New York vs. Los Angeles, 1973 (5-game series
   Golden State vs. Washington, 1975 (4-game series)
   Portland vs. Philadelphia, 1977 (6-game series)
   Seattle vs.Washington, 1979 (5-game series)
   Philadelphia vs. Los Angeles, 1983 (4-game series)
   Detroit vs. L.A. Lakers, 1989 (4-game series)
   Chicago vs. L.A. Lakers, 1991 (5-game series)
   Houston vs. Orlando, 1995 (4-game series)

Most consecutive games won at home, all championship series
7-Minneapolis, 1949-52
6-Boston, 1960-62
   Boston, 1964-65
   Syracuse/Philadelphia, 1955-67

Most consecutive games won at home, one championship series
4-Syracuse vs. Fort Wayne, 1955 (7-game series)

Most consecutive games won on road, all championship series
5-Detroit, 1989-90
4-Minneapolis, 1953-54
   Chicago, 1991-92
   Chicago, 1992-93

Most consecutive games won on road, one championship series
3-Minneapolis vs. New York, 1953 (5-game series)
   Detroit vs. Portland, 1990 (5-game series)
   Chicago vs. L.A. Lakers, 1991 (5-game series)
   Chicago vs. Phoenix, 1993 (6-game series)

Most consecutive games lost, all championship series
9-Baltimore/Washington, 1971-78
5-Minneapolis/Los Angeles, 1959-62
   New York, 1972-73
   Philadelphia, 1977-80

Most consecutive games lost at home, all championship series
5-L.A. Lakers, 1989-91 (current)
4-Baltimore/Washington, 1971-75
   Portland, 1990-92
   Phoenix, 1976-93

Most consecutive games lost on road, all championship series
7-Fort Wayne, 1955-56
5-Philadelphia, 1947-56
  St. Louis, 1960-61
  Syracuse/Philadelphia, 1954-67
  Los Angeles, 1968-70
  Baltimore/Washington, 1971-78

SCORING

Most points, game
148-Boston vs. L.A. Lakers (114), May 27, 1985
142-Boston vs. Los Angeles (110), April 18, 1965
141-Philadelphia vs. San Francisco (135), April 14, 1967 (OT)
    L.A. Lakers vs. Boston (122), June 4, 1987

Fewest points, game
71-Syracuse vs. Fort Wayne (74) at Indianapolis, April 7, 1955
74-Fort Wayne vs. Syracuse (71) at Indianapolis, April 7, 1955
78-New York at Houston (85), June 8, 1994

Most points, both teams, game
276-Philadelphia (141) vs. San Francisco (135), April 14, 1967 (OT)
263-L.A. Lakers (141) vs. Boston (122), June 4, 1987

Fewest points, both teams, game
145-Syracuse (71) vs. Fort Wayne (74) at Indianapolis, April 7, 1955
163-New York (78) at Houston (85), June 8, 1994

Largest margin of victory, game
35-Washington vs. Seattle, June 4, 1978 (117-82)
34-Boston vs. St. Louis, April 2, 1961 (129-95)
   Boston vs. L.A. Lakers, May 27, 1985 (148-114)
33-Boston vs. Los Angeles, April 25, 1965 (129-96)
   Philadelphia vs. Los Angeles, June 6, 1982 (135-102)
   Los Angeles vs. Boston, June 3, 1984 (137-104)
   Chicago vs. Portland, June 3, 1992 (122-89)

BY HALF

Most points, first half
79-Boston vs. L.A. Lakers, May 27, 1985
76-Boston vs. St. Louis, March 27, 1960

Fewest points, first half
30-Houston vs. Boston, May 9, 1981
31-Syracuse vs. Fort Wayne at Indianapolis, April 7, 1955

Most points, both teams, first half
140-San Francisco (72) vs. Philadelphia (68), April 24, 1967
138-Philadelphia (73) vs. San Francisco (65), April 14, 1967

Fewest points, both teams, first half
69-Syracuse (31) vs. Fort Wayne (38) at Indianapolis, April 7, 1955
71-Phoenix (33) vs. Boston (38), June 6, 1976
   Houston (30) vs. Boston (41), May 9, 1981

Largest lead at halftime
30-Boston vs. L.A. Lakers, May 27, 1985 (led 79-49; won 148-114)
27-New York vs. Los Angeles, May 8, 1970 (led 69-42; won 113-99)

Largest deficit at halftime, overcome to win game
21-Baltimore at Philadelphia, April 13, 1948 (trailed 20-41; won 66-63)
14-New York at Los Angeles, April 29, 1970 (trailed 42-56; won 111-108 in OT)
   Golden State at Washington, May 18, 1975 (trailed 40-54; won 101-95)
   Philadelphia at Los Angeles, May 31, 1983 (trailed 51-65; won 101-108)

Most points, second half
81-Philadelphia vs. Los Angeles, June 6, 1982
80-Los Angeles vs. Boston, June 3, 1984

Fewest points, second half
30-Washington vs.Seattle, May 24, 1979
31-St. Louis vs. Boston, April 2, 1960
   Houston vs. New York, June 8, 1994

Most points, both teams, second half
139-Boston (78) vs. Los Angeles (61), April 18, 1965
138-Los Angeles (71) at Boston (67), April 21, 1963
   Los Angeles (80) vs. Boston (58), June 3, 1984

Fewest points, both teams, second half
63-Houston (31) vs. New York (32), June 8, 1994
73-Washington (30) vs. Seattle (43), May 24, 1979

BY QUARTER, OVERTIME PERIOD

Most points, first quarter
43-Philadelphia vs. San Francisco, April 14, 1967
   Philadelphia at San Francisco, April 24, 1967
41-San Francisco vs. Philadelphia, April 24, 1967

Fewest points, first quarter
13-Fort Wayne at Syracuse, April 2, 1955
   Milwaukee at Boston, May 3, 1974
14-Houston at New York, June 15, 1994

Most points, both teams, first quarter
84-Philadelphia (43) at San Francisco (41), April 24, 1967
73-Philadelphia (43) vs. San Francisco (30), April 14, 1967

Fewest points, both teams, first quarter
31-Los Angeles (15) at Boston (16), April 29, 1969
33-Fort Wayne (13) at Syracuse (20), April 2, 1955
   Houston (14) at New York (19), June 15, 1994

Largest lead at end of first quarter
20-Los Angeles vs. New York, May 6, 1970 (led 36-16; won 135-113)
19-San Francisco vs. Boston, April 22, 1964 (led 40-21; won 115-91)
   Boston vs. Milwaukee, May 3, 1974 (led 32-13; won 95-83)

Largest deficit at end of first quarter, overcome to win
14-Los Angeles at Boston, April 17, 1966 (trailed 20-34; won 133-129 in OT)
12-Detroit at L.A. Lakers; June 13, 1989 (trailed 23-35; won 105-97)

Most points, second quarter
46-Boston vs. St. Louis, March 27, 1960
43-Los Angeles at Boston, April 8, 1962

Statistics

Fewest points, second quarter
12-Boston vs. Milwaukee, May 5, 1974
13-Syracuse vs. Fort Wayne at Indianapolis, April 7, 1955
   Phoenix vs. Boston, June 6, 1976
   Houston vs. Boston, May 9, 1981

Most points, both teams, second quarter
73-St. Louis (38) vs. Boston (35), April 8, 1961
   Boston (38) vs. Los Angeles (35), April 14, 1962
72-St. Louis (42) at Boston (30), March 29, 1958
   Boston (46) vs. St. Louis (26), March 27, 1960

Fewest points, both teams, second quarter
29-Syracuse (13) vs. Fort Wayne (16) at Indianapolis, April 7, 1955
31-Phoenix (13) vs. Boston (18), June 6, 1976

Most points, third quarter
47-Los Angeles vs. Boston, June 3, 1984
41-Portland vs. Philadelphia, May 31, 1977
   Los Angeles at Philadelphia, May 27, 1982

Fewest points, third quarter
11-New York at Los Angeles, April 30, 1972
12-Boston at St. Louis, April 7, 1960
   Boston at L.A. Lakers, June 14, 1987

Most points, both teams, third quarter
80-Los Angeles (47) vs. Boston (33), June 3, 1984
75-Boston (40) vs. Los Angeles (35), April 21, 1963

Fewest points, both teams, third quarter
31-Portland (15) vs. Chicago (16), June 7, 1992
33-Washington (14) vs. Seattle (19), May 24, 1979

Largest lead at end of third quarter
36-Chicago vs. Portland, June 3, 1992 (led 104-68; won 122-89)
31-Portland vs. Philadelphia, May 31, 1977, (led 98-67; won 130-98)

Largest deficit at end of third quarter, overcome to win
15-Chicago vs. Portland, June 14, 1992 (trailed 64-79; won 97-93)
12-San Francisco at Philadelphia, April 23; 1967 (trailed 84-96; won 117-109)

Most points, fourth quarter
44-Philadelphia vs. Los Angeles, June 6, 1982
42-Boston vs. Los Angeles, April 25, 1965
   Portland vs. Philadelphia, May 29, 1977

Fewest points, fourth quarter
12-Chicago at Phoenix, June 20, 1993
13-Philadelphia vs. San Francisco, April 23, 1967
   Milwaukee vs. Boston, April 30, 1974
   L.A. Lakers at Detroit, June 8, 1989
   Houston vs. New York, June 8, 1994

Most points, both teams, fourth quarter
76-Philadelphia (38) at Los Angeles (38), June 1, 1982
75-Boston (40) vs. L.A. Lakers (35), May 27, 1985

Fewest points, both teams, fourth quarter
28-Housuton (13) vs. New York (15), June 8, 1994
31-Chicago (12) at Phoenix (19), June 20, 1993

Most points, overtime period
22-Los Angeles vs. New York, May 1, 1970
18-Portland at Chicago, June 5, 1993

Fewest points, overtime period
4-Boston vs. Milwaukee, May 10, 1974
   Milwaukee at Boston, May 10, 1974
   L.A. Lakers vs. Chicago, June 7, 1991
   Chicago vs. Phoenix, June 13, 1993
   Phoenix at Chicago, June 13, 1993
6-Los Angeles vs. New York, April 29, 1970
   Boston at Milwaukee, April 30, 1974
   Boston vs. Phoenix, June 4, 1976
   Phoenix at Boston, June 4, 1976

Most points, both teams, overtime period
38-Los Angeles (22) vs. New York (16), May 1, 1970
30-Boston (16) vs. Phoenix (14), June 4, 1976

Fewest points, both teams, overtime period
8-Boston (4) vs. Milwaukee (4), May 10, 1974
   Chicago (4) vs. Phoenix (4), June 13, 1993
12-Boston (6) vs. Phoenix (6), June 4, 1976

100-POINT GAMES
Most consecutive games, 100 or more points,
all championship series
20-Minneapolis/Los Angeles, 1959-65
   L.A. Lakers, 1983-87
19-Boston, 1981-86
18-Philadelphia, 1977-83 (current)

Most consecutive games scoring fewer than 100 points,
all championship series
8-Houston, 1986-94
7-New York, 1994 (current)
6-Houston, 1981

PLAYERS SCORING
Most players, 30 or more points, game
2-Accomplished 27 times. Most recent:
Houston at Orlando, June 9, 1995
Orlando at Houston, June 9, 1995

Most players, 30 or more points, both teams, game
4-Houston (2) at Orlando (2), June 9, 1995
3-Occurred many times

Most players, 20 or more points, game
5-Boston vs. Los Angeles, April 19, 1965
   L.A. Lakers vs. Boston, June 4, 1987
   Boston vs. L.A. Lakers, June 11, 1987

Most players, 20 or more points, both teams, game
8-Boston (4) at Los Angeles (4), April 26, 1966
  L.A. Lakers (5) vs. Boston (3), June 4, 1987
7-Boston (5) vs. Los Angeles (2), April 19, 1965
  Philadelphia (4) vs. San Francisco (3), April 14, 1967
  Boston (4) vs. Los Angeles (3), April 30, 1968
  Philadelphia (4) at Los Angeles (3), May 31, 1983
  Los Angeles (4) vs. Boston (3), June 10, 1984
  Boston (4) at L.A. Lakers (3), June 7, 1985

Most players, 10 or more points, game
8-Boston vs. Los Angeles, May 31, 1984 (OT)
7-Accomplished 17 times. Most recent: Phoenix at Chicago, June 13, 1993

Most players, 10 or more points, both teams, game
14-Boston (7) vs. St. Louis (7), March 27, 1960
13-Los Angeles (7) at Boston (6), April 19, 1966
  Boston (8) vs. Los Angeles (5). May 31, 1984 (OT)

Fewest players, 10 or more points, game
Fort Wayne vs. Philadelphia, April 1, 1956
St. Louis at Boston, March 29, 1958
St. Louis vs. Boston, April 12, 1958
Los Angeles at Boston, April 29, 1969
Chicago vs. L.A. Lakers, June 2, 1991
Chicago vs. Portland, June 10, 1992

Fewest players, 10 or more points, both teams, game
5-Fort Wayne (2) vs. Philadelphia (3), April 1, 1956
  Los Angeles (2) at Boston (3), April 29, 1969
6-Boston (3) vs. Los Angeles (3), April 18, 1962 (OT)
  Boston (3) at Los Angeles (3), April 25, 1969
  Baltimore (3) at Milwaukee (3), April 21, 1971
  Golden State (3) vs. Washington (3), May 20, 1975
  Chicago (2) vs. L.A. Lakers (4), June 2, 1991
  Chicago (2) at Portland (4), June 10, 1992
  Chicago (3) at Phoenix (3), June 11, 1993

Field-Goal Percentage
Highest field-goal percentage, game
.617-Chicago vs. L.A. Lakers, June 5, 1991 (50/81)
.615-L.A. Lakers vs. Boston, June 4, 1987 (56-91)
.608-Boston vs. L.A. Lakers, May 27, 1985 (62-102)

Lowest field-goal percentage, game
.275-Syracuse vs. Fort Wayne at Indianapolis, April 7, 1955 (25-91)
.280-Fort Wayne vs. Syracuse at Indianapolis, April 7, 1955 (23-82)
.293-Boston at St. Louis, April 6, 1957 (29-99)
.295-San Francisco at Philadelphia, April 16, 1967 (38-129)
.302-Boston vs. St. Louis, April 9, 1958 (32-106)

Highest field-goal percentage, both teams, game
.582-L.A. Lakers (.615) vs. Boston (.548), June 4, 1987 (107-184)
.553 -L.A. Lakers (.556) vs. Boston (.549), June 2, 1987 (100-181)

Lowest field-goal percentage, both teams, game
.277-Syracuse (.275) vs. Fort Wayne (.280) at Indianapolis, April 7, 1955 (48-173)
.312-Boston (.304) at St. Louis (.320), April 11, 1957 (68-28)

Highest field-goal percentage, one half
.706-Philadelphia vs. Los Angeles, June 6, 1982 (36/51)
.667-Philadelphia vs. Los Angeles, May 7, 1980 (23/39)
    Philadelphia at Los Angeles, June 8, 1982 (26/39)
      Los Angeles vs. Boston, June 6, 1984 (28/42)
.659-Chicago vs. L.A. Lakers, June 5, 1991 (27/41)

Highest field-goal percentage, one quarter
.850-Chicago vs. L.A. Lakers, June 5, 1991 (17/20)
.824-Detroit vs. L.A. Lakers, June 6, 1989 (14/17)
.813-Los Angeles vs. Boston, June 6, 1984 (13/16)
    Boston at Houston, June 3, 1986 (13/16)

FIELD GOALS
Most field goals, game
62-Boston vs. L.A. Lakers, May 27, 1985
61-Boston vs. St. Louis, March 27, 1960

Fewest field goals, game
23 -Fort Wayne vs. Syracuse at Indianapolis, April 7, 1955
25-Syracuse vs. Fort Wayne at Indianpolis, April 7, 1955

Most field goals, both teams, game
112-Philadelphia (57) vs. San Francisco (55), April 14, 1967 (OT)
111-Boston (62) vs. L.A. Lakers (49), May 27, 1985

Fewest field goals, both teams, game
48-Fort Wayne (23) vs. Syracuse (25) at Indianapolis, April 7, 1955
57-Syracuse (26) vs. Fort Wayne (31) at Indianapolis, April 3, 1955

FIELD-GOAL ATTEMPTS
Most field-goal attempts, game
140-San Francisco at Philadelphia, April 14, 1967 (OT)
133-Boston vs. St. Louis, March 27, 1960

Fewest field-goal attempts, game
66-Los Angeles Lakers at New York, May 4, 1970
    L.A. Lakers at Chicago, June 2, 1991
      Houston vs. New York, June 19, 1994
69-New York at Houston, June 10, 1994

Most field-goal attempts, both teams, game
256-San Francisco (140) at Philadelphia (116), April 14, 1967 (OT)
250-Boston (130) vs. Minneapolis (120), April 4, 1959

Fewest field-goal attempts, both teams, game
146-L.A. Lakers (66) at Chicago (80), June 2, 1991
     Houston (66) vs. New York (80), June 19, 1994
149-Detroit (70) at L.A. Lakers (79), June 13, 1989

THREE-POIINT FIELD GOALS MADE
Most three-point field goals made, game
14-Houston at Orlando, June 7, 1995 (OT)
    Orlando at Houston, June 14, 1995
11-Houston at Orlando, June 14, 1995

Most three-point field goals made, both teams, game
25-Orlando (14) at Houston (11), June 14, 1995
23-Houston (14) at Orlando (9), June 7, 1995 (OT)

Most three-point field goals made, one half
9-Houston at Orlando, June 7, 1995
  Orlando at Houston, June 14, 1995

Most three-point field goals made, one quarter
7-Houston at Orlando, June 7, 1995
  Orlando at Houston June 14, 1995

THREE-POINT FIELD-GOAL ATTEMPTS

Most three-point field-goal attempts, game
32-Houston at Orlando, June 7, 1995 (OT)
31-Orlando at Houston, June 11, 1995
  Orlando at Houston, June 14, 1995

Most three-point field-goal attempts, both teams, game
62-Houston (32) at Orlando (30), June 7, 1995 (OT)
58-Orlando (31) at Houston (27), June 14, 1995

Most three-point field-goal attempts, one half
18-Orlando at Houston, June 11, 1995

FREE-THROW PERCENTAGE

Highest free-throw percentage, game
1.000-Portland at Chicago, June 14, 1992 (21-21)
.958-Boston vs. Houston, May 29, 1986 (23-24)

Lowest free-throw percentage, game
.444-Philadelphia vs. San Francisco, April 16, 1967 (16-36)
  Golden State at Washington, May 25, 1975 (8-18)
.476-Baltimore at Milwaukee, April 21, 1971 (10-21)

Highest free-throw percentage, both teams, game
.933-L.A. Lakers (.955) at Chicago (.875), June 5, 1991 (28-30)
.903-Boston (.926) vs. Los Angeles (.889), April 14, 1962 (65-72)

Lowest free-throw percentage, both teams, game
.538-Philadelphia (.444) vs. San Francisco (.655), April 16, 1967 (35-65)
.541-San Francisco (.478) at boston (.615), April 18, 1964 (46-85)

FREE THROWS MADE

Most free throws made, game
45-St. Louis at Boston, April 13, 1957 (2OT)
44-St. Louis at Boston, April 9, 1958

Fewest free throws made, game
3-Los Angeles at Philadelphia, May 26, 1983
6-Chicago vs. Phoenix, June 13, 1993 (3OT)

Most free throws made, both teams, game
80-St. Louis (44) at Boston (36), April 9, 1958
77-Syracuse (39) vs. Fort Wayne (38), April 9, 1955
  Boston (43) at St. Louis (34), April 12, 1958

Fewest free throws made, both teams, game
21-Phoenix (10) vs. Chicago (11), June 9, 1993
23-Milwaukee (9) vs. Boston (14), April 28, 1974

FREE-THROW ATTEMPTS

Most free-throw attempts
64-Philadelphia at San Francisco, April 24, 1967
62-St. Louis at Boston, April 13, 1957 (2OT)

Fewest free-throw attempts, game
5-Los Angeles at Philadelphia, May 26, 1983
8-Chicago vs. L.A. Lakers, June 5, 1991

Most free-throw attempts, both teams, game
116-St. Louis (62) at Boston (54), April 13, 1957 (2OT)
107-Boston (60) at St. Louis (47), April 2, 1958
 St. Louis (57) at Boston (50), April 9, 1958

Fewest free-throw attempts, both teams, game
30-Chicago (8) vs. L.A. Lakers (22), June 5, 1991
31-Milwaukee (13) vs. Boston (18), April 28, 1974

TOTAL REBOUNDS

Highest rebound percentage, game
.667-Boston vs. St. Louis, April 9, 1960 (78-117)
.632-Los Angeles vs. New York, May 7, 1972 (67-106)

Most rebounds, game
93-Philadelphia vs. San Francisco, April 16, 1967
86-Boston vs. Minneapolis, April 4, 1959

Fewest rebounds, game
29-L.A. Lakers vs. Chicago, June 7, 1991 (OT)
31-L.A. Lakers at Detroit, June 16, 1988
 Chicago at Portland, June 14, 1992

Most rebounds, both teams, game
169-Philadelphia (93) vs. San Francisco (76), April 16, 1967
159-San Francisco (80) at Philadelphia (79), April 14, 1967 (OT)

Fewest rebounds, both teams, game
69-Detroit (34) at L.A. Lakers (35), June 7, 1988
 Chicago (31) at Portland (38), June 14, 1992

Most rebounds, both teams, game
169-Philadelphia (93) vs. San Francisco (76), April 16, 1967
159-San Francisco (80) at Philadelphia (79), April 14, 1967 (OT)

Fewest rebounds, both teams, game
69-Detroit (34) at L.A. Lakers (35), June 7, 1988
 Chicago (31) at Portland (38), June 14, 1992
70-L.A. Lakers (34) at Chicago (36), June 5, 1991

OFFENSIVE REBOUNDS

Highest offensive rebound percentage, game
.556-Detroit vs. L.A. Lakers, June 16, 1988 (20-36)
.529-Seattle vs. Washington, June 7, 1978 (27-51)

Most offensive rebounds, game
28-Houston vs. Boston, May 10, 1981
27-Seattle vs. Washington, June 7, 1978
 Boston at Los Angeles, June 6, 1984

Fewest offensive rebounds, game
3-Boston vs. L.A. Lakers, May 30, 1985
   Houston vs. New York, June 22, 1994
5-Philadelphia at Los Angeles, May 7, 1980
   Philadelphia vs. Los Angeles, May 11, 1980
   Boston at L.A. Lakers, June 2, 1987
   L.A. Lakers vs. New York, June 1994

Most offensive rebounds, both teams, game
45-Houston (28) vs. Boston (17), May 10, 1981
44-Seattle (27) vs. Washington (17), June 7, 1978
   Boston (25) vs. Houston (19), May 5, 1981

Fewest offensive rebounds, both teams, game
15-L.A. Lakers (6) at Chicago (9), June 2, 1991
17-L.A. Lakers (14) at Boston (3), May 30, 1985
   L.A. Lakers (8) at Detroit (9), June 6, 1989
   Houston (3) vs. New York (14), June 22, 1994

DEFENSIVE REBOUNDS
Highest defensive rebound percentage, game
.921-L.A. Lakers at Boston, May 30, 1985 (35-38)
.897-New York at Houston, June 22, 1994 (26-29)

Most defensive rebounds, game
48-Portland at Philadelphia, June 3, 1977
46-Philadelphia vs. Portland, May 26, 1977

Fewest defensive rebounds, game
16-L.A. Lakers at Detroit, June 16, 1988
20-Philadelphia vs. Portland, May 22, 1977
   L.A. Lakers at Chicago, June 5, 1991
   L.A. Lakers vs. Chicago, June 7, 1991 (OT)

Most defensive rebounds, both teams, game
84-Portland (48) at Philadelphia (36), June 3, 1977
82-Philadelphia (46) vs. Portland (36), May 26, 1977

Fewest defensive rebounds, both teams, game
43-L.A. Lakers (21) at Detroit (22), June 8, 1989
45-L.A. Lakers (20) at Chicago (25), June 5, 1991

ASSISTS
Most assists, game
44-Los Angeles vs. New York, May 6, 1970
   L.A. Lakers vs. Boston, June 4, 1987
43-Boston vs. L.A. Lakers, May 27, 1985

Fewest assists, game
5-Boston at St. Louis, April 3, 1960
9-Los Angeles at Boston, April 28, 1966

Most assists, both teams, game
79-L.A. Lakers (44) vs. Boston (35), June 4, 1987
76-L.A. Lakers (40) vs. Boston (36), June 7, 1985

Fewest assists, both teams, game
21-Los Angeles (10) at Boston (11), April 29, 1969
24-Los Angeles (10) at Boston (14), May 3, 1969

PERSONAL FOULS
Most personal fouls, game
42-Minneapolis vs. Syracuse, April 23, 1950
40-Portland vs. Philadelphia, May 31, 1977

Fewest personal fouls, game
13-L.A. Lakers at Detroit, June 12, 1988
15-L.A. Lakers at Chicago, June 5, 1991

Most personal fouls, both teams, game
77-Minneapolis (42) vs. Syracuse (35), April 23, 1950
76-Minneapolis (39) at New York (37), April 18, 1952 (OT)

Fewest personal fouls, both teams, game
35-Boston (17) at Milwaukee (18), April 28, 1974
   Boston (17) at Houston (18), June 3, 1986
   L.A. Lakers (15) at Chicago (20), June 5, 1991
36-Baltimore (17) vs. Milwaukee (19), April 25, 1971
   Boston (17) vs. Houston (19), May 26, 1986
   L.A. Lakers (13) at Detroit (23), June 12, 1988
   Phoenix (19) vs. Chicago (17), June 9, 1993

DISQUALIFICATIONS
Most disqualifications, game
4-Minneapolis vs. Syracuse, April 23, 1950
   Minneapolis vs. New York, April 4, 1953
   New York vs. Minneapolis, April 10, 1953
   St. Louis at Boston, April 13, 1957 (2 OT)
   Boston vs. Los Angeles, April 18, 1962 (OT)

Most disqualifications, both teams, game
7-Boston (4) vs. Los Angeles (3), April 18, 1962 (OT)
6-St. Louis (4) at Boston (2), April 13, 1957 (2 OT)

STEALS
Most steals, game
17-Golden State vs. Washington, May 23, 1975
16-Philadelphia vs. Portland, May 22, 1977

Fewest steals, game
1-Milwaukee at Boston, May 10, 1974 (2 OT)
   Boston vs. Phoenix, May 23, 1976
2-Milwaukee at Boston, May 3, 1974
   Milwaukee at Boston, May 5, 1974
   Milwaukee vs. Boston, May 12, 1974
   Detroit vs. L.A. Lakers, June 6, 1989
   Detroit vs. Portland, June 7, 1990 (OT)

Most steals, both teams, game
31-Golden State (17) vs. Washington (14), May 23, 1975
28-Golden State (15) at Washington (13), May 25, 1975

Fewest steals, both teams, game
6-Detroit (3) vs. L.A. Lakers (3), June 8, 1989
   L.A. Lakers (3) vs. Detroit (3), June 13, 1989
8-Milwaukee (2) at Boston (6), May 5, 1974

Milwaukee (1) at Boston (7), May 10, 1974 (2 OT)
Seattle (4) vs. Washington (4), June 2, 1978
Seattle (4) vs. Washington (4), May 29, 1979 (OT)
Chicago (4) at L.A. Lakers (4), June 9, 1991

BLOCKED SHOTS
Most blocked shots, game
13-Seattle at Washington, May 28, 1978
   Philadelphia at Los Angeles, May 4, 1980
   Philadelphia vs. Los Angeles, June 6, 1982
   Philadelphia at Los Angeles, May 22, 1983
   Houston vs. Boston, June 5, 1986
12-Golden State vs. Washington, May 20, 1975
   Phoenix vs. Chicago, June 11, 1993

Fewest blocked shots, game
0-Boston vs. Milwaukee, May 5, 1974
   Boston vs. Milwaukee, May 10, 1974 (2 OT)
   Boston vs. Phoenix, June 4, 1976 (3 OT)
   Philadelphia vs. Portland, May 22, 1977
   Washington at Seattle, May 21, 1978
   Boston at Houston, May 14, 1981
   L.A. Lakers vs. Boston, June 5, 1985
   L.A. Lakers vs. Detroit, June 7, 1988

Most blocked shots, both teams, game
22-Philadelphia (13) at Los Angeles (9), May 4, 1980
   Philadelphia (13) vs. Los Angeles (9), June 6, 1982
21-Philadelphia (13) vs. Los Angeles (8), May 22, 1983

Fewest blocked shots, both teams, game
2-Boston (0) at Houston (2), May 14, 1981
3-Boston (0) vs. Milwaukee (3), May 5, 1974
   Boston (0) vs. Milwaukee (3), May 10, 1974 (2 OT)
   Boston (1) vs. Phoenix (2), May 23, 1976
   L.A. Lakers (1) vs. Detroit (2), June 21, 1988
   Chicago (1) vs. L.A. Lakers (2), June 5, 1991

TURNOVERS
Most turnovers, game
34- Portland at Philadelphia, May 22, 1977
31 -Golden State at Washington, May 25, 1975

Fewest turnovers, game
5-Chicago at L.A. Lakers, June 9, 1991
7-L.A. Lakers vs. Detroit, June 13, 1989

Most turnovers, both teams, game
60-Golden State (31) at Washington (29), May 25, 1975
54-Phoenix (29) at Boston (25), June 4, 1976 (3 OT)
   Portland (34) at Philadelphia (20), May 22, 1977

Fewest turnovers, both teams, game
15-Chicago (5) at L.A. Lakers (10), June 9, 1991
16-L.A. Lakers (7) vs. Detroit (9), June 13, 1989

Interviews

I want to thank the following people for granting interviews for this project: Red Auerbach, John McLendon, Jr., John Wooden, Bill Walton, Jim Pollard, Bob Kurland, Bobby Knight, John Havlicek, John Thompson, Guy Lewis, Pete Newell, Dick Harp, Frank Ramsey, George Senesky, Petey Rosenberg, Matt Goukas, Jr. and Sr., Howie Dallmar, Robert "Jake" Embry, Mike Bloom, Paul Seymour, Paul Hoffman, Buddy Jeannette, Vern Mikkelsen, John Kundla, Bones McKinney, Danny Biasone, Dolph Schayes, Al Cervi, Charlie Eckman, George King, K.C. Jones, Tom Heinsohn, Bob Cousy, Jerry West, Elgin Baylor, Fred Schaus, Johnny Most, Bailey Howell, Wali Jones, Oscar Robertson, Willis Reed, Dave DeBusschere, Walt Frazier, Sam Goldaper, Pat Riley, Rick Barry, Al Attles, Butch Beard, Elvin Hayes, Jamaal Wilkes, Magic Johnson, Larry Bird, Maurice Lucas, Michael Jordan, Scottie Pippen, Phil Jackson, John Paxson, Tex Winter, Jim Cleamons, Jack Haley, Dennis Rodman, Luc Longley, Steve Schanwald, Adrian Dantley, Dave Cowens, Sam Jones, Clifford Ray, Bob Ryan, Kevin McHale, Robert Parish, Gerald Henderson, Rick Mahorn, Joe Dumars II, Joe Dumars III, Ophelia Dumars, John Salley, Jack McCloskey, James Edwards, Rick Adelman, Mark Aguirre, Isiah Thomas, and Chuck Daly.

I want to acknowledge the work of the dozens of writers who have covered the NBA, including Mitch Albom, Terry Armour, Lacy J. Banks, Jesse Barkin, Terry Boers, Clifton Brown, Kelly Carter, Mitch Chortkoff, Robert Falkoff, Bill Gleason, Bill Halls, Scott Howard-Cooper, Mike Imrem, Melissa Isaacson, John Jackson, Paul Ladewski, Bernie Lincicome, Bob Logan, Jay Mariotti, Kent McDill, Corky Meinecke, Mike Mulligan, Skip Myslenski, Glenn Rogers, Steve Rosenbloom, Eddie Sefko, Gene Seymour, Sam Smith, Ray Sons, Paul Sullivan, Mike Tulumello, Mark Vancil, Bob Verdi, and many, many others. Without the front-line work of a variety of reporters and writers over the years, the compilation of this history would have been greatly hampered. In most cases in the text, these people are referred to as "the writers."

That group also includes the following:

Mitch Albom, Dave Anderson, Phil Berger, Frank DeFord, Bryan Burwell, David Dupree, Scott Ostler, Ira Berkow, Shelby Strother, Charlie Vincent, Cliff Brown, Bob Ryan, Joe Fitzgerald, Roy S. Johnson, Donald Hall, Alan Goldstein, Larry Donald, Jack Madden, Tony Kornheiser, Ted Green, Dave Kindred, Mitch Chortkoff, Pat Putnam, Sandy Padwe, Jack McCallum, Sam McManis, Doug Cress, Mike Littwin, John Papanek, Leonard Lewin, Leonard Koppett, Sam Goldaper, George Vecsey, Alex Wolff, Bruce Newman, Jackie MacMullen, Steve Bulpett, Peter May, Mike Fine, Frank Dell'Apa, Will McDonough, Ailene Voisin, Jim Fenton, Drew Sharp, Terry Foster, Steve Addy, Dean Howe, Bob Wojnowski, Corky Meinecke, Steve Kornacki, Bill Halls, Joe Falls, Jerry Green, Michelle Kaufmann, Mike Littwin, Allen Greenberg, and many others. Their work has been invaluable.

Extensive use was made of a variety of publications, including the *Baltimore Sun, Basketball Times, Boston Globe, Chicago Defender, Chicago Tribune, Chicago Sun-Times, Daily Southtown, The Detroit News, The Detroit Free Press, The Daily Herald, Hoop Magazine, Houston Post, Houston Chronicle, Inside Sports, Los Angeles Times, The National, New York Daily News, The New York Times, New York Post, The Charlotte Observer, USA Today, The Oregonian, Philadelphia Inquirer, San Antonio Express-News, Sport, Sports Illustrated, The Sporting News, Street & Smith's Pro Basketball Yearbook,* and *The Washington Post.*

Books

24 Seconds to Shoot by Leonard Koppett
50 Years of the Final Four by Billy Packer and Roland Lazenby
100 Greatest Basketball Players by Wayne Patterson and Lisa Fisher
1991 NCAA Basketball
A Century of Women's Basketball, Edited by Joan S. Hult and Marianna Trekell
A Sense of Where You Are by John McPhee
A Will to Win by Dwight Lewis and Susan Thomas
Above The Rim by Gary Tuell
All the Moves by Neil D. Isaacs
Bad Boys by Isiah Thomas and Matt Dobek
Basketball for the Player, the Fan and the Coach by Red Auerbach
Basketball's Greatest Games edited by Zander Hollander
Basketball's Hall of Fame by Sandy Padwe
Bird, The Making of An American Sports Legend by Lee Daniel Levine
Cages to Jump Shots by Robert Peterson
Championship NBA by Leonard Koppett
Coach by Ray Meyer and Ray Sons
Coaching Basketball edited by Jerry Krause
College Basketball's 25 Greatest Teams by Billy Packer and Roland Lazenby
Cousy on the Celtic Mystique by Bob Cousy and Bob Ryan
Drive, The Story of My Life by Larry Bird and Bob Ryan
Forty-Eight Minutes by Bob Ryan and Terry Pluto
From Muscular Christianity to the Market Place by Albert Gammon Applin II
From Set Shot to Slam Dunk by Charles Salzberg
Giant Steps by Kareem Abdul-Jabbar and Peter Knobler
Give 'Em The Hook by Tommy Heinsohn and Joe Fitzgerald
Heinsohn by Tommy Heinsohn and Leonard Lewin
Holzman on Hoops by Red Holzman and Harvey Frommer

377

Honey Russell by John Russell
Kareem by Kareem Abdul-Jabbar and Mignon McCarthy
Magic's Touch by Magic Johnson and Roy S. Johnson
March to the Top by Art Chansky and Eddie Fogler
Meadowlark by Meadowlark Lemon and Jerry B. Jenkins
Michael Jordan by Mitchell Krugel
Miracle on 34th Street by Phil Berger
Official Spalding Basketball Guide, various editions, 1898-1930
On and Off the Court with Red Auerbach and Joe Fitzgerald
Personal Fouls by Peter Golenbock
Pro Basketball Champions by George Vecsey
Raw Recruits by Alexander Wolff and Armen Keteyian
Rebound by K.C. Jones and Jack Warner
Red on Red by Red Holzman and Harvey Frommer
Rick Barry's Pro Basketball Scouting Report by Rick Barry and Jordan E. Cohn
Second Wind by Bill Russell and Taylor Branch
Showtime by Pat Riley and Byron Laursen
Sportswit by Lee Green
The Amazing Basketball Book by Bob Hill and Randall Baron
The Bird Era by Bob Schron and Kevin Stevens
The Bob Verdi Collection by Bob Verdi
The Boston Celtics by Bob Ryan
The Boston Celtics Greenbook, 1988-89 and 1989-90 by Roland Lazenby
The Breaks of the Game by David Halberstam
The Detroit Pistons, 1988-89, and 1989-90 by Roland Lazenby
The City Game by Pete Axthelm

The Final Four by Joe Gergen
The Franchise by Cameron Stauth
The Glory and the Dream by William Manchester
The History of Professional Basketball by Glenn Dickey
The Jim Murray Collection by Jim Murray
The Legend of Dr. J by Marty Bell
The Mickey Herskowitz Collection by Mickey Herskowitz
The Modern Basketball Encyclopedia by Zander Hollander
The Night Wilt Scored 100 by Eric Nadel
The Official NBA Basketball Encyclopedia edited by Zander Hollander and Alex Sachare
The Story of Basketball by Dave Anderson
The Story of Basketball by John Devaney
They Call Me Coach by John Wooden
They Were Number One by Robert Stern
Walt Frazier by Walt Frazier and Neil Offen
Where Are They Today? by John Devaney
Winnin' Times by Scott Ostler and Steve Springer
Winning Basketball by Gail Goodrich
Wilt by Wilt Chamberlain

Also:

Bull Session by Johnny Kerr and Terry Pluto
Long Time Coming by Chet Walker and Chris Messenger
Loose Balls by Terry Pluto
Maverick by Phil Jackson and Charlie Rosen
Pro Basketball Encyclopedia by David S. Neft and Richard M. Cohen
Rare Air by Michael Jordan with Mark Vancil
Tall Tales by Terry Pluto
The Bulls and Chicago by Bob Logan
The Jordan Rules by Sam Smith
Transition Game by Melissa Isaacson